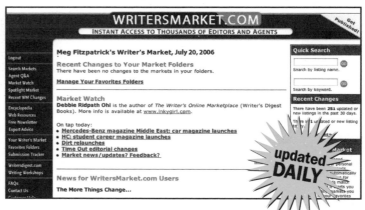

2007

Song Writer's Market®

Ian Bessler, Editor

W
WRITER'S DIGEST BOOKS
CINCINNATI, OH

If you would like to be considered for a listing in the next edition of *Songwriter's Market*, send a SASE (or SAE and IRC) with your request for a questionnaire to *Songwriter's Market—* QR, 4700 East Galbraith Road, Cincinnati OH 45236. Please indicate in which section you would like to be included.

Editorial Director, Writer's Digest Books: Jane Friedman
Managing Editor, Writer's Digest Market Books: Alice Pope

Writer's Digest Books Web site: www.writersdigest.com
Writer's Market Web site: www.writersmarket.com
Songwriter's Market Web site: www.songwritersmarket.com

2007 Songwriter's Market. Copyright © 2006 by Writer's Digest Books. Published by F+W Publications, 4700 East Galbraith Road, Cincinnati, Ohio 45236. Printed and bound in the United States of America. All rights reserved. No part of this book may be reproduced in any form or by any electronic or mechanical means including information storage and retrieval systems without written permission from the publisher, except by reviewers who may quote brief passages to be printed in a magazine or newspaper.

Distributed in Canada by Fraser Direct
100 Armstrong Avenue
Georgetown, ON, Canada L7G 5S4
Tel: (905) 877-4411

Distributed in the U.K. and Europe by David & Charles
Brunel House, Newton Abbot, Devon, TQ12 4PU, England
Tel: (+44) 1626 323200, Fax: (+44) 1626 323319
E-mail: postmaster@davidandcharles.co.uk

Distributed in Australia by Capricorn Link
P.O. Box 704, Windsor, NSW 2756 Australia
Tel: (02) 4577-3555

ISSN: 0161-5971
ISBN-13: 978-158297-431-6
ISBN-10: 1-58297-431-4

Cover design by Kelly Kofron/Claudean Wheeler
Interior design by Clare Finney
Production coordinated by Robin Richie/Kristen Heller

Attention Booksellers: This is an annual directory of F+W Publications. Return deadline for this edition is December 31, 2007.

Contents

From the Editor 1

GETTING STARTED

Quick-Start
New to *Songwriter's Market*? 2

Songwriter's Market
How Is It Put Together? 5

Songwriter's Market
How Do I Use It? 7

Where Should I Send My Songs? 9

Demo Recordings
What Should I Know? 13

How Do I Submit My Demo? 15

How Do I Avoid the Rip-Offs? 19

Submission Strategies 23

Quiz: Are You Professional? 26

MUSIC BIZ BASICS

Royalties
Where Does the Money Come From? 28

What About Copyright? 32

Career Songwriting
What Should I Know? 34

What About Contracts? 36

ADVANCED ARTICLES

Getting Ready to Face the Industry
by John Braheny 40

The Staff Writer Contract
by Randy Poe 49

Breaking in From Anywhere
by Brian Austin Whitney 54

Getting Started in Music Licensing
by Blake Althen with Paula Bellenoit 62
including interview: SONiA—Folk to Dance 67

David Lasley
Yesterday and Today, by Robin Renée 69

Brian Wilson
Ask Me Anything . . . , by Scott Mathews 73

MARKETS

Music Publishers 78

> **Insider Reports**
> **Allan Licht** of Allan Bradley Music
> *Allan Bradley Music seeks quality songs* 90
> **Ron Cornelius** of The Cornelius Companies
> *The Cornelius Companies build for the future* 98

Record Companies 138

> **Insider Reports**
> **Mr. Jimmi** of Ariana Records
> *Ariana Records follows muse to market* 146
> **Patrick Arn** of Gotham Records
> *Gotham Records pursues a diverse strategy* 162
> **Slim Moon** of Kill Rock Stars
> *Kill Rock Stars seeks artists with vision and drive* 168

Record Producers 192

Managers & Booking Agents 217

Music Firms
Advertising, Audiovisual & Commercial 250

Play Producers & Publishers 256

    Play Producers 257

    Play Publishers 260

Classical Performing Arts 264

Contests & Awards 276

    Insider Report
    Susan Greenbaum, independent singer-songwriter
    Singer-songwriter scores double contest win 286

RESOURCES

Organizations 293

    Insider Report
    Shawn Murphy of ASCAP
    ASCAP helps build music careers 296

Workshops & Conferences 321

Retreats & Colonies 332

State & Provincial Grants 336

Publications of Interest 340

Web Sites of Interest 347

Glossary 352

INDEXES

Category Indexes

    Look up companies by musical genre

    Music Publishers 358

    Record Companies 366

    Record Producers 371

    Managers & Booking Agents 376

Openness to Submissions Index 383

    Look up companies by openness to beginners

Film & TV Index 390

    Look up companies placing music in film and TV

Geographic Index 392

General Index 409

***Songwriter's Market* Feedback** 423

From the Editor

Over the years, I've had many readers ask how they might catch the attention of the music industry. Increasingly, I find myself saying, *"It helps if you're good."*

Although this often elicits a chuckle, it is also a serious message. If you write good songs, doors will open for you, provided your plan of approach is solid. If you are unrealistic about your level of talent, you will experience frustration. And make no mistake—*the standard is very high!*

So, what do you do?

First, *become a student of the craft of songwriting—for life!* No matter how good you are—or how good you *think* you are—there is always something new to learn. Read books on the subject, such as Sheila Davis' *The Craft of Lyric Writing*, or John Braheny's *The Craft & Business of Songwriting* (see page 40 for **Getting Ready to Face the Industry**, excerpted from Braheny's new 3rd edition revision).

Second, *you should join a songwriters organization.* (Go to the Organizations section on page 293.) You will learn a tremendous amount about how your songwriting measures up (or doesn't), and how you can take it further. Also see page 54 for **Breaking In From Anywhere**, by Brian Austin Whitney, for advice on making contacts no matter where you live.

Third, *seek out critiques from people inside the industry (and set aside your ego)*. You may not necessarily like what you hear. I have seen seminar participants—successful performing songwriters in their own right—walk away from critiques in disbelief and anger. They could not accept that the level of craft required to write for other artists is a step above, and they lost an opportunity to learn and improve.

Fourth, *take the leap and enter some song contests!* If you consistently have a good showing in song contests, you may consider it evidence that you are on to something with your songwriting. If not, many contests offer critiques and other feedback on your songs. (See page 286 for an interview with singer-songwriter Susan Greenbaum, winner of the most recent Mid-Atlantic Song Contest.)

So, if at first you don't succeed, consider that you may need some help, and go look for feedback. The resources and support available to you in today's songwriting world is a quantum leap beyond what anyone could have imagined even 10 years ago.

This book is an entryway to that world—use it to the fullest!

Ian C. Bessler
songmarket@fwpubs.com
www.songwritersmarket.com

Quick-Start

New to Songwriter's Market?

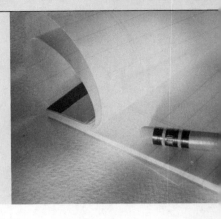

This "Quick-Start" guide is designed to lay it out for you step by step. Each step shows you where to find the information you need in *Songwriter's Market*, from basic to more advanced.

Use this as guide to launch your songwriting career. Look over the whole list once, then go back and read each article completely. They will show you new facets of the music industry and reinforce what you already know. Good luck!

1. Join a songwriting organization. Connecting with other songwriters and learning from their experience will save you a lot of trouble starting out. Organizations help you learn about the music business, polish your songwriting and help you make contacts who can take you to the next level.

- Organizations, page 293

2. Learn about the music business. Protect yourself with knowledge. Learn how money is really made in the music business and avoid scams. Go to songwriting workshops and music conferences.

- How Do I Avoid the Rip-Offs?, page 19
- Royalties: Where Does the Money Come From?, page 28
- What About Copyright?, page 32
- What About Contracts?, page 36
- Career Songwriting: What Should I Know?, page 34
- Workshops & Conferences, page 321
- Publications of Interest, page 340
- Getting Ready to Face the Industry, page 40
- The Staff Writer Contract, page 49
- Getting Started in Music Licensing, page 62
- Breaking In From Anywhere, page 54

3. Develop your songwriting skill. Get letterhead, have your songs critiqued, make contacts and subscribe to songwriting/music magazines. Start building your catalog of songs. If you also perform, start developing your performance skills and build a following.

- Organizations, page 293
- Workshops & Conferences, page 321
- Publications of Interest, page 340
- Web sites of Interest, page 347

4. Choose your best three songs and make a demo recording.

- Demo Recordings: What Should I Know?, page 13
- What About Copyright?, page 32

5. Learn how to spot rip-offs.
- How Do I Avoid the Rip-Offs?, page 19
- What About Copyright?, page 32
- What About Contracts?, page 36

6. Decide which arm(s) of the music business you will submit your songs to.
- Where Should I Send My Songs?, page 9
- Submission Strategies, page 23
- Music Publishers Section Introduction, page 78
- Record Companies Section Introduction, page 138
- Record Producers Section Introduction, page 192
- Managers & Booking Agents Section Introduction, page 217
- Advertising, Audiovisual & Commercial Music Firms Section Introduction, page 250
- Contests & Awards Section Introduction, page 276

7. Find companies open to your style of music and level of experience or use your contacts at Organizations and Performing Rights Organizations (ASCAP, BMI, SESAC) to get a referral and permission to submit. Be picky about where you send your material. Do not waste your time and effort submitting to every company listed in this book without regard to whether they want your style of music.
- Where Should I Send My Songs, page 9
- Openness to Submissions Index, page 383
- Category Indexes, page 358

8. Locate companies in your area.
- Geographic Index, page 392

9. Read the listings and decide which companies to submit to and whether they are appropriate for you (pay special attention to the **Music** subhead and also the royalty percentage they pay). Do additional research through trade publications, the Internet and other songwriters.
- Markets, beginning on page 78
- Publications of Interest, page 340
- Web sites of Interest, page 347

10. Find out how to submit. Read information under the How to Contact subhead of each listing. Learn the etiquette involved in contacting companies. Learn how to package your demo in a professional way. Learn how to avoid getting ripped off.
- *Songwriter's Market*: How Do I Use It?, page 7
- How Do I Submit My Demo?, page 15
- Quiz: Are You Professional?, page 26
- How Do I Avoid the Rip-Offs?, page 19
- Getting Ready to Face the Industry, page 40

11. Call the companies and verify their submission policy has not changed. Also check to make sure the contact person is still there.
- Getting Ready to Face the Industry, page 40

12. Send your submission package according to each company's directions. Read the information under the How to Contact subhead in each listing again.
- Quiz: Are You Professional?, page 26
- How Do I Submit My Demo?, page 15
- What About Copyright?, page 32

13. Decide whether to sign with a company.
- Royalties: Where Does the Money Come From?, page 28
- How Do I Avoid the Rip-Offs?, page 19

Getting Started

14. Have an entertainment attorney look over any contract before you sign.
- What About Contracts?, page 36
- How Do I Avoid the Rip-Offs?, page 19
- What About Copyright?, page 32
- Publishing Contracts, page 81
- Record Company Contracts, page 141

15. After signing, how do you get paid?
- Royalties: Where Does the Money Come From?, page 28

Songwriter's Market

How Is It Put Together?

The following articles are for songwriters who have never used this book before and are new to the music industry. This is all important information so don't skip straight to the listings. There's a lot to learn, but it's been rewritten for clarity and simplicity. Taking a little time now to educate yourself can save you from having to learn a lot of things the hard way.

How do I use *Songwriter's Market?*
First, take a minute to get to know the book and how it's put together. Here's a rundown of *what* is in the book:

What you'll find inside this book
Songwriter's Market is a big book and can seem overwhelming at first. But don't worry, it's not that tough to find your way around the book. Here's a quick look at how it's put together.
   The book has six basic parts:

1. Articles about the music business and songwriting craft
2. Introductions to each section of listings
3. Listings of music companies and organizations
4. Insider Reports
5. Indexes
6. Lists of Web sites, magazines, books, and other useful extras

Music biz and songwriting articles
These range from articles on the basics of how the music business works—the essentials, laid out in plain English, of how songwriters and artists make money and advance their careers—to articles with more detail and depth on business and creativity, written by music industry insiders with many years of experience in the trenches.

Section intros and listings—the "meat" of the book
There are 11 sections in the book, from Music Publishers and Record Companies to Contests & Awards. Each section begins with an introduction detailing how the different types of companies function—what part of the music industry they work in, how they make money, and what you need to think about when approaching them with your music.
   The listings are the heart of *Songwriter's Market*. They are the names, addresses and contact information of music biz companies looking for songs and artists, as well as descriptions of the types of music they are looking for.

What are Insider Reports?

Insider Reports are interviews with songwriters, performers and music industry honchos working at all levels in the music business. By showing how others have achieved success, you learn by example. By peeking behind the curtain of record labels, music publishers and others, you understand more about how the industry works. You learn how the businessmen think, and how to work that to your advantage. Reading these articles gives you an important edge over songwriters and performers who don't. Insider Reports are scattered throughout the listings and are listed in the Table of Contents.

Songwriter's Market

How Do I Use It?

The quick answer is that you should use the indexes to find companies who are interested in your type of music, then read the listings for details on how they want the music submitted. For support and help of all sorts, join a songwriting or other music industry association. Become a student of the music industry. (Also see the Quick-Start guide on page 2.)

How does *Songwriter's Market* "work"?

The listings in *Songwriter's Market* are packed with a lot of information. It can be intimidating at first, but they are put together in a structured way to make them easy to work with. Take a few minutes to get used to how the listings are organized, and you'll have it down in no time. For more detailed information about how the listings are put together, skip ahead to Where Should I Send My Songs? on page 9.

What are the general rules for working with listings?

Look at A Sample Listing Decoded on page 11 for an example of how a typical listing is put together. The following are general rules about how to use the listings.

1. **Read the entire listing** to decide whether to submit your music! Do not use this book as a mass mailing list! If you blindly mail out demos by the hundreds, you'll waste a lot of money on postage, irritate a lot of people, and your demos will wind up in the trash.

2. **Pay close attention to the "Music" section in each listing.** This will tell you what kind of music the company is looking for. If they want rockabilly only and you write heavy metal, don't submit.

3. **Pay close attention to submission instructions** shown under "How to Contact" and follow them to the letter. A lot of listings are very particular about how they want submissions packaged. Pay close attention. If you do not follow their instructions, they will probably throw your submission in the garbage. You have been warned! If you are confused about their directions, call, e-mail or write to the company for clarification.

4. **If in doubt, contact the company for permission to submit.** This is a good general rule. Many companies don't mind if you send an unsolicited submission, but some will want you to get special prior permission from them. Contacting a company first is also a good way to find out their latest music needs. This is also a chance to briefly make contact on a personal level.

5. **Be courteous, be efficient** and always have a purpose to your personal contact—

DO NOT WASTE THEIR TIME! If you call, always have a reason for making contact—permission to submit, checking on guidelines, following up on a demo, etc. These are solid reasons to make personal contact, but once you have their attention do not wear out your welcome! Always be polite! Always have an upbeat, pleasant attitude when you call (even if you are feeling frustrated or uptight at that particular moment)!

6. **Check for a preferred contact.** A lot of listings have a designated contact person shown after a bolded "**Contact**" in the heading. This is the person you should contact with questions or address you're submission to.

7. **Read the "Tips" section.** This part of the listing provides extra information on how to submit or what it might be like to work with the company.

This is just the beginning. For more detailed information about the listings, see Where Should I Send My Songs? on page 9 and the sidebar with the sample listing called A Sample Listing Decoded on page 11. Also see Quiz: Are You Professional? on page 26.

Frequently Asked Questions

1 **How do these companies get listed in the book anyway?** No company pays to be included—all listings are free. The listings come from a combination of research the editor does on the music industry and questionnaires requested by companies who want to be listed (many of them contact us to be included). All questionnaires are screened for known sharks and to make sure they meet our requirements (see How Do I Avoid the Rip-Offs? on page 19 for details of what makes us reject or remove a listing).

2 **Why aren't other companies I know about listed in the book?** We may have sent them a questionnaire, but they did not return it, were removed for complaints, went out of business, specifically asked not to be listed, could not be contacted for an update, etc.

3 **What's the deal with companies that don't take unsolicited submissions?** In the interest of completeness, the editor will sometimes include listings of crucial music companies he thinks you should be aware of. Major labels such as Capitol Records and Warner Bros. fall under this category. You want to at least have some idea of what their policies are, don't you? If a company is closed to unsolicited submissions, you can do either of two things: 1) don't submit to them; or 2) find a way around the roadblock by establishing a relationship or finding a backdoor of some kind (charming them on the phone, through managers, producers, artists, entertainment attorneys, or the fabled Seven Degrees of Separation—i.e. networking like crazy).

4 **A company said in their listing they take unsolicited submissions. My demo came back unopened. What happened?** Some companies needs change rapidly and may have changed since we contacted them for this edition of the book. This is another reason why it's often a good idea to contact a company before submitting.

Where Should I Send My Songs?

I t depends a lot on whether you write mainly for yourself as a performer, or if you only write and want someone else to pick up your song for their recording (usually the case in country music, for example). *Are you mainly a performing songwriter or a non-performing songwriter?* This is important for figuring out what kind of companies to contact, as well as how you contact them. (For more detail, skip to Submission Strategies on page 23.)

What if I'm a non-performing songwriter?

Many well-known songwriters are not performers in their own right. Some are not skilled instrumentalists or singers, but they understand melody, lyrics and harmony and how they go together. They can write great songs, but they need someone else to bring it to life through skilled musicianship. A non-performing songwriter will usually approach music publishers first for access to artists looking for songs, as well as artists' managers, their producers and their record companies. On the flip side, many incredibly talented musicians can't write to save their lives and need someone else to provide them with good songs to perform. (For more details on the different types of companies and the roles they play for performing songwriters, see the section introductions for Music Publishers on page 78, Record companies on page 138, Record Producers on page 192, and Managers & Booking Agents on page 217. Also see Submission Strategies on page 23.)

What if I am a performing songwriter?

Many famous songwriters are also famous as performers. They are skilled interpreters of their own material, and they also know how to write to their own particular talents as musicians. In this case, their intention is also usually to sell themselves as a performer in hopes of recording and releasing an album, or they have an album and want to find gigs and people who can help guide their careers. They will usually approach record companies or record producers first, on the basis of recording an album. For gigs and career guidance, they talk to booking agents and managers.

A smaller number also approach publishers in hopes of getting others to perform their songs, much like non-performing songwriters. Some music publishers in recent years have also taken on the role of developing artists as both songwriters and performers, or are connected to a major record label, so performing songwriters might go to them for these reasons. (For more details on the different types of companies and the roles they play for performing songwriters, see the section introductions for Music Publishers on page 78, Record companies on page 138, Record Producers on page 192, and Managers & Booking Agents on page 217. Also see Submission Strategies on page 23.)

Types of Music Companies

- **Music Publishers**—evaluate songs for commercial potential, find artists to record them, finds other uses for the songs such as film or TV, collects income from songs, protects copyrights from infringement
- **Record Companies**—sign artists to their labels, finance recordings, promotion and touring, releases songs/albums to radio and TV
- **Record Producers**—works in the studio and records songs (independently or for a record company), may be affiliated with a particular artist, sometimes develop artists for record labels, locates or co-writes songs if an artist does not write their own
- **Managers & Booking Agents**—works with artists to manage their careers, finds gigs, locates songs to record if the artist does not write their own

How do I use *Songwriter's Market* to narrow my search?

Once you've identified whether you are primarily interested in getting others to perform your songs (non-performing songwriter) or you perform your own songs and want a record deal, etc., there are several steps you can then take:

1. **Identify what kind of music company you wish to approach.** Based on whether you're a performing or non-performing songwriter, do you want to approach a music publisher for a publishing deal? Do you want to approach a record producer because you need somone to help you record an album in the studio? Maybe you want to approach a producer in hopes that an act he's producing needs songs to complete their album. Also see Submission Strategies on page 23 and the Section Introductions for Music Publishers on page 78, Record companies on page 138, Record Producers on page 192, and Managers & Booking Agents on page 217.
2. **Check for companies based on location.** Maybe you need a manager located close by. Maybe you need to find as many Nashville-based companies as you can because you write country and most country publishers are in Nashville. In this case start with the Geographic Index on page 392. You can also tell Canadian and Foreign listings by the icons in the listing (see A Sample Listing Decoded below and on page 11).
3. **Look for companies based on the type of music they want.** Some companies want country. Some record labels want only punk rock. Check the Category Indexes on page 358 for a list of music companies broken down by the type of music they are interested in.
4. **Look for companies based on how open they are to beginners.** Some companies are more open than others to beginning artists and songwriters. Maybe you are a beginner and it would help to approach these companies first. Some music publishers are hoping to find that wild card hit song and don't care if it comes from an unknown writer. Maybe you are just starting out looking for gigs or record deals, and you need a manager willing to help build your band's career from the ground up. Check the Openness to Submissions Index on page 383.

For more information on how to read the listings, see A Sample Listing Decoded on page 11.

A SAMPLE LISTING DECODED
What do the little symbols at the beginning of the listing mean?

Those are called "icons," and they give you quick information about a listing with one glance. Here is a list of the icons and what they mean:

Getting Started

Openness to submissions

☐ means the company is open to beginners' submissions, regardless of past success

◐ means the company is mostly interested in previously published songwriters/well-established acts*, but will consider beginners

◒ these companies do not want submissions from beginners, only from previously published songwriters/well-established acts*

⦸ companies with this icon only accept material referred by a reputable industry source**

*   Well-established acts are those with a following, permanent gigs or previous record deal

** Reputable industry sources include managers, entertainment attorneys, performing rights organizations, etc.

Other icons

🍁 means the listing is Canadian

🌐 means the listing is based overseas (Europe, Britain, Australia, etc.)

Ⓝ indicates a listing is new to this edition

✅ means there has been a change in the contact information: contact name, phone number, fax, e-mail or Web site

🏆 is for companies who have won an industry award of some sort

🎬 shows a company places songs in films or television shows (excluding commercials)

EASY-TO-USE
REFERENCE
ICONS

DETAILED
SUBMISSION
GUIDELINES

INSIDER
ADVICE

TERMS OF
AGREEMENT

WHAT THEY'RE
LOOKING FOR

Ⓝ◐🎬🏆 **METAL BLADE RECORDS**
2828 Cochran St., Suite 302, Simi Valley CA 93065. (805)522-9111. Fax: (805)522-9380. E-mail: metalblade@metalblade.com. Website: www.metalblade.com. Record company. Estab. 1982. Releases 20 LPs, 2 EPs and 20 CDs/year. Pays negotiable royalty to artists on contract.
How to Contact Submit demo CD by mail. Unsolicited submissions are OK. CD with 3 songs. Does not return material. Responds in 3 months.
Music Mostly **heavy metal** and **industrial**; also **hardcore**, **gothic** and **noise**. Released "Gallery of Suicide," recorded by Cannibal Corpse; "Voo Doo," recorded by King Diamond; and "A Pleasant Shade of Gray," recorded by Fates Warning, all on Metal Blade Records. Other artists include As I Lay Dying, The Red Chord, The Black Dahlia Murder, and Unearth.
Tips "Metal Blade is known throughout the underground for quality metal-oriented acts."

Additional Resources

For More Info

Songwriter's Market lists music publishers, record companies, producers and managers (as well as advertising firms, play producers and classical performing arts organizations) along with specifications on how to submit your material to each. If you can't find a certain person or company you're interested in, there are other sources of information you can try.

The Recording Industry Sourcebook, an annual directory published by Norris-Whitney Communications, lists record companies, music publishers, producers and managers, as well as attorneys, publicity firms, media, manufacturers, distributors and recording studios around the U.S. Trade publications such as *Billboard* or *Variety*, available at most local libraries and bookstores, are great sources for up-to-date information. These periodicals list new companies as well as the artists, labels, producers and publishers for each song on the charts.

CD booklets and cassette j-cards can also be valuable sources of information, providing the name of the record company, publisher, producer and usually the manager of an artist or group. Use your imagination in your research and be creative—any contacts you make in the industry can only help your career as a songwriter. See Publications of Interest on page 340.

Demo Recordings

What Should I Know?

What is a "demo"?

The demo, shorthand for *demonstration recording*, is the most important part of your submission package. They are meant to give music industry professionals a way to hear all the elements of your song as clearly as possible so they can decide if it has commercial potential.

Should I send a cassette or a CD?

More and more music industry people want CDs, although the cassette is still commonly accepted. A few companies want demos sent on CD only. It's getting cheaper and easier all the time to burn recordings onto CDR ("CD-Recordable"), so it is worth the investment to buy a burner or borrow one. Other formats such as DAT ("Digital Audio Tape") are rarely requested.

What should I send if I'm seeking management?

Some companies want a video of an act performing their songs. Most want VHS format videocassettes. A few ask for video on DVD. Check with the companies for specific requirements.

How many songs should I send, and in what order and length?

Most music industry people agree that three songs is enough. Most music professionals are short on time, and if you can't catch their attention in three songs, your songs probably don't have hit potential. Also, put three *complete songs* on your demo, not just snippets. Make sure to put your best, most commercial song first. An up-tempo number is usually best. If you send a cassette, *put all the songs on one side of the cassette and cue the tape to the beginning of the first song so no time is wasted fast-forwarding or rewinding.*

Should I sing my own songs on my demo?

If you can't sing well, you may want to find someone who can. There are many places to check for singers and musicians, including songwriters organizations, music stores, and songwriting magazines. Some aspiring professional singers will sing on demos in exchange for a copy they can use as a demo to showcase their singing.

Should I use a professional demo service?

Many songwriters find professional demo services convenient if they don't have time or the resources to put together musicians on their own. For a fee, a demo service will produce your songs in their studio using in-house singers and musicians (this is pretty common in

Nashville). Many of these advertise in music magazines, songwriting newsletters and bulletin boards at music stores. Make sure to hear samples of work they've done in the past. Some are mail-order businesses—you send a rough tape of your song or the sheet music, and they produce and record a demo within a month or two. Be sure you find a service that will let you have some control over how the demo is produced, and tell them exactly how you want your song to sound. As with studios, shop around for a service that fits your needs and budget. (Some will charge as low as $300 for three songs, while others may go as high as $3,000 and boast a high-quality sound—shop around and use your best judgment!)

Should I buy equipment and record demos myself?

If you have the drive and focus to learn good recording technique, yes. If not, it might be easier to have someone else do it. Digital multi-track recorders are now easily available and within reasonable financial reach of many people. For performing songwriters in search of record deals, the actual sound of their recordings can often be an important part of their artistic concept. Having the "means of production" within their grasp can be crucial to artists pursuing the independent route. But, if you don't know how to use the equipment, it may be better to go into a professional studio.

How elaborate and full should the demo production be if I'm a non-performing songwriter?

Many companies in *Songwriter's Market* tell you what they prefer. If in doubt, contact them and ask. In general, country songs and pop ballads can often be demoed with just a vocal plus guitar or piano, although many songwriters in those genres still prefer to get a more complete recording with drums, guitars and other backing instruments. Up-tempo pop, rock and dance demos usually need a more full production.

What kind of production do I need if I'm a performing songwriter?

If you are a band or artist looking for a record deal, you will need a demo that is as fully produced as possible. Many singer/songwriters record their demos as if they were going to be released as an album. That way, if they don't get a deal, they can still release it on their own. Professionally pressed CDs are also now easily within reach of performing songwriters, and many companies offer graphic design services for a professional-looking product.

How Do I Submit My Demo?

Y ou have three basic options for submitting your songs: submitting by mail, submitting in person and submitting over the Internet (the newest and least widely accepted option at this time).

SUBMITTING BY MAIL

Should I call, write or e-mail first to ask for permission or submission requirements?

This is always a good idea, and many companies ask you to contact them first. If you call, be polite, brief and specific. If you send a letter, make sure it is typed and to the point. Include a typed SASE they can use to reply. If you send an e-mail, again be professional and to the point. Proofread your message before you send it, and then be patient. Give them some time to reply. Do not send out mass e-mails or otherwise spam their e-mail account.

What do I send with my demo?

Most companies have specific requirements, but here are some general pointers:

- Read the listing carefully and submit *exactly* what they ask for, in the exact way they describe. It's also a good idea to call first, just in case they've changed their submission policies.
- Listen to each demo to make sure they sound right and are in the right order (see Demo Recordings: What Should I Know? on page 13).
- If you use cassettes, make sure they are cued up to the beginning of the first song.
- Enclose a *brief*, typed cover letter to introduce yourself. Tell them what songs you are sending and why you are sending them. If you are pitching your songs to a particular artist, say so in the letter. If you are an artist/songwriter looking for a record deal, you should say so. Be specific.
- Include *typed* lyric sheets or lead sheets, if requested. Make sure your name, address and phone number are on each sheet.
- Neatly label each tape or CD with your name, address and phone number, along with the names of the songs in the order they appear on the recording.
- Include a SASE with sufficient postage and large enough to return all your materials. **Warning: Many companies do not return materials, so read each listing carefully!**
- If you submit to companies in other countries, include a self-addressed envelope (SAE) and International Reply Coupon (IRC), available at most post offices. Make sure the envelope is large enough to return all of your materials.
- Pack everything neatly. Neatly type or write the company's address and your return

Getting Started

Submission Mailing Pointers

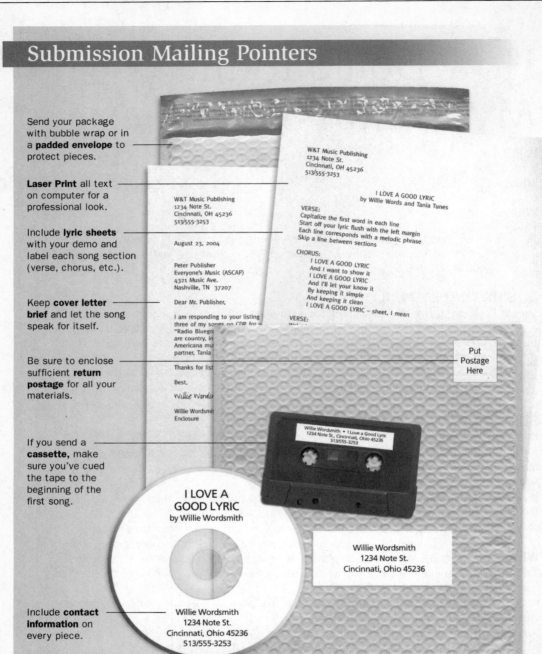

Send your package with bubble wrap or in a **padded envelope** to protect pieces.

Laser Print all text on computer for a professional look.

Include **lyric sheets** with your demo and label each song section (verse, chorus, etc.).

Keep **cover letter brief** and let the song speak for itself.

Be sure to enclose sufficient **return postage** for all your materials.

If you send a **cassette,** make sure you've cued the tape to the beginning of the first song.

Include **contact information** on every piece.

W&T Music Publishing
1234 Note St.
Cincinnati, OH 45236
513/555-3253

August 23, 2004

Peter Publisher
Everyone's Music (ASCAP)
4321 Music Ave.
Nashville, TN 37207

Dear Mr. Publisher:

I am responding to your listing
three of my songs on CDR for
"Radio Bluegra
are country, in
Americana mu
partner, Tania

Thanks for list

Best,

Willie Words

Willie Wordsmit
Enclosure

W&T Music Publishing
1234 Note St.
Cincinnati, OH 45236
513/555-3253

I LOVE A GOOD LYRIC
by Willie Words and Tania Tunes

VERSE:
Capitalize the first word in each line
Start off your lyric flush with the left margin
Each line corresponds with a melodic phrase
Skip a line between sections

CHORUS:
I LOVE A GOOD LYRIC
And I want to show it
I LOVE A GOOD LYRIC
And I'll let your know it
By keeping it simple
And keeping it clean
I LOVE A GOOD LYRIC – sheet, I mean

VERSE:

Put
Postage
Here

Willie Wordsmith • I Love a Good Lyric
1234 Note St., Cincinnati, Ohio 45236
513/555-3253

I LOVE A
GOOD LYRIC
by Willie Wordsmith

Willie Wordsmith
1234 Note St.
Cincinnati, Ohio 45236
513/555-3253

Willie Wordsmith
1234 Note St.
Cincinnati, Ohio 45236

address so they are clearly visible. Your package is the first impression a company has of you and your songs, so neatness counts!
- Mail first class. Stamp or write "First Class Mail" on the package and the SASE you enclose.
- **Do not use registered or certified mail unless requested!** Most companies will not accept or open demos sent by registered or certified mail for fear of lawsuits.
- Keep records of the dates, songs and companies you submit to.

Is it OK to send demos to more than one person or company at a time?
It is usually acceptable to make simultaneous submissions. One exception is when a publisher, artist or other industry professional asks to put your song "on hold."

What does it mean when a song is "on hold"?
This means they intend to record the song and don't want you to give the song to anyone else. This is not a guarantee, though. Your song may eventually be returned to you, even if it's been on hold for months. Or it may be recorded and included on the album. If either of these happens, you are free to pitch your song to other people again.

How can I protect myself from my song being put "on hold" indefinitely?
You can, and should, protect yourself. Establish a deadline for the person who asks for the hold (for example, "You can put my song on hold for [number of] months."), or modify the hold to specify you will still pitch the song to others but won't sign another deal without allowing the person with the song on hold to make you an offer. Once you sign a contract with a publisher, they have exclusive rights to your song and you may not pitch it to other would-be publishers.

SUBMITTING IN PERSON
Is a visit to New York, Nashville or Los Angeles to submit in person a good idea?
A trip to one of the major music hubs can be valuable if you are organized and prepared to make the most of it. You should have specific goals and set up appointments before you go. Some industry professionals are difficult to see and may not feel meeting out-of-town writers is a high priority. Others are more open and even encourage face-to-face meetings. By taking the time to travel, organize and schedule meetings, you can appear more professional than songwriters who submit blindly through the mail.

What should I take?
Take several copies of your demo and typed lyric sheets of each of your songs. More than one company you visit may ask you to leave a copy for them to review. You can expect occasionally to find a person has cancelled an appointment, but want you to leave a copy of your songs so they may listen and contact you later. (Never give someone the only or last copy of your demo if you absolutely want it returned, though.)

Where should I network while visiting?
Coordinate your trip with a music conference or make plans to visit ASCAP, BMI, or SESAC offices while you are there. For example, the South by Southwest Music Conference in Austin and the NSAI Spring Symposium often feature demo listening sessions, where industry professionals listen to demos submitted by songwriters attending the seminar. ASCAP, BMI, and SESAC also sometimes sponsor seminars or allow aspiring songwriters to make appointments with counselors who can give them solid advice.

How do I deal with rejection?

Many good songs have been rejected simply because they were not what the publisher or record company was looking for at that particular point. Do not take it personally. If few people like your songs, it does not mean they are not good. On the other hand, if you have a clear vision for what your particular songs are trying to get across, specific comments can also teach you a lot about whether your concept is coming across as you intended. If you hear the same criticisms of your songs over and over—for instance, the feel of the melody isn't right or the lyrics need work—give the advice serious thought. Listen carefully and use what the reviewers say constructively to improve your songs.

SUBMITTING OVER THE INTERNET

Is it OK to submit over the Internet?

It can be done, but it's not yet widely accepted. There can still be problems with audio file formats. Although e-mail is more common now if you look through the listings in *Songwriter's Market*, not all music companies are necessarily equipped with computers or Internet access sufficient to make the process easy. But it shows a lot of promise for the future. Web-based companies like Tonos.com or TAXI, among many others are making an effort to connect songwriters and industry professionals over the Internet. The Internet is proving important for networking. Tunesmith.net has extensive bulletin boards and allow members to post audio files of songs for critique. Stay tuned for future developments.

If I want to try submitting over the Internet, what should I do?

First, send an e-mail to confirm whether a music company is equipped to stream or download audio files properly (whether mp3 or real audio, etc.). If they do accept demos online, one strategy becoming common is build a Web site with audio files that can be streamed or downloaded. Then, when you have permission, send an e-mail with links to that Web site or to particular songs. All they have to do is click on the link and it launches their Web browser to the appropriate page. Do not try to send mp3s or other files as attachments. They are often too large for the free online e-mail accounts people commonly use, and they may be mistakenly erased as potential viruses.

How Do I Avoid the Rip-Offs?

The music industry has its share of dishonest, greedy people who will try to rip you off by appealing to your ambition, by stroking your ego, or by claiming special powers to make you successful—for a price, of course. Most of them use similar methods, and you can prevent a lot of heartbreak by learning to spot them and stay away.

What is a "song shark"?

"Song sharks," as they're called, prey on beginners—songwriters unfamiliar with how the music industry works and what the ethical standards are. Two general signs of a song shark are:

- Song sharks will take *any* songs—quality doesn't count.
- They're not concerned with future royalties, since they get their money up front from songwriters who think they're getting a great deal.

What are some of the more blatant rip-offs?

A request for money up front is the most common element. Song sharks may ask for money in the form of submission fees, an outright offer to publish your song for a fee or an offer to re-record your demo for a sometimes hefty price (with the implication that they will make your song wildly successful if you only pay to have it re-demoed in *their studio*). There are many variations on this theme.

If You Write Lyrics, But Not Music

- **You must find a collaborator.** The music business is looking for the complete package: music plus lyrics. If you don't write music, find a collaborator who does. The best way to find a collaborator is through songwriting organizations. Check the Organizations section (page 293) for songwriting groups near you.

- **Don't get ripped-off.** "Music mills" advertise in the back of magazines or solicit you through the mail. For a fee they will set your lyrics or poems to music. The rip-off is that they may use the same melody for hundreds of lyrics and poems, whether it sounds good or not. Publishers recognize one of these melodies as soon as they hear it.

Here is a list of rules that can help you avoid a lot of scams:

- **DO NOT SELL YOUR SONGS OUTRIGHT!** It's unethical for anyone to offer such a proposition. If your song becomes successful after you've sold it outright, you will never get royalties for it.
- **Never pay any sort of "submission fees," "review fees," "service fees," "filing fees," etc.** Reputable companies review material free of charge. If you encounter a company in this book who charges to submit, report them to the editor. If a company charges "only" $15 to submit your song, consider this: *if "only" 100 songwriters pay the $15, this company has made an extra $1,500 just for opening the mail!*
- **Never pay to have your songs published.** A reputable company interested in your songs assumes the responsibility and cost of promoting them, in hopes of realizing a profit once the songs are recorded and released. If they truly believe in your song, they will accept the costs involved.
- **Do not pay a company to pair you with a collaborator.** It's much better to contact a songwriting organization that offers collaboration services to their members.
- **Never pay to have your lyrics or poems set to music.** This is a classic rip-off. "Music mills"—for a price—may use the same melody for hundreds of lyrics and poems, whether it sounds good or not. Publishers recognize one of these melodies as soon as they hear it.
- **Avoid "pay-to-play" CD compilation deals.** It's totally unrealistic to expect this will open doors for you. These are mainly a money-maker for the music company. CDs are cheap to manufacture, so a company that charges $100 to include your recording on a CD is making a killing. They claim they send these CDs to radio stations, producers, etc., but they usually wind up in the trash or as drink coasters. Music industry professionals have no incentive to listen to them. Everybody on the CD paid to be included, so it's not like they were carefully screened for quality.
- **Avoid "songpluggers" who offer to "shop" your song for an upfront fee or retainer.** This practice is not appropriate for *Songwriter's Market* readers, many of whom are beginners and live away from major music centers like Nashville. Professional, established songwriters in Nashville are sometimes known to work on a fee basis with songpluggers they have gotten to know over many years, *but the practice is controversial even for professionals.* Also, the songpluggers used by established professionals are very selective about their clients and have their own reputation to uphold. Companies who offer you these services but barely know you or your work are to be avoided. Also, contracting a songplugger by long distance offers little or no accountability—you have no direct way of knowing what they're doing on your behalf.
- **Avoid paying a fee up front to have a publisher make a demo of your song.** Some publishers may take demo expenses out of your future royalties (a negotiable contract point usually meant to avoid endless demo sessions), but avoid paying up front for demo costs. Avoid situations where it is implied or expressed that a company will publish your song in return for you paying up front to use their demo services.
- **No record company should ask you to pay them or an associated company to make a demo.** The job of a record company is to make records and decide which artists to sign *after* listening to demo submissions.
- **Read all contracts carefully before signing.** And don't sign any contract you're unsure about or that you don't fully understand. It is well worth paying an attorney for the time it takes him to review a contract if you can avoid a bad situation that may cost you thousands of dollars.
- **Before entering a songwriting contest, read the rules carefully.** Be sure what you're

giving up in the way of entry fees, etc., is not more than what you stand to gain by winning the contest. See the Contests & Awards section on page 276.

- **Verify any situation about an individual or company if you have any doubts at all.** Contact the company's Performing Rights Society—ASCAP, BMI, SESAC, or SOCAN (in Canada). Check with the Better Business Bureau in the company's town, or contact the state attorney general's office. Contact professional organizations you're a member of and inquire about the reputation of the company.
- **If a record company or other company asks you to pay expenses up front, be careful.** Record producers commonly charge up front to produce an artist's album. Small indie labels sometimes ask a band to help with recording costs (but seek less control than a major label might). It's up to you to decide to whether or not it is a good idea. Talk to other artists who have signed similar contracts before you sign one yourself. Research companies to find out if they can deliver on their claims, and what kind of distribution they have. Visit their Web site, if they have one. Beware of any company that won't let you know what it has done in the past. If a company has had successes and good working relationships with artists, it should be happy to brag about them.

I noticed record producers charge to produce albums. Is this bad?

Not automatically. Just remember what your goals are. If you write songs, but do not sing or perform, you are looking for publishing opportunities with the producer instead of someone who can help you record an album or CD. If you are a performing artist or band, then you might be in the market to hire a producer, in which case you will most likely pay them up front (and possibly give them a share in royalties or publishing, depending on the specific deal you negotiate). For more information see the Record Producers section introduction on page 192 and Royalties: Where Does the Money Come From? on page 28.

How Do I File a Complaint?

Write to the *Songwriter's Market* editor at: 4700 E. Galbraith Rd., Cincinnati OH 45236. Include:

- A complete description of the situation, as best you can describe it.
- Copies of any materials a company may have sent you that we may keep on file.

If you encounter situations similar to any of the "song shark" scenarios described above, let us know about it.

Will it help me avoid rip-offs if I join a songwriting organization?

Yes. You will have access to a lot of good advice from a lot of experienced people. You will be able to research and compare notes, which will help you avoid a lot of pitfalls.

What should I know about contracts?

Negotiating a fair contract is important. You must protect yourself, and there are specific things you should look for in a contract (see What About Contracts? on page 36).

Are companies that offer demo services automatically bad?

No, but you are not obligated to make use of their services. Many music companies have their own or related recording studios, and with good recording equipment becoming so cheap and easy to use in recent years, a lot of them are struggling to stay afloat. This doesn't mean a company is necessarily trying to rip you off, but use your best judgment. In some cases, a company will submit a listing to *Songwriter's Market* for the wrong reasons—to pitch their demo services instead of finding songs to sign—in which case you should report them to the *Songwriter's Market* editor.

Submission Strategies

NON-PERFORMING SONGWRITERS

Here's a short list of avenues non-performing songwriters can pursue when submitting songs:

1. Submit to a music publisher. This is the obvious one. Look at the information under "Music" in the listing to see examples of a publisher's songs and the artists they've found cuts with. Do you recognize the songs? Have you heard of the artists? Who are the writers? Do they have cuts with artists you would like to get a song to?

2. Submit to a record company. Are the bands and artists on the record company's roster familiar? Do they tend to use outside songs on their albums? When pursuing this angle, it often helps to contact the record company first. Ask if they have a group or artist in development who needs material.

3. Submit to a record producer. Do the producer's credits in the listings show songs written by songwriters other than the artist? Does he produce name artists known for using outside material? Be aware that producers themselves often write with the artists, so your song might also be competing against the producer's songwriting.

4. Submit to an artist's manager. If an artist needs songs, their manager is a prime gateway for your song. Contact the manager and ask if he has an act in need of material.

5. Join a songwriting organization. Songwriting organizations are a good way to make contacts. You'll discover opportunities through the contacts you make that others might not hear about. Some organizations can put you in direct contact with publishers for song critique sessions. You can increase your chances of a hit by co-writing with other songwriters. Your songs will get better because of the feedback from other members.

6. Approach Performing Rights Organizations (PROs). PROs like ASCAP and BMI have writer relations representatives who can sometimes (if they think you're ready) give you a reference to a music company. This is one of the favored routes to success in the Nashville music scene.

PERFORMING SONGWRITERS

This is a bit more complicated, because there are a lot of different avenues available.

Finding a record deal.

This is often a performing songwriter's primary goal—to get a record deal and release an album. Here are some possible ways to approach it:

1. Approach a record company for a record deal. This is another obvious one. Independent labels will be a lot more approachable than major labels, who are usually deluged with demos. Independent labels give you more artistic freedom, while major labels will demand more compromise, especially if you do not have a previous track record. A compromise

Getting Started

between the two is to approach one of the "fake indie" labels owned by a major. You'll get more of the benefits of an indie, but with more of the resources and connections of a major label.

2. Approach a record producer for a development deal. Some producers sign artists, produce their album and develop them like a record company, and then approach major labels for distribution deals. This has advantages and drawbacks. For example, the producer gives you guidance and connections, but it can also be harder to get paid because you are signed to the producer and not the label.

3. Get a manager with connections. The right manager with the right connections can make all the difference in getting a record deal.

4. Ask a music publisher. Publishers are taking on more and more of a role of developing performing songwriters as artists. Many major publishers are sister companies to record labels and can shop you for a deal when they think you're ready. They do this in hopes of participating in the mechanical royalties from an album release, and these monies can be substantial when it's a major label release.

5. Approach an entertainment attorney. Entertainment attorneys are a must when it comes to negotiating record contracts, and some moonlight by helping artists make connections for record deals (they will get their cut, of course).

6. Approach PROs. ASCAP and BMI can counsel you on your career and possibly make a referral. They also commonly put on performance showcases where A&R ("artist and repertoire") people from record labels attend to check out new artists.

Finding a producer to help with your album

Independently minded performing songwriters often find they need help navigating the studio when it comes time to produce their own album. In this case, the producer often works for an upfront fee from the artist, for a percentage of the royalty when the album is released and sold (referred to as "points," as in "percentage points"), or a combination of both.

Things to keep in mind when submitting a demo to a producer on this basis:

1. Is the producer known for a particular genre or "sound"? Many producers have a signature sound to their studio productions and are often connected to specific genres. Phil Spector had the "Wall of Sound." Bob Rock pioneered a glossy metal sound for Metallica and The Cult. Daniel Lanois and Brian Eno are famous for the atmospheres they created on albums by U2. Look at your favorite CDs to see who produced. Use these as touchstones when approaching producers to see if they are on your wavelength.

2. What role does a particular producer like to take in the studio? The "Tips" section of *Songwriter's Market* Record Producers listings often have notes from the producer about how they like to work with performing songwriters in the studio. Some work closely as a partner with the artist on developing arrangements and coaching performances. Some prefer final authority on creative decisions. Think carefully about what kind of working relationship you want.

Finding a manager

Many performing songwriters eventually find it necessary to find a manager to help with developing their careers and finding gigs. Some things to keep in mind when looking:

1. Does the manager work with artists in my genre of music? A manager who typically works with punk rock bands may not have as many connections useful to an aspiring country singer-songwriter. A manager who mainly works with gospel artists might not know what to do with a hedonistic rock band.

2. How big is the manager's agency? If a manager is working with multiple acts, but has a small (or no) staff, you might not get the attention you want. Some of the listings have information in the heading about the agency's staff size.

3. Does the manager work with acts from my region? You can check the Geographic Index on page 392 to check for management agencies located near your area. Many of the listings also have information in their headings provided by the companies describing whether they work with regional acts only or artists from any region.

4. Does the manager work with name acts? A manager with famous clients could work wonders for your career. Or you could get lost in the shuffle. Use your best judgment when sizing up a potential manager and be clear with yourself about the kind of relationship you would like to have and the level of attention you want for your career.

5. If I'm a beginner, will the manager work with me? Look in the Openness to Submissions Index on page 383 to find companies open to beginners. Some may suggest extensive changes to your music or image. On the other hand, you may have a strong vision of what you want to do and need a manager who will work with you to achieve that vision instead of changing you around. Decide for yourself how much you are willing to compromise in good faith.

Remember that a relationship between you and a manager is a two-way street. You will have to earn each other's trust and be clear about your goals for mutual success.

Quiz: Are You Professional?

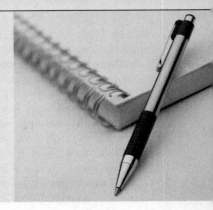

Okay, everybody! Take out your submission package and let's take a look. Hmm . . . very interesting. I think you're well on your way, but you should probably change a few things.

We asked record companies, music publishers and record producers, "What do songwriters do in correspondence with your company (by phone, mail or demo) that screams 'amateur'?" Take this quiz and find out how professional you appear to those on the receiving end of your submission. The following are common mistakes songwriters make all the time. They may seem petty, but, really, do you want to give someone an excuse not to listen to your demo? Check off the transgressions you have committed.

BY MAIL YOU SENT:

☑ anything handwritten (lyrics, cover letters, labels for cassettes). Today there is no excuse for handwritten materials. Take advantage of your local library's typewriters or businesses that charge by the hour to use a computer. And don't even think about using notebook paper.

☑ materials without a contact name *and* phone number. Put this information on *everything*.

☑ lyrics only. Music companies want music and words. See the If You Write Lyrics, But Not Music sidebar on page 19.

☑ insufficient return postage, an envelope too small to return materials, no SASE at all, or a "certified mail" package. If you want materials returned, don't expect the company to send it back on their dime with their envelope—give them what they need. Certified mail is unnecessary and annoying; first class will suffice.

☑ long-winded, over-hyped cover letters, or no cover letter at all. Companies don't need (or want) to hear your life story, how many instruments you play, how many songs you've written, how talented you are or how all your songs are sure-fire hits. Briefly explain why you are sending the songs (e.g., your desire to have them published) and let the songs speak for themselves. Double check your spelling too.

☑ over-packaged materials. Do not use paper towels, napkins, foil or a mountain of tape to package your submission. Make the investment in bubble wrap or padded envelopes.

☑ photos of your parents or children. As much as you love them, your family's pictures or letters of recommendation won't increase your chances of success (unless your family is employed by a major music company).

☑ songs in the style the company doesn't want. Do not "shotgun" your submissions. Read the listings carefully to see if they want your style of music.

YOU CALLED THE CONTACT PERSON:

☑ to check on the submission only a couple days after it was received. Read the listings to see how soon (or if) they report back on submissions. Call them only after that time has elapsed. If they are interested, they will find a way to contact you.

☑ excessively. It's important to be proactive, but check yourself. Make sure you have given them enough time to respond before you call again. Calling every week is inappropriate.

☑ armed with an angry or aggressive tone of voice. A bad attitude will get you nowhere.

WITH THE DEMO YOU PROVIDED:

☑ no lyric sheet. A typed sheet of lyrics for each song is required.

☑ poor vocals and instrumentation. Spending a little extra for professionals can make all the difference.

☑ a poor-quality cassette. The tape should be new and have a brand name.

☑ long intros. Don't waste time—get to the heart of the song.

☑ buried vocals. Those vocals should be out front and clear as a bell.

☑ recordings of sneezes or coughs. Yuck.

SCORING

If you checked 1-3: Congratulations! You're well within the professional parameters. Remedy the unprofessional deeds you're guilty of and send out more packages.

If you checked 4 or more: Whoa! Overhaul your package, let someone check it over, and then fire away with those impeccably professional submissions!

Royalties

Where Does the Money Come From?

NON-PERFORMING SONGWRITERS

How do songwriters make money?

The quick answer is that songwriters make money through rights available to them through the copyright laws. For more detail, keep reading and see the article What About Copyright? on page 32.

What specific rights make money for songwriters?

There are two primary ways songwriters earn money on their songs: Performance Royalties and Mechanical Royalties.

What is a performance royalty?

When you hear a song on the radio, on television, in the elevator, in a restaurant, etc. the songwriter receives royalties, called "Performance Royalties." Performing Rights Organizations (ASCAP, BMI and SESAC in the U.S.A.) collect payment from radio stations, television, etc. and distribute those payments to songwriters (see below).

What is a mechanical royalty?

When a record company puts a song onto a CD, cassette, etc. and distributes copies for sale, they owe a royalty payment to the songwriter for each copy they press of the album. It is called a "mechanical royalty" because of the mechanical process used to mass produce a copy of a CD, cassette or sheet music. The payment is small per song (see the "Royalty Provisions" subhead of the Basic Song Contract Pointers sidebar on page 38), but the earnings can add up and reach massive proportions for songs appearing on successful major label albums. ****Note: This royalty is totally different from the artist royalty on the retail price of the album.****

Who collects the money for performance and mechanical royalties?

Performing Rights Organizations collect performance royalties. There are three organizations that collect performance royalties: ASCAP, BMI, and SESAC. These organizations arose many years ago when songwriters and music publishers gathered together to press for their rights and improve their ability to collect fees for the use of their songs. ASCAP, BMI, and SESAC collect fees for the use of songs and then pass along the money to their member songwriters and music publishers.

Mechanical rights organizations collect mechanical royalties. There are three organizations that collect mechanical royalties: The Harry Fox Agency (HFA), The American Mechanical Rights Agency (AMRA), and The Songwriters Guild of America (SGA). These three organizations collect mechanical royalties from record companies of all sizes—major labels, mid-size and independents—and pass the royalties along to member music publishers and songwriters.

MUSIC PUBLISHING ROYALTIES

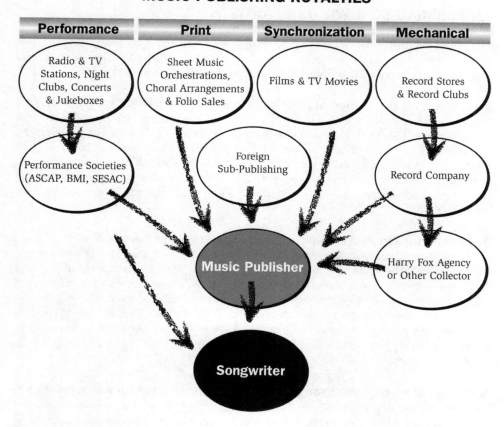

| Performance | Print | Synchronization | Mechanical |

- Radio & TV Stations, Night Clubs, Concerts & Jukeboxes
- Sheet Music Orchestrations, Choral Arrangements & Folio Sales
- Films & TV Movies
- Record Stores & Record Clubs
- Performance Societies (ASCAP, BMI, SESAC)
- Foreign Sub-Publishing
- Record Company
- Music Publisher
- Harry Fox Agency or Other Collector
- Songwriter

Music Biz Basics

How do songwriters hook up with this system to earn royalties?

For **Performance Royalties**, individual songwriters **affiliate** with a Performing Rights Organization of their choice, and register their songs in the PRO database. Each PRO has a slightly different method of calculating payment, different ownership, and different membership structure, so choosing a PRO is an individual choice. Once a songwriter is affiliated and has registered their songs, the PROs then collect fees as described above and issue a check to the songwriter.

For **Mechanical Royalties**, three different things can happen:

1. The songwriter is signed to a publisher that is affiliated with The Harry Fox Agency. The Harry Fox Agency collects the mechanical royalties and passes them along to the publisher. The publisher then passes these along to the songwriter within 30 days. This case usually happens when a songwriter is signed to a major publisher and has a song on a major label album release.

2. The songwriter is not signed to a publisher and owns exclusive rights to his songs, and so works with AMRA or The Songwriters Guild of America, who cut a check directly to the songwriter instead of passing them to the publisher first.

3. They are signed to a publisher, but the songs are being released on albums by independent labels. In this case, the songwriter often works with AMRA since they have a focus on the independent music publishing market.

PERFORMING SONGWRITERS/ARTISTS
How do performing songwriters make money?

Performing songwriters and artists (if they write their own songs) make money just like non-performing songwriters, as described above, but they also make money through royalties made on the retail price of an album when it is sold online, in a store, etc.

What about all the stories of performing songwriters getting into bad deals?

The stories are generally true, but if they're smart, performing songwriters usually can hold on to the money they would be owed as songwriters (performing and mechanical royalties). But when it comes to retail sale royalties, all they will usually see is an "advance"—essentially a loan—which must then be paid off from record sales. You will not see a royalty check on retail sales until you're advance is paid off. If you are given a $600,000 advance, you will have to pay back the record company $600,000 out of your sales royalties before you see any more money.

Do performing songwriters and artists get to keep the advance?

Not really. If you have a manager who has gotten you a record deal, he will take his cut. You will probably be required in the contract to pay for the producer and studio time to make the album. Often the producer will take a percentage of subsequent royalties from album sales, which comes out of your pocket. Then there are also music video costs, promotion to radio stations, tour support, paying sidemen, etc. Just about anything you can think of is eventually paid for out of your advance or out of sales royalties. There are also deductions to royalties usually built in to record company contracts that make it harder to earn out an advance.

What should a performing songwriter wanting to sign with a major label do?

Their best option is to negotiate a fair contract, get as big of an advance as possible, and then manage that advance money the best they can. A good contract will keep the songwriting royalties described above completely separate from the flow of sales royalties, and will also cut down on the number of royalty deductions the record company builds into the contract. And because of the difficulty in earning out any size advance or auditing the record company, it makes sense to get as much cash up front as you can, then to manage that as best you can. You will need a good lawyer.

RECORD COMPANIES, PRODUCERS AND MANAGERS & BOOKING AGENTS
How do music publishers make money?

A publisher works as a songwriter's agent, looks for profitable commercial uses for the songs he represents, and then takes a percentage of the profits. This is typically 50% of all earning from a particular song—often referred to as the *publisher's share*. A successful publisher stays in contact with several A&R reps, finding out what upcoming projects are in need of new material, and whether any songs he represents will be appropriate.

How do record companies make money?

Record companies primarily make their money from profits made selling CDs, cassettes, DVDs, etc. Record companies keep most of the profit after subtracting manufacturing costs, royalties to recording artists, distribution fees and the costs of promoting songs to radio (which for major labels can reach up to $300,000 per song). Record companies also usually have music publishing divisions that make money performing all the functions of publishers.

How do record producers make money?

Producers mostly make their money by charging a flat fee up front to helm a recording project, by sharing in the royalties from album sales, or both. A small independent producer might charge $10,000 (or sometimes less) up front to produce a small indie band, while a "name" producer such as Bob Rock, who regularly works with major label bands, might charge $300,000. Either of these might also take a share in sales royalties, referred to as "points"— as in "percentage points." A producer might say, "I'll produce you for $10,000 and 2 points." If an artist is getting a 15% royalty an album sales, then two of those percentage points will go to the producer instead. Producers also make money by co-writing with the artists to get publishing royalties, or they may ask for part of the publishing from songs written by outside songwriters.

How do managers make money?

Most managers make money by taking a percentage commission of their clients' income, usually 10-25%. If a touring band finishes a show and makes a $2,000 profit, a manager on 15% commission would get $300. If an artist gets a $40,000 advance from a mid-size label, the manager would get $6,000. Whether an artist's songwriting income is included in the manager's commission comes down to negotiation. *The commission should give the manager incentive to make things happen for your career, so avoid paying flat fees up front.*

What About Copyright?

How am I protected by the copyright laws?

Copyright protection applies to your song the instant you it them down in fixed form—a recording, sheet music, lead sheet, etc. This protection lasts for your lifetime plus 70 years (or the lifetime of the last surviving writer, if you co-wrote the song with somebody else). When you prepare demos, place notification of copyright on all copies of your song—the lyric sheets, lead sheets and labels for cassettes, CDs, etc. The notice is simply the word "copyright" or the symbol © followed by the year the song was created (or published) and your name: © 2007 by John Q. Songwriter.

What parts of a song are protected by copyright?

Traditionally, the melody line and the lyrics are eligible for copyright. Period. Chords and rhythms are virtually never protected. An incredibly original arrangement can sometimes qualify, but the original copyright owner of the song must agree to it (and they usually don't). Sound recordings can also be copyrighted, but this applies strictly to the actual sounds on the recording, not the song itself (this copyright is usually owned by record companies).

What songs are not protected?

Song titles or mere ideas for music and lyrics cannot be copyrighted. Very old songs in the "public domain" are not protected. You could quote a melody from a Bach piece, but you could not then stop someone else from quoting the same melody in their song.

When would I lose or have to share the copyright?

If you *collaborate* with other writers, they are assumed to have equal interests unless you state some other arrangement, in writing. If you write under a *work-for-hire* arrangement, the company or person who hired you to write the song then owns the copyright. Sometimes your spouse may automatically be granted an interest in your copyright as part of their *spousal rights*, which might then become important if you got divorced.

Should I register my copyright?

Registering your copyright with the Library of Congress gives the best possible protection. Registration establishes a public record of your copyright—even though a song is legally protected whether or not it is registered—and could prove useful in any future court cases involving the song. Registration also entitles you to a potentially greater settlement in a copyright infringement lawsuit.

How do I register my song?

To register your song, request government form PA from the Copyright Office. Call the 24-hour hotline at (202)707-9100 and leave your name and address on the messaging system. Once you receive the PA form, you must return it, along with a registration fee and a CD (or tape) and lead sheet of your song. Send these to the Register of Copyrights, Copyright Office, Library of Congress, Washington DC 20559. It may take several months to receive your certificate of registration from the Copyright Office, but your songs are protected from the date of creation (the date of registration will reflect the date you applied). For more information, call the Copyright Office's Public Information Office at (202)707-3000 or visit their Web site at www.copyright.gov.

Government Resources

For More Info

The Library of Congress's copyright website is your best source for current, complete information on the subject of copyright. Not only can you learn all you could possibly wish to know about intellectual property rights and U.S. copyright law (the section of the U.S. Code dealing with copyright is reprinted there in its entirety), but you can also download copyright forms directly from the site. The site also includes links to other copyright-related web pages, many of which will be of interest to songwriters, including ASCAP, BMI, SESAC, and the Harry Fox Agency. Check it out at **www.copyright.gov**.

How likely is it that someone will try to steal my song?

Copyright infringement is very rare. But, if you ever feel that one of your songs has been stolen—that someone has unlawfully infringed on your copyright—you must prove that you created the work and that the person you are suing had access to your song. Copyright registration is the best proof of a date of creation. You *must* have your copyright registered in order to file a lawsuit. Also, it's helpful if you keep your rough drafts and revisions of songs, either on paper or on tape.

Why did song sharks start soliciting me after I registered my song?

This is one potential, unintended consequence of registering your song with the Library of Congress. The copyright indexes are a public record of your songwriting, and song sharks often search the copyright indexes and mail solicitations to songwriters who live out away from major music centers such as Nashville. They figure these songwriters don't know any better and are easy prey. *Do not allow this possibility to stop you from registering your songs!* Just be aware, educate yourself, and then throw the song sharks' mailings in the trash.

What if I mail a tape to myself to get a postmark date on a sealed envelope?

The "poor man's copyright" has not stood up in court, and is not an acceptable substitute for registering your song. If you feel it's important to shore up your copyright, register it with the Library of Congress.

Career Songwriting

What Should I Know?

What career options are open to songwriters who do not perform?

The possibilities range from a beginning songwriter living away from a music center like Nashville who lands an occasional single-song publishing deal, to a staff songwriter signed to a major publishing company. And then there are songwriters like Desmond Child who operate independently, have developed a lot of connections, work with numerous artists, and have set up their own independent publishing operations.

What is "single-song" songwriting about?

In this case, a songwriter submits songs to many different companies. One or two songs gain interest from different publishers, and the songwriter signs separate contracts for each song with each publisher. The songwriter can then pitch other songs to other publishers. In Nashville, for instance, a single-song contract is usually the first taste of success for an aspiring songwriter on his way up the ladder. Success of this sort can induce a songwriter to move to a music center like Nashville (if they haven't already), and is a big boost for a struggling songwriter already living there. A series of single-song contracts often signals a songwriters' maturing skill and marketability.

What is a "staff songwriter"?

A staff songwriter usually works for a major publisher and receives a monthly stipend as an advance against the royalties he is likely to earn for the publisher. The music publisher has exclusive rights to everything the songwriter writes while signed to the company. The publisher also works actively on the writer's behalf to hook him or her up with co-writers and other opportunities. A staff songwriting position is highly treasured by many because it offers a steady income, and in Nashville is a sign the songwriter has "arrived."

What comes after the staff songwriting position?

Songwriters who go to the next level have a significant reputation for their ability to write hit songs. Famous artists seek them out, and they often write actively in several markets at once. They often write on assignment for film and television, and commonly keep their own publishing companies to maximize their income.

As my career grows what should I do about keeping track of expenses, etc.?

You should keep a ledger or notebook with records on all financial transactions related to your songwriting—royalty checks, demo costs, office supplies, postage, travel expenses, dues to organizations, class and workshop fees, plus any publications you purchase pertaining to songwriting. You may also want a separate checking account devoted to your songwriting activities. This will make record keeping easier and help to establish your identity as a business for tax purposes.

What should I know about taxes related to songwriting income?

Any royalties you receive will not reflect taxes or any other mandatory deductions. It is your responsibility to keep track of income and file the correct tax forms. For specific information, contact the IRS or talk to an accountant who serves music industry clients.

What About Contracts?

CO-WRITING
What kind of agreements do I need with co-writers?

You may need to sign a legal agreement between you and a co-writer to establish percentages you will each receive of the writer's royalties. You will also have to iron out what you will do if another person, such as an artist, wants to change your song and receive credit as a co-writer. For example, in the event, a major artist wants to cut your song for her album—but also wants to rewrite some lyrics and take a share of the publishing—you and your co-writer need to agree whether it is better to get a song on an album that might sell millions (and make a lot of money) or pass on it because you don't want to give up credit. The situation could be uncomfortable if you are not in sync on the issue.

When do I need a lawyer to look over agreements?

When it comes to doing business with a publisher, producer, or record company, you should always have the contract reviewed by a knowledgeable entertainment attorney. As long as the issues at stake are simple, the co-writers respect each other, and they discuss their business philosophies before writing a song together, they can probably write up an agreement without the aid of a lawyer.

SINGLE-SONG CONTRACTS
What is a single-song contract?

A music publisher offers a single-song contract when he wants to sign one or more of your songs, but doesn't want to hire you as a staff songwriter. You assign your rights to a particular song to the publisher for an agreed-upon number of years, so that he may represent the song and find uses profitable for both of you. This is a common contract and will probably be the first you encounter in your songwriting career.

What basic elements should every single-song contract contain?

Every contract should have the publisher's name, the writer's name, the song's title, the date, and the purpose of the agreement. The songwriter also declares the song is a original work and he is creator of the work. The contract *must* specify the royalties the songwriter will earn from various uses of the song, including performance, mechanical, print and synchronization royalties.

How should the royalties usually be divided in the contract?

The songwriter should receive no less than 50% of the income his song generates. That means the songwriter and publisher split the total royalties 50/50. The songwriter's half is

When Does 50% Equal 100%?

NOTE: the publisher's and songwriter's share of the income are sometimes referred to as each being 100%—for 200% total! You might hear someone say, "I'll take 100% of the publisher's share." **Do not be needlessly confused!** If the numbers confuse you, ask for the terms to be clarified.

Tip

called the "writer's share" and the publisher's half is called the "publisher's share." If there is more than one songwriter, the songwriters split the writer's share. Sometimes, successful songwriters will bargain for a percentage of the publisher's share, negotiating what is basically a co-publishing agreement. For a visual explanation of how royalties are collected and flow to the songwriter, see the chart called Music Publishing Royalties on page 29.

What should the contract say about a "reversion clause"?

Songwriters should always negotiate for a "reversion clause," which returns all rights back to the songwriter if some provision of the contract is not met. Most reversion clauses give a publisher a set amount of time (usually one or two years) to work the song and make money with it. If the publisher can't get the song recorded and released during the agreed-upon time period, the songwriter can then take his song to another publisher. The danger of *not* getting some sort of reversion clause is that you could wind up with a publisher sitting on your song for the entire life-plus-70-years term of the copyright—which may as well be forever.

Is a reversion clause difficult to get?

Some publishers agree to it, and figure if they can't get any action with the song in the first year or two, they're not likely to ever have much luck with it. Other publishers may be reluctant to agree to a reversion clause. They may invest a lot of time and money in demoing and pitching a song to artists and want to keep working at it for a longer period of time. Or, for example, a producer might put a song on hold for a while and then go into a lengthy recording project. A year can easily go by before the artist or producer decides which songs to release as singles. This means you may have to agree to a longer time period, be flexible and trust the publisher has your best mutual interests in mind. Use your best judgment.

What other basic issues should be covered by a single-song contract?

The contract should also address these issues:

- will an advance be paid, and if so, how much will the advance be?
- when will royalties be paid (annually or semiannually)?
- who will pay for demos—the publisher, songwriter or both?
- how will lawsuits against copyright infringement be handled, including the cost of lawsuits?
- will the publisher have the right to sell its interest in the song to another publisher without the songwriter's consent?
- does the publisher have the right to make changes in a song, or approve changes by someone else, without the songwriter's consent?
- the songwriter should have the right to audit the publisher's books if he feels it is necessary and gives the publisher reasonable notice.

Music Biz Basics

Basic Song Contract Pointers

Tips

The following list, taken from a Songwriters Guild of America publication, enumerates the basic features of an acceptable songwriting contract:

1. **Work for Hire.** When you receive a contract covering just one composition, you should make sure the phrases "employment for hire" and "exclusive writer agreement" are *not* included. Also, there should be no options for future songs.

2. **Performing Rights Affiliation.** If you previously signed publishing contracts, you should be affiliated with either ASCAP, BMI, or SESAC. All performance royalties must be received directly by you from your performing rights organization and this should be written into your contract.

3. **Reversion Clause.** The contract should include a provision that if the publisher does not secure a release of a commercial sound recording within a specified time (one year, two years, etc.), the contract can be terminated by you.

4. **Changes in the Composition.** If the contract includes a provision that the publisher can change the title, lyrics or music, this should be amended so that only with your consent can such changes be made.

5. **Royalty Provisions.** You should receive fifty percent (50%) of all publisher's income on all licenses issued. If the publisher prints and sells his own sheet music, your royalty should be ten percent (10%) of the wholesale selling price. The royalty should not be stated in the contract as a flat rate ($.05, $.07, etc.).

6. **Negotiable Deductions.** Ideally, demos and all other expenses of publication should be paid 100% by the publisher. The only allowable fee is for the Harry Fox Agency collection fee, whereby the writer pays one half of the amount charged to the publisher for mechanical rights. The current mechanical royalty collected by the Harry Fox Agency is 9.1 cents per cut for songs under 5 minutes; and 1.75 cents per minute for songs over 5 minutes.

7. **Royalty Statements and Audit Provision.** Once the song is recorded, you are entitled to receive royalty statements at least once every six months. In addition, an audit provision with no time restriction should be included in every contract.

8. **Writer's Credit.** The publisher should make sure that you receive proper credit on all uses of the composition.

9. **Arbitration.** In order to avoid large legal fees in case of a dispute with your publisher, the contract should include an arbitration clause.

10. **Future Uses.** Any use not specifically covered by the contract should be retained by the writer to be negotiated as it comes up.

Where else can I go for advice on contracts?

The Songwriters Guild of America has drawn up a Popular Songwriter's Contract which it believes to be the best minimum songwriter contract available (see the Ten Basic Points Your Contract Should Include sidebar above). The Guild will send a copy of the contract at no charge to any interested songwriter upon request (see the Songwriters Guild of America listing in the Organizations section on page 293). SGA will also review—free of charge—any contract offered to its members, and will check it for fairness and completeness. Also see these two books published by Writer's Digest Books: *The Craft and Business of Songwriting*, by John Braheny and *The New Songwriter's Guide to Music Publishing, 3rd Edition*, by Randy Poe.

Getting Ready to Face the Industry

by John Braheny

Now that you understand how the business operates, you're ready to venture out and start making some contacts. Even when you feel physically prepared, like a soldier going into battle, you need to prepare yourself mentally. No matter which approach you take to get your songs heard and no matter whom you decide to contact, knowing what to expect will give you a lot more confidence. There is a professional way to approach the industry and the more professionally you present yourself, the more professionally you will be treated.

ETHICS IN THE BIZ

Discussions about ethics in the music business frequently expose a great variety of feelings about it. A business like this that seems so blatant about its powers, pleasures, and extravagance draws many people who are greedy for those most visible things. I always loved that great Hunter S. Thompson quote, "The music business is a cruel and shallow money trench, a long plastic hallway where thieves and pimps run free, and good men die like dogs. There's also a negative side." Now *that's* a cynic! I'm not there yet, but I've come close a time or two.

As a creative industry, it also draws very creative *business* people (for better or worse). Most songwriters and musicians, though they're certainly enticed by the high stakes involved, are much more wrapped up in the music itself and seem to want to keep "The Biz" at a distance. Managers, attorneys, and others on the business end will say, "You shouldn't worry about anything but the music. Leave all the business stuff to us." It's exactly what a lot of musicians want to hear. They'll say, "I don't want to even know about that! Just go ahead and do it!" Both lines are candidates for "famous last words."

I can't count the number of times I've heard musicians and writers say, after a sour business deal, "I should have checked him out before I signed . . ." or "I should have seen an attorney . . ." or "But the vibes really felt right! He told me we'd split the publishing; he'd record masters; he'd get me a record deal; we'd get paid right after the gig; we'd split the advance 50/50 . . ."—and a list of other famous music biz lies. But it wasn't *written* in the contracts.

In many of those cases, I'm sure the businesspeople were quite well intentioned and, at the time, really wanted to do what they promised. (But I'm the kind of guy who'll give anybody the benefit of the doubt at least once.) Others chronically take advantage of people and earn bad reputations. Save yourself a lot of grief by doing some research and talking to others who have dealt with them.

• **Don't feel obligated to work with the first people who show interest in you.** Even when the voice of that poor, trampled part of you says, "Oh, thank you, thank you! I'm *so* glad you like me—show me where to sign." Get a grip on yourself! This may indeed be someone you'll want to work with, but if you go into a deal with that frame of mind, you're begging to be victimized. Calm down, check him out, and don't sign anything without legal advice.

• **Make sure there's a "performance clause" in the contract,** which states that if the terms of the contract are not fulfilled within X amount of time or in X manner, the contract becomes void. This can quite literally save you years of your creative productivity. Without a performance clause, it's possible for someone to pick up one-year options for five or more years (whatever's in the contract) without doing anything he's supposed to do. Meanwhile, someone else may want to sign you but can't without paying some exorbitant amount of money to buy you out of the deal. According to you, you were ripped off. According to him, he made a good business deal. He recognized good talent, got you to sign, and made some bucks. That's his gig. You may not consider him to be ethical, but you *did* sign the contract.

• **Remember, *they* work for you. You don't work for *them*.** Of course, not everyone does business this way. There are lots of straightforward, honest, up-front people in the business who believe that, in the long run, a good reputation will make them more successful than a bad one. No rigid set of ethics governs practices in the music business short of what's actually illegal. Some industry people follow "situational ethics" and follow the credo, "it seemed like the right thing to do at the time." Some subscribe to the basic greed philosophy that "anything goes if it gets me what I want." Others hold the "everybody else is doing it" and "do it unto others before they do it unto you" philosophies. You're likely to run into any of these in *any* business, and the best protection you can have is to get to know enough about the business that you have some idea about whether you're hearing straight talk or jive. If you turn your business over to someone, you should know enough about what he ought to be doing to know whether or not he *is* getting it done.

• **The type of people you associate with in the industry can have a great effect on your reputation, peace of mind, and creative future.** Take it very seriously and find good people to work with. Journalist Paul Lawrence once asked Ken Kravitz of Hit City West recording studio if he felt that "nice guys finish last." "Maybe nice guys sometimes finish last in the rat race," Ken answered, "but that's not the only race there is."

EGO

Get a grip on your ego and leave it at the door when you go in to show your wares. As you approach industry pros, keep in mind that though your songs may be very personal and expose delicate parts of your being, people in the business must look at them as a *product* or as *content*. They, in turn, must try to sell your product to someone else on the merits of its commercial potential alone. It's understandably difficult for a writer to keep from feeling that it's her who's being rejected, rather than the song. Some of the most powerful songs written are very personal statements and confessional revelations that make the writer's ego vulnerable to destruction when rejected. Don't stop writing those kinds of songs, and don't let your ego get in the way of criticism.

Before you can successfully pitch your songs to the industry, you need to be a good self-critic. Those of you who write songs that you hope will be recorded by other artists will need to be a bit more self-critical than independent artists and bands whose performance and sound are a more important part of the mixture of ingredients that makes for their success. But the quality of your songs is still a major ingredient. There's a point while writing a song where you need to step away from it and try to look at the song as though you were another person—a publisher, a recording artist, a radio program director, or J.Q. Public. Sometimes, in order to get that perspective, writers put a song away for a few days or weeks so they can later get a fresh look at it. If you're a solo artist or in a band, sometimes an important part of the process is to play the song live a few times.

Ask yourself the same questions that, consciously or unconsciously, others will ask. Is this a song about an event or feeling that many people can relate to? Will the people who most likely relate to the lyric be in a certain age group? Will the music appeal to the same age group? Can the lyrics be understood by everyone? Is there a better, more powerful, more graphic way to say what I've said? Is every line of the song important? Is this a song that can compete with the best songs that I hear on the radio (not the worst songs)?

Doing this kind of self-critique will help you in important ways. It will help you write better songs. It will help you choose from among your songs the ones most commercially viable and therefore the least subject to rejection. It will help you develop that professional detachment to look at your own work more objectively, like someone who makes omelets or clothes or anything else. In accomplishing that, you'll find it easier to approach buyers and to welcome their positive and negative comments. They, in turn, will find it easier to work with you.

Play your songs for friends before approaching the buyers. Even if they can't or won't give you honest criticism, it gives you some instant perspective. I've written songs I was perfectly happy with until I read the lyric or sang the song to someone else and it suddenly sounded trite or unclear. Back to the drawing board!

Put yourself in the industry professionals' shoes. It also helps in dealing with rejection if you can sympathize with the publisher or producer's side of the business. It does neither of you any good if he publishes a song he's not enthusiastic about or sees little commercial potential in. He'll have to invest in promoting it and put up with your continued questions about what he's done with your song. He'll have to keep telling you nothing's happened or avoid taking your calls altogether. So if he can't get really excited about your song as a product, he *has* to reject it.

You shouldn't want someone to publish your song unless she's very enthusiastic about it. When *she* gets rejections on your song, you want her to retain enough enthusiasm for the song to continue to pitch it. Several publishers have told me that they had songs in their catalogue that had been rejected over a hundred times! In spite of that, they continued pitching them because they totally believed in those songs.

Sometimes songs or styles are simply ahead of their time. In the late 1970s, for instance, it was common for Los Angeles writers (the Eagles, for example) to get rejections because their "country" songs were "too country" for L.A. and "too pop" for Nashville. There have been black artists whose songs were too rock for R&B airplay (like Prince). Who in Nashville could have predicted Big & Rich? Times and radio formats change but sometimes not until a previously unclassifiable artist becomes a major money-maker.

There are more reasons why you're more likely to be in the wrong place at the wrong time with the wrong song than vice versa. Probably 99 percent of those reasons have nothing to do with you personally, but with the marketplace, your product, and the buyer's ability and inclination to deal with it. Actors say it's like auditioning—"Sorry, you're too: tall/short/ethnic/blonde/etc." and generally, "You just don't have the 'look' we need."

It's a certainty that no matter how good your songs are, they *will* be rejected. If you don't adopt some attitudes that help you to deal with that rejection, you can get too discouraged to persevere, and if you quit, nobody's hurt but you. There will always be more writers out there to take your place.

DEALING WITH REJECTION

It might comfort you to know that, at all levels, a substantial part of what happens in the music industry involves rejection—rejection of songs, rejection of finished master recordings that people have sunk thousands of dollars into, rejection of record company product by radio stations, and, ultimately, rejection of individual records or styles by consumers.

Every day, for hundreds of different reasons, people in every facet of the industry are facing rejection. They may accept it as inevitable—an everyday occurrence, but it is never easy for anyone to deal with. Egos are bent, reputations are questioned, jobs are lost, and friendships are damaged or ended. There are hundreds of rejection stories of major songs and artists. Elton John was turned down by 22 record companies. The Beatles and Billy Joel were each turned down early in their careers by every major record company. Mariah Carey was paid millions of dollars to *leave* her label after a failed film and album but she came back big time. The list goes on and on and continues today. I would venture to say that every major artist has been rejected numerous times before attaining any success. In fact, even after an artist is successful and subsequently goes through an unproductive period, he may again face those rejections. There's even an industry joke about being fortunate to be turned down by certain record execs, because they've rejected so many successful artists that you should worry if they *like you*.

For songwriters it's particularly difficult, though, because you're usually creating in isolation, and it's difficult to find good critical feedback. Often your only artistic validation comes from friends and family who are so excited that you're doing something *they* don't have the talent for that the last thing they want is to criticize your efforts. They'll be supportive and keep you in that bubble until you smash up against the "real world" of the music business. Songs that your friends liked because they saw you reflected in them (and they like you), songs that audiences seemed to like ("They clapped, didn't they?") are meeting with "Sorry, not strong enough/not appropriate/no hook," and other standard lines.

There *are* some ways that you can deal with rejection that will keep you from totally losing your self-esteem.

• **Cultivate a support group.** Yes, there is life outside the music business. Sometimes you can get in a rut, take the whole thing far too seriously, and fail to take comfort in your family and friends who love you whether you're successful in a music career or not. Cultivate friends outside the music business so you can tap into some other worlds and keep yourself from getting too isolated and tunnel-visioned. That cross-fertilization of experiences and ideas is also creatively stimulating. It also helps to hang out with other songwriters who understand what you're going through and can help you get back up when you're down. Stay away from those who will trivialize even your smallest successes or surround you with that "ain't the biz awful" vibe. You don't need negativity.

• **Develop short-term payoffs.** It usually takes a very long time for anything to happen in the music business. So that big reward—the recording, the record deal, the hit, the royalty check, the film score—that's somewhere in the unseen future isn't always enough to make you feel like a valuable human being today. Yes, you should be able to get that by just writing a good song and feeling good about it. But after you've written the song, you're likely to set another goal for it that requires the validation of others and a dependence on a timetable and circumstances you don't have much control over. So it helps to be actively involved in hobbies, sports, another job, volunteering for a cause, or even something as mundane as cleaning the garage or organizing your CDs that gives you a sense of accomplishment and immediate positive payoff.

• **Don't let rejection stop you from writing.** There's a particular song you keep pitching and it keeps getting turned down. You've already rewritten it twice. You're now so totally obsessed with getting it published or produced that you stop writing altogether. A little self-destructive voice inside you says, "This is the best thing I've ever done. If I can't get anything happening with this one, I might as well hang it up because if they don't like this, they won't like anything." So you stop writing "just 'til I get this one cut." Meanwhile, you're forgetting several important things. The next song you write may be much better than this one, or at least more interesting to the industry. You won't become a better writer, or a more successful writer, unless you continue writing. A song you haven't written yet may be just the song that gets everybody interested in everything else you've done. Just the process of writing can make you feel good about yourself. If you're also a performer, work on getting some more gigs. Doing a great show will give you some instant gratification.

- **Stay healthy.** A depressed body begets a depressed mind. Nothing like a decent diet and a good physical workout to help you get rid of those pent-up frustrations.
- **Only the "yes" is important.** There is an old line that salesmen use to keep themselves going in the face of rejection: It's only another "no" on the way to "yes." The "no's aren't important.
- **Honestly assess your strengths and schedule time** to discipline yourself to work on the areas you could improve. A schedule keeps you looking forward and gives you the feeling that you're actually accomplishing something, no matter how small, to keep you moving ahead.
- **Have additional plans of attack** so if you strike out on one, you're ready to try something else right away and you don't have time to feel sorry for yourself. My wife, JoAnn, worked for several years in Creative Development at Walt Disney Imagineering, Disney's theme park think-tank. A common problem among the designers there was a sort of depression after a big project was completed. The company helped to counteract this by giving them information about the next project so they had something to look forward to after the current project ended. Bands often experience that same "down" after a tour.

SURVIVAL

Getting through the door involves continuously and consistently making contacts and being able to support yourself while you're doing it. If you're a writer who isn't working as a performer, don't assume you'll be making it "any day now" and borrow from friends and family to survive until your big break comes.

Get a day job so you can spend your evenings writing with others who have day jobs, and attend industry events, workshops, and clubs. And just as important, get a day job so you'll be able to afford to eat and pay rent, and to embark on a songwriting career. You'll need money for demos and other songwriting expenses, as well.

Try to get a job in some aspect of the industry. It's tough because everyone else wants those jobs, too. Don't be afraid or too proud to start on the bottom rung. If you have good typing or other office skills, get work with temporary employment agencies that specialize in the entertainment industry.

MARKETING YOUR LYRICS

The situation for lyricists in the marketplace has its positives and negatives. On the plus side, it's necessary for you to collaborate to have a suitable melody for your words. I know that doesn't really sound like a plus, but if you're a prolific lyricist, finding several collaborators represents an opportunity to produce a great number of finished songs. Those who insist on writing both lyrics and music, in my experience, are rarely so prolific. As a lyricist, you can develop your lyric skills in a variety of styles without needing to restrict yourself for marketing purposes, as many writer/performers do.

On the minus side, it's very difficult for you to get a staff-writing deal. You really have to be an extraordinary lyricist with some commercial success under your belt to get an exclusive staff-writing situation. *And it's virtually impossible to make a single-song deal on a lyric with no melody*. There are audio-visual firms that commission lyricists to write material for them. Check with local firms to see what their needs are, and find additional contacts listed in *Songwriter's Market*.

So, outside of that, what can a lyricist do? Find collaborators. Pay particular attention to political strategy. Find co-writers who are further ahead in their careers than you and still moving forward. Among collaborators to consider are new bands that are getting some industry attention or at least drawing great audiences locally. Good lead singers and keyboard players are usually worth considering because they're more likely to write exciting melodies that may need equally exciting lyrics. Find other writers who are starting to get their songs recorded or those who are already on staff at a publishing company. Find writers in strong positions to make contacts with artists, such as studio musicians and recording engineers. With all the above you have the advantage of writing with people who could get good demos made at a reasonable cost, a big plus for you.

If those situations are just not available to you, look for skilled musicians in bands, college music departments, churches, theaters, and so on.

If you speak another language fluently, gather samples of your song translations from, and into, the language. Contact publishers both here and in the countries where the language is spoken. They can be found in directories like *Songwriter's Market* and *Billboard International Buyer's Guide*. The Spanish-speaking market, for example, is enormous. I have a client who's written several English lyrics for a wonderful South American composer.

Make contact with as many potential co-writers as possible and enter lyric writing contests. *American Songwriter* magazine (www.americansongwriter.com) has a lyric contest every two months and they publish the winners in the magazine. Put notices in music stores, schools, and magazines and music Web sites. I'm proud to be a mentor for Just Plain Folks (www.jpfolks.com), a major online music community with over 50,000 members. It's free to join. They have a songwriters' forum where members can post notices that they're looking for collaborators and post a sample of their lyrics. Let everyone know what you're looking for and you'll find that your opportunities will grow quickly.

Caution: Do not send your lyrics to companies who advertise in magazines for "song poems" and ask you to pay a fee to have them write melodies to your lyrics.

ORGANIZE YOUR SONG SHOPPING

If you plan to actively "plug" your own songs, it's important to keep track of what's going on. You'll want to be as professional as the successful music publishers who are out there pitching their writers' songs to some of your same contacts. You'll need to develop a list of producers and recording artists for whom your songs may be appropriate. Keep a good database. Print a hard copy file on everything in case you forget to back up your computer and lose your database. Every time you make contact, you can note who he's producing, what type of material he needs for the upcoming LP, where he's recording, what kind of demos he prefers, whether he usually asks for a percentage of publishing, and so on. If you're also shopping for publishers, keep a similar file for them.

SETTING UP YOUR DATABASE

Your database should have plenty of information on artists, producers, managers, and collaborators—whatever will help you to better work for them, pitch to them, or write for them.

The information you keep on an artist should include vocal range, what style he or she prefers, and personal idiosyncrasies like "hates sexist songs" or "positive lyrics only." This information can be obtained from the producer, consumer and trade magazines, tip sheets, radio and TV interviews, or, if you're one of the more fortunate ones, from the artist personally.

Submission Software Packages

Here are good computer programs available for keeping track of songs, writers, contacts, casting, contracts, forms, and more. Go to their Web sites and check them out in detail. The inefficiency of file card systems doesn't quite make sense anymore when computers can run software that gives you the kind of comprehensive control over your business that these programs do.

SongTracker
Working Solutionz Software
www.bizbasics.net
111 Main St., Simi Valley, CA 93065
Tel: (805) 522-2170; Fax: (805) 527-7787
E-mail: sales@bizbasics.net

The original, started in 1975 and still going strong. SongTracker 3.0 manages the business side of your songwriting or music-industry company with an economical and easy-to-use office database system, designed in FileMaker Pro 6 (version 8 in the works) for Macintosh (OSX compatible) and Windows. SongTracker is a comprehensive contact manager that automates and prepares copyrights, ASCAP/BMI registration forms, DAT/CD/cassette inserts, contracts, songplugging correspondence, and more. Digital sounds may easily be stored or played with a mouse click. An optional "PRO" version offers your network of coworkers a set of sophisticated management/tracking modules for the "contract," "licensing," "administration," and "royalty" aspects of your publishing or record company needs. Over 130 reports provide powerful music industry information. SongTracker 3.0 is $249; SongTracker PRO 3.0 is $798.

Music Publisher
YEAH! Solutions
www.yeahsolutions.com
P.O. Box 163507, Austin, TX 78716
Tel: (512) 347-9324 or 1-800-593-9324; Fax: (512) 347-9325

The high-end Music Publisher software suite is for Windows only. It has features for A&R, business affairs, copyright, licensing, royalties, and sub-publishing, all for approximately $2,000. (With support packages it would be about $3,000.)

The Music Review
Network Marketing, Inc.
www.musreview.com/musicdata.html
P.O. Box 41635, Nashville, TN 37204-1635
Tel: (615) 599-5793

"The Music Industry Search Engine." If you want to promote your CD project, here's a series of databases that that you can download to your system. They say they update daily. Radio Station Data Base has over 15,000 stations for $139.95; Distributors has 1,500 plus distributors for $79.95; Retailers, Book Stores is $89.95; Booking Agents has 2,000 plus listings for $79.95; and access to All Data Bases is $269.95. Explore this site. It's good for research.

It's smart to keep a record in the "notes" field of your database of personal items about the producer (or anyone else), such as "plays golf," "anti-nuke activist," "just had a baby," "going to England in August," and so forth. This type of information is useful in all businesses where personal contact is important. It allows you an instant recap when you call someone or set up a meeting, it gives you an idea for opening a conversation to break the ice, and it lets him know that you're concerned about him as a person. It doesn't take the place of having good songs, though, since many producers have little time for "small talk" and are best served by a brief presentation of your material. However, it can create a better climate for you to get feedback on your songs and help you develop as both a writer and publisher.

After every meeting or phone call, make notes regarding the outcome, such as "Loved 'Don't Take That Away,' doesn't feel it's right for [artist's name] but wants to keep demo for future reference—remind him," "Didn't like 'Do It Again' but maybe if the hook were stronger, re-write," or "Will be producing (artist's name) in September—start writing."

Set up file folders (yes, it *is* a good idea to keep hard copies, even if you have a database that you back up frequently) with the name of each song you're working on, one song per folder (alphabetical by title, if you have several songs). Each folder will contain:

- **The lyric sheets and lead sheets for that song.** If you keep your rough drafts and rewrites, mark them accordingly, so you don't send out the unfinished versions by mistake!
- **The names, phone numbers, and addresses of each co-writer** on that song *and* their performing rights affiliation (BMI, ASCAP, or SESAC).
- **The names, addresses, and phone numbers of any co-publishers on that song for reference.**
- **Photocopies or printouts of any correspondence that pertain to that song.** If a letter you receive mentions more than one of your songs, make a photocopy for each respective file.
- **Photocopies or printouts of any contracts or legal documents that pertain to that song,** for example, a co-writer's agreement, a co-publisher's agreement, or an assignment of copyright agreement. You don't want any unpleasant surprises looming over your future about anyone who has ties to your song without your knowledge.
- **The copyright registration certificate** (or the letter saying you've sent for it), or any forms from other song protection services.
- **The performing rights clearance forms** (BMI, ASCAP, or SESAC) and any correspondence with them.
- **Any correspondence or forms from the Harry Fox Agency** or other agency collecting your mechanical royalties (or reports from the record company about these).

The value of these files will become apparent after you've called about 30 producers and are preparing for another call or visit when you discover you can't remember whether it was producer X or Y who already "passed" on the song you want to present.

Aside from the obvious value in being able to keep track of what you have or haven't done with a song, this organizational process is psychologically valuable in helping you view your songs as products in the marketplace. It takes a little of the edge off rejection by keeping you constantly involved in pitching your songs to many industry people on an ongoing basis.

- **Keep your CD copies well labeled with the song titles on each.** Once more, don't forget to put your name, address, and phone number on the CD, the insert, and your lyric sheets. Have everything ready so you don't need to delay if someone asks you for a copy.
- **It's also a good idea to keep a small notebook** with you (or a PDA handheld such as Palm Pilot, Handspring, or BlackBerry) at all times so you can jot down any info you pick up "on the street." The notebook is better than little scraps of paper or matchbook covers

because they don't get lost. The street information you pick up is usually about who's recording now, a new producer with an unknown act who might give you the opportunity to get in on the ground floor, or a valuable Web site or service.

• **Always remember that this is a "people" business.** As in most other businesses, maintaining your personal relationships, networking for new contacts, taking advantage of your memberships in organizations that can put you in touch with the industry, doing favors for your colleagues, researching the trade magazines, and being ready immediately to take advantage of opportunities are all things that will contribute to your success.

The Staff Writer Contract

by Randy Poe

The *staff writer contract* (also referred to as an *exclusive contract*) is an agreement in which the writer is signed exclusively to a particular publishing company. Staff writer contracts are usually offered when a publisher believes, based on a writer's past success, that the songwriter's talents warrant a deal granting the publisher the rights to all of the songs written by the writer during the term of the contract.

Sometimes these contracts are offered even when a writer's track record consists of only one or two recorded songs. In fact, this is usually the best time (from the publisher's point of view) to get a songwriter to sign such a deal. A songwriter with no previous success and a handful of songs might be considered too much of a risk by most publishers. A writer with several hits under her belt would demand a large weekly advance and a contract heavily in her favor. However, a writer with only a cut or two to her name is the perfect type for a publisher to approach with an offer of a staff writer agreement.

A songwriter who has a staff writer contract with a publisher is like an artist contracted to a particular record label. As long as the artist is signed to that label, she can't go out and make a record for a rival company.

ADVANCES

One of the major differences between the single-song contract and the staff writer contract is the amount of advance money involved and the manner in which the advance is paid. When a writer signs a single-song contract, she is paid a one-time recoupable advance. Advances are paid to the staff writer weekly, monthly, or (in rare instances) quarterly. A staff writer can sometimes draw, weekly, an amount equal to the one-time advance for a single-song contract. (But it should be noted that the weekly or monthly advances paid to a staff writer are recoupable, just as is the advance paid under the terms of a single-song contract.) The weekly advance paid to a staff writer is similar to the weekly draws paid to salespeople against commissions on future sales. The amount of the songwriter's weekly draw (or advance) will usually depend on the writer's (or the writer's lawyer's) negotiating power.

For example, a nonperforming songwriter with a minimal number of recorded songs generally has very little negotiating power. She is probably looking for a publisher willing to sign her to a staff writer agreement for a few hundred dollars a week so that she can make ends meet for the duration of the agreement while she writes full-time.

On the other hand, a writer who also has a recording contract will be offered a very high advance (potentially thousands of dollars per week). The publishing company knows that it has an excellent chance of recouping the advance and making a profit from an agreement with a writer/performer, since the writer is already planning to release an album filled entirely with her own songs.

Somewhere in between is the writer/performer who hasn't yet acquired a recording contract. Music publishing is no longer just a matter of finding a great song and trying to get it recorded. Granted, this is still an important part of the business, especially in Nashville. However, many music publishers (including those in Nashville) are on the lookout for the songwriter/performer who can be taken into the recording studio, where professional artist demos or even finished masters of the songwriter's original material can be made. The music publisher can then pitch the finished product to record labels in an attempt to turn the performing songwriter into a recording act. Thus, the publisher will often sign the writer/artist to a staff writer contract and attempt to get a recording contract for her so that the publisher will, once again, be in a position to reap a profit from the situation.

Publishers are almost always open to signing a writer who has a built-in guarantee that her songs will be recorded. This guarantee can come in the form of a signed or soon-to-be-signed recording contract, but a songwriter who is also a record producer with the power to get her own songs cut also carries a guarantee. Of course, as I said earlier, writers in these positions can demand a great deal of money and very favorable contract terms. They are also, in many cases, able to demand that all of the money they expect to receive during the term of the agreement be paid up front—an enviable situation to be in. (As we will see, writers in such powerful positions are much more likely to sign co-publishing or administration agreements than staff writer agreements.)

TERM OF THE STAFF WRITER CONTRACT

There are generally three types of terms included in most staff writer agreements. The first of these three is the term of the contract itself. This is usually a one-year term with a specific series of one-year options. For example, a contract might call for a one-year deal with three one-year options, which means the publisher has the option to decide if she wishes to continue her relationship with the writer at the end of each year, for a maximum total contractual term of four years (the original one-year term plus the three options).

The second type of term is the length of time the publisher will retain ownership of the copyrights acquired during the term of the staff writer contract. In some cases this will be the same as in a single-song contract (approximately 35 years). In many modern-day staff writer agreements, publishers agree to shorter terms of five to 25 years. At the end of this term, the copyrights revert to the writer, who can sign a new deal with the publisher, assign the copyrights to another publisher, or assign the copyrights to her own publishing company.

The third term is the amount of time the publisher is allowed to try to get the songs in question recorded. Often this term will be the length of the staff writer agreement plus anywhere from one to five years. If there are songs that remain unrecorded after that time, many staff writer agreements allow the writer to "buy back" those copyrights for the amount of any unrecouped advances and the costs of the demos of the unrecorded songs.

WORKS MADE FOR HIRE

A work made for hire is "a work prepared by an employee within the scope of his or her employment . . . ." Some publishers consider songs written by a staff writer to be works made for hire, and therefore claim actual authorship of the work as the employer under the copyright law. These publishers' staff writer agreements usually state that all songs written during the term of the agreement will be considered works made for hire. Despite the fact that the copyright law says the employer will be considered the author of a work made for hire, the publisher will usually agree to credit the writer in the appropriate instances and allow the writer to receive the usual writer's share of all types of royalties. However, the copyright doesn't revert to the writer at the end of 35 years, since the copyright law clearly states that the employer is considered to be the author.

A songwriter who is offered a staff writer agreement should always have such language removed from the agreement. In fact, the writer should ask that the contract specifically state that any songs written during the term of the contract are not works made for hire.

OTHER DEAL POINTS COMMON TO THE STAFF WRITER CONTRACT

Most of the other topics covered in the staff writer contract are similar to those in a single-song contract. A couple of other items common to the staff writer agreement are: (1) a statement of the specific number of songs required to be written, and (2) inclusion of back catalog.

1. A staff writer deal will usually require that the writer turn over to the publisher a certain number of acceptable songs each year. The number of songs will vary, depending on the writer. However, the number of songs the writer agrees to turn out may affect the amount of advance money she is offered. Also, it's important to note that the concept of writing a certain number of songs isn't as straightforward as it might seem.

If a writer agrees to write 20 songs a year, she is agreeing that her share of the writing will total 20 complete songs. In other words, if that writer composes the melody to 20 songs, but someone else writes the lyrics, the contracted songwriter has only written 20 half-songs, or the equivalent of 10 complete songs. She will have to write either 20 more melodies or 10 more complete songs—or some combination of the two—so that the total amount of songs for the year will equal 20 complete songs.

You may also have noticed that I specified that a songwriter is expected to turn in a certain amount of *acceptable* songs each year. What this means is that the songs must be deemed acceptable *by the publisher*. If a writer submits a song the publisher considers too weak to exploit, the writer will not be able to count it against the total number of songs required in her contract. Of course, the writer who is also a recording artist is an exception to this rule. If she records the song and it's released on an album, it will obviously count in the total number of songs, no matter how bad the publisher might think it is.

2. The other topic common to staff writer agreements is the writer's back catalog. These are songs written prior to the signing of the staff writer contract. Often a writer will agree to include these titles in the contract if they are available and if they will count against the total number of songs required by the agreement. However, the writer obviously can't agree to include songs that are already signed to another publisher. Also, if the writer owns the publishing rights to a song that has already been successfully recorded, she is not likely to want to give up that song to another publisher.

THE *RECORDED AND RELEASE* COMMITMENT

One of the most complicated and tempting conditions that many publishers include in their staff writer agreements is the awkwardly named *recorded and release* commitment.

In fact, it's so complex that only a very good entertainment lawyer could possibly explain it. That being the case, here's attorney Jeffrey S. Sacharow's breakdown of precisely what this clause entails, and why you as a songwriter should be careful if a publisher asks you to sign an agreement containing *recorded and release* commitment language.

One way that publishers structure song delivery requirements under exclusive songwriter agreements is to provide for a *recorded and release* commitment. The *recorded and release* commitment is typically used by publishers when signing writer/producers or other songwriters who are not themselves recording artists.

A recorded and release commitment obligates the writer to deliver to the publisher an agreed-upon number of musical compositions that will be recorded and commercially released nationally by a major record company.

Since whether a record ends up being released is largely out of your (and your publisher's) control—and getting others to record your songs is usually a Herculean feat—most writers who have publishing deals containing release commitments do not guarantee the release of each of the songs they are required to deliver. A typical delivery requirement might be 10 whole songs, of which four or five have to be recorded and commercially released.

Publishers usually base the advances they are willing to pay you, in large part, on an estimate of what they think they will earn from your songs. Therefore, the more songs that you are willing to commit to being recorded and released, the higher your advance will likely be. Now, before you think, *Heck! I'll agree to 20 songs being released if I can get that big check*, know that most publishers will not require or accept a completely unrealistic release commitment.

Now, this all seems easy, right? No sweat. You can easily crank out 10 super smashes each year that anyone in her right mind would want to record. Not so fast. Even if you could write amazing songs each day, all day, getting them to count as part of your release commitment is difficult.

Most publishers will only count your songs as one full released song under certain conditions.

1. You must be the only writer of that song. If you are not the only writer of that song, most publishers will count the song as a partial song in proportion to your writer interest in that song. So, for example, if you have a five-song release commitment and you usually write with one other person, you will have to release 10 of those co-written songs to fulfill your release commitment.

2. The song has to be contained on an album that is released throughout the United States by a so-called major record company. Again, this is not something in your control. Even if an artist signed to a major record deal agrees to record your song, there is no guarantee that the song will actually make the album, or that the album will ever be released.

3. The major record company must actually pay the publisher a full mechanical royalty rate. The latter requirement seems especially easy, but it is not. Various factors, including samples and controlled composition provisions, often reduce the mechanical royalty rate payable for the use of a particular song.

Now, after reading all this, you are probably totally discouraged and thinking to yourself, *Wait a minute. This is dang near impossible. Even if I can write all those amazing songs under the pressure of an agreement that requires me to write those songs, what's the point? There is no way I can control which songs get cut or even released.* You're right. You can't. But if you want the big (or bigger) advances, you are going to have to be willing to take the risk that you will be able to meet your release commitment. Be cautious, however, in determining what you realistically will be able to accomplish and what you agree to. If you cannot fulfill your commitment in the time period required under your publishing agreement, one of the remedies typically available to the publisher is to place you in what will seem like an indefinite limbo: They can extend the term of their agreement with you-with no further obligation to pay you any additional advances-until you have met your release commitment (which means, among other things, that you cannot write for any other publisher during this period of time).

Breaking in From Anywhere

by Brian Austin Whitney

There was a time when the standard advice someone would give a songwriter was to move to one of the big three music cities to pursue their career. Though there are still some advantages to living in Nashville, Los Angeles or New York City, (as well as other music centers such as Memphis, Boston, Atlanta, Miami, Minneapolis, Austin, Chicago, Detroit, or Seattle), as technology and communication tools progress, there are many successful strategies to build your network and find success no matter where you live.

BREAKING IN FROM ANYWHERE

It's clear that the big three music centers offer advantages (and a few disadvantages) over other places to live in the U.S. and Canada. But with the advent of the Internet and the digital music boom, you can successfully get your start no matter where you live.

Next, we'll discuss eight important strategies, resources, and techniques to use no matter where you live.

PRO and major organization offices

If you live in or near a town that has a Performance Rights Organization office (check the Web for a complete list), you should make appointments to meet with a writer relations representative. This will typically be a relaxed and friendly chat with a rep who can often offer you feedback on a sample of your material, as well as offer ideas and suggestions where you can find resources to develop your skills, or if they feel you are ready, help you find people who might be interested in what you write. There's an endless debate about which PRO is the best in the U.S. (it's obviously not a factor in countries where there is only one organization to choose from) but rather than delve into that, I strongly recommend that you visit with representatives in person and get a feel for who you think is the best fit for what you do and what you want. Face to face meetings are always better than simple second hand opinion.

If you live in a city where a major organization in the music industry has offices or is headquartered, find out if you can visit and talk to staff members in person. This isn't always possible (especially for Internet-based groups) but it's always worth asking

BRIAN AUSTIN WHITNEY is the founder of the Just Plain Folks Music Organization. Starting with 60 members in 1998, JPF has grown to become the largest grassroots music organization in the world with 50,000 members in over 100 countries. For more info on JPF, check their listing in the 2007 Songwriters Market.

about. If you can visit and get to know staff members directly, it will always give you an advantage both with that organization as well as putting you in the loop with the others they often do business with. Though it's common for large organizations to have offices in music centers, you'll also find them located all over the U.S. and Canada, sometimes in non-music centers.

Publishers, labels and producers

It's long been a rite of passage for songwriters to trek to music centers to meet with publishers, especially in Nashville. If you live near a city with active music publishers in your genre, I highly recommend you call and set up appointments to meet with them. There's nothing more helpful than a friendly publisher who will take a little time to give honest feedback and suggestions on your material and where you are in your career and talent level. It's always important to be professional, show up on time, have multiple copies of your material that you can leave with them if requested, and that you keep a very open mind to the feedback you will receive. It won't always be positive, but even top-level professionals get negative feedback from honest publishers on their material in many cases. The pros know how to take that feedback and use it productively. It will never be productive to argue or try to explain away a weakness that has been identified. In fact, it's the quickest way to get a friendly publisher to avoid you like the plague the next time.

If you don't live in a music center, you may be surprised to still find a small number of active music publishers in your town, or a town nearby. Do a search (*Songwriter's Market* is a good start) and find anyone located within a reasonable drive. Set up appointments in advance (that is always better than walking in unannounced) and you might be surprised how welcoming publisher in less busy music cities will be. Don't assume that because you don't live in the "big three" music cities, there isn't plenty of music business going on in your town.

Depending on the genre of music you write, it can also be worthwhile to check out the label and producer scene in your town. There is life beyond country music if you're a non-performing songwriter, but you have to go to the people who need what you do. If you write R&B or rap lyrics, for example, finding a hot producer who likes your writing can be a gigantic connection, since these genres of music are driven by producers who often write or co-write the material themselves for the artists they produce. How do you find producers? Aside from the standard Web searches and questions to PRO's, check out recording studios, labels, hot music clubs (if they do dance music, for example) and other places where music heavy in production is performed. Few beginning songwriters are savvy enough to reach out to these resources, so you might find a more receptive audience than you expect simply based on the novelty of your efforts. The less beaten path is often the best one to take if you want to cut through the masses.

Local organizations, chapters and open mics

Some large organizations have local chapters where members can meet and network. The two largest in this area are the Nashville Songwriters Association International and Just Plain Folks. Both organizations have information on their Web sites about where they have local chapters. There are often chapters even in smaller cities, so it's worth checking out. In the case of JPF, anyone can start a chapter with as little as ten interested individuals. NSAI is more specifically songwriter oriented, and they also have more requirements to start a regional workshop (which is their term for local chapters). In some cities, members from both groups may be involved with both, and both organizations welcome all genres and all levels of ability. If there isn't a chapter of either near you, it's well worth considering starting your own.

You should also check out all the local organizations that already exist. I travel North America a great deal and it's rare to visit any average or larger sized city without one or more local music organizations. These are usually similar to the chapters mentioned above, but are simply run by and for the locals. You should get involved and become well known in your town as a mover and shaker. Helping out with a local organization and being a resource for others always puts you in the know. What better position can you be in?

There are very few towns in North America without at least one open mic. Most writers assume this is the domain of the performing artist, but that is shortsighted. Instead, it is a fertile meeting place of musicians and fellow writers (who may also be performers) you need to know. It's been proven over and over that writers as well as performers often rise in success alongside their peers, rather than making a jump directly from obscurity to the top ranks of their profession. A healthy local network, no matter where it is located, exponentially increases everyone's contacts, connections and opportunities. Working together with your peers really works. Since open mics are the places people go to get started if they are performers, if you're getting started as a writer, it's the place for you to be as well. Even advanced writers may find some great new talent who would be perfect to record their songs. It's always better to catch a rising star on the way up than to travel to a music center and beg them for attention once they are famous.

Internet resources and tools

Songwriters working today have a great advantage over their brethren from any other era to date. The Internet alone has done more to open up opportunities for songwriters than any other invention since the advent of recording. Beyond just being a place to buy and sell music, it's truly shrunk the entire world within reach from any computer terminal in your home, office, or even your lap. Now you can learn how to write songs, you can find like-minded collaborators, you can get feedback on your work from around the world, and if you're so inclined, you can post and market the results of your work for the world to hear. Most importantly, it's a quick and efficient communication tool that allows you to make progress at lightning speed no matter what you're trying to do.

Some of the tools at your disposal:

E-mail lists of all your contacts. Regular communication with your growing network of friends, collaborators, business contacts, and online resources is as simple as a click. Instead of trying to manage a big pile of business cards or hand scribbled mailing addresses, you can just update your e-mail list, contact them instantly any time you need and follow up better than before. E-mail is as important to songwriters today as the telephone was 10 years ago. If you aren't comfortable with e-mail and Web sites, you need to learn. It's as critical as any other songwriting tool you'll ever use. If you aren't currently computer savvy, have a friend help you sign up for one of the many free e-mail services such as hotmail.com or yahoo.com and you can send and receive e-mails from libraries and schools around the world even without your own computer.

Search Engines. The Internet has made it easier than ever to do background checks on companies or individuals who want you to conduct business with them. Google.com is the king of all search engines today. A quick search on Google might save you from years of misery by learning that someone is not who they say they are, or that they've ripped off hundreds of other songwriters before you. There are more scams out there than ever before (a downside of the Internet) but if you use due diligence, you should

Inside the "Big Three" Music Centers

We consulted with some well-known educators in the "big three" cities to get their take on the advantages to living in a well-established music center.

NASHVILLE

The king of songwriting meccas has long been Nashville. With its concentrated Music Row neighborhood, the long tradition of educational efforts by groups like the Nashville Songwriters Association International, and the continuing opportunities for non-performing songwriters, it's still the place to be in terms of songwriting. We asked two of our favorite Nashvillians—Sara Light, hit songwriter and co-founder of SongU.-com, and Mike Dunbar, a long time educator and session player—to give us the scoop on what makes Nashville a bit different than other cities for songwriters.

Sara Light: "The one big advantage to living in any music city, especially Nashville, is the serendipitous encounters that can create immediate results. Just today I spoke with an aspiring songwriter here who mentioned she was eating lunch at a local shop and bumped into a well-known writer and struck up a conversation. Before lunch was over, she was invited to play a gig with him and has a co-writing appointment scheduled for the next week. A lot of deals happen and a lot of songs get recorded simply because someone literally bumped into someone at the right moment. These opportunities and face to face meetings with someone who might not return your phone calls normally is a benefit you won't find living outside of Nashville or other leading music cities."

Mike Dunbar: "You'll find the majority of major release songwriters either living full time in Nashville or visiting frequently enough that they might as well be. Songs are rarely cut through A&R departments or by being pitched face to face. Mostly, songs are brought into an office and placed in the "right" basket which only a songwriter who has an existing relationship with the office recognizes. Gatekeepers and decision makers often prefer to listen to songs alone, usually in their cars. Developing songwriters are well served by living here or visiting periodically so they can spend time at writer's nights, hangouts and offices to network and develop relationships. A lot of co-writing goes on which serves as a stepping stone to working with more successful writers. It's very rare for a complete outsider to get a cut simply via a publisher or agent. At the very least, they'll need to develop some type of relationship with the locals."

Light: "Another unique thing about Nashville is that you can literally go out seven nights a week to a variety listening rooms where live original music is being played by emerging and professional songwriters and bands. Most of the venues are near each other or easy to get to, and most places have a very low cover charge or are free. There are a ton of opportunities for writers to listen to great music being played all the time, and to play their own songs out as well. It builds the kind of community and camaraderie among songwriters that Nashville is known for."

But with the benefits of living in Nashville, also come some predatory dangers, especially for entry-level writers.

Dunbar: "Nashville has an entire industry devoted to developing songwriters, which includes publishers, demo houses, songwriter organizations, critics and teachers. Unfortunately some of these services are havens for 'shady' types who prey on beginners, often flattering them with unwarranted praise of their songs

Advanced Articles

and promising 'access' of which they can't truthfully deliver. Out-of-town writers conducting business via mail and the Internet are especially easy targets. Few entities can truly offer outsiders access and opportunity that locals enjoy. There's no shortcut available that a few hundred dollars to some promotional or demo company will make possible. Writers beware!''

LOS ANGELES

Los Angeles is well known for its connection to the TV and Film industry as well as a vibrant Rock and Pop scene. L.A. is a definite creative destination for starry-eyed dreamers in all artistic disciplines, but it's sheer size and spread create challenges not shared with it's country music cousin.

Legendary songwriting advocate and educator John Braheny explains:

John Braheny: ''For songwriters, L.A. is unlike Nashville in that the crucial networking takes a little more effort because of the size of the city. Consequently, L.A. has developed a lot of organizations dedicated to helping writers and industry professionals meet each other. They all function online as information resources as well as providing street-level networking and showcasing opportunities. These include SongsAlive.net, Songnet.org, Songwriterscoop.com, L.A. Music Network (lamn.com) and important chapters of the Nashville Songwriters Association International (nashvillesongwriters.com), The Songwriters Guild (songwritersguild.com) and Just Plain Folks (justplainfolks.org). The PRO's (BMI, ASCAP and SESAC) also host showcases and networking events dedicated to different musical styles. Their meetings are held in various parts of the city and, in L.A., dedicated songwriters rarely give a second thought to driving 20 miles or more to a meeting where they can meet industry folks who are guest speakers at the meetings.

''Night-time songwriting and music industry classes at UCLA Extension are great places to not only learn about the business from active pros, but to meet collaborators and industry guests. Publications such as *Music Connection* and *L.A. Weekly* keep the pulse of the entire L.A. music scene and often list who's playing at the myriad of clubs around town. A disadvantage is that L.A. is not a great place to make a living as a performing songwriter or band because most clubs are pay-to-play in which the artist has to guarantee ticket sales to their gigs. The chances of 'discovery' are slim and it takes sustained effort and savvy to build the connections and attention to get noticed.

''A unique advantage to living in L.A. is the Film and TV industry. The city is flush with film/TV supervisors, music libraries, song placement companies, and publishers who serve that industry's constant appetite for new music. Performing songwriters/bands with original songs who own their own master recordings can do very well in that arena. This year a very successful ASCAP 'I Create Music' Expo was added to the short list of L.A.'s major songwriting events along with TAXI's already successful and well-established Road Rally (members only).''

NEW YORK CITY

The Big Apple shares many of the benefits of Nashville and Los Angeles, as well as some of the drawbacks. Daylle Deanna Schwartz, NYC-based music industry consultant and author of several *Billboard* books, explains:

Daylle Deanna Schwartz: ''New York City has many of the benefits found in Nashville and Los Angeles. There are regular events sponsored by the large organizations with offices in NYC. ASCAP, BMI, and Songwriters Hall of Fame have workshops and showcases. The NY Chapter of the FilmMusic Network (www.filmmusic.net) has monthly events that are quite valuable to songwriters. Many include panels with music supervisors, producers, and other people who use music for TV, video games, advertising and more.

"There are songwriting resources and opportunities for all musical disciplines. NYC is more compact than L.A.—most events are a short subway or taxi ride away—so it's easier to get to multiple events. Often a songwriter on a budget can walk. This makes it more conducive to meet and work with a variety of songwriters for collaborations.

"New York also offers unparalleled exposure to the theatre world. Just as country music thrives in Nashville, and film and TV opportunities are concentrated in Los Angeles, there's no place like NYC for songwriters who write for musical theatre. It's also a hotbed for advertising agencies and other media."

be able to navigate the landmine pretty well. You no longer have to take someone's word for it, or be falsely impressed by their name dropping or past or present fame. Scam artists come in all shapes and sizes. The old axiom "In God we trust, all others we check references" should apply here. Don't proceed on blind faith or a great sales pitch—verify, verify, verify!

Online Message Boards. You can meet people from around the world on message boards. These are simply a public place to post questions, comments, and have discussions with whoever else is interested in the topic. You need to understand that just as there are people who are full of BS in regular life, those same people also post on message boards, so you must always research any information you get from a message board. But that danger aside, you'll also come up with more ideas, information and leads to great opportunities and resources through message boards than with any other thing you can do on the Net or in real life. It's that powerful a tool.

Most "boards" require you to register (you can use your real name, or a user name of your creation) but do keep in mind it's never a good idea to give out personal info like address or phone number over the Internet. I've personally always used my real name and it helps with your own credibility and the veracity of what you are saying if you are willing to stand behind it with your own name. Some sites with popular message boards for Songwriters include Just Plain Folks (justplainfolks.org), Muses Muse (musesmuse.com), and TAXI (taxi.com) and there are many others out there. Often, local organizations will also have Web sites for their area members to networking and share info. One example of a great local music resource and message board site is Indianapolismusic.net. If your city doesn't have a similar site, you can always start one yourself! Take advantage of this powerful tool no matter where you live!

Face to face versus Internet

The Internet is a powerful research and communication tool, but it can't substitute for that handshake and look into someone's eyes to solidify a professional and personal bond. Though running one of the largest and most active Internet Music Organizations, I've learned there's never anything better than face-to-face contact with others. You can solidify a friendship (or learn who to avoid for that matter) in face-to-face situations far more quickly and effectively than you can on the Internet where there's often a different language and a different culture to adapt to. The smart songwriter will use the power of both to their advantage. Find people and resources on the Net. Break the ice via e-mail or on message boards and in chat rooms. But then take the next step and meet these people in person. Even if people live far away, a few well-placed friends in a certain area can make it worth taking a weekend trip to visit your contacts and meet all of *their* local musical friends at the same time.

Use international resources to find local contacts

There are some very large Web sites that can help you find very local contacts. Two that are popular as of this writing are MySpace.com and CDBaby.com. You can do a search on MySpace by city to find artists and individuals who make and love music, and you can use the site to develop fans for your own work (especially if you're also a performer). CDBaby.com is the top site for independent music in the world, and you can search their database by location and genre to find people who make the kind of music you write, read about what they do and hear samples of their album releases that might lead you to new candidates to record your music or new resources in your genre. You can even e-mail the artists directly from the Web page. Use these and other convenient international resources to find people near you. It works!

I also highly recommend a visit to SongU.com. This educational site is run very similarly to any college or university, but with the convenience of being on your computer. They have a friendly and knowledgeable staff of songwriting educators (many of which are behind some of the most popular books on the subject) and even better, you get to interact with your fellow students in a variety of ways. If you live near a university that has an actual program for songwriting, definitely check it out. But if not (or if you work during class hours) check out SongU. You'll learn a lot, meet some great people, and further expand your network around the world. Knowledge is power no matter where you get it!

Borrow ideas from the DIY artist community

The songwriting community is well developed in Nashville and some of the other major music cities. It's not as well developed everywhere else. But that's okay. Find out what the "Do It Yourself" artist community is doing and borrow their ideas. How do they network and develop contacts in your area? How do they get the word out about what they are doing? What tools are they using in your town? Usually, you can find use for those same techniques and tools yourself. You can also look to other artistic disciplines for help and ideas. Have a photography club nearby? How about a theater workshop? Are there any college courses that deal with songwriting? Take a class or request that the school offer one. You could even help find resources to make the class happen. The DIY philosophy is all about finding ways to create your own success. Songwriters need to use that same tenacity. You don't need an existing organization or "entity" to succeed. You can often do everything they do yourself. This leads us to the next topic.

Create your own scene

The major music centers weren't always that. They sprung up because like-minded people started working together and more and more joined them. Often a "scene" will be genre driven. Whether it's alternative music in Seattle, or rap music in Atlanta or the Latin scene in Miami, the Country empire in Nashville, the Blues communities in Chicago and Memphis, the singer-songwriter factory in Boston, or the live music capital of the world in Austin, just plain people invented and created those scenes, and what one man (or woman) can do, any man can do. If you can afford to move to a major music center

Musical Links

For More Info

To learn more about the people quoted in the article above, visit these sites:

Mike Dunbar: www.justplainfolks.org
John Braheny: www.johnbraheny.com
Sara Light: www.songu.com
Daylle Deanna Schwartz: www.daylle.com
Brian Austin Whitney: www.brianaustinwhitney.com

and it makes sense for you personally, that's great. There are a lot of shortcuts you can take advantage of when there's already an active industry in a given town. But you can create a scene anywhere you live using the tools above and others you'll discover on your own.

Here is one final thought to summarize how to succeed doing what you love wherever you may live. If it's there, use it. If it's not there, create it. Isn't that what songwriters have always done?

Getting Started in Music Licensing

by Blake Althen with Paula Bellenoit

At every music conference, you will hear someone say, "Licensing, that's where the money is." Licensing can be a great income source. However, many people who quietly nod their heads during discussions of music licensing are actually just pretending to understand the world of licensing. Music licensing is a confusing and complicated part of the music business. It took me years to appreciate many of the key elements of licensing, and I am still learning.

Many music business books explain the technical aspects of licensing (synchronization licenses, mechanical licenses, etc.).I will not go into those details here. Instead, I'll share my experience about the players in music licensing: who is looking for music, who is buying it, and who is selling it. Then, I will offer some ideas on how to reach these folks and expose your music to them.

WHO USES MUSIC?

Everyone is aware that there is music in movies, and many songwriters have dreamed of having their songs play during the end credits of their favorite blockbuster. But if you pay attention, you'll notice there are many other places where you hear licensed music every day.

- TV/radio shows
- TV/radio commercials
- TV/radio station promos
- in-store/office "muzak"
- corporate/government training videos
- trade show booths
- Web sites
- live presentations
- educational videos
- theater
- amusement parks
- video games

BLAKE ALTHEN and **PAULA BELLENOIT** are also the record production duo known as Human Factor. They've worked with artists such as DJ Logic and Michael Manring, as well as Pale Beneath the Blue, Michelangelo, and Abby Someone. They are also known for their interactive production seminars and clinics both at music conferences and independently. Visit www.hfproductions.com.

This is by no means an all-inclusive list, but it makes the point—music is licensed to a vast and diverse market.

HOW CAN YOU REACH THE MUSIC USERS?

If you can find the right person who uses music in any of these applications, you can license your recordings directly to them. More often, though, you will be dealing with one of the "middlemen" who stand between the artist and the user. They find music and then place the music with end users. They are:

- Advertising Agencies
- Music Supervisors (I am going to lump Independent Films, Major Films, and Directors under this one)
- Music Libraries
- Publishers
- Agents (or "Morphs," as I like to call them)

These people get music licensed. The defining lines between these different types of middlemen is often fuzzy and overlapping. Moreover, in the rapidly changing music industry, I expect there to be an ongoing erosion of differences and overlapping of roles among the middlemen. However, for now, it's useful to understand what these different types of firms and music industry professionals do.

Advertising agencies

Ad agencies help businesses plan advertising strategies, and make the ads or hire the producers that make the ads. Obviously, TV and radio commercials use music. The agencies use many avenues to get their music, and not all ad agencies do it the same way. However, every ad agency doing commercials with music—including movies, TV, Internet, and radio—has a source or sources where it gets music. Some may have a "go to" music production company they use for every spot. Others may have a music library they use for every ad. Some have an in-house music supervisor or an in-house composer. Some use all of these and other sources for music.

An ad agency's needs may change from project to project. One week it may be working on a flower commercial and need a heartfelt sentimental song. The next week it may be doing a car commercial and need a hard-hitting heavy metal song. One thing is always true—the producer of the project for an agency has *many* things on his plate (not just the music). The producer is concerned with the message of the commercial, actors, camera people, location, animation, graphics, and more. He/she does not have time to go through thousands of songs. The agency also does not want to worry about making sure that it can use the song legally. Therefore, 9 times out of 10 the ad agency has a person that will give it 5-10 options. If that person is in-house, they are normally called a music supervisor or music director.

Submission Tip

There are companies who put out something called a "tip sheet." A tip sheet is a list of requests from the people who use music compiled and sent (by fax or over the Internet) containing what is essentially a classified ad sheet full of requests for music. They usually charge a monthly fee for a subscription. These can be an effective way of getting in the door with music supervisors. You have to be persistent to make this pay off.

Music supervisors

A music supervisor is somebody who takes the responsibility of getting the music and the copyright clearance for a project. Whether it be a major movie studio, a TV show, or a radio commercial, if there is a music supervisor on the project, that is the person you need to know. Although music supervisors may not be the end decision makers, they can have great influence. Their job essentially is to worry about finding and clearing ("clearing" is making sure that it is all legal) the perfect music for the project. Of course, they can be harassed on a daily basis by publishers, music libraries, songwriters, composers, and musicians. At the same time, they may be on numerous projects at one time. Consequently, a number of movie producers or directors may be harassing them at one time. The point is that they can be extremely busy and, if you can become the person that always has the perfect track, you will get called more and more often.

Submission Tip

Send the music supervisor the type of music he/she asks for. If a music supervisor asks you for a specific type of song, "Alt country, with a lyric about cars", and you do not have that type song, DO NOT SEND them a rap song about cars. This irritates most supervisors, and they probably will not call again. Instead, say something like, "I don't have any thing like that right now but my catalog is always growing, thanks for thinking of me, and keep me in mind next time."

Production music libraries

One of the easiest sources for music users is pre-cleared music libraries. A music library gathers a catalog of different types of music, gains the rights to license it, and provides it to the music users in a series of CDs, an on-line catalog, or now, a searchable hard drive or similar technology. The music user picks out a song from the library and uses it in his/her project. Users then report to the library about where and how they used it, and they pay the applicable fee. Typically, fees are based on how important the music is to the project and how many people will hear it once the project is distributed. How many people hear it depends on the exposure the piece will get, where and how many times it will be played, and for how long. In some cases, libraries negotiate a "blanket fee" up front, instead of getting a fee each time. This kind of fee allows the user to use whatever they want from the library for as often as they want during a specified time period, something like an all-you-can-eat buffet.

Submission Tip

When submitting your music to a library, recognize that they are looking to fill holes in their catalog. Send them something they do not already have. Importantly, never send poor quality recordings. Libraries need ready-to-license tracks that already sound great.

Major publishers

What if the customer wants a specific title, i.e. "Smells Like Teen Spirit" by Nirvana? The short answer is that they call one of the major publishers. Like major labels, there are relatively few major publishers. Their job is to find "homes" for the songs in their catalog. Publishers, like music libraries, have large catalogs full of different kinds of music. The major publishers typically have the most popular songs from the most popular artists and songwriters. Unlike production music libraries, publishers can use songs without a good recording because part of their function is to match songwriters with performing artists. They are not limited to selling the music "as is" from the shelf.

Submission Tip

Because popular songs have a high demand, the major publishers can charge very high license fees to the music users. You can use this to your advantage by offering "sound-alikes" to popular songs and charge a lesser fee to the music users who do not have a major publisher budget.

"Morphs"

With the changes in the music industry such as cheaper recording methods and the internet, we are seeing many new kinds of middlemen popping up. We now may have an Agent who has a database set up for production music, two recording artists signed, and on staff composers. They are essentially a record label, music publisher and a music library all rolled into one.

HOW TO GET LICENSED?

"There is no simple answer to the question of how best to approach agencies with music. Obviously we can't listen to every disc we receive. Persistence is important, but even more important is to only submit material that is truly worthy of consideration.

Initially what draws us to considering a licensed song is the familiarity of a certain master performance, and the lyrics, emotion and image the song evokes. From there we would decide if it's actually necessary to have that performance, or if a re-record would provide the same appeal and recognition to the viewer/listener of our commercials so that we will have a successful campaign. In the case of Slum Village, it was the right act, with the right song at the right time, and they worked with us to make it a win for everyone."

—*Kathi Strace of Campbell-Ewald Advertising*

Now you know about a few of the people who are looking for music. The tricky part is how to get them to listen and then choose work with you. If there were an easy way to do this, everybody would do it. The fact is that it is extremely difficult to get the decision maker to hear your music. It requires a mix of persistence, "getting out there," money, and skill. Take these one at a time.

Persistence. This is the trait where most people fail. Instead of calling it persistence, you might think of this as "getting used to rejection." Learning the craft of music, songwriting, composing, etc., takes many years. Learning how to market it will take just as long. Take learning to play guitar. The beginning was the hardest. At first, your fingers hurt, your muscles were sore, and you had blisters on your fingertips. Your hand had to learn all kinds of new motor patterns. Then once you were past that, you had to practice, practice, practice. Gradually, you got better and better.

The persistence in marketing is much the same. In the beginning, you will not be used to people saying no, doors slamming in your face, and not being called back. Your ego might get blisters and your motivation might get sore. You must learn not to take it personally. Think about this like an actor thinks about auditioning for a play. No actor is right for every play. A 20-year-old, six-foot-five, 220 pound guy cannot play the part of the grandmother no matter how much he practiced acting and how excellent a performer he is. It is the same in music licensing. Sometimes, artists simply do not have the music a user needs. So move on and look for more opportunities.

Networking. One of the ways of getting out there is to find out what music, film, and TV associations are in your area. Many of them have networking events, learning seminars, award ceremonies, Internet job boards, and more. My advice to someone who is just beginning is to attend as many of these events as possible, *not just music oriented events*. If there is a seminar on lighting, you need to be there with your business cards. You may not run into a music supervisor, but you may hit it off with a camera person. A few years later that camera person may have moved up the ladder to producer. If you have befriended that person, now you have an in. You'll notice that I said "a few years later." Networking can take a long time to pay off. This is where persistence comes in. "Getting out there" may sound easy but it can be very hard, even if you have an outgoing personality. It is all that much harder for introverts. Also when you start out, you usually still have a day job, and networking events create late hours on work nights. Be sure to pace yourself to avoid burnout. And again, persistence.

Networking Tip

Bring a friend with you to the networking event. The hardest part is walking in the door and talking to the first stranger, and it's easier to do with two than on your own. But don't just stick with your friend the whole night. Make it a game to see how many business cards you can get.

The follow up is also very important. If you want that camera person you met to call you in three years when he needs music, you have to stay on his mind. At an event you will meet many people. You need to create a database of contacts. You will need a way to log and file who, what, when, where, and if possible, a little personal detail about the person you met. You can make it as simple as writing the info on the back of the person's card or creating an elaborate spreadsheet. This will make contacting that person in the future that much easier if you can say, "Hey Ed, remember me, Blake? We met at the Washington Press Club at the Writers Workshop back in May. We talked about fishing in Canada, remember? I was wondering if you would have a minute to give me some advice."

Money. Part of pacing yourself means watching your budget. Belonging to many associations can get very expensive. However, you can often attend a single event as a non-member for minimal cost. At the event, ask around to see what the members think of the association before you decide to join. See if you can get a schedule of events. Compare all of them and pick those that you can afford and you think will benefit you the most.

Skill. Finally, never lose site of what you are actually selling—your music. Remember that, in the end, you are a songwriter or musician. While attending events, making phone calls, and sending out packages you can lose your focus on the music and become caught up in the marketing. Whatever your musical style, you should constantly be improving it. Whether you are writing country music, classical crossover, or commercial jingles, there is always room for improvement.

Career Tip

Compare your craft with the people with whom you'd like to compete, instead of the people at your current level. This will help you see where you need to improve to get past where you are now. For example, you may be the very best musical lyricist in your small town in Indiana, so try comparing your lyrics to Tim Rice's instead of your neighboring competitor's.

SONiA—Folk to Dance

Internationally acclaimed road warrior SONiA of disappear fear is a very successful and prolific singer songwriter out of the Baltimore area. Last year, we contributed an article on re-mixing entitled "The Power of the Re-Mix" to the 2006 *Songwriter's Market*. At the same time, SONiA was looking for a re-mixer, and she hired us to do the re-mixing, culminating in SONiA's *No Bomb Is Smart: Dance Mix Singles* EP. This year, *Songwriter's Market* has asked us to tell the tale with this interview:

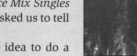

Human Factor: What gave you the idea to do a re-mix?

SONiA: Well I had this vision of people dancing to my music in Israel (particularly the song "No Bomb Is Smart") because it's a place ridden with so much violence and wars and strife all the time. [And] because I knew I was going there in August, I thought "Wow, wouldn't it be cool if I can get people dancing to this music? OK, how do I get people dancing to this music? Well, it has to become a dance song! Laura [Cerulli, my drummer] highly recommended [you as] this great re-mixer that she knew, this crazy producer guy in DC. She said he's amazing and he can make you jump, so that's what I wanted and when I first heard the beginning of [your re-mix] I thought, "This is incredible!" So I was very, very, very excited—great energy.

Human Factor: Did you know anything about dance music before you did it?

SONiA: No. Other than my own likes and dislikes, I don't really follow that kind of thing very much. Except if I'm in a club or something and hear something that's got a cool beat, I just get out there on the dance floor like everybody else, I think. You know?

Human Factor: Yeah, I do. (Laughs) How was the process of making it?

SONiA: It was really thrilling actually. It was different in that I didn't know [much about the process]. First of all I was worried about speeding up my vocals. I'd never heard it done so that I didn't sound like Minnie Mouse. And when I heard it done on this I actually liked it. The integrity of my vocals was still there even though it was there at a higher speed, which is complimentary to both the producer, and probably partially to technology. That was [a] really great thing.

Human Factor: What did you think when you first heard it?

SONiA: I loved it, I was really surprised—it really kept my interest. The only thing I had to do for myself (because I wrote the song and I sang the song) was just take a step back. Just let go and let it be the creation of someone else. And then and now I'm really pleased with it. I'm really jazzed, thrilled actually, that my name is on it— that it says SONiA and disappear fear. But it's really very much the creation of the producer because it's really his vision and that's really cool. It's some of the best ear candy I've heard, and it makes you dance! So I love it.

Human Factor: You have a folk audience for a fan base, so how did your fans react to it?

SONiA: The people who like dance music in addition to folk music have said it was the greatest thing ever and I'm not kidding. The people who don't really like dance music that much but still like my music like it a lot, so I think it's really positive, really cool. And because the song itself takes a theme that's not necessarily a romantic theme on the dance floor, it speaks to a whole other realm of songwriting, of protest music in a sense. It's a whole other universe of possibilities. You know, you're dancing on the floor, you're having fun with the sound, fun with the grooves, and then you realize that the lyric is ''No Bomb Is Smart'' and that's like ''Woah . . . well that's true, no bomb *is* smart!'' It's sort of like enrolling people in something they already know. It feels really good.

The only thing I would have done differently, and if it ever comes down to this, because art, if it is good art, you never want to abandon it, you just want to keep playing with it. If I ever get a chance to put some other words in it, I would put in ''Ain Pi Z a Z a Cha'' which means ''No Bomb Is Smart'' in Hebrew. And I would learn how to say those exact same words in Arabic as well, and have that in there as well. But we were able to put the Hebrew on the liner notes, so that was cool.

Human Factor: So far would you consider it a success?

SONiA: Absolutely. It got listed as a #1 breakout mix in *Billboard*. So we're hoping it keeps on moving, which I think is amazing for an independent song.

Human Factor: Anything else you want to say to the person considering getting a re-mix?

SONiA: I can't wait to do more work like this and I really encourage other songwriters to break out of their own writing prisons and experiment with different genres and dance beats, 'cause it's really fun.

Advanced Articles

David Lasley

Yesterday and Today

by Robin Renée

David Lasley was born and raised in Michigan about 250 miles from Detroit in surroundings beyond rural—he attended school with an enrollment of 28 kids. His musically-inclined family lead him to form his first group with his sisters, The Utopias, who released 3 records to regional success. When his younger sister left the group to return to school, Lasley remained in Detroit and in 1970, landed a part in a touring production of the musical *Hair*. His traveling took him to New York City, and by November of 1972 he found himself with no job and no money, but with the sheer determination to work as a session singer and songwriter. You might say that sticking to it paid off.

Well known as a backing vocalist for James Taylor, Bonnie Raitt, Luther Vandross, and many more, his talent as a solo artist and most prominently as a songwriter stands on its own. His albums include the critically-acclaimed *Missin' Twenty Grand* (EMI, 1982), *Soldiers on the Moon* (Agenda/Pony Canyon, 1990), and his latest, *Demos Vol. 2—Take a Look* (Cool Sound—Japan, 2005). The list of classic performers who have covered Lasley's material is a long one—Dionne Warwick, Sheena Easton, Whitney Houston, Pablo Cruise, Tina Turner, Dusty Springfield, Peter Allen, and Peaches and Herb are just a few. Lasley-penned hits include "Lead Me On," performed by Maxine Nightingale and "You Bring Me Joy," performed by Anita Baker.

I'll start at the obvious beginning. How do your songs generally originate? Do you write from piano?

I don't play guitar at all. I wish I did. I would say that the older things I wrote started sitting at the piano, noodling, finding some chords, or sometimes I'd have a title or a line. I remember "You Bring Me Joy" was a title I had in my head for a short time. It was either "You Bring Me Joy" or "You Brought Me Joy," and when I finally figured it out, it was present tense. Anita Baker recorded that, and had the version that people know.

A lot of singer/songwriters will want to know how you get from point A to point B, that is, from having an idea to getting Anita Baker to hear it.

I was signed to a publisher, Almo Music, part of A&M. In 1976, I was in the studio singing background for Garland Jeffries with Arnold McCuller and Lynn Pitney. James Taylor came

---

Performing songwriter and freelance writer **ROBIN RENÉE** has contributed to *Elmore Magazine*, *PanGaia*, and *WeirdoMusic.com*. Her most recent CD is *All Six Senses*, and she continues to develop her own style of Mantra-Pop. Visit www.robinrenee.com.

in and added to our trio on a song called "Cool Down Boy." We exchanged numbers because he really liked our voices, and he said maybe one day we'd get the chance to work together. We thought that would never happen in a million years. Then sure enough, I got a call from him in May of '77 and he said, "I have this new album coming out"—which happened to be *JT*—"and I'm gonna need singers." Within about 3 weeks, we were in Texas and we did the summer tour. We had six or ten shows in the fall in California.

I stayed [in California] and started to write some things with my friend Allee Willis. She wrote all the great Earth, Wind & Fire stuff, and we actually co-wrote "Lead Me On" for Maxine Nightingale. I was writing with Allee and that's what got me introduced to the publisher. Finally, by the summer of '78 they signed me to a deal. Brenda Andrews was the vice president there. She was a big believer in my music and got me almost all of my covers. They were a really hard-working company. They really pushed your stuff. The salary wasn't huge, maybe $200 a week plus a $5,000 advance at the beginning of the year, which was still pretty good for the late '70s or early '80s. In those days, we'd just write, write, write. For the most part, I'd either write with Allee at her apartment or just on my own.

So you were paid a regular rate to write songs, like a job?

Like a staff writer. $15,000 or maybe 20 would have been a big year, total. I didn't understand all of it at the time, but they'd charge pretty much three quarters of the demo cost, or sometimes all of it, and your travel stuff, and your pianos—you'd wind up owing a pretty large amount of money whenever you did leave, which in my case was about six or seven years later. I left owing a lot of money. [Allee Willis and I] had a lot of records, but we just wrote all the time. Maybe we wrote 160 or 200 songs, so we were charged the cost of that, plus the hotels and cars and things. Not that we were living high on the hog or anything, but before I moved out to L.A., it was very expensive to be traveling back and forth. All that stuff had to be paid back.

But eventually with "You Bring Me Joy" and "Lead Me On," I got out of the red and into the beginnings of royalties. It took me quite a long time, into the late '0s or maybe even 1990 before I saw any money. The song that got me out of the red was by Taylor Dayne, actually. She did a cover version of a song on my *Raindance* album called "Where Does That Boy Hang Out."

I never really begrudged [my financial situation]. Brenda Andrews really had a sense of my music, knew all the producers, and really believed in my songs. Some songpluggers just send anything to people whether it's right or wrong. If she really thought it was right, she'd send it. I actually miss those days of someone running my stuff. I'm not as good at plugging my own songs as people might think.

Over the years, you've gotten to know so many people. Do you ever call someone up personally and say, "Hey I have this song . . ."

Very rarely. I would say more so in the last 10 years, but very rarely now because the business has changed so much. There are so few slots open on an album, it's very tough. These days, it just comes down to producers who know you or who you've worked with over the years. I was always able to separate that background singer cap and that songwriter hat. I never went into a background session loaded with cassettes of my latest songs. I thought that was really tacky.

Do you craft a song with a mind toward it being an "evergreen," one that could be covered again and again by multiple artists?

I don't think I consciously think of that. I'm pretty lucky in that my music tends to be fairly melodic. For my solo singer/songwriter stuff, it tends to be a little more esoteric and word-heavy, but I think my pop songs, the ballads especially, tend to be songs that can be covered by people in different genres. Things like "I Don't Go Shopping (For Love)," that I wrote with Peter Allen, was first done by Patti LaBelle, then he recorded it, then a girl in Japan recorded it, and then Lulu, who I absolutely love, did a fabulous version. "The Blue Side" was done first by Valerie Carter as pop/R&B, and then Crystal Gayle did it in a total country arrangement. I might set out to write for a specific person if they're looking, to tailor-make it to something they'd like, but I don't ever say "Let's try to write a standard." What is a standard anymore (melodies being a thing of the past in certain types of music)?

What do you mean by "melodies being a thing of the past?"

Even though you watch *American Idol* and people are singing standards—or at least attempting to—I think music overall is less and less melodic than it used to be. I tend to like people like Mariah Carey. Her big song, "We Belong Together," has a melody. You can sing it, even though it has a groove.

I don't get all the boy singers—what people are calling melodic—the Elton John sound-alikes. They're OK, but to me they're very non-original. We already have an Elton John. I'd rather hear something more sincere.

I write from the heart. If it does well, great. If it doesn't, I have to suffer the consequences. I've never been that super-competitive. I find you just end up chasing your tail a lot and spinning in place. You're safest to just write a song and let somebody grab onto it if they're hearing it.

Who have been some of your favorite writing partners? Were you sometimes put together by publishers?

Yes, put together by publishers back in the day, not always with good results. They were always the biggest and the hottest people around. Peter Allen was one of my favorite people to write with because he was just so talented. He had a great memory. He would edit as he wrote. At the end of the writing session, he could play it from bottom to top. I really liked working with Gary Wright, who had the song "Dream Weaver," though I never got any covers with him. I liked writing with Kiki Dee, Boz Scaggs, Sophie B. Hawkins, Josh Kadison—he was very sincere. He is more like an old-school writer, like a Neil Sedaka or Carole King.

Which songs did you write with Luther Vandross?

Such a great loss. At least he has that huge body of work that we can listen to. We actually wrote probably five songs together. Only one of them was recorded. We wrote a song for Paula Abdul, but it never came out. The one that came out, though, was a number one R&B hit for Donna Washington called "'Scuse Me While I Fall In Love." When we did the demo, Luther played piano on it. That was fun that we had a hit together.

Tell me about the business aspect of co-writing.

It's pretty understood that if there are two people it's 50/50, even though you may do a little bit more, or vice versa. It may come back on another song on another day. If you just split it, it's easier for book keeping and what you might lose on one song, you gain on another. There were a couple instances where, it's wasn't a matter of getting less than you deserve, but getting nothing. Once with one song, they were just going to leave me off. At the last minute, I got a very small percent. So there are instances when you have to go to your publisher and say, "This is really not cool." At the time, I was just happy to be credited.

You've worked with so many great songwriters. Any memorable conversations of advice given or received?

Not consciously, but at recording sessions, we'd get into conversations like "What are you listening to lately?" People are definitely conscious of that—"Who will be the next hot thing?"

They really want to know if there are songs they should hear or writers they should know about. At the MusicCares benefit honoring James Taylor (February 2006), I remember Bonnie Raitt coming to practice really stoked about Maia Sharp, a really good songwriter.

It's interesting with iTunes and all the downloads, kids can go buy a song and they get just the song, no artwork. Maybe it's like going back to the '60s. It was sound, and I wouldn't know if they were black or if they were white—it was the music that was on the grooves of that record. Maybe it's come back to when somebody downloads a song, they are getting what they want, the sound of that song.

Now, I've heard you talk about how you've felt your lead vocals don't fit well into most pop worlds, that it's "too white to be black and too black to be white." Has that also been true of your writing? Does it help that you're enigmatic, or has it been a hindrance in any way?

I think it's very much the same as I feel about my voice. It's good to be versatile and to write all genres, but I think it has hurt me a little bit. In the late '70s and early '80s, it was like the kiss of death—Once you had a big pop hit like "Lead Me On," then people couldn't take you seriously if you wrote more of a confessional, singer-songwriter solo record. I never felt that that was fair. I love the fact that Laura Nyro, who was a big inspiration to me, had her solo records, but she had her big hits like "Stone Soul Picnic," and "Wedding Bell Blues"—so many hits for other people. For me, songwriting is songwriting.

What would you say today to someone who is a songwriter and either wants to be a performer or to have songs recorded by other artists?

It's ironic—I never wanted to be a solo artist and never thought I was good enough to be a professional songwriter, but I just kept doing it and I would get records in spite of myself. It's almost unrealistic in a way, but it's just the nature of a kid who's young and trying to make it and stay in the business.

If you really want to be a writer today, go to workshops and go to hear other writers speak. Just talk to each other and meet each other. I know that it sounds so simple, but write and continue to write. Most of all, you have to believe in yourself. I find that for just about anybody I've ever known, if they hang in and if they've stayed in it, they do get some sort of success either as a producer or a background singer or a songwriter or an artist. The thing that I think it sort of bad about *American Idol* is that it's saying be like somebody else and you'll have a better shot at making it. To me, that sends out a bad signal. I think it's still best to be unique.

Brian Wilson

Ask Me Anything . . .

by Scott Mathews

My obsession with all things Brian Wilson began in Sacramento, California back in early 1963, a time when it was still very common to have "regional" hits climb the charts on local radio stations. My relatively small hometown of Sacramento was the first (outside of Los Angeles) to salute the primitive sounds on the demos-turned-records that Brian Wilson was making as well as book his otherwise little known surf band from four hundred miles due south in Hawthorne into 4,000 seaters as headliners up north. Sacramento proved huge in jump-starting The Beach Boys' career. The residents of this land-locked capitol city were drawn to the Beach Boys' unique sound—Chuck Berry rhythms and chord structures married to the Four Freshmen modern vocal harmony blend—but perhaps even more importantly, they were captivated by the dream these SoCal boys were singing about. With lyrics full of surf and sand, the message of freedom was at the heart of every song by The Beach Boys and we wanted it—vicariously, we got it. They got it too. After their first show at the Sacramento Memorial Auditorium, The Beach Boys returned to their motel to celebrate their new-found success by sitting on a bed, counting the several thousands of dollars they had made that evening, and throwing all the money up in the air. Their lives would never be the same again.

ENDLESS SUMMER

The Beach Boys' sunny California mythology of endless summers was heard, seen, and felt from coast to coast and, before long, continent to continent. Everybody wanted a piece of that dream. Who knew the writer of this carefree lifestyle was terrified of the ocean and rarely ventured outdoors himself, unless perhaps to cruise over to the Foster Freeze on Hawthorne Boulevard (which is still there today) to pick up on some cheeseburgers and inspiration?

Since they lived close to the beach and Dennis Wilson was the only member of the musical Wilson family who surfed, an inquisitive Brian Wilson got all of his information about the new craze through his brothers' animated exploits and tales of adventure. It drove their strict, disciplinarian father Murry Wilson mad and inspired Brian to write about Dennis' lifestyle in first person. The result was that Brian Wilson and The Beach Boys—brothers Brian, Dennis, and Carl Wilson, along with cousin Mike Love, and their neighbor Al Jardine—developed an image and musical concept that endured in the public imagination (for better or worse) well beyond their first albums and singles.

SCOTT MATHEWS can be heard on several of The Beach Boys releases on Capitol Records including *Good Vibrations—the Box Set*, *The Endless Harmony Soundtrack* and *Greatest Hits—The Best of the Brother Years*

TEENAGE SYMPHONIES TO GOD

Later in their career when Brian felt held back by the limited scope of subject matter and musical exploration the band (especially cousin Mike Love) was known for, his response was to write some of the most timeless and creative music ever heard. He cut all the tracks without any band members (except for his able brother, Carl Wilson) and sang all of their parts with perfection and grace. When the band came in to do their vocals, some of the innocence and beauty began to fade into bitterness and greed. "Where are the surf songs, Brian? These songs are only for your ego." Maybe his cousin and company bean counters didn't quite get it, but The Beatles sure did. John Lennon and Paul McCartney were notorious for studying Brian's records and then going into the studio to "respond" in an open dialogue of music with a healthy dash of competition for good measure. Thus, Brian would do the same when he heard the next Beatles record. It is common knowledge that the classic *Sgt. Pepper's Lonely Hearts Club Band* was an ambitious attempt to rise up to Brian's level, set by the challenging and breathtaking *Pet Sounds* LP.

Following the initial displeasure from the label and one or two band members regarding *Pet Sounds*, Capitol Records rush released a "best of" compilation and did virtually nothing to promote Brian's masterpiece. Another throwaway record, *Beach Boys Party* deflected any of the progressive music and forward motion Brian's heart and soul were dedicated to.

Bravely, he pursued a now legendary project called, *Smile* and spent months recording beautiful and experimental music, collaborating with the brilliant Van Dyke Parks as a lyricist. Van Dyke had never written lyrics before but Brian liked to hear him talk so he thought it made sense. Of course, it did. And of course, Love and others with conservative tastes ridiculed it—so this time Brian folded and shelved the project after working on it for nearly a full year. He had practically single-handedly pushed that stone all the way up the hill but let it crush him by letting it go at the end.

The classic "Good Vibrations" was released as a single and went straight to number one all over the world, but the hurt and loss caused by his disloyal, lowest common denominator-type business associates cut Brian to the core. He would retire to his room and not get out of bed for the better part of three years.

Some of Brian's deepest works come from the period of time following these events, when (on the rare occasion) he felt compelled to share his music and vision again. "Surf's Up" and "Till I Die" are two gorgeous pieces that will never be heard anywhere near a Beach Boys concert, but are flawless high water marks of composition and sound.

SMILE

In recent years, Brian has revived both *Pet Sounds* and *Smile* to unprecedented raves on record and in concert with his band of able, devoted fans who play and sing his music with the conviction of true disciples. He has proven himself and his music triumphant over any and all negative physical, mental, business obstacles and and the naysayers in his life.

By virtue of our working together both onstage and in the studio, I have been close to Brian Wilson for nearly 30 years (as well as forming strong personal relationships with his late, great brothers Dennis and Carl Wilson), but then again, I'm not sure how close anyone actually gets. He is by nature open, forthcoming with a charming naïveté that is not usually seen in adults while at the same time, obviously damaged and scarred by his life's events and the demons he struggles with on a daily basis. Courage has always been one of his strongest points—be it in the '60s, with his asking people to try avant-garde ideas in the recording studio (that nobody could comprehend for decades to come) or these days, fighting off the life-long stage fright that forced him to retire from the road in 1964, and touring with his own band to adoring crowds all over the world.

ASK ME ANYTHING, SCOTT

When I sat down to talk with Brian Wilson for the record, he said, "Ask me about anything at all, Scott—I'll tell you everything about anything you want to talk about."

Scott Mathews: Brian, people finally know you for the incredible music you made after you stopped riding the surf hits and got into some deeper waters.

Brian Wilson: *Pet Sounds* was a big departure from surf music and from there it was just one album at a time that we just squeezed out over the years. Now we're quite a legend, you know?

SM: You're being compared to Beethoven, George Gershwin . . .

BW: Oh, come on! Really? Gershwin and Beethoven? Well does Bach have anything to do with it?

SM: Sure, Bach, rock—bring it all!

BW: Yeah! Ha!

SM: I know you are a modest guy. How much are you buying all these types of comparisons?

BW: Well, I'm buying them because I think I am an original musician. I write original music. And Beethoven and Bach were very original. Gershwin was very original and their origins were very, very, very original. So, I am proud to be considered an original person.

SM: And those cats only wrote music . . . I say you are highly underrated in the lyric department.

BW: Oh, I am a good lyricist—I have to admit that. But I prefer to collaborate.

SM: I really love the pure, unadulterated Brian Wilson songs that you wrote alone but for the most part you have collaborated with a lyricist. You have used wild wordsmiths like Van Dyke Parks and meat and potato guys like Mike Love.

BW: Mike's best was "Do It Again"—that was the one. [*sings*] "It's automatic when I talk with old friends/the conversation turns to girls we knew/when their hair was soft and long . . ." You know, just great lyrics.

SM: Yeah, and that simple chorus. [*sings*] *"Did did did—did did did—did did did did did did did did did—did did did—dum de do do ron"* Nothing sings better than that!

BW: Right, exactly!

SM: What did you do to the drum on the intro of that track? It's an instant hook . . .

BW: Oh, that's a real heavy one. That drum was sent to a reverberation unit that had 50 or 100 notes per second—like dddddd, real fast. That's how we got that sound.

SM: Your attention to detail on the sounds you use and the imaginative blend of unconventional groups of instruments as well as voices . . . you know, most people don't use banjos, accordions and Theremins on rock and roll records!

BW: "California Girls" is my biggest achievement in sound.

SM: Again, just the intro alone!

BW: Aahhh . . . I wrote the introduction on my piano then I had Carl go direct through the board instead of going through an amplifier in the studio. We had him plug directly into the console in the booth with the electric 12-string and that's how we got that sound. Put a little echo on it, ya know—made it swim a little bit. It took me to another world.

SM: I have a special fondness for *Beach Boys Love You* and *15 Big Ones*, both done right before I started working with you guys. People are just now finding out about them.

BW: Oh yeah, those were great albums.

I've been writing songs! I have written about eight songs now in the last month. And they're all really interesting little songs. They're not throwaway shit songs. I'm not going for the throwaway; I'm going for the goods.

SM: And it's always there—you just have to tap into it, right?

BW: Yeah, yeah, it's just right there and I have just recorded (earlier this afternoon) a song that I wrote that's really cool called "Mexican Girl." It's gonna be really cool.

SM: Are you rockin' it?

BW: Oh . . . it's got a driving beat with one of the great bass lines. It's really good. The songs are coming, one by one . . . I'm telling ya, it's really good stuff. It's like when you are writing a song, you are looking for gold and then you find yourself some gold, ya know? When you write a song, it's gold. That's the gold.

SM: I dig.

BW: Yeah. Ha!

SM: Working in the studio with you, I notice not everyone can keep up with your ideas.

BW: Sometimes it'll end up a little bit off the wall.

SM: Well, this may sound off the wall and I know it's a sensitive area, but do you think there is any correlation between your ability to hear glorious music—have it just pop into your head and the auditory hallucinations you sometimes experience? I mean on a yin/yang level, is it a blessing and a curse to get the gifts, but also have some tough things come with the package?

BW: You know . . . I never thought about it that way but I guess . . . Your art reflects the mood you are in, ya know? It's reflective of the bag that your head is in. If I was in a real serious mood, I'd write a serious song, like "Till I Die."

SM: This may sound a bit morbid but if they played that song at my funeral (a long long time from now), I think I'd love it. I might not hear it but . . .

BW: Wow, that is a far out thing to say but it is interesting. I think vocally, it expressed a lot of soul, ya know? A lot of my soul and our souls. I think that was one of my better vocal sessions.

SM: How about "Don't Worry Baby"?

BW: Oh, that was sweet. A very sweet and loving song. Yeah . . .

SM: "The Warmth of the Sun"?

BW: The vocal on that was cool. Sweet.

SM: When you are on the piano writing, how do you capture the essence of the songs? Do you have a process?

BW: Well, we just follow through with our feelings, you know. When the ideas come, I put 'em on tape right away so I don't forget it.

SM: Do you think your best compositions are usually the quick ones to write?

BW: I think some of the most inspired ones come quicker so I guess so . . . the one's that come quicker are a little more inspired. "God Only Knows" took about 45 minutes.

SM: Have mercy!

BW: Really! That's all it took. It was the moment. We got all jazzed up on the title "God Only Knows" and we just started crankin' out on the melody and put the lyrics together real fast. It took about 45 minutes to an hour.

SM: How about "Good Vibrations"—was that written more as a production piece than most songs? Since you were the writer, producer and visionary, I can see how the roles can overlap, especially on that cut.

BW: First it was a production kind of idea. We wrote it as we went from studio to studio. It took six weeks overall to get it done. It was written as a production. It's a pop symphony.

SM: What makes a song timeless in general and your songs in particular?

BW: I think the melodies have a catchiness to 'em . . . ah let me think . . . the harmonies are very, very loving and beautiful. I think the harmonies and the melodies are what make people still love our music. Now I wanna get into some rock and roll that will make people wanna get out of their seats and clap and yell. Yell and clap, ya know? If not stand up and cheer, at least listen. I just want to make music that makes people feel good!

SM: Kids, grandparents . . .

BW: Yeah, yep.

SM: Talk about getting out of our seats and yelling, I took my family and a ton of friends to your recent Bay Area show and wow! Also, you were most kind to say hello to me from the stage . . . thanks . . .

BW: You are very welcome, Scott. Did your kids have fun?

SM: They flipped. I have always sung "Mama Says" to them. [*sings*] "Eat a lot—sleep a lot—brush 'em like crazy . . ." They recognized a lot of the *Smile* stuff. Geez, the band was picture perfect too.

BW: They are among some of the better musicians that I've bumped into.

SM: And The Beach Boys?

BW: Oh, I think when Carl and Denny left us they stopped rockin'.

SM: Carl was the engine and Denny was the fossil fuel.

BW: Denny was a hell of a singer too, you know. And Carl . . . I'm really glad you knew him so well.

SM: Many people reading this book are starting out and to a large degree are relatively new so what advice do you have for folks who are trying to break into the music industry these days?

BW: Well, I would say if you get about half way through a project—don't back down from the project. Keep following through until you've finished your songs. And don't ever stop writing a song until you have finished it.

SM: Given *Smile* took something like 35 years to complete, are you sort of talking to yourself when you recommend this to others?

BW: Yeah . . . well, I've lived that myself. Now, I always follow through with songs that I'm writing.

SM: Where do you pull it from when the light bulb isn't over your head?

BW: Ha! God Only Knows! [*laughs*]

SM: When are you going to do that comedy record? You are one of the funniest guys . . .

BW: I got my sense of humor from my Mother. I think my Dad gave me the balls. You know as they say, "the balls" in it? But my Mother gave me lovingness and humor so that was a good combination.

SM: Did your Father instill a competitive spirit in you? I mean this is a tough business . . .

BW: Yeah, I was competitive. Subtly. I wasn't like a Paul McCartney competitive or a Phil Spector competitive. I went a little easier on it.

SM: That Spector's a pretty funny one . . .

BW: Well yeah, he's a character. He pulls guns on people. A little scary and a little funny both put together.

SM: The three of us were talking at a party in L.A. some years back and I guess I was living dangerously when I mentioned that I thought you had taken modern music the furthest.

BW: Well, I tried to!

SM: So if you hadn't gone into music, what would you have done?

BW: I would have tried out as a Major League baseball player. Yeah, I was a big New York Yankee, Boston Red Sox fan, and I wanted to be a baseball player, you know, Major Leagues. But I made a left turn [*laughs*] into the music business. And it has turned out great.

SM: What position would you have played?

BW: Centerfield.

SM: I get it . . . not too left field . . . kind of mono.

BW: OK.

Advanced Articles

Music Publishers

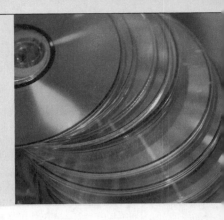

Music publishers find songs and then get them recorded. In return for a share of the money made from your songs, they work as an agent for you by plugging your songs to recording artists, taking care of paperwork and accounting, setting you up with co-writers (recording artists or other songwriters), and so on.

HOW DO MUSIC PUBLISHERS MAKE MONEY FROM SONGS?

Music publishers make money by getting songs recorded onto albums, Film and TV soundtracks, commericals, etc.and other areas. While this is their primary function, music publishers also handle administrative tasks such as copyrighting songs; collecting royalties for the songwriter; negotiating and issuing synchronization licenses for use of music in films, television programs and commercials; arranging and administering foreign rights; auditing record companies and other music users; suing infringers; and producing new demos of new songs. In a small, independent publishing company, one or two people may handle all these jobs. Larger publishing companies are more likely to be divided into the following departments: creative (or professional), copyright, licensing, legal affairs, business affairs, royalty, accounting and foreign.

HOW DO MUSIC PUBLISHERS FIND SONGS?

The *creative department* is responsible for finding talented writers and signing them to the company. Once a writer is signed, it is up to the creative department to develop and nurture the writer so he will write songs that create income for the company. Staff members often put writers together to form collaborative teams. And, perhaps most important, the creative department is responsible for securing commercial recordings of songs and pitching them for use in film and other media. The head of the creative department—usually called the "professional manager"—is charged with locating talented writers for the company.

HOW DO MUSIC PUBLISHERS GET SONGS RECORDED?

Once a writer is signed, the professional manager arranges for a demo to be made of the writer's songs. Even though a writer may already have recorded his own demo, the publisher will often re-demo the songs using established studio musicians in an effort to produce the highest-quality demo possible.

Once a demo is produced, the professional manager begins shopping the song to various outlets. He may try to get the song recorded by a top artist on his or her next album or get the song used in an upcoming film. The professional manager uses all the contacts and leads he has to get the writer's songs recorded by as many artists as possible. Therefore, he must be able to deal efficiently and effectively with people in other segments of the music industry, including A&R personnel, recording artists, producers, distributors, managers and lawyers. Through these contacts, he can find out what artists are looking for new material, and who may be interested in recording one of the writer's songs.

HOW IS A PUBLISHING COMPANY ORGANIZED?

After a writer's songs are recorded, the other departments at the publishing company come into play.

- The *licensing and copyright departments* are responsible for issuing any licenses for use of the writer's songs in film or TV and for filing various forms with the copyright office.
- The *legal affairs department and business affairs department* works with the professional department in negotiating contracts with its writers.
- The *royalty and accounting departments* are responsible for making sure that users of music are paying correct royalties to the publisher and ensuring the writer is receiving the proper royalty rate as specified in the contract and that statements are mailed to the writer promptly.
- Finally, the *foreign department*'s role is to oversee any publishing activities outside of the United States, to notify sub-publishers of the proper writer and ownership information of songs in the catalogue and update all activity and new releases, and to make sure a writer is being paid for any uses of his material in foreign countries.

LOCATING A MUSIC PUBLISHER

How do you go about finding a music publisher that will work well for you? First, you must find a publisher suited to the type of music you write. If a particular publisher works mostly with alternative music and you're a country songwriter, the contacts he has within the industry will hardly be beneficial to you.

Each listing in this section details, in order of importance, the type of music that publisher is most interested in; the music types appear in **boldface** to make them easier to locate. It's also very important to submit only to companies interested in your level of experience (see A Sample Listing Decoded on page 11). You will also want to refer to the Category Indexes on page 358, which list companies by the type of music they work with. Publishers placing music in film or TV will be proceded by a 🎬 (see the Film & TV Index on page 390 for a complete list of these companies).

Do your research!

It's important to study the market and do research to identify which companies to submit to.

- Many record producers have publishing companies or have joint ventures with major publishers who fund the signing of songwriters and who provide administration services. Since producers have an influence over what is recorded in a session, targeting the producer/publisher can be a useful avenue.
- Since most publishers don't open unsolicited material, try to meet the publishing representative in person (at conferences, speaking engagements, etc.) or try to have an intermediary intercede on your behalf (for example, an entertainment attorney; a manager, an agent, etc.).
- As to demos, submit no more than 3 songs.
- As to publishing deals, co-publishing deals (where a writer owns part of the publishing share through his or her own company) are relatively common if the writer has a well-established track record.

- Are you targeting a specific artist to sing your songs? If so, find out if that artist even considers outside material. Get a copy of the artist's latest album, and see who wrote most of the songs. If they were all written by the artist, he's probably not interested in hearing material from outside writers. If the songs were written by a variety of different writers, however, he may be open to hearing new songs.
- Check the album liner notes, which will list the names of the publishers of each writer. These publishers obviously have had luck pitching songs to the artist, and they may be able to get your songs to that artist as well.
- If the artist you're interested in has a recent hit on the *Billboard* charts, the publisher of that song will be listed in the "Hot 100 A-Z" index. Carefully choosing which publishers will work best for the material you write may take time, but it will only increase your chances of getting your songs heard. "Shotgunning" your demo packages (sending out many packages without regard for music preference or submission policy) is a waste of time and money and will hurt, rather than help, your songwriting career.

Once you've found some companies that may be interested in your work, learn what songs have been successfully handled by those publishers. Most publishers are happy to provide you with this information in order to attract high-quality material. As you're researching music publishers, keep in mind how you get along with them personally. If you can't work with a publisher on a personal level, chances are your material won't be represented as you would like it to be. A publisher can become your most valuable connection to all other segments of the music industry, so it's important to find someone you can trust and feel comfortable with.

Independent or major company?

Also consider the size of the publishing company. The publishing affiliates of the major music conglomerates are huge, handling catalogs of thousands of songs by hundreds of songwriters. Unless you are an established songwriter, your songs probably won't receive enough attention from such large companies. Smaller, independent publishers offer several advantages. First, independent music publishers are located all over the country, making it easier for you to work face-to-face rather than by mail or phone. Smaller companies usually aren't affiliated with a particular record company and are therefore able to pitch your songs to many different labels and acts. Independent music publishers are usually interested in a smaller range of music, allowing you to target your submissions more accurately. The most obvious advantage to working with a smaller publisher is the personal attention they can bring to you and your songs. With a smaller roster of artists to work with, the independent music publisher is able to concentrate more time and effort on each particular project.

SUBMITTING MATERIAL TO PUBLISHERS

When submitting material to a publisher, always keep in mind that a professional, courteous manner goes a long way in making a good impression. When you submit a demo through the mail, make sure your package is neat and meets the particular needs of the publisher. Review each publisher's submission policy carefully, and follow it to the letter. Disregarding this information will only make you look like an amateur in the eyes of the company you're submitting to.

Listings of companies in Canada are preceded by a ⬇ , and international markets are designated with a 🌐 . You will find an alphabetical list of these companies at the back of the book, along with an index of publishers by state in the Geographic Index (see page 392).

Icons

For more instructional information on the listings in this book, including explanations of symbols (Ⓝ✔️☡🔫🍁🌐◯◑◐⊘), read the article *Songwriter's Market: How Do I Use It?* on page 7.

For More Info

PUBLISHING CONTRACTS

Once you've located a publisher you like and he's interested in shopping your work, it's time to consider the publishing contract—an agreement in which a songwriter grants certain rights to a publisher for one or more songs. The contract specifies any advances offered to the writer, the rights that will be transferred to the publisher, the royalties a songwriter is to receive and the length of time the contract is valid.

- When a contract is signed, a publisher will ask for a 50-50 split with the writer. *This is standard industry practice*; the publisher is taking that 50% to cover the overhead costs of running his business and for the work he's doing to get your songs recorded.
- It is always a good idea to have a publishing contract (or any music business contract) reviewed by a competent entertainment lawyer.
- There is no "standard" publishing contract, and each company offers different provisions for their writers.

Make sure you ask questions about anything you don't understand, especially if you're new in the business. Songwriter organizations such as the Songwriters Guild of America (SGA) provide contract review services, and can help you learn about music business language and what constitutes a fair music publishing contract. Be sure to read What About Contracts? on page 36 for more information on contracts. See the Organizations section, beginning on page 293 of this book, for more information on the SGA and other songwriting groups.

When signing a contract, it's important to be aware of the music industry's unethical practitioners. The "song shark," as he's called, makes his living by asking a songwriter to pay to have a song published. The shark will ask for money to demo a song and promote it to radio stations; he may also ask for more than the standard 50% publisher's share or ask you to give up all rights to a song in order to have it published. Although none of these practices is illegal, it's certainly not ethical, and no successful publisher uses these methods. *Songwriter's Market* works to list only honest companies interested in hearing new material. (For more on "song sharks," see How Do I Avoid the Rip-Offs? on page 19.)

ADDITIONAL PUBLISHERS

There are **more publishers** located in other sections of the book! On page 136 use the list of Additional Publishers to find listings within other sections who are also music publishers.

Music Publishers

ABALORN MUSIC (ASCAP)

P.O. Box 5537, Kreole Station, Moss Point MS 39563-1537. (601)914-9413. "No collect calls." Estab. 1974. **Contact:** Joe F. Mitchell, executive vice president/general manager. First Vice President: Justin F. Mitchell. Second Vice President: Jayvean F. Mitchell. Music publisher and record company (Missile Records).

• Also see the listing for Bay Ridge Publishing in this section and the listing for Missile Records in the Record Companies section.

Affiliate(s) Bay Ridge Publishing Co. (BMI).

How to Contact *"Please don't send us anything until you contact us by phone or in writing and receive submission instructions. You must present your songs the correct way to get a reply.* **No registered mail—no exceptions! You may send a UPS or FedEx tracking number, but do not ask us to travel to the post office to sign for packages!** Always whenever you write to us, be sure you include a #10 business-size envelope addressed back to you with a first class USA postage stamp on the envelope. We reply back to you from the SASE you send to us. All songs sent for review must include sufficient return postage. No reply made back to you without SASE or return of material without sufficient return postage. **Absolutely no reply postcards—only SASE.** If you only write lyrics, do not submit. We only accept completed songs, so you must find a collaborator. We are not interested in reviewing homemade recordings." Prefers CD (first choice) or cassette with 3-8 songs and lyrics to songs submitted. Responds in 2 months. "A good quality demo recording will always get preference over a poor recording."

Music All types and styles of songs. "Mixed Up Love Affair," "Sweet Sexy Lady," and "My Love Just Fell Again" (singles) from *album title TBD* (album), written and recorded by Herb Lacy (blues);and "My First Kiss," and "Moving On" (singles by Evan Webb), as well as "My Own Paradise" (single by Brad Adams) from *album title TBD* (album), recorded by Kenny Ray (modern pop country), released on Missile Records.

Tips "Our doors are always open to young recording artists who are exceptional talented and want to make a name for themselves in the music business. Your success is our success. We will work with you to reach your goal. We also are in the business of getting your professionally-recorded album of 10-12 well-produced and well-written, radio-ready songs placed with record companies in the USA and foreign countries for the possibility of record deals. Here is what we have gotten for some artists: $850,000 record deal for Charity (religious singing group) on Big Easy (USA) in 2001; $500,000 record deal for Vance Greek on Dime-A-Dozen (Germany) in 2002; a $150,000 record deal for Randell Ruthledge (country) on Dime-A-Dozen (Germany) in 2003; and a record deal for Karen Frazier (pop) of Ren & T. (mother-daughter act) from Hyattsville, MD on Mr. Wonderful Productions in Louisville, KY. Missile Records, Abalorn Music (ASCAP) and Bay Ridge Publishing Co. (BMI) are listed in some well-known publications such as the *Billboard International Buyer's Guide*, *Mix Master Directory*, *Industrial Source Book*, *Pollstar*, *Yellow Pages of Rock* and other publications. Some well-known recording artists born and raised in Mississippi include Elvis Presley, Conway Twitty, B.B. King and Faith Hill. The Moss Point, MS area music scene is also home to nationally-known rock group Three Doors Down, who sold more than 10 million of their CD albums and singles. Singers and songwriters thinking about doing professional recording, give us a call before you make that move. We can save you money, time, headaches, heartaches and troubles you may run into. We know what to do and how to do it to benefit you and get the best results."

ABEAR PUBLISHING (BMI)/SONGTOWN PUBLISHING (ASCAP)

323 N. Walnut St., Murfreesboro TN 37130. (615)890-1878. Fax: (615)890-3771. E-mail: ron@icofm .com. **Contact:** Ron Hebert.

ACUFF-ROSE MUSIC (BMI)

• Acuff-Rose Music has been sold to Sony Music and is not accepting submissions.

ALEXANDER SR. MUSIC (BMI)

PMB 364, 7100 Lockwood Blvd., Boardman OH 44512. (330)726-8737. Fax: (330)726-8747. E-mail: dap@netdotcom.com. Web site: www.dapentertainment.com. **Contact:** LaVerne Chambers, promotions. Owner: Darryl Alexander. Music publisher, record company (DAP Entertainment), music consulting, distribution and promotional services and record producer. Estab. 1992. Publishes 12-22 songs/year; publishes 2-4 new songwriters/year. Staff size: 3. Pays standard royalty.

• Also see the listing for DAP Entertainment in the Record Producers section of this book.

How to Contact *Write first and obtain permission to submit.* Prefers cassette with 4 songs and lyric sheet. "We will accept finished masters (CD) for review." Include SASE. Responds in 2 months. "No phone calls or faxes please."

Film & TV Places 2 songs in TV/year. Music Supervisor: Darryl Alexander. Recently published "Love Never Fails in Saturday Night Live" (through DSM); "Feel Your Love" and "You Are So Beautiful" for the film *The Doctor Is Upstairs*, both written and recorded by Darryl Alexander.

Music Mostly **contemporary jazz** and **urban gospel**; also **R&B**. Does not want rock, gangsta rap, heavy metal or country. Published "Plumb Line" (single by Herb McMullan/Darryl Alexander) from *Diamond In The Sky* (album), recorded by Darryl Alexander (contemporary jazz); "3rd Eye" and "Too Late For Love" (singles) from *Diamond In The Sky* (album), written and recorded by Darryl Alexander (contemporary jazz), all released 2004 on DAP Entertainment.

Tips "Send only music in styles that we review. Submit your best songs and follow submission guidelines. Finished masters open up additional possibilities. Lead sheets may be requested for material we are interested in. Must have SASE if you wish to have CD returned. No phone calls, please."

☐ ALIAS JOHN HENRY TUNES (BMI)

11 Music Square E., Suite 607, Nashville TN 37203. (615)255-4437. E-mail: bobbyjohnhenry@bellso uth.net. **Contact:** Bobby John Henry, owner. Music publisher and record producer. Publishes 3 songs/year; publishes 1 new songwriter/year. Staff size: 3. Pays standard royalty.

How to Contact Send by mail. Prefers cassette or CD with 3 songs and lyric sheet. Does not return material. Responds in 6 months only if interested.

Music Mostly **country**, **rock** and **alternative**; also **inspirational**, **gospel**, **Christian** and **jazz**. Does not want rap. Published *Mr. Right Now* (album by Kari Jorgensen), recorded by "Hieke" on Warner Bros. (rock); and *Nothing to Me* (album by B.J. Henry), recorded by Millie Jackson on Spring.

Tips "Focus and rewrite, rewrite, rewrite. We are looking into inspirational material, any style, also gospel and Christian music, any style. I like when the story is so good you don't even realize it's a spiritual or inspirational song. I'm not crazy about the 'glory be, glory be' type of song. I'm all gloried out! I'm also interested in hearing jazz standard types of songs that might be done with a big band. I don't know what I'll do with them, but if you have them, let me hear them. I don't know if anyone knows what to do with them, but I know some great singers that are singing new material in the Cole Porter/Johnny Mercer tradition. What have ya got?"

✸ ☐ ALL ROCK MUSIC

(31) 186-604266. Fax: (32) 0186-604366. Web site: www.collectorrecords.nl. **Contact:** Cees Klop, president. Music publisher, record company (Collector Records) and record producer. Estab. 1967. Publishes 40 songs/year; publishes several new songwriters/year. Staff size: 3. Pays standard royalty.

Affiliate(s) All Rock Music (United Kingdom).

• Also see the listings for Collector Records in the Record Companies and Record Producers sections of this book.

How to Contact Submit demo by mail. Unsolicited submissions are OK. Prefers cassette. SAE and IRC. Responds in 2 months.

Music Mostly **'50s rock**, **rockabilly** and **country rock**; also **piano boogie woogie**. Published *Rock Crazy Baby* (album), written and recorded by Art Adams (1950s rockabilly), released 2004; *Marvin Jackson* (album), by Marvin Jackson (1950s rockers), released 2005; *Western Australian Snake Pit R&R* (album), recorded by various (1950s rockers), released 2005, all on Collector Records.

Tips "Send only the kind of material we issue/produce as listed."

☐ ALLEGHENY MUSIC WORKS (ASCAP, BMI)

1611 Menoher Blvd., Johnstown PA 15905. E-mail: TunedOnMusic@aol.com. Web site: www.alleg henymusicworks.com. **Contact:** Al Rita, managing director. Music publisher and record company (Allegheny Records). Estab. 1991. Staff size: 2. Pays standard royalty.

Affiliate(s) Allegheny Music Works Publishing (ASCAP) and Tuned on Music (BMI).

• Also see the listings for Allegheny Music Works in the Record Companies section and The Leads Sheet in Publications of Interest section of this book.

How to Contact *Does not accept unsolicited submissions. Write first and obtain permission to submit.* Include SASE for reply. "E-mail queries are acceptable; we respond ASAP to e-mail queries. However, we will not open e-mail containing attachments or pictures. NO Phone Call queries or solicitations. We will not reply to voice mail requests."

Music Mostly **radio-ready masters of Halloween songs** in any genre except rap and metal. "100% publishing must be open—no exceptions—and control of all rights for releasing the said masters must also be available. Songs can be for either children or adults. However, even with songs having more appeal to adults, we will not consider any material we think parents would want to screen from their children. We also do not want any material with any lyric content that suggests or makes light of cruelty to animals." Published "The Pumpkin Twist" (single), written and recorded by Ben Brown; "It's Halloween" (single by Al Rita), recorded by Victor R. Vampire; and "Halloween Is in the Air" (single by Carlon Miller/T.D. Bayless), recorded by Phil Coley, all released 2006 on Allegheny Music Works.

Tips "Bookmark our Web site and check it regularly, clicking on *Songwriter Opportunities*. Each month, as a free service to songwriters, we list a new artist or company looking for songs. Complete contact information is included."

☑ ☑ ALPHA MUSIC INC. (BMI)

747 Chestnut Ridge Rd., Chestnut Ridge NY 10977. (845)356-0800. Fax: (845)356-0895. E-mail: alpha@trfmusic.com. Web site: www.trfmusic.com. **Contact:** Michael Nurko. Music publisher. Estab. 1931. Pays standard royalty.

Affiliate(s) Dorian Music Publishers, Inc. (ASCAP) and TRF Music Inc.

• Also see listing for TRF Production Music Libraries in the Advertising, Audiovisual & Commercial Music Firms section of this book.

How to Contact "We accept submissions of new compositions. Submissions are not returnable."

Music **All categories**, mainly **instrumental** and **acoustic** suitable for use as **production music**, including **theme and background music for television and film**. "Have published over 50,000 titles since 1931."

☑ AMERICATONE INTERNATIONAL (ASCAP)

1817 Loch Lomond Way, Las Vegas NV 89102-4437. (702)384-0030. Fax: (702)382-1926. E-mail: jjj@americatone.com. Web site: www.americatone.com. **President:** Joe Jan Jaros. Estab. 1975. Publishes 25 songs/year. Pays variable royalty.

Affiliate(s) Americatone Records International, Christy Records International USA, Rambolt Music International (ASCAP).

• Also see the listing for Americatone Records International in the Record Companies section of this book.

How to Contact Submit demo by mail. Unsolicited submissions OK. Prefers CDs, "studio production with top sound recordings." Include SASE. Responds in 1 month.

Music Mostly **country**, **R&B**, **Spanish** and **classic ballads**. Published *Explosion* (album), recorded by Sam Trippe; *A New Life Start* (album), by Gabriel Oscar Rosati; *Many Ways to Go* (album), by Bill Perkins; and *Jazz in the Rain* (album), by the Rain Jazz Band; all on Americatone International Records.

☐ ANTELOPE PUBLISHING INC. (BMI)

P.O. Box 55, Rowayton CT 06853. **Contact:** Tony LaVorgna, owner/president. Music publisher. Estab. 1982. Publishes 5-10 new songs/year; publishes 3-5 new songwriters/year. Pays standard royalty.

How to Contact Submit demo by mail. Unsolicited submissions are OK. Prefers cassette with lead sheet. Does not return material. Responds in 1 month "only if interested."
Music Only **bebop** and **1940s swing**. Does not want anything electronic. Published *Inspiration* (album), written and recorded by T. LaVorgna (jazz); *Please Stay* (album by Nicole Pasternak), recorded by Cathy Gale (1940s swing), both on Antelope; *Nightcrawler* (album by Tommy Dean), recorded by Swing Fever on Alto Sound (jazz); and "Latin Blues," recorded by David Budway.
Tips "Put your best song first with a short intro."

☐ AUDIO MUSIC PUBLISHERS (ASCAP)

449 N. Vista St., Los Angeles CA 90036. (818)362-9853. Fax: (323)653-7670. E-mail: parlirec@aol.com. Web site: www.parliamentrecords.com. **Contact:** Len Weisman, professional manager. Owner: Ben Weisman. Music publisher, record company and record producer (The Weisman Production Group). Estab. 1962. Publishes 25 songs/year; publishes 10-15 new songwriters/year. Staff size: 10. Pays standard royalty.
• Also see the listings for Queen Esther Music Publishers in the Music Publishers section of this book; the Weisman Production Group in the Record Producers section of this book and Parliament Records in the Record Companies section of this book.
How to Contact Submit demo by mail. Unsolicited submissions are OK. "No permission needed." Prefers cassette with 3-10 songs and lyric sheet. "We do not return unsolicited material without SASE. Don't query first; just send tape." Responds in 6 weeks. "We listen; we don't write back. If we like your material we will telephone you."
Music Mostly **pop**, **R&B** and **rap**; also **dance**, **funk**, **soul** and **gospel**. Does not want heavy metal. "Crazy About You" (single) and *Where Is Love* (album), both written by Curtis Womack; and *Don't Make Me Walk Away* (album by Debe Gunn), all recorded by Valerie (R&B) on Kon Kord.

☑ BAIRD MUSIC GROUP (BMI)

P.O. Box 42, 1 Main St., Ellsworth PA 15331. **Contact:** Ron Baird, president. Music publisher, record company (La Ron Ltd. Records), record producer (Ron Baird Enterprises). Estab. 1999. Publishes 5-12 songs/year. Pays standard royalty.
Affiliate(s) Baird Family Music (ASCAP).
• Also see the listing for Ron Baird Enterprises in the Record Producers section of this book.
How to Contact Submit demo by mail. Unsolicited submissions are OK. "No certified mail." Prefers cassette only with 2-4 songs and lyric sheet. Does not return submissions. Responds only if interested.
Music Mostly **country** and **country rock**. Does not want hip-hop, gospel/religious or R&B.
Tips "Don't give up!"

☑ BAITSTRING MUSIC, (ASCAP)

2622 Kirtland Rd., Brewton AL 36426. (251)867-2228. **Contact:** Roy Edwards, president. Music publisher and record company (Bolivia Records). Estab. 1972. Publishes 20 songs/year; publishes 10 new songwriters/year. Hires staff songwriters. Pays standard royalty.
Affiliate(s) Cheavoria Music Co. (BMI).
• Also the listings for Cheavroia Music in this section, Bolivia Records in the Record Companies section, and Known Artist Productions in the Record Producers section of this book.
How to Contact Submit demo by mail. Unsolicited submissions are OK. Prefers CD with 3 songs and lyric sheet. Does not return material. Responds in 1 month.
Music Mostly **R&B**, **pop** and **easy listening**; also **country**. Published "Forever and Always," written and recorded by Jim Portwood (pop); and "Make Me Forget" (by Horace Linsley) and "Never Let Me Go" (by Cheavoria Edwards), both recorded by Bobbie Roberson (country), all on Bolivia Records.

☐ BARKIN' FOE THE MASTER'S BONE (ASCAP)

405 Broadway St. Suite 900, Cincinnati OH 45202-3329. (513)241-6489. Fax: (513)241-9226. E-mail: autoredcurtis@aol.com. Web site: www.1stbook.com. Company Owner (rock, R&B): Kevin Curtis.

Professional Managers: Shonda Barr (country, jazz, pop, rap); Betty Barr (gospel, soul, soft rock). Music publisher. Estab. 1989. Publishes 4 songs/year; publishes 1 new songwriter/year. Staff size: 4. Pays standard royalty.

Affiliate(s) Beat Box Music (ASCAP) and Feltstar (BMI).

How to Contact Submit demo by mail. Unsolicited submissions are OK. Prefers CD (or VHS video-cassette) with 3 songs. Include SASE. Responds in 2 weeks.

Music Mostly **top 40** and **pop**; also **soul**, **gospel**, **rap** and **jazz**. Does not want classical. Published "Lover, Lover" (single by J Tea/Jay B./Skylar) from The Time Has Come (album), recorded by J-Trey (rap), released 2003 on East Side Records; "Been A Long Time" (single by J Tea/Jay B./Skylar), from The Time Has Come (album), recorded by J-Trey (rap), released 2003 on East Side Records; "No Worries" (single by Mejestic/7-Starr/D-Smooy/Hardhead), from Home Grown (album), recorded by Low Down Boyz (rap), released 2002 on Untamed Records.

✦ BAY RIDGE PUBLISHING CO. (BMI)

P.O. Box 5537, Kreole Station, Moss Point MS 39563-1537. (601)914-9413. "No collect calls." Estab. 1974. **Contact**: Joe F. Mitchell, executive vice president/general manager. First Vice President: Justin F. Mitchell. Second Vice President: Jayvean F. Mitchell. Music publisher and record company (Missile Records).

• Also see the listing for Abalorn Music in this section and the listing for Missile Records in the Record Companies section of this book.

Affiliate(s) Abalorn Music (ASCAP).

How to Contact *"Please don't send us anything until you contact us by phone or in writing and receive submission instructions. You must present your songs the correct way to get a reply.* **No registered mail—no exceptions! You may send a UPS or FedEx tracking number, but do not ask us to travel to the post office to sign for packages!***" Always whenever you write to us, be sure you include a #10 business-size envelope addressed back to you with a first class USA postage stamp on the envelope. We reply back to you from the SASE you send to us. All songs sent for review must include sufficient return postage. No reply made back to you without SASE or return of material without sufficient return postage. **Absolutely no reply postcards—only SASE.** If you only write lyrics, do not submit. We only accept completed songs, so you must find a collaborator. We are not interested in reviewing homemade recordings." Prefers CD (first choice) or cassette with 3-8 songs and lyrics to songs submitted. Responds in 2 months. "A good quality demo recording will always get preference over a poor recording."

Music All types and styles of songs. "Mixed Up Love Affair," "Sweet Sexy Lady," and "My Love Just Fell Again" (singles) from *album title TBD* (album), written and recorded by Herb Lacy (blues);and "My First Kiss," and "Moving On" (singles by Evan Webb), as well as "My Own Paradise" (single by Brad Adams) from *album title TBD* (album), recorded by Kenny Ray (modern pop country), released on Missile Records.

Tips "Our doors are always open to young recording artists who are exceptional talented and want to make a name for themselves in the music business. Your success is our success. We will work with you to reach your goal. We also are in the business of getting your professionally-recorded album of 10-12 well-produced and well-written, radio-ready songs placed with record companies in the USA and foreign countries for the possibility of record deals. Here is what we have gotten for some artists: $850,000 record deal for Charity (religious singing group) on Big Easy (USA) in 2001; $500,000 record deal for Vance Greek on Dime-A-Dozen (Germany) in 2002; a $150,000 record deal for Randell Ruthledge (country) on Dime-A-Dozen (Germany) in 2003; and a record deal for Karen Frazier (pop) of Ren & T. (mother-daughter act) from Hyattsville, MD on Mr. Wonderful Productions in Louisville, KY. Missile Records, Abalorn Music (ASCAP) and Bay Ridge Publishing Co. (BMI) are listed in some well-known publications such as the *Billboard International Buyer's Guide*, *Mix Master Directory*, *Industrial Source Book*, *Pollstar*, *Yellow Pages of Rock* and other publications. Some well-known recording artists born and raised in Mississippi include Elvis Presley, Conway Twitty, B.B. King and Faith Hill. The Moss Point, MS area music scene is also home to nationally-known rock group Three Doors Down, who sold more than 10 million of their CD albums and singles. Singers and songwriters thinking about doing professional recording, give us a call before you make that move. We can save you money, time, headaches, heartaches and troubles you may run into. We know what to do and how to do it to benefit you and get the best results.''

⊕ BEARSONGS (PRS)

Box 944, Birmingham B16 8UT United Kingdom. 44-121-454-7020. E-mail: jim@bigbearmusic.com. Web site: www.bigbearmusic.com. Managing Director: Jim Simpson. Professional Manager: Juliet Kenny. Music publisher and record company (Big Bear Records). Member PRS, MCPS. Publishes 25 songs/year; publishes 15-20 new songwriters/year. Pays standard royalty.
- Also see the listings for Big Bear Records in the Record Companies section and Big Bear in the Record Producers section of this book.

How to Contact Submit demo by mail. Unsolicited submissions are OK. Prefers CD. Does not return material. Responds in 3 months.

Music Mostly **blues**, **swing** and **jazz**. Published *Blowing With Bruce* and *Cool Heights* (by Alan Barnes), recorded by Bruce Adams/Alan Barnes Quintet; and *Blues For My Baby* (by Charles Brown), recorded by King Pleasure & The Biscuit Boys, all on Big Bear Records.

Tips ''Have a real interest in jazz, blues, swing.''

◖ BEAVERWOOD AUDIO-VIDEO (BMI)

133 Walton Ferry, Hendersonville TN 37075. (615)824-2820. Fax: (615)824-2833. E-mail: beaverwd @bellsouth.net. Web site: www.beaverwoodaudiovideo.com. **Owner:** Clyde Beavers. Music publisher, record company (Kash Records, JCL Records), record producer, 32 track studio, audio-video duplication. Estab. 1976. Pays standard royalty.

Affiliate(s) Jackpot Music (BMI).

How to Contact Submit demo by mail. Unsolicited submissions are OK. Prefers CD, DAT or video-cassette with 1-5 songs. Does not return material.

Music Mostly **gospel** and **country**. Published ''Mary Had a Little Lamb,'' ''Listen to My Story'' and ''I Heard His Call'' (singles), all written and recorded by Lawrence Davis (gospel) on JCL Records; ''A Last Lap'' (single—tribute to Dale Earnhardt), written and recorded by Jay Powell (country); and ''My Brother'' (single—tribute to Johnny Cash), recorded by Tommy Cash.

▣ ◲ BIG FISH MUSIC PUBLISHING GROUP (ASCAP, BMI)

11927 Magnolia Blvd., Suite 3, N. Hollywood CA 91607. (818)984-0377. President, CEO and Music Publisher: Chuck Tennin. Producer: Gary Black (country, pop, adult contemporary, rock, crossover songs, other styles). Professional Music Manager: Lora Sprague (jazz, New Age, instrumental, pop rock, R&B). Professional Music Manager: B.J. (pop, TV, film and special projects). Professional Music & Vocal Consultant: Zell Black (country, pop, gospel, rock, blues). Producer Independent Artists: Darryl Harrelson—Major Label Entertainment (country, pop and other genres). Music publisher, record company (California Sun Records) and production company. Estab. 1971. Publishes 10-20 songs/year; publishes 5-10 new songwriters/year. Staff size: 7. Pays standard royalty. ''We also license songs and music copyrights to users of music, especially TV and film.''

Affiliate(s) Big Fish Music (BMI) and California Sun Music (ASCAP).

How to Contact *Write first and obtain permission to submit*. Include SASE for reply. ''*Please do not call*. After permission to submit is confirmed, we will assign and forward to you a submission code number allowing you to submit up to 4 songs maximum, preferably on CD or cassette. Include a properly addressed cover letter, signed and dated, with your source of referral (*Songwriter's Market*) with your assigned submission code number and SASE for reply and/or return of material. Include lyrics. *Unsolicited material will not be accepted*. That is our Submission Policy to review outside and new material.'' Responds in 2 weeks.

Film & TV Places 6 songs in TV/year. Recently published ''Even the Angels Knew'' (by Cathy Carlson/Craig Lackey/Marty Axelrod); ''Stop Before We Start'' (by J.D. Grieco); ''Oh Santa'' (by Christine Bridges/John Deaver), all recorded by The Black River Girls in *Passions* (NBC); licensed ''A Christmas Wish'' (by Ed Fry/Eddie Max), used in *Passions* (NBC); ''Girls Will Be Girls'' (by Cathy Carlson/John LeGrande), recorded by The Black River Girls, used in *All My Children* (ABC); ''The Way You're Drivin' Me'' and ''Ain't No Love 'Round Here'' (by Jerry Zanandrea), both recorded by The Black River Girls, used in *Passions* (NBC).

Music Country, including **country pop**, **country A/C** and **country crossover** with a cutting edge; also **pop**, **pop ballads**, **adult contemporary**, **uplifting**, **praise**, **worship**, **spiritual**, and **inspirational adult contemporary gospel** with a powerful message, **instrumental background and theme music** for TV & films, **New Age/instrumental jazz** and **novelty, orchestral classical, R&B** and **Children's music** for all kinds of commercial use. Published ''If Wishes Were Horses'' (single by Billy O'Hara); ''Purple Bunny Honey'' (single by Robert Lloyd/Jim Love); ''Leavin' You For Me'' (single by J.D. Grieco); ''Move That Train'' (single by Robert Porter); ''Happy Landing'' (by T. Brawley/B. Woodrich); ''Girls Will Be Girls'' (single by Cathy Carlson/John LeGrande); ''You Should Be Here With Me'' (single by Ken McMeans); ''Stop Before We Start'' (single by J.D. Grieco); ''The Way You're Drivin' Me'' and ''Ain't No Love 'Round Here'' (singles by Jerry Zanandrea), all recorded by Black River Girls on California Sun Records; ''Let Go and Let God'' and ''There's A Power in Prayer'' (singles by Corinne Porter/Molly Finkle), recorded by Molly Pasutti, released on California Sun Records.

Tips ''Demo should be professional, high quality, clean, simple, dynamic, and must get the song across on the first listen. Good clear vocals, a nice melody, a good musical feel, good musical arrangement, strong lyrics and chorus—a unique, catchy, clever song that sticks with you. Looking for unique country and pop songs with a different edge that can crossover to the mainstream market for ongoing Nashville music projects and songs for a hot female country trio that crosses over to adult contemporary and pop with great lush, warm harmonies that reach out to middle America and baby boomers and their grown up children (25 to 65). Also, catchy up-tempo songs with an attitude, meaningful lyrics (Shania Twain style), and unique pop songs (Celine Dion style) for upcoming album projects and song pitches. Also, soundtrack music of all types (melodic, uplifting, moody, mystique, orchestral, mind soothing, pretty, action packed, etc.) for new film production company and upcoming film and TV projects. Demo should be broadcast quality.''

☑ ▣ ◯ BLACK MARKET ENTERTAINMENT RECORDINGS (ASCAP, BMI)

2144 Hills Ave. Suite D-2, Atlanta GA 30318. (404)367-8130. Fax: (404)367-8630. E-mail: demos@bmerecording.com. **Contact:** D. Searcy, A&R. Music publisher and record company (B.M.E. Records). Estab. 1992. Staff size: 10.
Affiliate(s) SWOLE Music (ASCAP).
How to Contact Submit demo by mail at P.O. Box 20084, Atlanta GA 30325. Unsolicited submissions are OK. Prefers CD/CDR with cover letter. ''Please do not call; enclose mailing and e-mail address.'' Does not return material. Responds in 1 month.
Film & TV Places 3 songs in film and 1 song in TV/year. Music Supervisor: Vincent Phillips. Recently published ''I Like Dem'' (by J. Smith/S. Norris), recorded by Li'l Jon and the Eastside Boyz; ''Kissable Spot'' (by Jonathan Smith), recorded by Devon, both placed in Big Momma's House; and ''Trick Busta'' (by Hardnett/Anderson/Bryon), recorded by Lyrical Giants, placed in Sex and the City.
Music Mostly **rap** and **R&B**; also **rock** and **alternative**. Published ''Bia, Bia'' (single by J. Smith/S. Norris/T. Shaw/S. Martin) from *Put Yo Hood Up* (album), recorded by Lil Jon and the Eastside Boyz (rap), released 2001 on BME/TVT; ''Shut Up'' (single by R. McDowell/J. Jones/D. Green/R. Lewis) from *Right Quick* (album), recorded by Jim Crow (rap), released 2001 on Noontime/Interscope; and ''I Like Dem'' (single by J. Smith/S. Norris) from *We Still Crunk* (album), recorded by Lil Jon and the Eastside Boyz (rap), released 2000 on BME Recordings.
Tips ''Put your best foot forward. Submit only the best stuff you have. First impressions are important.''

☑ ⊘ BMG MUSIC PUBLISHING (ASCAP)

245 5th Ave. 8th Floor, New York NY 10016. (212)287-1300. Fax: (212)930-4263. Web site: www.bmgmusicsearch.com. **Contact:** Adam Epstein (pop/rock). **Beverly Hills office:** 8750 Wilshire Blvd., Beverly Hills CA 90211. (310)358-4700. Fax: (310)358-4727. **Contact:** Monti Olson (pop/rock), Brad Aarons (pop/rock), or Derrick Thompson (urban). **Nashville office:** 1600 Division St. Suite 225, Nashville TN 37203. (615)687-5800. Fax: (615)687-5839. Music publisher.
How to Contact *BMG Music Publishing does not accept unsolicited submissions.*

Music Published works by Maroon 5, Christina Aguilera, Coldplay, Nelly, Britney Spears, Keane, R. Kelly, Ne-Yo, and The All-American Rejects.

⊘ BOURNE CO. MUSIC PUBLISHERS (ASCAP)

5 W. 37th St., New York NY 10018. (212)391-4300. Fax: (212)391-4306. E-mail: bourne@bournemu sic.com. Web site: www.bournemusic.com. **Contact:** Professional Manager. Music publisher. Estab. 1919. Publishes educational material and popular music.

Affiliate(s) ABC Music, Ben Bloom, Better Half, Bogat, Burke & Van Heusen, Goldmine, Harborn, Lady Mac and Murbo Music.

How to Contact *Does not accept unsolicited submissions.*

Music Piano/vocal, **band pieces** and **choral pieces**. Published "Amen" and "Mary's Little Boy Child" (singles by Hairston); "When You Wish Upon a Star" (single by Washington/Harline); and "San Antonio Rose" (single by Bob Willis, arranged John Cacavas).

⊡ ALLAN BRADLEY MUSIC (BMI)

835 E. Buckeyewood Ave., Orange CA 92865. (714)685-9958. E-mail: melodi4ever@earthlink.net. Web site: www.ablmusic.com. **Contact:** Allan Licht, owner. Music publisher, record company (ABL Records) and record producer. Estab. 1993. Publishes 10 songs/year; publishes 5 new songwriters/ year. Staff size: 2. Pays standard royalty.

Affiliate(s) Lichtenfeld Music (ASCAP).

• Also see the listing for ABL Records in the Record Companies section of this book.

How to Contact Submit demo by mail. Unsolicited submissions are OK. Prefers CD with 3 songs and lyric sheet. "Send only unpublished works." Does not return material. Responds in 2 weeks only if interested.

Music Mostly **A/C**, **pop** and **R&B**; also **country** and **Christian contemporary**. Does not want hard rock. Published *Time to Go* (album), written and recorded by Alan Douglass; *The Sun that Follows the Rain* (album by R.K. Holler/Rob Driggers), recorded by Michael Cavanaugh (pop), released 1999; *Only In My Mind* (album by Jonathon Hansen), recorded by Allan Licht, all on ABL Records.

Tips "Be open to suggestions from well-established publishers. Please send only songs that have Top 10 potential. Only serious writers are encouraged to submit."

⊡ BRANDON HILLS MUSIC, LLC (BMI)/HEATH BROWN MUSIC (ASCAP)

N. 3425 Searle County Line Rd., Brandon WI 53919. (920)398-3279 or (cell) (920)570-1076. E-mail: marta@dotnet.com. **Contact:** Marsha Brown, president. Music publisher. Estab. 2005. Publishes 4 new songwriters/year. Staff size: 2. Pays standard royalty of 50%.

How to Contact Submit demo by mail. Unsolicited submissions are OK. Prefers CD with 1-4 songs and cover letter. Does not return submissions. Responds in 5 weeks.

Music Mostly **country (traditional, modern, country rock)**, **contemporary Christian**, **blues**; also **children's** and **bluegrass**. Does not want rap or hip-hop.

Tips "We prefer studio-produced CDs. The lyrics and the CD must match. Cover letter, lyrics, and CD should have a professional look. Demos should have vocals up front and every word should be distinguishable. Submit only your best. The better the demo, the better of chance of getting your music published and recorded."

ℕ ⊡ BRANSON COUNTRY MUSIC PUBLISHING (BMI)

P.O. Box 2527, Broken Arrow OK 74013. (918)455-9442. Fax: (918)451-1965. E-mail: bransoncm@a ol.com. **Contact:** Betty Branson, A&R. Music publisher. Estab. 1997. Publishes 5 songs/year; publishes 4-5 new songwriters/year. Pays standard royalty.

Affiliate(s) High Lonesome Country (ASCAP).

How to Contact Submit demo by mail with lyric sheet. Unsolicited submissions are OK. Prefers CD or cassette with 3-5 songs and lyric sheet. Does not return material. Responds in 3 weeks only if interested.

Music Mostly **traditional country** and **upbeat country**. Published "Sharin Sharon" (CD single),

Music publisher Allan Licht of Allan Bradley Music (BMI)/ABL Records began his musical career as a lounge singer in 1974 and performed in Cleveland, Ohio area supper clubs. By 1981, he had achieved his dream of performing in Las Vegas, and began to develop dreams of becoming a successful songwriter. In 1984, he signed a publishing deal with Buried Treasure Music (BMI) in Nashville, Tennessee. Buried Treasure owner Scott Turner signed Licht for his musical skills and introduced the budding songwriter to lyricist Diane Baumgartner, and the two formed a long-running, successful collaboration.

Licht formed his own publishing company in the early '90s to pursue cuts with artists in the pop/rock, adult contemporary, country, and Christian genres, and has published songs by songwriters Marilyn Oakley, Jonathan Hansen, and Benny Ray. He also produces, and as of this writing is in the producer's chair for contemporary Christian artist Bree Noble.

Several months prior to this interview, Licht held a pitch session with the San Diego Songwriter's Guild, his first such meeting with a songwriters organization, and our conversation begins there.

Referring to the San Diego Songwriters Guild and the meetings you had with them, would you say the songs tend to be stronger when you're dealing with a songwriters organization?
The songs were magnificent. I have never experienced so many great writers in one place in my entire career. So the answer is yes, I would say that 95% of the 50 songs sent to me were top-notch commercial hit potential songs. I was blown away. Because usually through the mail I get 20 CDs a week, and I would say out of a thousand songs, there's maybe one song. But this, everything I was hearing was a slam-dunk. It was brilliant work.

Tell me a little about some of the writers you have published, and what sort of things caught you about their music, either through the book or by whatever means you've gotten to know them.
Sure. For me, I don't meet with people one-on-one because time doesn't permit it, so when I hear a song, and this is the truth, I give a song 15 seconds. And if a song doesn't wow me in 15 seconds or less, then I move on. And what attracts me to song is: does it have a musical hook immediately? Is the demo of good quality, because I need to hear a near-finished master. So, I think the things that really grab my ear are the hookiness of the music and what's coming at me—I don't care what style it is, whether it's country or Christian contemporary, or if it's a rock or hip-hop song, but is it moving me? Am I having some kind of visceral experience? And I need to have that in 15 seconds.

In terms of the near-finished master, for those who are just writers, do you generally recommend that people *not* sing on their own demos?

I always recommend that, unless they're amazing. What I tell people is, if you want to spend money, the place you spend your money is on getting the greatest vocalist that ever walked the planet, because that is what moves most people, and that's what sells the song. So, if someone has to choose whether they get a full production and get a so-so singer, or just do a piano or guitar with vocal, you get the greatest singer possible to sing your song. I believe that is the most important thing with presenting your demo.

So even with a smaller artist on a smaller label, for songwriters who are building a career, simply getting something cut and out there has got to be a good thing.

It is a great thing, but what I tell the people I work with is make certain, though, that the cut is with a quality artist, because in my early years I had many cuts with artists that were inferior to the original demos I had sent in. But I think it's really paramount that whoever cuts your song, that they are a superior artist, because otherwise they'll be in the same situation, they'll have a song just cut by someone else that won't get the attention.

When you were with Buried Treasure Music, were you living in Nashville at the time?

No, I was living in Orange County, California. I've actually never been to Nashville. And that's the beauty nowadays with the Internet and with mailing, wherever you live, you can make it. Some say people say you have to be in a major hub—Chicago, L.A., New York—and that's not true. You don't have to be anywhere. You just have to be great at what you do.

Since you take Christian contemporary, what do people need to know about that genre to write what the market accepts?

About 50% of what I write is Christian contemporary, so you approach it just as you would the secular market. You approach it from a musical point of view. You can either write crossover-potential songs that are universal, or you can write songs that are more scripturally steeped, and that will perhaps appeal to a more evangelical crowd. Like Amy Grant. She crossed over. And a lot of Christian artists today will do secular songs as long as the lyric is inspirational. There's that real fine line, but approach it business-wise just as if you were writing a big pop ballad for Whitney Houston or Celine Dion, because the artists are of that ilk, and they are looking for songs that are just as strong, and the criteria is just as strong as it is for the secular market.

What are some of the big no-nos you see from people who submit to you through *Songwriter's Market*?

One definite no-no, before I even hear the song, is to send packages by registered mail that I have to go the Post Office to get. That is the biggest no-no. I know it makes me angry because it takes a lot of my time. Don't try to be fancy with what you're going to be sending your song in. I just feel that they're trying to make their package seem more special than what it is. It's taking my time to go to the post office to pick it up, and I don't go to the post office usually to pick stuff up, so it's an inconvenience.

Have you almost always done single-song contracts? I assume since you're a smaller operation, the idea of signing staff writers is not realistic.

It's not. I always do single-song contracts, and although I'll look for artists once in a while, I look for that hit potential song. That's my thing. I just want that Top 10-potential hit song, and when I get it, I call the individual immediately. I also don't ask for envelopes to reply, because I only reply if interested. And if I'm interested, they'll hear from me in five minutes. I will just call.

I saw that you were producing occasionally. Do you take submissions for the projects you produce, or do you typically co-write with the artist you're producing?

I do both. Currently I'm working on an album with a young lady named, Bree Noble, and I'm co-writing with her, and I also am taking outside material for her. So, I do look for outside material for the artists I work with. Definitely.

As a producer, are you always looking for the hit single, or do you sometimes choose a song because it seems suitable to be an album track and add depth to the album overall?

Most of the time, I am looking for that hit song. However I will take a song, and have recently published a song that is fantastic. It is so well written. It's a slow song and doesn't necessarily hook you write away, but it is so well written that I would definitely include it on an album. So, yes, I do look for fillers, but those songs have to be very strong songs in themselves.

Are there are a lot of people who don't get the distinction between poetry and lyrics?

I think so. In this market today and with this music nowadays, the rhymes have changed with the times. But I still think a poetic lyric that is well done has a very important place, along with the conversational lyric and the slang lyric. But I just thing it's being able to paint pictures with their words. I tell any aspiring writer that they are creating a map for someone to follow. You're painting a picture, and where are you taking me? A lot of times, they know where they're going, but they aren't able to take us with them. And so that's the craft of writing—take everyone with you on this journey.

—Ian Bessler

written and recorded by Roger Wayne Manard (country), released 2001; "Odds Are" (video single by Dale Ray/Allison Rae), recorded by Chris Lowther and the Sidewinder Band (country), released 2004; "Toy Soldier" (CD single by Teena Eaton), recorded by Carol Shull (country), released 2004 ; "Happy Mother's Day, Momma" (CD single), written and recorded by Jerry James, released 2006; and "Sharin' the Love," "She Goes Out," and "Miss Wonderful" (singles), written and recorded by Jackson Ray, released 2006.

Tips "Send good quality demo capable of competing with airplay top 40. Put your 'attention getter' up front and build from that point as the listener will give you about 10-15 seconds to continue listening or turn you off. Use a good hook and keep coming back to it."

BSW RECORDS (BMI)

P.O. Box 2297, Universal City TX 7814. (210)599-0022. E-mail: bswr18@txdirect.net. **Contact:** Frank Willson, president. Music publisher, record company and record producer (Frank Willson). Estab. 1987. Publishes 26 songs/year; publishes 14 new songwriters/year. Staff size: 5. Pays standard royalty.

Affiliate(s) WillTex Music and Universal Music Marketing (BMI).

• This company has been named Record Label of the Year ('94-'01) by the Country Music Association of America. Also see the listings for BSW Records in the Record Companies section, Frank Wilson in the Record Producers section, and Universal Music Marketing in the Managers & Booking Agents section of this book.

How to Contact Submit demo by mail. Unsolicited submissions are OK. Prefers cassette or CD with 3 songs, lyric sheet and cover letter. Include SASE. Responds in 2 months.

Film & TV Places 2 songs in film/year.

Music Mostly **country**, **blues** and **soft rock**. Does not want rap. Published *These Four Walls* (album), written and recorded by Dan Kimmel (country); and *I Cried My Last Tear* (album by T. Toliver), recorded by Candeeland (country), both released 1999 on BSW Records.

BUCKEYE MUSIC GROUP (ASCAP)

5695 Cherokee Rd., Cleveland OH 44124-3047. (440)442-7777. Fax: (440)442-1904. **Contact:** John J. Selvaggio (country) or Joseph R. Silver (rock and roll). Music publisher. Estab. 1998. Publishes 1 song/year. Staff size: 4. Pays standard royalty.

How to Contact Submit demo by mail. Unsolicited submissions are OK. Prefers cassette or CD/CDR along with VHS videocassette. "Send your best three songs with a lead sheet." Include SASE. Responds in 3 weeks.

Music Mostly **country**, **rock** and **R&B**; also **jingles** and **ballads**.

Tips "Write from the heart, not from the head. Strive to be different."

BUG MUSIC, INC. (ASCAP, BMI)

7750 Sunset Blvd., Los Angeles CA 90046. (323)969-0988. Fax: (323)969-0968. E-mail: buginfo@bugmusic.com. Web site: www.bugmusic.com. Vice President of Creative: Eddie Gomez. Creative Manager: Mara Schwartz. Creative Assistant: Nissa Pedraza. **Nashville:** 1910 Acklen Ave., Nashville TN 37212. (615)279-0180. Fax: (615)279-0184. Creative Director: John Allen; Creative Manager: Drew Hale. **New York:** 347 W. 36th St., Suite 1203, New York NY 10018. (212)643-0925. Fax: (212)643-0897. Senior Vice President: Garry Valletri. Music publisher. Estab. 1975. "We handle administration."

Affiliate(s) Bughouse (ASCAP).

How to Contact *Does not accept unsolicited submissions.*

Music **All genres**. Published "You Were Mine" (by E. Erwin/M. Seidel), recorded by Dixie Chicks on Monument.

BURIED TREASURE MUSIC (ASCAP)

524 Doral Country Dr., Nashville TN 37221. **Contact:** Scott Turner, owner/manager. Music publisher and record producer (Aberdeen Productions). Estab. 1972. Publishes 30-50 songs/year; publishes 3-10 new songwriters/year. Pays standard royalty.

Affiliate(s) Captain Kidd Music (BMI).

• Also see the listing for Aberdeen Productions in the Record Producers section of this book.

How to Contact Submit demo by mail. Unsolicited submissions are OK. Prefers cassette or VHS videocassette with 1-4 songs and lyric sheet. Responds in 2 weeks. "Always enclose SASE if answer is expected."

Music Mostly **country**, **country/pop** and **MOR**. Does not want rap, hard rock, metal, hip-hop or alternative. Published "I Still Can't Say Goodbye" (single by Bunn/Moore) from *Chicago Wind* (album), recorded by Merle Haggard (country), released 2005 on Capitol; "Please Mr. Music Man" (single by Scott Turner/Audie Murphy) and "My Baby's Coming Home" (Scott Turner/Buddy Holly/Harry Nilsson) from *Hollywood Dreamer* (album), recorded by Harry Nilsson (rock/pop), released 2006 on E-Music.

Tips "*DO NOT* send songs in envelopes that are 15×20, or by registered mail. The post office will not accept tapes in regular business-size envelopes. Also, always enclose a SASE. Submission without same aren't answered because of the wealth of tapes that come in."

◻ CALIFORNIA COUNTRY MUSIC (BMI)

112 Widmar Pl., Clayton CA 94517. (925)833-4680. **Contact:** Edgar J. Brincat, owner. Music publisher and record company (Roll On Records). Estab. 1985. Staff size: 1. Pays standard royalty.
Affiliate(s) Sweet Inspirations Music (ASCAP).
  ● Also see the listing for Roll On Records in the Record Companies section of this book.
How to Contact Submit demo by mail. Unsolicited submissions are OK. "Do not call or write. Any calls will be returned collect to caller." Prefers CD or cassette with 3 songs and lyric sheet. Include SASE. Responds in 6 weeks.
Music Mostly **MOR, contemporary country** and **pop**. Does not want rap, metal or rock. Published *For Realities Sake* (album by F.L. Pittman/R. Barretta) and *Maddy* (album by F.L. Pittman/M. Weeks), both recorded by Ron Banks & L.J. Reynolds on Life & Bellmark Records; and *Quarter Past Love* (album by Irwin Rubinsky/Janet Fisher), recorded by Darcy Dawson on NNP Records.

◻ ◻ ◻ CHERRI/HOLLY MUSIC (BMI)

1859 Acton Court, Simi Valley CA 93065-2205. (805)527-4082. E-mail: hollyrose@netscape.com. Web site: www.whirlwindrecords.com. Professional Managers: John G. Goske (MOR, top 40, jazz); Holly Rose Lawrence (R&B, new and traditional country, dance/pop); Pat (Big Red) Silzer (Southern gospel, Christian contemporary). Vice President: Helen Goske. Music publisher, record company (Whirlwind Label) and record producer (Helen and John G. Goske). Estab. 1961. Publishes 200-300 songs/year; publishes 75-100 new songwriters/year. Staff size: 3-4. Pays standard royalty.
Affiliate(s) Blue Sapphire Music (ASCAP).
How to Contact Submit professional studio demo by mail with SASE. Unsolicited submissions are OK. Prefers cassette or CD with 3 songs and typed lyric sheet and cover letter. Must be copyrighted. "Absolutely no phone calls. Put name, address and phone number on everything. Important to hear lyrics above music! "Please submit cover letter overview with demo. Lyrics should be typed. Photo would be good. Please include SASE." Does not return material. Responds in 2 months only if interested.
Music Mostly **traditional country, contemporary country with crossover edge, honky-tonk country, pop ballads** ala Diane Warren; also **Southern Christian** and **contemporary Christian gospel, salsa** and **film and TV music**. No grunge or gangster rap. Published "One Night in Nashville" and "Lone Star" (singles by Le Carol Goins), "One Lonely Teardrop" (single by Don Fields), "I Can Hear Old Dixie Call My Name" (single by David Holiday/Bert Swanson), and "Angel in Tight Blue Jeans" (single by Steven Cooper/Beverly Fisher), all recorded by Brian Curtis (country), released 2006 on Whirlwind Records; "Dance Like You Love Her" (single by Ron McManaman), recorded by Ronnie Kimball (country), released 2006 on WIR Records; "I Can Hear Kentucky Calling" (single by Beverly Fisher/Steven Cooper) from *From the Heart of Hannah Erin* (album), recorded by Hannah Erin (country bluegrass); "Maybe Next Time (single by Beverly J. Fisher) from *Holly Wassell* (album), recorded by Holly Wassell (country pop/crossover), all released 2003 on Whirlwind Records.
Tips "Submit well-crafted songs with killer hooks ala hits on radio. Must be copyrighted with symbol and year. Also looking for radio-ready masters. Whirlwind/Attitude Studios now offer songwriter demo services by some of the country's best musicians and state-of-the-art facilities—e-mail redrose511g@aol.com."

◻ ◻ CHRISTMAS & HOLIDAY MUSIC (BMI)

24351 Grass St., Lake Forest CA 92630. (949)859-1615. E-mail: justinwilde@christmassongs.com. Web site: www.christmassongs.com. **Contact:** Justin Wilde, president. Music publisher. Estab. 1980. Publishes 8-12 songs/year; publishes 8-12 new songwriters/year. Staff size: 1. "All submissions must be complete songs (i.e., music and lyrics)." Pays standard royalty.
Affiliate(s) Songcastle Music (ASCAP).
How to Contact Submit demo CD or cassette by mail. Unsolicited submissions are OK. *Do not call. Do not send unsolicited mp3s or links to Web sites.* See Web site for submission guidelines. "First class mail only. Registered or certified mail not accepted." Prefers CD or cassette with no more than 3 songs with lyric sheets. Do not send lead sheets or promotional material, bios, etc." Include SASE but does not return material out of the US. Responds only if interested.

Film & TV Places 4-5 songs in TV/year. Published "Mr. Santa Claus" in *Casper's Haunted Christmas*. **Music** Strictly **Christmas**, **Halloween**, **Hanukkah**, **Mother's Day**, **Thanksgiving**, **Father's Day** and **New Year's Eve music** in every style imaginable: easy listening, rock, R&B, pop, blues, jazz, country, reggae, rap, children's secular or religious. *Please do not send anything that isn't a holiday song.* Published "It Must Have Been the Mistletoe" (single by Justin Wilde/Doug Konecky) from *Christmas Memories* (album), recorded by Barbra Streisand (pop Christmas), released 2001 by Columbia; "What Made the Baby Cry?" (single by Toby Keith) and "You've Just Missed Christmas" (single by Penny Lea/Buzz Smith/Bonnie Miller) from *The Vikki Carr Christmas Album* (album), recorded by Vikki Carr (holiday/Christmas), released 2000 on Delta; and "Mr. Santa Claus" (single by James Golseth) from *Casper's Haunted Christmas* soundtrack (album), recorded by Scotty Blevins (Christmas), released 2000 on Koch International.

Tips "We only sign one out of every 100 submissions. Please be selective. If a stranger can hum your melody back to you after hearing it twice, it has 'standard' potential. Couple that with a lyric filled with unique, inventive imagery, that stands on its own, even without music. Combine the two elements, and workshop the finished result thoroughly to identify weak points. Submit to us only when the song is polished to perfection. Submit positive lyrics only. Avoid negative themes like 'Blue Christmas'."

☑ SONNY CHRISTOPHER PUBLISHING (BMI)

P.O. Box 9144, Ft. Worth TX 76147-2144. (817)685-8343. E-mail: ebbycondra@aol.com. **Contact:** Sonny Christopher, CEO. Music publisher, record company and record producer. Estab. 1974. Publishes 20-25 new songs/year; publishes 3-5 songwriters/year. Staff size: 1. Pays standard royalty.

How to Contact *Write first, then call and obtain permission to submit.* Prefers cassette with lyric sheet. Include SASE (#10 or larger). Responds in 3 months.

Music Mostly **country**, **rock** and **blues**. Published Did They Judge Too Hard (album by Sonny Christopher), recorded by Ronny Collins (condraebby@aol.com) on Sonshine Records.

Tips "Be patient. I will respond as soon as I can. A songwriter should have a studio-cut demo with a super vocal. I am one who can hear a song with just acoustic guitar. Don't be hesitant to do a rewrite. To the young songwriter: *never, never* quit."

☑ CHRYSALIS MUSIC GROUP (ASCAP, BMI)

8500 Melrose Ave., Suite 207, Los Angeles CA 90069. (310)652-0066. Fax: (310)652-5428. Web site: www.chrysalismusic.com. **Contact:** Mark Friedman, vice president of A&R. Music publisher. Estab. 1968.

How to Contact *Chrysalis Music does not accept any submissions.*

Music Published "Sum 41" (single), written and recorded by OutKast; "Light Ladder" (single), written and recorded by David Gray. Administer, David Lee Roth, Andrea Boccelli, Velvet Revolver, and Johnta Austin.

☑ COAL HARBOR MUSIC (BMI)

P.O. Box 148027, Nashville TN 37214-8027. (616)883-2020. E-mail: info@coalharborbmusic.com. Web site: www.coalharbormusic.com. **Contact:** Jerry Ray Wells, president. Music publisher, Record company (Coal Harbor Music), Record producer (Jerry Ray Wells), also recording studio, demo services, sheet music, number charts, management and booking services, artist development. Estab. 1990. Publishes 28 songs/year; publishes 3 new songwriters/year. Staff size: 2. Pays standard royalty.

● Also see the listing for Coal Harbor Music in the Record Companies Record section of this book.

How to Contact *Contact first via e-mail to obtain permission to submit a demo.* Send CD and SASE with lyric sheet and cover letter. Does not return submissions. Only responds if interested.

Music Mostly **country**, **gospel** and **bluegrass**; also **contemporary Christian**, **Christmas**, **patriotic**, **comedy** and **pop/rock**. Does not want heavy metal, rap, hard rock/grunge. Released "Forever True" (single) written by Ogie De Guzman, recorded by Back on Track (contemporary Christian) released 2005 on Tribute Family Corporation label; "So Good to Know" (single) from *All I Need* (album), written and recorded by Damon Westfaul (country Gospel), released 2004 on Coal Harbor/Shoreline Music; "You" (single) from *Unraveled* (album), written and recorded by Anne Borgen (contemporary Christian), released 2004 on Coal Harbor.

Tips "Write from the heart—the listener knows. Join songwriter organizations, go to seminars, co-write, etc. When submitting material send everything on one cassette or CD. Don't send two CDs and one cassette and tell us what song or track numbers to listen to. We don't have time. Put your best song first, even if it is a ballad. Keep writing; we ARE looking for GREAT songs!"

☑ COME ALIVE COMMUNICATIONS, INC. (ASCAP)

348 Valley Rd., Suite 1, West Grove PA 19390-0436. (610)869-3660. Fax: (610)869-3660. E-mail: info@comealivemusic.com. Web site: www.comealivemusic.com. Professional Managers: Joseph L. Hooker (pop, rock, jazz); Bridget G. Hylak (spiritual, country, classical). Music publisher, record producer and record company. Estab. 1985. Publishes 4 singles/year. Staff: 7. Pays standard royalty of 50%.

• Come Alive Communications received a IHS Ministries Award in 1996.

How to Contact *Call first to obtain permission to submit a demo.* For song publishing submissions, prefers CD/CDR with 3 songs, lyric sheet, and cover letter. Does not return submissions. Responds only if interested.

Music Mostly **pop**, **easy listening**, **contemporary Christian**, and **patriotic**; also **country** and **spiritual**. Does not want obscene, suggestive, violent, or morally offensive lyrics. Produced "In Search of America" (single) from *Long Road to Freedom* (album), written and recorded by J. Hooker (patriotic), released 2003 on ComeAliveMusic.com.

☑ ☑ COPPERFIELD MUSIC GROUP/PENNY ANNIE MUSIC (BMI)/TOP BRASS MUSIC (ASCAP)/BIDDY BABY MUSIC (SESAC)

1400 South St., Nashville TN 37212. (615)726-3100. Web site: www.copperfieldmusic.com. **Contact:** Ken Biddy, president/CEO.

How to Contact Contact first and obtain permission to submit a demo. Does not return submissions. Responds only if interested.

Music Mostly **country**; also **pop**, **contemporary gospel**, and **modern bluegrass**. Does not want rap or heavy/metal/rock. Recently published "Daddy Won't Sell the Farm" from *Tattoos and Scars* (album), recorded by Montgomery Gentry (country).

☑ ☐ CORELLI MUSIC GROUP (BMI/ASCAP)

P.O. Box 2314, Tacoma WA 98401-2314. (253)735-3228. E-mail: corellismusicgroup@yahoo.com. Web site: www.CorelliMusicGroup.com. **Contact:** Jerry Corelli, owner. Music publisher, record company (Omega III Records), record producer (Jerry Corelli/Angels Dance Studio) and booking agency (Tone Deaf Booking). Estab. 1996. Publishes 12 songs/year; publishes 6 new songwriters/year. Staff size: 3. Pays standard royalty.

Affiliate(s) My Angel's Songs (ASCAP); Corelli's Music Box (BMI).

How to Contact Submit demo by mail. Unsolicited submissions are OK. "No phone calls, e-mails, or letters asking to submit." Prefers CD with 3 songs, lyric sheet and cover letter. "We DO NOT accept mp3s via e-mail. We want songs with a message and overtly Christian. Make sure all material is copyrighted. *You must include SASE or we DO NOT respond!*" Responds in 2 months.

Music Mostly **contemporary Christian**, **soft rock Christian** and **Christmas**; also **love songs**, **ballads** and **new country**. Does not want songs without lyrics. Published "Did You See Him" (single by Rich Green), "Jesus Is His Name" (single by Carolyn Swayze), and "All He Ever Wanted" (single by Rich Green/Jerry Corelli), all from *Righteous Man* (album), released 2006 on Omega III Records.

Tips "Success is obtained when opportunity meets preparation! If a SASE is not sent with demo, we don't even listen to the demo. Be willing to do a rewrite. Don't send mat erial expecting us to place it with a Top Ten artist. Be practical. Do your songs say what's always been said, except differently? Don't take rejection personally."

☑ ⬛ THE CORNELIUS COMPANIES (BMI, ASCAP, SESAC)

Dept. SM, 1710 Grand Ave., Nashville TN 37212. (615)321-5333. E-mail: corneliuscomps@aol.com. Web site: www.corneliuscompanies.com. **Contact:** Ron Cornelius, owner/manager. Music publisher and record producer (Ron Cornelius). Estab. 1986. Publishes 60-80 songs/year; publishes 2-3 new songwriters/year. Occasionally hires staff writers. Pays standard royalty.

Affiliate(s) RobinSparrow Music (BMI), Strummin' Bird Music (ASCAP) and Bridgeway Music (SESAC).

How to Contact *Contact by e-mail or call for permissions to submit material.* Submit demo by mail. Unsolicited submissions are OK. Prefers CD, DAT or cassette with 2-3 songs. Include SASE. Responds in 2 months.

Music Mostly **country** and **pop**; also **positive country**, **gospel** and **alternative**. Published songs by Confederate Railroad, Faith Hill, David Allen Coe, Alabama and over 50 radio singles in the positive Christian/country format.

Tips "Looking for material suitable for film."

🌐 CRINGE MUSIC (PRS, MCPS)

The Cedars, Elvington Lane, Folkestone Kent CT18 7AD United Kingdom. (01)(303)893-472. Fax: (01)(303)893-833. E-mail: info@cringemusic.co.uk. Web site: www.cringemusic.co.uk. **Contact:** Christopher Ashman, CEO. Music publisher and record company (Red Admiral Records). Estab. 1979. Staff size: 2.

How to Contact Submit demo by mail. Unsolicited submissions are OK. Prefers CD with unlimited number of songs and lyric sheet, lead sheet. Include SASE or SAE and IRC for outside United States. Responds in approximately 3 months.

Music All styles.

🌐 🖼 ⬛ CTV MUSIC (GREAT BRITAIN)

Television Centre, St. Helier, Jersey JE1 3ZD Channel Islands Great Britain. (1534)816816. Fax: (1534)816817. E-mail: gordon.destecroix@channeltv.co.uk. Web site: www.channeltv.co.uk. **Contact:** Gordon De Ste. Croix, director of special projects. Music publisher of music for TV commercials, TV programs and corporate video productions. Estab. 1986. Staff size: 1. Pays standard royalty.

How to Contact *Does not accept unsolicited submissions.*

Music Mostly **instrumental**, for TV commercials and programs.

⬛ CURB MUSIC (ASCAP, BMI, SESAC)

48 Music Square East, Nashville TN 37203. Web site: www.curb.com.

Affiliates Mike Curb Music (BMI); Curb Songs (ASCAP); and Curb Congregation Songs (SESAC).

• *Curb Music only accepts submissions through reputable industry sources and does not accept unsolicited demos.*

⬛ JOF DAVE MUSIC (ASCAP)

1055 Kimball Ave., Kansas City KS 66104. (913)593-3180. **Contact:** David Johnson, CEO. Music publisher, record company (Cymbal Records). Estab. 1984. Publishes 30 songs/year; publishes 12 new songwriters/year. Pays standard royalty.

How to Contact *Contact first and obtain permission to submit.* Prefers cassette or CD. Include SASE. Responds in 1 month.

Music Mostly **gospel** and **R&B**. Published "The Woman I Love" (single) from *Sugar Bowl* (album), written and recorded by King Alex, released 2001 on Cymbal Records.

🖼 ⬛ THE EDWARD DE MILES MUSIC COMPANY (BMI)

28 E. Jackson Bldg., 10th Floor, #S627, Chicago IL 60604-2263. (773)509-6381. Fax: (312)922-6964. Web site: www.edmsahara.com. **Contact:** Professional Manager. Music publisher, record company (Sahara Records), record producer, management, bookings and promotions. Estab. 1984. Publishes 50-75 songs/year; publishes 5 new songwriters/year. Hires staff songwriters. Pays standard royalty.

Ron Cornelius

*The Cornelius Companies
build for the future*

Ron Cornelius, head of Nashville's Cornelius Companies music publishing and production firm, has had a long and varied career in the music industry as songwriter, recording artist, studio musician, producer, and music publisher. He has served as a backing musician, both in and out of the studio, for artists as varied as Bob Dylan, Chubby Checker, Leonard Cohen, Smoky Robinson, Johnny Cash, and Hoyt Axton. He has been signed to five different major labels as a recording artist, including the band West, who signed to Epic Records in 1967, recorded three albums, and charted nationally with a cover version of Bob Dylan's "Just Like Tom Thumb's Blues." Not surprisingly, he later contributed guitar work to seven multi-platinum albums by Bob Dylan, as well as contributing to four albums by Leonard Cohen, and serving as Cohen's bandleader for six world tours. He also contributed music to several films during this period, including two songs in *I Walk the Line*, starring Gregory Peck and Tuesday Weld.

In 1980, Cornelius moved to Nashville with the aim of becoming a record producer, but made a detour into the world of music publishing. This move into music publishing was a contingent career move on the way to being a producer, but, says Cornelius, "Little did I know, I would absolutely fall in love with publishing music and working with writers."

He held positions at Drake Music Group and ATV Music Corporation (where he administered the catalogue of Lennon and McCartney, as well as a massive catalogue of great country songs) before forming The Cornelius Companies and striking out on his own. The Cornelius Companies have had cuts with such artists as Faith Hill, Alabama, David Allen Coe, and Confederate Railroad, as well as making inroads into licensing songs for film and television. In 1995, Cornelius formed Gateway Entertainment to serve as a production and record label wing within The Cornelius Companies aimed at the "Positive Country" format. This division racked up several Top 10 hits and awards, including two #1 hits and several *Cashbox* magazine awards for Top Label for the Positive Country format.

Cornelius has strong feelings about the direction of the music industry in Nashville and the health of songwriting as an art form, as seen through the lens of his wide-ranging career, and agreed to share his thoughts with us on these and other topics.

Do songwriters tend to have common misconceptions about what it takes to be a successful music publisher?

Oh, definitely! The main thing being that a lot of writers don't realize that publishing is a full-time job. Paul Overstreet, five years in a row BMI Writer of the Year, was with Tree for a long time and at that end of his agreement decided he wanted to have his own publishing company. And I think that lasted a year or so, and before you know it, he folded that tent and signed back with a big publisher. And the reason for that is if you're going to be a publisher, if you're going to make sure and take care of things and police copyrights on a worldwide basis, it truly is a full-time job, just like being a writer is a full-time job. They don't realize there is a whole segment of people out there that truly are full-time writers, and those people are in direct competition with each other, and if you take time out of your work-week to worry about the publishing side of it while you're [also] trying to write songs, you're cheating yourself. You need to choose one or the other, in my estimation.

Having worked directly with Bob Dylan and Leonard Cohen, did you experience a culture shock when you moved to Nashville? How has Music City changed?
Actually, I found Nashville was more appreciative of the craft of songwriting, but I've watched over the years as the level of the quality of songs in Nashville, Tennessee simply has descended. Now, there's an exception to every rule, such as "I Hope You Dance." What a wonderful song! It may be there are quite a lot of those still being written, however because of what I always call "political cannibalism," which appears constantly, daily in the major labels, disc jockeys on the radio are constantly saying stuff like, "When is Nashville going to stop with this every-song-sounds-alike-type thing?" Well, I just keep praying that something will come along.

And it seems to have started in that direction with iPods, and things like that. People can go back to just buying what *is* good, and they don't have to buy an album because they really are in love with one or two songs and the rest they could care less about. And if that really does take hold, what we're going to see is the major labels are definitely going to have to start saying, "OK, we've got to steer away from this cannibalistic atmosphere, and put ten great songs on a record, or we're not going to be selling them."

So the downward pressure is coming from the label end?
That's right. As far as your big-time writers go, I've heard several of them say, "I need to write down to the labels nowadays. I'm not trying to do by best all the time." And that's a shame, just to earn a living. People like Max D. Barnes and Larry Kingston and Harlan Sanders, who wrote "If Drinkin' Don't Kill Me, Her Memory Will," people that wrote great country standards that will be here as long as country music is around, found themselves in the last few years actually having to *write down* to the labels, because radio is only going to get what the labels give them.

Some performing singer-songwriters outside Nashville have aspirations to write for others, but their work is idiosyncratic to their own abilities as performers. Do they generally understand the level of craft needed to succeed in writing songs for other artists?
I don't think they do to tell you the truth, because you just used the correct term—it is a real "craft," and it is something that can be learned. Now, when you speak of someone like a Leonard Cohen, or a Bob Dylan, or a Loudon Wainwright III, they merely use music as a forum to speak to the people. The people who write songs for a living here in Nashville, Tennessee, which is the Tin Pan Alley of our time, are tremendously concerned with what is known as "radio-programmable current country music." This is way, way different than being emotionally driven to speak to the masses about something.

Let's say you're talking about trying to get someone as big as Faith Hill or Alan Jackson, somebody who is one of the true superstars of the industry. I think that a writer needs to take only their very strongest stuff, and develop it after those people. That doesn't mean they can't also through their craft, and through networking here in Nashville with other people, write songs that I would call an "across the board pitch"—a good radio current programmable song that you could pitch to nine different artists.

What should these songwriters keep in mind so that a song intended for Faith Hill not only expresses something meaningful for her, but is also congruent with the public image she cultivates as a recording artist?

I'm looking at four or five gold and platinum albums by Faith Hill that our company has here for music of ours that she's recorded, but the camp that surrounds her is a very hard wall to get over. I know a lot of great songs that have gone at that camp and couldn't get over the brick wall. But as far as what Faith actually hears, I think that she does have good ears, because the things that seem to speak to aspects of her own life, she's not afraid to get up and record those, and I respect that a lot. When you see her on TV, she has a lot to say about her husband and her kids, and the family atmosphere in her home, and that should give writers and publishers a pretty good view on what is going to touch her if it gets all the way in there.

Is there really a big advantage to moving to Nashville and being there in the songwriting scene?

If somebody has it in their mind that they only want to be a successful songwriter—they don't have any aspirations to be onstage in the limelight, in a record deal and all that— that person needs to move to Nashville. If someone wants to be a recording artist, I think it's a mistake to move to Nashville, because after a while they become sort of like furniture. Even though somebody might really have something going, somebody in some label is going to go, "Oh, yeah, I saw them. They're always down at the Broken Spoke."

What are the requirements versus radio, for getting songs licensed to film? Should demos be of broadcast quality?

Yes, that's help a lot, because what our company is doing here regarding film and TV is a little different than most publishers. Because of the production side of our company, we're sitting on two or three million dollars worth of masters, so when it comes to dealing with film and television, this is a "one-stop" situation. You'll find that the user, whether Paramount Pictures or Warner Bros., whoever it is, when they decide on a piece they really can't live without, normally they now have to get legal access to that piece of music from the publisher, and if they want to use what they're listening to, now they also have to turn around and go to that label that put that record out, and negotiate a deal with them.

Once in a while, that's a smooth thing. So often, one or the other wants so much for it that it queers the deal. And the reason I like to see things that we put in our film package nicely done, is so that it is a one-stop situation. If they want to re-record the song, fine I can deal with that on a publisher level and work out a synch license that we're all happy with. If they want to use what they're holding in their hands, they don't have to go to anybody else. This company can license the music, the master, whatever they want. If they want us to take the vocal off and put a saxophone on it, we can do that.

Have you ever had a writer work on assignment for a film?

No, I haven't.

Does your own career suggest any across-the-board strategy for success in the music industry?

If I pull my profile on my Web site up and look back over it myself, I even go "Jeez, I ought to be 200 years old to have done all that." But if there is one thing I could leave to anybody inquisitive about being a writer or being an artist, I would have to say that it's a rollercoaster situation if you want to make a life out of music. You can have a year or so where you have more travel, more money, more of everything than you ever thought you would have, followed directly by, "How in the world did I ever choose to do this for a living?"

But looking back at the best years, the curve at the top of each of those ups and downs, I would say the best times, the most successful times, were when I'd had enough of trying to figure out the business of all this crap and I said, "To heck with it, I'm just going to do my music!" That's seems to be when the best things happen for people.

—Ian Bessler

• Also see the listings for Edward De Miles in the Record Producers and Managers & Booking Agents sections, and Sahara Records And Filmworks Entertainment in the Record Companies section of this book.

How to Contact *Write first and obtain permission to submit.* Prefers cassette with 1-3 songs and lyric sheet. Does not return material. Reponds in 1 month.

Music Mostly **top 40 pop/rock**, **R&B/dance** and **country**; also **musical scores for TV, radio, films** and **jingles**. Published "Dance Wit Me" and "Moments" (singles), written and recorded by Steve Lynn on Sahara Records (R&B).

Tips "Copyright all songs before submitting to us."

☑ DELEV MUSIC COMPANY (ASCAP, BMI)

7231 Mansfield Ave., Philadelphia PA 19138-1620. (215)276-8861. Fax: (215)276-4509. E-mail: delevmusic@msn.com. President/CEO: William L. Lucas. A&R: Darryl Lucas. Music publisher. Publishes 6-10 songs/year; publishes 6-10 new songwriters/year. Pays standard royalty.

Affiliate(s) Sign of the Ram Music (ASCAP) and Delev Music (BMI).

How to Contact *Does not accept unsolicited material. Write or call first to obtain permission to submit.* Prefers CD with 1-8 songs and lyric sheet. "We will not accept certified mail or SASE." Does not return material. Responds in 1-2 months.

Music Mostly **R&B ballads** and **dance-oriented**; also **pop ballads, christian/gospel, crossover** and **country/western**. No gangsta rap. Published "Angel Love" (single by Barbara Heston/Geraldine Fernandez) from *The Silky Sounds of Debbie G* (album), recorded by Debbie G (light R&B/easy listening), released 2000 on Blizzard Records; *Variety* (album), produced by Barbara Heston and Carment Lindsay, released on Luvya Records; and "Ever Again" by Bernie Williams, released 2003 on SunDazed Records.

Tips "Persevere regardless if it is sent to our company or any other company. Most of all, no matter what happens, believe in yourself."

☑ DISNEY MUSIC PUBLISHING, (ASCAP, BMI)

500 S. Buena Vista St., Burbank CA 91521-6182. (818)569-3228. **Contact:** Brian Rawlings or Ashley Saunig, DMP creative department.

Affiliate(s) Seven Peaks Music and Seven Summits Music.

How to Contact *Call first and obtain permission to submit.* Does not return material.

☐ DREAM SEEKERS PUBLISHING (BMI)

21 Coachlight Dr., Danville IL 61832-8240. (615)822-1160. President: Sally Sidman. Music publisher. Estab. 1993. Publishes 25-50 songs/year; publishes 15-20 new songwriters/year. Pays standard royalty.

Affiliate(s) Dream Builders Publishing (ASCAP).

How to Contact Submit demo by mail. Unsolicited submissions are OK. "Please do not call to request permission—just submit your material. There are no code words. We listen to everything." Prefers cassette or CD with 2 songs and lyric sheet. "If one of your songs is selected for publishing, we prefer to have it available on CD for dubbing off copies to pitch to artist." Include SASE. Responds in 6 weeks.

Music Mostly **country**. "All types of **country** material, but mostly in need of up -tempo songs, preferably with positive lyrics." Does not want rap, jazz, classical, children's, hard rock, instrumental or blues. Published "Not Done Yet" (single by Coley McCabe/Mark Collie) from *Alabama Love Story* (album), recorded by Mark Collie (country), released 2004; "A Dad Like That" (single by Jamie Champa) from *Ken Mahon* (album), recorded by Ken Mahon (country), released 2003; and "City Lights" (single by Kim Caudill) from *So Far So Good* (album), recorded by Avery Lovey (country), released 2004.

Tips "Be willing to work hard to learn the craft of songwriting. Be persistent. Nobody is born a hit songwriter. It often takes years to achieve that status."

☑ DREAMWORKS SKG MUSIC PUBLISHING

331 N. Maple Dr., Suite 300, Beverly Hills CA 90210. Web site: www.dreamworkspublishing.com. Music publisher and record company (DreamWorks Records).

 • Dreamworks SKG Music Publishing has been bought out by Universal Music Publishing.

☑ DUANE MUSIC, INC. (BMI)

382 Clarence Ave., Sunnyvale CA 94086. (408)739-6133. **Contact:** Garrie Thompson, President. Music publisher and record producer. Publishes 10-20 songs/year; publishes 1 new songwriter/year. Pays standard royalty.

Affiliate(s) Morhits Publishing (BMI).

How to Contact Submit demo by mail. Unsolicited submissions are OK. Prefers CD with 1-2 songs. Include SASE. Responds in 2 months.

Music Mostly **blues**, **country**, **disco** and **easy listening**; also **rock**, **soul** and **top 40/pop**. Published "Little Girl" (single), recorded by The Syndicate of Sound & Ban (rock); "Warm Tender Love" (single), recorded by Percy Sledge (soul); and "My Adorable One" (single), recorded by Joe Simon (blues).

☑ EARITATING MUSIC PUBLISHING (BMI)

P.O. Box 1101, Gresham OR 97030. Music publisher. Estab. 1979. Pays individual per song contract, usually greater than 50% to writer.

How to Contact Submit demo by mail. Unsolicited submissions are OK. Prefers CD or CD-R with lyric sheet. "Submissions should be copyrighted by the author. We will deal for rights if interested." Does not return material. Responds only if interested.

Music Mostly **rock**, **country** and **folk**. Does not want rap.

Tips "Melody is most important, lyrics second. Style and performance take a back seat to these. A good song will stand with just one voice and one instrument. Also, don't use staples on your mailers."

☑ EARTHSCREAM MUSIC PUBLISHING CO., (BMI)

8377 Westview Dr., Houston TX 77055. (713)464-GOLD. E-mail: sarsjef@aol.com. Web site: www.s oundartsrecording.com. **Contact:** Jeff Wells; Peter Verheck. Music publisher, record company and record producer. Estab. 1975. Publishes 12 songs/year; publishes 4 new songwriters/year. Pays standard royalty.

 • Also see the listings for Surface Records in the Record Companies section and Sound Arts Recording Studio in the Record Producers section of this book.

Affiliate(s) Reach For The Sky Music Publishing (ASCAP).

How to Contact Submit demo by mail. Unsolicited submissions are OK. Prefers cassette or videocassette with 2-5 songs and lyric sheet. Does not return material. Responds in 6 weeks.

Music Mostly **new rock**, **country**, **blues** and **top 40/pop**. Published "Baby Never Cries" (single by Carlos DeLeon), recorded by Jinkies on Surface Records (pop); "Telephone Road" (single), written and recorded by Mark May(blues) on Icehouse Records; "Do You Remember" (single by Barbara Pennington), recorded by Perfect Strangers on Earth Records (rock), and "Sherly Crow" (single), recorded by Dr. Jeff and the Painkillers (pop).

☑ ELECTRIC MULE PUBLISHING COMPANY (BMI)/NEON MULE MUSIC (ASCAP)
1500 Clifton Ln., Nashville TN 37215. E-mail: emuleme@aol.com. **Contact**: Jeff Moseley, President.

◐ EMANDELL TUNES (ASCAP, BMI, SESAC)
10220 Glade Ave., Chatsworth CA 91311. (818)341-2264. Fax: (818)341-1008. **Contact:** Leroy C. Lovett, Jr., president/administrator. Music Publisher. Estab. 1979. Publishes 6-12 songs/year; publishes 3-4 new songwriters/year. Pays standard royalty.
Affiliate(s) Ben-Lee Music (BMI), Birthright Music (ASCAP), Em-Jay Music (ASCAP), Northworth Songs, Chinwah Songs, Gertrude Music (all SESAC), Andrask Music, Australia (BMI), Nadine Music, Switzerland.
How to Contact *Write first and obtain permission to submit.* Prefers CD, cassette or videocassette with 4-5 songs and lead or lyric sheet. Include bio of writer, singer or group. Include SASE. Responds in 6 weeks.
Music Mostly **inspirational**, **contemporary gospel** and **choral**; also **strong country** and **light top 40**. Published "Under My Skin" and "Colorada River" (singles by Diana/Kim Fowley), recorded by Diana, released 2001 on WFL Records; and "Runaway Love" (single by Gil Askey), recorded by Linda Clifford (new gospel), released 2001 on Sony Records.
Tips "We suggest you listen to current songs. Imagine how that song would sound if done by some other artist. Keep your ear tuned to new groups, bands, singers. Try to analyze what made them different, was it the sound? Was it the song? Was it the production? Ask yourself these questions: Do they have that 'hit' feeling? Do you like what they are doing?"

☑ EMF PRODUCTIONS (ASCAP)
1000 E. Prien Lake Rd., Suite D, Lake Charles LA 70601. E-mail: emfprod@aol.com. Web site: www.emfproductions.com. President: Ed Fruge. Music publisher and record producer. Estab. 1984. Pays standard royalty.
How to Contact Submit demo by mail. Unsolicited submissions are OK. Prefers CD or VHS videocassette with 4 songs and lyric sheet. Does not return material. Responds in 6 weeks.
Music Mostly **R&B**, **pop** and **rock**; also **country** and **gospel**.

☑ EMI CHRISTIAN MUSIC PUBLISHING (ASCAP, BMI, SESAC)
P.O. Box 5085, Brentwood TN 37024. (615)371-6800. Web site: www.emicmg.com. Music publisher. Publishes 100 songs/year; publishes 2 new songwriters/year. Hires staff songwriters. Pays standard royalty.
Affiliate(s) Birdwing Music (ASCAP), Sparrow Song (BMI), His Eye Music (SESAC), Ariose Music (ASCAP), Straightway Music (ASCAP), Shepherd's Fold Music (BMI), Songs of Promise (SESAC), Dawn Treader Music (SESAC), Meadowgreen Music Company (ASCAP), River Oaks Music Company (BMI), Stonebrook Music Company (SESAC), Bud John Songs, Inc. (ASCAP), Bud John Music, Inc. (BMI), Bud John Tunes, Inc. (SESAC).
How to Contact *"We do not accept unsolicited submissions."*
Music Published "Concert of the Age" (by Jeffrey Benward), recorded by Phillips, Craig & Dean; "God Is In Control," written and recorded by Twila Paris, both on StarSong Records; and "Faith, Hope and Love" (by Ty Lacy), recorded by Point of Grace on Word Records.
Tips "Come to Nashville and be a part of the fastest growing industry. It's nearly impossible to get a publisher's attention unless you know someone in the industry that is willing to help you."

☑ EMI MUSIC PUBLISHING
1290 Avenue of the Americas, 42nd Floor, New York NY 10104. (212)492-1200. Web site: www.emi musicpub.com. Music publisher.

How to Contact *EMI does not accept unsolicited material.*

Music Published "All Night Long" (by F. Evans/R. Lawrence/S. Combs), recorded by Faith Evans featuring Puff Daddy on Bad Boy; "You" (by C. Roland/J. Powell), recorded by Jesse Powell on Silas; and "I Was" (by C. Black/P. Vassar), recorded by Neal McCoy on Atlantic.

Tips "Don't bury your songs. Less is more—we will ask for more if we need it. Put your strongest song first."

◻ EMSTONE MUSIC PUBLISHING (BMI)

Box 398, Hallandale FL 33008. (305)936-0412. E-mail: webmaster@emstonemusicpublishing.com. **Contact:** Michael Gary, creative director. President: Mitchell Stone. Vice President: Madeline Stone. Music publisher. Estab. 1997. Pays standard royalty.

How to Contact Submit demo CD by mail with any number of songs. Unsolicited submissions are OK. Does not return material. Responds only if interested.

Music Everything except classical and opera. Published "www.history" (single by Tim Eatman) and "Gonna Recall My Heart" (single by Dan Jury) from *No Tears* (album), recorded by Cole Seaver and Tammie Darlene, released on CountryStock Records; and "I Love What I've Got" (single by Heather and Paul Turner) from *The Best of Talented Kids* (compilation album) recorded by Gypsy.

Tips "We only offer publishing contracts to writers whose songs exhibit a spark of genius. Anything less can't compete in the music industry."

◻ ◻ FAMOUS MUSIC PUBLISHING LLC (ASCAP, BMI)

10635 Santa Monica Blvd., Suite 300, Los Angeles CA 90025. (310)441-1300. Fax: (310)441-4722. President: Ira Jaffe. Vice President, Film and TV: Stacey Palm. Senior Creative Director: Carol Spencer (rock/pop/alternative). Senior Creative Director/Latin: Claribell Cuevas. **New York office:** 1633 Broadway, 11th Floor, New York NY 10019. (212)654-7433. Fax: (212)654-4748. Chairman and CEO: Irwin Z. Robinson. Executive Vice President, Finance and Administration: Margaret Johnson. Vice President Catalogue Development: Mary Beth Roberts. Creative Director: Britt Morgan-Saks. **Nashville office:** 65 Music Square East, Nashville TN 37212. (615)329-0500. Fax: (615)321-4121. Senior Creative Director: Curtis Green. Music Publisher. Estab. 1929.

Affiliate(s) Famous Music (ASCAP) and Ensign Music (BMI).

How to Contact *Famous Music does not accept unsolicited submissions.*

Film & TV Famous Music is a Paramount Pictures' company. Music Supervisor: Stacey Palm.

◻ FIFTH AVENUE MEDIA, LTD. (ASCAP)

1208 W. Broadway, Hewlett NY 11557. (212)691-5630. Fax: (212)645-5038. E-mail: thefirm@thefir m.com. Web site: www.thefirm.com. Professional Managers: Bruce E. Colfin(rootsy bluesy rock/ reggae, Jam Bands/alternative rock/heavy metal); Jeffrey E. Jacobson (hip-hop/R&B/dance). Music publisher and record company (Fifth Avenue Media, Ltd.). Estab. 1995. Publishes 2 songs/year. Staff size: 4. Pays standard royalty.

Music Published "Analog" (single by Paul Byrne) from Paul Byrne & the Bleeders (album), recorded by Paul Byrne (pop rock), released 2001 on Independent.

◻ ◻ ◻ ◻ FIRST TIME MUSIC (PUBLISHING) U.K. (PRS, MCPS)

Sovereign House, 12 Trewartha Road, Praa Sands, Penzance, Cornwall TR20 9ST United Kingdom. (01736)762826. Fax: (01736)763328. E-mail: panamus@aol.com. Web site: www.panamamusic.co .uk. **Contact:** Roderick G. Jones, managing director. Music publisher, record company (Rainy Day Records, Mohock Records, HepCat Records, Pure Gold Records). Estab. 1986. Publishes 500-750 songs/year; 20-50 new songwriters/year. Staff size: 6. Hires staff writers. Pays standard royalty; "50-60% to established and up-and-coming writers with the right attitude."

Affiliate(s) Scamp Music Publishing, Panama Music Library, Musik Image Library, Caribbean Music Library, Psi Music Library, ADN Creation Music Library, Promo Sonor International, Eventide Music, Melody First Music Library, Piano Bar Music Library, Corelia Music Library, Panama Music Ltd.

How to Contact Submit demo by mail. Unsolicited submissions are OK. Submit on CD only, "of professional quality'' with unlimited number of songs and lyric or lead sheets. Responds in 1 month. SAE and IRC required for reply.

Film & TV Places 200 songs in film and TV/year. ''Copyrights and phonographic rights of Panama Music Limited and its associated catalogue idents have been used and subsist in various productions broadcasts and adverts produced by major and independent production companies, television, film/video companies, radio broadcasters (not just in the UK, but in various countries world-wide) and by commercial record companies for general release and sale. In the UK & Republic of Ireland they include the BBC networks of national/regional television and radio, ITV network programs and promotions (Channel 4, Border TV, Granada TV, Tyne Tees TV, Scottish TV, Yorkshire TV, HTV, Central TV, Channel TV, LWT, Meridian TV, Grampian TV, GMTV, Ulster TV, Westcountry TV, Channel TV, Carlton TV, Anglia TV, TV3, RTE (Ireland), Planet TV, Rapido TV, VT4 TV, BBC Worldwide, etc.), independent radio stations, satellite Sky Television (BskyB), Discovery Channel, Learning Channel, National Geographic, Living Channel, Sony, Trouble TV, UK Style Channel, Hon Cyf, CSI, etc., and cable companies, GWR Creative, Premier, Spectrum FM, Local Radio Partnership, Fox, Manx, Swansea Sound, Mercury, 2CRFM, Broadland, BBC Radio Collection, etc. Some credits include copyrights in programs, films/videos, broadcasts, trailers and promotions such as Desmond's, One Foot in the Grave, EastEnders, Hale and Pace, Holidays from Hell, A Touch of Frost, 999 International, and Get Away.''

Music All styles. Published ''Truly'' (single) from *Innocence* (album), recorded by Rik Waller (soul music), released 2005 on Red Admiral Records; ''Blitz'' (single) from *Heavy Rock Spectacular* (album), recorded by Bram Stoker (Gothic rock music), released 2004 on Windmill Records, Arkama Records, Black Widow Records, Comet Records and Panama Music Library Records in 2006; and ''Dreaming Fields'' (single) from *Winter* (album), recorded by Kevin Kendle (New Age instrumental), released 2004 on Eventide Records and Panama Music Library Records in 2006.

Tips ''Have a professional approach—present well produced demos. First impressions are important and may be the only chance you get. Writers are advised to join the Guild of International Songwriters and Composers in the United Kingdom.''

🖼 ▢ FRESH ENTERTAINMENT (ASCAP)

1315 Simpson Rd., Atlanta GA 30314. E-mail: whunter1122@yahoo.com. **Contact:** Willie W. Hunter, managing director. Music publisher and record company. Publishes 5 songs/year. Staff size: 4. Hires staff songwriters. Pays standard royalty.

Affiliate(s) !Hserf Music (ASCAP), Blair Vizzion Music (BMI), Santron Music (BMI), G.I. Joe Muzick Publishing (BMI), and Bing-O Productions.

How to Contact Submit demo by mail. Unsolicited submissions are OK. Prefers cassette or videocassette with 3 songs and lyric sheet. ''Send photo if available.'' Include SASE. Responds in 6 weeks.

Film & TV Places 1 song in TV/year. Published the theme song for BET's *Comic Vue* (by Charles E. Jones), recorded by Cirocco.

Music Mostly **rap**, **R&B** and **pop/dance**. Published *Ancestral Spirits* (album), written and recorded by Robert Miles (jazz), released 2004 on Sheets of Sound/Fresh Entertainment; *My Life My Hustle* (album), written and recorded by Jamal Smith (rap/hip-hop), released 2004 on Vision Vibe/Fresh Entertainment; ''Go Sit Down'' (single), by Maceo, released 2005 on Quick Flip/Fresh Entertainment.

✓ ▨ FRICON MUSIC COMPANY (BMI)

1050 S. Ogden Dr., Los Angeles CA 90019. (323)931-7323. Fax: (323)938-2030. E-mail: fricon@com cast.net. President: Terri Fricon. **Contact:** Madge Benson, professional manager. Music publisher. Estab. 1981. Publishes 25 songs/year; publishes 1-2 new songwriters/year. Staff size: 6. Pays standard royalty.

Affiliate(s) Fricout Music Company (ASCAP) and Now and Forever Songs (SESAC).

How to Contact *Contact first and obtain permission to submit.* Prefers CD with 3-4 songs and lyric or lead sheet. ''Prior permission must be obtained or packages will be returned.'' Include SASE. Responds in 2 months.

Music Mostly **country**.

☐ FURROW MUSIC (BMI)

P.O. Box 4121, Edmond OK 73083-4121. E-mail: furromusic@sbcglobal.net. **Contact:** G.H. Derrick, owner/publisher. Music publisher, record company (Gusher Records) and record producer. Estab. 1984. Publishes 10-15 songs/year. Staff size: 1. Pays standard royalty.

How to Contact Submit demo by mail. Unsolicited submissions are OK. Prefers CD with no more than 5 songs or cassette with 1 song and lyric sheet. "One instrument and vocal is OK for demo." Include SASE. Responds in 2 weeks.

Music Mostly **country** and **cowboy**. Prefer up -tempo; no drinking or cheating songs.

Tips "Have your song critiqued by other writers (or songwriter organizations) prior to making the demo. Only make and send demos of songs that have a universal appeal. Make sure the vocal is out front of the music. Never be so attached to a lyric or tune that you can't rewrite it. Don't forget to include your SASE and lyric sheet with all submissions."

☑ G MAJOR MUSIC (BMI)

P.O. Box 3331, Fort Smith AR 72913-3331. E-mail: JerryGlidewell@juno.com. **Owner:** Jerry Glidewell. Professional Managers: Alex Hoover. Music publisher. Estab. 1992. Publishes 10 songs/year; publishes 2 new songwriters/year. Staff size: 2. Pays standard royalty.

How to Contact Submit inquiry by mail. No unsolicited submissions. Prefers CD. Submit up to 3 songs. Include SASE. Responds in 3 weeks.

Music Mostly **country** and **contemporary Christian**. Published *Set The Captives Free* (album by Chad Little, Jeff Pitzer, Ben Storie), recorded by Sweeter Rain for Cornerstone Television (contemporary Christian); "Don't Talk About Love" (single by Chad Little and Jerry Glidewell), recorded by Carrie Underwood (country); and "Competition with a Track" (by Elaine Wooslsey), recorded by Libby Benson (Christian contemporary), all on MBS.

Tips "We are looking for 'smash hits' to pitch to the Country and Christian markets."

☐ ALAN GARY MUSIC (ASCAP, BMI)

P.O. Box 179, Palisades Park NJ 07650. President: Alan Gary. Creative Director: Fran Levine. Creative Assistant: Harold Green. Music publisher. Estab. 1987. Publishes a varying number of songs/year. Staff size: 3. Pays standard royalty.

How to Contact Submit demo by mail. Unsolicited submissions are OK. Prefers cassette or VHS videocassette with lyric sheet. Include SASE.

Music Mostly **pop**, **R&B** and **dance**; also **rock**, **A/C** and **country**. Published "Liberation" (single by Gary/Julian), recorded by Les Julian on Music Tree Records (A/C); "Love Your Way Out of This One" (single by Gary/Rosen), recorded by Deborah Steel on Bad Cat Records (contemporary country); and "Dueling Rappers" (single by Gary/Free), recorded by Prophets of Boom on You Dirty Rap! Records (rap/R&B).

☐ GLAD MUSIC CO. (ASCAP, BMI, SESAC)

14340 Torrey Chase, Suite 380, Houston TX 77014. (281)397-7300. Fax: (281)397-6206. E-mail: hwesdaily@gladmusicco.com. Web site: www.gladmusicco.com. **Contact:** Wes Daily, A&R Director (country). Music publisher, record company and record producer. Estab. 1958. Publishes 10 songs/year; publishes 10 new songwriters/year. Staff size: 4. Pays standard royalty.

Affiliate(s) Bud-Don (ASCAP) and Rayde (SESAC).

How to Contact *Write first and obtain permission to submit.* Prefers CD with 3 songs, lyric sheet and cover letter. Does not return material. Responds in 6 weeks. SASE or e-mail address for reply.

Music Mostly **country**. Does not want weak songs. Published *Love Bug* (album by C. Wayne/W. Kemp), recorded by George Strait, released 1995 on MCA; *Walk Through This World With Me* (album), written and recorded by George Jones and *Race Is On* (album by D. Rollins), recorded by George Jones, both released 1999 on Asylum.

☑ ☒ ☐ GOODNIGHT KISS MUSIC (BMI, ASCAP)

10153½ Riverside Dr. #239, Toluca Lake CA 91602. (831)479-9993. Web site: www.goodnightkiss.com. **Contact:** Janet Fisher, managing director. Music publisher, record company and record producer. Estab. 1986. Publishes 6-8 songs/year; publishes 4-5 new songwriters/year. Pays standard royalty.

• Goodnight Kiss Music specializes in placing music in movies and TV.

Affiliate(s) Scene Stealer Music (ASCAP).

How to Contact "Check our Web site or subscribe to free newsletter (www.goodnightkiss.com) to see what we are looking for and to obtain codes. Packages must have proper submission codes, or they are discarded." Only accepts material that is requested on the Web site. Prefers CD or with 1-3 songs and lyric sheet. Send SASE for reply. Does not return material. Responds in 6 months.

Film & TV Places 3-5 songs in film/year. Published "I Do, I Do, Love You" (by Joe David Curtis), recorded by Ricky Kershaw in Road Ends; "Bee Charmer's Charmer" (by Marc Tilson) for the MTV movie Love Song; "Right When I Left" (by B. Turner/J. Fisher) in the movie Knight Club.

Music **All modern styles.** Published and produced Addiction: Highs & Lows (CD), written and recorded by various artists (all styles), released 2004; Tall Tales of Osama Bin Laden (CD), written and recorded by various artists (all styles parody), released 2004; and Rythm of Honor (CD), written and recorded by various artists (all styles), slated release 2005, all on Goodnight Kiss Records.

Tips "The absolute best way to keep apprised of the company's needs is to subscribe to the online newsletter. Only specifically requested material is accepted, as listed in the newsletter (what the industry calls us for is what we request from writers). We basically use an SGA contract, and there are never fees to be considered for specific projects or albums. However, we are a real music company, and the competition is just as fierce as with the majors."

⒩ ◻ R.L. HAMMEL ASSOCIATES, INC. (ASCAP/BMI)

"Consultants to the Music, Recording & Entertainment Industries," P.O. Box 531, Alexandria IN 46001-0531. E-mail: info@rlhammel.com. Web site: www.rlhammel.com. **Contact:** A&R Department. President: Randal L. Hammel. Music publisher, record producer and consultant. Estab. 1974. Staff size: 3-5. Pays standard royalty.

Affiliate(s) LADNAR Music (ASCAP) and LEMMAH Music (BMI).

How to Contact Submit demo by mail. Unsolicited submissions are OK. Prefers CD, DAT or VHS/8mm videocassette with a maximum of 3 songs and typed lyric sheets. "Please notate three (3) best songs—no time to listen to a full project." Does not return material. Responds ASAP. "No fixed timeline."

Music Mostly **pop** and **Christian R&B**; also **MOR**, **light rock**, **pop country** and **feature film title cuts**. Published Lessons For Life (album by Kelly Hubbell/Jim Boedicker) and I Just Want Jesus (album by Mark Condon), both recorded by Kelly Connor, released on iMPACT Records.

⊕ ◿ HAPPY MELODY

VZW, Paul Gilsonstraat 31, St-Andries 8200 Belgium. 00 32 50-316380. Fax: 00 32 50-315235. E-mail: happymelody@skynet.be. **Contact:** Eddy Van Mouffaert, general manager. Music publisher, record company (Jump Records) and record producer (Jump Productions). Member SABAM S.V., Brussels. Publishes 100 songs/year; publishes 8 new songwriters/year. Staff size: 2. Pays standard royalty via SABAM S.V.

How to Contact Submit demo CD or tape by mail. Unsolicited submissions are OK. Prefers CD. Does not return material. Responds in 2 weeks.

Music Mostly **easy listening**, **disco** and **light pop**; also **instrumentals**. Published "Football Mania" (single by R. Mondes/J. Towers/D. Winters), recorded by Le Grand Julot (accordion), released 2005 on Scorpion; Don't Give Up Your Dream (album), written and recorded by Chris Clark (pop), released 2004 on 5 Stars; and Instrumental Delight (album), written and recorded by various artists (pop), released 2005 on Belstar.

Tips "Music wanted with easy, catchy melodies (very commercial songs)."

☑ ⠶ ⊘ HICKORY LANE PUBLISHING AND RECORDING (ASCAP, SOCAN)

2713 Oakridge Crescent, Prince George BC V2K 3Y2 Canada. (250)962-5135. E-mail: cmupublishing @aol.com. **Contact:** Chris Urbanski, president. Music publisher, record company and record producer. Estab. 1988. Hires staff writers. Publishes 30 songs/year; publishes 5 new songwriters/year. Pays standard royalty.

How to Contact *Does not accept unsolicited submissions.*

Music Mostly **country** and **country rock**. Published "Just Living For Today" (single by Chris Urbanski), recorded by Chris Michaels (country), released 2005 on Hickory Lane Records; "This is My Sons" (single by Tyson Avery/Chris Urbanski/Alex Bradshaw), recorded by Chris Michaels (country), released 2005 on Hickory Lane Records; "Stubborn Love" (single by Owen Davies/Chris Urbanski/John Middleton), recorded by Chris Michaels (country), released 2005 on Hickory Lane Records.

Tips "Send us a professional quality demo with the vocals upfront. We are looking for hits, and so are the major record labels we deal with. Be original in your approach, don't send us a cover tune."

☑ HIGH-MINDED MOMA PUBLISHING & PRODUCTIONS (BMI)

P.O. Box 487, Myrtle Point OR 97458. **Contact:** Kai Moore Snyder, president. Music publisher and production company. Pays standard royalty.

How to Contact Prefers 7½ ips reel-to-reel, CD or cassette with 4-8 songs and lyric sheet. Include SASE. Responds in 1 month.

Music Mostly **country, MOR, rock (country), New Age** and **top 40/pop**.

☑ ☑ ☐ HIS POWER PRODUCTIONS AND PUBLISHING (ASCAP, BMI)

1304 Canyon, Plainview TX 79072-4740. (806)296-7073. Fax: (806)296-7111. E-mail: dcarter@hisp ower.net. Professional Managers: T.D. (Darryl) Carter (R&B, gospel, country rock, jazz, pop, new rock, classic rock) . Music publisher, record company (Lion and Lamb), record producer, artist and song development, agent for placement and representation (End-Time Management & Booking Agency). Estab. 1995. Publishes 0-3 songs/year; publishes 0-3 new songwriters/year. Staff size: 3. May hire staff songwriters. Pays negotiable royalty.

Affiliate(s) Love Story Publishing (BMI).

• The song "Heal Me," published by His Power, was awarded ASCAP Popular Award from 1998-2005.

How to Contact *E-mail or call first and obtain permission to submit.* Prefers mp3, CD or DAT with 1-4 songs and lyric sheet. "No material returned. Send copies only." Responds if interested.

Music Mostly **gospel, pop, inspirational, black, new rock, classic rock, country/rock** and **adult contemporary gospel**; also **R&B, jazz, Christ-oriented Christmas music, pro-life and family**. Looking for unconventional styles and structure. Does not want negative-based lyrics of any kind. Published "It's His Life" (single) and "Bible Thumpers Blues" (single), written and recorded by Mike Burchfield (country gospel), released on Lion and Lamb Records, produced by T.D. Carter.

Tips "Be serious. We are only interested in those who have meaning and substance behind what is created. Music is an avenue to change the world. Submit what comes from the heart. Don't be in a hurry. Good music has no time limits. And yet, time will reward the desire you put into it. Be willing to embark on newly designed challenges that will meet a new century of opportunity and needs never before obtainable through conventional music companies."

☐ HITSBURGH MUSIC CO. (BMI)

P.O. Box 1431, 233 N. Electra, Gallatin TN 37066. (615)452-0324. Promotional Director: Kimolin Crutcher. A&R Director: K'leetha Gilbert. Executive Vice President: Kenneth Gilbert. **Contact:** Harold Gilbert, president/ general manager. Music publisher. Estab. 1964. Publishes 12 songs/year. Staff size: 4. Pays standard royalty.

Affiliate(s) 7th Day Music (BMI).

How to Contact Submit demo by mail. Unsolicited submissions are OK. Prefers cassette or quality videocassette with 2-4 songs and lead sheet. Prefers studio produced demos. Include SASE. Responds in 6 weeks.

Music Mostly **country gospel** and **MOR**. Published "That Kind'a Love" (single by Kimolin Crutchet and Dan Serafini), from *Here's Cissy* (album), recorded by Cissy Crutcher (MOR), released 2005 on Vivaton; and "Disorder at the Border" (single), written and recorded by Donald Layne, released 2001 on Southern City.

☐ HOME TOWN HERO'S PUBLISHING (BMI)

112 West Houston, Leonard TX 75452. (903)587-2767. **Contact:** Tammy Wood, owner. Music publisher. Estab. 2003. Staff size: 2. Pays standard royalty.

How to Contact Submit demo by mail. Unsolicited submissions are OK. Prefers cassette or CD with 3-6 songs, lyric sheet, and cover letter. Does not return submissions. Responds only if interested.

Music Mostly **country (all styles)**, **pop**, **Southern rock**; also **ballads**, **gospel**, and **blues**. Does not want heavy metal and rap.

Tips "Most of all, believe in yourself. The best songs come from the heart. Don't get discouraged, be tough, keep writing, and always think positive."

[N] ⊕ ☐ INSIDE RECORDS/OK SONGS

St.-Jacobsmarkt 76, Antwerp 6 2000 Belgium. (32) + 3 + 226-77-19. Fax: (32) + 3 + 226-78-05. **Contact:** Jean Ney, MD. Music publisher and record company. Estab. 1989. Publishes 50 songs/year; publishes 30-40 new songwriters/year. Hires staff writers. Royalty varies "depending on teamwork."

How to Contact Submit demo by mail. Unsolicited submissions are OK. Prefers cassette with complete name, address, telephone and fax number. SAE and IRC. Responds in 2 months.

Music Mostly **dance, pop** and **MOR contemporary**; also **country, reggae** and **Latin**. Published *Fiesta De Bautiza* (album by Andres Manzana); *I'm Freaky* (album by Maes-Predu'homme-Robinson); and *Heaven* (album by KC One-King Naomi), all on Inside Records.

[N] ⊕ ☒ ☐ INTOXYGENE SARL

283 Fbg St. Antoine, Paris 75011 France. 011(33)1 43485151. Fax: 011(33)1 43485753. Web site: www.intoxygene.com or www.intoxygene.net. E-mail: infos@intoxygene.com. **Contact:** Patrick Jammes, managing director. Music publisher and record company. Estab. 1990. Staff size: 1. Publishes 30 songs/year. Pays 50% royalty.

How to Contact *Does not accept unsolicited submissions.*

Film & TV Places 3/5 songs in film and in TV/year.

Music Mostly **new industrial** and **metal**, **lounge**, **electronic**, and **ambient**. Does not want country, pop or jazz. Publisher and label for Peeping Tom (trip-hop), Djaimin (house), Missa Furiosa by Thierry Zaboitzeff (progressive), and The Young Gods (alternative) amongst others.

☒ ☐ IVORY PEN ENTERTAINMENT (ASCAP)

P.O. Box 1097, Laurel MD 20725. (301)490-4418. Fax: (301)490-4635. E-mail: ivorypen@comcast.net. Web site: www.ivorypen.com. Professional Managers: Steven Lewis (R&B, hip-hop, inspirational); Sonya Lewis (pop/rock, A/C). Music publisher. Estab. 2003. Publishes 10 songs/year. Staff size: 4. Pays standard royalty.

How to Contact Submit demo by mail. Unsolicited submissions are OK. Prefers CD with 3-5 songs and cover letter. Include SASE. Does not return material. Responds in 3 months. "Don't forget contact info with e-mail address for faster response! Always be professional when you submit your work to any company."

Music Mostly **R&B**, **hip-hop**, and **inspirational/gospel**; also **jazz**, **adult contemporary**, and **pop/rock**. Published *V.I. Professa* (album), written and recorded by Marvin Davis Jr. Project (R&B/Caribbean), released on Ivory Pen Entertainment; and "All Healed" (single), by Angel Demone, on Vox Angel Inc./Ivory Pen Entertainment.

Tips "Learn your craft and don't steal from other musicians. Be original. Ivory Pen Entertainment is a music publishing company that caters to the new songwriter, producer and aspiring artist. We also place music tracks (no vocals) with artists for release."

⊕ ☐ JA/NEIN MUSIKVERLAG GMBH (GEMA)

Oberstr. 14 A, D-20144, Hamburg Germany. Fax: (49)(40)448 850. E-mail: janeinmv@aol.com. General Manager: Mary Dostal. Music publisher, record company and record producer. GEMA.

Publishes 50 songs/year; publishes 5 new songwriters/year. Staff size: 3. Pays 60% royalty.
Affiliate(s) Pinorrekk Mv., Star-Club Mv. and Wunderbar Mv. (GEMA).
How to Contact Submit audio (visual) carrier by mail. Unsolicited submissions are OK. Prefers CDR or VHS videocassette. Enclose e-mail address. Responds in 2 months.
Music Mostly **jazz**, **klezmer**, **pop**, **rap** and **rock**. Published *Groovology* (album) written and recorded by Axel Zwingenberger and Gottfried Boettger (boogie woogie & blues), released 2004 on Vagabond; *Horizons* (album) written and recorded by Gottfried Boettger (ragtime/jazz), released 2004 on Vagabond.
Tips "We do not return submitted material. Send A-Side songs or extraordinary works/ideas only, please. Write what you expect from collaboration. If artist, enclose photo. If CS, leave three seconds between tracks. Enclose lyrics. Be fantastic!"

JAELIUS ENTERPRISES (ASCAP, BMI)
P.O. Box 459, Royse City TX 75189. (972)636-9230. Fax: (972)636-0036. E-mail: jaelius@flash.net. Web site: www.jaelius.com. **Contact:** James Cornelius, managing director. Music publisher. Staff size: 2. Pays standard royalty.
Affiliate(s) Jaelius Music (ASCAP), Hitzgalore Music (BMI), Air Rifle Music (ASCAP) and Bee Bee Gun Music (BMI).
How to Contact *Write or call first and obtain permission to submit.* Prefers CD. Include SASE. Responds in 6 weeks.
Film & TV Places 2 songs in film/year. Recently published "Night Has a Thousand Eyes" (by Wayne/Weisman/Garrett), recorded by Anita Kelsey in Dark City; and "Feeling in Love," written and recorded by J.J. Cale in Lawn Dogs.
Music Mostly gospel. Published "Where Would I Be Without Your Love" (single), recorded by Lee Mays (gospel); "God Gives His Love International" (single), recorded by Michelle Deck (gospel).
Tips "Today's market requires good demos. Strong lyrics are a must."

JERJOY MUSIC, (BMI)
P.O. Box 1264, 6020 W. Pottstown Rd., Peoria IL 61654-1264. (309)673-5755. Fax: (309)673-7636. E-mail: uarltd@A5.com. Web site: www.unitedcyber.com. **Contact:** Jerry Hanlon, professional manager. Music publisher and record company (UAR Records). Estab. 1978. Publishes 6 songs/year; publishes 6 new songwriters/year. Staff size: 3. Pays standard royalty.
Affiliate(s) Kaysarah Music (ASCAP); Abilite Music (BMI).
   • Also see the listing for Kaysarah Music in this section and UAR Records in the Record Companies section of this book.
How to Contact *Write first and obtain permission to submit.* "WE DO NOT RESPOND TO TELEPHONE CALLS. We are currently accepting only a limited number of submissions, *so please write for permission before sending.* Unsolicited submissions are OK, but be sure to send SASE/and or postage or mailing materials if you want a reply and/or a return of all your material. WE DO NOT OFFER CRITIQUES OF YOUR WORK UNLESS SPECIFICALLY ASKED. Simple demos—vocal plus guitar or keyboard are acceptable. We DO NOT require a major demo production to interpret the value of a song." Prefers CD with 4-8 songs and lyric sheet. Responds in 2 weeks.
Music Mostly **country**. Published "For Old Loves Sake," "Never Mind" and "You Don't Have to Tell Me" (singles by Norma Owen) and "Just An Ordinary Woman" (single by J.J. Jan Cole), recorded by Melanie Hiatt (country); "All Your Little Secrets" and "The Girl From Central High" (singles by Ron Czikall), recorded by Tracy Wells (country); "Inching My Way Toward Heaven" and "Rainbows in Heaven" (singles by J.W. Rhea/Marilyn Westerhoff/Danny Blakey), recorded by Danny Blakey (country), all released on UAR Records.
Tips "Don't submit any song that you don't honestly feel is well constructed and strong in commercial value. Be critical of your writing efforts. Be sure you use each and every one of your lyrics to its best advantage. 'Think Big!' Make your songs tell a story and don't be repetitive in using the same or similar ideas or words in each of your verses. Would your musical creation stand up against the major hits that are making the charts today? Think of great hooks you can work into your song ideas."

JODA MUSIC (BMI)

P.O. Box 100, Spirit Lake IA 51360. (712)336-2859. E-mail: jdsenn@mchsi.com. President: John Senn. Music publisher and record company. Estab. 1970. Publishes 10 songs/year. Pays standard royalty.

Affiliate(s) Okoboji Music (BMI).

How to Contact Prefers CD with no more than 4 songs and lyric sheet. "Keep demos short." Include SASE. Responds in 3 weeks.

Music Mostly light rock, country and gospel. Published "Beer & Popcorn" (single by Dave Peterson), recorded by Ralph Lundquist (country); "Change is Going to Come" (single by Roger Hughes), recorded by Silver $ Band (pop); and *Ain't Like it Used to Be* (album by Dave Petersen and John Senn), recorded by Brent (pop), all on IGL Records.

QUINCY JONES MUSIC (ASCAP)

6671 Sunset Blvd., #1574A, Los Angeles CA 90028. (323)957-6601. E-mail: info@quincyjonesmusic.com. Music publisher.

How to Contact *Quincy Jones Music does not accept unsolicited submissions.*

JPMC MUSIC INC. (BMI, ASCAP)

P.O. Box 526, Burlington VT 05402. (802)860-7110. Fax: (802)860-7112. E-mail: music@jpmc.com. Web site: www.jpmc.com. **Contact:** Jane Peterer, president. Music publisher, record company (JPMC Records) and book publisher. Estab. 1989. Publishes 20 songs/year; publishes 10 new songwriters/year. Pays standard royalty.

Affiliate(s) GlobeSound Publishing (ASCAP) and GlobeArt Publishing Inc. .

How to Contact Submit a demo by mail. Unsolicited submissions are OK. Prefers "professional" DAT, CD or cassette with 3 songs and lyric sheet. "If submitting a CD, indicate which three tracks to consider, otherwise only the first three will be considered." Include SASE. Responds in 2 months. See Web site for complete guidelines.

Music Mostly **pop/R&B**, **jazz** and **gospel**; also **country** and **instrumental**. Published "Ode to Ireland" (single by Breschi), recorded by Breschi/Cassidy on Pick Records (instrumental); and "Ici Paris" (single), written and recorded by Michael Ganian.

Tips "We are in constant communication with record and film producers and will administer your work on a worldwide basis. We also publish songbooks for musicians and fans, as well as educational and method books for students and teachers."

JUKE MUSIC (BMI)

P.O. Box 120277, Nashville TN 37212. **Contact:** Becky Gibson, songwriter coordinator. Music publisher. Estab. 1987. Publishes 60-150 songs/year; publishes 3-25 new songwriters/year. Pays standard royalty.

How to Contact Submit demo by mail. Unsolicited submissions are OK. Prefers CD with 3 songs and lyric sheet. "Send only radio-friendly material." Does not return material. Responds only if interested.

Music Mostly **country/pop** and **rock**; also **alternative adult** and **Christian**. Does not want theatrical, improperly structured, change tempo and feel, poor or no hook. Published "Cross on the Highway" (single) from *Sumner Country Drive Inn* (album), written and recorded by Ronnie McDowell, released 2001 on Portland; "Wichita Woman" (single), written and recorded by Buddy Jewell (country), released 2006 on Sony; "Living the American Dream" (single) from *Kansas Storm* (album), written and recorded by Dave Parks (country), released 2006 on DayDreamer.

Tips "Do your homework, craft the song, be sure you're willing to gamble your songwriting integrity on this song or songs you're sending. We recommend songwriters attend workshops or conferences before submitting material. Help us cut through the junk. Send positive, up -tempo, new country for best results. It seems most of our submitters read what we do not want and send that! Please listen to country radio."

◻ **KAYSARAH MUSIC (ASCAP, BMI)**
P.O. Box 1264, 6020 W. Pottstown Rd., Peoria IL 61654-1264. (309)673-5755. Fax: (309)673-7636. E-mail: uarltd@A5.com. Web site: www.unitedcyber.com. **Contact:** Jerry Hanlon, owner/producer. Music Publisher, record company (UAR Records), and record producer. Estab. 2000. Publishes 2 new songwriters/year. Staff size: 3. Pays standard royalty.
Affiliate(s) Jerjoy Music (BMI); Abilite Music (BMI).
● Also see the listing for Jerjoy Music in this section and UAR Records in the Record Companies section of this book.
How to Contact *Write first and obtain permission to submit. "WE DO NOT RESPOND TO TELE-PHONE CALLS. We are currently accepting only a limited number of submissions, so please write for permission before sending.* Unsolicited submissions are OK, but be sure to send SASE/and or postage or mailing materials if you want a reply and/or a return of all your material. *WE DO NOT OFFER CRITIQUES OF YOUR WORK UNLESS SPECIFICALLY ASKED."* Prefers CD with 4 songs and lyric sheet and cover letter. Include SASE. Responds in 2 weeks.
Music Mostly **traditional country** and **country gospel**; also **Irish country**, **Irish ballads** and **Irish folk/traditional**.
Tips "Be honest and self critical of your work. Make every word in a song count. Attempt to create work that is not over 2:50 minutes in length. Compare your work to the songs that seem to be what you hear on radio. A good A&R person or professional recording artist with a creative mind can determine the potential value of a song simply by hearing a melody line (guitar or keyboard) and the lyrics. DON'T convince yourself that your work is outstanding if you feel that it will not be able to compete with the tough competition of today 's market."

◪ **LAKE TRANSFER PRODUCTIONS & MUSIC (ASCAP, BMI)**
11300 Hartland St., North Hollywood CA 91605. (818)508-7158. **Contact:** Jim Holvay, professional manager (pop, R&B, soul); Tina Antoine (hip-hop, rap); Steve Barri Cohen (alternative rock, R&B). Music publisher and record producer (Steve Barri Cohen). Estab. 1989. Publishes 11 songs/year; publishes 3 new songwriters/year. Staff size: 6. Pay "depends on agreement, usually 50% split."
Affiliate(s) Lake Transfer Music (ASCAP) and Transfer Lake Music (BMI).
How to Contact *Does not accept unsolicited submissions.*
Music Mostly **alternative pop**, **R&B/hip-hop** and **dance**. Does not want country & western, classical, New Age, jazz or swing. Published "Tu Sabes Que Te Amo (Will You Still Be There)" (single by Steve Barri Cohen/Rico) from *Rico: The Movement II* (album), recorded by Rico (rap/hip-hop), released 2004 on Lost Empire/Epic-Sony; "When Water Flows" (single by Steve Barri Cohen/Sheree Brown/Terry Dennis) from *Sheree Brown "83"* (album), recorded by Sheree Brown (urban pop), released 2004 on BBEG Records (a division of Saravels, LLC); and "Fair Game" (single by LaTocha Scott/Steve Barri Cohen) soundtrack from the movie *Fair Game* (album), recorded by LaTocha Scott (R&B/hip-hop), released 2004 on Raw Deal Records, College Park, Georgia. "All our staff are songwriters/producers. Jim Holvay has written hits like 'Kind of a Drag' and 'Hey Baby They're Playin our Song' for the Buckinghams. Steve Barri Cohen has worked with every one from Evelyn 'Champagne' King (RCA), Phantom Planets (Epic), Mer edith Brooks (Capitol) and Dre (Aftermath/Interscope)."
Tips "Trends change, but it's still about the song. Make sure your music and lyrics have a strong (POV) point of view."

◪ **LARI-JON PUBLISHING (BMI)**
P.O. Box 216, Rising City NE 68658. (402)542-2336. **Contact:** Larry Good, owner. Music publisher, record company (Lari-Jon Records), management firm (Lari-Jon Promotions) and record producer (Lari-Jon Productions). Estab. 1967. Publishes 20 songs/year; publishes 2-3 new songwriters/year. Staff size: 1. Pays standard royalty.
How to Contact Submit demo by mail. Unsolicited submissions are OK. Prefers CD with 5 songs and lyric sheet. "Be professional." Include SASE. Responds in 2 months.
Music Mostly **country**, **Southern gospel** and **'50s rock**. Does not want rock, hip-hop, pop or heavy metal. Published "Bluegrass Blues" and "Carolina Morning" (singles by Larry Good) from *Carolina*

Morning (album), recorded by Blue Persuasion (country), released 2002 by Bullseye; ''Those Rolling Hills of Glenwood'' (single by Tom Campbell) from *Single* (album), recorded by Tom Campbell (country), released 2001 by Jeffs-Room-Productions.

▢ LCS MUSIC GROUP (ASCAP, BMI, SESAC)

P.O. Box 7809, Dallas TX 75209. E-mail: chris@dallastexas.cc. Web site: www.ccentertainment.c om. Professional Managers: Chris Christian (pop/Christian); Gina Madrigal. Music publisher, record company and record producer. Estab. 1981. Publishes 2,000 songs/year. Staff size: 3. Hires staff songwriters. Pays standard royalty.

Affiliate(s) Home Sweet Home Music/Bug and Bear Music (ASCAP), Chris Christian Music (BMI) and Monk and Tid (SESAC).

How to Contact Submit demo by mail. Unsolicited submissions are OK. Prefers CD, DAT or video-cassette. Include name, phone number and e-mail on CD or tape. Does not return material. Responds if interested.

Music Does not want quartet music.

Tips ''Keep writing until you get good at your craft. Co-write with the best you can—always put phone number on tape or CD's.''

◩ ◪ ▢ LILLY MUSIC PUBLISHING (SOCAN)

61 Euphrasia Dr., Toronto ON M6B 3V8 Canada. (416)782-5768. Fax: (416)782-7170. E-mail: panfilo @sympatico.ca. **Contact:** Panfilo Di Matteo, president. Music publisher and record company (P. & N. Records). Estab. 1992. Publishes 20 songs/year; publishes 8 new songwriters/year. Staff size: 3. Pays standard royalty.

Affiliate(s) San Martino Music Publishing and Paglieta Music Publishing (CMRRA).

How to Contact Submit demo by mail. Unsolicited submissions are OK. Prefers CD (or videocassette if available) with 3 songs and lyric and lead sheets. ''We will contact you only if we are interested in the material.'' Responds in 1 month.

Film & TV Places 12 songs in film/year.

Music Mostly **dance**, **ballads** and **rock**; also **country**. Published ''I'd Give It All'' (single by Glenna J. Sparkes), recorded by Suzanne Michelle (country crossover), released 2005 on Lilly Records.

◪ LINEAGE PUBLISHING CO. (BMI)

P.O. Box 211, East Prairie MO 63845. (573)649-2211. **Contact:** Tommy Loomas, professional manager. Staff: Alan Carter and Joe Silver. Music publisher, record producer, management firm (Staircase Promotions) and record company (Capstan Record Production). Pays standard royalty.

How to Contact Submit demo by mail. Unsolicited submissions are OK. Prefers cassette with 2-4 songs and lyric sheet; include bio and photo if possible. Include SASE. Responds in 2 months.

Music Mostly **country**, **easy listening**, **MOR**, **country rock** and **top 40/pop**. Published ''Let It Rain'' (single by Roberta Boyle), recorded by Vicarie Arcoleo on Treasure Coast Records; ''Country Boy'' (single), written and recorded by Roger Lambert; and ''Boot Jack Shuffle'' (single by Zachary Taylor), recorded by Skid Row Joe, both on Capstan Records.

◪ LITA MUSIC, (ASCAP)

2831 Dogwood Place, Nashville TN 37204. (615)269-8682. Fax: (615)269-8929. Web site: http:// songsfortheplanet.com. **Contact:** Justin Peters, president. Music publisher. Estab. 1980.

Affiliate(s) Justin Peters Music, Platinum Planet Music and Tourmaline (BMI).

How to Contact Submit demo by mail. Unsolicited submissions are OK. Prefers CD with 5 songs and lyric sheet. Does not return material. ''Place code '2007' on each envelope submission.''

Music Mostly **Southern gospel/Christian**, **country**, **classic rock** and **worship songs**. Published ''No Less Than Faithful'' (single by Don Pardoe/Joel Lyndsey), recorded by Ann Downing on Daywind Records, Jim Bullard on Genesis Records and Melody Beizer (#1 song) on Covenant Records; ''No Other Like You'' (single by Mark Comden/Paula Carpenter), recorded by Twila Paris and Tony Melendez (#5 song) on Starsong Records; ''Making A New Start'' and ''Invincible Faith'' (singles by Gayle Cox), recorded by Kingdom Heirs on Sonlite Records; and ''I Don't Want To Go

Back'' (single by Gayle Cox), recorded by Greater Vision on Benson Records; ''Lost In The Shadow of the Cross'' (single by James Elliott and Steven Curtis Chapman) recorded by Steven Curtis Chapman on Spawn Records.

☐ M & T WALDOCH PUBLISHING, INC. (BMI)

4803 S. Seventh St., Milwaukee WI 53221. (414)482-2194. VP, Creative Management (rockabilly, pop, country): Timothy J. Waldoch. Professional Manager (country, top 40): Mark T. Waldoch. Music publisher. Estab. 1990. Publishes 2-3 songs/year; publishes 2-3 new songwriters/year. Staff size: 2. Pays standard royalty.

How to Contact Submit demo by mail. Unsolicited submissions are OK. Prefers CD with 3-6 songs and lyric or lead sheet. ''We prefer a studio produced demo.'' Include SASE. Responds in 3 months.

Music Mostly **country/pop**, **rock**, **top 40 pop**; also **melodic metal**, **dance**, **R&B**. Does not want rap. Published ''It's Only Me'' and ''Let Peace Rule the World'' (by Kenny LePrix), recorded by Brigade on SBD Records (rock).

Tips ''Study the classic pop songs from the 1950s through the present time. There is a reason why good songs stand the test of time. Today's hits will be tomorrow's classics. Send your *best* well-crafted, polished song material.''

Ⓝ Ⓐ MAKERS MARK GOLD PUBLISHING (ASCAP)

534 W. Queen Lane, Philadelphia PA 19144. (215)849-7633. E-mail: MakersMark@verizon.net. **Contact:** Paul Hopkins, producer/publisher. Music publisher and record producer. Estab. 1991. Pays standard royalty.

How to Contact Submit demo CD or tape by mail. Unsolicited submissions are OK. Prefers 2-4 songs. Does not return material. Responds in 6 weeks if interested.

Music Mostly **R&B**, **hip-hop**, **gospel**, **pop** and **house**. Published ''Silent Love,'' ''Why You Want My Love'' and ''Something for Nothing,'' (singles), written and recorded by Elaine Monk, released on Black Sands Records/Metropolitan Records; ''Get Funky'' (single), written and recorded by Larry Larr, released on Columbia Records; and ''He Made A Way'' (single by Kenyatta Arrington), ''We Give All Praises Unto God'' (single by Jacqueline D. Pate), ''I Believe He Will'' (single by Pastor Alyn E. Waller), and ''Psalms 146'' (single by Rodney Roberson), all songs recorded by The Enon Tabernacle Mass Choir from *Pastor Alyn E. Waller Presents: The Enon Tabernacle Mass Choir*, released on ECDC Records (www.enontab.org). Also produces and publishes music for Bunim/Murray productions network television, MTV's *Real World*, *Road Rules*, *Rebel Billionaire*, *Simple Life*, and movie soundtracks worldwide. Also produced deep soul remixes for Brian McKnight, Musiq Souchild, Jagged Edge, John Legend, and Elaine Monk.

Tips ''Love is all.''

☑ 🖼 Ⓐ MANUITI L.A. (ASCAP)

% Rosen Music Corp. (310)230-6040. Fax: (310)230-4074. E-mail: assistant@rosenmusiccorp.com. **Contact:** Steven Rosen, president. Music publisher and record producer. ''The exclusive music publishing company for writer/producer Guy Roche.''

How to Contact *Does not accept unsolicited material.*

Film & TV Recently published ''Connected,'' recorded by Sara Paxton in *Aquamarine*; ''As If,'' recorded by Blaque in *Bring It On*; ''Turn the Page,'' recorded by Aaliyah in *Music of the Heart*; and ''While You Were Gone,'' recorded by Kelly Price in *Blue Streak*.

Music All genres. Published ''What A Girl Wants'' (single), recorded by Christina Aguilera (pop); ''Almost Doesn't Count'' (single), recorded by Brandy (R&B) on Atlantic; ''Beauty'' (single), recorded by Dru Hill (R&B) on Island; and ''Under My Tree'' (single), recorded by *NSync on RCA.

Tips ''Do your homework on who you are contacting and what they do. Don't waste yours or their time by not having that information.''

☒ Ⓐ MANY LIVES MUSIC PUBLISHERS (SOCAN)

RR #1, Kensington PE COB 1MO Canada. (902)836-1051. E-mail: paul.milner@summerside.ca. **Contact:** Paul C. Milner, publisher. Music publisher. Estab. 1997. Pays standard royalty.

● Chucky Danger's *Colour* album was named Winner Best Pop Recording at the East Coast Music Awards 2006, "Sweet Symphony" was nominated for Single of the Year, and Chucky Danger was nominated for Best New Group. The *Temptation* album won a SOCAN #1 award.

How to Contact Submit demo by mail. Unsolicited submissions are OK. Prefers CD and lyric sheet (lead sheet if available). Does not return material. Responds in 3 months if interested.

Music All styles. Released *Temptation* (album by various writers), arrangement by Paul Milner, Patrizia, Dan Cutrona (rock/opera), released 2003 on United One Records; *Six Pack EP* and *Colour* (album), written and recorded by Chucky Danger (pop/rock), released 2005 on Landwash Entertainment; *The Edge Of Emotion* (album by various writers), arrangement by Paul Milner, Patrizia, Dan Cutrona (rock/opera), released 2006 on Nuff entertainment/United One Records.

⌧ ◉ MARKEA MUSIC/GINA PIE MUSIC/SI QUE MUSIC (BMI, SESAD, ASCAP)

P.O. Box 121396, Nashville TN 37212. (615)386-0099. Fax: (615)386-0059. E-mail: chriskeaton@bel lsouth.net. Professional Managers: Kent Martin(folk/pop). President: Chris Keaton. Music publisher. Estab. 1995. Publishes 19 songs/year; publishes 1 new songwriter/year. Staff size: 2. Hires staff songwriters. Pays standard royalty.

Affiliate(s) Markea Music (BMI) and Gina Pie Music (SESAC).

How to Contact *Call first and obtain permission to submit.* Prefers cassette or CD with 3 songs and lyric sheet. Does not return material. Responds in 6 weeks.

Film & TV Places 1 song in film and 1 song in TV/year. Published "Keep Coming Back," written and recorded by Mike Younger in Time of Your Life; and "If By Chance . . .," written and recorded by Mike Younger in A Galaxy, Far, Far Away.

Music Mostly **country**, **folk** and **pop**; also **R&B**. Published "I'm Happy" (single by Ronna Reeves/ Tom McHugh) from *Ronna Reeves* (album), recorded by Ronna Reeves (pop/country), released 2000 on Hello.

Tips "Send your best."

☑ ◪ JOHN WELLER MARVIN PUBLISHING (ASCAP)

"View Web site for new submission address." (330)733-8585. Fax: (330)733-8595. E-mail: stephani e.arble@jwmpublishing.net. Web site: www.jwmpublishing.net. **Contact:** Stephanie Arble, president. Music Publisher. Estab. 1996. Pays standard royalty.

How to Contact Submit demo by mail. Unsolicited submissions are OK. Prefers cassette, CD or VHS and lyric or lead sheet. Responds in 6 weeks.

Music All genres, mostly **pop**, **R&B**, **rap**; also **rock**, and **country**. Published "Downloading Files" (single by S. Arble/R. Scott), recorded by Ameritech Celebration Choir (corporate promotional). "We work with a promoter, booking major label artists, and we're also involved in television and corporate promotional recordings."

☷ ◯ MATERIAL WORTH PUBLISHING (ASCAP)

46 First St., Walden NY 12586. (845) 283-0795. Fax: (678) 868-0743. E-mail: info@materialwothpub lishing.com. Web site: www.materialworthpublishing.com. **Contact:** Frank Sardella, owner. Music publisher. Estab. 2003. Staff size: 3. Pays standard royalty of 50%.

How to Contact *Call first and obtain permission to submit a demo.* Prefers CD and lyric sheet, lead sheet, cover letter. Does not return submissions. Responds in 1 weeks.

Music Mostly **pop**, **adult contemporary**, and **country**. Also **alternative**, **rock**, and **female singer-songwriter**.

☷ ◪ MAUI ARTS & MUSIC ASSOCIATION/SURVIVOR RECORDS/TEN OF DIAMONDS MUSIC (BMI)

120 Hana Hwy. #9, PMB 208, Paia HI 96779. (808)874-5900. E-mail: mamamaui@mac.com. Web site: www.dreammaui.com. Professional Manager: Greta Warren (pop). Director: Jason Schwartz. Music publisher and record producer. Estab. 1974. Publishes 2 songs/year plus compilations; publishes 2 new songwriters/year. Staff size: 4. Pays standard royalty.

Music Publishers

How to Contact *Prefers that submitters send a sound file submission via e-mail, maximum of 5 minutes in length.*

Music Mostly **pop**, **country**, **R&B** and **New Age**. Does not want rock. Published "In the Morning Light" (by Jack Warren), recorded by Jason (pop ballad); and "Before the Rain" (by Giles Feldscher), recorded by Jason (pop ballad), both on Survivor.

Tips "Looking for a great single only!"

◙ MAVERICK MUSIC (ASCAP)

3300 Warner Blvd., Burbank CA 91505. (310)385-7800. Web site: www.maverick.com. Music publisher and record company (Maverick).

How to Contact *Maverick Music does not accept unsolicited submissions.*

◙ MCA MUSIC PUBLISHING

12 Music Circle S., Nashville TN 37203.

- MCA music has been taken over by Universal, now functions only as a catalog of past music, and does not publish new material any longer.

◙ MCCLURE & TROWBRIDGE PUBLISHING, LTD. (ASCAP, BMI)

P.O. Box 70403, Nashville TN 37207. (615)902-0509. E-mail: manager@trowbridgeplanetearth.com. Web site: www.jiprecords.com. **Contact:** George McClure, president/CEO. Music publisher. Record company (JIP Records/Artist Choice CD) and record production company (George McClure, producer). Estab. 1983. Publishes 25 songs/year. Publishes 5 new songwriters/year. Staff size: 8. Pays standard royalty of 50%.

How to Contact *Contact first and obtain Control Number to submit a demo.* Requires CD with 1-5 songs, lyric sheet, and cover letter. Does not return submissions. Responds in 3 weeks.

Music Pop, country, gospel, Latin and swing. "We are very open-minded as far as genres. If it's good music, we like it!" Published "My Way or Hit the Highway" (single), written and recorded by Jacqui Watson (Americana), released 2005 on Artist Choice CD; and "I'm A Wild One" (single), recorded by Veronica Leigh, released 2006 on Artist Choice CD.

◻ ◙ JIM MCCOY MUSIC (BMI)

25 Troubadour Lane, Berkeley Springs WV 25411. (304)258-9381. E-mail: mccoytroubadour@aol.com. Web site: www.troubadourlounge.com. **Contact:** Bertha and Jim McCoy, owners. Music publisher, record company (Winchester Records) and record producer (Jim McCoy Productions). Estab. 1973. Publishes 20 songs/year; publishes 3-5 new songwriters/year. Pays standard royalty.

Affiliate(s) New Edition Music (BMI).

How to Contact Submit demo by mail with lyric sheet. Unsolicited submissions are OK. Prefers cassette or CD with 6 songs. Include SASE. Responds in 1 month.

Music Mostly **country**, **country/rock** and **rock**; also **bluegrass** and **gospel**. Published "Stand By Lover" (single by Earl Howard/Jim McCoy) from *Earl Howard Sings His Heart Out* (album), recorded by Earl Howard (country), released 2002 on Winchester; "Let Her" and "Same ole Town" (singles by Tommy Hill), recorded by R. Lee Gray (country), released 2002 on Winchester; and *Jim McCoy and Friends Remember Ernest Tubb* (album), recorded by Jim McCoy (country), released January 2003 on Winchester.

▨ ◙ MIDI TRACK PUBLISHING (BMI)/ALLRS MUSIC PUBLISHING CO. (ASCAP)

P.O. Box 1545, Smithtown NY 11787. (718)767-8995. E-mail: allrsmusic@aol.com. Web site: www.geocities.com/allrsmusic. **Contact:** Renee Silvestri, president. Music publisher, record company (MIDI Track Records), music consultant, artist management. Voting member of NARAS (The Grammy Awards), CMA, SGMA, SGA. Estab. 1994. Staff size: 5. Publishes 3 songs/year; publishes 2 new songwriters/year. Pays standard royalty.

Affiliate(s) Midi-Track Publishing Co. (BMI).

How to Contact *Write or e-mail first to obtain permission to submit.* "We do not accept unsolicited submissions." Prefers CD or cassette with 3 songs, lyric sheet and cover letter. "Make sure your

CD or cassette tape is labeled with your name, mailing address, telephone number, and e-mail address. We do not return material.'' Responds via e-mail in 3 months.

Film & TV Places 1 song in film/year. Published ''Why Can't You Hear My Prayer'' (single by F. John Silvestri/Leslie Silvestri), recorded by Iliana Medina in a documentary by Silvermine Films.

Music Mostly **country**, **gospel**, **top 40**, **R&B**, **MOR** and **pop**. Does not want showtunes, jazz, classical or rap. Published ''Why Can't You Hear My Prayer'' (single by F. John Silvestri/Leslie Silvestri), recorded by eight-time Grammy nominee Huey Dunbar of the group DLG (Dark Latin Groove), released on Trend Records (other multiple releases, also recorded by Iliana Medina and released 2002 on MIDI Track Records); ''Chasing Rainbows'' (single by F. John Silvestri/Leslie Silvestri), recorded by Tommy Cash (country), released on MMT Records (including other multiple releases); ''Because of You'' (single by F. John Silvestri/Leslie Silvestri), recorded by Iliana Medina, released 2002 on MIDI Track Records, also recorded by three-time Grammy nominee Terri Williams, released on KMA Records; also recorded by Grand Ole Opry member Ernie Ashworth, released 2004 on KMA Records; ''My Coney Island'' (single by F. John Silvestri/Leslie Silvestri), recorded by eight-time Grammy nominee Huey Dunbar, released 2005 on MIDI Track Records.

Tips '''Attend workshops, seminars, join songwriters organizations and keep writing, you will achieve your goal.''

MONTINA MUSIC (SOCAN)
Box 702, Snowdon Station, Montreal QC H3X 3X8 Canada. **Contact:** David P. Leonard, professional manager. Music publisher and record company (Monticana Records). Estab. 1963. Pays negotiable royalty.

Affiliate(s) Saber-T Music (SOCAN).

How to Contact Unsolicited submissions are OK. Prefers CD. SAE and IRC. Responds in 3 months.

Music Mostly **top 40**; also **bluegrass**, **blues**, **country**, **dance-oriented**, **easy listening**, **folk**, **gospel**, **jazz**, **MOR**, **progressive**, **R&B**, **rock** and **soul**. Does not want heavy metal, hard rock, jazz, classical or New Age.

Tips ''Maintain awareness of styles and trends of your peers who have succeeded professionally. Understand the markets to which you are pitching your material. Persevere at marketing your talents. Develop a network of industry contacts, first locally, then regionally, nationally and internationally.''

MOON JUNE MUSIC (BMI)
4233 SW Marigold, Portland OR 97219. (507)777-4621. Fax: (503)277-4622. **Contact:** Bob Stoutenburg, president. Music publisher. Estab. 1971. Staff size: 1. Pays standard royalty.

How to Contact Submit demo by mail. Unsolicited submissions are OK. Prefers cassette or CD with 2-10 songs.

Music Country.

THE MUSIC ROOM PUBLISHING GROUP (BMI)
P.O. Box 219, Redondo Beach CA 90277. (310)316-4551. E-mail: mrp@aol.com. **Contact:** John Reed, president/owner. Music publisher and record producer. Estab. 1982. Pays standard royalty.

Affiliate(s) MRP Music (BMI).

How to Contact *Not accepting unsolicited material.*

Music Mostly **pop/rock/R&B** and **crossover**. Published ''That Little Tattoo,'' ''Mona Lisa'' and ''Sleepin' with an Angel'' (singles by John E. Reed) from *Rock With An Attitude* (album), recorded by Rawk Dawg (rock), released 2002; ''Over the Rainbow'' and ''Are You Still My Lover'' (singles) from *We Only Came to Rock* (album), recorded by Rawk Dawg, released 2004 on Music Room Productions®.

NAKED JAIN RECORDS (ASCAP)
P.O. Box 4132, Palm Springs CA 92263-4132. (760)325-8663. Fax: (760)320-4305. E-mail: info@nakedjainrecords.com. Web site: www.nakedjainrecords.com. **Contact:** Dena Banes, vice president/A&R. Music publisher, record company and record producer (Dey Martin). Estab. 1991. Publishes

40 songs/year; publishes 2 new songwriters/year. Staff size: 5. Pays standard royalty.

Affiliate(s) Aven Deja Music (ASCAP).

How to Contact *Does not accept unsolicited material.*

Film & TV Places 10 songs in TV/year. Music Supervisors: Dey Martin (alternative). Recently published "Yea Right" (single), written and recorded by Lung Cookie in Fox Sports TV; "Just Ain't Me" (single), written and recorded by Lung Cookie in ESPN-TV; and "Speak Easy" (single), written and recorded by Lung Cookie in ESPN-TV.

Music Mostly **alternative rock**. Does not want country.

Tips "Write a good song."

◢ A NEW RAP JAM PUBLISHING

P.O. Box 683, Lima OH 45802. E-mail: just_chilling_2002@yahoo.com. Professional Managers: William Roach (rap, clean); James Milligan (country, 70s music, pop). **Contact:** A&R Dept. Music publisher and record company (New Experience/Grand Slam Records, Pump It Up Records, and Rough Edge Records). Estab. 1989. Publishes 30 songs/year; publishes 2-3 new songwriters/year. Hires staff songwriters. Staff size: 6. Pays standard royalty.

Affiliate(s) Party House Publishing (BMI), Creative Star Management, and Rough Edge Records.

How to Contact *Write first to arrange personal interview or submit demo by mail.* Unsolicited submissions are OK. Prefers cassette with 3-5 songs and lyric or lead sheet. Include SASE. Responds in up to weeks.

Music Mostly **R&B**, **pop**, **blues** and **rock/rap**; also **contemporary**, **gospel**, **country** and **soul**. Published "Lets Go Dancing" (single by Dion Mikel), recorded and released 2006 On Faze 4 Records/New Experience Records; "The Broken Hearted" (single) from *The Final Chapter* (album), recorded by T.M.C. the milligan conection (R&B/gospel), released 2003/2004 on New Experience/Pump It Up Records.

Tips "We are seeking hit artists of the 1970s and 1980s who would like to be re-signed, as well as new talent and female solo artists. Send any available information supporting the group or act. We are a label that does not promote violence, drugs or anything that we feel is a bad example for our youth. Establish music industry contacts, write and keep writing and most of all believe in yourself. Use a good recording studio but be very professional. Just take your time and produce the best music possible. Sometimes you only get one listen. Make sure you place your best song on your demo first. This will increase your chances greatly. If you're the owner of your own small label and have a finished product, please send it. And if there is interest we will contact you. Also be on the lookout for our new blues label Rough Edge Records and Rough Edge Entertainment now reviewing material. Please be aware of the new sampling laws and laws for digital downloading. It is against the law. People are being jailed and fined for this act. Do your homework. Read the new digital downloading contracts carefully or seek legal help if need be. Good luck and thanks for considering our company."

◢ NEWBRAUGH BROTHERS MUSIC (ASCAP, BMI)

228 Morgan Lane, Berkeley Springs WV 25411-3475. (304)258-3656. E-mail: Nbtoys@verizon.net. **Contact:** John S. Newbraugh, owner. Music publisher, record company (NBT Records, BMI/ASCAP). Estab. 1967. Publishes 124 songs/year. Publishes 14 new songwriters/year. Staff size: 1. Pays standard royalty.

Affiliates NBT Music (ASCAP) and Newbraugh Brothers Music (BMI).

How to Contact Submit demo by mail. Unsolicited submissions are OK. Prefers cassette or CD with any amount of songs, a lyric sheet and a cover letter. Include SASE. Responds in 6 weeks. "Please don't call for permission to submit. Your materials are welcomed."

Music Mostly **rockabilly**, **hillbilly**, **folk** and **bluegrass**; also **rock**, **country**, and **gospel**. "We will accept all genres of music except songs with vulgar language." Published "Blink Of An Eye" (single), by Steve Osheyack, released 2005; *Malcolm Arthur and the Knights* (album, from Australia), released 2005. "We also released and published many of the songs for *Ride The Train—Vol #13* in 2005, which brings the total of train/railroad related songs issued on this NBT series to 270 songs, with writers and artists from over half the states in the U.S.A., Canada, several countries in Europe, and Australia.

Tips "Find out if a publisher/record company has any special interest. NBT, for instance, is always hunting 'original' train songs. Our 'registered' trademark is a train and from time to time we release a compilation album of all train songs. We welcome all genres of music for this project."

⊠ ⊘ OLD SLOWPOKE MUSIC (BMI)

P.O. Box 52626, Tulsa OK 74152-0626. (918)742-8087. E-mail: ryoung@cherrystreetrecords.com. Web site: www.cherrystreetrecords.com. **Contact:** Steve Hickerson, professional manager. President: Rodney Young. Music publisher and record producer. Estab. 1977. Publishes 10- 20 songs/year; publishes 2 new songwriters/year. Staff size: 2. Pays standard royalty.

How to Contact *Does not accept unsolicited submissions.*

Film & TV Places 1 song in film/year. Recently published "Samantha," written and recorded by George W. Carroll in *Samantha*. Placed two songs for Tim Drummond in movies "Hound Dog Man" in *loving Lu Lu* and "Fur Slippers" in a CBS movie *Shake, Rattle & Roll*.

Music Mostly **rock**, **country** and **R&B**; also **jazz**. Published *Promise Land* (album), written and recorded by Richard Neville on Cherry Street Records (rock).

Tips "Write great songs. We sign only artists who play an instrument, sing and write songs."

⊘ ORCHID PUBLISHING (BMI)

Bouquet-Orchid Enterprises, P.O. Box 1335, Norcross GA 30091. Phone/fax: (770)339-9088. **Contact:** Bill Bohannon, president. Music publisher, record company, record producer (Bouquet-Orchid Enterprises) and artist management. Member: CMA, AFM. Publishes 10-12 songs/year; publishes 3 new songwriters/year. Pays standard royalty.

How to Contact Submit demo by mail. Unsolicited submissions are OK. Prefers cassette or CD with 3-5 songs and lyric sheet. "Send biographical information if possible—even a photo helps." Include SASE. Responds in 1 month.

Music Mostly **religious** ("Amy Grant, etc., contemporary gospel"); **country** ("Garth Brooks, Trisha Yearwood-type material"); and **top 100/pop** ("Bryan Adams, Whitney Houston-type material"). Published "Blue As Your Eyes" (single), written and recorded by Adam Day; "Spare My Feelings" (single by Clayton Russ), recorded by Terri Palmer; and "Trying to Get By" (single by Tom Sparks), recorded by Bandoleers, all on Bouquet Records.

⊘ PEERMUSIC (ASCAP, BMI)

5358 Melrose Ave., Suite 400, Los Angeles CA 90038. (323)960-3400. Fax: (323)960-3410. Web site: www.peermusic.com. Music publisher and artist development promotional label. Estab. 1928. Publishes 600 songs/year (worldwide); publishes 1-2 new songwriters/year. Hires staff songwriters. Royalty standard, but negotiable.

Affiliate(s) Peer Southern Organization (ASCAP) and Peer International Corporation (BMI).

How to Contact "We do NOT accept unsolicited submissions. We only accept material through agents, attorneys and managers." Prefers CD and lyric sheet. Does not return material. Responds in 6 weeks.

Music Mostly **pop**, **rock** and **R&B**. Published music by David Foster (writer/producer, pop); Andrew Williams (writer/producer, pop); Shelly Peiken (writer, pop); Christopher "Tricky" Stewart (R&B, writer/producer); and the Coma Boyz (R&B writers/producers). Also published music by the bands Over It and Bleed the Dream.

⋈ ⊕ ♥ PEGASUS MUSIC

P.O. Box 127, Otorohanga 2564. New Zealand. E-mail: peg.music@xtra.co.nz. Web site: www.pegasusmusic.biz. Professional Managers: Errol Peters (country, rock); Ginny Peters (gospel, pop). Music publisher and record company. Estab. 1981. Publishes 20-30 songs/year; publishes 5 new songwriters/year. Pays standard royalty.

How to Contact Submit demo by mail. Unsolicited submissions are OK. Prefers CD with 3-5 songs and lyric sheet. SAE and IRC. Responds in 1 month.

Music Mostly **country**; also **bluegrass**, **easy listening** and **top 40/pop**. Published "This Time" (single by Rob Innes), recorded by Mike D., released on MCK Records/Germany; "Beyond the

Reason'' (single by Ginny Peters), recorded by Reg Mctaggat, released on Discovery Records/New Zealand; and "The Journey" (single), written and recorded by Ginny Peters, released on Pegasus Records/New Zealand-Australia.

Tips "Get to the meat of the subject without too many words. Less is better."

🅽 ⊘ PERLA MUSIC, (ASCAP)

122 Oldwick Rd., Whitehouse Station NJ 08889-5014. (908)439-9118. Fax: (908)439-9119. E-mail: PerlaMusic@PMRecords.org. Web site: www.PMRecords.org. **Contact:** Gene Perla(jazz). Music publisher, record company (PMRecords.org), record producer (Perla.org), studio production (TheSystemMSP.com) and Internet Design (CCINYC.com). Estab. 1971. Publishes 5 songs/year. Staff size: 1. Pays 75%/25% royalty.

Music Mostly **jazz** and **rock**.

◻ JUSTIN PETERS MUSIC, (BMI)

P.O. Box 40251, Nashville TN 37204. (615)269-8682. Fax: (615)269-8929. Web site: http://songsfort heplanet.com. **Contact:** Justin Peters, president. Music publisher. Estab. 1981.

Affiliate(s) Platinum Planet Music, Tourmaline (BMI) and LITA Music (ASCAP).

How to Contact Submit demo by mail. Unsolicited submissions are OK. Prefers CD with 5 songs and lyric sheet. Does not return material. "Place code '2007' on each envelope submission."

Music Mostly **pop**, **reggae**, **country** and **comedy**. Published "Saved By Love" (single), recorded by Amy Grant on A&M Records; "Nothing Can Separate Us", recorded by Al Denson; "A Gift That She Don't Want" (single), recorded by Bill Engvall on Warner Brother Records; and "I Wanna Be That Man" (single), recorded by McKameys on Pamplin Records, all written by Justin Peters.

⊘ PHOEBOB MUSIC (BMI)

5181 Regent Dr., Nashville TN 37220. (615)832-4199. **Contact:** Phoebe Binkley.

How to Contact *"We do not want unsolicited submissions."*

Music **Country**, **Christian**, and **theatre**.

⊘ PIANO PRESS (ASCAP)

P.O. Box 85, Del Mar CA 92014-0085. (619)884-1401. Fax: (858)755-1104. E-mail: pianopress@pian opress.com. Web site: www.pianopress.com. **Contact:** Elizabeth C. Axford, M.A., owner. Music publisher. Publishes songbooks & CD's for music students and teachers. Estab. 1998. Licenses 32-100 songs/year; publishes 1-24 new songwriters/year. Staff size: 5. Pays standard print music and/or mechanical royalty; songwriter retains rights to songs.

How to Contact *Write or call first and obtain permission to submit.* Prefers cassette or CD with 1-3 songs, lyric and lead sheet, cover letter and sheet music/piano arrangements. "Looking for children's songs for young piano students and arrangements of public domain folk songs of any nationality." Currently accepting submissions for *Kidtunes II*. Include SASE. Responds in 2-3 months.

Music Mostly **children's**, **folk songs** and **funny songs**; also **teaching pieces**, **piano arrangements**, **lead sheets with melody, chords and lyrics** and **songbooks**. Does not want commercial pop, R&B, etc. Published "I Can" (single by Tom Gardner) from *Kidtunes* (album), recorded by The Uncle Brothers (children's), released 2002 by Piano Press; "Rock & Roll Teachers" (single by Bob King) from *Kidtunes* (album), recorded by Bob King & Friends (children's), released 2002 by Piano Press; and "It Really Isn't Garbage" (single by Danny Einbender) from *Kidtunes* (album), recorded by Danny Eibende/Pete Seeger/et al. (children's), released 2002 by Piano Press.

Tips "Songs should be simple, melodic and memorable. Lyrics should be for a juvenile audience and well-crafted."

◻ PLATINUM PLANET MUSIC, INC. (BMI)

2831 Dogwood Place, Nashville TN 37204. (615)269-8682. Fax: (615)269-8929. Web site: http:// songsfortheplanet.com. **Contact:** Justin Peters, president. Music publisher. Estab. 1997.

Affiliate(s) Justin Peters Music, Tourmaline (BMI) and LITA Music (ASCAP).

How to Contact Submit demo by mail. Unsolicited submissions are OK. Prefers CD with 5 songs

and lyric sheet. Does not return material. "Place code '2007' on each envelope submission."
Music Mostly **R& B, dance** and **country**; also represents many Christian artists/writers. Published "Happy Face" (single by Dez Dickerson/Jordan Dickerson), recorded by Squirt on Absolute Records; "Welcome To My Love" (single by Mike Hunter), recorded by Kyndl on PPMI; "Love's Not A Game" (single), written and recorded by Kashief Lindo on Heavybeat Rewards; "Dancing Singing" (single by A. Craig/Justin Peters) recorded by Dan Burda on Independent; and "Loud" (single), written and recorded by These Five Down on Absolute Records.

☑ POLLYBYRD PUBLICATIONS LIMITED (ASCAP, BMI, SESAC)
P.O. Box 261488, Encino CA 91426. (818)506-8533. Fax: (818)506-8534. E-mail: pplzmi@aol.com. Web site: www.pplzmi.com. Branch office: 468 N. Camden Drive Suite 200, Beverly Hills CA 90210. **Contact:** Dakota Hawk, vice president. Professional Managers: Cisco Blue (country, pop, rock); Tedford Steele (hip-hop, R&B). Music publisher, record company (PPL Entertainment) and Management firm (Sa'mall Management). Estab. 1979. Publishes 100 songs/year; publishes 25-40 new songwriters/year. Hires staff writers. Pays standard royalty.
Affiliate(s) Kellijai Music (ASCAP), Pollyann Music (ASCAP), Ja'Nikki Songs (BMI), Velma Songs International (BMI), Lonnvanness Songs (SESAC), PPL Music (ASCAP), Zettitalia Music, Butternut Music (BMI), Zett Two Music (ASCAP), Plus Publishing and Zett One Songs (BMI).
How to Contact *Write first and obtain permission to submit.* No phone calls. Prefers cassette or CD videocassette with 4 songs and lyric and lead sheet. Include SASE. Responds in 2 months.
Music Published "Return of the Players" (album) by Juz-Cuz 2004 on PPL; "Believe" (single by J. Jarrett/S. Cuseo) from *Time* (album), recorded by Lejenz (pop), released 2001 on PRL/Credence; *Rainbow Gypsy Child* (album), written and recorded by Riki Hendrix (rock), released 2001 on PRL/Sony; and "What's Up With That" (single by Brandon James/Patrick Bouvier) from *Outcast* (album), recorded by Condottieré; (hip-hop), released 2001 on Bouvier.
Tips "Make those decisions—are you really a songwriter? Are you prepared to starve for your craft? Do you believe in delayed gratification? Are you commercial or do you write only for yourself? Can you take rejection? Do you want to be the best? If so, contact us—if not, keep your day job."

☑ PORTAGE MUSIC (BMI)
16634 Gannon W., Rosemount MN 55068. (952)432-5737. E-mail: drivers@earthlink.net. President: Larry LaPole. Music publisher. Publishes 0-5 songs/year. Pays standard royalty.
How to Contact *Does not accept unsolicited submissions.*
Music Mostly **country** and **country rock**. Published "Lost Angel," "Think It Over" and "Congratulations to Me" (by L. Lapole), all recorded by Trashmen on Sundazed.
Tips "Keep songs short, simple and upbeat with positive theme."

☑ ☐ PRESCRIPTION COMPANY (BMI)
Box 222249, Great Neck NY 11021. (415)553-8540. E-mail: therxco@yahoo.com. President: David F. Gasman. Vice President of Sales: Bruce Brennan. Vice President of Finance: Robert Murphy. Music publisher and record producer. Staff size: 7. Pays standard royalty.
  ● Also see the listing for The Prescription Co. in the Record Producers section of this book.
How to Contact *Write or call first and obtain permission to submit.* Prefers cassette with any number of songs and lyric sheet. "Send all submissions with SASE (or no returns)." Responds in 1 month.
Music Mostly **bluegrass, blues, children's** and **country, dance-oriented**; also **easy listening, folk, jazz, MOR, progressive, R&B, rock, soul** and **top 40/pop**. Published "The World's Most Dangerous Man," "Here Comes Trouble" and "Automated People" (singles by D.F. Gasman) from *Special EP No. 1* (album), all recorded by Medicine Mike (rock), released 2003 on Prescription.
Tips "Songs should be good and written to last. Forget fads—we want songs that'll sound as good in ten years as they do today. Organization, communication and exploration of form are as essential as message (and sincerity matters, too)."

☒ ☒ ☐ QUARK, INC.
P.O. Box 7320, FDR Station, New York NY 10150. (917)687-9988. Fax: (845)708-0113. E-mail: quarkent@aol.com. **Contact:** Curtis Urbina, manager. Music publisher, record company (Quark

Records) and record producer (Curtis Urbina). Estab. 1984. Publishes 12 songs/year; 2 new song-writers/year. Staff size: 4. Pays standard royalty.

Affiliate(s) Quarkette Music (BMI), Freedurb Music (ASCAP) and Quark Records.

How to Contact Prefers CD only with 2 songs. No cassettes. Include SASE. Responds in 2 months.

Film & TV Places 10 songs in film/year. Music Supervisor: Curtis Urbina.

Music House music only. Does not want anything short of a hit. Published "All Because of You" (single), by Carolyn Harding; "He Moves" (single), by Big Brooklyn Red; and "Fever" (single), by Stephanie Renee.

QUEEN ESTHER MUSIC PUBLISHERS (ASCAP)

449 N. Vista St., Los Angeles CA 90036. (323)653-0693. E-mail: unclelenny@aol.com. **Contact:** Len Weisman, owner. Record producer, personal manager, music publisher. Estab. 1980. Publishes 30-50 songs/year.

• Also see the listings for Audio Music Publishers in the Music Publishers section of this book; Parliament Records in the Record Companies section and The Weisman Production Group in this section of this book.

How to Contact Send demo CD or cassette with 3-10 songs. Include SASE. We only return in prepaid large envelopes.

Music Mostly **R&B**, **soul**, **rap**, **blues** and **2nd gospel**. Just finished *E'morey* (album); *Jus van* (album); and *Jewel With Love* (album).

R.T.L. MUSIC

White House Farm, Shropshire TF9 4HA United Kingdom. (01630)647374. Fax: (01630)647612. **Contact:** Tanya Woof, international A&R manager. Professional Managers: Ron Dickson (rock/rock 'n roll); Katrine LeMatt (MOR/dance); Xavier Lee (heavy metal); Tanya Lee (classical/other types). Music publisher, record company (Le Matt Music) and record producer. Estab. 1971. Publishes approximately 30 songs/year. Pays standard royalty.

Affiliate(s) Lee Music (publishing), Swoop Records, Grenouille Records, Check Records, Zarg Records, Pogo Records, R.T.F.M. (all independent companies).

How to Contact Submit demo by mail. Unsolicited submissions are OK. Prefers CD, cassette, MDisc or DVD (also VHS 625/PAL system videocassette) with 1-3 songs and lyric and lead sheets; include still photos and bios. "Make sure name and address are on CD or cassette." Send IRC. Responds in 6 weeks.

Music All types. Published *I Hate School* (album), recorded by Suburban Studs; *Do You Wanna Dance* (album) and *F-B-I Rock Me* (album), recorded by Mike Sheridan; *Children of the Night* (album), recorded by Nightmare; and *I Do Love You* (album), recorded by Hush.

RAINBOW MUSIC CORP. (ASCAP)

45 E. 66 St., New York NY 10021. (212)988-4619. Fax: (212)861-9079. E-mail: fscam45@aol.com. **Contact:** Fred Stuart, vice president. Music publisher. Estab. 1990. Publishes 25 songs/year. Staff size: 2. Pays standard royalty.

Affiliate(s) Tri-Circle (ASCAP).

How to Contact *Only accepts material referred by a reputable industry source.* Prefers CD with 2 songs and lyric sheet. Include SASE. Responds in 1 week.

Film & TV Published "You Wouldn't Lie To An Angel, Would Ya?" (single by Diane Lampert/Paul Overstreet) from *Lady of the Evening* (album), recorded by Ben te Boe (country), released 2003 on Mega International Records; "Gonna Give Lovin' A Try" (single by Cannonball Adderley/Diane Lampert/Nat Adderley) from *The Axelrod Chronicles* (album), recorded by Randy Crawford (jazz), released 2003 on Fantasy Records; "Breaking Bread" (single by Diane Lampert/Paul Overstreet) from *Unearthed* (album), recorded by Johnny Cash (country), released 2003 on Lost Highway Records and "Gonna Give Lovin' A Try" (single by Cannonball Adderley/Diane Lampert/Nat Adderley) from *Day Dreamin'* (album), recorded by Laverne Butler (jazz), released 2002 on Chesky Records.

Music Mostly **pop**, **R&B** and **country**; also **jazz**. Published "Break It To Me Gently" (single by

Diane Lampert/Joe Seneca) from *TIME/LIFE* compilations *Queens of Country* (2004), *Classic Country* (2003), and *Glory Days of Rock 'n Roll* (2002), recorded by Brenda Lee.

☐ RED SUNDOWN MUSIC (BMI)

P.O. Box 609, Pleasant View TN 37212. (615)746-0844. E-mail: rsdr@bellsouth.net. Web site: www.redsundown.com. **Contact:** Ruby Perry.

How to Contact Does not accept unsolicited submissions. Submit CD and cover letter. Does not return submissions.

Music Country, **rock**, and **pop**. Does not want rap or hip-hop. Published "Take A Heart" (single by Kyle Pierce) from *Take Me With You*(album), recorded by Tammy Lee (country) released in 1998 on Red Sundown Records.

☑ ☒ ☒ REN ZONE MUSIC (ASCAP)

P.O. Box 3153, Huntington Beach CA 92605. (714)596-6582. Fax: (714)596-6577. E-mail: renzone@socal.rr.com. **Contact:** Renah Wolzinger, president. Music publisher. Estab. 1998. Publishes 14 songs/year; publishes 2 new songwriters/year. Staff size: 2. Pays standard royalty.

• This company won a Parents Choice 1998 Silver Honor Shield.

How to Contact *Does not accept unsolicited submissions.*

Music Mostly **klezmer** and **children's**. Does not want rap, punk or holiday music. Published "Walk Like the Animals" (single by Dayle Lusk) from *Tumble 'n' Tunes* (album), recorded by Dayle Lusk/Danielle Ganya (children's); "Surf Town" (single by Dayle Lusk) from *City Song at Huntington Beach* (album), recorded by Lisa Worshaw (pop); and "Snowboardin'" (single by Stephanie Donatoni) from *Sea Cliff Tunes* (album), recorded by Lisa Worshaw (children's), all released 2000 on Ren Zone. Recent klezmer releases include *Glazele Wine*, *Classic American Klezmer* and *Klezmer Coast to Coast*.

Tips "Submit well-written lyrics that convey important concepts to kids on good quality demos with easy to understand vocals."

☒ RHINESTONE COWBOY MUSIC (ASCAP)

P.O. Box 22971, Nashville TN 37202. (615)554-3400.

How to Contact *Contact first and obtain permission to submit a demo.* Submit demo CD with 5 songs. Responds only if interested.

☒ RHYTHMS PRODUCTIONS (ASCAP)

P.O. Box 34485, Los Angeles CA 90034. **Contact:** Ruth White, president. Music and multimedia publisher. Member NARAS. Publishes 4 titles/year. Pays negotiable royalty.

Affiliate(s) Tom Thumb Music.

How to Contact Submit tape with letter outlining background in educational children's music. Include SASE. Responds in 2 months.

Music "We're only interested in **children's songs** and interactive programs that have educational value. Our materials are sold in schools and homes, so artists/writers with an 'edutainment' background would be most likely to understand our requirements." Published "Professor Whatzit®" series including "Adventures of Professor Whatzit & Carmine Cat" (cassette series for children); "Musical Math," "Musical Reading" and "Theme Songs."

☒ ROCKFORD MUSIC CO. (ASCAP, BMI)

150 West End Ave., Suite 6-D, New York NY 10023. **Contact:** Danny Darrow, manager. Music publisher, record company (Mighty Records), record and video tape producer (Danny Darrow). Publishes 1-3 songs/year; publishes 1-3 new songwriters/year. Staff size: 3. Pays standard royalty.

Affiliate(s) Corporate Music Publishing Company (ASCAP), Stateside Music Company (BMI), Rockford Music Co. (BMI).

How to Contact Submit demo by mail. Unsolicited submissions are OK. "No phone calls and do not write for permission to submit." Prefers cassette with 3 songs and lyric sheet. Does not return material. Responds in 2 weeks.

Music Mostly **MOR** and **top 40/pop**; also **adult pop**, **country**, **adult rock**, **dance-oriented**, **easy listening**, **folk** and **jazz**. Does not want rap. Published "Let There Be Peace" (single by Danny Darrow) from *Falling In Love* (album), recorded by Danny Darrow (peace prayer/gospel); "Look to the Wind" (single by Peggy Stewart/Danny Darrow) from *Falling in Love* (album), recorded by Danny Darrow (movie theme); "Doomsday" (single by Robert Lee Lowery/Danny Darrow) from *Doomsday* (album), recorded by Danny Darrow (euro jazz), all released 2004 on Mighty Records.
Tips "Listen to Top 40 and write current lyrics and music."

Ⓜ RONDOR MUSIC INTERNATIONAL/ALMO/IRVING MUSIC, A UNIVERSAL MUSIC GROUP COMPANY (ASCAP,BMI)
2440 Sepulveda Blvd., Suite 119, Los Angeles CA 90064. (310)235-4800. Fax: (310)235-4801. Web site: www.universalmusicpublishing.com. **Contact:** Creative Staff Assistant. Nashville office: 1904 Adelicia St., Nashville TN 37212. (615)321-0820. Fax: (615)329-1018. Music publisher. Estab. 1965.
Affiliates Almo Music Corp. (ASCAP) and Irving Music, Inc. (BMI).
How to Contact *Does not accept unsolicited submissions.*

▢ RUSTIC RECORDS, INC. PUBLISHING (ASCAP,BMI,SESAC)
6337 Murray Lane, Brentwood TN 37027. (615)371-0646. Fax: (615)370-0353. E-mail: info@countr yalbums.com. Web site: www.countryalbums.com. **Contact:** Jack Schneider, president. Vice President: Claude Southall. Office Manager: Nell Tolson. Music publisher, record company (Rustic Records Inc.) and record producer. Estab. 1984. Publishes 20 songs/year. Pays standard royalty.
Affiliate(s) Covered Bridge Music (BMI), Town Square Music (SESAC), Iron Skillet Music (ASCAP).
How to Contact Submit demo by mail. Unsolicited submissions are OK. Prefers CD with 3-4 songs and lyric sheet. Include SASE. Responds in 3 months.
Music Mostly **country**. Published "In Their Eyes" (single by Jamie Champa); "Take Me As I Am" (single by Bambi Barrett/Paul Huffman); and "Yesterday's Memories" (single by Jack Schneider), recorded by Colte Bradley (country), released 2003.
Tips "Send three or four traditional country songs, novelty songs 'foot-tapping, hand-clapping' gospel songs with strong hook for male or female artist of duet. Enclose SASE (manilla envelope)."

▢ RUSTRON MUSIC PUBLISHERS (BMI) & WHIMSONG MUSIC (ASCAP)
1156 Park Lane, West Palm Beach FL 33417-5957. (561)686-1354. E-mail: rmp_wmp@bellsouth.n et. **Contact:** Sheelah Adams, office administrator (for current submission guidelines). Professional Managers: Rusty Gordon (adult contemporary, acoustic-electric, New Age instrumentals, folk fusions, children's, blues, cabaret, soft vocal & instrumental jazz fusions, soft rock, women's music, world music); Ron Caruso (all styles); Davilyn Whims (folk fusions, country, R&B). Music publisher, record company, management firm and record producer (Rustron Music Productions). Estab. 1972. Publishes 100-150 songs/year; publishes 10-20 new songwriters/year. Staff size: 9. Pays standard royalty.
Affiliate(s) Whimsong Publishing (ASCAP).
How to Contact Submit demo by mail. Cover letter should explain reason for submitting and what songwriter needs from Rustron-Whimsong. Unsolicited submissions are OK. Current submission guidelines will be sent by e-mail upon request. If requesting by snail mail, include SASE. All songs submitted must be copyrighted by the songwriter(s) on Form PA with the U.S. Library of Congress prior to submitting. For freelance songwriters we prefer CD with up to 10 songs or cassette with 1-3 songs and typed lyric sheets (1 sheet for each song). For performing songwriters we prefer CD with up to 15 songs. A typed lyric sheet for each song submitted is required. "Clearly label your tape container or jewel box. We don't review songs on Web sites." SASE or International Reply Coupons (IRC) required for all correspondence. No exceptions. Responds in 4 months.
Music Mostly **pop** (ballads, blues, theatrical, cabaret), **progressive country** and **folk/rock**; also **R&B** and **New Age** (instrumental fusions with classical, jazz or pop themes) and **women's music**, **children's music** and **world music**. Does not publish "youth music"—rap, hip-hop, new wave, hard rock, heavy metal or punk. Published "Hurricane Harassment" (single) from *Hurricane Harassment* (album), written and recorded by Continental Divide (topical), released 2006 on Rustron Records;

"The Baobab Tree and Me" (single) from *The Baobab Tree* (album) written and recorded by Tracie Mitchell & Ivory Coast (folk rock), released 2005 on Whimsong Records; "Resisting The Right" (single) from *Resisting The Right* (album), written and recorded by The Florida Rank & File (socio-political) released 2006 on Rustron Records.

Tips "Accepting performing and freelance songwriter's CD for full "Body of Work" product review of all songs on CD. Write strong hooks. For single-song marketing, songs should have definitive verse melody. Keep song length 3-3½ minutes or less. Avoid predictability—create original and unique lyric themes. Tell a story. Develop a strong chorus with well-planned phrasing that can build into song titles and/or tags. Tune in to the trends and fusions indicative of commercially viable new music for the new millennium. All songs reviewed for single-song marketing must be very carefully crafted. Album cuts can be eclectic."

⬛ ⬛ ⊘ S.M.C.L. PRODUCTIONS, INC.

P.O. Box 84, Boucherville QC J4B 5E6 Canada. (450)641-2266. **Contact:** Christian Lefort, president. Music publisher and record company. SOCAN. Estab. 1968. Publishes 25 songs/year. Pays standard royalty.

Affiliate(s) A.Q.E.M. Ltee, Bag Music, C.F. Music, Big Bazaar Music, Sunrise Music, Stage One Music, L.M.S. Music, ITT Music, Machine Music, Dynamite Music, Cimafilm, Coincidence Music, Music and Music, Cinemusic Inc., Cinafilm, Editions La Fete Inc., Groupe Concept Musique, Editions Dorimen, C.C.H. Music (PRO/SDE) and Lavagot Music.

How to Contact *Write first and obtain permission to submit.* Prefers CD with 4-12 songs and lead sheet. SAE and IRC. Responds in 3 months.

Film & TV Places songs in film and TV. Recently published songs in French-Canadian TV series and films, including *Young Ivanhoe, Twist of Terror, More Tales of the City, Art of War, Lance & Comte (Nouvelle Generation)*, *Turtle Island* (TV series), *Being Dorothy,* and *The Hidden Fortress.*

Music Mostly **dance, easy listening** and **MOR**; also **top 40/pop** and **TV and movie soundtracks**. Published *Always and Forever* (album by Maurice Jarre/Nathalie Carien), recorded by N. Carsen on BMG Records (ballad); *Au Nom De La Passion* (album), written and recorded by Alex Stanke on Select Records.

⬛ ⬛ ◯ SADDLESTONE PUBLISHING (BMI, SOCAN)

556 Amess St., New Westminster BC V3L 4A9 Canada. (604)930-9309. Fax: (604)523-9310. E-mail: saddlestone@shaw.ca. Web site: www.saddlestone.net. **Contact:** Candice James (country), CEO. President: Grant Lucas (rock). Professional Manager: Sharla Cuthbertson (pop, R&B). Music publisher, record company (Saddlestone) and record producer (Silver Bow Productions). Estab. 1988. Publishes 100 songs/year; publishes 12-30 new songwriters/year. Pays standard royalty.

Affiliate(s) Silver Bow Publishing (SOCAN, ASCAP).

How to Contact Submit demo by mail. Unsolicited submissions are OK. Prefers CD with any amount of songs and lyric sheet. "Make sure vocal is clear." Does not return material. Responds in 3 months.

Film & TV Places 1 song in film and 2 songs in TV/year. Music Supervisors: Janet York; John McCullough. Recently published "Midnite Ride" (by Cam Wagner), recorded by 5 Star Hillbillies in *North of Pittsburgh.*

Music Mostly **country, rock** and **pop**; also **gospel** and **R&B**. Published *That's Real Love* (album), written and recorded by Darrell Meyers (country), released 2000; *Silent River* (single by John Reilly), album recorded by Wolfe Milestone.

Tips "Submit clear demos, good hooks and avoid long intros or instrumentals. Have a great singer do vocals."

⬛ ◯ SALT WORKS MUSIC (ASCAP, BMI)

80 Highland Dr., Jackson OH 45640-2074. (740)286-1514 or (740)286-6561. Professional Managers: Jeff Elliott(country/gospel); Mike Morgan (country). Music publisher and record producer (Mike Morgan). Staff size: 2. Pays standard royalty.

Affiliate(s) Salt Creek Music (ASCAP) and Sojourner Music (BMI).

Music Publishers

How to Contact Submit demo by mail. Unsolicited submissions are OK. Prefers cassette or CD. Include SASE. Responds in 2 weeks.

Music Mostly **country, gospel** and **pop**. Does not want rock, jazz or classical. Published "The Tracks You Left On Me" (single by Ed Bruce/Jeff Elliott/MikeMorgan) and "Truth Is I'm A Liar" (single by Jeff Elliott/Mike Morgan) from *This Old Hat* (album), recorded by Ed Bruce (country), released 2002 on Sony/Music Row Talent.

☐ SANDALPHON MUSIC PUBLISHING (BMI)

P.O. Box 29110, Portland OR 97296. (503)957-3929. E-mail: jackrabbit01@sprintpcs.com. **Contact:** Ruth Otey, president. Music publisher, record company (Sandalphon Records), and management agency (Sandalphon Management). Estab. 2005. Staff size: 2. Pays standard royalty of 50%.

How to Contact Submit demo by mail. Unsolicited submissions are OK. Prefers cassette or CD with 1-5 songs, lyric sheet, and cover letter. Include SASE or SAE and IRC for outside United States. Responds in 1 month.

Music Mostly **rock, country**, and **alternative**; also **pop, blues**, and **gospel**.

☑ ☐ SDB MUSIC GROUP

- *SDB Music Group only accepts music through reputable industry sources.*

Music Mostly **country**. SDB has had cuts with artists including John Michael Montgomery, Leann Rimes, Don Williams, Steve Holy, and Trace Adkins.

☐ SEGAL'S PUBLICATIONS (BMI)

P.O. Box 507, Newton MA 02459. (617)969-6196. Web site: www.charlessegal.com. **Contact:** Charles Segal. Music publisher and record producer (Segal's Productions). Estab. 1963. Publishes 80 songs/year; publishes 6 new songwriters/year. Pays standard royalty.

- Look for *Instant Songwriting with the Piano*, by Charles and Colleen Segal, available from Writer's Digest Books in Spring 2006.

Affilate(s) Charles Segal's Publications (BMI) and Charles Segal's Music (SESAC).

How to Contact Submit demo by mail. Unsolicited submissions are OK. Prefers CD or VHS videocassette with 3 songs and lyric or lead sheet. Does not return material. Responds only if interested.

Music Mostly **rock, pop** and **country**; also **R&B, MOR** and **children's songs.** "Go to Bed" (by Colleen Segal), recorded Susan Stark (MOR); and "Only In Dreams" (by Chas. Segal), recorded by Melanie Reeve (MOR), all on Spin Records.

Tips "Besides making a good demo cassette, include a lead sheet of music—words, melody line and chords. Put your name and phone number on CD."

☑ ☐ SHAWNEE PRESS, INC.

1221 17th Avenue S., Nashville TN 37212. (615)320-5300. Fax: (615)320-7306. E-mail: shawnee-info@shawneepress.com. Web site: www.ShawneePress.com. **Contact:** Director of Church Music Publications (sacred choral music): Joseph M. Martin. Director of School Music Publications (secular choral music): Greg Gilpin. Music publisher. Estab. 1917. Publishes 150 songs/year. Staff size: 35. Pays negotiable royalty.

Affiliate(s) GlorySound, Harold Flammer Music, Mark Foster Music, Wide World Music, Concert Works.

How to Contact Submit manuscript. Unsolicited submissions are OK. See Web site for guidelines. Prefers manuscript; recording required for instrumental submissions; recordings optional for choral submissions. Include SASE. Responds in 4 months. "No unsolicited musicals or cantatas."

Music Mostly **church/liturgical, educational choral** and **instrumental**. No musicals or contatas.

Tips "Submission guidelines appear on our Web site."

☐ SILICON MUSIC PUBLISHING CO. (BMI)

222 Tulane St., Garland TX 75043-2239. President: Gene Summers. Vice President: Deanna L. Summers. Public Relations: Steve Summers. Music publisher and record company (Front Row Records).

Estab. 1965. Publishes 10-20 songs/year; publishes 2-3 new songwriters/year. Pays standard royalty.

• Also see the listing for Front Row Records in the Record Companies section of this book.

How to Contact Submit demo by mail. Unsolicited submissions are OK. Prefers cassette with 1-2 songs. Does not return material. Responds ASAP.

Music Mostly **rockabilly** and **'50s material**; also **old-time blues/country** and **MOR**. Published "Fancy Dan" (single by James McClung) from *High Class Baby* (album), recorded by Darrel Higham (rockabilly), released 1998 on Goofin' (Finland); "Rockaboogie Shake" (single by James McClung) from *Rebels and More* (album), recorded by Lennerockers (rockabilly), released 2002 on Lenne (Germany); and "Crazy Cat Corner" (single by Dea Summers/Gene Summers) from *Do Right Daddy* (album), released 2004 on Enviken (Sweden).

Tips "We are very interested in '50s rock and rockabilly *original masters* for release through overseas affiliates. If you are the owner of any '50s masters, contact us first! We have releases in Holland, Switzerland, United Kingdom, Belgium, France, Sweden, Norway and Australia. We have the market if you have the tapes! Our staff writers include James McClung, Gary Mears (original Casuals), Robert Clark, Dea Summers, Shawn Summers, Joe Hardin Brown, Bill Becker and Dan Edwards."

SILVER BLUE MUSIC/OCEANS BLUE MUSIC

3940 Laurel Canyon Blvd., Suite 441, Studio City CA 91604. (818)980-9588. E-mail: jdiamond20@aol.com. **Contact:** Joel Diamond, president. Music publisher and record producer (Joel Diamond Entertainment). Estab. 1971. Publishes 50 songs/year. Pays standard royalty.

How to Contact *Does not accept unsolicited material.* "No tapes returned."

Film & TV Places 4 songs in film and 6 songs in TV/year.

Music Mostly **pop** and **R&B**; also **rap** and **classical**. Does not want country or jazz. Published "After the Lovin'" (by Bernstein/Adams), recorded by Engelbert Humperdinck; "This Moment in Time" (by Alan Bernstein/Ritchie Adams), recorded by Engelbert Humperdinck. Other artists include David Hasselhoff, Kaci (Curb Records), Ike Turner, Andrew Dice Clay, Gloria Gaynor, Tony Orlando, Katie Cassidy and Vaneza.

SINUS MUSIK PRODUKTION, ULLI WEIGEL

Geitnerweg 30a, D-12209, Berlin Germany. +49-30-7159050. Fax: +49-30-71590522. E-mail: ulli.weigel@arcor.de. Web site: www.ulli-weigel.de. **Contact:** Ulli Weigel, owner. Music publisher, record producer and screenwriter. Wrote German lyrics for more than 500 records. Member: GEMA, GVL. Estab. 1976. Publishes 20 songs/year; publishes 6 new songwriters/year. Staff size: 3. Pays standard royalty.

Affiliate(s) Sinus Musikverlag H.U. Weigel GmbH.

How to Contact Submit demo or CD by mail. Unsolicited submissions are OK. Prefers cassette or CD-R with up to 10 songs and lyric sheets. Responds in 2 months. "If material should be returned, please send 2 International Reply Coupons (IRC) for cassettes and 3 for a CD. No stamps."

Music Mostly **rock**, **pop** and **New Age**; also **background music for movies**. Published "Simple Story" (single), recorded by MAANAM on RCA (Polish rock); *Die Musik Maschine* (album by Klaus Lage), recorded by CWN Productions on Hansa Records (pop/German), "Villa Woodstock" (film music/comedy) Gebrueder Blattschuss, Juergen Von Der Lippe, Hans Werner Olm (2005).

Tips "Take more time working on the melody than on the instrumentation. I am also looking for master-quality recordings for non-exclusive release on my label (and to use them as soundtracks for multimedia projects, TV and movie scripts I am working on)."

SIZEMORE MUSIC (BMI)

P.O. Box 210314, Nashville TN 37221. (615)356-3453. E-mail: gary@sizemoremusic.com. Web site: www.sizemoremusic.com. **Contact:** Gail Rhine. Music publisher, record company (The Gas Co.) and record producer (G.L. Rhine). Estab. 1960. Publishes 5 songs/year; 1 new songwriter/year. Pays standard royalty.

How to Contact Submit demo by mail. Unsolicited submissions are OK. Prefers CD, cassette or

VHS videocassette with lyric sheets. Does not return material. Responds in 3 months.
Music Mostly **hip-hop**, **soul**, **blues**, and **country**. Published "Liquor and Wine" and "The Wind," written and recorded by K. Shackleford on Heart Records (country); and "She's Tuff" (by Jerry McCain), recorded by The Fabulous Thunderbirds on Chrysalis Records (blues).

☑ ◎ SME PUBLISHING GROUP (ASCAP,BMI)

P.O. Box 1150, Tuttle OK 73089. Phone/fax: (405)381-3754. E-mail: smemusic@juno.com. Web site: www.smepublishinggroup.com. Professional Managers: Cliff Shelder (southern gospel); Sharon Kinard (country gospel). Music publisher. Estab. 1994. Publishes 6 songs/year; publishes 2 new songwriters/year. Staff size: 2. Pays standard royalty.
Affiliates Touch of Heaven Music (ASCAP) and SME Music (BMI).
How to Contact Submit demo by mail. Unsolicited submissions are OK. Prefers cassette or CD with 3 songs and lyric sheet. Make sure tapes and CDs are labeled and include song title, writer's name and phone number. Does not return material. Responds only if interested.
Music Mostly **Southern gospel**, **country gospel** and **Christian country**. Does not want Christian rap, rock and roll, and hard-core country. Released "Come See A Man" (single by Mike Spanhanks) from *God Writes Our Story* (album), recorded by The Jody Brown Indian Family (southern gospel) on Crossroads Records; and "I Love You Son" (single by Quint Randle, Patricia Smith and Jeff Hinton) from *Here I Come Again* (album) recorded by Jackie Cox (Christian country), released 2005 on Stonghouse Records.
Tips "Always submit good quality demos. Never give up."

◎ SONY/ATV MUSIC PUBLISHING (ASCAP, BMI, SESAC)

8 Music Square W., Nashville TN 37203. (615)726-8300. Fax: (615)242-3441. Web site: www.sonyatv.com. **Santa Monica:** 2100 Colorado Ave., Santa Monica CA 90404. (310)449-2100. **New York:** 550 Madison Ave., 5th Floor, New York NY 10022. (212)833-8000.
How to Contact *Sony/ATV Music does not accept unsolicited submissions.*

◎ SOUND CELLAR MUSIC (BMI)

703 N. Brinton Ave., Dixon IL 61021. (815)288-2900. E-mail: president@cellarrecords.com. Web site: www.cellarrecords.com. **Contact:** Todd Joos (country, pop, Christian), president. Professional Managers: James Miller (folk, adult contemporary); Mike Thompson (metal, hard rock, alternative). Music publisher, record company (Sound Cellar Records), record producer and recording studio. Estab. 1987. Publishes 15-25 songs/year. Publishes 5 or 6 new songwriters/year. Staff size: 7. Pays standard royalty.
How to Contact Submit demo by mail. Unsolicited submissions are OK. Prefers CD with 3 or 4 songs and lyric sheet. Does not return material. "We contact by phone in 3-4 weeks only if we want to work with the artist."
Music Mostly **metal**, **country** and **rock**; also **pop** and **blues**. Published "Problem of Pain" (single by Shane Sowers) from *Before the Machine* (album), recorded by Junker Jorg (alternative metal/rock), released 2000; "Vaya Baby" (single by Joel Ramirez) from *It's About Time* (album), recorded by Joel Ramirez and the All-Stars (latin/R&B), released 2000; and "X" (single by Jon Pomplin) from *Project 814* (album), recorded by Project 814 (progressive rock), released 2001, all on Cellar Records.

◎ STARBOUND PUBLISHING CO. (BMI)

Dept. SM, 207 Winding Rd., Friendswood TX 77546. E-mail: bb207@msn.com. **Contact:** Buz Hart, partner; Lonnie Wright, partner; Jack Duncan, partner. Music publisher, record company (Juke Box Records, Quasar Records and Eden Records) and record producers (Lonnie Wright, Buz Hart, Jack Duncan). Estab. 1970. Publishes 15-30 songs/year; publishes 5-10 new songwriters/year. Pays standard royalty.
How to Contact *Write or call first and obtain permission to submit.* Prefers CD with 3 songs and lyric sheet. Include SASE. Responds in 2 months.
Music Mostly **country**, **R&B** and **gospel**. Does not want rap. Published "If I Had Another Heart"

(single by Larry Wheeler/Buz Hart) from *Day One* (album), recorded by Waylon Adams (country), released 1999 on Jukebox Records; "My Biggest Thrill" and "Old Fashioned Girl" (singles by Phil Hamm/Buz Hart) from *This and That* (album), recorded by Raiders of the Lost Heart (country), released 2000 on MP3.com.

STILL WORKING MUSIC GROUP (ASCAP, BMI, SESAC)

1625 Broadway, Nashville TN 37203. (615)242-4201. Fax: (615)242-4202. Web site: www.stillworki ngmusic.com. **Owner:** Barbara Orbison. Music publisher and record company (Orby Records, Inc.). Estab. 1994.

Affiliate(s) Still Working for the Woman Music (ASCAP), Still Working for the Man Music (BMI) and Still Working for All Music (SESAC).

How to Contact *Does not accept unsolicited submissions.*

Film & TV Published "First Noel," recorded by The Kelions in *Felicity.*

Music Mostly **rock**, **country** and **pop**; also **dance** and **R&B**. Published "If You See Him/If You See Her" (by Tommy Lee James), recorded by Reba McIntire/Brooks & Dunn; "Round About Way" (by Wil Nance), recorded by George Strait on MCA; and "Wrong Again" (by Tommy Lee James), recorded by Martina McBride on RCA (country).

Tips "If you want to be a country songwriter you need to be in Nashville where the business is. Write what is in your heart."

SUCCES

Pijnderslaan 84, Dendermonde 9200 Belgium. (052)218 987. Fax: (052) 225 260. E-mail: deschuyten eer@hotmail.com. **Contact:** Deschuyteneer Hendrik, director. Music publisher, record company and record producer. Estab. 1978. Publishes 400 songs/year. Hires staff songwriters. Staff size: 4. Pays standard royalty.

How to Contact Submit demo by mail. Unsolicited submissions are OK. Prefers cassette or VHS videocassette with 3 songs. SAE and IRC. Responds in 2 months.

Film & TV Places songs in TV. Recently released "Werkloos" (by Deschuyteneer), recorded by Jacques Vermeire in Jacques Vermeire Show.

Music Mostly **pop**, **dance** and **variety**; also **instrumental** and **rock**. Published "Hoe Moet Dat Nou" (single by Henry Spider), recorded by Monja (ballad), released 2001 on MN; "Liefde" (single by H. Spider), recorded by Rudy Silvester (rock), released 2001 on Scorpion; and "Bel Me Gauw" (single by H. Spider), recorded by Guy Dumon (ballad), released 2001 on BM Records.

SUPREME ENTERPRISES INT'L CORP. (ASCAP, BMI)

12304 Santa Monica Blvd., 3rd Floor, Los Angeles CA 90025. (818)707-3481. Fax: (818)707-3482. E-mail: supreme2@earthlink.net. **Contact:** Lisa Lew, general manager copyrights. Music publisher, record company and record producer. Estab. 1979. Publishes 20-30 songs/year; publishes 2-6 new songwriters/year. Pays standard royalty.

Affiliate(s) Fuerte Suerte Music (BMI), Bigh Daddy G. Music (ASCAP).

How to Contact Submit demo by mail. Unsolicited submissions are OK. Prefers CD. Does not return material. **Mail Demos To:** P.O. Box 1373, Agoura Hills CA 91376. "Please copyright material before submitting and include e-mail." Responds in 3-4 months if interested.

Music Mostly **reggae**, **rap** and **dance**. Published "Paso La Vida Pensando," recorded by Jose Feliciano on Motown Records; "Cucu Bam Bam" (single by David Choy), recorded by Kathy on Polydor Records (reggae/pop); and "Mineaita" (single), recorded by Gaby on SEI Records.

Tips "A good melody is a hit in any language."

T.C. PRODUCTIONS/ETUDE PUBLISHING CO. (BMI)

121 Meadowbrook Dr., Hillsborough NJ 08844. (908)359-5110. Fax: (908)359-1962. E-mail: tcprodu ctions@rcn.com. Web site: www.vmgmusic.com. President: Tony Camillo. Music publisher and record producer. Estab. 1992. Publishes 25-50 songs/year; publishes 3-6 new songwriters/year. Pays negotiable royalty.

Affiliate(s) We Iz It Music Publishing (ASCAP) and Etude/Barcam (BMI).

How to Contact *Write or call first and obtain permission to submit.* Prefers CD or cassette with 3-4 songs and lyric sheet. Include SASE. Responds in 1 month.

Music Mostly **R&B** and **dance**; also **country** and **outstanding pop ballads**. Published "I Just Want To Be Your Everything" (single) from *A Breath of Fresh Air* (album), recorded by Michelle Parto (spiritual), released 2006 on Chancellor Records; and *New Jersey Jazz* (album).

Tips "Michelle Parto will soon be appearing in the film musical *Sing Out*, directed by Nick Castle and written by Kent Berhard."

☒ ◻ THISTLE HILL (BMI)

P.O. Box 707, Hermitage TN 37076. (615)320-6071. E-mail: acemusicgroup@hotmail.com. **Contact:** Arden Miller.

How to Contact Submit demo by mail. Unsolicited submissions OK. Prefers CD with 3-10 songs. *No* lyric sheets. Responds only if interested.

Music **Country**, **pop**, and **rock**; also **songs for film/TV**. Published "Angry Heart " (single) from *See What You Wanna See* (album), recorded by Radney Foster (Americana); and "I Wanna be Free" (single) from *I Wanna be Free* (album), recorded by Jordon MyCoskie (Americana), released 2003 on Ah! Records; "Que Vamos Hacer" (single) from *Rachel Rodriguez* (album), recorded by Rachel Rodriguez.

◍ TOURMALINE MUSIC, INC. (BMI)

2831 Dogwood Place, Nashville TN 37204. (615)269-8682. Fax: (615)269-8929. Web site: http://songsfortheplanet.com. **Contact:** Justin Peters, president. Music publisher. Estab. 1980.

Affiliate(s) Justin Peters Music (BMI), LITA Music (ASCAP) and Platinum Planet Music.

How to Contact Submit demo by mail. Unsolicited submissions are OK. Prefers CD with 5 songs and lyric sheet. Does not return material. "Place code '2007' on each envelope submissions."

Music Mostly **rock and roll, classy alternative, adult contemporary, classic rock,country** and some **Christmas music**. Published "Santa Can You Bring My Daddy Home" (single by D. Mattarosa); "The Hurt Is Worth The Chance" (single by Justin Peters/Billy Simon), recorded by Gary Chapman on RCA/BMG Records; and "For So Long" (single by Monroe Jones/Chris McCollum), recorded by GLAD on Benson Records (also recorded by DMB Band, Connie Scot).

☒ ◍ TOWER MUSIC GROUP (ASCAP, BMI)

30 Music Square W., Suite 102, Nashville TN 37203. (615)320-7003. Fax: (615)320-7006. E-mail: castlerecords@castlerecords.com. Web site: www.castlerecords.com. **Contact:** Dave Sullivan, A&R Director. Professional Managers: Ed Russell; Eddie Bishop. Music publisher, record company (Castle Records) and record producer. Estab. 1969. Publishes 50 songs/year; publishes 10 new songwriters/year. Staff size: 15. Pays standard royalty.

Affiliate(s) Cat's Alley Music (ASCAP) and Alley Roads Music (BMI).

How to Contact *See submission policy on Web site.* Prefers cassette with 3 songs and lyric sheet. Does not return material. "You may follow up via e-mail." Responds in 3 months only if interested.

Film & TV Places 2 songs in film and 26 songs in TV/year. Published "Run Little Girl" (by J.R. Jones/Eddie Ray), recorded by J.R. Jones in *Roadside Prey*.

Music Mostly **country** and **R&B**; also **blues**, **pop** and **gospel**. Published "If You Broke My Heart" (single by Condrone) from *If You Broke My Heart* (album), recorded by Kimberly Simon (country); "I Wonder Who's Holding My Angel Tonight" (single) from *Up Above* (album), recorded by Carl Butler (country); and "Psychedelic Fantasy" (single by Paul Sullivan/Priege) from *The Hip Hoods* (album), recorded by The Hip Hoods (power/metal/y2k), all released 2001 on Castle Records.

Tips "Please contact us via e-mail with any other demo submission questions."

⊕ ☒ ◍ TRANSAMERIKA MUSIKVERLAG KG

Wilhelmstrasse 10, Bad Schwartau 23611 Germany. (00) (49) 4512 1530. E-mail: transamerika@online.de. Web site: www.TRANSAMERIKAmusik.de. General Manager: Pia Kaminsky. **Hamburg**: Knauerstr 1, 20249 Hamburg, Germany. Phone: 0049-40-46 06 3394. E-mail: transamerika@t-online.de. License Manager: Kirsten Jung. Member: GEMA, PRS, KODA, NCB, APRA. Music publisher and administrator. Estab. 1978. Staff size: 3. Pays 50% royalty if releasing a record; 85% if only administrating.

Affiliate(s) Administrative agreements with: German Fried Music, Screen Music Services Ltd. (London), Cors Ltd. (London), MCI Ltd. (London), Origin Network PLC Australia Rty. Ltd. (Sydney), MCS Music Ltd. (USA, London), Native Tongue Music Pty. (New Zealand), Pacific Electric Music Publishing.

How to Contact "We accept only released materials—no demos!" Submit CD or VHS videocassette. Does not return material. Responds only if interested.

Film & TV Places several songs in film and 2 songs in TV/year.

Music Mostly **pop**; also **rock**, **country**, **film music** and **reggae**.

Tips "We are specializing in administering (filing, registering, licensing and finding unclaimed royalties, and dealing with counter-claims) publishers worldwide."

☐ TRANSITION MUSIC CORPORATION (ASCAP, BMI, SESAC)

11288 Ventura Blvd., #709, Studio City CA 91604. (323)860-7074. Fax: (323)860-7986. E-mail: info@transitionmusic.com. Web site: www.transitionmusic.com. Director of Film and Television Music: Jennifer Brown. President: Donna Ross-Jones. Vice President: David Jones. Administration: Mike Dobson. Music publisher. Estab. 1988. Publishes 250 songs/year; publishes 20 new songwriters/year. Variable royalty based on song placement and writer.

Affiliate(s) Pushy Publishing (ASCAP), Creative Entertainment Music (BMI) and One Stop Shop Music (SESAC).

How to Contact Address submissions to: New Submissions Dept. Submit demo by mail. Unsolicited submissions are OK. Prefers cassette, DAT or CD with 3 songs. Include SASE. Responds in 5 weeks.

Film & TV "TMC provides music for film, TV and commercials."

Music All styles.

Tips "Supply master quality material with great songs."

☑ TRIO PRODUCTIONS (BMI, ASCAP)

1026 15th Ave. S., Nashville TN 37212. (615)726-5810. E-mail: info@trioproductions.com. Web site: www.trioproductions.com. **Contact:** Robyn Taylor-Drake.

Affiliate(s) Birdseye Ranch Music (ASCAP), Unframed Music (ASCAP), and Whiskey Gap Music (BMI).

How to Contact *Contact first by e-mail to obtain permission to submit demo.* Submit CD with 3-4 songs and lyric sheet. "We do not return submissions. "

Music Country, **Americana**, and **bluegrass**.

☑ TWIN TOWERS PUBLISHING CO. (ASCAP)

8455 Beverly Blvd., Suite 400, Los Angeles CA 90048. (323)655-5007. President: Michael Dixon. Music publisher and booking agency (Harmony Artists, Inc.). Publishes 24 songs/year. Pays standard royalty.

How to Contact *Call first and get permission to submit.* Prefers CD's with 3 songs and lyric sheet. Include SASE. Responds only if interested.

Music Mostly **pop**, **rock**, and **R&B**. Published "Magic," from *Ghostbusters* soundtrack on Arista Records; and "Kiss Me Deadly" (by Lita Ford) on RCA Records.

☑ UNIVERSAL MUSIC PUBLISHING (ASCAP, BMI,SESAC)

2440 Sepulveda Blvd., Suite 100, Los Angeles CA 90064. (310)235-4700. **New York:** 1755 Broadway, 3rd Floor, New York NY 10019. (212)841-8000. **Tennessee:** 1904 Adelicia St., Nashville TN 37212. (615)340-5400. Web site: www.umusicpub.com or www.synchexpress.com.

• In 1999, MCA Music Publishing and PolyGram Music Publishing merged into Universal Music Publishing.

How to Contact *Does not accept unsolicited submissions.*

☑ UNKNOWN SOURCE MUSIC (ASCAP)

120-4d Carver Loop, Bronx NY 10475. E-mail: unknownsourcemusic@hotmail.com. **Contact:** James Johnson, A&R. Music publisher, record company (Smokin Ya Productions) and record producer. Estab. 1993. Publishes 5-10 songs/year; publishes 5-10 new songwriters/year. Hires staff songwriters. Staff size: 10. Pays standard royalty.

Affiliate(s) Sundance Records (ASCAP), Critique Records, WMI Records, and Cornell Entertainment.

How to Contact Send e-mail first then mail. Unsolicited submissions are OK. Prefers mp3s. Responds within 6 weeks.

Music Mostly **rap/hip-hop**, **R&B**, and **alternative**. Published ''LAH'' recorded by Force Dog; ''Changed My World'' recorded by Crysto.

Tips ''Keep working with us, be patient, be willing to work hard. Send your very best work.''

◙ VAAM MUSIC GROUP (BMI)

P.O. Box 29550, Hollywood CA 90029-0550. E-mail: pmarti3636@aol.com. Web site: www.VaamM usic.com. **Contact:** Pete Martin, president. Music publisher and record producer (Pete Martin/Vaam Productions). Estab. 1967. Publishes 9-24 new songs/year. Pays standard royalty.

Affiliate(s) Pete Martin Music (ASCAP).

  • Also see the listings for Blue Gem Records in the Record Companies section of this book and Pete Martin/Vaam Music Productions in the record Producers section of this book.

How to Contact Send CD or cassette with 2 songs and lyric sheet. Include SASE. Responds in 1 month. ''Small packages only.''

Music Mostly **top 40/pop**, **country**, and **R&B**. ''Submitted material must have potential of reaching top 5 on charts.''

Tips ''Study the top 10 charts in the style you write. Stay current and up-to-date with today's market.''

◙ VINE CREEK MUSIC (ASCAP)

P.O. Box 171143, Nashville TN 37217. (615)366-1326. Fax: (615)367-1073. E-mail: vinecreek1@aol. com. **Contact:** Darlene Austin, Brenda Madden. Administration: Jayne Negri. Creative Director: Brenda Madden. Song Plugger: Markham Brown.

How to Contact ''Only send material of good competitive quality. We do not return tapes/CDs unless SASE is enclosed.''

◙ WALKER PUBLISHING CO. L.L.C. (ASCAP/BMI)

P.O. Box 11084, Birmingham AL 35202-1084. (205)601-4420. E-mail: superior_marketing@msn.c om. Web site: www.walkerpublishingco.com. **Contact:** Gary Walker, owner. Professional Managers: Gary Walker (pop/R&B/ country), Charlie Craig (country/new country). Music Publisher, record producer (Charlie Craig Productions). Estab. 2000. Publishes 10 new songs/year; publishes 3 new songwriters/year. Staff size: 3. Hires staff songwriters. Pays standard royalty.

  • Also see the listing for Charlie Craig Productions in the Record Producers section of this book.

Affiliates Cryptogram Music (ASCAP) and Star Alliance Music (BMI).

How to Contact Submit demo by mail. Unsolicited submissions are OK. Prefers CD with 3 songs, lyric sheet and writer's e-mail address. Does not return material. Responds in 6 weeks if interested, via e-mail only. ''Submit only professional studio quality demos.''

Music Mostly **country** and **new country**. Does not want rap, hard rock or metal. Published ''Dallas Didn't Do It'' (single by Craig/Wilkinson/Crosby) from a yet-unnamed album recorded by The Wilkinsons (country); ''Tin Can'' (single by Charlie Craig/Jerry Cupid) from debut album recorded by Brad & Shelly (country), released on Cupid Records.

Tips ''Walker Publishing Co. L.L.C. has partnered with Charlie Craig Productions, owned by legendary writer/producer Charlie Craig—his writing credits include Alan Jackson's 'Wanted'; Travis Tritt's 'Between an Old Memory and Me'; Dolly Parton's 'Chicken Every Sunday'; and Johnny Cash's 'I Would Like to See You Again.' See www.charliecraig.com.''

☑ ◐ WALKERBOUT MUSIC GROUP (ASCAP, BMI, SESAC)

(formerly The Goodland Music Group Inc.), P.O. Box 24454, Nashville TN 37202. (615)269-7071. Fax: (615)269-0131. E-mail: info@walkerboutmusic.com. Web site: www.walkerboutmusic.com.

Contact: Matt Watkins, publishing coordinator. Estab. 1988. Publishes 50 songs/year; 5-10 new songwriters/year. Pays standard royalty.

Affiliate(s) Goodland Publishing Company (ASCAP), Marc Isle Music (BMI), Gulf Bay Publishing (SESAC), Con Brio Music (BMI), Wiljex Publishing (ASCAP), Concorde Publishing (SESAC).

How to Contact ''Please see Web site for submission information.''

Music Mostly **country/Christian** and **adult contemporary**.

◪ ⊘ WARNER/CHAPPELL MUSIC, INC.

10585 Santa Monica Blvd., Third Floor, Los Angeles CA 90025. (310)441-8600. Fax: (310)470-3232. **New York:** 1290 Avenue of the Americas, 23rd floor, New York NY 10104. (212)707-2600. Fax: (212)405-5428. **Nashville:** 20 Music Square E., Nashville TN 37203. (615)733-1880. Fax: (615)733-1885. Web site: www.warnerchappell.com. Music publisher.

How to Contact *Warner/Chappell does not accept unsolicited material.*

ℕ ◪ WEAVER OF WORDS MUSIC (BMI)

(administered by Bug Music), P.O. Box 803, Tazewell VA 24651. (276)988-6267. E-mail: cooksong@ver izon.net. Web site: www.weaverofmusic.com. **Contact:** H.R. Cook, president. Music publisher and record company (Fireball Records). Estab. 1978. Publishes 12 songs/year. Pays standard royalty.

Affiliate(s) Weaver of Melodies Music (ASCAP).

How to Contact Submit demo by mail. Unsolicited submissions are OK. Prefers CD with 3 songs and lyric or lead sheets. ''We prefer CD submissions but will accept submissions on cassette.'' Include SASE. Responds in 3 weeks.

Music Mostly **country, pop, bluegrass, R&B, film and television** and **rock**. Published ''Zero To Love'' (single by H. Cook/Brian James Deskins/Rick Tiger) from *It's Just The Night* (album), recorded by Del McCoury Band (bluegrass), released 2003 on McCoury Music; ''Muddy Water'' (single by Alan Johnston) from *The Midnight Call* (album), recorded by Don Rigsby (bluegrass), released 2003 on Sugar Hill; and ''Ol Brown Suitcase'' (single by H.R. Cook) from *Lonesome Highway* (album), recorded by Josh Williams (bluegrass), released 2004 on Pinecastle.

◻ ANGELA BAKER WELLS MUSIC (ASCAP)

P.O. Box 148027, Nashville TN 37214-8027. (615)883-2020. E-mail: angie@coalharbormusic.com. Web site: www.coalharbormusic.com. **Contact:** Angela Baker Wells, president/owner. Music publisher. Estab. 2004. Publishes 25 songs/year. Publishes 2 new songwriters/year. Staff size: 2. Pays standard royalty of 50%.

How to Contact *Contact first and obtain permission to submit a demo.* Prefers CD with 3-5 songs and cover letter. ''Put 'ATTN: Publ.' on submissions. Include SASE or stamped reply card for reply to submission'' Does not return submissions. Responds only if interested.

Music Mostly **Christian country, contemporary Christian, Southern gospel**; also **gospel (all forms), country,** and **bluegrass**. Does not want heavy metal, hard rock, rap, grunge, or punk. Published ''They Never Had You'' (single) from *Coal Harbor Gospel, Vol. 2*, written and recorded by Don Freeman (country/Christian country/AC); ''Storms of Life'' (single by Angela Renee Wells) from *Coal Harbor Gospel, Vol. 2*, recorded by Angela Baker Wells (Christian country/Southern gospel); ''The Anointing'' (single), written and recorded by Ray Holland (Southern gospel/inspirational), all released 2004 on Coal Harbor Music.

Tips ''We are actively seeking great songs to pitch to Christian and country artists. We are also interested in Christmas, patriotic, and children's songs. Please put all contact info on your cover letter, and include your name, phone, and e-mail on your CD. Do not send certified or registered mail!''

⊕ ◻ BERTHOLD WENGERT (MUSIKVERLAG)

Hauptstrasse 36, Pfinztal-Sollingen, D-76327 Germany. **Contact:** Berthold Wengert. Music publisher. Pays standard GEMA royalty.

How to Contact Prefers cassette and complete score for piano. SAE and IRC. Responds in 1 month. ''No cassette returns!''

Music Mostly **light music** and **pop**.

☑ WILCOM PUBLISHING (ASCAP)

Box 913, Cherokee Village AR 72525. (870)847-1721. Fax: (870)847-1721. E-mail: william@wilcom publishing.com. **Contact:** William Clark, owner. Music publisher. Estab. 1989. Publishes 10-15 songs/year; publishes 1-2 new songwriters/year. Staff size: 2. Pays standard royalty.

How to Contact *Write or call first and obtain permission to submit.* Prefers cassette with 1-2 songs and lyric sheet. Include SASE. Responds in 3 weeks.

Music Mostly **R&B**, **pop** and **rock**; also **country**. Does not want rap. Published "Girl Can't Help It" (single by W. Clark/D. Walsh/P. Oland), recorded by Stage 1 on Rockit Records (top 40).

☑ WINDSWEPT MUSIC (BMI)

33 Music Square W., #104B, Nashville TN 37203. (615)313-7676. Fax: (615)313-7670. Web site: www.windsweptpacific.com. **Contact:** Lisa Gamerts Selder.

▦ ☑ WINSTON & HOFFMAN HOUSE MUSIC PUBLISHERS (ASCAP, BMI)

P.O. Box 1415, Burbank CA 91507-1415. E-mail: sixties1@aol.com. **Contact:** Lynne Robin Green, president. Music publisher. Estab. 1958. Publishes 25 songs/year. Staff size: 2. Pays standard royalty.

Affiliate(s) Lansdowne Music Publishers (ASCAP), Bloor Music (BMI) and Ben Ross Music (AS-CAP), "also administers 30 other publishing firms."

How to Contact Submit demo by mail. Unsolicited submissions are OK. *"Do not query first.* Do not call. Do not send lyrics without completed music (or CD without lyric sheets)." Prefers cassette or CD with 3 songs maximum and lyric sheet. *"Must* include SASE or e-mail, or *NO* reply!" Responds in 1 month.

Film & TV Places 45 songs in film and 25 songs in TV/year. Recently published "Dooley" (by Dillard/Jayne) in *Baby Blues*; "Closer Walk With Thee" (by Craver/Henderson) in *Smiling Fish and Goat on Fire*; and "Born to Jump" (by Larry Dunn) in *Olympics 2000*, as well as songs placed in *Alias*, *Six Feet Under*, and on MTV, as well as Starz promo spot, *Los Tres Magos* DVD and soundtrack, *Saturday Night Live*, Comedy Central's *100 Greatest Comedy Moments*, *Malcolm in the Middle*, CMT's *20 Greatest Country Stars* and *Greatest Road Trips*, *The Best of Etta James*, and more.

Music Mostly **R&B**, **pop**, **ballads**, **hip-hop**, **vocal jazz**, **alternative rock**, and **R&B**; also **bluegrass**, **Spanish pop**, and **pop ballads**.

Tips "Be very selective in what you send. 'A' side hit quality single songs only. For film or TV submissions you must specify you own all the master rights yourself! Be interesting lyrically and strikingly original melodically. No metal or hard rock. No vague lyrics. No alternative, New Age, violent, or sexist lyrics. No novelty, kids music, or holiday songs. We don't work with lyrics only. No instrumental score-type synthy music, please. Independent artist's album material most welcome."

☑ YOUR BEST SONGS PUBLISHING (ASCAP)

1402 Auburn Way N, Suite 396, Auburn WA 98002. (877)672-2520. **Contact:** John Markovich, general manager. Music publisher. Estab. 1988. Publishes 1-5 songs/year; publishes 1-3 new songwriters/year. Query for royalty terms.

How to Contact *Write first and obtain permission to submit.* Prefers CD or cassette with 1-3 songs and lyric sheet. "Submit your 1-3 best songs per type of music. Use separate CDs or cassettes per music type and indicate music type on each CD or cassette." Include SASE. Responds in 3 months.

Music Mostly **country**, **rock/blues**, and **pop/rock**; also **progressive**, **A/C**, some **heavy metal** and **New Age**. Published "Sea of Dreams," written and recorded by J.C. Mark on Cybervoc Productions, Inc. (New Age).

Tips "We just require good lyrics, good melodies and good rhythm in a song. We absolutely do not want music without a decent melodic structure. We do not want lyrics with foul language or lyrics that do not inspire some form of imaginative thought."

▦ ☑ ZETTITALIA MUSIC INTERNATIONAL (ASCAP, BMI)

P.O. Box 261488, Encino CA 91426. (818)506-8533. Fax: (818)506-8534. E-mail: zettworks@aol.c om. Web site: www.pplzmi.com. **Contact:** Cheyenne Phoenix, A&R. Assistant . A&R: Kaitland

Diamond. Music publisher. Estab. 1995. Publishes 40 songs/year; publishes 2 new songwriters/year. Staff size: 2. Hires staff songwriters. Pays standard royalty.
Affiliate(s) Zett One Songs (ASCAP) and Zett Two Music (BMI).
How to Contact *E-mail or write to obtain permission to submit. No phone calls.* "Include SASE or e-mail." Prefers cassette or CD with 3 songs. Include SASE. Responds in 6 weeks.
Film & TV Places 2 songs in film and 4 songs in TV/year.
Music Mostly **pop**, **film music**, **country**, **instrumental**and **R&B**.
Tips "In art, be a good student and stay true to your instincts. In business, be thorough, realistic, flexible and straightforward. Finally, The Golden Rule rules."

☑ ◔ ZOMBA MUSIC PUBLISHING (ASCAP, BMI)

245 Fifth Ave., 8th Floor, New York NY 10001. (212)727-0016. Web site: www.zomba.com. **Contact:** Jennifer Blakeman (pop/rock), Peter Visvardis (pop/rock), or Tanya Brown (urban). **Beverly Hills:** 8750 Wilshire Blvd., Beverly Hills CA 90211. (310)358-4200. **Contact:** Andrea Torchia (pop/rock). Music publisher. Publishes 5,000 songs/year.
Affiliate(s) Zomba Enterprises, Inc. (ASCAP); Zomba Songs, Inc. (BMI).
How to Contact *Zomba Music Publishing does not accept unsolicited material.* "Contact us through management or an attorney."
Music Mostly **R&B**, **pop**, and **rap**; also **rock** and **alternative**. Published ". . . Baby One More Time" (single by M. Martin), recorded by Britney Spears on Jive; "Home Alone" (single by R. Kelly/K. Price/K. Murray), recorded by R. Kelly featuring Keith Murray on Jive; and "Taking Everything" (single by G. Levert/D. Allamby/L. Browder/A. Roberson), recorded by Gerald Levert on EastWest.

ADDITIONAL MUSIC PUBLISHERS

The following companies are also music publishers, but their listings are found in other sections of the book. Read the listings for submission information.

A

A.A.M.I. Music Group 142
''A'' Major Sound Corporation 194
ABL Records 142
ACR Productions 194
Apodaca Promotions Inc. 220
Ariana Records 144
Arkadia Entertainment Corp. 144
Atlan-Dec/Grooveline Records 145
Audio-Visual Media Productions 145
Avita Records 145

B

Banana Records 149
Blue Gem Records 150
Blue Wave 150
Blue Wave Productions 222
Blues Alley Records 196

C

Cacophony Productions 196
Cambria Records & Publishing 151
Capstan Record Production 152
Chattahoochee Records 153
Cherry Street Records 154
Circuit Rider Talent & Management
    Co. 223
Cosmotone Records 156
CPA Records 156

D

DaVinci's Notebook Records 198
DreamWorks Records 158

F

Final Mix Inc. 199
Fireant 159

G

Generic Records, Inc. 160
Gig Records 160

Goldwax Record Corporation 161
Groove Makers' Recordings 164

H

Hailing Frequency Music Productions 199
Hardison International Entertainment Corporation 230
Heads Up Int., Ltd. 165
Heart Consort Music 200
Hi-Bias Records Inc. 165
Huge Production, Inc., A 231

JE

J & V Management 232
Jay Jay Publishing & Record Co. 201

K

Knight Agency, Bob 233
Kuper Personal Management/
    Recovery Recordings 234

L

L.A. Entertainment, Inc. 202
Lazy Bones Productions/Recordings, Inc. 202
Levy Management, Rick 234
Lucifer Records, Inc. 167

M

Mac-Attack Productions 203
Mighty Records 171

O

On the Level Music! 237
Only New Age Music, Inc. 173

P

P. & N. Records 174
Philly Breakdown Recording Co. 207
Pierce, Jim 207

Precision Management 238
Presence Records 175

R
RAVE Records, Inc. 176
Riohcat Music 240
RN'D Distribution, LLC. 208
Robbins Entertainment LLC 177
Roll On Records® 178

S
Sahara Records and Filmworks Entertainment 179
Serge Entertainment Group 242
Sound Management Direction 243
Sound Works Entertainment Productions Inc. 210
SRS Productions/Hit Records Network 211
Stuart Audio Services 211
Studio Seven 211
Surface Records 182

T
Tangent® Records 182
Tari, Roger Vincent 212
Tas Music Co./Dave Tasse Entertainment 245
TMC Productions 212
TVT Records 184

U
UAR Records 185

W
Warehouse Creek Recording Corp. 186
Warner Productions, Cheryl K. 246
Westpark Music—Records, Production & Publishing 187
Winterland Entertainment Management & Publishing 247
World Wide Management 247

X
X.R.L. Records/Music 188

Record Companies

Record companies release and distribute records, cassettes and CDs—the tangible products of the music industry. They sign artists to recording contracts, decide what songs those artists will record, and determine which songs to release. They are also responsible for providing recording facilities, securing producers and musicians, and overseeing the manufacture, distribution and promotion of new releases.

MAJOR LABELS & INDEPENDENT LABELS

Major labels and independent labels—what's the difference between the two?

The majors

Major labels are defined as those record companies distributed by one of the "Big 5" distribution companies: BMG Distribution, EMI Music Distribution (EMD), Sony Music Distribution, Warner/Elektra/Atlantic Distribution (WEA) and Universal Music and Video Distribution (UMVD). Distribution companies are wholesalers that sell records to retail outlets. If a label is distributed by one of these major companies, you can be assured any release coming out on that label has a large distribution network behind it. It will most likely be sent to most major retail stores in the United States.

The independents

Independent labels go through smaller distribution companies to distribute their product. They usually don't have the ability to deliver records in massive quantities as the major distributors do. However, that doesn't mean independent labels aren't able to have hit records just like their major counterparts. A record label's distributors are found in the listings after the **Distributed by** heading.

Which do I submit to?

Many of the companies listed in this section are independent labels. They are usually the most receptive to receiving material from new artists. Major labels spend more money than most other segments of the music industry; the music publisher, for instance, pays only for items such as salaries and the costs of making demos. Record companies, at great financial risk, pay for many more services, including production, manufacturing and promotion. Therefore, they must be very selective when signing new talent. Also, the continuing fear of copyright infringement suits has closed avenues to getting new material heard by the majors. Most don't listen to unsolicited submissions, period. Only songs recommended by attorneys, managers and producers who record company employees trust and respect are being heard

The Case for Independents

Tip

If you're interested in getting a major label deal, it makes sense to look to independent record labels to get your start. Independent labels are seen by many as a stepping stone to a major recording contract. Very few artists are signed to a major label at the start of their careers; usually, they've had a few independent releases that helped build their reputation in the industry. Major labels watch independent labels closely to locate up-and-coming bands and new trends. In the current economic atmosphere at major labels—with extremely high overhead costs for developing new bands and the fact that only 10% of acts on major labels actually make any profit—they're not willing to risk everything on an unknown act. Most major labels won't even consider signing a new act that hasn't had some indie success.

But independents aren't just farming grounds for future major label acts; many bands have long term relationships with indies, and prefer it that way. While they may not be able to provide the extensive distribution and promotion that a major label can (though there are exceptions), indie labels can help an artist become a regional success, and may even help the performer to see a profit as well. With the lower overhead and smaller production costs an independent label operates on, it's much easier to "succeed" on an indie label than on a major.

by A&R people at major labels (companies with a referral policy have a Ø preceding their listing). But that doesn't mean all major labels are closed to new artists. With a combination of a strong local following, success on an independent label (or strong sales of an independently produced and released album) and the right connections, you could conceivably get an attentive audience at a major label.

But the competition is fierce at the majors, so you shouldn't overlook independent labels. Since they're located all over the country, indie labels are easier to contact and can be important in building a local base of support for your music (consult the Geographic Index at the back of the book to find out which companies are located near you). Independent labels usually concentrate on a specific type of music, which will help you target those companies your submissions should be sent to. And since the staff at an indie label is smaller, there are fewer channels to go through to get your music heard by the decision makers in the company.

HOW RECORD COMPANIES WORK

Independent record labels can run on a small staff, with only a handful of people running the day-to-day business. Major record labels are more likely to be divided into the following departments: A&R, sales, marketing, promotion, product management, artist development, production, finance, business/legal and international.

- The *A&R department* is staffed with A&R representatives who search out new talent. They go out and see new bands, listen to demo tapes, and decide which artists to sign. They also look for new material for already signed acts, match producers with artists

Record Companies

and oversee recording projects. Once an artist is signed by an A&R rep and a record is recorded, the rest of the departments at the company come into play.

- The *sales department* is responsible for getting a record into stores. They make sure record stores and other outlets receive enough copies of a record to meet consumer demand.
- The *marketing department* is in charge of publicity, advertising in magazines and other media, promotional videos, album cover artwork, in-store displays, and any other means of getting the name and image of an artist to the public.
- The *promotion department*'s main objective is to get songs from a new album played on the radio. They work with radio programmers to make sure a product gets airplay.
- The *product management department* is the ringmaster of the sales, marketing and promotion departments, assuring that they're all going in the same direction when promoting a new release.
- The *artist development department* is responsible for taking care of things while an artist is on tour, such as setting up promotional opportunities in cities where an act is performing.
- The *production department* handles the actual manufacturing and pressing of the record and makes sure it gets shipped to distributors in a timely manner.
- People in the *finance department* compute and distribute royalties, as well as keep track of expenses and income at the company.
- The *business/legal department* takes care of contracts, not only between the record company and artists but with foreign distributors, record clubs, etc.
- And finally, the *international department* is responsible for working with international companies for the release of records in other countries.

LOCATING A RECORD LABEL

With the abundance of record labels out there, how do you go about finding one that's right for the music you create? First, it helps to know exactly what kind of music a record label releases. Become familiar with the records a company has released, and see if they fit in with what you're doing. Each listing in this section details the type of music a particular record company is interested in releasing. You will want to refer to the Category Index on page 358 to help you find those companies most receptive to the type of music you write. You should only approach companies open to your level of experience (see A Sample Listing Decoded on page 11). Visiting a company's website can also provide valuable information about a company's philosophy, the artists on the label and the music they work with.

Networking

Recommendations by key music industry people are an important part of making contacts with record companies. Songwriters must remember that talent alone does not guarantee success in the music business. You must be recognized through contacts, and the only way to make contacts is through networking. Networking is the process of building an intercon-

Icons

For more instructional information on the listings in this book, including explanations of symbols ( ), read the article *Songwriter's Market: How Do I Use It?* on page 7.

For More Info

necting web of acquaintances within the music business. The more industry people you meet, the larger your contact base becomes, and the better are your chances of meeting someone with the clout to get your demo into the hands of the right people. If you want to get your music heard by key A&R representatives, networking is imperative.

Networking opportunities can be found anywhere industry people gather. A good place to meet key industry people is at regional and national music conferences and workshops. There are many held all over the country for all types of music (see the Workshops and Conferences section for more information). You should try to attend at least one or two of these events each year; it's a great way to increase the number and quality of your music industry contacts.

Creating a buzz

Another good way to attract A&R people is to make a name for yourself as an artist. By starting your career on a local level and building it from there, you can start to cultivate a following and prove to labels that you can be a success. A&R people figure if an act can be successful locally, there's a good chance they could be successful nationally. Start getting booked at local clubs, and start a mailing list of fans and local media. Once you gain some success on a local level, branch out. All this attention you're slowly gathering, this "buzz" you're generating, will not only get to your fans but to influential people in the music industry as well.

SUBMITTING TO RECORD COMPANIES

When submitting to a record company, major or independent, a professional attitude is imperative. Be specific about what you are submitting and what your goals are. If you are strictly a songwriter and the label carries a band you believe would properly present your song, state that in your cover letter. If you are an artist looking for a contract, showcase your strong points as a performer. Whatever your goals are, follow submission guidelines closely, be as neat as possible and include a top-notch demo. If you need more information concerning a company's requirements, write or call for more details. (For more information on submitting your material, see the article Where Should I Send My Songs? on page 9, Demo Recordings: What Should I Know? on page 13 and Quiz: Are You Professional? on page 26.)

RECORD COMPANY CONTRACTS

Once you've found a record company that is interested in your work, the next step is signing a contract. Independent label contracts are usually not as long and complicated as major label ones, but they are still binding, legal contracts. Make sure the terms are in the best interest of both you and the label. Avoid anything in your contract that you feel is too restrictive. It's important to have your contract reviewed by a competent entertainment lawyer. A basic recording contract can run from 40-100 pages, and you need a lawyer to help you understand it. A lawyer will also be essential in helping you negotiate a deal that is in your best interest.

Recording contracts cover many areas, and just a few of the things you will be asked to consider will be: What royalty rate is the record label willing to pay you? What kind of advance are they offering? How many records will the company commit to? Will they offer tour support? Will they provide a budget for video? What sort of a recording budget are they offering? Are they asking you to give up any publishing rights? Are they offering you a publishing advance? These are only a few of the complex issues raised by a recording contract, so it's vital to have an entertainment lawyer at your side as you negotiate.

ADDITIONAL RECORD COMPANIES

There are **more record companies** located in other sections of the book! On page 190 use the list of Additional Record Companies to find listings within other sections who are also record companies.

🌐 ☑ A.A.M.I. MUSIC GROUP

Maarschalklaan 47, 3417 SE Montfoort, The Netherlands. Fax: 31-384-471214. E-mail: aamimus@w xs.nl. Release Manager: Joop Gerrits; manager (dance, rap): Carlo Bonti. Labels include Associated Artists, Disco-Dance Records and Italo. Record company, music publisher (Hilversum Happy Music/BUMA-STEMRA, Intermedlodie/BUMA-STEMRA and Hollands Glorie Productions), record producer (Associated Artists Productions) and TV promotions. Estab. 1975. Releases 10 singles, 25 12'' singles, 6 LPs and 6 CDs/year. Pays 14% royalty to artists on contract; variable amount to publishers.

How to Contact Submit demo by mail. Unsolicited submissions are OK. Prefers CD or DVD with any number of songs and lyric or lead sheets. Records also accepted. SAE and IRC. Responds in 6 weeks.

Music Mostly **dance, pop, house, hip-hop**, and **rock**. Released ''Black Is Black'' (single by Gibbons/Hayes), recorded by Belle Epoque (dance); *Pocket Full of Whishes* (single by Robert Jones), recorded by Assault Team (dance), both on Movin' Novelties; and ''Let Me Be Free'' (single), written and recorded by Samantha Fox on LLP (pop). Other artists include Robert Ward, Yemisi, F.R. David and Black Nuss.

Tips ''We invite producers and independent record labels to send us their material for their entry on the European market. Mark all parcels as 'no commercial value—for demonstration only.' We license productions to record companies in all countries of Europe and South Africa. Submit good demos or masters.''

☐ ABL RECORDS

835 E. Buckeywood Ave., Orange CA 92865. (714)685-9958. E-mail: melodi4ever@earthlink.net. Web site: www.ABLmusic.com. **Contact:** Allan Licht, owner. Record company and music publisher (Allan Bradley Music/BMI and Lichtenfeld Music/ASCAP). Estab. 1993. Staff size: 2. Releases 10 singles/year. Pays 50% royalty to artists on contract; statutory rate to publisher per song on record.

● Also see the listing for Allan Bradley Music in the Music Publishers section of this book.

How to Contact Submit demo by mail. Unsolicited submissions are OK. Prefers CD with 3 songs and lyric sheet. Does not return material. Responds in 1 month.

Music Mostly **A/C, pop**, and **R&B**; also **country** and **Christian contemporary**. Released *I'll Keep the Change* (by Betty Kay Miller/Marcia McCaslin), recorded by Dakota Brad (country), released 1999 on ABL Records; ''22 Years Old'' (single), recorded by Donny Goldberg (pop/rock); ''I Trusted You'' (single), by Bree Noble/Linda Barbarino (A/C); ''Center of my Heart'' (single) by Tony Rooney (A/C); ''Impossibly Beautiful'' (single) by Daniel Goodman (A/C); ''His Own Hall of Fame'' (single) by Scott Ward/Chris Bradshaw (country); ''He Rolled The Stone Away'' (single) and ''A Dad Who Took The Time'' (single) by Jeff Knapp (Christian/country). Other artists include Tracy Todd, Sam Morrison, Donna West, Jill J. Switzer, Tony Rooney, Donny Goldberg, and Michael Cavanaugh.

Tips ''Submit top-notch material with great demos.''

☐ ALLEGHENY MUSIC WORKS

1611 Menoher Blvd., Johnstown PA 15905. E-mail: TunedOnMusic@aol.com. Web site: www.alleg henymusicworks.com. **Contact:** Al Rita, managing director. Labels include Allegheny Records. Record company and music publisher (Allegheny Music Works Publishing/ASCAP and Tuned on Music/BMI). Estab. 1991. Pays 10-12% royalty to artists on contract; statutory rate to publisher per song on record.

How to Contact *Does not accept unsolicited submissions. Write first and obtain permission to submit.* Include SASE for reply. ''E-mail queries are acceptable; we respond ASAP to e-mail queries. However, we will not open e-mail containing attachments or pictures. NO Phone Call queries or solicitations. We will not reply to voice mail requests.''

Music Mostly **radio-ready masters of Halloween songs** in any genre except rap and metal. ''100% publishing must be open—no exceptions—and control of all rights for releasing the said masters must also be available. Songs can be for either children or adults. However, even with songs having more appeal to adults, we will not consider any material we think parents would want to screen from their children. We also do not want any material with any lyric content that suggests or makes light of cruelty to animals." Released "The Pumpkin Twist" (single), written and recorded by Ben Brown; "It's Halloween" (single by Al Rita), recorded by Victor R. Vampire; and "Halloween Is in the Air" (single by Carlon Miller/T.D. Bayless), recorded by Phil Coley, all released 2006 on Allegheny Music Works.

Tips "Bookmark our Web site and check it regularly, clicking on *Songwriter Opportunities*. Each month, as a free service to songwriters, we list a new artist or company looking for songs. Complete contact information is included."

☑ AMERICAN RECORDINGS

8920 Sunset Blvd., 2nd Floor, W. Hollywood CA 90069. (310)288-5300. Web site: www.americanrecordings.com. A&R: Dino Paredes, George Drakoulias, Antony Bland, Brendon Mendoza. Labels include Too Pure, Infinite Zero, UBL, Venture and Onion. Record company.

Distributed by Sony.

How to Contact Submit demo by mail. Unsolicited submissions are OK. Prefers CD, cassette or videocassette with lyric and lead sheet.

Music Released *Unchained*, recorded by Johnny Cash on American Recordings. Other artists include Slayer, System of a Down, The Jayhawks, Rahat Feteh Ali Khan, Paloalto, Noise Ratchet, and The (International) Noise Conspiracy.

☑ AMERICATONE RECORDS INTERNATIONAL USA

1817 Loch Lomond Way, Las Vegas NV 89102-4437. (702)384-0030. Fax: (702)382-1926. E-mail: jjjamericatone@aol.com. Web site: www.americatone.com. Estab. 1985. **Contact:** A&R Director. Labels include The Rambolt Music International (ASCAP), Americatone Publishers (BMI) and Christy Records International. Record company, producer and music publisher. Releases 4-5 CDs and cassettes/year. Pays 10% royalty.

Distributed by Big Band Dist., Otter Music, North County, General, Harbor Export, International Dist., Twinbrook Dist., Gibson Dist.

How to Contact Submit demo by mail. Unsolicited submissions are OK. Prefers CD. Include SASE. Responds in 1 month.

Music Jazz and **Spanish jazz** only. Artists include Raoul Romero and His Jazz Stars Orchestra, Mark Masters and His Jazz Orchestra, Dick Shearer and His Stan Kenton Spirits, Sam Trippe and His Jazz Orchestra, Ladd McIntosh and His Orchestra, Caribbean Jazz, Jazz in the Rain Quintet, Bill Perkins and His Jazz Quintet, and the Eugene Shapiro Jazz Quintet. Americatone International USA is also a publisher of piano music and orchestrations.

Ⓝ ▦ ☑ AMP RECORDS & MUSIC

Box BM F.A.M.E., London WC1N 3XX United Kingdom. E-mail: markjenkins@beeb.net. Web site: www.markjenkins.net. **Contact:** Mark Jenkins, A&R (New Age, instrumental, ambient, progressive rock). Record company. Estab. 1985. Staff size: 10. Releases 12 CDs/year. Pays negotiable royalty to artists on contract; negotiable rate to publisher per song on record.

Distributed by Shellshock (UK), Eurock/ZNR/NSA (USA), MP (Italy) and Crystal Lake (France).

How to Contact Submit demo by mail. Unsolicited submissions are OK. Prefers cassette or CD with cover letter and press clippings. Does not return material. Responds in 2 months.

Music Mostly **New Age**, **instrumental** and **ambient**; also **progressive rock**, **synthesizer** and **ambient dance**. Does not want ballads, country or AOR. Released *Changing States*, recorded by Keith Emerson (progressive rock); *Tyranny of Beauty*, written and recorded by Tangerine Dream (synthesizer); and *Spirit of Christmas*, written and recorded by various artists (instrumental compilation), all on AMP Records.

Tips "Send a relevant style of music."

☑ ANGEL RECORDS

150 Fifth Ave., 6th Floor, New York NY 10011. (212)786-8600. Web site: www.angelrecords.com. Record company. Labels include EMI Classics, Manhattan Records, and Virgin Classics.

Distributed by EMI Music Distribution.

How to Contact *Angel/EMI Records does not accept unsolicited submissions.*

Music Artists include Sarah Brightman, Paul McCartney, and Bernadette Peters.

☻ ARIANA RECORDS

1312 S. Avenida Polar, Tucson AZ 85710. E-mail: jgasper1596@earthlink.net. Web site: www.cdba by.com/all/myko. **Contact:** James M. Gasper, president. Vice President (pop, rock): Tom Dukes. Partners: Tom Privett (funk, experimental, rock); Scott Smith (pop, rock, AOR). Labels include Egg White Records. Record company, music publisher (Myko Music/BMI) and record producer. Estab. 1980. Staff size: 4. Releases 5 CDs a year and 1 compilation/year. Pays negotiable royalty to artists on contract; negotiable rate to publisher per song on record.

Distributed by Impact Music Distributors and Care Free Music.

How to Contact "We are only interested in finished CD projects. *No tapes. No demos.* Unsolicited submissions are OK. Include SASE. Responds in 6 months.

Music Mostly **rock, funk, jazz, anything weird, strange,** or **lo-fi** (must be mastered to CD). Released "Bloated Floater" (single by Mr. Jimi/Trece Broline/Larry's Fault) from *Bloated Floater* (album), *PsychoPop* (Acidsoxx Musicks CD compilation), *Chuck & The Chair* (film soundtrack), recorded by Bloated Floater (space funk), released 2004 on Ariana Records; "Feel My Face" (single by James Gasper) from *Soledad* (album), recorded by Scuba Tails (electro rock), released 2004 on Ariana Records; and "Smak You Up" (single by Trece Broline/Mr. Jimi/Larry's Fault) from *Headphones Plez,*recorded by Beatnik Grip (trash euro funk), released 2004 on Ariana Records; *Just Arrived* (album), written and recorded by Gasper & Dukes (pop/rock), re-released 2005 on Ariana Records; *Songs From the Garden* (album), written and recorded by The Rakeheads, released 2006 on Ariana Records. New artist Goofy Boy Femroid is currently working on a CD for 2007. Other artists include Tom P., Big White Teeth, J. Tiom, Slim Taco Explosion, and The Miller Boys.

Tips "We're a small company, but working your material is our job. If we like it, we'll sell it! It's a tough business. Keep trying."

❷ ARISTA RECORDS

888 7th Ave., New York NY 10019. (212)489-7400. Fax: (212)977-9843. Web site: www.arista.com. Beverly Hills office: 8750 Wilshire Blvd., 3rd Floor, Beverly Hills CA 90211. (310)358-4600. Nashville office: 7 Music Circle North, Nashville TN 37203. (615)846-9100. Fax: (615)846-9192. Labels include Bad Boy Records, Arista Nashville and Time Bomb Recordings. Record company.

Distributed by BMG.

How to Contact *Does not accept unsolicited material.*

Music Artists include Outkast, Dido, Pink, Usher, Avril Lavigne, Babyface, and Sarah McLachlan.

☻ ARKADIA ENTERTAINMENT CORP.

34 E. 23rd St., New York NY 10010. (212)533-0007. Fax: (212)979-0266. E-mail: info@arkadiarecor ds.com. Web site: www.arkadiarecords.com. **Contact:** A&R Song Submissions. Labels include Arkadia Jazz, Arkadia Classical, Arkadia Now and Arkadia Allworld. Record company, music publisher (Arkadia Music), record producer (Arkadia Productions) and Arkadia Video. Estab. 1995.

How to Contact *Write or call first and obtain permission to submit.*

Music Mostly **jazz, classical,** and **pop/R&B**; also **world.**

☻ ASTRALWERKS

104 W. 29th St., 4th Floor, New York NY 10001. Web site: www.astralwerks.com/demo.html. **Contact:** A&R. Record company. Estab. 1979. Releases 10-12 12" singles and 100 CDs/year. Pays varying royalty to artists on contract; statutory rate to publisher per song.

How to Contact Send submissions to: "Alt: A&R" to address above. No unsolicited phone calls please.

Music Mostly **alternative/indie/electronic.** Artists include VHS or BETA, Badly Drawn boy, The Beta Band, Chemical Brothers, Turin Breaks, and Fatboy Slim.

Tips "We are open to artists of unique quality and enjoy developing artists from the ground up.

We listen to all types of 'alternative' music regardless of genre. It's about the aesthetic and artistic quality first. We send out rejection letters so do not call to find out what's happening with your demo.''

☐ ATLAN-DEC/GROOVELINE RECORDS

2529 Green Forest Court, Snellville GA 30078-4183. (770)985-1686. Fax: (877)751-5169. E-mail: atlandec@prodigy.net. Web site: www.ATLAN-DEC.com. President/Senior A&R Rep: James Hatcher. A&R Rep: Wiletta J. Hatcher. Record company, music publisher and record producer. Estab. 1994. Staff size: 2. Releases 3-4 singles, 3-4 LPs and 3-4 CDs/year. Pays 10-25% royalty to artists on contract; statutory rate to publisher per song on record.

Distributed by C.E.D. Entertainment Dist./Bayside Dist.—(407)679-6900.

How to Contact Submit demo by mail. Unsolicited submissions are OK. Prefers CD with lyric sheet. Does not return material. Responds in 3 months.

Music Mostly **R&B/urban**, **hip-hop/rap**, and **contemporary jazz**; also **soft rock**, **gospel**, **dance**, and **new country**. Released "Temptation" by Shawree, released 2004 on Atlan-Dec/Grooveline Records. Other artists include Furious D (rap/hip-hop), Tobias (rap/hip-hop) single due in 2005, and Mark Cocker (new country). Other artists include LowLife (rap/hip-hop).

◪ ⊘ ATLANTIC RECORDS

1290 Avenue of the Americas, New York NY 10104. (212)707-2000. Fax: (212)581-6414. Web site: www.atlanticrecords.com. **New York:** 1290 Avenue of the Americas, New York, NY 10104. **Los Angeles:** 3400 W. Olive Ave., 3rd Floor, Burbank CA 91505. (818)238-6800 Fax: (310)205-7411. **Nashville:** 20 Music Square East, Nashville TN 37203. (615)272-7990. Labels include Big Beat Records, LAVA, Nonesuch Records, Atlantic Classics, and Rhino Records. Record company. Pays negotiable royalty to artists on contract; negotiable rate to publisher per song on record.

Distributed by WEA.

How to Contact *Does not accept unsolicited material.* "No phone calls please."

Music Artists include Matchbox Twenty, Jewel, Sugar Ray, Kid Rock, Luna, P.O.D., The Darkness, and The Corrs.

⊕ ⊘ AUDIO-VISUAL MEDIA PRODUCTIONS

Sovereign House, 12 Trewartha Rd., Praa Sands, Penzance, Cornwall TR20 9ST England. (17)(36)762-826. Fax: (17)(36)763-328. E-mail: panamus@aol.com. Web site: www.songwriters-guild.co.uk and www.panamamusic.co.uk. **Contact:** Roderick G. Jones, managing director A&R. Labels include Pure Gold Records, Panama Music Library, Rainy Day Records, HepCat Records, Panama Records, Mohock Records. Registered members of Phonographic Performance Ltd. (PPL). Record company, music publisher (Panama Music Library, Melody First Music Library, Eventide Music Library, Musik Image Music Library, Promo Sonor International Music Library, Caribbean Music Library, ADN Creation Music Library, Piano Bar Music Library, Corelia Music Library, PSI Music Library, First Time Music Publishing U.K., registered members of the Mechanical Copyright Protection Society (MCPS) and the Performing Right Society (PRS), management firm and record producer (First Time Management & Production Co.). Estab. 1986. Staff size: 6. Pays variable royalty to artists on contract; statutory rate to publisher per song on record subject to deal.

Distributed by Media U.K. Distributors.

How to Contact Submit demo by mail. Unsolicited submissions are OK. Prefers CD with unlimited number of songs/instrumental themes and lyric or lead sheets. SAE and IRC. Responds in 3 months.

Music All styles. Released "Hot Popsicle" (single) from *Acid Jazz*(album), recorded by David Jones (urban jazz music), released 2006 on Panama Music Library; "Midwinter" (single) from *Winter* (album), recorded by Kevin Kendle (New Age), released 2006 on Panama Music Library and Eventide Music; "Fingal's Cave" (single) from *1970s Heavy Gothic Rock* (album), recorded by Bram Stoker (rock), released 2006 on Panama Music Library Records.

⊘ AVITA RECORDS

P.O. Box 764, Hendersonville TN 37077-0764. (615)824-9313. Fax: (615)824-0797. E-mail: tachoir@ bellsouth.net. Web site: www.tachoir.com. **Contact:** Robert Kayre, manager. Record company,

Mr. Jimmi

Ariana Records follows muse to market

James Gasper may not be a household name right now, but perhaps he just hasn't hit the right name yet. Along the course of his over 35 years in music, he's recorded and released projects under a variety of monikers including Dukes & Gasper, JTIOM, Scuba Tails, the Undercover Band, Beatnikgrip, Babyfishmouth, the Mobile Cubes, and others too numerous to mention. Most of this music has come out under the umbrella of Ariana Records, the Tucson-based label Gaspar founded in 1980 with sometime partner Tom Dukes, both of whom had grown up in Gary, Indiana, before eventually moving to Arizona—hence, Arizona + Indiana = Ariana.

Browsing over your extensive discography, it looks like you've got more names than maybe even Sean "P Diddy" Combs. What should I call you?
I prefer to be called Mr. Jimmi.

Okay, Mr. Jimmi it is. So tell me a little bit about Ariana Records—how did the label get started?
I had been signed to a major label in the 1970s. I was a member of a duo called Marshall & James, and we scored a recording contract with RCA records on the strength of a 15-song demo and a handful of live shows in Chicago. At the request of the record company, we added a third member and changed our name to SkyBlue. The band recorded an album, we did a tour of the Midwest—and then I found out one of my friends in the band was sleeping with my wife.

The whole thing fell apart. The record label tried to sue our management company, the management company tried to sue the band, and everybody left town.

I found out then that a record deal with a major isn't all that it's supposed to be—you end up either a slave or a tax deduction to them. The major record companies are into making money, they don't care about the music. It's not like being signed to a major label is going to make everything great. It's more like once you're signed to a major label they'll just tell you, "*This* is what you're going to sing, *this* is how you're going to sound, and *this* is what you're going to wear." I think the days of the big record deals are gone—but then so are the big rock stars.

The birth of Ariana Records was really because of an article I read. It was an interview with Frank Zappa where he said that artists and songwriters or anybody getting into the music industry should start their own label and form their own publishing company, so Tom Dukes and I formed Ariana Records in 1980. We wanted to retain the rights to all our own songs, so we formed the record label to release a four-song EP we had recorded called *Just Arrived*. We also formed Myko Music and signed with BMI.

As David Crosby once said, "First came the music . . . *then* came the business."

And how does the overall philosophy of Ariana Records differ from the major labels?

Our philosophy hasn't changed much over the years: write and record great songs, put together a cool looking CD package, and shoot it out there. It helps to play shows, but that's not always the way to sell records. Personally I've never wanted to be a rock star. I just wanted to make a living making music, and not have to play in a bar all the time. We are just a small label in the Southwest trying to reach a bigger audience, no matter what it takes. It's all about the music . . . I've always said music is my mistress.

Recently it seems you've been making inroads into licensing Ariana Records music for other media.

Yes, we are doing more as of late in licensing our music for film and video projects. We placed a song called "Bloated Floater" in a film called *Chuck & The Chair*, and the filmmakers recently contacted me and said the film has been picked up for distribution. Because of this project, I've been getting calls from other filmmakers who want to license more music for other projects. I just placed a song called "Little Mexico" in a documentary being shot in Mexico as we speak.

So in this case one film placement has led to other placements for you. What if you don't have that first placement to start off with?

Signing up with Versus Media helped to get our music in the hands of filmmakers. Versus has placed four of our songs in film productions in just the last two years. You just sign up with them, put up a profile sheet online and submit CDs of your music, and then they put you in touch with filmmakers looking to license your type of music for their projects.

What about online avenues for marketing and distribution—what kind of experiences have you had with these options?

Before the arrival of the Internet, the life of the independent musician was pretty much mailing out projects, making appointments, or going to Los Angeles, where maybe a friend has a friend who's a roadie, who knows such-and-such a guy. It was all pretty much a shot in the dark. A lot of my friends went to L.A., and now they're all either over there starving or they're sick and tired of the games.

The Internet has been great for us. We're selling CDs as well as downloads, and it's a great tool for building a fan base. And I *cannot* say enough good things about CD Baby— they rock!

Why do you like CD Baby so much? What is it specifically about them that has worked out so well for you?

The folks at CD Baby are musicians themselves, so they know how hard it is to get connected in the music industry. The last six years that Ariana Records has been involved with CD Baby has definitely helped to make us more visible. We do sell CDs of course, but we sell a lot more song downloads.

We also work with Strangevibes.com out of Michigan. Strangevibes is not as big as CD Baby, but they do keep you informed about what's happening with your projects.

The Strangevibes people are also musicians, like the CD Baby folks. It's funny to me how many musicians who got tired of waiting on the majors or who got rejected by the majors decided to do their own thing.

Does Ariana Records accept demos from "pure" songwriters?

We do accept material from outside songwriters and bands; we receive about 20 demos a month. But I've got to tell you, in 25 years I've probably come across about 15 packages total that really stood out.

What made those 15 good ones stand out from all the rest?

Most of the material that we listen to just isn't very professional. For me, personally, if I get a CD that has a great cover, is packaged well, and looks like the artist really cares about what he's doing, I'll give it a listen.

Want to get my attention with your music project? Then you have to know that when you get ready to put it in a mailer to Ariana Records that it's the very best you can do—that the songs are good, the recording is tight, the guitars are in tune, and the CD cover looks great. *That's* how you get my attention.

In this business it's all about persistence, you gotta keep after it. If you are a songwriter, take the time to learn your craft, read a lot, and *listen*. If you are in a band, work on your sound and write great songs. And please, if you're in it for the money, forget it. Have a passion for the music and it will be its own reward. I love music, and it's cost me more in my life than I would ever had expected. It's not like the industry owes me or anything, but sometimes I feel like maybe I didn't work hard enough, or maybe I have to work a little bit harder. In fact, I've been keeping a journal for 25 years, and I'm just about ready to start writing a book about my life in music. I think I'll call it *Keep on Tryin': Staying Sane in the Music Business*.

—*Aaron Poehler*

music publisher (Riohcat Music, BMI) and record producer (Jerry Tachoir). Estab. 1976. Staff size: 8. Releases 2 LPs and 2 CDs/year. Pays negotiable royalty to artists on contract; statutory rate to publisher per song on record.

• Also see the listing for Riohcat Music in the Managers & Booking Agents section of this book.
How to Contact *Contact first and obtain permission to submit.* We only accept material referred to us by a reputable industry source. Prefers cassette, CD, or DAT. Does not return materials. Responds only if interested.
Music Mostly **jazz**. Released *Improvised Thoughts* (album by Marlene Tachoir/Jerry Tachoir/Van Manakas), recorded by Jerry Tachoir and Van Manakas (jazz), released 2001 on Avita Records. Other artists include Van Manakas.

☑ ◢ AVITOR MUSIC INTERNATIONAL

P.O. Box 5537, Kreole Station, Moss Point MS 39563-1537. (601)914-9413. "No collect calls, please." **Contact:** Jemiah F. Mitchell, president/owner. Estab. 2003. Music publisher and record company (Avitor Music International Records).Releases 10 singles and 5 LPs/year. Pays negotable royalty to artists on contract; statutory rate to publisher per song on record. "Avitor Music has National and International distribution."
Distributed by Select-O-Hits, CD Baby, and Amazon.Com.
How to Contact *Write or call first for submission instructions.* "Always whenever you write, be sure you include a #10 business-size envelope addressed back to yourself with a first-class USA postage stamp on the envelope. A reply will come back to you using the SASE you include in your mailing when you write. *Absolutely no reply postcards—only SASE.* If you only write lyrics, do not submit; only complete songs reviewed, so you must find a collaborator. Not interested in reviewing homemade recordings." Prefers CD (first choice) or cassette with 3-10 songs along with lyrics to songs submitted. Responds in 2 months.
Music Mostly **alternative country, modern country, alternative rock, modern rock, mainstream rock, hip-hop, rap, R&B, Americana roots, bluegrass, hot A/C**, and **adult A/C**. Does not want

traditional country. "Recording artists with 10-12 professionally recorded and finished songs ready for release can contact Avitor Music International Records for release and National Distribution. Songs and artist must be outstanding in all respect." Released "Hellova," "Six O'Clock," "Along for the Ride," and "Just Drove Away" (singles) from album of 13 songs *Aron Dees* (album), written and recorded by Aron Dees (modern country).

Tips "We are reaching out to find undiscovered, talented writers and singers who deserve a chance to be heard, accepted, and appreciated. We are looking for serious-minded people who are hungry for success and filled with ambition. Singers and songwriters wanting to record professionally, contact Avitor Music before you make a move. Save time and money and problems you could run into. For the best results to benefit you call Avitor Music to get the job done right from the start."

☑ AWAL.COM

P.O. Box 879, Ojai CA 93024. (805)640-7399. Fax: (805)646-6077. E-mail: mike@awal.com. Web site: www.awal.com. **Contact:** A&R Department. President: Denzyl Feigelson. Record company. Estab. 1996. Staff size: 3.

Distributed by Primarily distributes via digital downloads but physical distribution available.

How to Contact Submit demo by mail. Unsolicited submissions are OK. Prefers CD with 5 songs, lyric sheet, cover letter and press clippings. Does not return materials.

Music Mostly **pop**, **world**, and **jazz**; also **techno**, **teen**, and **children's**. Released *Go Cat Go* (album by various), recorded by Carl Perkins on ArtistOne.com; *Bliss* (album), written and recorded by Donna Delory (pop); and *Shake A Little* (album), written and recorded by Michael Ruff, both on Awal Records.

☑ AWARE RECORDS

2336 W. Belmont Ave., Chicago IL 60618. (773)248-4210. E-mail: info@awarerecords.com. Web site: www.awarerecords.com. A&R: Steve Smith. President: Gregg Latterman. Record company. Distributed by Sony and Redeye. Estab. 1993. Staff size: 9. Releases 5 LPs, 1 EP and 3 CD/year. Pays negotiable royalty to artists on contract; statutory rate to publisher per song on record.

Distributed by Sony and RED.

How to Contact *Does not accept unsolicited submissions.*

Music Mostly **rock/pop**. Other artists include John Mayer, Five for Fighting, Kyle Riabko, Mat Kearney, and Bleu.

Ⓝ ☐ BANANA RECORDS

3115 Hiss Ave., Baltimore MD 21234. (410)663-5915. E-mail: theunholythree@yahoo.com. Web site: www.theunholythree.com. **Contact:** Ron Brown, President. Record company, music publisher (Infinite Publishing) and record producer (Ronald Brown). Estab. 1990. Releases 30 singles, 20 LPs and 20 CDs/year. Pays standard royalty to artists on contract; statutory rate to publisher per song on record.

How to Contact Submit demo by mail. Unsolicited submissions are OK. Prefers cassette with 3 songs and lyric sheet. Include SASE. Responds in 3 weeks.

Music Mostly **top 40/commercial**, **pop/ballads** and **alternative**. Released "Crack of the Universe," written and recorded by Jesse Brown (pop) on Global; *The Unholy Three* (album), written and recorded by Ronnie B. (commercial), released 2002 on Banana Records.

Tips "A good singer works hard at his craft. A hit song has good punch and a lot of talent."

⊞ ☑ BIG BEAR RECORDS

Box 944, Birmingham B16 8UT United Kingdom. 44-121-454-7020. Fax: 44-121-454-9996. E-mail: jim@bigbearmusic.com. Web site: www.bigbearmusic.com. A&R Director: Jim Simpson. Labels include Truckers Delight and Grandstand Records. Record company, record producer and music publisher (Bearsongs). Releases 6 LPs/year. Pays 8-10% royalty to artists on contract; 8¼% to publishers for each record sold. Royalties paid directly to songwriters and artists or through US publishing or recording affiliate.

• Big Bear's publishing affiliate, Bearsongs, is listed in the Music Publishers section, and Big Bear is listed in the Record Producers section of this book.

How to Contact Submit demo by mail. Unsolicited submissions are OK. Prefers CD. Does not return material. Responds in 3 weeks.

Music Blues and jazz. Released *I've Finished with the Blues* and *Blues for Pleasure* (by Skirving/ Nicholls), both recorded by King Pleasure and the Biscuit Boys (jazz); and *Side-Steppin'* (by Barnes), recorded by Alan Barnes/Bruce Adams Quintet (jazz), all on Big Bear Records. Other artists include Lady Sings the Blues, Drummin' Man, and Kenny Baker's Dozen.

☐ BLUE GEM RECORDS

P.O. Box 29550, Hollywood CA 90029. (323)664-7765. E-mail: pmarti3636@aol.com. Web site: www.VaamMusic.com. **Contact:** Pete Martin. Record company, music publisher (Vaam Music Group) and record producer (Pete Martin/Vaam Productions). Estab. 1981. Pays 6-15% royalty to artists on contract; statutory rate to publisher per song on record.

• Also see the listings for Vaam Music Group in the Music Publishers section of this book and Pete Martin/Vaam Music Productions in the Record Producers section of this book.

How to Contact Submit demo by mail. Unsolicited submissions are OK. Prefers CD or cassette with 2 songs. Include SASE. Responds in 3 weeks.

Music Mostly **country** and **R&B**; also **pop/top 40** and **rock**.

☐ BLUE WAVE

3221 Perryville Rd., Baldwinsville NY 13027. (315)638-4286. Fax: (315)635-4757. E-mail: bluewave @localnet.com. Web site: www.bluewaverecords.com. **Contact:** Greg Spencer, president/pro-ducer. Labels include Blue Wave/Horizon. Record company, music publisher (G.W. Spencer Music/ASCAP) and record producer (Blue Wave Productions). Estab. 1985. Staff size: 1. Releases 3 LPs and 3 CDs/year. Pays variable royalty to artists on contract; statutory rate to publisher per song on record.

Distributed by Select-O-Hits, Action Music, Burnside Dist.

• Also see the listing for Blue Wave Productions in the Managers & Booking Agents section of this book.

How to Contact Submit demo by mail. Unsolicited submissions are OK. Include SASE. Responds in 1 month only if interested. "Do not call."

Music Mostly **blues/blues rock**, **roots rock** and **roots R&B/soul**; also **roots country/rockabilly** or **anything with "soul."** Released "Leave Married Women Alone" (single by Jimmy Cavallo) from *The House Rocker* (album), recorded by Jimmy Cavallo (jump blues), released 2002 on Blue Wave; "Sometimes You Gamble" (single by Kim Simmonds) from *Blues Like Midnight* (album), recorded by Kim Simmonds (blues), released 2001 on Blue Wave; and "Motherless World" (single by Pete McMahon) from *Trouble on the Run* (album), recorded by The Kingsnakes (blues), released 2001 on Blue Wave.

Tips "Be able to put the song across vocally."

☒ ☐ BOLIVIA RECORDS

2622 Kirtland Rd., Brewton AL 36246. (251)867-2228. President: Roy Edwards. Labels include Known Artist Records. Record company, record producer (Known Artist Productions) and music publisher (Cheavoria Music Co.). Estab. 1972. Releases 10 singles and 3 LPs/year. Pays 5% royalty to artists on contract; statutory rate to publishers for each record sold.

• Also see ths listings for Baitstring Music and Chearovia Music in the Music Publishers section and Known Artist Productions in the Record Producers section of this book.

How to Contact Submit demo by mail. Unsolicited submissions are OK. Prefers CD with 3 songs and lyric sheet. Include SASE for reply. All tapes will be kept on file. Responds in 1 month.

Music Mostly **R&B**, **country** and **pop**; also **easy listening**, **MOR** and **soul**. Released "If You Only Knew" (single by Horace Linsley), recorded by Roy Edwards; "Make Me Forget" (single by Horace Linsley), recorded by Bobbie Roberson, both on Bolivia Records; and "We Make Our Reality" (single), written and recorded by Brad Smiley on Known Artist Records. Other artists include Jim Portwood.

Tips "We need some good gospel."

☑ BOUQUET RECORDS

Bouquet-Orchid Enterprises, P.O. Box 1335, Norcross GA 30091. Phone/fax: (770)339-9088. **Contact:** Bill Bohannon, president. Record company, music publisher (Orchid Publishing/BMI), record producer (Bouquet-Orchid Enterprises) and management firm (Bouquet-Orchid Enterprises). Releases 3-4 singles and 2 LPs/year. Pays 5-8% royalty to artists on contract; pays statutory rate to publishers for each record sold.

How to Contact Submit demo by mail. Unsolicited submissions are OK. Prefers cassette or CD with 3-5 songs and lyric sheet. Include SASE. Responds in 1 month.

Music Mostly **religious** (contemporary or country-gospel, Amy Grant, etc.), **country** ("the type suitable for Kenny Chesney, George Strait, Carrie Underwood, Patty Loveless, etc.") and **top 100** ("the type suitable for Billy Joel, Whitney Houston, R.E.M., etc."); also **rock**, and **MOR**. Released *Blue As Your Eyes* (by Bill Bohannon), recorded by Adam Day (country); *Take Care of My World* (by Bob Freeman), recorded by Bandoleers (top 40); and *Making Plans* (by John Harris), recorded by Susan Spencer (country), all on Bouquet Records.

Tips "Submit 3-5 songs on a cassette tape or CD with lyric sheets. Include a short biography and perhaps a photo. Enclose SASE."

ⓝ ☑ BROKEN RECORDS INTERNATIONAL

940 S. Grace St., Lombard IL 60148. (630)693-0719. E-mail: roy@mcguitar.com. Web site: www.mc guitar.com/BrokenRecords.htm. International A&R: Roy Bocchieri. Vice President: Jeff Murphy. Record company. Estab. 1984. Payment negotiable.

How to Contact *Write first and obtain permission to submit.* Prefers cassette or CD with at least 2 songs and lyric sheet. Does not return material. Responds in 2 months.

Music Mostly **rock**, **pop** and **dance**; also **acoustic** and **industrial**. Released *Figurehead* (album by LeRoy Bocchieri), recorded by Day One (pop/alternative); and *Eitherway* (album by Jeff Murphy/ Herb Eimerman), recorded by The Nerk Twins (pop/alternative), both on Broken Records.

☑ BSW RECORDS

P.O. Box 2297, Universal City TX 78148. E-mail: bswr18@wmconnect.com. Web site: www.bswrec ords.com. President: Frank Willson. Vice Presidents: Frank Weatherly (country, jazz); Regina Willson (blues). Record company, music publisher (BSW Records/BMI), management firm (Universal Music Marketing) and record producer (Frank Willson). Estab. 1987. Staff size: 5. Releases 18 albums/year. Pays standard royalty to artists on contract; statutory rate to publisher per song on record.

- Also see the listings for BSW Records in the Music Publishers section, Frank Wilson in the Record Producers section and Universal Music Marketing in the Managers & Booking Agents section of this book.

How to Contact Submit demo by mail. Unsolicited submissions are OK. Prefers CD (or ¾" videocassette) with 3 songs and lyric sheet. Include SASE. Responds in 6 weeks.

Music Mostly **country**, **rock**, and **blues**. Released *Memories of Hank Williams, Sr.* (album), recorded by Larry Butler and Willie Nelson. Other artists include Candee Land, Crea Beal, John Wayne, Sonny Marshall, and Bobby Mountain.

☑ CAMBRIA RECORDS & PUBLISHING

P.O. Box 374, Lomita CA 90717. (310)831-1322. Fax: (310)833-7442. E-mail: admin@cambriamus.c om. **Contact:** Lance Bowling, director of recording operations. Labels include Charade Records. Record company and music publisher. Estab. 1979. Staff size: 3. Pays 5-8% royalty to artists on contract; statutory rate to publisher for each record sold.

Distributed by Albany Distribution.

How to Contact *Write first and obtain permission to submit.* Prefers cassette. Include SASE. Responds in 1 month.

Music Mostly **classical**. Released *Songs of Elinor Remick Warren* (album) on Cambria Records. Other artists include Marie Gibson (soprano), Leonard Pennario (piano), Thomas Hampson (voice), Mischa Leftkowitz (violin), Leigh Kaplan (piano), North Wind Quintet , and Sierra Wind Quintet.

☑ CANDYSPITEFUL PRODUCTIONS

2051 E. Cedar St., #8, Tempe AZ 85281. (480)968-7017. E-mail: mandrakerocks@yahoo.com. Web site: www.candyspiteful.com. President: William Ferraro. Professional Managers: Maxwell Frye (jazz, rock). Record company, music publisher (Candyspiteful Productions), record producer (William Ferraro). Estab. 2000. Staff size: 2. Produces 30 demo projects, 12 albums per year. Charges producer/engineer fee's, other fees are negotiable.

- Also see the listings for Candyspiteful Productions in the Record Producers section of this book.

How to Contact Submit demo by mail. Unsolicited submissions are OK. Prefers CD with 3 songs, lyric sheet, and cover letter. "Please include a fact sheet, bio, current play dates, etc." Does not return material. Responds only if interested.

Music Mostly **hard rock**, **radio-friendly rock** and **hip-hop**.

Tips "We are out in the trenches with our artists and fight hard for them. Often in N.Y. and L.A. and we just may be that person standing in the back checking you out."

☑ CAPITOL RECORDS

1750 N. Vine St., Hollywood CA 90028-5274. (323)462-6252. Fax: (323)469-4542. Web site: www.hollywoodandvine.com. **Nashville:** 3322 West End Ave., 11th Floor, Nashville TN 37203. (615)269-2000. Labels include Blue Note Records, Grand Royal Records, Pangaea Records, The Right Stuff Records and Capitol Nashville Records. Record company.

Distributed by EMD.

How to Contact *Capitol Records does not accept unsolicited submissions.*

Music Artists include Coldplay, Beastie Boys, Liz Phair, and Auf der Maur.

☑ ☑ CAPP RECORDS

P.O. Box 150871, San Rafael CA 94915-0871. Phone/fax: (415)457-8617. E-mail: manus@capprecords.com. Web site: www.capprecords.com. CEO/International Manager: Dominique Toulon (pop, dance, New Age); Creative Manager/A&R: Manus Buchart (dance, techno). President: Rudolf Stember. Vice President/Publisher: Marc Oshry (pop, rock, dance). Music publisher (Lappster music/ASCAP and CIDC Music/BMI) and record company. Member: NARAS, NCSA, Songwriter's Guild of America. Estab. 1993. Publishes 100 songs/year; publishes 25 new songwriters/year. Staff size: 8. Pays standard royalty.

Affiliate(s) Cary August Publishing Co./CAPP Company (Germany)/Capp Company (Japan).

How to Contact Submit demo by mail. Unsolicited submissions are OK. Prefers CD or NTSC videocassette with 3 songs and cover letter. "E-mail us in advance for submissions, if possible." Include SASE. Only responds if interested.

Film & TV Places 20 songs in film and 7 songs in TV/year. Music Supervisors: Dominique Toulon (pop, dance, New Age); Mark D. D'Elicio (dance, techno). Published "Wish You Were Here" (by Cary August/Marc Oshry/Brian Wood/Tom Finch), recorded by Cary August for "Cafe Froth" TV/ad; "Indian Dream" and "Song For the Earth," both written and recorded by Steven Buckner in "Deep Encounters."

Music Mostly **pop**, **dance**, and **techno**; also **New Age**. Does not want country. Released "It's Not a Dream" (single by Cary August/Andre Pessis), recorded by Cary August on CAPP Records (dance).

☑ CAPSTAN RECORD PRODUCTION

P.O. Box 211, East Prairie MO 63845. (575)649-2211. **Contact:** Joe Silver or Tommy Loomas. Labels include Octagon and Capstan Records. Record company, music publisher (Lineage Publishing Co.), management firm (Staircase Promotion) and record producer (Silver-Loomas Productions). Pays 3-5% royalty to artists on contract.

How to Contact Unsolicited submissions are OK. Prefers cassette or VHS videocassette with 2-4 songs and lyric sheet. "Send photo and bio." Include SASE. Responds in 1 month.

Music Mostly **country**, **easy listening**, **MOR**, **country rock**, and **top 40/pop**. Released "Country Boy" (single by Alden Lambert); and "Yesterday's Teardrops" (single) and "Round & Round" (single), written and recorded by The Burchetts. Other artists include Bobby Lee Morgan, Skidrow Joe, Vicarie Arcole, and Fleming and Scarlett Britoni.

☑ CASE ENTERTAINMENT GROUP/C.E.G. RECORDS, INC.

102 E. Pikes Peak Ave., #200, Colorado Springs CO 80903. (719)632-0227. Fax: (719)634-2274. E-mail: rac@hpi.net. Web site: www.newpants.com and www.oldpants.com. **Contact:** Robert A. Case, president. Record company and music publisher (New Pants Publishing/ASCAP, Old Pants Publishing/BMI). Estab. 1989. Releases 3-4 LPs and 3-4 CDs/year. Pays negotiable royalty to artists on contract.

How to Contact Submit demo by mail. Unsolicited submissions are OK. Prefers CD with 3-5 songs and lyric sheet. "Include a brief history of songwriter's career. Songs submitted must be copywritten or pending with copyright office." Does not return material. "Our representative will contact you if interested in material."

Music Mostly **pop**, **rock**, and **country**. Released *James Becker* (album), recorded by James Becker (folk), released 2001 on New Pants; *Romancing the Blues* (album), by Kathy Watson (pop), released 2001 on New Pants; and *Stephanie Aramburo* (album), recorded by Stephanie Aramburo (pop), released 2001 on Old Pants.

Tips "Think of the music business as a job interview. You must be able to sell yourself and the music is your baby. You have to be strong and not deal with rejection as a personal thing. It is not a rejection of you, it's a rejection of the music. Most songwriters don't know how to communicate with labels. The best way is to start a friendship with people at the label."

☑ CELLAR RECORDS

703 N. Brinton Ave., Dixon IL 61021. (866)287-4997. E-mail: president@cellarrecords.com. Web site: www.cellarrecords.com. **Contact:** Todd Joos, president. A&R Department: Bob Brady, Albert Hurst, Jim Miller, Mark Summers, Jon Pomplin. Record company, music publisher (Sound Cellar Music/BMI) and record producer (Todd Joos). Estab. 1987. Staff size: 6. Releases 6-8 CDs/year. Pays 15-100% royalty to artists on contract; statutory rate to publisher per song on record. Charges in advance "if you use our studio to record."

Distributed by "We now service retail and online (Apple iTunes, etc.) direct from Cellar Records."

How to Contact Submit demo by mail. Unsolicited submissions are OK. Prefers CD with 3-4 songs and lyric sheet. Does not return material. Responds in 1 month only if interested. "If we like it we will call you."

Music Mostly **metal**, **country**, **rock**, **pop**, and **blues**. "No rap." Released "With Any Luck at All" (single by Tony Stampley/Randy Boudreaux/Joe Stampley) from *With Any Luck At All* (album), recorded by Cal Stage (pop/country); "Sleeping With a Smile" (single by Tony Stampley/Melissa Lyons/Tommy Barnes) from *With Any Luck At All* (album), recorded by Cal Stage (pop/country); and "Speed of My Life" (single by Jon Pomplin/Todd Joss) from *Declassified* (album), recorded by Project 814 (rock), all released 2001 on Cellar Records. Other artists include Eric Topper, Snap Judgment, Ballistic, Dago Red, Sea of Monsters, Rogue, Kings, James Miller, Vehement, Noopy Wilson, Dual Exhaust, Junker Jorg, The Unknown, Joel Ramirez & the Allstars, Tracylyn, Junk Poet, Cajun Anger, Roman, Flesh Pilgrims, LYZ, and Justice4.

Tips "Make sure that you understand your band is a business and you must be willing to self-invest time, effort and money just like any other new business. We can help you, but you must also be willing to help yourself."

☐ CHATTAHOOCHEE RECORDS

2544 Roscomare Rd., Los Angeles CA 90077. (818)788-6863. Fax: (310)471-2089. E-mail: cyardum @prodigy.net. **Contact:** Robyn Meyers, Music Director/A&R. Music Director: Chris Yardum. Record company and music publisher (Etnoc/Conte). Member NARAS. Releases 4 singles/year. Pays negotiable royalty to artists on contract.

How to Contact Submit demo by mail. Unsolicited submissions are OK. Prefers CD with 2-6 songs and lyric sheet. *Does not return material.* Responds in 2 months only if interested.

Music Mostly **rock**. Released *Don't Touch It Let It Drip* (album), recorded by Cream House (hard rock), released 2000 on Chattahoochee Records. Artists include DNA, Noctrnl, and Vator.

● CHERRY STREET RECORDS

P.O. Box 52626, Tulsa OK 74152. (918)742-8087. Fax: (918)742-8003. E-mail: info@cherrystreetmu sic.com. Web site: www.cherrystreetrecords.com. President: Rodney Young. Vice President: Steve Hickerson. Record company and music publisher. Estab. 1990. Staff size: 2. Releases 2 CD/year. Pays 50% royalty to artists on contract; statutory rate to publisher per song on record.

Distributed by Internet.

How to Contact *Write first and obtain permission to submit.* Prefers cassette or videocassette with 4 songs and lyric sheet. Include SASE. Responds in 4 months.

Music Rock, **country**, and **R&B**; also **jazz**. Released *Promised Land* (album), written and recorded by Richard Neville on Cherry Street (rock). Other artists include George W. Carroll and Chris Blevins.

Tips ''We sign only artists who play an instrument, sing, and write songs. Send only your best four songs.''

☑ ● CHIAROSCURO RECORDS

180 Mundy St., Wilkes Barre PA 18702. (570) 826-5553 or 1-800-528-2582 Web site: www.Chiarosc uroJazz.com. **Contact:** Jon Bates, A&R/operations manager. Labels include Downtown Sound. Record company and record producer (Hank O'Neal, Andrew Sordoni, Jon Bates). Estab. 1973. Releases 12 CDs/year. Pays negotiable royalty to artists on contract; statutory rate to publisher per song on record.

Distributed by Allegro. Also distributed digitally by iTunes, Napster, Rhapsody, MusicMatch, Audio Lunchbox, MusicNow, MSN Music Service, Sony Connect, MusicNet, Liquid Audio, and Musicstream.

How to Contact Submit demo by mail. Unsolicited submissions are OK. Prefers cassette, CD, DAT or videocassette with 1-3 songs. Include SASE. Responds in 6 weeks.

Music Mostly **jazz** and **blues**. ''A full catalog listing is available on the web at www.chiarascurojazz .com or by calling (800)528-2582. Reissues and new recordings for 2003 by the following artists: Earl Hines, Junior Nance & Joe Temperly, Abdullah Ibrahim, and Bobby Hackett.''

Tips ''We are not a pop label. Our average release sells between 3,000-5,000 copies in the first three years. We do not give cash advances or tour support, and our average budget per release is about $15,000 including all production, printing, and manufacturing costs.''

● CKB RECORDS/HELAPHAT ENTERTAINMENT

527 Larry Court, Irving TX 75060. (214)223-5181. E-mail: spoonfedmusik@juno.com. **Contact:** Tony Briggs, CEO. Record company and production company. Estab. 1999. Staff size: 5. Pays negotiable royalty to artists on contract.

Distributed by Crystal Clear Distribution.

How to Contact Submit demo by mail. Unsolicited submissions are OK. Prefers CD with 4 songs, cover letter and press clippings. Does not return materials. Responds only if interested.

Music Mostly **rap**, **hip-hop**, and **R&B**. Released ''Body, Body'' (single), recorded by T-Spoon (hip-hop), released 2002 on CKB Records; and ''We Can't Be Stopped'' (single) from *Ouncified* (album), written and recorded by Tha 40 Clique (hip-hop), released 2002 on CKB. Other artists include Baby Tek, Lil' Droop, Shampoo, Deuce Loc, Tre and Laticia Love.

Tips ''Be confident, honest and open to ideas.''

Ⓝ ● CLEOPATRA RECORDS

11041 Santa Monica Blvd., PMB 703, Los Angeles CA 90025. (310)477-4000. Fax: (310)312-5653. **Contact:** Jason Myers, A&R. Labels include Hypnotic, Deadline, X-Ray, Cult, Stardust and Purple

Pyramid. Record company. Estab. 1991. Releases 5 singles, 10 LPs, 5 EPs and 100 CDs/year. Pays 10-14% royalty to artists on contract; negotiable rate to publisher per song on record.

How to Contact Submit demo by mail. Unsolicited submissions are OK. Prefers CD with 3 songs. Does not return material. Responds in 1 month.

Music Mostly **industrial**, **gothic** and **trance**; also **heavy metal**, **space rock** and **electronic**.

COAL HARBOR MUSIC

P.O. Box 148027, Nashville TN 37214-8027. (615)883-2020. E-mail: info@coalharborbmusic.com. Web site: www.coalharbormusic.com. President/Owner: Jerry R. Wells (country/pop/rock). Vice President: Angela R. Wells (gospel/contemporary Christian). Labels include Coal Harbor. Record company, music publisher (Coal Harbor Music/BMI), record producer (Jerry R. Wells), radio promotion agency, management firm, booking agency, demo services, recording studio, artist development. Estab. 1990. Staff size: 2. Releases 16 singles/year and 4 CDs/year. Pays negotiable royalty to artists on contract; statutory royalty to publisher per song on record.

● Also see the listing for Coal Harbor Music in the Music Publishers section of this book.

Distributed by Self distribution.

How to Contact *Contact first by e-mail to obtain permission to submit a demo.* Send CD with 3-5 songs, lyric sheet, and cover letter. Does not return submissions. Responds only if interested.

Music Mostly **country**, **gospel**, and **contemporary Christian**; also **pop**, **rock**, and **jazz/bluegrass instrumental**. Does not want hard rock, rap, heavy metal, or grunge.

COLLECTOR RECORDS

P.O. Box 1200, 3260 AE oud beyerland Holland. (31)186 604266. Fax: (31)186 604366. E-mail: cees@collectorrec.com. Web site: www.collectorrecords.nl. **Contact:** Cees Klop, president. Manager: John Moore. Labels include All Rock, Downsouth, Unknown, Pro Forma and White Label Records. Record company, music publisher (All Rock Music Publishing) and record producer (Cees Klop). Estab. 1967. Staff size: 4. Release 25 LPs/year. Pays 10% royalty to artist on contract.

How to Contact Submit demo by mail. Unsolicited submissions are OK. Prefers cassette. SAE and IRC. Responds in 2 months.

Music Mostly **'50s rock**, **rockabilly**, **hillbilly boogie** and **country/rock**; also **piano boogie woogie**. Released *Rock Crazy Baby* (album), by Art Adams (1950s rockabilly), released 2005; *Marvin Jackson* (album), by Marvin Jackson (1950s rockers), released 2005; *Western Australian Snake Pit R&R* (album), recorded by various (1950s rockers), released 2005, all on Collector Records. Other artists include Henk Pepping, Rob Hoeke, Eric-Jan Overbeek, and more. See our Web site.

COLUMBIA RECORDS

550 Madison Ave., 24th Floor, New York NY 10022. (212)833-4000. Fax: (212)833-4389. E-mail: sonymusiconline@sonymusic.com. Web site: www.columbiarecords.com. **Santa Monica:** 2100 Colorado Ave., Santa Monica CA 90404. (310)449-2100. Fax: (310)449-2743. **Nashville:** 34 Music Square E., Nashville TN 37203. (615)742-4321. Fax: (615)244-2549. Labels include So So Def Records and Ruffhouse Records. Record company.

Distributed by Sony.

How to Contact *Columbia Records does not accept unsolicited submissions.*

Music Artists include Aerosmith, Marc Anthony, Beyonce, Bob Dylan, and Patti Smith.

COMPADRE RECORDS

708 Main St, Suite 720, Houston TX 77002. (713)228-3847. Fax: (713)228-3843. E-mail: info@comp adrerecords.com. Web site: www.compadrerecords.com. **Contact:** Brad Turcotte, president. **Tennessee Office:** 806 Centeroak Dr., Knoxville TN 37920. (615)423-2038. Fax: (615)726-8601. Record company. Estab. 2001.

Distributed by RED/Sony Music.

How to Contact "We can't promise that we will listen to every demo that is sent to us, but we welcome any submission. We enjoy listening to new material and support the creative process. Keep writing, sing loud and keep the spirit alive."

Music Mostly **Americana**. Released *Billy and the Kid* (album), recorded by Billy Joe Shaver (Americana); and *James McMurtry—Live* (album), recorded by James McMurtry (Americana), both released 2004 on Compadre. Other artists include Suzy Bogguss, Flaco Jimenez, Kate Campbell, and Kevin Kinney.

☑ COMPENDIA MUSIC

210 25th Ave. N., Suite 1200, Nashville TN 37203. (615)277-1800. Web site: www.compendiamusic .com. Vice President/General Manager, Compendia Label & Intersound: Mick Lloyd (country/rock; contemporary jazz); Vice President/General Manager, Light Records: Phillip White (black gospel). Record company. Labels include Compendia, Light Records, Life², Intersound. Pays negotiable royalty to artists on contract; negotiable rate to publisher per song on record.

How to Contact *Write or call first and obtain permission to submit.* Prefers CD with 3 songs. "We will contact the songwriter when we are interested in the material." Does not return material. Responds only if interested.

Music Mostly **country**, **rock**, **gospel**, and **classical**. Artists include Joan Osborne and Mighty Clouds of Joy.

☑ ☑ COSMOTONE RECORDS

2951 Marina Bay Dr., Suite 130, PMB 501, League City TX 77573-2733. E-mail: marianland@earthlin k.net. Web site: www.marianland.com/music.html. Record company, music publisher (Cosmotone Music, ASCAP) and record producer (Rafael Brom). Estab. 1984.

Distributed by marianland.com.

How to Contact "We do not accept material at this time." Does not return materials.

Music Christian pop/rock. Released *Dance for Padre Pio*, *Peace of Henry*, *Music for Peace of Mind*, *The Sounds of Heaven*, *The Christmas Songs*, *Angelophany*, *The True Measure of Love*, *All My Love to You Jesus* (albums), and *Rafael Brom Unplugged* (live concert DVD), by Rafael Brom.

☑ CPA RECORDS

15104 Golden Eagle Way, Tampa FL 33625-1545. (813)920-4605. Fax: (813)926-0846. E-mail: al@cp arecords.com. Web site: www.cparecords.com. **Contact:** Al McDaniel, president. Labels include Coffee's Productions and Associates. Record company and music publisher (CPA Music Publishing). Estab. 1999. Staff size: 5. Releases 3 singles and 2 albums/year. Pays negotiable royalty to artists on contract; negotiable royalty to publisher per song on record.

How to Contact *Write or call first and obtain permission to submit a demo.* Prefers CD/CDR and VHS videocassette with 3 songs, lyric sheet, lead sheet, and cover letter. Include SASE. Responds in 2 weeks.

Music Mostly **gospel/Christian**, **rhythm**, **blues**, and **jazz**; also **pop** and **rap**. Does not want country. Released "Somewhere" (single by Al McDaniel) from **"Coffee" Greatest Oldies** (album), recorded by Al "Coffee" McDaniel (jazz), released 2002 on CPA Records; and "The Last Dance" (single by Al McDaniel) from **"Coffee" Greatest Oldies** (album), recorded by Al "Coffee" McDaniel (R&B), released 2002 on CPS Records. Other artists include Sax Kari, Anthony "Big Lou" McDaniel, and Mike and Anita.

Tips "Be marketable, creative, committed to achieving success, and willing to work hard to accomplish your goals."

☐ CRANK! A RECORD COMPANY

Attn: New Rock, 1223 Wilshire Blvd. #823, Santa Monica CA 90403. E-mail: fan@crankthis.com. Web site: www.crankthis.com. **Contact:** Jeff Matlow. Record company. Estab. 1994. Releases 6 singles, 5 LPs, 2 EPs and 5 CDs/year. Pays negotiable royalty to artists on contract.

Distributed by Southern, Revolver, Lumberjack, and Nail.

How to Contact Submit demo by mail. Unsolicited submissions are OK. Prefers CD. "Send whatever best represents your abilities." Does not return material. Responds in 6 weeks.

Music Mostly **indie/alternative rock** and **pop**. Released *Neva Dinova* (album), written and recorded by Neva Dinova; *Mono* (album), written and recorded by The Icarus Line (rock/punk);

Down Marriott Lane! (album), written and recorded by the Get Set (rock/pop); *The Power of Failing*, written and recorded by Mineral (rock); *Boys Life*, written and recorded by Boys Life (rock); and *Such Blinding Stars for Starving Eyes*, written and recorded by Cursive (rock), all on Crank! Other artists include Fireside, Errortype:11, Onelinedrawing, The Regrets, Sunday's Best, and Gloria Record.

◻ CREATIVE IMPROVISED MUSIC PROJECTS (CIMP) RECORDS

CIMP LTD, Cadence Building, Redwood NY 13679. (315)287-2852. Fax: (315)287-2860. E-mail: cimp@cadencebuilding.com. Web site: www.cimprecords.com. **Contact:** Bob Rusch, producer. Labels include Cadence Jazz Records. Record company and record producer (Robert D. Rusch). Estab. 1980. Releases 25-30 CDs/year. Pays negotiable royalty to artists on contract; pays statutory rate to publisher per song on record.

Distributed by North Country Distributors.

  • CIMP specializes in jazz and creative improvised music.

How to Contact Submit demo by mail. Unsolicited submissions are OK. Prefers cassette or CD. ''We are not looking for songwriters but recording artists.'' Include SASE. Responds in 1 week.

Music Mostly **jazz** and **creative improvised music**. Released *The Redwood Session* (album), recorded by Evan Parker, Barry Guy, Paul Lytton , and Joe McPhee; *Sarah's Theme* (album), recorded by the Ernie Krivda Trio, Bob Fraser , and Jeff Halsey; and *Human Flowers* (album), recorded by the Bobby Zankel Trio, Marily Crispell , and Newman Baker, all released on CIMP (improvised jazz). Other artists include Arthur Blyme, John McPhee, David Prentice, Anthony Braxton, Roswell Rudd, Paul Smoker, Khan Jamal, Odean Pope, etc.

Tips ''CIMP Records are produced to provide music to reward repeated and in-depth listenings. They are recorded live to two-track which captures the full dynamic range one would experience in a live concert. There is no compression, homogenization, eq-ing, post-recording splicing, mixing, or electronic fiddling with the performance. Digital recording allows for a vanishingly low noise floor and tremendous dynamic range. This compression of the dynamic range is what limits the 'air' and life of many recordings. Our recordings capture the dynamic intended by the musicians. In this regard these recordings are demanding. Treat the recording as your private concert. Give it your undivided attention and it will reward you. CIMP Records are not intended to be background music. This method is demanding not only on the listener but on the performer as well. Musicians must be able to play together in real time. They must understand the dynamics of their instrument and how it relates to the others around them. There is no fix-it-in-the-mix safety; either it works or it doesn't. What you hear is exactly what was played. Our main concern is music not marketing.''

◉ CURB RECORDS

47 Music Square E., Nashville TN 37203. (615)321-5080. Fax: (615)327-1964. Web site: www.curb.com. **Contact:** John Ozler, A&R coordinator. Record company.

How to Contact Curb Records does not accept unsolicited submissions; accepts previously published material only. *Do not submit without permission.*

Music Released *Everywhere* (album), recorded by Tim McGraw; *Sittin' On Top of the World* (album), recorded by LeAnn Rimes; and *I'm Alright* (album), recorded by Jo Dee Messina, all on Curb Records. Other artists include Mary Black, Merle Haggard, Kal Ketchum, David Kersh, Lyle Lovett, Tim McGraw, Wynonna, and Sawyer Brown.

◻ DEEP SOUTH ENTERTAINMENT

P.O. Box 17737, Raleigh NC 27619-7737. (919)844-1515. Fax: (919)847-5922. E-mail: info@deepsouthentertainment.com. Web site: www.deepsouthentertainment.com. Director of Artist Relations: Melissa Embry. Manager: Amy Cox. Record company and management company. Estab. 1996. Staff size: 10. Pays negotiable royalty to artists on contract; statutory rate to publisher per song on record.

Distributed by Redeye Distribution, Valley, Select-O-Hits, City Hall, AEC/Bassin, Northeast One Stop, Pollstar, and Koch International.

How to Contact Submit demo by mail. Unsolicited submissions are OK. Prefers cassette or CD with

3 songs, cover letter, and press clippings. Does not return material. Responds only if interested. **Music** Mostly **pop**, **modern rock**, and **alternative**; also **swing**, **rockabilly**, and **heavy rock**. Does not want rap or R&B. Artists include Bruce Hornsby, Little Feat, Mike Daly, SR-71, Stretch Princess, Darden Smith, and many more.

✓ ☐ DENTAL RECORDS

P.O. Box 20058, New York NY 10017. E-mail: info@dentalrecords.com. Web site: www.dentalrecor ds.com. **Contact:** Rick Sanford, owner. Record company. Estab. 1981. Staff size: 2. Releases 1-2 CDs/year. Pays negotiable royalty to artists on contract; statutory rate to publisher per song on record.

Distributed by Dutch East India Trading.

How to Contact Submit demo by mail. Unsolicited submissions are OK. Prefers CD with any number of songs, lyric sheet, and cover letter. "Check our Web site to see if your material is appropriate." Include SASE. Responds only if interested.

Music Pop derived structures, jazz-derived harmonies and neo-classic-wannabee-pretenses. Does not want urban, heavy metal, or hard core. Released *Perspectivism*, written and recorded by Rick Sanford (instrumental), released 2003 on Dental Records. Other artists include Les Izmor.

☑ ☑ DREAMWORKS RECORDS

2220 Colorado Ave., Santa Monica CA 90404. (310)365-1000. Fax: (310)865-8059. Web site: www.d reamworksrecords.com. **Nashville:** 60 Music Sq. E., Nashville TN 37203. (615)463-4600 Fax: (615)463-4601. Record company and music publisher (DreamWorks SKG Music Publishing). Labels include Interscope, Geffen, and A&M.

How to Contact Material must be submitted through an agent or attorney. *Does not accept unsolicited submissions.*

Ⓝ ☑ DRUMBEAT INDIAN ARTS, INC.

4143 N. 16th St., Suite 1, Phoenix AZ 85016. (602)266-4823. **Contact:** Bob Nuss, president. Labels include Indian House and Sweet Grass. Record company and distributor of American Indian recordings. Estab. 1984. Staff size: 8. Releases 50 cassettes and 50 CDs/year. Royalty varies with project.

 ● Note that Drumbeat Indian Arts is a very specialized label, and only wants to receive submissions by Native American artists.

How to Contact *Call first and obtain permission to submit.* Include SASE. Responds in 2 months.

Music Music by American Indians—any style (must be enrolled tribal members). Does not want New Age "Indian style" material. Released *Pearl Moon* (album), written and recorded by Xavier (native Amerindian). Other artists include Black Lodge Singers, R. Carlos Nakai, Lite Foot, and Joanne Shenandoah.

Tips "We deal only with American Indian performers. We do not accept material from others. Please include tribal affiliation."

☑ ELEKTRA RECORDS

75 Rockefeller Plaza, 17th Floor, New York NY 10019. Web site: www.elektra.com. Labels include Elektra Records, Eastwest Records, and Asylum Records. Record company.

Distributed by WEA.

How to Contact *Elektra does not accept unsolicited submissions.*

Music Mostly **alternative/modern rock**. Artists include Phish, Jason Mraz, Bjork, Busta Rhymes, and Metallica.

Ⓝ ☑ EMF RECORDS & AFFILIATES

633 Post, Suite #145, San Francisco CA 94109. (415)273-1421. Fax: (415)752-2442. E-mail: onelinkgl obal1@aol.com. **Contact:** Steven Lassiter, director of operations. Vice President, A&R (all styles): Michael Miller. A&R Supervisor (commercial): Robin Taylor. International Producer (world artists): Kimberly Nakamori. Producer/Writer (all or most styles): Joe Tsongo. Labels include Richland Communications, Sky Bent and Urbana Sounds. Record company. Estab. 1994. Staff size: 9. Re-

leases 5 CDs/year. Pays negotiable royalty to artists on contract; statutory rate to publisher per song on record.

Distributed by GTI Marketing and Songo Publishing International.

How to Contact Submit demo CD by mail. Unsolicited submissions are OK. Prefers CD with 3 songs and lyric and lead sheets. Does not return material. Responds in 4 months.

Music Mostly **urban/pop/rock**, **jazz/Latin** and **New Age/classical (crossover)**; also **country**, **world beat** and **ethnic (world)**. Released *Mutual Impact*, written and recorded by Joe Tsongo on EMF Records (New Age); *If I Had Your Love*, written and recorded by Flame on Richland Communications (soft jazz); and *From The Source* (by B. Flores/A. Jiminez), recorded by Orchestra de Sabor on Urbana Sounds (salsa/Latin jazz). Other artists include Slam Jam.

Tips "Build your fan base and present good images or professional packages as much as possible. Market focus in your genre is a must. Beware of trends in music and film."

⚊ EPIC RECORDS

550 Madison Ave., 21st Floor, New York NY 10022. (212)833-8000. Fax: (212)833-4054. Web site: www.epicrecords.com. Senior Vice Presidents A&R: Ben Goldman, Rose Noone. **Santa Monica:** 2100 Colorado Ave., Santa Monica CA 90404. (310)449-2100 Fax: (310)449-2848. A&R: Pete Giberga, Mike Flynn. Labels include Epic Soundtrax, LV Records, Immortal Records, and Word Records. Record company.

Distributed by Sony Music Distribution.

How to Contact *Write or call first and obtain permission to submit* (New York office only). Does not return material. Responds only if interested. *Santa Monica and Nashville offices do not accept unsolicited submissions.*

Music Artists include Celine Dion, Macy Gray, Modest Mouse, Audioslave, Fuel, Jennifer Lopez, B2K, Incubus, Ben Folds.

Tips "Do an internship if you don't have experience or work as someone's assistant. Learn the business and work hard while you figure out what your talents are and where you fit in. Once you figure out which area of the record company you're suited for, focus on that, work hard at it and it shall be yours."

⚊ FIREANT

2009 Ashland Ave., Charlotte NC 28205. E-mail: lewh@fireantmusic.com. Web site: www.fireantm usic.com. **Contact:** Lew Herman, owner. Record company, music publisher (Fireant Music) and record producer (Lew Herman). Estab. 1990. Releases several CDs/year. Pays negotiable royalty to artists on contract; statutory royalty to publisher per song on record.

Distributed by City Hall and North Country.

How to Contact Submit demo by mail. Unsolicited submissions are OK. Prefers cassette, DAT, or videocassette. Does not return material.

Music Mostly **progressive**, **traditional**, and **musical hybrids**. "Anything except New Age and MOR." Released *Loving the Alien: Athens Georgia Salutes David Bowie* (album), recorded by various artists (rock/alternative/electronic), released 2000 on Fireant; and *Good Enough* (album), recorded by Zen Frisbee. Other artists include Mr. Peters' Belizean Boom and Chime Band.

⚊ ⚊ FRESH ENTERTAINMENT ✓

1315 Simpson Rd. NW, Suite 5, Atlanta GA 30314. E-mail: whunter1122@yahoo.com. **Contact:** Willie W. Hunter, managing director. Record company and music publisher (Hserf Music/ASCAP, Blair Vizzion Music/BMI). Releases 5 singles and 2 LPs/year. Pays 7-10% royalty to artists on contract; statutory rate to publisher per song on record.

Distributed by Ichiban International and Intersound Records.

How to Contact Submit demo by mail. Unsolicited submissions are OK. Prefers cassette or VHS videocassette with at least 3 songs and lyric sheet. Include SASE. Responds in 2 months.

Music Mostly **R&B**, **rock** and **pop**; also **jazz**, **gospel** and **rap**. Released "We Hate Pastor Troy" (single by W. Jackson/Javou/Chosen One) from *Ready For War*, recorded by Swat Team (rap/hip-hop), released 2000 on Armageddon/Milltyme; "Erase The Color Line" (single by M. Warner/J.

Smith/J. Lewis) from *EMG-Non Pilation*, recorded by Michael Warner/JS-1/Noray (R&B/hip-hop), released 2000 on EMQ Entertainment; *Ancestral Spirits* (album), written and recorded by Bob Miles (jazz), released 2004 on Sheets of Sound/Fresh Entertainment; *My Life—My Hustle* (album), written by Jamal Smith and recorded by JS-1 (rap/hip-hop), released 2004 on Vision Vibe/Fresh Entertainment; "Go Sit Down" (single), by Maceo, released 2005 on Quick Flip/Fresh Entertainment. Other artists include Cirocco and Invisible Men.

☐ FRONT ROW RECORDS

Ridgewood Park Estates, 222 Tulane St., Garland TX 75043. **Contact:** Gene or Dea Summers. Public Relations/Artist and Fan Club Coordinator: Steve Summers. A&R: Shawn Summers. Labels include Juan Records. Record company and music publisher (Silicon Music/BMI). Estab. 1968. Releases 5-6 singles and 2-3 LPs/year. Pays negotiable royalty to artists on contract; standard royalty to songwriters on contract.

Distributed by Crystal Clear Records.

 • Also see the listing for Silicon Music Publishing Co. in the Music Publishers section of this book.

How to Contact Submit demo by mail. Unsolicited submissions are OK. Prefers cassette or VHS videocassette with 1-3 songs. "*We request a photo and bio with material submission.*" Does not return material. Responds ASAP.

Music Mostly **'50s rock/rockabilly**; also **country**, **bluegrass**, **old-time blues**, and **R&B.** Released "Domino" (single), recorded by Gene Summers on Pollytone Records (rockabilly); "Goodbye Priscilla" and "Cool Baby" (singles), both recorded by Gene Summers on Collectables Records.

Tips "If you own masters of 1950s rock and rockabilly, contact us first! We will work with you on a percentage basis for overseas release. We have active releases in Holland, Switzerland, Belgium, Australia, England, France, Sweden, Norway, and the US at the present. We need original masters. You must be able to prove ownership of tapes before we can accept a deal. We're looking for little-known, obscure recordings. We have the market if you have the tapes! We are also interested in country and rockabilly *artists* who have not recorded for awhile but still have the voice and appeal to sell overseas."

☐ GENERIC RECORDS, INC.

433 Limestone Rd., Ridgefield CT 06877. (203)438-9811. Fax: (203)431-3204. E-mail: hifiadd@aol.com. President (pop, alternative, rock): Gary Lefkowith. A&R (pop, dance, adult contemporary): Bill Jerome. Labels include Outback, GLYN. Record company, music publisher (Sotto Music/BMI) and record producer. Estab. 1976. Staff size: 2. Releases 6 singles and 2 CDs/year. Pays 15% royalty to artists on contract; statutory rate to publisher per song on record.

Distributed by Dutch East India.

How to Contact Submit demo by mail. Unsolicited submissions are OK. Prefers cassette with 2-3 songs. Include SASE. Responds in 2 weeks.

Music Mostly **alternative rock**, **rock**, and **pop**; also **country** and **rap**. Released "Young Girls" (by Eric Della Penna/Dean Sharenow), recorded by Henry Sugar (alternative/pop); "Rock It," written and recorded by David Ruskay (rock/pop); and *Tyrus*, written and recorded by Tyrus (alternative), all on Generic Records, Inc. Other artists include Hifi, Honest, Loose Change, and John Fantasia.

Tips "Love what you're doing. The music comes first."

☑ ☐ GIG RECORDS

520 Butler Ave., Point Pleasant NJ 08742. (732)598-7586. E-mail: lenny@gigrecords.com. Web site: www.gigrecords.com. **Contact:** Lenny Hip, A&R. Labels include AMPED. Record company and music publisher (Gig Music). Estab. 1998. Staff size: 8. Releases 2 singles, 2 EPs and 15 CDs/year. Pays negotiable royalty to artists on contract; statutory rate to publisher per song on record.

Distributed by Amazon, E-Music, CD Now, Nail, and Sumthing.

How to Contact Submit demo by mail. Unsolicited submissions are OK. Prefers cassette, CD, or VHS videocassette with lyric sheet and cover letter. Does not return materials. Responds ASAP if interested.

Music Mostly **rock** and **electronic**; also **drum & bass**, **trip-hop**, and **hip-hop**. Does not want country. Released *Hungry* (album), recorded by Gum Parker (electronico), released 2003 on Gig Records; *Waiting For You* (album), recorded by Nick Clemons Band (alternative rock/pop), released 2003 on Groove Entertainment; and 3 new releases to come from Michael Ferentino, Amazing Meet Project, Love in Reverse. Other artists include Ned's Atomic Dustbin, Virginia, The Vibrators, Groundswell UK, Nebula Nine, The Youth Ahead, Dryer, and Red Engine Nine.

Tips "No egos."

N ▣ ◯ GOLDWAX RECORD CORPORATION ✓

P.O. Box 54700, Atlanta GA 30308-0700. (770)316-7454. Fax: (770)454-8088. E-mail: goldwaxrec@ aol.com. Web site: www.goldwax.com. **Contact:** Jimmy McClendon, A&R. Labels include Abec, Bandstand USA and Beale Street USA. Record company and music publisher (Stellar Music Industries). Estab. 1963. Staff size: 4. Releases 15 singles, 12 LPs, 4 EPs and 2 CDs/year. Pays negotiable royalty to artists on contract; statutory rate to publisher per song on record.

Distributed by City Hall Records, Goldwax Distributing.

• Also see the listing for Stellar Music Industries in the Music Publishers section of this book.

How to Contact *Write or call first and obtain permission to submit.* Prefers cassette, CD, DAT or VHS videocassette with 4 songs and lyric sheet. Include SASE. Responds in 6 weeks.

Music Mostly **R&B/hip-hop**, **pop/rock** and **jazz**; also **blues**, **contemporary country** and **contemporary gospel**. Released *Clifford & Co.* (album) (soul) on Beale Street Records and *Double Deuce* (album) (rap) on Urban Assault Records. Other artists include Double Deuce, Elvin Spenser and Margie Alexander.

Tips "Songwriters need to provide great melodies; artists need to have commercial appeal."

N ✉ ◯ GONZO! RECORDS INC.

5757 E. Erin Ave., Fresno CA 93727. (559)269-2244. Fax: (559)452-9694. E-mail: gonzorcrds@aol.c om. Web site: members.aol.com/gonzorcrds. **Contact:** Jeffrey Gonzalez, president. Record company. Estab. 1993. Staff size: 3. Releases 3 singles and 1-6 CDs/year. Pays negotiable royalty to artists on contract; statutory rate to publisher per song on record.

• Gonzo! Records was awarded Best Indie Label, and Full Frequency was awarded Best Techno/ Industrial Band at the 1999 Los Angeles Music Awards.

How to Contact Submit demo by mail. Unsolicited submissions are OK. Prefers cassette or CD. "When submitting, please specify that you got the listing from *Songwriter's Market*." Does not return material. Responds in 6 weeks.

Music Mostly **commercial industrial**, **dance** and **techno**; also **commercial alternative** and **synth pop**. Released *Hate Breeds Hate* (album), written and recorded by BOL (hard industrial); *Momentum* (album), written and recorded by Full Frequency (commerical industrial); and *Ruth in Alien Corn* (album), written and recorded by Pinch Point (alternative pop), all on Gonzo! Records. Other artists include Turning Keys.

Tips "If you're going to submit music to me, it must be because you love to write music, not because you want to be a rockstar. That will eventually happen with a lot of hard work."

◯ GOTHAM RECORDS

Attn: A&R, P.O. Box 237067, New York NY 10023. E-mail: ar@gothamrecords.com. Web site: www.gothamrecords.com. **Contact:** John Cross, vice president A&R/retail. Record company. Estab. 1994. Staff size: 3. Releases 8 LPs and 8 CDs/year. Pays negotiable royalty to artists on contract; statutory rate to publisher per song on record.

Distributed by Dutch East India and MS Distributing.

How to Contact Submit demo by mail "in a padded mailer or similar package." Unsolicited submissions are OK. Prefers cassette or CD and bios, pictures, and touring information. Does not return material. Responds in 6 weeks.

Music Mostly **rock**, **pop**, **alternative**, and **AAA**. Released *Nineteenth Soul*, recorded by Liquid Gang (rock); *Supafuzz*, written and recorded by Supafuzz (rock); and *Oh God! Help Our Fans!*, written and recorded by The Loose Nuts (ska), all on Gotham Records. Other artists include Love Huskies, Flybanger, and The Booda Velvets.

Patrick Arn

*Gotham Records pursues
a diverse strategy*

Patrick Arn, President of New York-based Gotham Records, has kept an sharp eye out for rising talent in the music industry, and his patience and effort seems to be paying off. Since 1994, Gotham Records has released the debuts of several acts that have gone on to sign with major labels including Flybanger, Liquid Gang, and the Loose Nuts. More recently, the label has brought Boston singer-songwriter Mike Previti and San Diego metallers Scar'd Sanity on board. Time will tell whether these acts follow in the paths of those who came before them and confirm Arn's discerning eye once again.

Here Arn speaks about the route Gotham Records has taken to get to their current position, as well as where he sees the label headed in the near future.

Gotham Records has been operating since 1994, a fairly impressive lifespan for an independent label—especially during a time when the music industry has undergone such substantial, sweeping changes. What kicked it all off for you and for Gotham?

I was always intrigued by the business and marketing side of the music business, so in 1994, after working at the William Morris Agency, I started Gotham Records. The first band I signed was called John Monopoly, a fun band from Rhode Island. At first, I ran the label out of my apartment. I spent most of my time booking the band and visiting retail stores everywhere, giving them CDs on consignment.

The next band I signed was the Love Huskies, whose first album was distributed via Ichiban Records. Then I signed their friends Liquid Gang, who [eventually] got signed by Jason Flom, who was the head of LAVA/Atlantic at the time. Flom thought that Gotham Records was a great platform for new artists, so he pulled Gotham Records into the Warner Brothers family by offering us a wonderful distribution deal through their indie label distributor Alternative Distribution Alliance, who we were with for eight years [Gotham is currently distributed throughout North America by Koch Entertainment Distribution]. From there on, it just continued to grow.

How do you relate to Gotham Records artists, and how does it differ from the kind of relationship one might expect at a major label?

My relationship with my artists is my specialty. Though I run a record label, the truth is that probably 60 percent of what I do falls more in the category of management. There is *never* a time when my artists can't reach me. I am up every night until at least 2 a.m. If I am not working on my computer, I am speaking on the phone with my West Coast artists. It's what I love to do.

In the past, Gotham Records has acted as something of a link between upcoming talent and the major distribution channels, by signing acts that end up signing major-label deals. Do you generally aim towards the mainstream audience, or are you seeking to target a more specialized niche market? Are these aims mutually exclusive?

I have always stated that I want Gotham Records to be an indie label with major-label diversity. We have released rock, Americana, and even country artists.

However, times are changing. I have come to realize that in this extremely competitive marketplace, label identification is an intricate part of success. Take Victory Records, Vagrant Records, and Epitaph, for example; each has established a unique label identity that has served them well. As Gotham continues to grow, we will begin to create sub-genre labels within the corporation. However, I believe we will always stay true to rock—I just have no interest in hip-hop or dance.

What do you look for in new acts? What things can would-be submitters do to stand out from the pack when they approach Gotham Records?

The most important things to remember are *professionalism* and *etiquette*. As for submissions, if a package contains a hand-written letter or is full of arrogant statements such as "We are the best," then out it goes. Professionalism is *key*.

Music and performance are important, but if I need to rely on the artist to book gigs and promote themselves, they'd better be professional and understand the business. Unfortunately, too few do.

Do you usually fund album recording with an advance, or do you mainly license already-finished masters provided by the acts? What kind of financial arrangements do you generally set up in these cases?

Our artists are generally paid somewhere in the area of 30% post-recoupment. I do this for two reasons: I consider this a very fair setup, and it provides extra incentive for the band to not attempt to "rape" the label. This way, if an artist has already recorded their material, it would be in their best interest to simply give it to the label and allow us to spend more of the budget on the marketing of the album and the artist, instead of putting on an attempt to milk more money out of the label by claiming they need more funds for recording than they really do.

Does Gotham Records seek out uses for its artists' music in film, TV, or commercials?

We have had tremendous success with music placement over our 12 years in existence—the Loose Nuts' single "Wishen" earned us our first gold record when it was chosen for the soundtrack to the Universal Pictures film *American Pie*. A few of our other successes include getting Fear The Clown's single "Inside the Memories" featured on the WB's series premiere of Smallville; TNN licensing four tracks by Midline for use on their program *The Re:Evolution of Sports*; and ESPN licensing the title track of Tony Justice's Gotham debut *Rockin' Rusty* for the 2006 NASCAR season. Also, the Booda Velvets' music has been featured in a variety of projects including NBC's coverage of the Xbox Pipeline Masters, MTV's *The Osbournes*, *Road Rules*, *Laguna Beach*, and most recently Sony Pictures' *The Fog*.

Because of this, I do state that in order to provide me with the desire to spend my time, effort and money attempting to secure placement, I expect the artist to provide me with a co-publishing opportunity. I don't ask for it to hold back payments on record sales or anything like that.

Do you accept demos from songwriters who wish to pitch their songs to Gotham Records acts?
No, we don't really look for songs. We prefer acts that are self-contained.

Since Gotham was founded in 1994, the music industry has undergone a range of changes with the rise of the Internet, digital downloads, and the importance of online presence. How have your methods of working changed during that time, and what will you be doing in the future to help prepare yourselves and your artists for what other changes might be to come?
Since digital is quickly becoming a staple of music retail, we are really focusing on signing bands to digital deals. We have a wonderful arrangement with SONY-RED. They are able to get any of our releases up on iTunes, Napster, Rhapsody, MSN, etc. We view this as a great platform to expand our catalog, test the marketability and determination of new artists, and not have to worry about manufacturing, in-store promotion, and everything else that goes along with promoting actual CDs at the store level.

—Aaron Poehler

Tips "Send all submissions in regular packaging. Spend your money on production and basics, not on fancy packaging and gift wrap."

☑ ⊘ GROOVE MAKERS' RECORDINGS
P.O. Box 271170, Houston TX 77227-1170. E-mail: drathoven@yahoo.com. Web site: www.paidnp hull.com. **Contact:** Drathoven, A&R . Labels include Paid In Full Entertainment. Record company, music publisher, and record producer (Crazy C). Estab. 1994. Staff size: 4. Releases 3 singles, 2 LPs, and 2 CDs/year. Pays negotiable royalty to artists on contract; statutory rate to publisher per song on record.
Distributed by S.O.H.
How to Contact *Write first and obtain permission to submit.* Prefers cassette or CD. Does not return material.
Music Mostly **rap** and **R&B**. Released "They Don't Know" (single by Paul Wall/Mike Jones) from *Chick Magnet* (album), recorded by Paul Wall (rap), released 2004 on Paid In Full; "Down South Pt. II" (single by Ben Thompson III) from *Supa Thugz Pt. II* (album), recorded by Mista MADD (rap), released 2004 on Paid In Full; and "Ballin Is A Habit" (single) from *Grown Man Style* (album), recorded by 50/50 Twin (rap), released 2004 on Paid in Full. Other artists include S.O.U.L., Yung Ro, and Shei Atkins.

⃝ HACIENDA RECORDS & RECORDING STUDIO
1236 S. Staples St., Corpus Christi TX 78404. (361)882-7066. E-mail: info@haciendarecords.com. Web site: www.haciendarecords.com. **Contact:** Rick Garcia, executive vice president. Founder/CEO: Roland Garcia. Record company, music publisher, and record producer. Estab. 1979. Staff size: 10. Releases 12 singles and 15 CDs/year. Pays negotiable royalty to artists on contract; negotiable rate to publisher per song on record.
How to Contact Submit demo by mail. Unsolicited submissions are OK. Prefers CD or cassette with cover letter. Does not return material. Responds in 6 weeks.
Music Mostly **tejano**, **regional Mexican**, **country** (Spanish or English), and **pop**. Released "Chica Bonita" (single), recorded by Albert Zamora and D.J. Cubanito, released 2001 on Hacienda Records; "Si Quieres Verme Llorar" (single) from *Lisa Lopez con Mariachi* (album), recorded by Lisa Lopez

(mariachi), released 2002 on Hacienda; "Tartamudo" (single) from *Una Vez Mas* (album), recorded by Peligro (norteno); and "Miento" (single) from *Si Tu Te Vas* (album), recorded by Traizion (tejano), both released 2001 on Hacienda. Other artists include Ricky Naramzo, Gary Hobbs, Steve Jordan, Grammy Award nominees Mingo Saldivar and David Lee Garza, Michelle, Victoria Y Sus Chikos, La Traizion.

◖ HEADS UP INT., LTD.

23309 Commerce Park Dr., Cleveland OH 44122. (216)765-7381. Fax: (216)464-6037. E-mail: dave @headsup.com. Web site: www.headsup.com. **Contact:** Dave Love, president. Record company, music publisher (Heads Up Int., Buntz Music, Musica de Amor), and record producer (Dave Love). Estab. 1980. Staff size: 57. Releases 10 LPs/year. Pays negotiable royalty to artists on contract. **Distributed by** Telarc Int. Corp.

How to Contact Submit demo by mail. Unsolicited submissions are OK. Prefers CD. Does not return material. Responds in one month.

Music Mostly **jazz**, **R&B**, and **pop**. Does not want anything else. Released *Keeping Cool* (album), written and recorded by Joyce Cooling (jazz); *Another Side of Midnight* (album), written and recorded by Marion Meadows (jazz); and *Love Letters* (album), written and recorded by Gerald Veasley (jazz). Other artists include Philip Bailey, Joe McBride, Richard Smith, Robert Perera, Spyro Gyra, and Pieces of a Dream.

◖◗ HI-BIAS RECORDS INC.

Attn: A&R Dept., 20 Hudson Dr. (side entrance), Maple ON L6A 1X3 Canada. (905)303-9611. Fax: (905)303-6611. E-mail: info@hibias.ca. Web site: www.hibias.ca. **Contact:** Nick Fiorucci, director. Labels include Tilt, Riff, Toronto Underground, Remedy, and Club Culture. Record company, music publisher (Bend 60 Music/SOCAN), and record producer (Nick Fiorucci). Estab. 1990. Staff size: 5. Releases 20-30 singles and 2-5 CDs/year. Pays negotiable royalty to artists on contract; statutory rate to publisher per song on record.

Distributed by EMI.

How to Contact Submit demo by mail. Unsolicited submissions are OK. Prefers cassette or DAT with 3 songs and lyric sheet. Does not return material. Responds in 6 weeks.

Music Mostly **dance**, **house**, **club**, **pop**, and **R&B**. Released "Hands of Time" (single by N. Fiorucci/ B. Cosgrove), recorded by Temperance; "Now That I Found You" (single by B. Farrinco/Cleopatra), recorded by YBZ; and "Lift Me Up" (single), written and recorded by Red 5, all on Hi-Bias (dance/ pop). Other artists include DJ's Rule.

◖◗ IDOL RECORDS PUBLISHING

P.O. Box 720043, Dallas TX 75372. (214)321-8890. E-mail: info@idolrecords.com. Web site: www.I dolRecords.com. **Contact:** Erv Karwelis, president. Record company. Estab. 1992. Releases 30 singles, 80 LPs, 20 EPs and 10-15 CDs/year. Pays negotiable royalty to artists on contract; negotiable rate to publisher per song on record.

Distributed by Navarre.

How to Contact See Web site at www.idolrecords.com for submission policy. No phone calls or e-mail follow-ups.

Music Mostly **rock**, **pop**, and **alternative**. Released *The Man* (album), recorded by Sponge (alternative); *Movements* (album), recorded by Black Tie Dynasty (alternative); and *The Fifth of July* (album), recorded by Watershed (alternative), all released 2006 on Idol Records. Other artists include Flickerstick, the Fags, DARYL, Old 97's, Centro-matic, The Deathray Davies, and GBH.

◖◗ INTERSCOPE/GEFFEN/A&M RECORDS

2220 Colorado Ave., Santa Monica CA 90404. (310)865-1000. Fax: (310)865-7908. Web site: www.i nterscoperecords.com. Labels include Death Row Records, Nothing Records, Rock Land, Almo Sounds, Aftermath Records, and Trauma Records. Record company.

• As a result of the PolyGram and Universal merger, Geffen and A&M Records have been folded into Interscope Records.

How to Contact *Does not accept unsolicited submissions.*

Music Released *Worlds Apart*, recorded by . . . And You Will Know Us By The Trail Of Dead; and *Guero*, recorded by Beck. Other artists include U2, M.I.A, Keane, and Marilyn Manson.

⊘ ISLAND/DEF JAM MUSIC GROUP

825 Eighth Ave., 29th Floor, New York NY 10019. (212)333-8000. Fax: (212)603-7654. Web site: www.islanddefjam.com. **Los Angeles:** 8920 Sunset Blvd, 2nd Floor, Los Angeles CA 90069. (310)276-4500. Fax: (310)242-7023. Executive A&R: Paul Pontius. Labels include Mouth Almighty Records, Worldly/Triloka Records, Blackheart Records, Private Records, Slipdisc Records, Thirsty Ear, Blue Gorilla, Dubbly, Little Dog Records, Rounder, and Capricorn Records. Record company.
How to Contact *Island/Def Jam Music Group* does not accept unsolicited submissions. Do not send material unless requested.
Music Artists include Bon Jovi, Ja Rule, Jay-Z, and Ludacris.

⊘ J RECORDS

745 Fifth Ave., 6th Floor, New York NY 10151. (646)840-5600. Web site: www.jrecords.com.
How to Contact *J Records does not accept unsolicited submissions.*
Music Artists include Faithless, Alicia Keys, and Annie Lennox.

Ⓝ ⊘ JUDGMENT ENTERTAINMENT INC.

(formerly Judgment/RCA Records), 129 Rayette St., Conshohocken PA 19428. (610)940-9589. Fax: (610)940-9886. E-mail: judgrecs@aol.com. Web site: www.judgment-records.com. President: Joe Nicolo. General Manager: Thad Shirey. Record company, music publisher (Judgment Publishing). Estab. 1999. Pays negotiable royalty to artists on contract.
   ● This label was previously Ruffhouse/Sony whose artist, Lauryn Hill, won 5 Grammys.
How to Contact Submit demo by mail. Unsolicited submissions are OK. Prefers cassette, CD with lyric sheet, cover letter and press clippings. Include SASE. Responds only if interested.
Music Mostly **urban r&b**, **rap**, **pop** and **rock**; also **country** and **alternative rock**.
Tips "Put your best songs first. We are radio driven; we need strong hooks."

✔ ⊘ KILL ROCK STARS

120 N.E. State #418, Olympia WA 98501. E-mail: krs@killrockstars.com. Web site: www.killrocksta rs.com. **Contact:** Slim Moon, CEO or Maggie Vail, VP of A&R. Record company. Estab. 1991. Releases 4 singles, 10 LPs, 4-6 EPs and 35 CDs/year. Pays 50% of net profit to artists on contract; negotiated rate to publisher per song on record.
Distributed by Touch and Go.
How to Contact *Write first and obtain permission to submit.* Prefers link to Web page or EPK. Does not return material.
Music Mostly **punk rock**, **neo-folk or anti-folk** and **spoken word**. Artists include Deerhoof, Xiu Xiu, Mary Timony, The Gossip, Frase Errata, and Two Ton Boa
Tips "Send a self-released CD or link. NEVER EVER send unsolicited mp3s. We will not listen. We will only work with touring acts, so let us know if you are playing Olympia, Seattle or Portland. Particularly interested in young artists with indie-rock background."

⊘ LARI-JON RECORDS

P.O. Box 216, Rising City NE 68658. (402)542-2336. **Contact:** Larry Good, owner. Record company, management firm (Lari-Jon Promotions), music publisher (Lari-Jon Publishing/BMI) and record producer (Lari-Jon Productions). Estab. 1967. Staff size: 1. Releases 15 singles and 5 LPs/year. Pays varying royalty to artists on contract.
How to Contact Submit demo by mail. Unsolicited submissions are OK. Prefers CD with 5 songs and lyric sheet. Include SASE. Responds in 2 months.
Music Mostly **country**, **Southern gospel**, and **'50s rock**. Released "Glory Bound Train" (single), written and recorded by Tom Campbell; *The Best of Larry Good* (album), written and recorded by Larry Good (country); and *Her Favorite Songs* (album), written and recorded by Johnny Nace (country), all on Lari-Jon Records. Other artists include Kent Thompson and Brenda Allen.

◎ LUCIFER RECORDS, INC.

P.O. Box 263, Brigantine NJ 08203-0263. (609)266-2623. Fax: (609)266-4870. **Contact:** Ron Luciano, president. Labels include TVA Records. Record company, music publisher (Ciano Publishing and Legz Music), record producer (Pete Fragale and Tony Vallo), management firm and booking agency (Ron Luciano Music Co. and TVA Productions). "Lucifer Records has offices in South Jersey; Palm Beach, Florida; and Las Vegas, Nevada."

How to Contact *Call or write to arrange personal interview*. Prefers cassette with 4-8 songs. Include SASE. Responds in 3 weeks.

Music Mostly **dance**, **easy listening**, **MOR**, **rock**, **soul**, and **top 40/pop**. Released "I Who Have Nothing," (single), by Spit-N-Image (rock); "Lucky" (single), by Legz (rock); and "Love's a Crazy Game" (single), by Voyage (disco/ballad). Other artists include Bobby Fisher, Jerry Denton, FM, Zeke's Choice, Al Caz, Joe Vee, and Dana Nicole.

☑ ◎ MAKOCHE RECORDING COMPANY

208 N. Fourth St., Bismarck ND 58501. (701)223-7316. Fax: (701)255-8287. E-mail: info@makoche. com. Web site: www.makoche.com. **Contact:** Lisa Dowhaniuk, A&R assistant. Labels include Makoche and Chairmaker's Rush. Record company and recording studio. Estab. 1995. Staff size: 5. Releases 4 CDs/year. Pays negotiable royalty to artists on contract; statutory rate to publisher per song on record.

Distributed by DNA, Music Design, Four Winds Trading, Zango Music, and New Leaf Distribution.
   • Makoche is noted for releasing quality music based in the Native American tradition. Recognized by the Grammys, Nammys, New Age Voice Music Awards, Indian Summer Music Awards, and C.O.V.R. Music Awards.

How to Contact *Call first and obtain permission to submit*. "Please submit only fiddle and American Indian-influenced music." Include SASE. Responds in 2 months.

Music Mostly **Native American**, **flute** and **fiddle**. Released *Edge of America* (album), written and recorded by Annie Humphrey (folk), released 2004 on Makoche; and *Togo* (album), written and recorded by Andrew Vasquez (Native American flute), released on Makoche 2004; *Way of Life* (album), recorded by Lakota Thunder (drum group), released on Makoche 2004. Other artists include Gary Stroutsos, Bryan Akipa, Keith Bear, Andrew Vasquez, Lakota Thunder, Sissy Goodhouse, and Kevin Locke.

Tips "We are a small label with a dedication to quality."

▦ ☑ ◎ MAVERICK RECORDS

9348 Civic Center Dr., Beverly Hills CA 90210. Web site: www.maverick.com. CEO/Head of A&R: Guy Oseary. A&R: Russ Rieger, Jason Bentley, Danny Strick, Berko Weber, Michael Goldberg. Record company.

Distributed by WEA.

Music Released *Under Rug Swept* (album); *Supposed Former Infatuation Junkie* (album) and *Jagged Little Pill* (album), both recorded by Alanis Morissette; *The Spirit Room* (album), recorded by Michelle Branch; *Tantric* (album), recorded by Tantric; and *Ray of Light* (album), recorded by Madonna. Other artists include Deftones, Home Town Hero, Mest, Michael Lee, Me'shell Ndegeocello, Muse, Onesidezero, Prodigy and Paul Oakenfold.

☑ ◎ MCA NASHVILLE

(formerly MCA Records), 60 Music Square E., Nashville TN 37203. (615)244-8944. Fax: (615)880-7447. Web site: www.mca-nashville.com. Record company and music publisher (MCA Music).

How to Contact MCA Nashville cannot accept unsolicited submissions.

Music Artists include Tracy Byrd, George Strait, Vince Gill, The Mavericks, and Trisha Yearwood.

☑ ◻ MEGAFORCE RECORDS

P.O. Box 63584, Philadelphia PA 19147. **New York office**: P.O. Box 1955, New York NY 10113. (212)741-8861. Fax: (509)757-8602. E-mail: gregaforce@aol.com. Web site: www.megaforcerecord s.com. **Contact:** Robert John, President. General Manager: Missi Callazzo. Record company. Estab.

Slim Moon

*Kill Rock Stars seeks artists
with vision and drive*

Founded in 1991 by Slim Moon, the Olympia, Washington-based independent record label Kill Rock Stars was originally intended simply to release nothing but spoken word punk "wordcore" seven-inch vinyl records. However, the label's purview quickly expanded to encompass punk bands such as Unwound, Bikini Kill, and Bratmobile, and later to include artists such as Elliott Smith, Sleater-Kinney, and The Decemberists—though some felt KRS may have strayed too far from their dyed punk roots when they released an album by Linda Perry, former leader of major-label act 4 Non Blondes and writer/producer for major-label acts including Christina Aguilera, Britney Spears, Pink, and Gwen Stefani. Despite this, KRS continues to release relatively non-mainstream music such as Amps For Christ and The Paper Chase, and has even spun off 5RC (5 Rue Christine), a sister label intended for "harsher-sounding indie rock," including more noise and experimental music than KRS releases.

Here, label founder Slim Moon talks about what he's learned during his 15 years on the edge and discusses some of the changes he's seen in the music industry—especially over the last few years.

Was there a specific moment that led to the birth of Kill Rock Stars?

I can't actually remember any specific moment that led to its birth as a spoken word label. There was in fact a specific moment that led to the transformation to a music label—Unwound's first show. They were really good, and I got inspired that they ought to have a record immediately, but then felt dejected because I knew no label would sign them for years. So I decided to do it myself.

Has the label's overall philosophy changed over the intervening years?

Yes, there has been some evolution: partly because of my experience, learning what is real and what is fantasy; partly because my interests and values have changed; partly because just in a practical way, the philosophy of an established mid-sized label can't be the same as a young up-and-comer. It could be argued that we were locally focused at first, which cannot be argued anymore. We have a roster of 36 bands now, and only two are local. We have employees, contracts, and a warehouse now, none of which we had at the beginning, but our focus as artist-friendly and artist-centric has not changed.

So as far as your experience goes, what have you learned is real and what have you learned is fantasy?

I found that my vision of cultivating long-term relationships with career artists and being a home for their recordings for a long, long time was a naive vision. I found that loyalty from a label towards artists is not repaid by the artists with loyalty to the label, and I've grown up enough to understand that there is no reason it should be. It might be about art, but it *is* still a business, after all.

What are you looking for in new acts?

I am looking primarily for innovative artists making great, interesting, creative music, but in some cases I am looking for less creative artists who have mastered a genre I find meaningful and who can be described as "the cream of the crop" in their field. Either way, they must be hard workers with vision, patience, drive, and a willingness to be actively engaged in promoting their music to an audience. In terms of "songwriters" even though we do some loud crazy rock and roll (those kids are songwriters too, of course), I do have a soft spot for pure songwriters in the traditional sense, or performing singer/songwriters.

Does Kill Rock Stars accept demos from songwriters who wish to pitch to KRS acts?

We haven't had any reason to do that yet, but we might in the future. In particular, Beth Ditto (of The Gossip) is thinking of making a solo record, and that might be the time.

How can would-be submitters help themselves stand out?

Most submissions we get are really passive. I appreciate evidence of the kind of drive and vision that we are looking for. It helps us know some important things about the band other than what the music sounds like.

Demonstrating knowledge of the backgrounds of KRS and 5RC and our rosters and values, then describing why the band would be a good fit is very helpful. Photos of the band, live video footage, and a log of tour history are all very helpful. I will be sure to check out any artist who has played a hundred-plus shows in the last calendar year.

What kinds of things do submitters do that end up hurting them?

The number one turnoff for me is the statement that "We would love to tour, but we aren't actually ever going to tour unless someone releases our record and gives us tour support." Bands who start with that kind of attitude show a lack of patience, drive, and vision, and they tend to be easily demoralized. I've increasingly lost my patience for bands who are easily demoralized over time.

Do you usually fund album recording with an advance, or do you mainly license already-finished masters provided by the acts?

There is no set rule for the debut, but after the first album, we generally provide the recording funds.

In terms of dealing with an act's publishing, will KRS seek out uses in film, TV, or commercials?

Yes.

What kind of successes have you had with placing KRS music in other media? Have you ever found that the label's philosophy has interfered or aided in this process?

I guess I have two salient things to say about that one: we've had a lot of artists say no to placements over the years, and as an artist-friendly label, we have respected this. Also, because we look for innovative music that frequently fits in no easy genre, a lot of our stuff is difficult to place in movies and TV.

The music industry has changed a lot since you founded KRS. Do you see a major difference between selling 7-inch vinyl records and selling digital downloads?
The biggest difference is all the copies people are acquiring without paying us for them.

Do you find the amount of sales through venues such as iTunes help compensate for this kind of copyright infringement at all?
Definitely not. In comparing ratios between a band's live draw and its sales, digital or otherwise, sales are inexplicably down even though our artists are drawing more people than ever to their shows. It seems like when we sell a CD now we are selling it to the buyer and all her friends, instead of to just one person.

I do think that kids burning CD-Rs or instant messaging tracks to their friends are a much bigger culprit than the peer-to-peer networks, though. Every day in every city in America, a kid walks up to a merch table, checks out a CD, then tells the person behind the counter, "My friend has this, I'll just burn it from him." It is the norm these days, not the exception.

Have you considered implementing anti-copying measures on KRS releases?
No, this is not something we would do unless it was an industry trend or supported by regulatory/legal policy.

How do you feel about the RIAA's efforts to fight copyright infringement?
The RIAA is one of the most backward and ineffective institutions I've ever seen when it comes to stating its case, winning a public relations battle, or gaining the ear and respect of the legislature and relevant regulatory authorities. I really have been stunned at how unhelpful and regressive their efforts have been.

So I'm guessing you don't expect current anti-infringement efforts to curb this trend any time soon, then.
I'm not an expert and feel helpless to predict the trend. I believe it will only change with policy change. Unless copyright law changes, or new court decisions set new precedents, or the industry as a whole comes up with a viable solution, consumers are not likely to stop liking free stuff.

If no policy change ever happens, I personally see myself migrating towards artist management and away from the business of selling copies of recordings.

—Aaron Poehler

1983. Staff size: 5. Releases 6 CDs/year. Pays various royalties to artists on contract; ¾ statutory rate to publisher per song on record.
Distributed by Red/Sony Distribution.
How to Contact *Contact first and obtain permission to submit.* Submissions go to the Philadelphia office.
Music Mostly **rock**. Artists include Ministry, Clutch, S.O.D. and Blackfire Revelation.

METAL BLADE RECORDS
2828 Cochran St., Suite 302, Simi Valley CA 93065. (805)522-9111. Fax: (805)522-9380. E-mail: metalblade@metalblade.com. Web site: www.metalblade.com. Record company. Estab. 1982. Releases 20 LPs, 2 EPs and 20 CDs/year. Pays negotiable royalty to artists on contract.

How to Contact Submit demo CD by mail. Unsolicited submissions are OK. CD with 3 songs. Does not return material. Responds in 3 months.

Music Mostly **heavy metal** and **industrial**; also **hardcore, gothic** and **noise**. Released "Gallery of Suicide," recorded by Cannibal Corpse; "Voo Doo," recorded by King Diamond; and "A Pleasant Shade of Gray," recorded by Fates Warning, all on Metal Blade Records. Other artists include As I Lay Dying, The Red Chord, The Black Dahlia Murder, and Unearth.

Tips "Metal Blade is known throughout the underground for quality metal-oriented acts."

⊘ MIGHTY RECORDS

150 West End, Suite 6-D, New York NY 10023. Manager: Danny Darrow. Labels include Mighty Sounds & Filmworks. Record company, music publisher (Rockford Music Co./BMI, Stateside Music Co./BMI and Corporate Music Publishing Co./ASCAP) and record producer (Danny Darrow). Estab. 1958. Releases 1-2 singles, 1-2 12" singles and 1-2 LPs/year. Pays standard royalty to artists on contract; statutory rate to publisher per song on record.

Distributed by Amazon.com and CDBaby.com.

How to Contact Submit demo by mail. Unsolicited submissions are OK. "No phone calls." Prefers cassette or CD with 2 songs and lyric sheet. Does not return material. Responds in 1 month only if interested.

Music Mostly **pop, country** and **dance**; also **jazz**. Released "Let There Be Peace" (single by Danny Darrow) from *Falling In Love* (album), recorded by Danny Darrow (peace prayer/gospel); "Look to the Wind" (single by Peggy Stewart/Danny Darrow) from *Falling in Love* (album), recorded by Danny Darrow (movie theme); "Doomsday" (single by Robert Lee Lowery/Danny Darrow) from *Doomsday* (album), recorded by Danny Darrow (euro jazz), all released 2004 on Mighty Records.

⊘ MINOTAUR RECORDS

P.O. Box 620, Redwood Estates CA 95044. Estab. 1987. (408)353-1006. E-mail: dminotaur@hotmail.com. **Contact:** A&R. Record company. Estab. 1987. Staff size: 2. Releases 2 CDs/year. Pays statutory royalty to publishers per song on record. Distributed by CDbaby.com. Member of BMI, ASCAP, NARAS, TAXI.

How to Contact We only accept material referred to us by a reputable industry source (manager, entertainment attorney, etc.). Does not return submissions. Responds only if interested.

Music Mostly **adult contemporary, country, dance.** Also **easy rock, pop.** Does not want rap, heavy metal, jazz, hip-hop, hard rock and instrumentals. "Maybe Love" written by D. Baumgartner and Steven Worthy,from the *Dancing in the Dark* (album) recorded by Andrew Ceglio (pop/dance); "That Was A Great Affair" written by Tab Morales and Ron Dean Tomich, from *This Side of Heaven* (album), recorded by Doug Magpiong (adult contemporary); "Baby Blue Eyes and Tight Levis" written by Ron Dean Tomich, from *This Side of Nashville* (album) recorded by Candy Chase (country).

☑ ⊘ MISSILE RECORDS FILM & TV, INC.

P.O. Box 5537, Kreole Station, Moss Point MS 39563-1537. (601)914-9413. "No collect calls!" Estab. 1974. **Contact:** Joe F. Mitchell, executive vice president/general manager. First Vice President: Justin F. Mitchell. Second Vice President: Jayvean F. Mitchell. Record company and music publisher (Abalorn Music/ASCAP, Bay Ridge Publishing/BMI) and record producer. Releases 28 singles and 10 LPs/year. Pays "negotiable royalty to new artists on contract"; statutory rate to publisher for each record sold. "Missile Records has National and International Distribution."

• Also see the listing for Bay Ridge Publishing and Abalorn Music in the Music Publishers section.

Distributed by Star Sound Music Distributors, Hits Unlimited, Action Music Sales, Inc., Allegro Corp., Big Easy Distributing, Select-O-Hits, Total Music Distributors, Music Network, Impact Music, Universal Record Distributing Corporation, Dixie Rak Records & Tapes, Navaree Corporation, Curtis Wood Distributors, Big Daddy Music Distribution Co., ATM Distributors, HL Distribution, Bayside Distribution, Blue Sky Distribution, Alamo Record Distributors and MDI Distribution.

How to Contact *"Please don't send us anything until you contact us by phone or in writing and* *receive submission instructions. You must present your songs the correct way to get a reply.* **No registered mail—no exceptions! You may send a UPS or FedEx tracking number, but do not ask us to travel to the post office to sign for packages!**" Always whenever you write to us, be sure you include a #10 business-size envelope addressed back to you with a first class USA postage stamp on the envelope. We reply back to you from the SASE. All songs sent for review must include sufficient return postage. No reply made back to you without SASE or return of material without sufficient return postage. **Absolutely no reply postcards—only SASE.** If you only write lyrics, do not submit. We only accept completed songs, so you must find a collaborator. We are not interested in reviewing homemade recordings." Prefers CD (first choice) or cassette with 3-8 songs and lyrics to songs submitted. Responds in 2 months. A good quality demo recording will always get preference over a poor recording.

Music All types and styles of songs. Released "Mixed Up Love Affair," "Sweet Sexy Lady," and "My Love Just Fell Again" (singles) from *album title TBD* (album), written and recorded by Herb Lacy (blues); "Excuse Me Lady" and "When She Left Me" (singles by Rich Wilson); "Everyone Gets A Chance (To Lose In Romance)" and "I'm So Glad We Found Each Other" (singles by Joe F. Mitchell), from Excuse Me Lady (album), recorded by Rich Wilson (country/western); "My First Kiss," and "Moving On" (singles by Evan Webb), as well as "My Own Paradise" (single by Brad Adams) from *album title TBD* (album), recorded by Kenny Ray (modern pop country); "Southern Born" and "Old Folks Know" (singles by Christian Ramsey); "Innocent Little One" (single by Bob Levy), "Pretty Lady Come Closer" (single by David L. Resler) and "She Was Sittin' Pretty" (single by Jim Hendricks) all from If *It Takes All Night* (album), recorded by Christian Ramsey (modern pop country), all released on Missile Records. Other artists include Moto (reggae), Jackie Lambarella (country pop), Sarah Cooper (pop/R&B), Della Reed (contemporary Christian), Metellica (heavy metal), Coco Hodge (alternative) and Lady Love (rap).

Tips "Our doors are always open to young recording artists who are exceptionally talented and want to make a name for themselves in the music business. Your success is our success. We will work with you to reach your goal. We also are in the business of getting your professionally-recorded album of 10-12 well-produced and well-written, radio-ready songs placed with record companies in the USA and foreign countries for the possibility of record deals. Here is what we have gotten for some artists: $850,000 record deal for Charity (religious singing group) on Big Easy (USA) in 2001; $500,000 record deal for Vance Greek on Dime-A-Dozen (Germany) in 2002; a $150,000 record deal for Randell Ruthledge (country) on Dime-A-Dozen (Germany) in 2003; and a record deal for Karen Frazier (pop) of Ren & T. (mother-daughter act) from Hyattsville, MD on Mr. Wonderful Productions in Louisville, KY. Missile Records, Abalorn Music (ASCAP) and Bay Ridge Publishing Co. (BMI) are listed in some well-known publications such as the *Billboard International Buyer's Guide*, *Mix Master Directory*, *Industrial Source Book*, *Pollstar*, *Yellow Pages of Rock* and other publications. Some well-known recording artists born and raised in Mississippi include Elvis Presley, Conway Twitty, B.B. King and Faith Hill. The Moss Point, MS area music scene is also home to nationally-known rock group Three Doors Down, who sold more than 10 million of their CD albums and singles. Singers and songwriters thinking about doing professional recording, give us a call before you make that move. We can save you money, time, headaches, heartaches and troubles you may run into. We know what to do and how to do it to benefit you and get the best results."

☐ MODAL MUSIC, INC.™

P.O. Box 6473, Evanston IL 60204-6473. (847)864-1022. E-mail: info@modalmusic.com. Web site: www.modalmusic.com. President: Terran Doehrer. Assistant: J. Distler. Record company and agent. Estab. 1988. Staff size: 2. Releases 1-2 LPs/year. Pays negotiable royalty to artists on contract; negotiable rate to publisher per song on record.

How to Contact Submit demo by mail. Unsolicited submissions are OK. Prefers CD or cassette with bio, PR, brochures, any info about artist and music. Does not return material. Responds in 4 months.

Music Mostly **ethnic** and **world**. Released *St. James Vet Clinic* (album by T. Doehrer/Z. Doehrer), recorded by Wolfpak, released 2005; *Dance The Night Away* (album by T. Doehrer), recorded by Balkan Rhythm Band™; *Sid Beckerman's Rumanian (D. Jacobs)* (album), recorded by Jutta & The

Hi-Dukes™; and *Hold Whatcha Got* (album), recorded by Razzemetazz™, all on Modal Music Records. Other artists include Ensemble M'chaiya™, Nordland Band™ and Terran's Greek Band™.
Tips "Please note our focus is ethnic. You waste your time and money by sending us any other type of music. If you are unsure of your music fitting our focus, please call us before sending anything. Put your name and contact info on every item you send!"

⬩ ◐ MONTICANA RECORDS
P.O. Box 702, Snowdon Station, Montreal QC H3X 3X8 Canada. **Contact:** David P. Leonard, general manager. Record company, record producer (Monticana Productions) and music publisher (Montina Music/SOCAN). Estab. 1963. Staff size: 1. Pays negotiable royalty to artists on contract.
How to Contact Submit demo by mail. Unsolicited submissions are OK. Prefers CD. Include SASE.
Music Mostly **top 40**, **blues**, **country**, **dance-oriented**, **easy listening**, **folk** and **gospel**; also **jazz**, **MOR**, **progressive**, **R&B**, **rock** and **soul**.
Tips "Be excited and passionate about what you do. Be professional."

◻ NBT RECORDS
228 Morgan Lane, Berkeley Springs WV 25411-3475. (304)258-3656. E-mail: nbtoys@verizon.net. **Contact:** John S. Newbraugh, owner. Record company, music publisher (Newbraugh Brothers Music/BMI, NBT Music/ASCAP). Estab. 1967. Staff size: 1. Releases 4 singles and 52 CDs/year. Pays negotiable royalty to artists on contract; statutory royalty to publishers per song on record.
Distributed by "Distribution depends on the genre of the release. Our biggest distributor is perhaps the artists themselves, for the most part, depending on the genre of the release. We do have product in some stores and on the Internet as well."
How to Contact Submit demo by mail. Unsolicited submissions are OK. Prefers CD or cassette with any amount of songs, lyric sheet and cover letter. Include SASE. Responds in 4-6 weeks. "Please don't call for permission to submit. Your materials are welcomed."
Music Mostly **rockabilly**, **hillbilly**, **folk** and **bluegrass**; also **rock**, **country** and **gospel**. Does not want any music with vulgar lyrics. "We will accept all genres of music except songs that contain vulgar language." Released *Meandered Lakes Presents Songs By John Wiggins* (album), released 2006; "Set Your Eyes On The Son" (single), by Shelly Champion released 2005. "We also released and published many of the songs for *Ride The Train—Vol #13* in 2005, which brings the total of train/railroad related songs issued on this NBT series to 270 songs, with writers and artists from over half the states in the U.S.A., Canada, several countries in Europe, and Australia."
Tips "We are best known for our rockabilly releases. Reviews of our records can be found on both the American and European rockabilly Web sites. Our 'registered' trademark is a train. From time to time, we put out a CD with various artists featuring original songs that use trains as part of their theme. We use all genres of music for our train releases. We have received train songs from various parts of the world. All submissions on this topic are welcomed."

◔ NEURODISC RECORDS, INC.
3801 N. University Dr., Suite 403, Ft. Lauderdale FL 33351. (954)572-0289. Fax: (954)572-2874. E-mail: info@neurodisc.com. Web site: www.neurodisc.com. President: Tom O'Keefe. Label Manager: John Wai. Record company and music publisher. Estab. 1992. Releases 6 singles and 10 CDs/year. Pays negotiable royalty to artists on contract; 75% "to start" to publisher per song on record.
Distributed by Capital Records/EMI.
How to Contact Submit demo CD by mail. Unsolicited submissions are OK. Prefers CD, DAT or DVD. Include SASE and contact information. Responds only if interested.
Music Mostly **electronic**, **dance**, **New Age**, and **electro-bass**; also **rap**. Released albums from Sleepthief, Blue Stone Peplab, Etro Anime, Tastexperience, Ryan Farish & Amethystium, as well as Bass Lo-Ryders and Bass Crunk. Other artists include Eric Hansen, Bella Sonus and NuSound as well as DJ's Suzy Solar, Vicious Vic, Andy Hughes and Scott Stubbs.

◻ ONLY NEW AGE MUSIC, INC.
8033 Sunset Blvd. #472, Hollywood CA 90046. (323)851-3355. Fax: (323)851-7981. E-mail: info@newagemusic.com. Web site: www.newagemusic.com or www.newageuniverse.com. **Contact:** Su-

zanne Doucet, president. Record company, music publisher and consulting firm. Estab. 1987.
How to Contact *Call first and obtain permission to submit*. Does not return material.
Music Mostly **New Age**; also **world music**.
Tips "You should have a marketing strategy and at least a small budget for marketing your product."

OUTSTANDING RECORDS

P.O. Box 2111, Huntington Beach CA 92647. (714)377-7447 or (800)749-8469. Fax: (714)377-7468. Web site: www.outstandingmusic.com. **Contact:** Earl Beecher, owner. Labels include Morrhythm (mainstream/commercial), School Band (educational/charity), Church Choir (religious charity), and Empowerment (educational CDs and DVDs). Record company, music publisher (Earl Beecher Publishing/BMI and Beecher Music Publishing/ASCAP) and record producer (Earl Beecher). Estab. 1968. Staff size: 1. Releases 100 CDs/year. Pays $2/CD royalty to artists on contract; statutory rate to publisher per song on record.
Distributed by Sites on the Internet and "through distribution companies who contact me directly, especially from overseas."
How to Contact Submit demo by mail. Unsolicited submissions are OK. Prefers CD (full albums), lyric sheet, photo and cover letter. Include SASE. Responds in 3 weeks.
Music Mostly **jazz**, **rock** and **country**; also **everything else especially Latin**. Does not want music with negative, anti-social or immoral messages. Released *I've Seen It All* (album), recorded by John Buttram (country); *Everyday Life of Kids* (album), recorded by Cheryl Edelman (children's); *Live at the Bamboo Terrace* (album), recorded by The Lively Ones (surf), all released 2006 on Outstanding; and *Let's Get Funky* (album), recorded by Date Line 5 (rap), released 2005 on Outstanding.
Tips "We prefer to receive full CDs, rather than just three numbers. A lot of submitters suggest we release their song in the form of singles, but we just can't bother with singles at the present time. Especially looking for performers who want to release their material on my labels. Some songwriters are pairing up with performers and putting out CDs with a 'Writer Presents the Performer' concept. No dirty language. Do not encourage listeners to use drugs, alcohol or engage in immoral behavior. I'm especially looking for upbeat, happy, danceable music."

P. & N. RECORDS

61 Euphrasia Dr., Toronto ON M6B 3V8 Canada. (416)782-5768. Fax: (416)782-7170. E-mail: panfilo @sympatico.ca. **Contact:** Panfilo Di Matteo, president, A&R. Record company, record producer and music publisher (Lilly Music Publishing). Estab. 1993. Staff size: 2. Releases 10 singles, 20 12" singles, 15 LPs, 20 EPs and 15 CDs/year. Pays 25-35% royalty to artists on contract; statutory rate to publisher per song on record.
How to Contact Submit demo by mail. Unsolicited submissions are OK. Prefers CD or videocassette with 3 songs and lyric or lead sheet. Does not return material. Responds in 1 month only if interested.
Music Mostly **dance**, **ballads** and **rock**. Released Only This Way (album), written and recorded by Angelica Castro; *The End of Us* (album), written and recorded by Putz, both on P. & N. Records (dance); and "Lovers" (single by Marc Singer), recorded by Silvana (dance), released 2001 on P. and N. Records.

PARLIAMENT RECORDS

449 N. Vista St., Los Angeles CA 90036. (323)653-0693. E-mail: parlirec@aol.com. Web site: www.p arlirec.com. **Contact:** Ben Weisman, owner. Record company, record producer (Weisman Production Group) and music publisher (Audio Music Publishers, Queen Esther Music Publishing). Estab. 1965. Produces 30 singles/year. Fee derived from sales royalty when song or artist is recorded.
   ● Also see the listings for Audio Music Publishers and Queen Esther Music Publishing in the Music Publishers section and Weisman Production Group in the Record Producer section.
How to Contact Submit demo by mail. Unsolicited submissions are OK. Prefers CD or cassette with 3-10 songs and lyric sheet. Include SASE. "Mention *Songwriter's Market*. Please make return envelope the same size as the envelopes you send material in, otherwise we cannot send everything back." Responds in 6 weeks.

Music Mostly **R&B**, **soul**, **dance**, **rap**, and **top 40/pop**; also **gospel** and **blues**. Arists include Rapture 7 (gospel), Wisdom (male gospel singers), and chosen Recovery Ministry (female gospel group).
Tips "Parliament Records will also listen to 'tracks' only. If you send tracks, please include a letter stating what equipment you record on—ADAT, Protools or Roland VS recorders."

POP RECORD RESEARCH
10 Glen Ave., Norwalk CT 06850. E-mail: horar@earthlink.net. Director: Gary Theroux. Estab. 1962. Pays statutory rate to publisher per song on record.
• Also see their listing in the Organizations section.
How to Contact Submit demo by mail. Unsolicited submissions are OK. Prefers CD, cassette or VHS videocassette. Does not return material.
Music Mostly **pop**, **country** and **R&B**. Released "The Declaration" (single by Theroux-Gilbert), recorded by An American; "Thoughts From a Summer Rain" (single), written and recorded by Bob Gilbert, both on Bob Records; and "Tiger Paws" (single), written and recorded by Bob Gilbert on BAL Records. Other artists include Gary and Joan, The Nightflight Singers and Ruth Zimmerman.
Tips "Help us keep our biographical file on you and your career current by sending us updated bios/press kits, etc. They are most helpful to writers/researchers in search of accurate information on your success."

PPL ENTERTAINMENT GROUP
P.O. Box 261488, Encino, CA 91426. (818)506-8533. Fax: (818)506-8534. E-mail: a&r/labels@pplzm i.com. Web site: www.pplentertainmentgroup.com. **Contact:** Cisco Crowe, vice president A&R. Vice President A&R: Dakota Kelly. Vice President, A&R: Kaitland Diamond. General Manager: Jim Sellavain. President, Creative: Suzette Cuseo. Labels include Bouvier, Credence and JBK. Record company, music publisher (Pollybyrd Publications), management firm (Sa'mall Management) and distributor (Malibu Trading Company). Estab. 1979. Staff size: 15. Releases 10-30 singles, 12 12" singles, 6 LPs and 6 CDs/year. Pays 10-15% royalty to artists on contract; statutory rate to publisher per song on record.
Distributed by Sony and The Malibu Trading Company.
How to Contact *E-mail and obtain permission to submit.* "Only interested in professional full-time artists who tour and have fan bases. No weekend warriors, please." Prefers CD, cassette or videocassette with 3 songs. Include SASE. Responds in 6 weeks.
Music Released "The Return of the Players" (album) by Juz-Cuz on PPL2004; "Bigg Leggeded Woman" (single by Buddy Wright) from *Destiny* (album), recorded by Buddy Wright (blues), released 2003 on PPL; *Ghost* (album), recorded by The Band AKA, written and produced by J. James Jarrett; "Step Aside" (single by Gary Johnson) from *Step Aside* (album), recorded by Gary J., released 2003 on PPL/Sony. Other artists include Phuntaine, Condottiere and Gary J.

PRESENCE RECORDS
67 Candace Lane, Chatham NJ 07928-1115. (201)701-0707. **Contact:** Paul Payton, president. Record company, music publisher (Paytoons/BMI) and record producer (Presence Productions). Estab. 1985. Staff size: 1. Pays 1-2% royalty to artists on contract; statutory rate to publisher per song on record.
Distributed by Clifton Music.
How to Contact Submit demo by mail. Unsolicited submissions are OK. "No phone calls." Prefers cassette or CD with 2-4 songs and lyric sheet. Include SASE. Responds in 1 month. "Tapes and CDs not returned without prepaid mailer."
Music Mostly **doo-wop ('50s)**, **rock** and **new wave rock**. "No heavy metal, no 'Christian' or religious rock." Released "Ding Dong Darling," "Bette Blue Moon" and "Davilee/Go On" (singles by Paul Payton/Peter Skolnik), recorded by Fabulous Dudes (doo-wop), all on Presence Records.
Tips "Would you press and distribute it if it was your money? Only send it here if the answer is yes."

◐ QUARK RECORDS

P.O. Box 7320, FDR Station, New York NY 10150. (917)687-9988. E-mail: quarkent@aol.com. **Contact:** Curtis Urbina. Record company and music publisher (Quarkette Music/BMI and Freedurb Music/ASCAP). Estab. 1984. Releases 3 singles and 3 LPs/year. Pays negotiable royalty to artists on contract; ³/₄ statutory rate to publisher per song on record.

How to Contact Prefers CD with 2 songs (max). Include SASE. "Must be an absolute 'hit' song!" Responds in 6 weeks.

Music House music only.

☑ ◻ RADICAL RECORDS

77 Bleecker St., Suite C2-21, New York NY 10012. (212)475-1111. Fax: (212)475-3676. E-mail: info@radicalrecords.com. Web site: www.radicalrecords.com. **Contact:** Bryan Mechutano. Record company. "We also do independent retail distribution for punk, hardcore music." Estab. 1986. Staff size: 7. Releases 1 single and 6 CDs/year. Pays 14% royalty to artists on contract; statutory rate to publisher per song on record.

Distributed by City Hall, Revelation, Select-O-Hits, Choke. Southern, Carrot Top, and other indie distributors.

How to Contact *E-mail first for permission to submit demo.* Prefers CD. Does not return material. Responds in 1 month.

Music Mostly **punk**, **hardcore**, **glam** and **rock**. Released *New York City Rock N Roll* (compilation album featuring 22 NYC bands); *Too Legit for the Pit—Hardcore Takes the Rap* (compilation album), recorded by various; *Punk's Not Dead—A Tribute to the Exploited* (compilation album), recorded by various; *East Coast of Oi!* (compilation album), recorded by various; *Ramones Forever* (compilation album), recorded by various; *Sex Pistols Tribute—Never Mind The Sex Pistols, Here's The Tribute* (compilation album), recorded by various; and *3 volumes of OI!/Skampilation* (compilation albums, recorded by various shi and oi! punk bands. Artists include Sex Slaves, 5¢ Deposit, Blanks 77, Speadealer, The Agents, Inspector 7 and ICU.

Tips "Create the best possible demos you can and show a past of excellent self-promotion."

◐ RAVE RECORDS, INC.

Attn: Production Dept., 13400 W. Seven Mile Rd., Detroit MI 48235. E-mail: info@raverecords.com. Web site: www.raverecords.com. **Contact:** Carolyn and Derrick, production managers. Record company and music publisher (Magic Brain Music/ASCAP). Estab. 1992. Staff size: 2. Releases 2-4 singles and 2 CDs/year. Pays various royalty to artists on contract; statutory rate to publisher per song on record.

Distributed by Action Music Sales.

How to Contact *"We do not accept unsolicited materials."* Submit demo CD by mail. Prefers CD with 3 songs, lyric sheet. "Include any bios, fact sheets, and press you may have. We will contact you if we need any further information." Does not return materials.

Music Mostly **alternative rock** and **dance**. Artists include Cyber Cryst, Dorothy, Nicole and Bukimi 3.

◐ RAZOR & TIE ENTERTAINMENT

214 Sullivan St., Suite 4A, New York NY 10012. (212)473-9173. E-mail: info@razorandtie.com. Web site: www.razorandtie.com. Record company.

How to Contact *Does not accept unsolicited material.*

Music Released *The Beauty of the Rain* (album) by Dar Williams; *The Sweetheart Collection* by Frankie & The Knockouts; *Everybody's Normal But Me* by Stuttering John; and *Marigold* (album) by Marty Lloyd, all on Razor & Tie Entertainment. Other artists include Graham Parker, Marshall Crenshaw, Sam Champion and Toshi Reagon.

☒ ◐ RCA RECORDS

1540 Broadway, 36th Floor, New York NY 10036. (212)930-4936. Fax: (212)930-4447. Web site: www.rcarecords.com. A&R: Donna Pearce. **Beverly Hills:** 8750 Wilshire Blvd., Beverly Hills CA

90211. (310)358-4105 Fax: (310)358-4127. Senior Vice President of A&R: Jeff Blue. **Nashville:** 1400 18th Ave. S., Nashville TN 37212. A&R Director: Jim Catino. Labels include Loud Records, Deconstruction Records and Judgment/RCA Records. Record company.
Distributed by BMG.
How to Contact *RCA Records does not accept unsolicited submissions.*
Music Artists include The Strokes, Dave Matthews Band, Clay Aiken, Christina Aguilera, and Velvet Revolver.

🌐 🔾 RED ADMIRAL RECORDS
The Cedars, Elvington Lane, Folkestone Kent CT18 7AD United Kingdom. Estab. 1979. (01)(303)893-472. Fax: (01)(303)893-833. E-mail: info@redadmiralrecords.com. Web site: www.re dadmiralrecords.com. **Contact:** Chris Ashman, CEO. Registered members of MCPS, PRS, and PPL. Record company and music publisher (Cringe Music (MCPS/PRS)). Estab. 1979.
How to Contact Submit demo by mail. Unsolicited submissions are OK.Include CD with unlimited number of songs. Responds in 3 months.
Music Mostly **AOR**, **MOR**, and **pop**. Also **soul**, **R&B**, **reggae/ska**. Artists include Rik Waller's Mighty Soul Band, The Sharpee's, Rhythm of Blues.

🔾 REDEMPTION RECORDS
P.O. Box 10238, Beverly Hills CA 90213. E-mail: info@redemption.net. Web site: www.redemption. net. A&R Czar: Ryan D. Kuper (indie rock, power pop, rock, etc.). Record company. Estab. 1990. Staff size: varies. Releases 2-3 singles, 2-3 EPs and 2-3 CDs/year. Pays standard royalty to artists on contract; statutory rate to publisher per song on record.
Distributed by Navarre and others.
How to Contact Does not accept unsolicited material. *E-mail to obtain permission to submit.* Submit demo CD by mail or send mp3 link by e-mail. "Include band's or artist's goals." Does not return material. Responds only if interested.
Music Mostly **indie rock** and **power pop**. Artists include Vicious Vicious, The Working Title, Race For Titles, Schatzi, Motion City Soundtrack, Nolan, and the Redemption Versus Series featuring indie rock bands from different geographical locations.
Tips "Be prepared to tour to support the release. Make sure the current line-up is secure."

⊘ REPRISE RECORDS
3300 Warner Blvd., 4th Floor, Burbank CA 91505. (818)846-9090. Fax: (818)840-2389. Web site: www.repriserecords.com. Labels include Duck and Sire. Record company.
Distributed by WEA.
How to Contact *Reprise Records does not accept unsolicited submissions.*
Music Artists include Eric Clapton, Guster, Josh Groban, The Distillers, and Neil Young.

☑ ROBBINS ENTERTAINMENT LLC
159 W. 25th St., 4th Floor, New York NY 10001. (212)675-4321. Fax: (212)675-4441. E-mail: info@r obbinsent.com. Web site: www.robbinsent.com. **Contact:** John Parker, vice president, A&R/dance promotion. Record company and music publisher (Rocks, No Salt). Estab. 1996. Staff size: 8. Releases 25 singles and 12-14 CDs/year. Pays negotiable royalty to artists on contract; statutory rate to publisher per song on record.
Distributed by BMG.
How to Contact Accepts unsolicited demos as long as it's dance music. Prefers CD with 2 songs or less. "Make sure everything is labeled with the song title information and our contact information. t his is important in case the CD and the jewel case get separated. Do not call us and ask if you can send your package. The answer is yes."
Music Commercial **dance** only. Released top 10 pop smashes, "Heaven" (single), recorded by DJ Sammy; "Everytime We Touch" (single), recorded by Cascada; "Listen To Your Heart" (single), recorded by DHT; as well as Hot 100 records from Rockell, Lasgo, Reina and K5. Other artists include Ian Van Dahl, Andain, Judy Torres, Marly, Dee Dee, Milky, Kreo and many others.

Tips "Do not send your package 'Supreme-Overnight-Before-You-Wake-Up' delivery. Save yourself some money. Do not send material if you are going to state in your letter that, 'If I had more (fill in the blank) it would sound better.' We are interested in hearing your best and only your best. Do not call us and ask if you can send your package. The answer is yes. We are looking for dance music with crossover potential."

☐ ROLL ON RECORDS®

112 Widmar Pl., Clayton CA 94517. (925)833-4680. E-mail: rollonrecords@aol.com. **Contact:** Edgar J. Brincat, owner. Record company and music publisher (California Country Music). Estab. 1985. Pays 10% royalty to artists on contract; statutory rate to publisher per song on record. Member of Harry Fox Agency.
Distributed by Tower.
How to Contact Submit demo CD by mail. Unsolicited submissions are OK. "Do not call or write for permission to submit, if you do you will be rejected." Prefers CD or cassette with 3 songs and lyric sheet. Include SASE and phone number. Responds in 6 weeks.
Music Mostly **contemporary/country** and **modern gospel**. Released "Broken Record" (single by Horace Linsley/Dianne Baumgartner), recorded by Edee Gordon on Roll On Records; *Maddy* and *For Realities Sake* (albums both by F.L. Pittman/Madonna Weeks), recorded by Ron Banks/L.J. Reynolds on Life Records/Bellmark Records.
Tips "Be patient and prepare to be in it for the long haul. A successful songwriter does not happen overnight. It's rare to write a song today and have a hit tomorrow. If you give us your song and want it back, then don't give it to us to begin with."

☑ ☐ ROTTEN RECORDS

Attn: A&R Dept., P.O. Box 56, Upland CA 91786. E-mail: rotten@rottenrecords.com. Web site: www.rottenrecords.com. President: Ron Peterson. Promotions/Radio/Video: Andi Jones. Record company. Estab. 1988. Releases 3 LPs, 3 EPs and 3 CDs/year.
Distributed by RIOT (Australia), Sonic Rendezvous (NL), RED (US) and PHD (Canada).
How to Contact Submit demo by mail. Unsolicited submissions are OK. Prefers CD. Does not return material.
Music Mostly **rock**, **alternative** and **commercial**; also **punk** and **heavy metal**. Released *Paegan Terrorism* (album), written and recorded by Acid Bath; *Kiss the Clown* (album by K. Donivon), recorded by Kiss the Clown; and *Full Speed Ahead* (album by Cassidy/Brecht), recorded by D.R.T., all on Rotten Records.
Tips "Be patient."

☑ RUSTIC RECORDS

6337 Murray Lane, Brentwood TN 37027. (615)371-0646. Fax: (615)370-0353. E-mail: rusticrecordsinc@aol.com. Web site: www.rusticrecordsinc.com. President: Jack Schneider. Office Manager: Nell Schneider. Traditional country independent music record label and music publisher (Iron Skillet Music/ASCAP, Covered Bridge/ BMI, Town Square/SESAC). Estab. 1979. Staff size: 3. Releases 2-3 albums/year. Pays negotiable royalty to artists on contract; statutory royalty to publisher per song on record.
   • Also see the listings for Rustic Records, Inc. Publishers in the Music Publishers section of this book.
Distributed by CDBaby.com, BathtubMusic.com and available on iTunes, MSN Music, Rhapsody, and more.
How to Contact Submit professional demo by mail. Unsolicited submissions are OK. Prefers CD or cassette; no mp3s or e-mails. Include no more than 3-4 songs with corresponding lyric sheets and a cover letter. Include appropriately-sized SASE. Responds in 6-8 weeks.
Music Mostly **traditional country**, **novelty**, and **old-time gospel**. 2005 releases include "Drankin Business" (single from Colte Bradley); "Love Don't Even Know My Name" (single) from Beckey Burr's debut album; and "Was It Good for You" (single) from Lloyd Knight's upcoming album.
Tips "Submit a professional demo."

☐ RUSTRON-WHIMSONG MUSIC PRODUCTIONS

1156 Park Lane, West Palm Beach FL 33417-5957. (561)686-1354. E-mail: rmp_wmp@bellsouth.net. **Contact:** Sheelah Adams, office administrator. Executive Director: Rusty Gordon (folk fusions, blues, women's music, adult contemporary, electric, acoustic, New Age instrumentals, children's, cabaret, pop ballads). Director A&R: Ron Caruso (all styles). Associate Director of A&R: Kevin Reeves (pop, country, blues, R&B, jazz, folk). Labels include Rustron Records and Whimsong Records. "Rustron administers 20 independent labels for publishing and marketing." Record company, record producer, management firm and music publisher (Whimsong Music Publishing/ASCAP and Rustron Music Publishing/BMI). Estab. 1970. Releases 5-10 CDs/year. Pays variable royalty to artists on contract. "Artists with history of product sales get higher percent than those with no sales track record." Pays statutory rate to publisher.

How to Contact *Songwriters may write or call first to discuss your submission.* You may send a snail-mail request for current submission guidelines. Include a SASE or International Response Coupon (IRC) for all correspondence, including sending submissions. No Exceptions. E-mail gets the quickest response. Song submissions should include a cover letter that explains why you are submitting and what type of review you want. You may want a combined publishing and record company review. If your songs are already published, let us know what publishing company you signed with. Tell us about your intentions for the future and if you are a performing or a freelance songwriter. Tell us if you are collaborating on some or all of your songs. All songwriters who creatively contributed to a song must sign the cover letter authorizing the review. Copyrighting the songs in your submission with The U.S. Library of Congress is essential before sending them to us. We do not review uncopyrighted original songs. Songwriter's must officially own the exclusive rights to their songs by copyrighting them. As soon as you have mailed the Copyright Form PA to the Library of Congress, the songs are "Copyright Pending," and you can send them. Submit 1 CD or several CDs, requesting a "body of work review" by snail-mail. You may present up to 15 songs on each CD you submit. Unsolicited submissions are OK. We prefer a CD with up to 15 songs and typed 8½ X 11 lyric sheets, one song per sheet. Cassettes are limited to 3 songs. Responds in 4 months.

Music Mostly **mainstream** and **women's music, adult contemporary electric acoustic, pop (cabaret, blues)** and **blues (R&B, country and folk)**; also **soft rock** (ballads), **New Age fusions** (instrumentals), **modern folk fusions** (environmental, socio-political), **children's music** and **light jazz.** Released "Hurricane Harassment" (single) from *Hurricane Harassment* (album), written and recorded by Continental Divide (topical), released 2006 on Rustron Records; "The Baobab Tree and Me" (single) from *The Baobab Tree* (album) written and recorded by Tracie Mitchell & Ivory Coast (folk rock), released 2005 on Whimsong Records; "Resisting The Right" (single) from *Resisting The Right* (album), written and recorded by The Florida Rank & File (socio-political) released 2006 on Rustron Records.

Tips "Find your own unique style; write well crafted songs with unpredictable concepts, strong hooks and definitive verse melody. New Age composers: evolve your themes and add multi-cultural diversity with instruments. Don't be predictable. Don't over-produce your demos and don't drown vocals. Carefully craft songs for single-song marketing. An album can have 9 eclectic songs that are loosely crafted and not very commercially viable individually. It takes only one carefully crafted 'radio ready' song with the right arrangement to get your album the exposure it needs."

☒ ⊘ SAHARA RECORDS AND FILMWORKS ENTERTAINMENT

28 E. Jackson Bldg., 10th Floor #S627, Chicago IL 60604-2263. (773)509-6381. Fax: (312)922-6964. Web site: www.edmsahara.com. **Contact:** Edward De Miles, president. Record company, music publisher (EDM Music/BMI, Edward De Miles Music Company) and record producer (Edward De Miles). Estab. 1981. Releases 15-20 CD singles and 5-10 CDs/year. Pays 9½-11% royalty to artists on contract; statutory rate to publishers per song on record.

How to Contact *Does not accept unsolicited submissions.*

Music Mostly **R&B/dance, top 40 pop/rock** and **contemporary jazz**; also **TV-film themes, musical scores** and **jingles.** Released "Hooked on U," "Dance Wit Me" and "Moments" (singles), written and recorded by Steve Lynn (R&B) on Sahara Records. Other artists include Lost in Wonder, Dvon Edwards and Multiple Choice.

Tips ''We're looking for strong mainstream material. Lyrics and melodies with good hooks that grab people's attention.''

☑ ⊘ SALEXO MUSIC

P.O. Box 18093, Charlotte NC 28218-0093. (704)563-8775. E-mail: salexo@bellsouth.net. **Contact:** Samuel Obie, president. Record company. Estab. 1992. Releases 1 CD/year.
How to Contact *Write first and obtain permission to submit.*
Music Mostly **contemporary gospel** and **jazz**. Released *A Joyful Noise* (album), recorded by Samuel Obie with J.H. Walker Unity Choir (gospel), released 2003, Macedonia Baptist Church; and ''Favor'' (single) from *Favor*, written and recorded by Samuel Obie (contemporary gospel), released 2004 on Salexo Music.
Tips ''Make initial investment in the best production.''

◻ SANDALPHON RECORDS

P.O. Box 29110, Portland OR 97296. (503)957-3929. E-mail: jackrabbit01@sprintpcs.com. **Contact:** Ruth Otey, president. Record company, music publisher (Sandalphon Music/BMI), and management agency (Sandalphon Management). Estab. 2005. Staff size: 2. Pays negotiable royalty to artists on contract; statutory royalty to publisher per song on record.
Distributed by ''We are negotiating for a distributor.''
How to Contact Submit demo by mail. Unsolicited submissions are OK. Prefers cassette or CD with 1-5 songs with lyric sheet and cover letter. Returns submissions if accompanied by a SASE or SAE and IRC for outside the United States. Responds in 1 month.
Music Mostly **rock**, **country**, and **alternative**; also **pop**, **gospel**, and **blues**.

⊘ SILVER WAVE RECORDS

P.O. Box 7943, Boulder CO 80306. (303)443-5617. Fax: (303)443-0877. E-mail: info@silverwave.c om. Web site: www.silverwave.com. **Contact:** James Marienthal. Record company. Estab. 1986. Releases 3-4 CDs/year. Pays varying royalty to artists on contract and to publisher per song on record.
How to Contact *Call first and obtain permission to submit.* Prefers CD. Include SASE. Responds only if interested.
Music Mostly **Native American** and **world**.

Ⓝ ⊘ SILVERTONE RECORDS

137-139 W. 25th St., New York NY 10001. (212)727-0016. Fax: (212)620-0048. Label Director: Michael Tedesco. Hollywood office: 9000 Sunset Blvd., Suite 300, W. Hollywood CA 90069 Fax:(213)247-8366. Labels include Essential Records. Record company.
Distributed by BMG.
How to Contact *Does not accept unsolicited materials.* ''Contact us through management or an attorney.''
Music Released *Jars of Clay* (album), recorded by Jars of Clay on Essential Records. Other artists include Chris Duarte, Buddy Guy, Hed, Livingstone, John Mayall, Metal Molly and Solar Race.

⊘ SMALL STONE RECORDS

P.O. Box 02007, Detroit MI 48202. (248)219-2613. Fax: (248)541-6536 E-mail: sstone@smallstone.c om. Web site: www.smallstone.com. **Owner:** Scott Hamilton. Record company. Estab. 1995. Staff size: 1. Releases 2 singles, 2 EPs and 10 CDs/year. Pays negotiable royalty to artists on contract; statutory rate to publisher per song on record.
Distributed by AEC, Allegro/Nail.
How to Contact Submit CD/CD Rom by mail. Unsolicited submissions are OK. Does not return material. Responds in 2 months.
Music Mostly **alternative**, **rock** and **blues**; also **funk (not R&B)**. Released *Fat Black Pussy Cat*, written and recorded by Five Horse Johnson (rock/blues); *Wrecked & Remixed*, written and recorded by Morsel (indie rock, electronica); and *Only One Division*, written and recorded by Soul

Clique (electronica), all on Small Stone Records. Other artists include Acid King, Perplexa, and Novadriver.

Tips "Looking for esoteric music along the lines of Bill Laswell to Touch & Go/Thrill Jockey records material. Only send along material if it makes sense with what we do. Perhaps owning some of our records would help."

☐ SOLANA RECORDS
2440 Great Highway, #5, San Francisco CA 94116. (415)566-0411. E-mail: info@solanarecords.com. Web site: www.solanarecords.com. **Contact:** Eric Friedmann, president. Record company, music publisher (Neato Bandito Music) and record producer (Eric Friedmann). Estab. 1992. Staff size: 1. Releases 1 single and 2 CDs/year. Pays negotiable royalty to artists on contract; statutory rate to publisher per song on record.

How to Contact Submit demo by mail but please e-mail permissions first. Prefers CD with 3-5 songs, photo and cover letter. Include SASE. Responds in 1 month.

Music Mostly any kind of guitar/vocal-based **rock/pop** and **country**. Does not want rap, hip-hop. Released *Spacious* (by Valerie Moorhead), recorded by Enda (alternative rock); *Livin' the High Life* (by James Cook), recorded by The Wags (yardcore); and *The Grain* (by Rick Ordin), recorded by The Grain (progressive rock). *To Hell with the Road*; *Live at the Sandbox*, recorded b Delectric (Skiffle).Other artists include The Detonators, Eric Friedman and the Lucky Rubes, The Mudkats, Emily Hickey, and Doormouse.

Tips "Be honest and genuine. Know how to write a good song, and know how to sing. Don't send my your résumé or life story please. Big bonus points for Telecaster players."

☒ ☐ SONIC UNYON RECORDS CANADA
P.O. Box 57347, Jackson Station, Hamilton ON L8P 4X2 Canada. (905)777-1223. Fax: (905)777-1161. E-mail: jerks@sonicunyon.com. Web site: www.sonicunyon.com. Co-owners: Tim Potocic; Mark Milne. Record company. Estab. 1992. Releases 2 singles, 2 EPs and 6-10 CDs/year. Pays negotiable royalty to artists on contract; statutory rate to publisher per song on record.

Distributed by Caroline Distribution.

How to Contact *Call first and obtain permission to submit.* Prefers cassette or CD. "Research our company before you send your demo. We are small; don't waste my time and your money." Does not return material. Responds in 4 months.

Music Mostly **rock**, **heavy rock** and **pop rock**. Released *Doberman* (album), written and recorded by Kittens (heavy rock); *What A Life* (album), written and recorded by Smoother; and *New Grand* (album), written and recorded by New Grand on sonic unyon records (pop/rock). Other artists include Tricky Woo, Danko Jones, Crooked Fingers, Frank Black and the Catholics, Jesus Lizard, Chore, Sectorseven, The Dirtmitts, Sianspheric, gorp, Hayden and Poledo.

Tips "Know what we are about. Research us. Know we are a small company. Know signing to us doesn't mean that everything will fall into your lap. We are only the beginning of an artist's career."

☑ SONY MUSIC
550 Madison Ave., New York NY 10022. Web site: www.sonymusic.com.

How to Contact *For specific contact information see the listings in this section for Sony subsidiaries Columbia Records, Epic Records and Sony Nashville.*

☑ SONY MUSIC NASHVILLE
34 Music Square E., Nashville TN 37203. (615)742-4321. Labels include Columbia, Epic, Lucky Dog Records, Monument.

How to Contact *Sony Music Nashville does not accept unsolicited submissions.*

☑ SOUND GEMS
P.O. Box 801, Southeastern PA 19399. Web site: www.soundgems.com. CEO: Frank Fioravanti. A&R Director: Trish Wassel. Record company and music publisher (Melomega Music, Meloman

Music). Estab. 1972. Staff size: 3. Pays negotiable royalty to artists on contract; statutory rate to publisher per song on record.

Distributed by EMI, Sony, Warner.

How to Contact Submit demo by mail. Unsolicited submissions are OK. Prefers cassette, CD with lyric sheet, cover letter and press clipping. "Do not send registered or certified mail. Your contact details (full name, address, telephone, email, Web site etc) should be printed onto the CD as well as any documentation just in case the two are separated" Does not return material. Responds only if interested.

Music R&B only. Released "Be Thankful" (single by William Devaughn) from *Bones* (soundtrack album), recorded by William DeVaughn (r&b), released 2001 on PRI; and "Limo Dream" (single by Hopkins/Rakes/Fioravanti), recorded by Corey (r&b), released 2001 on Sound Gems; and "Girl I Wanna Take You Home" (single by Rueben Cross), recorded by Corey Wims (R&B/neo-soul), released 2002 on Sound Gems.

Tips "Be sure your style fits our catagory. Submit R&B material only."

☑ SUGAR HILL RECORDS

P.O. Box 55300, Durham NC 27717-5300. E-mail: info@sugarhillrecords.com. Record company. Estab. 1978.

- Welk Music Group acquired Sugar Hill Records in 1998.

How to Contact *No unsolicited submissions*. "If you are interested in having your music heard by Sugar Hill Records or the Welk Music Group, we suggest you establish a relationship with a manager, publisher, or attorney that has an ongoing relationship with our company. We do not have a list of such entities."

Music Mostly **Americana**, **bluegrass**, and **country**. Artists include Nickel Creek, Allison Moorer, The Duhks, Sonny Landreth, Scott Miller, Reckless Kelly, Tim O'Brien, The Gibson Brothers, and more.

ℕ ☑ SURFACE RECORDS

8377 Westview, Houston TX 77055. (713)464-4653. Fax: (713)464-2622. E-mail: jeffwells@soundar tsrecording.com. Web site: www.soundartsrecording.com. **Contact:** Jeff Wells, president. A&R: Peter Verkerk. Record company, music publisher (Earthscream Music Publishing Co./BMI) and record producer (Jeff Wells). Estab. 1996. Releases 4 CDs/year. Pays negotiable royalty to artists on contract; statutory rate to publisher per song on record.

Distributed by Earth Records.

How to Contact Submit demo by mail. Unsolicited submissions are OK. Prefers cassette or CD with 4 songs and lyric sheet. Does not return material. Responds in 6 weeks.

Music Mostly country, blues and pop/rock. Released *Everest* (album), recorded by The Jinkies; Joe "King" Carrasco (album), recorded by Joe "King" Carrasco; *Perfect Strangers* (album), recorded by Perfect Strangers, all on Surface Records (pop); and "Sherly Crow" (single) recorded by Dr. Jeff and the Painkillers. Other artists include Rosebud.

☐ TANGENT® RECORDS

P.O. Box 383, Reynoldsburg OH 43068-0383. (614)751-1962. Fax: (614)751-6414. E-mail: info@tang entrecords.com. Web site: www.tangentrecords.com. **Contact:** Andrew Batchelor, president. Director of Marketing: Elisa Batchelor. Record company and music publisher (ArcTangent Music/BMI). Estab. 1986. Staff size: 3. Releases 10-12 CDs/year. Pays negotiable royalty to artists on contract; statutory rate to publisher per song on record.

How to Contact Submit demo or CD by mail. Unsolicited submissions are OK. Prefers CD, with minimum of 3 songs and lead sheet if available. "Please include a brief biography/history of artist(s) and/or band, including musical training/education, performance experience, recording studio experience, discography and photos (if available)." Does not return material. Responds in 3 months.

Music Mostly **artrock** and **contemporary instrumental/rock instrumental**; also **contemporary classical**, **world beat**, **jazz/rock**, **ambient**, **electronic**, and **New Age**.

Tips "Take the time to pull together a quality CD or cassette demo with package/portfolio, including such relevant information as experience (on stage and in studio, etc.), education/training, biography, career goals, discography, photos, etc. Should be typed. We are *not* interested in generic sounding or 'straight ahead' music. We are seeking music that is innovative, pioneering and eclectic with a fresh, unique sound.''

☑ ☑ TEXAS ROSE RECORDS

2002 Platinum St., Garland TX 75042. (972)272-3131. Fax: (972)272-3155. E-mail: txrr1@aol.com. Web site: www.texasroserecords.com. **Contact:** Nancy Baxendale, president. Record company, music publisher (Yellow Rose of Texas Publishing) and record producer (Nancy Baxendale). Estab. 1994. Staff size: 3. Releases 3 CDs/year. Pays negotiable royalty to artists on contract; statutory rate to publisher per song on record.

Distributed by Self distribution.

How to Contact *Call, write or e-mail first for permission to submit.* Submit maximum of 2 songs on CD and lyrics. Does not return material. Responds only if interested.

Music Mostly **country**, **soft rock** and **blues**; also **pop** and **gospel**. Does not want hip-hop, rap, heavy metal. Released *Flyin' High Over Texas* (album), recorded by Dust Martin (country); *High On The Hog* (album), recorded by Steve Harr (country); *Time For Time to Pay* (album), recorded by Jeff Elliot (country); and *Pendulum Dream* (album), written and recorded by Maureen Kelly (alternative/americana), and ''Cowboy Super Hero'' (single) written and recorded by Robert Mauldin.

Tips ''We are interested in songs written for today's market with a strong hook. Always use a good vocalist.''

☑ TOMMY BOY RECORDS

120 Fifth Avenue, 7th Floor, New York NY 10011. (212)388-8300. Fax: (212)388-8431. E-mail: info@tommyboy.com. Web site: www.tommyboy.com. Record company. Labels include Penalty Recordings, Outcaste Records, Timber and Tommy Boy Gospel.

Distributed by WEA.

How to Contact *Call to obtain current demo submission policy.*

Music Artists include Chavela Vargas, Afrika Bambaataa, Biz Markie, Kool Keith, and INXS.

☐ TON RECORDS

4474 Rosewood Ave., Los Angeles CA 90004. E-mail: tonmusic@earthlink.net. Web site: www.tonr ecords.com. Vice President: Jay Vasquez. Labels include 7'' collectors series and Ton Special Projects. Record company and record producer (RJ Vasquez). Estab. 1992. Releases 6-9 LPs, 1-2 EPs and 10-11 CDs/year. Pays negotiable royalty to artists on contract; statutory rate to publisher per song on record.

Distributed by MS, Com Four, Rotz, Subterranean, Revelation, Get Hip, Impact, Page Canada and Disco Dial.

How to Contact Submit demo by mail. Unsolicited submissions are OK. Prefers cassette or CD. Include SASE. Responds in 1 month.

Music Mostly **new music**; also **hard new music**. Released *Intoxicated Birthday Lies*, recorded by shoegazer (punk rock); *The Good Times R Killing Me*, recorded by Top Jimmy (blues); and *Beyond Repair*, recorded by Vasoline Tuner (space rock), all on Ton Records. Other artists include Why? things burn, Hungry 5 and the Ramblers.

Tips ''Work as hard as we do.''

☑ TOPCAT RECORDS

P.O. Box 670234, Dallas TX 75367. (972)484-4141. Fax: (972)620-8333. E-mail: info@topcatrecords. com. Web site: www.topcatrecords.com. President: Richard Chalk. Record company and record producer. Estab. 1991. Staff size: 3. Releases 4-6 CDs/year. Pays 10-15% royalty to artists on contract; statutory rate to publisher per song on record.

Distributed by City Hall.

How to Contact *Call first and obtain permission to submit.* Prefers CD. Does not return material. Responds in 1 month.

Music Mostly **blues**, **swing** and **R&B**. Released *If You Need Me* (album), written and recorded by Robert Ealey (blues); *Texas Blueswomen* (album by 3 Female Singers), recorded by various (blues/R&B); and *Jungle Jane* (album), written and recorded by Holland K. Smith (blues/swing), all on Topcat. Released CDs: *Jim Suhler & Alan Haynes—Live*; Bob Kirkpatrick *Drive Across Texas; Rock My Blues to Sleep* by Johnny Nicholas; *Walking Heart Attack*, by Holland K. Smith; *Dirt Road* (album), recorded by Jim Suhler; *Josh Alan Band* (album), recorded by Josh Alan; *Bust Out* (album), recorded by Robin Sylar. Other artists include Grant Cook, Muddy Waters, Big Mama Thornton, Big Joe Turner, Geo. "Harmonica" Smith, J.B. Hutto and Bee Houston.

Tips "Send me blues (fast, slow, happy, sad, etc.) or good blues oriented R&B. No pop, hip-hop, or rap."

☑ TRANSDREAMER RECORDS

P.O. Box 1955, New York NY 10113. (212)741-8861. E-mail: gregaforce@aol.com. Web site: www.transdreamer.com. **Contact:** Greg Caputo, marketing savant. President: Robert John. Record company. Estab. 2002. Staff size: 5. Released 4 CDs/year. Pays negotiable rate to artists on contract; 3/4 statutory rate to publisher per song on record.

  ● Also see the listing for Megaforce in this section of the book.

Distributed by Red/Sony.

How to Contact *Contact first and obtain permission to submit.*

Music Mostly **alternative/rock**. Artists include The Delgados, Arab Strap, Dressy Bessy, Bill Richini, and Wellwater Conspiracy.

☑ TVT RECORDS

A&R Dept. 23 E. Fourth St., 3rd Floor, New York NY 10003. Web site: www.tvtrecords.com. **Contact:** A&R. Labels include Tee Vee Toons, TVT Soundtrax, 1001 Sundays. Record company and music publisher (TVT Music). Estab. 1986. Releases 25 singles, 20 12" singles, 40 LPs, 5 EPs and 40 CDs/year. Pays varying royalty to artists on contract; statutory rate to publisher per song on record.

How to Contact Send e-mail to demo-help@tvtrecords.com to receive information on how to submit your demo.

Music Mostly **alternative rock**, **rap** and **techno**; also **jazz/R&B**. Released *Home*, recorded by Sevendust; *Hoopla*, recorded by Speeches; and *Retarder*, recorded by The Unband.

Tips "We look for seminal, ground breaking, genre-defining artists of all types with compelling live presentation. Our quest is not for hit singles but for enduring important artists."

ℕ ☐ 28 RECORDS

4571 Haskell Ave., Suite 8, Encino CA 91436. E-mail: rec28@aol.com. **Contact:** Eric Diaz, president/CEO/A&R. Record company. Estab. 1994. Staff size: 1. Releases 2 LPs and 4 CDs/year. Pays 12% royalty to artists on contract; statutory rate to publisher per song on record.

Distributed by Rock Bottom-USA.

How to Contact *Contact first and obtain permission to submit.* Submit demo by mail. Unsolicited submissions are OK. Prefers cassette, VHS videocassette or CD (if already released on own label for possible distribution or licensing deals). If possible send promo pack and photo. "Please put Attn: A&R on packages." Does not return material. Responds in 6 weeks.

Music Mostly **hard rock/modern rock**, **metal** and **alternative**; also **punk** and **death metal**. Released *Julian Day* (album), recorded by Helltown's Infamous Vandal (modern/hard rock); *Fractured Fairy Tales* (album), written and recorded by Eric Knight (modern/hard rock); and *Mantra*, recorded by Derek Cintron (modern rock), all on 28 Records.

Tips "Be patient and ready for the long haul. We strongly believe in nurturing you, the artist/songwriter. If you're willing to do what it takes, and have what it takes, we will do whatever it takes to get you to the next level. We are looking for artists to develop. We are a very small label but we are giving the attention that is a must for a new band as well as developed and established acts. Give us a call."

☐ UAR RECORDS (Universal-Athena Records)

Box 1264, 6020 W. Pottstown Rd., Peoria IL 61654-1264. (309)673-5755. Fax: (309)673-7636. E-mail: uarltd@A5.com. Web site: www.unitedcyber.com. **Contact:** Jerry Hanlon, A&R director. Record company and music publisher (Jerjoy Music/BMI and Kaysarah Music/ASCAP). Estab. 1978. Staff size: 3. Releases 3 or more CDs/year.

- Also see the listings for Kaysarah Music (ASCAP) and Jerjoy Music (BMI) in the Music Publishers section of this book.

How to Contact "If you are an artist seeking a record deal, please send a sample of your vocal and/or songwriting work—guitar and vocal is fine, no more than 4 songs. Fully produced demos are NOT necessary. Also send brief information on your background in the business, your goals, etc. If you are NOT a songwriter, please send 4 songs maximum of cover tunes that we can use to evaluate your vocal ability. If you wish a reply, please send a SASE, otherwise, you will not receive an answer. If you want a critique of your vocal abilities, please so state as we DO NOT offer critiques. Unsolicited submissions are OK. If you wish all of your material returned to you, be sure to include mailing materials and postage. WE DO NOT RETURN PHONE CALLS."

Music Mostly **country**. Released "Kingdom I Call Home," "We Could" (counry), recorded by Danny Blakey; "Millionaires in Love" and "Since I've Found You" (country and religious), recorded by Micah Spayer; "For Old Loves Sake" recorded by new artist Melanie Hiatt.

Tips "We are a small independent company, but our belief is that every good voice deserves a chance to be heard and our door is always open to new and aspiring artists."

⊘ UNIVERSAL RECORDS

1755 Broadway, 7th Floor, New York NY 10019. (212)373-0600. Fax: (212)373-0726. Web site: www.universalrecords.com. Universal City office: 70 Universal City Plaza, 3rd Floor, Universal City CA 91608. (818)777-1000. Vice Presidents A&R: Bruce Carbone, Tse Williams. Labels include Uptown Records, Mojo Records, Republic Records, Bystorm Records and Gut Reaction Records. Record company.

- As a result of the 1998 PolyGram and Universal merger, Universal is the world's largest record company.

How to Contact *Universal Records in California does not accept unsolicited submissions.* The New York office *only* allows you to call first and obtain permission to submit.

Music Artists include India Arie, Erykah Bad, Godsmack, Kaiser Chiefs, and Lindsey Lohan.

Ⓝ ⊘ VALTEC PRODUCTIONS

721 E. main St., #206, Santa Maria CA 93454. (805)928-8559. E-mail: info@valtec.net. Web site: www.valtec.net. **Contact:** J. Andersonand J. Valenta, owner/producers. Record company and record producer (Joe Valenta). Estab. 1986. Releases 20 singles, 15 LPs and 10 CDs/year. Pays negotiable royalty to artists on contract; statutory rate to publisher per song on record.

How to Contact Submit demo by mail. Unsolicited submissions are OK. Prefers DAT with 4 songs and lyric sheet. Does not return material. Responds in 2 months.

Music Mostly **country, top 40** and **A/C**; also **rock**. Released *Just Me* (album by Joe Valenta) and *Hold On* (album by Joe Valenta/J. Anderson), both recorded by Joe Valenta (top 40); and *Time Out (For Love)* (album by Joe Valenta), recorded by Marty K. (country), all on Valtec Records.

Ⓥ ⊘ THE VERVE MUSIC GROUP

1755 Broadway, 3rd Floor, New York NY 10019. (212)331-2000. Fax: (212)331-2064. Web site: www.vervemusicgroup.com. A&R Director: Dahlia Ambach. A&R Coordinator: Heather Buchanan. **Los Angeles:** 100 N. First St., Burbank CA 91502. (818)729-4804 Fax: (818)845-2564. Vice President A&R: Bud Harner. A&R Assistant: Heather Buchanan. Record company. Labels include Verve, GRP, Blue Thumb and Impulse! Records.

• Verve's Diana Krall won a 1999 Grammy Award for Best Jazz Vocal Performance; Wayne Shorter won Best Jazz Instrumental Solo; and the Charlie Haden Quartet West won Best Instrumental Arrangement with Vocals.

How to Contact *The Verve Music Group* does not accept unsolicited submissions.

Music Artists include Roy Hargrove, Diana Krall, George Benson, Al Jarreau, John Scofield, Natalie Cole, David Sanborn.

☑ ✺ VIDEO ARTISTS INTERNATIONAL DISTRIBUTION

(formerly VAI Distribution), 109 Wheeler Ave., Pleasantville NY 10570. 1-800-477-7146 or (914)769-3691. Fax: (914)769-5407. E-mail: inquiries@vaimusic.com. Web site: www.vaimusic.com. President: Ernest Gilbert. Record company, video label and distributor. Estab. 1983. Pays negotiable royalty to artists on contract; other amount to publisher per song on record.

How to Contact *Does not accept unsolicited material.*

Music Mostly **opera (classical vocal)**, **classical (orchestral)** and **classical instrumental/piano**. Released *Susannah* (album by Carlisle Floyd), recorded by New Orleans Opera Orchestra and Chorus, on VAI Audio. Other artists include Jon Vickers, Rosalyn Tureck, Evelyn Lear and Thomas Stewart.

✺ VIRGIN RECORDS

5750 Wilshire Blvd., Los Angeles CA 90036. (323)692-1100. Fax: (310)278-6231. Web site: www.virginrecords.com. New York office: 150 5th Ave., 3rd Floor, New York NY 10016. (212)786-8200 Fax:(212)786-8343. Labels include Rap-A-Lot Records, Pointblank Records, SoulPower Records, AWOL Records, Astralwerks Records, Cheeba Sounds and Noo Trybe Records. Record company.

Distributed by EMD.

How to Contact Virgin Records does not accept recorded material or lyrics unless submitted by a reputable industry source. "If your act has received positive press or airplay on prior independent releases, we welcome your written query. Send a letter of introduction accompanied by all pertinent artist information. Do not send a tape until requested. All unsolicited materials will be returned unopened." Artists include Lenny Kravitz, Janet Jackson, Mick Jagger, Nikka Costa, Ben Harper, and Boz Scaggs.

✺ WAREHOUSE CREEK RECORDING CORP.

P.O. Box 102, Franktown, VA 23354. (757)442-6883. E-mail: warehouse@esva.net. Web site: www.warehousecreek.com. President: Billy Sturgis. Record company, music publisher (Bayford Dock Music) and record producer (Billy Sturgis). Estab. 1993. Staff size: 1. Releases 11 singles and 1 CD/year. Pays negotiable royalty to artists on contract; statutory rate to publisher per song on record.

Distributed by City Hall Records.

How to Contact Submit demo by mail. Unsolicited submissions are OK. Prefers cassette, CD, DAT or VHS videocassette with lyric sheet. Does not return material.

Music Mostly **R&B**, **blues** and **gospel**. Released *Greyhound Bus* (album), by Arthur Crudup; *Going Down in Style* (album), by Tim Drummond; and *Something On My Mind* (album), by George Crudup, all released on Warehouse Creek Records (blues).

☒ ✺ WARNER BROS. RECORDS

3300 Warner Blvd., 3rd Floor, Burbank CA 91505. (818)846-9090. Fax: (818)953-3423. Web site: www.wbr.com. **New York:** 75 Rockefeller Plaza, New York NY 10019. (212)275-4500 Fax:(212)275-4596. A&R: James Dowdall, Karl Rybacki. **Nashville:** 20 Music Square E., Nashville TN 37203. (615)748-8000 Fax:(615)214-1567. Labels include American Recordings, Eternal Records, Imago Records, Mute Records, Giant Records, Malpaso Records and Maverick Records. Record company.

Distributed by WEA.

How to Contact *Warner Bros. Records does not accept unsolicited material.* All unsolicited material will be returned unopened. Those interested in having their tapes heard should establish a relationship with a manager, publisher or attorney that has an ongoing relationship with Warner Bros. Records.

Music Released *Van Halen 3* (album), recorded by Van Halen; *Evita* (soundtrack); and *Dizzy Up the Girl* (album), recorded by Goo Goo Dolls, both on Warner Bros. Records. Other artists include Faith Hill, Tom Petty & the Heartbreakers, Jeff Foxworthy, Porno For Pyros, Travis Tritt, Yellowjackets, Bela Fleck and the Flecktones, Al Jarreau, Joshua Redmond, Little Texas and Curtis Mayfield.

N ⊘ WATERDOG MUSIC

(a.k.a. Waterdog Records), 329 W. 18th St., #313, Chicago IL 60616-1120. (312)421-7499. Fax: (312)421-1848. E-mail: waterdog@waterdogmusic.com. Web site: www.waterdogmusic.com. **Contact:** Rob Gillis, label manager. Labels include Whitehouse Records. Record company. Estab. 1991. Staff size: 2. Releases 2 CDs/year. Pays negotiable royalty to artists on contract; statutory rate to publisher per song on record.

Distributed by Big Daddy Music.

How to Contact "Not accepting unsolicited materials, demos at this time. If submission policy changes, it will be posted on our Web site."

Music Mostly **rock** and **pop**. Released *Good Examples of Bad Examples: The Best of Ralph Covert & The Bad Examples, Vol. 2* (album), released 2005. Other artists have included Middle 8, Al Rose & The Transcendos, Kat Parsons, Torben Floor (Carey Ott), MysteryDriver, Joel Frankel, Dean Goldstein & Coin, and Matt Tiegler.

Tips "Ralph Covert's children's music (*Ralph's World*) is released in Disney Sound. We are not looking for any other children's music performers or composers."

✔ ⊕ ⊘ WESTPARK MUSIC—RECORDS, PRODUCTION & PUBLISHING

P.O. Box 260227, Rathenauplatz 4, 50515 Cologne Germany. (49)221 247644. Fax: (49)221 4535846. E-mail: westparkmusic@netcologne.de. Web site: www.westparkmusic.de. **Contact:** Ulli Hetscher. Record company and music publisher. Estab. 1986. Staff size: 3. Releases 10-12 CDs/year.

Distributed by Indigo (Germany), Music & Words (Netherlands), Musik Ver Trieb (Switzerland), Ixthucu (Austria), Resistencia (Spain), Mega Musica (Italy), Digelius (UK, Finland).

How to Contact "*Check Web site first to find out if your music fits into our repertoire.*" Unsolicited submissions are OK. Does not return material.

Music "Check Web site."

Tips "Don't send country, mainstream rock/pop or MOR. Mark your material clearly with brief description first."

✔ ⊘ WINCHESTER RECORDS

25 Troubadour Lane, Berkeley Springs WV 25411. (304)258-9381. E-mail: mccoytroubadour@aol.com. Web site: www.troubadourlounge.com. **Contact:** Jim or Bertha McCoy, owners. Labels include Master Records and Real McCoy Records. Record company, music publisher (Jim McCoy Music, Clear Music, New Edition Music/BMI), record producer (Jim McCoy Productions) and recording studio. Releases 20 singles and 10 LPs/year. Pays standard royalty to artists; statutory rate to publisher for each record sold.

How to Contact *Write first and obtain permission to submit.* Prefers CD with 5-10 songs and lead sheet. Include SASE. Responds in 1 month.

Music Mostly **bluegrass**, **church/religious**, **country**, **folk**, **gospel**, **progressive** and **rock**. Released "Runaway Girl" (single by Earl Howard/Jim McCoy) from *Earl Howard Sings His Heart Out* (album), recorded by Earl Howard (country), released 2002 on Winchester; *Jim McCoy and Friends Remember Ernest Tubb* (album), recorded by Jim McCoy (country), released January 2003 on Winchester; *The Best of Winchester Records* (album), recorded by RileeGray/J.B. Miller/Jim McCoy/ Carroll County (country), released 2002 on Winchester.

⊘ WIND-UP ENTERTAINMENT

72 Madison Ave., 8th Floor, New York NY 10016. (212)251-9665. Web site: www.winduprecords.com. Contact: A&R. Record company. Estab. 1997. Releases 6-7 CDs/year. Pays negotiable royalty to artists on contract; statutory rate to publisher per song on record.

Distributed by BMG.

How to Contact *Write first and obtain permission to submit.* Prefers cassette, CD, DAT or videocassette. Does not return material or respond to submissions.

Music Mostly **rock**, **folk** and **hard rock**. Artists include Seether, Scott Stapp, Evanescence, and People In Planes.

Tips "We rarely look for songwriters as opposed to bands, so writing a big hit single would be the rule of the day."

⊘ WORD RECORDS & MUSIC

25 Music Square W, Nashville TN 37203. Web site: www.wordrecords.com. Record company.

Distributed by Epic/Sony.

How to Contact *Word Records does not accept unsolicited submissions.*

Music Released *Blaze*, recorded by Code of Ethics; *Steady On*, recorded by Point of Grace; and *Past the Edges*, recorded by Chris Rice, all on Word. Other artists include Amy Grant, Building 429, and Sixpence None The Richer

☑ ⬚ WORLD BEATNIK RECORDS

20 Amity Lane, Rockwall TX 75087. (972) 771-3797. Fax: (972)771-0853. E-mail: tropikal@juno.com. Web site: www.tropikalproductions.com/label.html. Producers: J. Towry (world beat, reggae, ethnic, jazz); Jimbe (reggae, world beat, ethnic); Arik Towry (ska, pop, ragga, rock). Labels include World Beatnik Records. Record company and record producer (Jimi Towry). Estab. 1983. Staff size: 4. Releases 6 singles, 6 LPs, 6 EPs and 6 CDs/year. Pays negotiable royalty to artists on contract; statutory rate to publisher per song on record.

Distributed by Midwest Records, Southwest Wholesale, Reggae OneLove, Ejaness Records, Ernie B's, CD Waterhouse and Borders.

How to Contact Submit demo by mail. Unsolicited submissions are OK. Prefers cassette, DAT, mini disk or VHS videocassette with lyric sheet. Include SASE. Responds in 2 weeks.

Music Mostly **world beat, reggae** and **ethnic**; also **jazz, hip-hop/dance** and **pop**. Released *I and I* (album by Abby I/Jimbe), recorded by Abby I (African pop); *Rastafrika* (album by Jimbe/Richard Ono), recorded by Rastafrika (African roots reggae); and *Vibes* (album by Jimbe/Bongo Cartheni), recorded by Wave (worldbeat/jazz), all released 2001/2002 on World Beatnik. Other artists include Ras Richi (Cameroon), Wisdom Ogbor (Nigeria), Joe Lateh (Ghana), Dee Dee Cooper, Ras Lyrix (St. Croix), Ras Kumba (St. Kitts), Gary Mon, Darbo (Gambia), Ricki Malik (Jamaica), Arik Miles, Narte's (Hawaii), Gavin Audagnotti (South Africa) and Bongo (Trinidad).

⊕ ⬚ X.R.L. RECORDS/MUSIC

White House Farm, Shropshire TF9 4HA England. (01630)647374. Fax: (01630)647612. **Contact:** Xavier Lee, International A&R Manager. A&R: Tanya Woof. UK A&R Manager: Cathrine Lee. Labels include Swoop, Zarg Records, Genouille, Pogo and Check Records. Record company, record producer and music publisher (Le Matt Music, Lee Music, R.T.F.M. and Pogo Records). Member MPA, PPL, PRS, MCPS, V.P.L. Estab. 1972. Staff size: 11. Releases 30 12" singles, 20 LPs and 20 CDs/year. Pays negotiable royalty to artists on contract; negotiable rate to publisher for each record sold. Royalties paid to US songwriters and artists through US publishing or recording affiliate.

Distributed by Lematt Music.

How to Contact Submit demo by mail. Unsolicited submissions are OK. Prefers CD, cassette, MD, DVD, or VHS 625 PAL standard videocassette with 1-3 songs and lyric sheet. Include bio and still photos. IRC only. Responds in 6 weeks.

Music Mostly **pop/top 40**; also **bluegrass, blues, country, dance-oriented, easy listening, MOR, progressive, R&B, '50s rock, disco, new wave, rock** and **soul**. Released *Love on the Lichfield Line* (album), by Orphan, released 2005; *Now and Then* (album), by D. Boone, released 2005; *'60s Rock* (album), by Mike Sheriden, released 2006; *Country Blues* (album), by Emmitt Till, released 2005. Other artists include Orphan, The Chromatics, Mike Sheriden and the Nightriders, Johnny Moon, Dead Fish, Sight 'N' Sound, Hush, and Emmitt Till.

Tips "Be original."

☑ XEMU RECORDS

19 W. 21st St., Suite 503, New York NY 10010. (212)807-0290. Fax: (212)807-0583. E-mail: xemu@xemu.com. Web site: www.xemu.com. **Contact:** Dr. Claw, vice president A&R. Record company. Estab. 1992. Staff size: 4. Releases 4 CDs/year. Pays negotiable royalty to artists on contract; statutory rate to publisher per song on record.

Distributed by Redeye Distribution.

How to Contact *Write first and obtain permission to submit.* Prefers cassette with 3 songs. Does not return material. Responds in 2 months.

Music Mostly **alternative**. Released *Guess What* (album), recorded by Mikki James (alternative rock); *A is for Alpha* (album), recorded by Alpha Bitch (alternative rock); *Hold the Mayo* (album), recorded by Death Sandwich (alternative rock); *Stockholm Syndrom* (album), recorded by Trigger Happy (alternative rock); and *The Evolution of Despair* (album), recorded by The Love Kills Theory (alternative rock), all released on Xemu Records. Other artists include Malvert P. Redd, The Fifth Dementia, and the Neanderthal Spongecake.

ADDITIONAL RECORD COMPANIES

The following companies are also record companies, but their listings are found in other sections of the book. Read the listings for submission information.

A
ACR Productions 194
Alert Music, Inc. 219
Alexander Sr. Music 82
Atch Records and Productions 220

B
Barrett Rock 'n' Roll Enterprises, Paul 221
Big Fish Music Publishing Group 87
Black Market Entertainment Recordings 88
Blues Alley Records 196
Bouquet-Orchid Enterprises 223
BSW Records 92

C
California Country Music 94
Cherri/Holly Music 94
Christopher Publishing, Sonny 95

D
DaVinci's Notebook Records 198

E
EAO Music Corporation of Canada 227

F
Fifth Avenue Media, Ltd. 104
Final Mix Inc. 199
First Time Music (Publishing) U.K. 104
Fresh Entertainment 105
Furrow Music 106

G
Glad Music Co. 106

H
Hailing Frequency Music Productions 199

Hale Enterprises 229
Happy Melody 107
Hardison International Entertainment Corporation 230
Heart Consort Music 200
Hickory Lane Publishing and Recording 107
His Power Productions and Publishing 108
Huge Production, Inc., A 231

I
Inside Records/OK Songs 109

J
Ja/Nein Musikverlag GmbH 109
Jay Jay Publishing & Record Co. 201
Jerjoy Music 110
JPMC Music Inc. 111

K
Kaysarah Music 112
Kickstart Music Ltd. 232
Kuper Personal Management/Recovery Recordings 234

L
L.A. Entertainment, Inc. 202
Lazy Bones Productions/Recordings, Inc. 202
LCS Music Group 113
Levy Management, Rick 234
Lineage Publishing Co. 113

M
Makers Mark Music Productions 203
McCoy Music, Jim 116
Mega Truth Records 205

N
Naked Jain Records 117
Neu Electro Productions 205

New Experience Records/Faze 4 Records 206

P

Pegasus Music 119
Philly Breakdown Recording Co. 207
Pierce, Jim 207
Pollybyrd Publications Limited 121

R

R.T.L. Music 122
Rockford Music Co. 123
Rustic Records, Inc Publishing 124

S

Saddlestone Publishing 125
Satkowski Recordings, Steve 209
Segal's Productions 209
Silicon Music Publishing Co. 126
Sound Cellar Music 128
Sound Works Entertainment Productions Inc. 210

SRS Productions/Hit Records Network 211
Starbound Publishing Co. 128
Still Working Music Group 129
Studio Seven 211
Succes 129
Supreme Enterprises Int'l Corp. 129
Swift River Productions 211

T

Tari, Roger Vincent 212
Tas Music Co./Dave Tasse Entertainment 245
TMC Productions 212
Tower Music Group 130

U

Unknown Source Music 131

W

Warner Productions, Cheryl K. 246
World Records 214

Record Producers

The independent producer can best be described as a creative coordinator. He's often the one with the most creative control over a recording project and is ultimately responsible for the finished product. Some record companies have in-house producers who work with the acts on that label (although, in more recent years, such producer-label relationships are often non-exclusive). Today, most record companies contract out-of-house, independent record producers on a project-by-project basis.

WHAT RECORD PRODUCERS DO

Producers play a large role in deciding what songs will be recorded for a particular project and are always on the lookout for new songs for their clients. They can be valuable contacts for songwriters because they work so closely with the artists whose records they produce. They usually have a lot more freedom than others in executive positions and are known for having a good ear for potential hit songs. Many producers are songwriters and musicians themselves. Since they wield a great deal of influence, a good song in the hands of the right producer at the right time stands a good chance of being cut. And even if a producer is not working on a specific project, he is well-acquainted with record company executives and artists and can often get material through doors not open to you.

SUBMITTING MATERIAL TO PRODUCERS

It can be difficult to get your tapes to the right producer at the right time. Many producers write their own songs and even if they don't write, they may be involved in their own publishing companies so they have instant access to all the songs in their catalogs. Also, some genres are more dependent on finding outside songs than others. A producer working with a rock group or a singer-songwriter will rarely take outside songs.

It's important to understand the intricacies of the producer/publisher situation. If you pitch your song directly to a producer first, before another publishing company publishes the song, the producer may ask you for the publishing rights (or a percentage thereof) to your song. You must decide whether the producer is really an active publisher who will try to get the song recorded again and again or whether he merely wants the publishing because it means extra income for him from the current recording project. You may be able to work out a co-publishing deal, where you and the producer split the publishing of the song. That means he will still receive his percentage of the publishing income, even if you secure a cover recording of the song by other artists in the future. Even though you would be giving up a little bit initially, you may benefit in the future.

Some producers will offer to sign artists and songwriters to "development deals." These can range from a situation where a producer auditions singers and musicians with the intention of building a group from the ground up, to development deals where a producer signs a band or singer-songwriter to his production company with the intention of developing the act and producing an album to shop to labels (sometimes referred to as a "baby record deal").

You must carefully consider whether such a deal is right for you. In some cases, such a deal can open doors and propel an act to the next level. In other worst-case scenarios, such a deal can result in loss of artistic and career control, with some acts held in contractual bondage for years at a time. Before you consider any such deal, be clear about your goals, the producer's reputation, and the sort of compromises you are willing to make to reach those goals. If you have any reservations whatsoever, don't do it.

The listings that follow outline which aspects of the music industry each producer is involved in, what type of music he is looking for, and what records and artists he's recently produced. Study the listings carefully, noting the artists each producer works with, and consider if any of your songs might fit a particular artist's or producer's style. Then determine whether they are open to your level of experience (see the A Sample Listing Decoded on page 11).

Consult the Category Index on page 358 to find producers who work with the type of music you write, and the Geographic Index at the back of the book to locate producers in your area.

Icons

For more instructional information on the listings in this book, including explanations of symbols (N ✔ �ू ❋ ⊕ ◯ ◐ ◑ ⊘), read the article *Songwriter's Market: How Do I Use It?* on page 7.

For More Info

ADDITIONAL RECORD PRODUCERS

There are **more record producers** located in other sections of the book! On page 215 use the list of Additional Record Producers to find listings within other sections who are also record producers.

☑ ☒ ☑ "A" MAJOR SOUND CORPORATION

RR #1, Kensington PE COB 1MO Canada. (902)836-1051. E-mail: info@amajorsound.com. Web site: www.amajorsound.com. **Contact:** Paul C. Milner, producer. Record producer and music publisher. Estab. 1989. Produces 8 CDs/year. Fee derived in part from sales royalty when song or artist is recorded, and/or outright fee from recording artist or record company, or investors.

How to Contact Submit demo CD by mail. Unsolicited submissions are OK. Prefers CD with 5 songs and lyric sheet (lead sheet if available). Does not return material. Responds only if interested in 3 months.

Music Mostly **rock**, **A/C**, **alternative** and **pop**; also **Christian** and **R&B**. Produced *COLOUR* (album written by J.MacPhee/R. MacPhee/C.Buchanan/D. MacDonald), recorded by The Chucky Danger Band(pop/rock), released 2006; *Rock Classics* (album, by various writers), recorded by Phe Cullen with Randy Waldman Trio (jazz), released 2002 on United One Records; *Jazz Standards* (album, by various writers), recorded by Phe Cullen with the Norm Amadio Trio (jazz), to be released in 2003 on United One Records; "Temptation" (single by Verdi, Paul Milner and Patrizia Pomeroy) from *Edge of Emotion* (album), recorded by Patrizia, released 2005 on Nuff Entertainment; and *Fury* (album, adapted from public domain), recorded by Patricia Pomeroy, Paul Milner and Dan Cutrona, released 2003 on B&B/Edel/Nuff Entertainment.

☐ ABERDEEN PRODUCTIONS

524 Doral Country Dr., Nashville TN 37221. (615)646-9750. **Contact:** Scott Turner, executive producer. Record producer and music publisher (Buried Treasure Music/ASCAP, Captain Kidd/BMI). Estab. 1971. Produces 10 singles, 15-20 12″ singles, 8 LPs and 8 CDs/year. Fee derived from outright fee from recording artist.

• Also see the listing for Buried Treasure Music in the Music Publishers section of this book.

How to Contact Submit demo by mail. Unsolicited submissions OK. Prefers cassette with maximum 4 songs and lead sheet. Include SASE. "No SASE, no reply." Responds in 2 weeks. No "lyrics only."

Music Mostly **country**, **MOR** and **rock**; also **top 40/pop**. Produced "All of the Above" (single by Douglas Bush) from *The Entrance* (album), recorded by Lea Brennan (country/MOR), released 2000. Other artists include Jimmy Clanton.

Tips "Start out on an independent basis because of the heavy waiting period to get on a major label."

☐ ACR PRODUCTIONS

P.O. Box 5636, Midland TX 79704. (432)687-2702. E-mail: dwaine915@cox.net. **Contact:** Dwaine Thomas, owner. Record producer, music publisher (Joranda Music/BMI) and record company (ACR Records). Estab. 1986. Produces 120 singles, 8-15 12″ singles, 25 LPs, 25 EPs and 25 CDs/year. Fee derived from sales royalty when song or artist is recorded. "We charge for in-house recording only. Remainder is derived from royalties."

How to Contact Submit demo by mail. Unsolicited submissions are OK. Prefers cassette or VHS videocassette with 5 songs and lyric sheet. Does not return material. Responds in 6 weeks if interested.

Music Mostly **country swing**, **pop** and **rock**; also **R&B** and **gospel**. Produced *Bottle's Almost Gone* (album) and "Black Gold" (single), written and recorded by Mike Nelson (country), both released 1999 on ACR Records; and *Nashville Series* (album), written and recorded by various (country), released 1998 on ProJam Music.

Tips "Be professional. No living room tapes!"

☑ ☐ AIF MUSIC PRODUCTIONS

P.O. Box 691, Mamaroneck NY 10543. (914)381-3559. E-mail: aifrecords@verizon.net. Web site: www.robertjackson.net/aif%20records.htm. **Contact:** Robert Jackson, president. Record producer. Estab. 1995. Produces 3 singles and 4 CDs/year. Fee derived from sales royalty when song or artist is recorded or outright fee from recording artist. "We work on a combination of fee basis, plus a percentage after the deal is made."

How to Contact Submit demo by mail. Unsolicited submissions are OK. Prefers CD or cassette. "Don't send photos, lyrics or press. We work on a fee plus percentage basis." Responds in 2-3 weeks.

Music Mostly **rock**, **hard rock** and **alternative**; also **metal**, **blues**, **folk**, **pop** and **country**. Does not want rap, dance, hip-hop, death/black metal, industrial or house. Produced "Much Better" (single by Nard) from *Highways, Biways* (album), recorded by Liquor Daddies (rock/alternative), released 2002 on PA/AIF; "Found A Way" (single by M. Lough) from *Spankin' America* (album), recorded by Young Spank (rock/alternative), released 2002 on Core; and "Eastern Sands" (single by R. Zucker) from *Time Waltz* (album), recorded by Rob Zucker (rock/instrumental), released 2002 on Grease/AIF. Other artists include First Spawn.

Tips "Contact us. If you like what we say, and we are compatible, we will work with you, period. For producing, you must travel to NY/NJ/CT tri-state area or pay for my transportation. My role in a project is to coach, coordinate and oversee music, lyrics, instrumentation, arrangements, restructuring of songs (if need be), and selection of studio musicians and facilities for recording, mixing and mastering. If you want a fantastic producer, contact me. I can hear everything, including your out-of-tune instrument."

✪ STUART J. ALLYN

250 Taxter Rd., Irvington NY 10533. (212)486-0856. Fax: (914)591-5617. E-mail: adrstudios@adrinc .org. Web site: www.adrinc.org/arzell2.html. Associate: Jack Walker. **Contact:** Jack Davis, general manager. President: Stuart J. Allyn. Record producer. Estab. 1972. Produces 6 singles and 3-6 CDs/ year. Fee derived from sales royalty and outright fee from recording artist and record company.

How to Contact *Does not accept unsolicited submissions.*

Music Mostly **pop**, **rock**, **jazz** and **theatrical**; also **R&B** and **country**. Produced *Thad Jones Legacy* (album), recorded by Vanguard Jazz Orchestra (jazz), released 2000 on New World Records. Other artists include Billy Joel, Aerosmith, Carole Demas, Michael Garin, The Magic Garden, Bob Stewart, The Dixie Peppers, Nora York, Buddy Barnes and various video and film scores.

☑ ✪ AUDIO 911

(formerly Steve Wytas Productions), P.O. Box 212, Haddam CT 06438. (860)345-3300. E-mail: songwritersmarket@audio911.com. Web site: www.audio911.com. **Contact:** Steven J. Wytas. Record producer. Estab. 1984. Produces 4-8 singles, 3 LPs, 3 EPs and 4 CDs/year. Fee derived from outright fee from recording artist or record company.

How to Contact Submit demo by mail. Unsolicited submissions are OK. Prefers CD or VHS videocassette with several songs and lyric or lead sheet. "Include live material if possible." Does not return material. Responds in 3 months.

Music Mostly **rock**, **pop**, **top 40** and **country/acoustic**. Produced *Already Home* (album), recorded by Hannah Cranna on Big Deal Records (rock); *Under the Rose* (album), recorded by Under the Rose on Utter Records (rock); and *Sickness & Health* (album), recorded by Legs Akimbo on Joyful Noise Records (rock). Other artists include King Hop!, The Shells, The Gravel Pit, G'nu Fuz, Tuesday Welders and Toxic Field Mice.

Ⓝ ✪ RON BAIRD ENTERPRISES

P.O. Box 42, 1 Main St., Ellsworth PA 15331. **Contact:** Ron Baird, executive producer. Record producer, record company (La Ron Ltd. Records), music publisher (Baird Music Group). Estab. 1999. Produces 2-5 singles and 1-2 LPs/year.

• Also see the listing for Baird Music Group in the Music Publishers section of this book.

How to Contact Submit demo by mail. Unsolicited submissions are OK. "No certified mail." Prefers cassette only with 2-4 songs and lyric sheet. Does not return submissions. Responds only if interested.

Music Mostly **country** and **country rock**. Does not want hip-hop, gospel/religious or R&B. Produced "Big Time Dreams" (single by Ron Baird), recorded by Corey Christie (country), released

2004; "Back to Nashville" (single by Ron Baird) from *Here's Kim Early* (album), recorded by Kim Early (country), released 2004; and "My Texas Girl" (single by Ron Baird), recorded by Dale Such (country), released 2004, all on LaRon Ltd.

Tips "Our goal is to produce finished masters and shop these for major label deals. We want to produce legitimate hits."

🌐 🖉 BIG BEAR

Box 944, Birmingham B16 8UT United Kingdom. 44-121-454-7020. E-mail: jim@bigbearmusic.com. Web site: www.bigbearmusic.com. Managing Director: Jim Simpson. Record producer, music publisher (Bearsongs) and record company (Big Bear Records). Produces 10 LPs/year. Fee derived from sales royalty.

• Also see the listings for Bearsongs in the Music Publishers section of this book and Big Bear Records in the Record Companies section of this book.

How to Contact Write first about your interest, then submit demo and lyric sheet. Does not return material. Responds in 2 weeks.

Music Blues, swing and jazz.

🅝 ⃝ BLUES ALLEY RECORDS

Rt. 1, Box 288, Clarksburg WV 26301. (304)598-2583. Web site: www.bluesalleymusic.com. **Contact:** Joshua Swiger, producer. Record producer, record company and music publisher (Blues Alley Publishing/BMI). New Christian record label (Joshua Tree Records/BMI). Produces 4-6 LPs and 2 EPs/year. Fee derived from sales royalty when song or artist is recorded.

How to Contact Submit demo by mail. Unsolicited submissions are OK. Prefers CD with 4 songs and lyric and lead sheets. Does not return material. Responds in 6 weeks.

Music Mostly **Christian**, **alternative** and **pop**. Produced *Hard Road* (album), recorded by The New Relics (acoustic rock), released 2003; *Sons of Sirens* (album), recorded by Amity (rock), released 2004; and *It's No Secret* (album), recorded by Samantha Caley (pop country), released 2004, all on Blues Alley Records.

🅜 CACOPHONY PRODUCTIONS

2400 Vasanta Way, Los Angeles CA 90068. (917)856-8532. Producer: Steven Miller. Record producer and music publisher (In Your Face Music). Estab. 1981. Fee derived from sales royalty when song or artist is recorded, or outright fee from recording artist or record company.

How to Contact *Call first and obtain permission to submit.* Prefers CD with 3 songs and lyric sheet. "Send a cover letter of no more than three paragraphs giving some background on yourself and the music. Also explain specifically what you are looking for Cacophony Productions to do." Does not return material. Responds only if interested.

Music Mostly **progressive pop/rock**, **singer/songwriter** and **progressive country**. Produced Dar Williams, Suzanne Vega, John Gorka, Michael Hedges, Juliana Hatfield, Toad the Wet Sprocket and Medeski-Martin & Wood.

🅙 CANDYSPITEFUL PRODUCTIONS

2051 E. Cedar St., #8, Tempe AZ 85281. (480)468-7017. E-mail: mandrakerocks@yahoo.com. Web site: www.candyspiteful.com. **Contact:** William Ferraro, president. Record producer, record company (Candyspiteful Productions), music publisher (Candyspiteful Productions). Estab. 2000. Produces 30 singles, 12 albums per year. Fee derived from outright fee from recording artist.

• Also see the listings for Candyspiteful Productions in the Record Companies section of this book.

How to Contact Submit demo by mail. Unsolicited submissions are OK. Prefers CD with 3 songs and lyric sheet and cover letter. Does not return material. Responds only if interested.

Music Mostly **hard rock**, **radio-friendly rock** and **hip-hop**. Produced 11 full length albums in 2005.

⃝ COACHOUSE MUSIC

P.O. Box 1308, Barrington IL 60011. (847)382-7631. Fax: (847)382-7651. E-mail: coachouse1@aol.com. **Contact:** Michael Freeman, president. Record producer. Estab. 1984. Produces 6-8 CDs/year. Fee derived from sales royalty when song or artist is recorded.

How to Contact *Write or e-mail first and obtain permission to submit.* Prefers CD, cassette, with 3-5 songs and lyric sheet. Include SASE. Responds in 6 weeks.
Music Mostly **rock**, **pop** and **blues**; also **alternative rock** and **country/Americana/roots**. Produced *Casque Nu* (album), written and recorded by Charlelie Couture on Chrysalis EMI France (contemporary pop); *Time Will Tell*, recorded by Studebaker John on Blind Pig Records (blues); *Where Blue Begins* (album by various/D. Coleman), recorded by Deborah Coleman on Blind Pig Records (contemporary blues); *A Man Amongst Men* (album), recorded by Bo Diddley (blues); and *Voodoo Menz* (album), recorded by Corey Harris and Henry Butler. Other artists include Paul Chastain, Candi Station, Eleventh Dream Day, Magic Slim, The Tantrums, The Pranks, The Bad Examples, Mississippi Heat and Sharrie Williams.
Tips "Be honest, be committed, strive for excellence."

☐ COAL HARBOR MUSIC
P.O. Box 148027, Nashville TN 37214-8027. (615)883-2020. E-mail: jerry@coalharbormusic.com. Web site: www.coalharbormusic.com. **Contact:** Jerry Ray Wells, producer. Record producer, record company (Coal Harbor Music), music publisher (Coal Harbor Music), and radio promotion company. Estab. 1990. Produces 10-15 singles/year and 3-5 albums/year. Fee derived from sales royalty when song or artist is recorded, outright fee from recording artist, outright fee from record company, or from investors (depending on situation/artist/project).
How to Contact Submit a demo by mail. Unsolicited submissions are OK.with 3-5 songs, cover letter. We do not return submissions.Responds only if interested.
Music Mostly **country**, **Christian (all forms)**, **bluegrass**; also **pop/AC**, **jazz/blues**, **Christmas/novelty**. Does not want hard rock, heavy metal, or rap. Produced "It Overwhelms Me" (single by Sara Aten/Vicky Schneider) from *The Cross of Christ* (album), recorded by Sara Aten (contemporary Christian), released 2005 on Coal Harbor Music; "You" (single) from *Unraveled* (album), written and recorded by Anne Borgen (contemporary Christian), released 2004 on Coal Harbor Music; and "So Good To Know" (single) from *All I Need* (album), written and recorded by Damon Westfaul (southern gospel), released 2004 on Coal Harbor Music.
Tips "Other artists include Angela Baker Wells, Holly Norman, Don Freeman, and Teri Garrison."

⊞ ☑ COLLECTOR RECORDS
P.O. Box 1200, 3260 AE Oud Beyerland, Holland, The Netherlands. (31)(18)660-4266. Fax: (32)(18)660-4366. E-mail: info@collectorrecords.nl. Web site: www.collectorrecords.nl. **Contact:** Cees Klop, president. Record producer and music publisher (All Rock Music). Produces 25 CDs/year. Fee derived from outright fee from record company.
• Also see the listings for All Rock Music in the Music Publishers section and Collector Records in the Record Companies section of this book.
How to Contact Submit demo by mail. Unsolicited submissions are OK. Prefers cassette. SAE and IRC. Responds in 2 months.
Music Mostly **'50s rock**, **rockabilly** and **country rock**; also **piano boogie woogie**. Produced *When You Rock And Roll* (album), recorded by Marvin Jackson (1950s rockers); *Bobby Crown & The Kapers* (album), recorded by Bobby Crown (1950s rockers); and *Rock, Rock, Rockin' Tonight* (album), recorded by various artists (1950s rockers), all released 2004 on Collector Records.
Tips "Only send the kind of music we produce."

☑ CHARLIE CRAIG PRODUCTIONS
P.O. Box 1448, Mt. Juliet TN 37121-1448. Web site: www.charliecraig.com. **Contact:** Charlie Craig, producer. Record producer and music publisher (Song Machine/BMI, Walker Publishing Co. L.L.C./ASCAP/BMI). Estab. 2001. Produces 5 singles and 5 CDs/year. Fee derived from sales royalty and/or outright fee from recording artist.
• Charlie Craig Productions received a Grammy nomination in 1991 and Song of the Year nominations in 1986 and 1991. Was inducted into the South Carolina Entertainment Hall of Fame in 1998.
How to Contact *Write or call first to arrange personal interview.* For song publishing submissions,

prefers CD with 3 songs, lyric sheet and lead sheet. "Include e-mail address for response." Does not return submissions. Responds in 3 weeks via e-mail only.

Music Mostly **traditional country, new country** and **country pop**. Co-produced *The Nashville Super Pickers* (album), recorded by The Nashville Super Pickers Band (country), released 1972 on Royal American Records. "First Nashville writer to work with Alan Jackson. Extensively involved in getting a record deal for the Wilkinsons with Giant Records."

Tips "Be prepared to record only the best songs, even if it takes an extended length of time. We won't go into the studio until we have great songs. Vocals should be memorized before going into the studio. You need to express as much emotion as possible. Suggestions are welcome from artists and musicians, but final decisions are made by the Producer. We will make sure the vocals are perfect no matter how many takes are necessary. Be prepared to work."

☑ ○ DAP ENTERTAINMENT

PMB 364, 7100 Lockwood Blvd., Boardman OH 44512. (330)726-8737. Fax: (330)726-8747. Web site: www.dapentertainment.com. **Contact:** Darryl Alexander, producer. Record Producer and music publisher (Alexander Sr. Music, BMI). Estab. 1997. Produces 12 singles and 2-4 CDs/year. Fee derived from sales royalty (producer points) when song or artist is recorded or outright fee from recording artist or record company.

• Also see the listing for Alexander Sr. Music in the Music Publishers section of this book.

How to Contact *Write first and obtain permission to submit.* Prefers CD with 2-4 songs and lyric sheet. Include SASE. Responds in 1 month. "No phone calls or faxes will be accepted."

Music Mostly **contemporary jazz, urban contemporary gospel**; also **R&B**. Produced "Plumb Line" (single by Herb McMullen/Darryl Alexander) from *Diamond In the Sky* (album); "Cafe Rio" and "Garden of My Heart" (singles) from *Diamond In the Sky*, written and recorded by Darryl Alexander (contemporary jazz), all released 2004 on DAP Entertainment. Other artists include Kathryn Williams.

☑ ✤ ✐ DAVINCI'S NOTEBOOK RECORDS

10070 Willoughby Dr., Niagara Falls ON L2E 6S6 Canada. E-mail: admin@davincismusic.com. Web site: www.davincismusic.com. **Owner:** Kevin Richard. Record producer, record company, music publisher, distributor and recording studio (The Sound Kitchen). Estab. 1992. Produces 1 cassette and 1 CD/year. Fee derived from outright fee from artist or commission on sales. "Distribution is on consignment basis. Artist is responsible for all shipping, taxes, and import/export duties."

How to Contact E-mail first for postal details then submit demo CD by mail. Unsolicited submissions are OK. Prefers CD and bio. Does not return material. Responds in 6 weeks.

Music Mostly **rock, instrumental rock, New Age** and **progressive-alternative**; also **R&B**, **pop** and **jazz**. Produced *Windows* (album by Kevin Hotte/Andy Smith), recorded by Musicom on DaVinci's Notebook Records (power New Age); *Inventing Fire*, *Illumination*, *A Different Drum* (albums), written and recorded by Kevin Richard on DNR/Independent (instrumental rock); and *The Cunninghams* (album), written and recorded by The Cunninghams on Independent (gospel).

Tips "DNR is an artist-run label. Local bands and performers will receive priority. Be more interested in getting a-foot-in-the-door exposure as opposed to making a fortune. Be satisfied with conquering the world using 'baby steps.' Indie labels don't have large corporate budgets for artist development. We are more about online distribution than artist development. Being a local act means that you can perform live to promote your releases. For indie artist, selling from the stage is probably going to bring you the biggest volume of sales."

▨ ✐ EDWARD DE MILES

28 E. Jackson Bldg., 10th Floor #S627, Chicago IL 60604-2263. (773)509-6381. Fax: (312)922-6964. Web site: www.edmsahara.com. **Contact:** Edward De Miles, president. Record producer, music publisher (Edward De Miles Music Co./BMI) and record company (Sahara Records and Filmworks Entertainment). Estab. 1981. Produces 5-10 CDs/year. Fee derived from sales royalty when song or artist is recorded.

- Also see the listing for Edward De Miles in the Music Publishers and Managers & Booking Agents sections, as well as Sahara Records and Filmworks Entertainment in the Record Companies section of this book.

How to Contact *Does not accept unsolicited submissions.*

Music Mostly **R&B/dance**, **top 40 pop/rock** and **contemporary jazz**; also **country, TV and film themes—songs** and **jingles**. Produced "Moments" and "Dance Wit Me" (singles) (dance), both written and recorded by Steve Lynn; and "Games" (single), written and recorded by D'von Edwards (jazz), all on Sahara Records. Other artists include Multiple Choice.

Tips "Copyright all material before submitting. Equipment and showmanship a must."

☑ ☒ ◎ AL DELORY AND MUSIC MAKERS

E-mail: aldelory@mn.rr.com. Web site: www.aldelory.com. **Contact:** Al DeLory, president. Record producer and career consultant (MUSIC MAKERS/ASCAP). Estab. 1987. Fee derived from outright fee from recording artist.

- Al DeLory has won two Grammy Awards and has been nominated five times.

How to Contact *E-mail first and obtain permission to submit.* Prefers CD or cassette. Include SASE. Responds in 2-3 months only if interested.

Music Mostly **pop** and **Latin**. Produced "Gentle On My Mind" (single), "By the Time I Get to Phoenix" (single) and "Wichita Lineman" (single), all recorded by Glen Campbell. Other artists include Lettermen, Wayne Newton, Bobbie Gentry and Anne Murray.

Tips "Seek advice and council only with professionals with a track record and get the money up front."

◎ JOEL DIAMOND ENTERTAINMENT

Dept. SM, 3940 Laurel Canyon Blvd., Suite 441, Studio City CA 91604. (818)980-9588. Fax: (818)980-9422. E-mail: jdiamond20@aol.com. Web site: www.joeldiamond.com. **Contact:** Joel Diamond. Record producer, music publisher and manager. Fee derived from sales royalty when song is recorded or outright fee from recording artist or record company.

- Also see the listing for Silver Blue Music/Oceans Blue Music in the Music Publishers section of this book.

How to Contact Does not return material. Responds only if interested.

Music Mostly **dance**, **R&B**, **soul** and **top 40/pop**. Produced "One Night In Bangkok" (single by Robey); "I Think I Love You," recorded by Katie Cassidy (daughter of David Cassidy) on Artemis Records; "After the Loving" (single), recorded by E. Humperdinck; "Forever Friends," recorded by Vaneza (featured on Nickelodeon's *The Brothers Garcia*); and "Paradise" (single), recorded by Kaci.

ℕ ◑ FINAL MIX INC.

(formerly Final Mix Music), 2219 W. Olive Ave., Suite 102, Burbank CA 91506. (818)970-8717. E-mail: finalmix@aol.com. **Contact:** Theresa Frank, A&R. Record producer/remixer/mix engineer, independent label (3.6 Music, Inc.) and music publisher (Ximlanif Music Publishing). Estab. 1989. Releases 12 singles and 3-5 LPs and CDs/year. Fee derived from sales royalty when song or artist is recorded.

How to Contact *Does not accept unsolicited submissions.*

Music Mostly **pop**, **rock**, **dance**, **R&B** and **rap**. Produced and/or mixer/remixer for Will Smith, Hilary Duff, Jesse McCartney, Christina Aguilera, *American Idol*, Ray Charles, Quincy Jones, Michael Bolton, K-Ci and Jo Jo (of Jodeci), Janet Jackson, Ice Cube, Queen Latifah, Jennifer Paige and The Corrs.

◎ HAILING FREQUENCY MUSIC PRODUCTIONS

7438 Shoshone Ave., Van Nuys CA 91406. (818)881-9888. Fax: (818)881-0555. E-mail: blowinsmokeband@ktb.net. Web site: www.blowinsmokeband.com. President: Lawrence Weisberg. Vice President: Larry Knight. Record producer, record company (Blowin' Smoke Records), management firm (Blowin' Smoke Productions) and music publisher (Hailing Frequency Publishing). Estab. 1992.

Produces 3 LPs and 3 CDs/year. Fee derived from sales royalty when song or artist is recorded or outright fee from artist.

● Also see the listing for Blowin' Smoke Productions/Records in the Managers & Booking Agents section of this book.

How to Contact *Write or call first and obtain permission to submit.* Prefers cassette or VHS ½″ videocassette. "Write or print legibly with complete contact instructions." Include SASE. Responds in 1 month.

Music Mostly **contemporary R&B**, **blues** and **blues-rock**; also **songs for film**, **jingles for commercials** and **gospel (contemporary)**. Produced "Beyond the Blues Horizon" (single), recorded by Blowin' Smoke Rhythm & Blues Band, released 2004. Other artists include the Fabulous Smokettes.

☑ HEART CONSORT MUSIC

410 First St. W., Mt. Vernon IA 52314. E-mail: mail@heartconsortmusic.com. Web site: www.heart consortmusic.com. **Contact:** Catherine Lawson, manager. Record producer, record company and music publisher. Estab. 1980. Produces 2-3 CDs/year. Fee derived from sales royalty when song or artist is recorded.

How to Contact Submit demo by mail. Unsolicited submissions are OK. Prefers CD or cassette with 3 songs and 3 lyric sheets. Include SASE. Responds in 3 months.

Music Mostly **jazz**, **New Age** and **contemporary**. Produced *New Faces* (album), written and recorded by James Kennedy on Heart Consort Music (world/jazz).

Tips "We are interested in jazz/New Age artists with quality demos and original ideas. We aim for an international audience."

☑ HUMAN FACTOR

P.O. Box 3742, Washington DC 20027. (202)415-7748. E-mail: info@hfproductions.com. Web site: www.hfproductions.com. **Contact:** Blake Althen or Paula Bellenoit, producers/owners. Estab. 2001. Record producer. "Human Factor Productions is a full service music production team offering a range of music production services, including composition, arranging, recording, remixing, and more."

● See the article written by Blake Althen with Paula Bellenoit on pg. 62 about music licensing, entitled " Getting Started in Music Licensing," also featuring an interview with contemporary folk artist SONiA of disappear fear about her foray into dance remixes.

How to Contact *Please call or e-mail to get permission to submit.* "Solicited material only."

Music Mostly **adult contemporary**, **pop**, **singer/songwriter**, **rock (all types)**, **world/ethnic**, **techno/electronica**, **rap** and **soundtrack/film score**. Produced dance remixes of "No Bomb Is Smart" (single), written and recorded by SONiA of disappear fear (contemporary folk); "Fall Down," and "Without Light" (by S. Bitz), recorded by Abby Someone (heartland rock). Other artists include Jennifer Cutting's Ocean Orchestra (contemporary folk rock, celtic), Rachel Panay (dance), Pale Beneath the Blue (adult contemporary/singer/songwriter), Paul Kawabori (classical crossover), and Michelangelo (adult contemporary), and more.

Tip "Get your goals clear in your mind and on paper. What do you want a producer to do for you? Know the answer to this question, and it will guide you to the industry professionals who are right for you. And really work hard on your live show. The best-produced recording in the world will not be worth what you paid for it if no one wants to come to your shows and buy it."

☑ INTEGRATED ENTERTAINMENT

1815 JFK Blvd., #1612, Philadelphia PA 19103. (215)563-7147. E-mail: gelboni@aol.com. **Contact:** Gelboni, president. Record producer. Estab. 1991. Produces 6 EPs and 6 CDs/year. Fee derived from sales royalty when song or artist is recorded or outright fee from recording artist or record company.

How to Contact Submit demo CD by mail. Solicited submissions only. CD only with 3 songs. "Draw a guitar on the outside of envelope so we'll know it's from a songwriter." Responds in 2 months.

Music Mostly **rock** and **pop**. Produced *Gold Record* (album), written and recorded by Dash Rip Rock (rock) on Ichiban Records; *Virus* (album), written and recorded by Margin of Error (modern rock) on Treehouse Records; and *I Divide* (album), written and recorded by Amy Carr (AAA) on Evil Twin Records. Other artists include Land of the Blind, Gatlin, Ash Wednesday, Playing for Audrey, Three Miles Out and others.

☐ JAY JAY PUBLISHING & RECORD CO.
P.O. Box 41-4156, Miami Beach FL 33141. (305)758-0000. Owner: Walter Jagiello. Associate: J. Kozak. Record producer, music publisher (BMI) and record company (Jay Jay Record, Tape and Video Co.). Estab. 1951. Produces 12 singles, 12 LPs and 12 CDs/year. Fee derived from sales royalty when song or artist is recorded.

How to Contact Submit demo by mail. Prefers CD or cassette or VHS videocassette with 6 songs and lyric and lead sheet. "Quality cassette or reel-to-reel, sheet music and lyrics." Does not return material. Responds in 2 months.

Music Mostly **ballads**, **love songs**, **country music** and **comedy**; also **polkas**, **hymns**, **gospel** and **waltzes**. Produced seven Christmas albums in English and Polish, recorded by the S.P. Stanislaus Choral Group of Michigan City, IN and the Lucky Harmony Boys Orchestra. Other artists include Eddie & The Slovenes, Johnny Vandal, Wisconsin Dutchmen and Eddie Zima.

⊕ ☐ JUMP PRODUCTIONS
31 Paul Gilsonstraat, 8200 St-Andries Belgium. (050)31-63-80. E-mail: happymelody@skynet.be. **Contact:** Eddy Van Mouffaert, general manager. Record producer and music publisher (Jump Music). Estab. 1976. Produces 25 singles and 2 CDs/year. Fee derived from sales royalty when song or artist is recorded.

- Also see the listing for Happy Melody in the Music Publishers section of this book.

How to Contact Submit demo CD or tape by mail. Unsolicited submissions are OK. Prefers CD. Does not return material. Responds in 2 weeks.

Music Mostly **ballads**, **up-tempo**, **easy listening**, **disco** and **light pop**; also **instrumentals**. Produced "De Club Is Kampioen" (single by H. Spider/E. Govert), recorded by Benny Scott (light pop), released 2005 on Scorpion; *A Christmas of Hope* (album), recorded by Chris Clark (pop), released 2004 on 5 Stars; and *The Best of Le Grand Julot* (album), recorded by Le Grand Julot (accordion), released 2000 on Happy Melody.

☑ ⊕ ☐ JUNE PRODUCTIONS LTD.
The White House, 6 Beechwood Lane, Warlingham, Surrey CR6 9LT England. Phone: 44(0) 1883 622411Fax: 44(0)1883 652457. E-mail: david@mackay99.plus.com. **Contact:** David Mackay, producer. Record producer and music producer (Sabre Music). Estab. 1970. Produces 6 singles, 3 LPs and 3 CDs/year. Fee derived from sales royalty.

How to Contact Submit demo by mail. Unsolicited submissions are OK. Prefers CD or cassette with 1-2 songs and lyric sheet. SAE and IRC. Responds in 2 months.

Music Mostly **MOR**, **rock** and **top 40/pop**. Produced *Web of Love* (by various), recorded by Sarah Jory on Ritz Records (country rock). Other artists include Bonnie Tyler, Cliff Richard, Frankie Miller, Johnny Hallyday, Dusty Springfield, Charlotte Henry and Barry Humphries.

Tips "I am currently producing the music for the America 2007 celebrtions and two new musicals. I am happy to review songs, but on the understanding that it is less likely I can deliver cuts based on the fact I am currently rarely recording for single releases."

Ｎ ☐ KAREN KANE PRODUCER/ENGINEER
(910)681-0220. E-mail: mixmama@total.net. Web site: www.mixmama.com. **Contact:** Karen Kane, producer/engineer. Record producer and recording engineer. Estab. 1978. Produces 3-5 CDs/year. Fee derived from sales royalty when song or artist is recorded or outright fee from recording artist or record company.

How to Contact *E-mail first and obtain permission to submit.* Unsolicited submissions are *not* OK. "Please note: I am not a song publisher. My expertise is in album production." Does not return material. Responds in 1 week.

Music Mostly **rock**, **blues**, **pop**, **alternative**, **R&B/reggae**, **acoustic**, **country**, and **bluegrass**. Pro-

duced *Independence Meal* (album), recorded by Alix Olson (blues), released on Subtle Sister Records; *Topless* (Juno-nominated album), recorded by Big Daddy G, released on Reggie's Records. Mixed *Wise and Otherwise* (Juno-nominated album), recorded by Harry Manx (blues). Other artists include Tracy Chapman (her first demo), Chad Mitchell, Ember Swift, Laura Bird, Wishing Chair, Blue Mule, Barenaked Ladies (live recording for a TV special), and Ron Wiseman.
Tips "Get proper funding to be able to make a competitive, marketable product."

☐ L.A. ENTERTAINMENT, INC.
7095 Hollywood Blvd., #826, Hollywood CA 90028. (323)467-1496. Fax: (323)467-0911. E-mail: info@warriorrecords.com. Web site: www.WarriorRecords.com. **Contact:** Jim Ervin, A&R. Record producer, record company (Warrior Records) and music publisher (New Entity Music/ASCAP, New Copyright Music/BMI, New Euphonic Music/SESAC). Estab. 1988. Fee derived from sales royalty when song or artist is recorded.
How to Contact Submit demo by mail. Unsolicited submissions are OK. Prefers CD and/or videocassette with original songs, lyric and lead sheet if available. Does not review Internet sites. "Do not send MP3s, unless requested. All written submitted materials (e.g., lyric sheets, letter, etc.) should be typed." Does not return material unless SASE is included. Responds in 2 months only via e-mail or SASE.
Music All styles. "All genres are utilized with our music supervision company for Film & TV, but our original focus is on **alternative rock** and **urban genres** (e.g., **R&B**, **rap**, **gospel**)."

Ⓝ ☐ LARI-JON PRODUCTIONS
P.O. Box 216, Rising City NE 68658. (402)542-2336. **Contact:** Larry Good, owner. Record producer, music publisher (Lari-Jon Publishing/BMI), management firm (Lari-Jon Promotions) and record company (Lari-Jon Records). Estab. 1967. Produces 10 singles and 5 LPs/year. Fee derived from sales royalty when song or artist is recorded.
  • Also see the listings for other Lari-Jon companies in the Music Publishers, Record Companies, and Managers & Booking Agents sections of this book.
How to Contact Submit demo CD by mail. Unsolicited submissions are OK. "Must be a professional demo." Include SASE. Responds in 2 months.
Music Mostly **country, Southern gospel** and **'50s rock**. Produced *Jesus is my Hero* (album), written and recorded by Larry Good on Lari-Jon Records (gospel). Other artists include Brenda Allen, Tom Campbell and Tom Johnson.

☐ LAZY BONES PRODUCTIONS/RECORDINGS, INC.
9594 First Ave. NE, Suite 449, Seattle WA 98115-2012. (310)281-6232. Fax: (425)821-5720. E-mail: lbrinc@earthlink.net. Web site: www.lazybones.com. **Contact:** Scott Schorr, president. Record producer, record company and music publisher (Lazy Bones Music/BMI, Cat from Guatemala Music/ASCAP). Estab. 1992. Produces 4-6 CDs/year. Fee derived from sales royalty when song or artist is recorded or outright fee from recording artist (if unsigned) or outright fee from record company (if signed) or publishing royalties when co-songwriting with artist.
How to Contact Submit demo by mail. Unsolicited submissions are OK. Prefers cassette, DAT or CD with 3 songs (minimum) and lyric sheet. "If you honestly believe you can do better, improve your project to its greatest potential before submitting. With the number of projects received, if the material is not truly special and unique, it will not be taken seriously by a legitimate company." Does not return material. Responds in 1 month only if interested.
Music Mostly **alternative** and **rock**; also **hip-hop**. Produced *No Samples* (album by Da Blasta/Ratboy), recorded by Turntable Bay (hip-hop); and *Headland II* (album by Dave Hadland), recorded by Headland (pop), both on Lazy Bones. Other artists include Blackhead, MFTJ, B. Chestnut and Alan Charing.
Tips "Have outstanding and unique talent!"

☐ LINEAR CYCLE PRODUCTIONS
P.O. Box 2608, Sepulveda CA 91393-2608. E-mail: LCP@wgn.net. Web site: www.westworld.com/lcp/. **Contact:** Manny Pandanceski, producer. Record producer. Estab. 1980. Produces 15-25 sin-

gles, 6-10 12″ singles, 15-20 LPs and 10 CDs/year. Fee derived from sales royalty when song or artist is recorded.

How to Contact Submit demo by mail. Unsolicited submissions are OK. Prefers cassette, 7 3/8 ips reel-to-reel or ½″ VHS or ¾″ videocassette. Include SASE. Responds in 6 months.

Music Mostly **rock/pop**, **R&B/blues** and **country**; also **gospel** and **comedy**. Produced ''Lost In a Fog 4U'' (single by B. Hitte/N. Nigle/P. Grippe, etc.), recorded by L'il Shette (pop/dance), released 2003 on WIPie; ''Noz No Fippos'' (single by G. Juan) from his self titled album, recorded by Glax Aleart (alternative), released 2003 on Swip; and ''I Wanna F'' (single by Washington/''P''/Jaletyme/Supick) from *Bitty & Beans* (album), recorded by Y78H 22A (3W) (rap/hip-hop), released 2004 on Blyacke.

Tips ''We only listen to songs and other material recorded on quality tapes and CDs. We will not accept anything that sounds distorted, muffled and just plain bad! If you cannot afford to record demos on quality stock, or in some high aspects, shop somewhere else!''

☐ MAC-ATTACK PRODUCTIONS
868 NE 81st St., Miami FL 33138. (305)949-1422. E-mail: GoMacster@aol.com. **Contact:** Michael McNamee, engineer/producer. Record producer and music publisher (Mac-Attack Publishing/ASCAP). Estab. 1986. Fee derived from outright fee from recording artist or record company.

How to Contact Submit demo by mail. Unsolicited submissions are OK. Prefers CD or cassette or VHS videocassette with 3-5 songs, lyric sheet and bio. Does not return material. Responds in up to 3 months.

Music Mostly **pop**, **alternative rock** and **dance**. Produced and engineered *Tuscan Tongue* (album by Caution Automatic), recorded by Caution Automatic (rock), released 2005 on C.A. Records; Produced and engineered ''Never Gonna Let You Go'' (single by Bruce Jordan/John Link/Michael McNamee), recorded by Bruce Jordan (pop), released 2002 on H.M.S. Records; Produced and engineered ''They Don't Want This'' (single by Rip the Mic), recorded by Rip the Mic (hip-hop), released 2002 on Mac-Attack. Other artists include Blowfly, Tally Tal, Nina Llopis, The Lead, Girl Talk, Tyranny of Shaw and Jacobs Ladder.

N ☐ MAKERS MARK MUSIC PRODUCTIONS
534 W. Queen Lane, Philadelphia PA 19144. (215)849-7633. E-mail: Makers.Mark@verizon.net. Web site: www.mp3.com/paulhopkins. **Contact:** Paul E. Hopkins, producer/publisher. Record producer, music publisher and record company (Prolific Records). Estab. 1991. Produces 15 singles, 5 12″ singles and 4 LPs/year. Fee derived from outright fee from recording artist or record company. ''We produce professional music videos in VHS and DVD format.''

• Also see the listing for Makers Mark Gold in the Music Publishers section of this book.

How to Contact Submit demo or CD with bio by mail. Unsolicited submissions are OK. ''Explain concept of your music and/or style, and your future direction as an artist or songwriter.'' Does not return material. No need to call or send SASE. Responds in 6 weeks if interested.

Music Mostly **R&B**, **gospel**, **dance** and **pop**. Produced ''Because You Love Me'' (single by Anita Clement McCloud), recorded by Jacque Pate and Anita McCloud. Other artists include Larry Larr, Ruffhouse/Columbia, Nardo Ranks (international Jamaican artist), Elaine Monk (R&B), New Jerusalem (drama ministry), up-and-coming artists Tatiana (R&B), SAGE (R&B) and Christin McHenry (pop artist). Also produced *Pastor Alyn E. Waller Presents: The Enon Tabernacle Mass Choir* concert album and digital video (*Live from the Tabernacle*), released on ECDC Records/Universal Distributors (www.ebontab.org), Enon Mass Choir (from *Philadelphia Live at the Tabernacle*), New Jerusalem (drama ministry) and Tatiana (R&B). Produces music for Bunim/Murray productions network television, MTV's *Real World*, *Road Rules*, *Rebel Billionaire*, *Simple Life*, and movie soundtracks worldwide. Also produced deep soul remixes for Brian McKnight, Musiq Souchild, Jagged Edge, John Legend, and Elaine Monk.

☑ ☐ COOKIE MARENCO
P.O. Box 874, Belmont CA 94002. E-mail: cojemamusic@yahoo.com. (650)591-6857. Record producer/engineer. Over 20 years experience, 5 Grammy nominations, 2 gold rewards, proprietary

surround recording techniques. Estab. 1981. Produces 10 CDs/year. $2,000 per day payable in advance.

How to Contact Contact only if interested in production. Does not accept unsolicited material.

Music Mostly **alternative modern rock**, **country**, **folk**, **rap**, **ethnic** and **avante-garde**; also **classical**, **pop** and **jazz**. *Winter Solstice II* (album), written and recorded by various artists; *Heresay* (album by Paul McCandless); and *Deep At Night* (album by Alex DeGrassi), all on Windham Hill Records (instrumental). Other artists include Tony Furtado Band, Praxis, Oregon, Mary Chapin Carpenter, Max Roach and Charle Haden & Quartet West.

Tips "If you're looking for Beat Detective and Autotune, please call someone else. We still believe in analog recording and great musicianship."

☑ ◑ PETE MARTIN/VAAM MUSIC PRODUCTIONS

P.O. Box 29550, Hollywood CA 90029-0550. (323)664-7765. E-mail: pmarti3636@aol.com. Web site: www.VaamMusic.com. **Contact:** Pete Martin, president. Record producer, music publisher (Vaam Music/BMI and Pete Martin Music/ASCAP) and record company (Blue Gem Records). Estab. 1982.

   • Also see the listings for Vaam Music Group in the Music Publishers section of this book and Blue Gem Records in the Record Companies section of this book.

How to Contact Send CD or cassette with 2 songs and a lyric sheet. Send small packages only. Include SASE. Responds in 1 month.

Music Mostly **top 40/pop**, **country** and **R&B**.

Tips "Study the market in the style that you write. Songs must be capable of reaching top 5 on charts."

☑ ◌ SCOTT MATHEWS, D/B/A HIT OR MYTH PRODUCTIONS INC.

246 Almonte Blvd., Mill Valley CA 94941. Fax: (415)389-9682. E-mail: hitormyth@aol.com. Web site: www.ScottMathews.com. **Contact:** Mary Ezzell, A&R Director. President: Scott Mathews. Assistant: Tom Luekens. Record producer, song doctor, studio owner and music publisher (Hang On to Your Publishing/BMI). Estab. 1990. Produces 6-9 CDs/year. Fee derived from recording artist or record company (with royalty points).

   • Scott Mathews has several gold and platinum awards for sales of over 13 million records. He has worked on several Grammy and Oscar winning releases. In 2005, Scott Mathews-produced a full length album by The Rock and Roll Soldiers released on Atlantic records. In 2006 he was nominated for another Grammy.

How to Contact *"No phone calls or publishing submissions, please."* Submit demo CD by mail or an mp3 by email. "Unsolicited submissions are often the best ones and readily accepted." Include SASE and include your e-mail address on the CD. Responds in 2 months.

Music Mostly **rock/pop**, **alternative** and **singer/songwriters of all styles**. Produced 4 tracks on *Anthology (Best of)*, recorded by John Hiatt (rock/pop), released 2001 on Hip-O. Has produced Elvis Costello, Roy Orbison, Rosanne Cash, Jerry Garcia, Huey Lewis, and many more. Has recorded records with everyone from Barbra Streisand to John Lee Hooker, including Keith Richards, George Harrison, Mick Jagger, Van Morrison, Bonnie Raitt and Eric Clapton to name but a few.

Tips "These days if you are not independent, you are dependent. Sadly, to be dependent on a major label to develop, nurture, and stand by you in the early stages of your career is skating on thin ice at best. The new artists that are coming up and achieving success in the music industry are the ones that prove they have a vision and can make incredible records without the huge financial commitment of a major label. When an emerging artist makes great product for the genre they are in, they are in the driver's seat to be able to make a fair and equitable deal for distribution—be it with a major or independent label. My philosophy is to go where you are loved. The truth is, a smaller label that is completely dedicated to you and shares your vision may help your career far more than a huge label that will not keep you around if you don't sell millions of units. I feel too much pressure is put on the emerging artist when they have to pay hundreds of thousands of dollars back to the label in order to see their first royalty check—we all know those records can be made for a fraction of that cost without compromising quality or commercial appeal. I still believe in potential. It is up to us as record makers to take that potential into the studio and come out with music that can compete with anything else on the market. Discovering, developing and producing artists that can sustain long careers is our main focus at Hit or Myth Productions. Our artists own their own masters and publishing rights. If you love making music, don't let anyone dim that light. We look forward to hearing from you. (Please check out www.ScottMathews.com for more info, and also www.allmusic.com—keyword: Scott Mathews.)''

☒ ◪ MEGA TRUTH RECORDS

P.O. Box 4988, Culver City CA 90231. E-mail: jonbare@aol.com. Web site: www.jonbare.net. **Contact:** Jon Bare, CEO. Record producer and record company. Estab. 1994. Produces 2 CDs/year. Fee negotiable.

How to Contact Submit demo by mail. Unsolicited submissions are OK. Prefers CD. ''We specialize in recording world-class virtuoso musicians and bands with top players.'' Does not return material. Responds in 2 weeks only if interested.

Music Mostly **rock**, **blues** and **country rock**; also **swing**, **dance** and **instrumental**. Produced *Party Platter* recorded by Hula Monsters (swing); and *Killer Whales, Shredzilla and Orcastra* (by Jon Bare and the Killer Whales) (rock), all on Mega Truth Records. Other artists include The Rich Harper Blues Band, Aeon Dream & the Dream Machine and Techno Dudes.

Tips ''Create a unique sound that blends great vocals and virtuoso musicianship with a beat that makes us want to get up and dance.''

☒ ◪ MONTICANA PRODUCTIONS

P.O. Box 702, Snowdon Station, Montreal QC H3X 3X8 Canada. **Contact:** David Leonard, executive producer. Record producer, music publisher (Montina Music) and record company (Monticana Records). Estab. 1963. Fee derived from sales royalty when song or artist is recorded.

• Also see the listings for Monticana Records in the Record Companies section and Montina Music in the Music Publishers section of this book.

How to Contact Submit demo by mail. Unsolicited submissions are OK. Prefers CD with maximum 4 songs. ''Demos should be as tightly produced as a master.'' Include SASE.

Music Mostly **top 40**; also **bluegrass**, **blues**, **country**, **dance-oriented**, **easy listening**, **folk**, **gospel**, **jazz**, **MOR**, **progressive**, **R&B**, **rock** and **soul**.

Tips ''Work creatively and believe passionately in what you do and aspire to be. Success comes to those who persevere, have talent, develop their craft and network.''

◪ MUSTROCK PRODUCTIONZ WORLDWIDE

Office: 167 W. 81st St., Suite 5C, New York NY 10024-7200. (212)799-9268. E-mail: recordmode@ho tmail.com. President: Ivan ''Doc'' Rodriguez. Record producer and recording/mixing/mastering engineer. Estab. 1987. Produces 5 singles, engineers 6 CDs/year. Fee derived from sales royalty when song or artist is recorded. *''We provide services for a fee—we do not sign or represent artists.''*

How to Contact *E-mail first and obtain permission to submit.* Prefers CD, DVD and lyric sheet. Does not return material. Responds in 2 months.

Music Mostly **hip-hop**, **R&B** and **pop**; also **soul**, **ballads** and **soundtracks**. Produced ''Poor Georgie'' (by MC Lyte/DJ DOC), recorded by MC Lyte on Atlantic Records (rap). Other artists include Caron Wheeler, The Hit Squad, The Awesome II, Black Steel Music, Underated Productions, EPMD, Redman, Dr. Dre & Ed-Lover, Das-EFX, Biz Markie, BDP, Eric B & Rakim, The Fugees, The Bushwackass, Shai and Pudgee, Alisha Keys, 50 cent, Tiro de Garcia, etc.

Tips ''Services provided include ProTools production (pre/post/co), digital tracking, mixing, remixing, live show tapes, jingles, etc. For additional credits, go to www.allmusic.com, type 'Ivan Doc Rodriguez' under 'artist' and enter, or send e-mail.''

◯ NEU ELECTRO PRODUCTIONS

P.O. Box 1582, Bridgeview IL 60455. (630)257-6289. E-mail: neuelectro@email.com. Web site: www.neuelectro. com. **Contact:** Bob Neumann, owner. Record producer and record company.

Estab. 1984. Produces 16 singles, 16 12″ singles, 20 LPs and 4 CDs/year. Fee derived from outright fee from record company or recording artist.

How to Contact Submit demo by mail. Unsolicited submissions are OK. Prefers cassette or CD with 3 songs and lyric sheet or lead sheet. "Provide accurate contact phone numbers and addresses, promo packages and photos." Include SASE for reply. Responds in 2 weeks. "A production fee estimate will be returned to artist."

Music Mostly **dance**, **house**, **techno**, **rap** and **rock**; also **experimental**, **New Age** and **top 40**. Produced "Juicy" (single), written and recorded by Juicy Black on Dark Planet International Records (house); "Make Me Smile" (single), written and recorded by Roz Baker (house); *Reactovate-6* (album by Bob Neumann), recorded by Beatbox-D on N.E.P. Records (dance); and *Sands of Time* (album), recorded by Bob Neumann (New Age). Other artists include Skid Marx and The Deviants.

☑ ◿ NEW EXPERIENCE RECORDS/FAZE 4 RECORDS

P.O. Box 683, Lima OH 45802. E-mail: just_chilling_2002@yahoo.com. Web site: www.faze4record s.com. **Contact:** A&R Department. Music Publisher: James L. Milligan Jr. Record producer, music publisher (A New Rap Jam Publishing/ASCAP), management firm (Creative Star Management) and record company (New Experience Records, Grand-Slam Records and Pump It Up Records). Estab. 1989. Produces 15-20 12″ singles, 2 LPs, 3 EPs and 2-5 CDs/year. Fee derived from sales royalty when song or artist is recorded or outright fee from record company, "depending on services required."

> • Also see the listings for A New Rap Jam Publishing in the Music Publishers section of this book.

How to Contact *Write first to arrange personal interview.* Address material to A&R Dept. or Talent Coordinator. Prefers CD with a minimum of 3 songs and lyric or lead sheet (if available). "If tapes are to be returned, proper postage should be enclosed and all tapes and letters should have SASE for faster reply." Responds in 6-8 weeks.

Music Mostly **pop**, **R&B** and **rap**; also **gospel**, **contemporary gospel** and **rock**. Produced "The Son of God" (single by James Milligan/Anthony Milligan/Melvin Milligan) from *The Final Chapter* (album), recorded by T.M.C. Milligan Conection (R&B, Gospel), released 2002 on New Experience/Pump It Up Records. Other artists include Dion Mikel, Paulette Mikel, Melvin Milligan and Venesta Compton.

Tips "Do your homework on the music business. Be aware of all the new sampling laws. There are too many sound alikes. Be yourself. I look for what is different, vocal ability, voice range and sound stage presence, etc. Be on the look out for our new blues label Rough Edge Records/Rough Edge Entertainment. blues material is now being reviewed. Send your best studio recorded material. Also be aware of the new sampling laws and the New Digital downloading laws. People are being jailed and fined for recording music that has not been paid for. Do your homework. We have also signed Diamond Sound Productions, located in Fresno, CA and Ground Breakers Records. Now we can better serve our customers on the East and West Coast. You can also visit our Web site at www.faze4records.com for further information on our services. We are also seeking artists and groups singers from the '60s, '70s, and '80s who would like to be re-signed. Please contact us. Please state your intentions when submitting your material and contact information. We have had submissions from artists who could have received a possible record deal from one of our labels, but we had no contact information. Once again, do your homework, please. Good luck!"

☑ ◻ NIGHTWORKS RECORDS

355 W. Potter Dr., Anchorage AK 99518. (907)562-3754. Fax: (907)561-4367. E-mail: kurt@nightwo rks.com. Web site: www.surrealstudios.com. **Owner:** Kurt Riemann. Record producer. Produces 16 CDs/year. Fees derived from sales royalty when song or artist is recorded.

How to Contact Submit demo by mail. Unsolicited submissions are OK. Prefers CD with 2-3 songs "produced as fully as possible. Send jingles and songs on separate CDs." Does not return material. Responds in 1 month.

Music Produces a variety of music from **native Alaskan** to **Techno** to **Christmas**.

◻ PHILLY BREAKDOWN RECORDING CO.

216 W. Hortter St., Philadelphia PA 19119. (215)848-6725. E-mail: mattcozar@juno.com. **Contact:** Matthew Childs, president. Music Director: Charles Nesbit. Record producer, music publisher (Philly Breakdown/BMI) and record company. Estab. 1974. Produces 3 singles and 2 LPs/year. Fee derived from sales royalty when song or artist is recorded.

How to Contact *Contact first and obtain permission to submit.* Prefers cassette with 4 songs and lead sheet. Does not return material. Responds in 2 months.

Music Mostly **R&B**, **hip-hop** and **pop**; also **jazz**, **gospel** and **ballads**. Produced "Lonely River" (single by Clarence Patterson/M. Childs) from *Lonely River* (album), recorded by Gloria Clark; and *Taps* (album), recorded by H Factor, both released 2001 on Philly Breakdown. Other artists include Leroy Christy, Gloria Clark, Jerry Walker, Nina Bundy, Mark Adam, Emmit King, Betty Carol, The H Factor and Four Buddies.

Tips "If you fail, just learn from your past experience and keep on trying, until you get it done right. Never give up."

◪ JIM PIERCE

Dept. SM, 101 Hurt Rd., Hendersonville TN 37075. Phone/fax: (615)824-5900. E-mail: jim@jimpierce.net. Web site: www.jimpierce.net. **Contact:** Jim Pierce, president. Record producer, music publisher (Strawboss Music/BMI) and record company (Round Robin Records). Estab. 1974. Fee derived from sales royalty or outright fee from recording artist. "Many artists pay me in advance for my services." Has had over 200 chart records to date.

How to Contact *E-mail first and obtain permission to submit.* Prefers CD with 3 songs and lyric sheet. Will accept cassettes. Does not return material. Responds only if interested. "All submissions should include their contact phone number and/or e-mail address."

Music Mostly **contemporary and traditional country**, **pop** and **gospel**. Have produced projects with George Jones, Waylon Jennings, Willie Nelson, Tommy Cash, Johnny Cash, Jimmy C. Newman, Bobby Helms, Sammi Smith, Charlie Louvin and Melba Montgomery, and many others.

Tips "Industry is seeking good singers who can write songs. Viewing our Web site is highly recommended."

◪ ◻ THE PRESCRIPTION CO.

P.O. Box 222249, Great Neck NY 11021. (415)553-8540. E-mail: therxco@yahoo.com. **Contact:** David F. Gasman, president. San Francisco office: 525 Ashbury St., San Francisco CA 94117. (415)553-8540. VP Sales (West Coast warehouse): Bruce Brennan. Record producer and music publisher. Fee derived from sales royalty when artist or song is recorded or outright fee from record company.

• Also see the listing for Prescription Company in the Music Publishers section of this book.

How to Contact *Write or call first about your interest then submit demo.* Prefers cassette with any number of songs and lyric sheet. Include SASE. "Does not return material without SASE and sufficient postage."

Music Mostly **bluegrass**, **blues**, **children's**, **country**, **dance**, **easy listening**, **jazz**, **MOR**, **progressive**, **R&B**, **rock**, **soul** and **top 40/pop**. Produced "The World's Most Dangerous Man," "Here Comes Trouble" and "Automated People" (singles by D.F. Gasman) from *Special EP No. 1* (album), all recorded by Medicine Mike (rock), all released 2003 on Prescription.

◻ REEL ADVENTURES

9 Peggy Lane, Salem NH 03079. (603)898-7097. Web site: www.reeladventures1.homestead.com. **Contact:** Rick Asmega, chief engineer/producer. Record producer. Estab. 1972. Produces 100 12" singles, 200 LPs, 5 EPs and 40 CDs/year. Fee derived from sales royalty when song or artist is recorded, or outright fee from recording artist or record company.

How to Contact Submit demo by mail. Unsolicited submissions are OK. Prefers cassette or CD. Include SASE. Responds in 6 weeks.

Music Mostly **pop**, **funk** and **country**; also **blues**, **Christian reggae** and **rock**. Produced *Funky Broadway* (album), recorded by Chris Hicks; *Testafye* (album), recorded by Jay Williams; and

"Acoustical Climate" (single by John G.). Other artists include Nicole Hajj, The Bolz, Second Sinni, Larry Sterling, Broken Men, Melvin Crockett, Fred Vigeant, Monster Mash, Carl Armand, Cool Blue Sky, Ransome, Backtrax, Push, Too Cool for Humans and Burn Alley.

RN'D DISTRIBUTION, LLC.

(formerly RN'D Productions), P.O. Box 540102, Houston TX 77254-0102. (713)521-2616, ext. 10. Fax: (713)529-4914. E-mail: AandR@aol.com. Web site: www.rnddistribution.com. **Contact:** Caudell Baham, A&R director. National Sales Director: Ramon Smith. Record producer, record company (Albatross Records), distributor (labels distributed include Suavehouse Records, Albatross Records, TDA Music and Ball In' Records) and music publisher (Ryedale Publishing). Estab. 1986. Produces 25 singles, 20 LPs, 4 EPs and 21 CDs/year.

• Also see the listing for Albatross Records in the Record Companies section of this book.

How to Contact Submit demo by mail. Unsolicited submissions are OK. Prefers CD with 4 songs and lyric sheet. Does not return material. Responds in 1 month.

Music All types.

RUSTRON MUSIC PRODUCTIONS

1156 Park Lane, West Palm Beach FL 33417-5957. (561)686-1354. E-mail: rmp_wmp@bellsouth.net. **Contact:** Sheelah Adams, office administrator. Executive Director: Rusty Gordon. Director of A&R: Ron Caruso. Assistant A&R Director: Kevin Reeves. Record producer, record company, manager and music publisher (Rustron Music Publishers/BMI and Whimsong Publishing/ASCAP). Estab. 1970. Produces 10 CDs/year. Fee derived from sales royalty when song or artist is recorded or outright fee from record company. "This branch office reviews all material submitted for the home office in Connecticut."

• Also see the listings for Rustron Music Publishers in the Music Publishers section and Rustron Music Productions in the Record Companies and Managers & Booking Agents sections of this book.

How to Contact *Songwriters may write, call or e-mail first to discuss your submission.* We prefer you e-mail a request for current submission guidelines. Include a SASE or International Response Coupon (IRC) if requesting guidelines or other information by snail-mail. All correspondence should include SASE or International Response Coupon (IRC), no exceptions. Submit CD or cassette demo by snail-mail. Prefers CD with up to 15 songs. We will do a "body of work" review for multiple CDs that were produced to sell at performing songwriter's gigs. 1-3 songs on cassette tape submissions. Include 8½ × 11 typed lyric sheets, 1 sheet per song. Also include cover letter clearly explaining your reason for submitting. Tell us about you and if you are a freelance or performing songwriter. Do you create songs with collaborators? Songs for single-song marketing should be 3-3½ minutes long or less and must be commercially viable and carefully crafted with definitive verse melody. New Age fusion or World Music Instrumentals 3-10 minutes each, 1 hour maximum for all songs. Responds in 4 months.

Music Mostly **mainstream**, **progressive country**, **pop** (ballads, blues, theatrical, cabaret), **soft rock**, **folk/rock**, and **adult contemporary**, **electric acoustic**; also **R&B**, **New Age/world music**, **instrumental fusions**, **children's music**, **women's music**, **African or Native American synthesis**, **reggae** and **light jazz**. Produced "Hurricane Harassment" (single) from *Hurricane Harassment* (album), written and recorded by Continental Divide (topical), released 2006 on Rustron Records; "The Baobab Tree and Me" (single) from *The Baobab Tree* (album) written and recorded by Tracie Mitchell & Ivory Coast (folk rock), released 2005 on Whimsong Records; "Resisting The Right" (single) from *Resisting The Right* (album), written and recorded by The Florida Rank & File (sociopolitical) released 2006 on Rustron Records. Other artists include Haze Coates, Star Smiley, Jayne Margo-Reby, Stacie Jubal, Deb Criss, Robin Plitt, Boomslang Swampsinger.

Tips "Be open to developing your own unique style. Write well-crafted songs with unpredictable concepts, strong hooks and definitive verse melodies. New Age and world music composers: evolve your themes and use multiculturally diverse instruments to embellish your compositions/arrangements. Don't be predictable. Experiment with instrumental fusion with jazz and/or classical themes, pop themes and international styles. Don't overproduce your demos or drown the vocals.

Craft songs carefully for single-song marketing. On a 10 song album, 9 songs can be eclectic/loosely crafted, it takes only 1 carefully crafted 'radio-ready' song, with the right arrangement to get your album the exposure it needs.''

☐ STEVE SATKOWSKI RECORDINGS

P.O. Box 3403, Stuart FL 34995. (772)225-3128. Web site: www.clearsoulproductions.com/stevesatkowski.html. Engineer/producer: Steven Satkowski. Record producer, recording engineer, management firm and record company. Estab. 1980. Produces 20 CDs/year. Fee derived from outright fee from recording artist or record company.

How to Contact Submit demo by mail. Unsolicited submissions are OK. Prefers CD or cassette. Does not return material. Responds in 2 weeks.

Music Mostly **classical**, **jazz** and **big band**. Produced recordings for National Public Radio and affiliates. Engineered recordings for Steve Howe, Patrick Moraz, Kenny G and Michael Bolton.

◖ SEGAL'S PRODUCTIONS

16 Grace Rd., Newton MA 02459. (617)969-6196. Fax: (617)969-6614. Web site: www.charlessegal. com. **Contact:** Charles Segal. Record producer, music publisher (Segal's Publications/BMI and Samro South Africa) and record company (Spin Records). Produces 6 singles and 6 LPs/year. Produced 21 CD's in 2005. Fee derived from sales royalty when song or artist is recorded.

• Also see the listing for Segal's Publications in the Music Publishers section of this book.

• Charles and Colleen Segal have also been commissioned to write a ''Quick and Easy Songwriting'' book for beginners.

How to Contact *Write first and obtain permission to submit or to arrange personal interview.* Prefers cassette, CD or videocassette with 3 songs and lyric sheet or lead sheet of melody, words, chords. ''Please record keyboard/voice or guitar/voice if you can't get a group.'' Does not return material. Do not send originals. Responds in 3 months only if interested.

Music Mostly **rock**, **pop** and **country**; also **R&B** and **comedy.** ''You're not alone'' (single by Barbera Brilliant), *African Fantasy* (album by Charles Segal), ''Animal Concepts'' (single by Lindsy Duplesey), *My Way* (LP by Rick Shrider) ''Michelle meets Mark'' (single), ''Reeve's Song'' (single), *Steve's Favorites* (album) and *Magical Mystery Man* and *Everyday things* (albums by Colleen Segal, produced by Collen and Charles Segal). Other artists include Art Heatley, Dan Hill and Melanie. Has also published songbooks which include *Opus Africa* and *Songs of Africa.*

Tips ''Make a good and clear production of cassette even if it is only piano rhythm and voice. Also do a lead sheet of music, words and chords.''

◼ ◪ ☐ SILVER BOW PRODUCTIONS

556 Amess St., New Westminster BC V3L 4A9 Canada. (604)930-9309. Fax: (604)523-9310. E-mail: saddlestone@shaw.ca. Web site: www.saddlestone.net. **Contact:** Candice James, Rex Howard, Grant Lucas—A&R. Record producers. Estab. 1986. Produces 16 singles, and 6 CDs/year. Fee derived from outright fee from recording artist.

• Also see the listings for Saddlestone Publishing in the Music Publishers section and Silver Bow Management in the Managers & Booking Agents section of this book.

How to Contact Prefers cd or cassette with 2 songs and lyric sheet. Does not return material. Responds in 6 weeks.

Music Mostly **country**, **pop**, and **rock**; also **gospel**, **blues** and **jazz.** Produced *Fragile-Handle With Care*, recorded by Razzy Bailey on SOA Records (country); *High Society*, written and recorded by Darrell Meyers (country); and *Man I Am*, written and recorded by Stang Giles (country crossover), both released 2000 on Saddlestone Records. Other artists include Rex Howard, Gerry King, Joe Lonsdale, Barb Farrell, Dorrie Alexander, Peter James, Matt Audette and Cordel James.

◪ ⊘ SOUL CANDY PRODUCTIONS

176-B Woodridge Crescent, Ottawa ON K2B 7S9 Canada. (613)820-5715. Fax: (613)820-8736. E-mail: jshakka@hotmail.com. Web site: www.jonesshakka.com. **Contact:** Jon E. Shakka, co-president. Record producer. Estab. 1988. Produces 1 album/year. Fee derived from sales royalty when song or artist is recorded.

How to Contact *Does not accept unsolicited submissions.*

Music Mostly **funk**, **rap** and **house music**; also **pop**, **ballads** and **funk-rock**. Produced *I'm My Brother's Keeper* (album), recorded by The Jon E. Shakka Project (funk rap), released 2001 on Poku Records. Other artists include Uncut Records, Double F, and LY.

✒ SOUND ARTS RECORDING STUDIO

8377 Westview Dr., Houston TX 77055. (713)464-GOLD. E-mail: sarsjef@aol.com. Web site: sound artsrecording.com. **Contact:** Jeff Wells, president. Record producer and music publisher (Earths-cream Music). Estab. 1974. Produces 12 singles and 3 LPs/year. Fee derived from sales royalty when song or artist is recorded.

- Also see the listings for Earthscream Music Publishing in the Music Publishers section and Surface Records in the Record Companies section of this book.

How to Contact Submit demo by mail. Unsolicited submissions are OK. Prefers cassette with 2-5 songs and lyric sheet. Does not return material. Responds in 6 weeks.

Music Mostly pop/rock, country and blues. Produced *Texas Johnny Brown* (album), written and recorded by Texas Johnny Brown on Quality (blues); and "Sherly Crow" (single), recorded by Dr. Jeff and the Painkillers. Other artists include Tim Nichols, Perfect Strangers, B.B. Watson, Jinkies, Joe "King" Carasco (on Surface Records), Mark May (on Icehouse Records), The Barbara Penning-ton Band (on Earth Records), Tempest Under the Sun, and Attitcus Finch.

✓ ◯ SOUND WORKS ENTERTAINMENT PRODUCTIONS INC.

P.O. Box 30, Virginia City NV 89440. (775)315-3255. E-mail: mike@musicjones.com. Web site: www.musicjones.com. **Contact:** Michael E. Jones, president. Record producer, record company (Sound Works Records) and music publisher (Sound Works Music). Estab. 1989. Produces 16 singles, 2 LPs and 20 CDs/year. Fee derived from sales royalty when song or artist is recorded or outright fee from recording artist or record company.

How to Contact Submit demo by mail. Unsolicited submissions are OK. Prefers cassette with 3-6 songs and lyric sheet. "Please include short bio and statement of goals and objectives." Does not return material. Responds in 6 weeks.

Music Mostly **country**, **folk** and **pop**; also **rock**. Produced "Lonelyville," and "Alabama Slammer" (singles), both written and recorded by Wake Eastman; and "Good Looking Loser" (single), written and recorded by Renee Rubach, all on Sound Works Records (country). Other artists include Matt Dorman, Steve Gilmore, The Tackroom Boys, The Los Vegas Philharmonic and J.C. Clark.

Tips "Put your ego on hold. Don't take criticism personally. Advice is meant to help you grow and improve your skills as an artist/songwriter. Be professional and business-like in all your dealings."

✓ ✒ SPHERE GROUP ONE

795 Waterside Dr., Marco Island FL 34145. (239)398-6800. Fax: (239)394-9881. E-mail: spheregroup one@att.net. **Contact:** Tony Zarrella, president. Talent Manager: Janice Salvatore. Record producer, artist development and management firm. Produces 5-6 singles and 3 CDs/year. Estab. 1986.

How to Contact Submit CD/video by mail. Unsolicited submissions are OK. Prefers CD or DVD with 3-5 songs and lyric sheets. "Must include: photos, press, résumé, goals and specifics of project submitted, etc." Does not return material.

Music Mostly **pop/rock (mainstream)**, **progressive/rock**, **New Age** and **crossover country/pop**; also **film soundtracks**. Produced song titles: *Rock to the Rescue, Sunset At Night, Double Trouble, Take This Heart, It's Our Love* and *You and I* (by T. Zarrella), recorded by 4 of Hearts (pop/rock) on Sphere Records and/or various labels. Other associated artists include Frontier 9, Oona Falcon, Myth, Survivor and Wicked Lester/Kiss.

Tips "Take direction, have faith in yourself, producer and manager. Currently seeking artists/ groups incorporating various styles into a focused mainstream product. Groups with a following are a plus. Artist development is our expertise and we listen! In the pocket, exceptional songs, experienced performers necessary."

N ☐ SRS PRODUCTIONS/HIT RECORDS NETWORK

6633 Yucca St., Suite #311, Hollywood CA 90028. (323)467-4082. E-mail: GLB@hotmail.com. **Contact:** Greg Lewolt, Ernie Orosco and J.C. Martin, producers. Record producer, record company (Night City Records, Warrior Records and Tell International Records), radio and TV promotion and music publisher. Estab. 1984. Produces 4 singles, 2 12″ singles, 4 LPs, 2 EPs and 2-4 CDs/year. Fee derived from outright fee from record company.

How to Contact Submit demo by mail. Unsolicited submissions are OK. Prefers cassette, CD or VHS videocassette with 4-8 songs, photos, bio and lyric sheet. Does not return material. Include SASE. Responds in 2 months.

Music Mostly **pop-rock**, **country** and **top 40**; also **top 40 funk**, **top 40 rock** and **top 40 country**. Produced "Do You Remember When" (single by Liehengood/B. Faith) from *Legends of Rock* (album), recorded by Bobby Harris (Drifters) and Greg Munford (Strawberry Alarm Clock) (pop), released 2002 on Hit Records Network; "Blond Adventure" (single by JC Martin) from *Blond Adventure* (album), recorded by Black Angel (r&b rock), released 2002 on Outsider-Hit Records Network; "Michael" (single by B. Faith/F. Towles/K. Dyer) from *Anthology* (album), recorded by Brian Faith/Nic St. Nicholas (Steppenwolf) (pop rock), released 2002 on All American Records. Other artists include New Vision, Jade, Ernie and the Emperors, Hollywood Heros, Tim Bogert (Vanilla Fudge, Jeff Beck), Peter Lewis, Jim Calire (America), Mike Kowalski, Greg Munford (Strawberry Alarm Clock), Bobby Harris (Drifters), Ernie Knapp (Beach Boys) and Jewel.

Tips "Keep searching for the infectious chorus hook and don't give up."

☐ STUART AUDIO SERVICES

134 Mosher Rd., Gorham ME 04038. (207)892-0960. E-mail: js@stuartaudio.com. Web site: www.stuartaudio.com. **Contact:** John A. Stuart, producer/owner. Record producer and music publisher. Estab. 1979. Produces 5-8 CDs/year. Fee derived from sales royalty when song or artist is recorded, outright fee from recording artist or record company, or demo and consulting fees.

How to Contact *Write or call first and obtain permission to submit or to arrange a personal interview.* Prefers CD with 4 songs and lyric sheet. Include SASE. Responds in 2 months.

Music Mostly **alternative folk-rock**, **rock** and **country**; also **contemporary Christian**, **children's** and **unusual**. Produced *One of a Kind* (by various artists), recorded by Elizabeth Boss on Bosco Records (folk); *Toad Motel*, written and recorded by Rick Charrette on Fine Point Records (children's); and *Holiday Portrait*, recorded by USM Chamber Singers on U.S.M. (chorale). Other artists include Noel Paul Stookey, Beavis & Butthead (Mike Judge), Don Campbell, Jim Newton and John Angus.

☐ STUDIO SEVEN

417 N. Virginia, Oklahoma City OK 73106. (405)236-0643. Fax: (405)236-0686. E-mail: cope@okla.net. Web site: www.lunacyrecords.com. **Contact:** Dave Copenhaver, producer. Record producer, record company (Lunacy Records) and music publisher (Lunasong Music). Estab. 1990. Produces 10 LPs and CDs/year. Fee is derived from sales royalty when song or artist is recorded or outright fee from recording artist or record company. "All projects are on a customized basis."

How to Contact *Contact first and obtain permission to submit.* Prefers cassette with lyric sheet. Include SASE. Responds in 6 weeks.

Music Mostly **rock**, **jazz-blues** and **world-Native American**; also **country** and **blues**. Produced "Like A Lifetime" (single) from *Where the Wind Blows* (album), written and recorded by Stephanie Musser (easy listening), released 2004 on Passio Productions; "Wouldn't Be the First Time" (single) from *Picasso's Clouds* (album), written and recorded by Dustin Pittsley (rock), released 2004 on Lunacy Records; and "On My Way" (single) from *On My Way* (album), written and recorded by Joe Merrick (country), all released 2004 on Lunacy Records. Other artists include Harvey Shelton, Steve Pryor, Ken Taylor, Albert Aguilar, 2 A.M., and Curt Shoemaker.

☐ SWIFT RIVER PRODUCTIONS

P.O. Box 231, Gladeville TN 37071. (615)316-9479. E-mail: office@andymay.com. Web site: www.swiftrivermusic.com. **Contact:** Andy May, producer/owner. Record producer and record company.

Estab. 1979. Produces 40 singles and 4 CDs/year. Fee paid by artist or artist's management. Works with recording client to come up with budget for individual project. Provides world-class backing musicians and thorough pre-studio preparation as needed.

How to Contact *Write or call first and obtain permission to submit.* "Let us know your background, present goals and reason for contacting us so we can tell if we are able to help you. Demo should be clear and well thought out. Vocal plus guitar or piano is fine." Does not return material. Responds in up to 1 months.

Music Mostly **country**, **singer/songwriters** and **"roots" (folk, acoustic, bluegrass and rock)**; also **instrumental**. Produced *Natick, There's Talk About a Fence* and *Look What Thoughts Will Do* (albums), by Rick Lee (folk/Americana); *Second Wind* (album), by Bill Mulroney (contemporary folk/Americana); *Dreamin' the Blues* (album), by Henry May (blues guitar); and *Flyin' Fast* (album), by Brycen Fast (country), released 2003 on Swift River. Other artists include Marinda Flom and Curtis McPeake.

Tips "I'm interested in artists who are accomplished, self-motivated, and able to accept direction. I'm looking for music that is intelligent, creative and in some way contributes something positive. We are a production house; we accept song submissions from our production clients only."

☑ ○ ROGER VINCENT TARI

P.O. Box 576, Piscataway NJ 08855. E-mail: rogervtari@earthlink.net. Office: (732)529-4808. Voice: (908)338-7299. Web site: http://home.earthlink.net/~rogervtari/index.html. **Contact:** Roger Vincent Tari, president/producer. Vice President: Mike Roze. A&R: Joe Tasi. Live Booking Department: Mike Bino. Record producer, record company (VT Records), music publisher (Vintari Music/ASCAP) and magazine publisher (*Music of the World for Youth Culture*). Estab. 1979. Produces 6-8 singles/year. Fee derived from sales royalty when song or artist is recorded, statutory for mechanical and negotiated license agreement for all distribution, etc.

How to Contact Submit demo by mail. Unsolicited submissions are OK. Prefers CD, vinyl, cassette, DVD, or VHS videocassette with 3 songs and lyric sheet (videocassette is optional). "The artist should send any relevant literature and a simple black and white picture along with the 3-song CD/cassette and lyric sheet." Include SASE. Responds in 1 month.

Music Mostly **female pop**, **new wave**, **art rock**, **synth-pop**, **R&B** and **innovative hip-hop**; also **world pop, J-pop, 80's style hair rock bands, visual melodic hard rock** and **avant jazz**. Produced "Bad Apple" (single by Reiko Lai/Chung Ho J Lee), recorded by Flush (indie-pop/rock), released 2002 on VT Music/VR Records; "Notice of Death" (single by Scott Cheng), recorded by Scott Cheng (hard rock), released 2002 on VT Music/VT Records; and "Rocket Adventure To Jupiter" written and recorded by John Paul Immordino (synth-pop) released 2005 on VT Music/VT Records. Other artists include Neko Zhang, Trippin on Dolls, Fractured Glass, The Subterraneans, Tin Pan Alley, Smol, and The Last Patrol.

Tips "We seek Pop artists from around the world. Especially female-oriented artists and bands, etc. The music should be new and creative regardless of style. VT Records and Music of the World are distributed by Seven Gods/Benten in Tokyo and the 7″ record label in Taiwan. We are distributor for the 7″ record label and Benten/Sister Records in the East Coast of the U.S.A. VT Music are also exclusive distributor/licenser for all Canadian-American and Caprice International recordings and their affiliate labels throughout Asia and the Pacific rim. Canadian-American Artists include: Reese N Rhythm, B-4-Real, Keenan Baxter, and Noble Gas, as well as legendary Canadian-American/ Caprice artists; Janie Grant, Linda Scott, and Joey Welz, etc. This year VT Music also added 'Dagger' Promotions into its distribution ring. Distributing classic punk releases including artists 'Dennis Most & The Instigators and the compilation (vinyl) album, *Hardcore From The Early Days*, etc."

○ TMC PRODUCTIONS

P.O. Box 12353, San Antonio TX 78212. (210)829-1909. E-mail: axbar@STIC.net. Web site: www.ax barmusic.com. **Contact:** Joe Scates, producer. Record producer, music publisher (Axbar Productions/BMI, Scates & Blanton/BMI and Axe Handle Music/ASCAP), record company (Axbar, Trophy, Jato, Prince and Charro Records) and record distribution and promotion. Produces 2-3 CDs/year. Fee derived from sales royalty.

How to Contact *Please write or call first and obtain permission to submit.* Prefers CD and accepts cassettes with 1-5 songs and lyric sheet. Does not return material. Responds "as soon as possible, but don't rush us."

Music Mostly **traditional country**; also **blues**, **novelty** and **rock (soft)**. Produced "Chicken Dance" (single) (traditional), recorded by George Chambers and "Hobo Heart" (single), written and recorded by Juni Moon, both on Axbar Records. Other artists include Jim Marshall, Caroll Gilley, Rick Will, Wayne Carter, Kathi Timm, Leon Taylor, Mark Chestnutt, Kenny Dale and Britney Hendrickson.

Tips "We are in the business of making good music."

☐ THE TRINITY STUDIO

P.O. Box 1417, Corpus Christi TX 78403. (361)854-SING. E-mail: info@trinitystudio.com. Web site: www.trinitystudio.com. **Contact:** Jim Wilken, owner. Record producer and recording studio. Estab. 1988. Fee derived from outright fee from recording artist or record company.

How to Contact Submit demo by mail. Unsolicited submissions are OK. Accepts demos in all formats. Does not return material. Responds in 1 month.

Music Mostly **Christian-country**. Produced *Miracle Man* (album), written and recorded by Merrill Lane (country Christian) on TC Records; and *Higher Love* (album by Merrill Lane/Becky Redels), recorded by Becky Redels (country Christian). Other artists include Kerry Patton, Patty Walker, Leah Knight, Lofton Kline, Rockports Gospel Force, and Jackie Cole.

☑ VALTEC PRODUCTIONS

P.O. Box 6018, Santa Maria CA 93456. (805)928-8559. Web site: www.valtec.net. **Contact:** Joe Valenta, producer. Record producer. Estab. 1986. Produces 20 singles and 10 CDs/year. Fee derived from sales royalty when song or artist is recorded.

How to Contact Submit demo by mail. Unsolicited submissions are OK. Prefers CD or DVD with 3 songs and lyric or lead sheet. Send photo. Does not return material (kept on file for 2 years). Responds in 6 weeks.

Music Mostly **country**, **Christian**, **pop/AC** and **rock**.

☐ THE WEISMAN PRODUCTION GROUP

449 N. Vista St., Los Angeles CA 90036. (323)653-0693. E-mail: parlirec@aol.com. **Contact:** Ben Weisman, owner. Record producer and music publisher (Audio Music Publishers). Estab. 1965. Produces 10 singles/year. Fee derived from sales royalty when song or artist is recorded.

- Also see the listings for Audio Music Publishers and Queen Esther Music Publishers in the Music Publishers section of this book.

How to Contact Submit demo CD or tape by mail. Unsolicited submissions are OK. Prefers CD or cassette with 3-10 songs and lyric sheet. Include SASE. "Mention *Songwriter's Market*. Please make return envelope the same size as the envelopes you send material in, otherwise we cannot send everything back. Just send tape." Responds in 6 weeks.

Music Mostly **R&B**, **soul**, **dance**, **rap** and **top 40/pop**; also **gospel** and **blues**.

☑ WESTWIRES RECORDING

(formerly Westwires Digital USA), 1042 Club Ave., Allentown PA 18109. (610)435-1924. E-mail: info@ westwires.com. Web site: www.westwires.com. **Contact:** Wayne Becker, owner/producer. Record producer and production company. Fee derived from outright fee from record company or artist retainer.

How to Contact *Contact via e-mail for permission to submit.* Submit demo by mail. Unsolicited submissions are OK. Prefers CD, DVD, or VHS videocassette with 3 songs and lyric sheet. Does not return material. Responds in 1 month.

Music Mostly **rock**, **R&B**, **dance**, **alternative**, **folk** and **eclectic**. Produced Ye Ren (Dimala Records), Weston (Universal/Mojo), Zakk Wylde (Spitfire Records). Other artists include Ryan Asher, Paul Rogers, Anne Le Baron, and Gary Hassay

Tips "We are interested in singer/songwriters and alternative artists living in the mid-Atlantic area. Must be able to perform live and establish a following."

FRANK WILLSON

P.O. Box 2297, Universal City TX 78148. (210)653-3989. E-mail: bswr18@wmconnect.com. **Contact:** Frank Willson, producer. Record producer, management firm (Universal Music Marketing) and record company (BSW Records/Universal Music Records). Estab. 1987. Produces 20-25 albums/year. Fee derived from sales royalty when song or artist is recorded.

- Also see the listings for BSW Records in the Music Publishers and Record Companies sections and Universal Music Marketing in the Managers & Booking Agents section of this book.

How to Contact Submit demo by mail. Unsolicited submissions are OK. Prefers CD with 3-4 songs and lyric sheets. Include SASE. Responds in 1 month.

Music Mostly **country**, **blues**, **jazz** and **soft rock**. Produced *Follow the Roses* (album), written and recorded by Larry Butler on BSW Records (country). Other artists include Candee Land, Dan Kimmel, Brad Lee, John Wayne, Sonny Marshall, Bobby Mountain and Crea Beal.

WLM MUSIC/RECORDING

2808 Cammie St., Durham NC 27705-2020. (919)471-3086. Fax: (919)471-4326. E-mail: wlm-musicr ecording@nc.rr.com or wlm-band@nc.rr.com. **Contact:** Watts Lee Mangum, owner. Record producer. Estab. 1980. Fee derived from outright fee from recording artist. "In some cases, an advance payment requested for demo production."

How to Contact Submit demo by mail. Unsolicited submissions are OK. Prefers CD with 2-4 songs and lyric or lead sheet (if possible). Include SASE. Responds in 6 months.

Music Mostly country, country/rock and blues/rock; also pop, rock, blues, gospel and bluegrass. Produced "911," and "Petals of an Orchid" (singles), both written and recorded by Johnny Scoggins (country); and "Renew the Love" (single by Judy Evans), recorded by Bernie Evans (country), all on Independent. Other artists include Southern Breeze Band and Heart Breakers Band.

WORLD RECORDS

5798 Deer Trail Dr., Traverse City MI 49684. E-mail: jack@worldrec.org. Web site: www.worldrec.o rg. **Contact:** Jack Conners, producer. Record producer, engineer/technician and record company (World Records). Estab. 1984. Produces 1 CD/year. Fee derived from outright fee from recording artist.

How to Contact *Write first and obtain permission to submit.* Prefers CD with 1 or 2 songs. Include SASE. Responds in 6 weeks.

Music Mostly **classical**, **folk** and **jazz**. Produced *Have You Heard?* (album by Traverse Symphony Orchestra), (classical), released 2003, and *Music From the Monastery* (album by Nancy Larson), (classical), released 2002. Other artists include The Murphy Brothers and The Camerata Singers.

ADDITIONAL RECORD PRODUCERS

The following companies are also record producers, but their listings are found in other sections of the book. Read the listings for submission information.

A

A.A.M.I. Music Group 142
Alexander Sr. Music 82
Alias John Henry Tunes 83
Ariana Records 144
Arkadia Entertainment Corp. 144
Atlan-Dec/Grooveline Records 145
Audio Music Publishers 85
Audio-Visual Media Productions
    (formerly First Time Records) 145
Avita Records 145

B

Bacchus Group Productions, Ltd.
    220
Banana Records 149
Barrett Rock 'n' Roll Enterprises,
    Paul 221
Big Fish Music Publishing Group 87
Blue Gem Records 150
Blue Wave 150
Blue Wave Productions 222
BSW Records 92

C

Capstan Record Production 152
Cellar Records 153
Cherri/Holly Music 94
Chiaroscuro Records 154
Christopher Publishing, Sonny 95
CKB Records/Helaphat Entertain-
    ment 154
Cornelius Companies, The 97
Cosmotone Records 156

D

Duane Music, Inc. 102

E

EMF Productions 103

F

Fireant 159
First Time Music (Publishing) U.K.
    104

Furrow Music 106

G

Generic Records, Inc. 160
Glad Music Co. 106
Groove Makers' Recordings 164

H

Hammel Associates, Inc., R.L. 107
Hardison International Entertain-
    ment Corporation 230
Heads Up Int., Ltd. 165
Hi-Bias Records Inc. 165
Hickory Lane Publishing and Re-
    cording 107
His Power Productions and Publish-
    ing 108

J

Ja/Nein Musikverlag GmbH 109

K

Kaysarah Music 112

L

Lake Transfer Productions & Music
    112
LCS Music Group 113
Loggins Promotion 235
Lucifer Records, Inc. 167

M

Makers Mark Gold 114
Manuiti L.A. 114
Martin Productions 235
Maui Arts & Music Association/Sur-
    vivor Records/Ten of Diamonds
    Music 115
McCoy Music, Jim 116
Mega Music Productions 236
Mighty Records 171

Music Room Publishing Group, The 117

N
Naked Jain Records 117

P
P. & N. Records 174
Perla Music 120
Presence Records 175

Q
QUARK, Inc. 121

R
R.T.L. Music 122
Rockford Music Co. 123
Rustic Records, Inc Publishing 124

S
Sahara Records and Filmworks Entertainment 179
Salt Works Music 125
Segal's Publications 126
Sinus Musik Produktion, Ulli Weigel 127

Sound Cellar Music 128
Sound Management Direction 243
Starbound Publishing Co. 128
Succes 129
Supreme Enterprises Int'l Corp. 129
Surface Records 182

T
T.C. Productions/Etude Publishing Co. 129
Ton Records 183
Topcat Records 183
Tower Music Group 130
Twentieth Century Promotions 245

U
Unknown Source Music 131

W
Wagner Agency, William F. 246
Warehouse Creek Recording Corp. 186
Warner Productions, Cheryl K. 246
World Beatnik Records 188

X
X.R.L. Records/Music 188

Managers & Booking Agents

Before submitting to a manager or booking agent, be sure you know exactly what you need. If you're looking for someone to help you with performance opportunities, the booking agency is the one to contact. They can help you book shows either in your local area or throughout the country. If you're looking for someone to help guide your career, you need to contact a management firm. Some management firms may also handle booking; however, it may be in your best interest to look for a separate booking agency. A manager should be your manager—not your agent, publisher, lawyer or accountant.

MANAGERS

Of all the music industry players surrounding successful artists, managers are usually the people closest to the artists themselves. The artist manager can be a valuable contact, both for the songwriter trying to get songs to a particular artist and for the songwriter/performer. A manager and his connections can be invaluable in securing the right publishing deal or recording contract if the writer is also an artist. Getting songs to an artist's manager is yet another way to get your songs recorded, since the manager may play a large part in deciding what material his client uses. For the performer seeking management, a successful manager should be thought of as the foundation for a successful career.

The relationship between a manager and his client relies on mutual trust. A manager works as the liaison between you and the rest of the music industry, and he must know exactly what you want out of your career in order to help you achieve your goals. His handling of publicity, promotion and finances, as well as the contacts he has within the industry, can make or break your career. You should never be afraid to ask questions about any aspect of the relationship between you and a prospective manager.

Always remember that a manager works *for the artist*. A good manager is able to communicate his opinions to you without reservation, and should be willing to explain any confusing terminology or discuss plans with you before taking action. A manager needs to be able to communicate successfully with all segments of the music industry in order to get his client the best deals possible. He needs to be able to work with booking agents, publishers, lawyers and record companies.

Keep in mind that you are both working together toward a common goal: success for you and your songs. Talent, originality, professionalism and a drive to succeed are qualities that will attract a manager to an artist—and a songwriter.

BOOKING AGENTS

The function of the booking agent is to find performance venues for their clients. They usually represent many more acts than a manager does, and have less contact with their acts. A booking agent charges a commission for his services, as does a manager. Managers usually ask for a 15-20% commission on an act's earnings; booking agents usually charge around 10%. In the area of managers and booking agents, more successful acts can negotiate lower percentage deals than the ones set forth above.

SUBMITTING MATERIAL TO MANAGERS & BOOKING AGENTS

The firms listed in this section have provided information about the types of music they work with and the types of acts they represent. You'll want to refer to the Category Index on page 358 to find out which companies deal with the type of music you write, and the Geographic Index at the back of the book to help you locate companies near where you live. Then determine whether they are open to your level of experience (see A Sample Listing Decoded on page 11). Each listing also contains submission requirements and information about what items to include in a press kit and will also specify whether the company is a management firm or a booking agency. Remember that your submission represents you as an artist, and should be as organized and professional as possible.

Icons

For More Info

For more instructional information on the listings in this book, including explanations of symbols (N ✓ ☟ ✿ ⊕ ◯ ⊘ ◐ ∅), read the article *Songwriter's Market: How Do I Use It?* on page 7.

ADDITIONAL MANAGERS & BOOKING AGENTS

There are **more managers & booking agents** located in other sections of the book! On page 249 use the list of Additional Managers & Booking Agents to find listings within other sections who are also managers/booking agents.

☑ AIR TIGHT MANAGEMENT
115 West Rd., P.O. Box 113, Winchester Center CT 06094. (860)738-9139. Fax: (860)738-9135. E-mail: mainoffice@airtightmanagement.com. Web site: www.airtightmanagement.com. **Contact:** Jack Forchette, president. Management firm. Estab. 1969. Represents individual artists, groups or songwriters from anywhere; currently handles 8 acts. Receives 15-20% commission. Reviews material for acts.
How to Contact *Write e-mail first and obtain permission to submit.* Prefers CD or VHS videocassette. If seeking management, press kit should include photos, bio and recorded material. "Follow up with a fax or e-mail, not a phone call." Does not return material. Responds in 1 month.
Music Mostly **rock**, **country** and **jazz**. Current acts include P.J. Loughran (singer/songwriter), Johnny Colla (songwriter/producer, and guitarist/songwriter for Huey Lewis and the News), Jason Scheff (lead singer/songwriter for the group "Chicago"), Gary Burr (Nashville songwriter/producer), Nathan East (singer/songwriter/bassist—Eric Clapton, Michael Jackson, Madonna, 4-Play and others), Rocco Prestia (legendary R&B musician, "Tower of Power" bassist), Steve Oliver (contemporary jazz/pop songwriter/guitarist/vocalist, recording artist), and Kal David (blues).

☑ ☒ ☑ ALERT MUSIC INC.
51 Hillsview Ave., Toronto ON M6P 1J4 Canada. (416)364-4200. Fax: (416)364-8632. E-mail: contact@alertmusic.com. Web site: www.alertmusic.com. **Contact:** W. Tom Berry, president. Management firm, record company and recording artist. Represents local and regional individual artists and groups; currently handles 5 acts. Reviews material for acts.
How to Contact *Write first and obtain permission to submit.* Prefers CD. If seeking management, press kit should include finished CD, photo, press clippings and bio. Include SASE.
Music All types. Works primarily with bands and singer/songwriters. Current acts include Holly Cole (jazz vocalist), Kim Mitchell (rock singer/songwriter), Gino Vannelli (singer/songwriter), Crystal Pistol (rock, singer/songwriter), and Roxanne Potvin (blues, singer/songwriter).

☑ ALL STAR MANAGEMENT
3142 Rainier Ave., Columbus OH 43231-3145. (614)794-2102. Fax: (614)794-2103. E-mail: allstarmanage@msn.com. **Contact:** John or Mary Simpson, owners. Management firm. Estab. 1980. Represents individual artists, groups and songwriters from anywhere; currently handles 3 acts. Receives 20% commission. Reviews material for acts.
• Also see the listing for All Star Record Promotions in the Record Companies section of this book.
How to Contact Submit demo by mail. Unsolicited submissions are OK. Prefers cassette or videocassette with 3 songs and lyric or lead sheet. If seeking management, press kit should include CD with 3 songs, bio, 8×10 photo or any information or articles written about yourself or group, and video if you have one. Does not return material. Responds in 2 months.
Music Mostly **country**, **Christian**, **adult contemporary**, **smooth jazz** and **pop rock**. Works primarily with bands and singers/songwriters. Current acts include Debbie Robins (singer/songwriter, Christian contemporary), Allen Austin (singer/songwriter, country rock) and Leon Seiter (country singer/songwriter).

☑ MICHAEL ALLEN ENTERTAINMENT DEVELOPMENT
P.O. Box 111510, Nashville TN 37222. (615)754-0059. E-mail: michael@michaelallencreates.com. Web site: www.michaelallencreates.com. **Contact:** Michael Allen. Management firm and public relations. Represents individual artists, groups and songwriters; currently handles 2 acts. Receives 15-25% commission. Reviews material for acts.
How to Contact Submit demo by mail. Unsolicited submissions are OK. Prefers CD or cassette or VHS videocassette with 3 songs and lyric or lead sheets. If seeking management, press kit should include photo, bio, press clippings, letter and tape. Include SASE. Responds in 3 months.
Music Mostly **country** and **pop**; also **rock** and **gospel**. Works primarily with vocalists and bands. Currently doing public relations for Sheri Pedigo, Amy Jordyn, Two Hearts N Him, and Randy Roberts.

Managers & Agents

□ AMERICAN BANDS MANAGEMENT

P.O. Box 840607, Houston TX 77284. (713)785-3700. Fax: (713)785-4641. E-mail: johnblomstrom@aol.com. President: John Blomstrom . Sr. Vice President: Cheryl Byrd. Management firm. Estab. 1973. Represents groups from anywhere; currently handles 3 acts. Receives 15-25% commission. Reviews material for acts.

How to Contact Submit demo by mail prior to making phone contact. Unsolicited submissions are OK. Prefers cassette or CD. If seeking management, press kit should include cover letter, bio, photo, demo/CD, press clippings, video, résumé and professional references with names and numbers. Does not return material. Responds in 1 month.

Music Mostly **rock (all forms)** and **modern country**. Works primarily with bands. Current acts include Captain Pink (Motown), Vince Vance & the Valiants (show band) and Rachel (guitarist/singer/modern folk).

□ APODACA PROMOTIONS INC.

717 E. Tidwell Rd., Houston TX 77022. (713)691-6677. Fax: (713)692-9298. E-mail: houston@apodacapromotions.com. Web site: www.apodacapromotions.com. Manager: Domingo A. Barrera. Management firm, booking agency, music publisher (Huina Publishing, Co. Inc.). Estab. 1991. Represents songwriters and groups from anywhere; currently handles 40 acts. Receives 15% commission. Reviews material for acts.

How to Contact Submit demo by mail. Unsolicited submissions are OK. Prefers CD and lyric and lead sheet. Include SASE. Responds in 2 months.

Music Mostly **international** and **Hispanic**; also **rock**. Works primarily with bands and songwriters. Current acts include Bobby Pulido (Tex-Mex music) Kubia Kings, Alicia Billarreal, Atrapado, Jenniffer Pena and Ninelconde.

□ ARTIST REPRESENTATION AND MANAGEMENT

1257 Arcade St., St. Paul MN 55106. (651)483-8754. Fax: (651)776-6338. E-mail: ra@armentertainment.com. Web site: www.armentertainment.com. **Contact:** Roger Anderson, agent/manager. Management firm and booking agency. Estab. 1983. Represents artists from anywhere; currently handles 10 acts. Receives 15% commission. Reviews material for acts.

How to Contact Submit CD and video by mail. Unsolicited submissions are OK. Please include minimum 3 songs. If seeking management, references, current schedule, bio, photo, press clippings should also be included. "Priority is placed on original artists with product who are currently touring." Does not return material. Responds only if interested within 30 days.

Music Mostly **melodic rock**. Current acts include Warrant, Firehouse, Jesse Lang, Scarlet Haze, Head East, Frank Hannon of Tesla, The Family Stone, and Austin Healy.

☑ □ ATCH RECORDS AND PRODUCTIONS

P.O. Box 330067, Houston TX 77233-0067. (832)978-2742. Web site: www.atchrecords.com. Chairman/CEO: Charles Atchison. Management firm, recording studio and record company. Estab. 1989. Represents local, regional and international individual artists, groups and songwriters; currently handles 2 acts. Receives 20% commission. Reviews material for acts.

How to Contact Submit demo by mail. Unsolicited submissions are OK. Prefers CD with 2 songs and lyric sheet. If seeking management, include cover letter, bio, photo, demo and lyrics. Does not return material. Responds in 3 weeks.

Music Mostly **R&B** and **gospel**; also **pop**, **rap** and **hip-hop**. Works primarily with vocalists and groups. Current acts include Prime Flo and Joy (rap).

Tips "Send a good detailed demo with good lyrics. Looking for wonderful love stories, dance music."

☑ BACCHUS GROUP PRODUCTIONS, LTD.

5701 N. Sheridan Rd., Suite 8-U, Chicago IL 60660. (773)334-1532. Fax: (773)334-1531. E-mail: bacchusgrp@uron.cc. Web site: www.BacchusGroup.com. **Contact:** D. Maximilian, Managing Director and Executive Producer. Director of Marketing: M. Margarida Rainho. Management firm and

record producer (D. Maximilian). Estab. 1990. Represents individual artists or groups from any-where; currently handles 9 acts. Receives 15-25% commission. Reviews material for acts.
How to Contact *Does not accept unsolicited submissions.*
Music Mostly **pop**, **R&B/soul** and **jazz**; also **Latin** and **world beat**. Works primarily with singer/songwriters, composers, arrangers, bands and orchestras. "Visit our Web site for current acts."

⊘ BARNARD MANAGEMENT SERVICES (BMS)

228 Main St., Suite 3, Venice CA 90291. (310)399-8886. Fax: (310)450-0470. E-mail: bms@barnardu s.com. **Contact:** Russell Barnard, president. Management firm. Estab. 1979. Represents artists, groups and songwriters; currently handles 2 acts. Receives 10-20% commission. Reviews material for acts.
How to Contact *Write first and obtain permission to submit.* Prefers cassette or CD with 3-10 songs and lead sheet. Artists may submit VHS videocassette (15-30 minutes) by permission only. If seeking management, press kit should include cover letter, bio, photo, demo/CD, lyric sheets, press clippings, video and résumé. Does not return material. Responds in 2 months.
Music Mostly **country crossover**, **blues**, **country**, **R&B**, **rock** and **soul**. Current acts include Mark Shipper (songwriter/author) and Sally Rose (R&B band).
Tips "Semi-produced demos are of little value. Either save the time and money by submitting material 'in the raw,' or do a finished production version."

⊕ ⊍ PAUL BARRETT ROCK 'N' ROLL ENTERPRISES

16 Grove Place, Penarth, Vale of Glamorgan CF64 2ND United Kingdom. 02920-704279. E-mail: barrettrocknroll@amserve.com. **Contact:** Paul Barrett, director. Management firm, booking agency, record company (Rock 'n' Roll Records) and record producer (Paul Barrett). Estab. 1969. Represents individual artists and groups from anywhere; currently handles 37 acts. Receives 10% commission. Reviews material for acts.
• This company only represents acts who perform '50s rock 'n' roll.
How to Contact "We are not actively looking for songs, as most of our performers/musicians write their own material." Submit demo by mail. Unsolicited submissions are OK. Prefers CD or DAT with picture and bio (for performers). SAE and IRC. Responds in 3 weeks.
Music Mostly **'50s rock 'n' roll**. Works primarily with "performers plus some writers." Current acts include The Jets (trio), Matchbox (rockabilly) and Crazy Caravan & The Rhythm Rockers (rockabilly).
Tips "Paul Barrett Rock 'N' Roll Enterprises is, more than anything else, a specialist booking agency dealing on an international basis on with pre-Beatles rock 'n' rollers."

☑ ◻ BASSLINE ENTERTAINMENT, INC.

P.O. Box 2394, New York NY 10185. E-mail: talent@basslineinc.com. Web site: www.basslineinc.c om. **Contact:** Talent Relations Dept. Management firm. Estab. 1993. Represents local and regional vocalists, producers and songwriters. Receives 20-25% commission. Reviews material for acts.
How to Contact Submit demo package by mail. Unsolicited submissions are OK. Prefers CD, mp3, VHS or cassette. If seeking management, press kit should include cover letter, press clippings and/or reviews, bio, demo (in appropriate format), picture and accurate contact telephone number. Include SASE. Responds in 3 weeks.
Music Mostly **pop**, **R&B**, **club/dance** and **hip-hop/rap**; some **Latin**. Works primarily with singer/songwriters, producers, rappers and bands. Current acts include Iceman (hip hop), Shylon (R&B/pop), FWZ (rap/hip-hop), and Novacane (rap).

⊘ BIG J PRODUCTIONS

2516 S. Sugar Ridge, Laplace LA 70068. (504)652-2645. **Contact:** Frankie Jay, agent. Booking agency. Estab. 1968. Represents individual artists, groups and songwriters; currently handles over 50 acts. Receives 15-25% commission. Reviews material for acts.
How to Contact *Call first and obtain permission to submit (office hours Monday-Friday: noon-5 pm).* Prefers cassette or VHS videocassette with 3-6 songs and lyric or lead sheet. "It would be best

for an artist to lip-sync to a prerecorded track. The object is for someone to see how an artist would perform more than simply assessing song content.'' Artists seeking management should include pictures, biography, tape or CD and video. Does not return material. Responds in 2 weeks.

Music Mostly **rock**, **pop** and **R&B**. Works primarily with groups with self-contained songwriters. Current acts include Zebra (original rock group), Crowbar (heavy metal) and Kyper (original dance).

☑ BLANK & BLANK

1 Belmont Ave., Suite 320, Bala Cynwyd PA 19004-1604. (610)664-8200. Fax: (610)664-8201. **Contact:** E. Robert Blank, manager. Management firm. Represents individual artists and groups. Reviews material for acts.

How to Contact *Contact first and obtain permission to submit.* Prefers CD, DVD, or videocassette. If seeking management, press kit should include cover letter, demo/CD and video. Does not return material.

☑ BLOWIN' SMOKE PRODUCTIONS/RECORDS

7438 Shoshone Ave., Van Nuys CA 91406-2340. (818)881-9888. Fax: (818)881-0555. E-mail: blowin smokeband@ktb.net. Web site: www.blowinsmokeband.com. **Contact:** Larry Knight, president. Management firm and record producer. Estab. 1990. Represents local and West Coast individual artists and groups; currently handles 6 acts. Receives 15-20% commission. Reviews material for acts.

• Also see the listing for Hailing Frequency Music Productions in the Record Producers section of this book.

How to Contact *Write or call first and obtain permission to submit.* Prefers cassette or CD. If seeking management, press kit should include cover letter, demo/CD, lyric sheets, press clippings, video if available, photo, bios, contact telephone numbers and any info on legal commitments already in place. Include SASE. Responds in 1 month.

Music Mostly **R&B**, **blues** and **blues-rock**. Works primarily with single and group vocalists and a few R&B/blues bands. Current acts include Larry ''Fuzzy'' Knight (blues singer/songwriter), King Floyd (R&B artist), The Blowin' Smoke Rhythm & Blues Band, The Fabulous Smokettes, and Joyce Lawson.

☑ THE BLUE CAT AGENCY

E-mail: bluecat_agency@yahoo.com. Web site: www.geocities.com/bluecat_agency. **Contact:** Karen Kindig, owner/agent. Management firm and booking agency. Estab. 1989. Represents individual artists and/or groups from anywhere; currently handles 2 acts. Receives 10-15% commission. Reviews material for acts.

How to Contact *E-mail only for permission to submit.* Prefers cassette or CD. If seeking management, press kit should include demo, CD or tape, bio, press clippings and photo. SASE. Responds in 2 months.

Music Mostly **rock/pop** ''en espanol '' and **jazz/latin jazz**. Works primarily with bands. Current acts include Kai Eckhardt, Alejandro Santos, Ania Paz, Gabriel Rosati.

☐ BLUE WAVE PRODUCTIONS

3221 Perryville Rd., Baldwinsville NY 13027. (315)638-4286. Fax: (315)635-4757. E-mail: bluewave @localnet.com. Web site: www.bluewaverecords.com. **Contact:** Greg Spencer, owner/president. Management firm, music publisher (G.W. Spencer Music/ASCAP), record company (Blue Wave Records) and record producer (Blue Wave Productions). Estab. 1985. Represents individual artists and/or groups and songwriters from anywhere; currently handles 5 acts. Receives 10% commission. Reviews material for acts.

• Also see the listing for Blue Wave in the Record Companies section of this book.

How to Contact Submit demo by mail. Unsolicited submissions are OK. Prefers CD or VHS videocassette with 3-6 songs. ''Just the music first, reviews and articles are OK. No photos or lyrics until later.'' If seeking management, press kit should include cover letter and demo/CD. Include SASE. Responds in 1 month. No phone calls.

Music Mostly **blues**, **blues/rock** and **roots rock**. Current acts include Kim Lembo (female blues vocalist), Kim Simmonds (blues guitarist and singer/songwriter) and Downchild Bluesband (blues). **Tips** ''I'm looking for great singers with soul. Not interested in pop/rock commercial material.''

☑ ☑ BOUQUET-ORCHID ENTERPRISES

P.O. Box 1335, Norcross GA 30091. (770)339-9088. **Contact:** Bill Bohannon, president. Management firm, booking agency, music publisher (Orchid Publishing/BMI) and record company (Bouquet Records). Represents individuals and groups; currently handles 3 acts. Receives 10-15% commission. Reviews material for acts.

• Also see the listing for Orchid Publishing in the Music Publishers section of this book.

How to Contact Submit demo by mail. Unsolicited submissions are OK. Prefers cassette, CD or videocassette with 3-5 songs, song list and lyric sheet. Include brief résumé. If seeking management, press kit should include current photograph, 2-3 media clippings, description of act, and background information on act. Include SASE. Responds in 1 month.

Music Mostly **country**, **rock** and **top 40/pop**; also **gospel** and **R&B**. Works primarily with vocalists and groups. Current acts include Susan Spencer, Jamey Wells, Adam Day and the Bandoleers.

☐ BREAD & BUTTER PRODUCTIONS

P.O. Box 1539, Wimberley TX 78676. (512)301-7117. E-mail: sgladson@gmail.com. **Contact:** Steve Gladson, managing partner. Management firm and booking agency. Estab. 1969. Represents individual artists, songwriters and groups from anywhere; currently handles 6 acts. Receives 10-20% commission. Reviews material for acts.

How to Contact Submit demo by mail. Unsolicited submissions OK. Prefers cassette, videocassette or CD and lyric sheet. If seeking management, press kit should include cover letter, demo/CD, lyric sheets, press clippings, video, résumé, picture and bio. Does not return material. Responds in 1 month.

Music Mostly **alternative rock**, **country** and **R&B**; also **classic rock**, **folk** and **Americana**. Works primarily with singer/songwriters and original bands. Current acts include Lou Cabaza (songwriter/producer/manager), Duck Soup (band) and Gaylan Ladd (songwriter/singer).

Tips ''Remember why you are in this biz. The art comes first.''

☑ BROTHERS MANAGEMENT ASSOCIATES

141 Dunbar Ave., Fords NJ 08863. (732)738-0880. Fax: (732)738-0970. E-mail: bmaent@yahoo.c om. Web site: www.bmaent.com. **Contact:** Allen A. Faucera, president. Management firm and booking agency. Estab. 1972. Represents artists, groups and songwriters; currently handles 25 acts. Receives 15-20% commission. Reviews material for acts.

How to Contact *Write first and obtain permission to submit.* Prefers CD or DVD with 3-6 songs and lyric sheets. Include photographs and résumé. If seeking management, include photo, bio, tape and return envelope in press kit. Include SASE. Responds in 2 months.

Music Mostly **pop**, **rock**, **MOR** and **R&B**. Works primarily with vocalists and established groups. Current acts include Nils Lofgren and Danny Federici.

Tips ''Submit very commercial material—make demo of high quality.''

⊕ ☑ CIRCUIT RIDER TALENT & MANAGEMENT CO.

123 Walton Ferry Rd., Hendersonville TN 37075. (615)824-1947. Fax: (615)264-0462. E-mail: dotwo ool@bellsouth.net. **Contact:** Linda S. Dotson, president. Consultation firm, booking agency and music publisher (Channel Music, Cordial Music, Dotson & Dotson Music Publishers, Shalin Music Co.). Represents individual artists, songwriters and actors; currently handles 10 acts. Works with a large number of recording artists, songwriters, actors, producers. (Includes the late multi-Grammy-winning producer/writer Skip Scarborough.) Receives 10-15% commission (union rates). Reviews material for acts (free of charge).

How to Contact *Write or call first and obtain permission to submit.* Prefers cassette or videocassette with 3 songs and lyric sheet. If seeking consultation, press kit should include bio, cover letter, résumé, lyric sheets if original songs, photo and tape with 3 songs. Videocassettes required of artist's submissions. Include SASE. Responds in 2 months.

Music Mostly **Latin blues**, **pop**, **country** and **gospel**; also **R&B** and **comedy**. Works primarily with vocalists, special concerts, movies and TV. Current acts include Razzy Bailey (award winning blues artist/writer), Clint Walker (actor/recording artist), Ben Colder (comedy/novelty), and Freddy Weller (formerly Paul Revere & The Raiders/hit songwriter).

Tips "Artists, have your act together. Have a full press kit, videos and be professional. Attitudes are a big factor in my agreeing to work with you (no egotists). This is a business, and we will be building your career."

☑ CLASS ACT PRODUCTIONS/MANAGEMENT

P.O. Box 55252, Sherman Oaks CA 91413. (818)980-1039. E-mail: pkimmel@gr8gizmo.com. **Contact:** Peter Kimmel, president. Management firm. Estab. 1985. Currently handles 2 acts. Receives 20% commission. Reviews material for acts.

How to Contact Submit demo CD by mail. Unsolicited submissions are OK. Include cover letter, bio, lyric sheets (essential), CD in press kit. Include SASE. Responds in 1 month.

Music All styles. Current acts include Terpsichore (cyber dance/pop), Karma (high energy bluesy rock), and Don Cameron (pop/rock).

Ⓝ ☐ CLOCKWORK ENTERTAINMENT MANAGEMENT AGENCY

227 Concord St., Haverhill MA 01830. (978)373-5677. E-mail: wjm227@hotmail.com. **Contact:** William J. Macek, esq., entertainment attorney, president. Management firm. Represents groups and songwriters throughout New England with mastered product who are looking for label deals and licensing in US and internationally. Fee is negotiated individually; currently handles multiple acts. Commissions vary. Reviews material for acts.

How to Contact Submit demo by mail. Unsolicited submissions are OK. Prefers cassette or CD with 3-12 songs. "Also submit promotion and cover letter with interesting facts about yourself." If seeking management, press kit should include cover letter, tape or CD, photo, bio and press clippings. Include SASE. Responds in 1 month.

Music Mostly **rock (all types)** and **top 40/pop**. Works primarily with bar bands and original acts.

☑ CLOUSHER PRODUCTIONS

P.O. Box 1191, Mechanicsburg PA 17055. (717)766-7644. Fax: (717)766-1490. E-mail: clousher@we btv.net. Web site: www.clousherentertainment.com. **Contact:** Fred Clousher, owner. Booking agency and production company. Estab. 1972. Represents groups from anywhere; currently handles over 100 acts.

How to Contact Submit demo by mail. Unsolicited submissions are OK. Prefers VHS videocassette. If seeking management, press kit should include press clippings, testimonials, credits, glossies, video demo, references, cover letter, résumé and bio. Does not return material. "Performer should check back with us!"

Music Mostly **country**, **old rock** and **ethnic** (German, Hawaiian, etc.); also **dance bands** (regional) and **classical musicals**. "We work mostly with country, old time R&R, regional variety dance bands, tribute acts, and all types of variety acts." Current acts include Jasmine Morgan (country/pop vocalist), Robin Right (country vocalist) and Island Breeze (ethnic Hawaiian group).

Tips "The songwriters we work with are entertainers themselves, which is the aspect we deal with. They usually have bands or do some sort of show, either with tracks or live music. We engage them for stage shows, dances, strolling, etc. We DO NOT publish music or submit performers to recording companies for contracts. We strictly set up live performances for them."

☑ COAL HARBOR MUSIC

P.O. Box 148027, Nashville TN 37214-8027.(615)883-2020. E-mail: info@coalharbormusic.com. Web site: www.coalharbormusic.com. **Contact:** Jerry Ray Wells, President/Owner. Management firm, booking agency, music publisher (Coal Harbor Music), record company (Coal Harbor Music), record producer (Jerry Ray Wells), and radio promoter ("We promote clients' single released songs to radio stations." Estab. 1990. Represents individual artists, groups. Works with artists from anywhere. Receives 10-20% commission. Reviews material for acts.

How to Contact *Write or call first and obtain permission to submit a demo.* Prefers CD/CDR with 2-3 songs and cover letter. Include SASE or stamped reply postcard. If seeking management representation send CD, photo, bio, VHS videocassette or DVD (if possible), letters of recommendation, newspaper articles, and/or reviews.Be prepared to furnish extra press kits if interested in booking. Put what you are interested in on outside of submission, for example "ATTN: Mgmt," "ATTN: Booking," "ATTN: Songs," etc. Does not return material.

Music Mostly **country**, **Christian (all forms)**, and **bluegrass**. Also **Christmas**, **patriotic**, and **comedy**. Does not want hard rock, heavy metal, or rap. Works primarily with country and Christian. "We are a company that strives to seek the best, most profitable business deal for both parties involved, both our clients and ourselves. We are looking for talent that we can market." Current acts include Don Freeman (country/Christian singer-songwriter), Anne Borgen (contemporary Christian singer-songwriter), Back On Track (contemporary Christian group).

Tips "Send us your very best work and state clearly in your cover letter your career goals along with exactly what it is you want us to do with you or your material. We work with a lot of singer-songwriters, but are open to any talent that can be marketed and booked. A career is something you have to build. Don't expect us, or anyone, to make you an overnight sensation!"

☑ CONCEPT 2000 INC.

P.O. Box 2950, Columbus OH 43216-2950. (614)276-2000. Fax: (614)275-0163. E-mail: info2k@con cept2k.com. Web site: www.concept2k.com. **Florida office:** P.O. Box 2070, Largo FL 33779-2070. (727)585-2922. Fax: (727)585-3835. **Contact:** Brian Wallace, president. Management firm and booking agency. Estab. 1981. Represents international individual artists, groups and songwriters; currently handles 4 acts. Receives 20% commission. Reviews material for acts.

How to Contact Submit demo by mail. Unsolicited submissions are OK. Prefers cassette with 4 songs. If seeking management, include demo, press clips, photo and bio. Does not return material. Responds in 2 weeks.

Music Mostly **country**, **gospel** and **pop**; also **jazz**, **R&B** and **soul**. Current acts include Bryan Hitch (contemporary gospel), Shades of Grey (R&B/soul), Dwight Lenox (show group) and Gene Walker (jazz).

Tips "Send quality songs with lyric sheets. Production quality is not necessary."

☑ CONCERTED EFFORTS, INC./FOGGY DAY MUSIC

P.O. Box 600099, Newtonville MA 02460. (617)969-0810. Fax: (617)969-6761. Web site: www.conc ertedefforts.com. **Owner:** Paul Kahn. Management firm, booking agency and music publisher (Foggy Day Music). Represents individual artists, groups and songwriters from anywhere. Commission varies. Reviews material for acts.

How to Contact Submit demo by mail. Unsolicited submissions are OK "but call first!" Prefers CD, will accept cassette, with lyric sheet. "No management submissions." Does not return material.

Music Mostly **folk**, **country** and **rock**; also **world music**, **zydeco** and **blues**. Current acts include Luther Johnson (blues singer), Holmes Brothers, Roseanne Cash and Orchestra Baobab.

Tips "Simple recorded demo is OK, with lyrics."

☑ ☑ COUNTRYWIDE PRODUCERS

2466 Wildon Dr., York PA 17403. (717)741-2658. E-mail: cwpent@wmconnect.com. **Contact:** Bob Englar, president. Booking agency. Represents individuals and groups; currently handles 8 acts. Receives 15% commission. Reviews material for acts.

How to Contact Query or submit demo by mail. Unsolicited submissions are OK. If seeking management, press kit should include photo and demo. Include SASE. Responds in 1 week.

Music Bluegrass, **blues**, **classical**, and **country**; also **folk**, **gospel**, **polk a**, **rock (light)**, and **top 40/pop**. Works primarily with show bands. Current acts include The Walls of Time (bluegrass), Shilha Ridge (bluegrass) and Iron Ridge (bluegrass).

▢ STEPHEN COX PROMOTIONS & MANAGEMENT

6708 Mammoth Ave., Van Nuys CA 91405. (818)377-4530. Fax: (818)782-5305. E-mail: stephencox @earthlink.net. **Contact:** Stephen Cox, president. Management firm. Estab. 1993. Represents individual artists, groups or songwriters from anywhere; currently handles 5 acts. Receives 15% commission. Reviews material for acts.

How to Contact *Call first and obtain permission to submit.* Prefers CD. If seeking management, press kit should include biographies, performance history and radio play. "Include a clear definition of goals in a thoughtful presentation." Include SASE. Responds in 2 weeks.

Music Mostly **rock**, **New Age/world** and **alternative**; also **blues**, **folk** and **progressive**. Works primarily with bands. Current acts include Joe Sherbanee (jazz), Val Ewell & Pulse (blues rock), Paul Micich & Mitch Espe (New Age/jazz), Covet (metal) and Jill Cohn (folk rock).

Tips "Establish goals based on research, experience and keep learning about the music business. Start the business as though it will always be you as an independent. Establish a foundation before considering alternative commitments. We aim to educate and consult to a level that gives an artist the freedom of choice to choose whether to go to the majors etc., or retain independence. Remember, promote, promote and promote some more. Always be nice to people, treat them as you would wish to be treated."

▨ ▧ ▢ CRANIUM MANAGEMENT

P.O. Box 240, Annandale NSW 2038 Australia. E-mail: cranium@smartchat.net.au. **Manager:** Peter "Skip" Beaumont-Edmonds. Management firm. Estab. 1992. Represents individual artists, groups and songwriters from anywhere; currently handles 4 acts. Receives 20% commission. Reviews material for acts.

How to Contact *E-mail first and obtain permission to submit.* Send "The minimum number of best songs—don't waste money on being elaborate. Talent will show through. Be sensible—if it doesn't suit us don't send it." If seeking management, press kit should include photo (optional), demo, press clippings (minimal), bio and cover letter. Does not return material. Responds in 1 month.

Music Mostly **alternative**, **pop** and **country**. Works primarily with pop/rock, alternative bands and singer/songwriters. Current acts include Dog Trumpet (alternative roots), Adam Harvey (country singer), David Mason-Cox (singer/songwriter), and Karl Broadie (singer/songwriter).

✔ ▢ D&R ENTERTAINMENT

302 Tanglewood Dr., Broken Bow OK 74728. (580)584-9429. **Contact:** Don Walton, president. Management firm. Estab. 1985. Represents individual artists from anywhere; currently handles 2 acts. Receives 15% commission. Reviews material for acts. Also reviews for other country singers.

How to Contact Submit demo by mail. Unsolicited submissions are OK. Prefers CD, cassette, or videocassette, with lyric and lead sheet. If seeking management, press kit should include brief background of artist, videotape of performance, cover letter, résumé, photo, press clippings, and cassette or CD. "Indicate whether you have any financial or prospective financial backing." Does not return material. Responds in 3 months.

Music Mostly **contemporary Christian**; also **country** and **pop**. Works primarily with young beginning singers. Current acts include Kristi Reed (positive country) and Thomas Wells (contemporary Christian).

Tips "I need songs (country) that would fit a young adult singer. In other words no drinking, cheating, marrying songs. A pretty tough choice. Also Christian contemporary songs."

◑ DAS COMMUNICATIONS, LTD.

83 Riverside Dr., New York NY 10024. (212)877-0400. Fax: (212)595-0176. Management firm. Estab. 1975. Represents individual artists, groups and producers from anywhere; currently handles 25 acts. Receives 20% commission.

How to Contact *Does not accept unsolicited submissions.*

Music Mostly **rock**, **pop**, **R&B**, **alternative** and **hip-hop**. Current acts include Joan Osborne (rock), Wyclef Jean (hip-hop), Black Eyed Peas (hip-hop), John Legend (R&B), Spin Doctors (rock), The Bacon Brothers (rock).

DCA PRODUCTIONS

676A 9th Ave., #252, New York NY 10036. (212)245-2063. Fax: (212)245-2367. Web site: www.dca productions.com. **Contact:** Suzanne Perotta, office manager. President: Daniel Abrahamsen. Vice President: Geraldine Abrahamsen. Management firm. Estab. 1975. Represents individual artists, groups and songwriters from anywhere; currently handles 14 acts.

How to Contact If seeking management, press kit should include cover letter, bio, photo, demo/ CD and video. Prefers cassette or VHS videocassette with 2 songs. "All materials are reviewed and kept on file for future consideration. Does not return material. We respond only if interested."

Music Mostly **acoustic**, **rock** and **mainstream**; also **cabaret** and **theme**. Works primarily with acoustic singer/songwriters, top 40 or rock bands. Current acts include Gabrielle (singer/songwriter), Sean Altman (singer/songwriter) and 1910 Fruitgum Company (oldies band). Visit our Web site for a current roster of acts.

Tips "Please do not call for a review of material."

THE EDWARD DE MILES COMPANY

28 E. Jackson Bldg., 10th Floor, #S627, Chicago IL 60604-2263. (773)509-6381. Fax: (312)922-6964. Web site: www.edmsahara.com. **Contact:** Edward de Miles, president. Management firm, booking agency, entertainment/sports promoter and TV/radio broadcast producer. Estab. 1984. Represents film, television, radio and musical artists; currently handles 15 acts. Receives 10-20% commission. Reviews material for acts. Regional operations in Chicago, Dallas, Houston and Nashville through marketing representatives. Licensed A.F. of M. booking agent.

• Also see listings for Edward De Miles in the Music Publishers and Record Producers sections, and Sahara Records and Filmworks Entertainment in the Record Companies section of this book.

How to Contact *Does not accept unsolicited materials.* Prefers cassette with 3-5 songs, 8×10 b&w photo, bio and lyric sheet. "Copyright all material before submitting." If seeking management, include cover letter, bio, demo cassette with 3-5 songs, 8×10 b&w photo, lyric sheet, press clippings and video if available in press kit. Include SASE. Does not return material. Responds in 1 month.

Music Mostly **country**, **dance**, **R&B/soul**, **rock**, **top 40/pop** and **urban contemporary**; also looking for material for television, radio and film productions. Works primarily with dance bands and vocalists. Current acts include Steve Lynn (R&B/dance), Multiple Choice (rap) and D'von Edwards (jazz).

Tips "Performers need to be well prepared with their presentations (equipment, showmanship a must)."

EAO MUSIC CORPORATION OF CANADA

P.O. Box 1240, Station "M," Calgary AB T2P 2L2 Canada. (403)228-9388. Fax: (403)229-3598. E-mail: edmund@oliverio.ca. Web site: www.oliverio.ca. **Contact:** Edmund A. Oliverio, president. Management firm and record company. Estab. 1985. Represents individual artists, groups and songwriters from western Canada (aboriginal artists); currently handles 52 acts. Receives 15-20% commission. Reviews material for acts.

How to Contact Submit demo by mail. Unsolicited submissions are OK. Prefers cassette with 3 songs and lyric and lead sheets. If seeking management, press kit should include cover letter, résumé, b&w glossy photo, cassette tape, bio, media clippings and list of venues and festivals performed. SAE and IRC. Responds in 2 weeks.

Music Mostly **folk** and **native (aboriginal)**; also **rock**. Works primarily with singer/songwriters. Current acts include Activate (funky reggae), Feeding Like Butterflies (folk rock/Celtic), Katrina (country/folk) and Gloria K. MacRae (adult contemporary).

Tips "Be upfront and honest. Establish your long term goals and short term goals. Have you joined your music associations (i.e., CMA, etc.)?"

SCOTT EVANS PRODUCTIONS

P.O. Box 814028, Hollywood FL 33081-4028. (954)963-4449. E-mail: evansprod@aol.com. Web site: www.theentertainmentmall.com. **Contact:** Ted Jones, new artists, or Jeanne K., Internet marketing and sales. Management firm and booking agency. Estab. 1979. Represents local, regional or international individual artists, groups, songwriters, comedians, novelty acts and dancers; currently handles over 200 acts. Receives 10-50% commission. Reviews material for acts.

How to Contact New artists can make submissions through the 'auditions' link located on the Web site. Unsolicited submissions are OK. "Please be sure that all submissions are copyrighted and not your original copy as we do not return material."

Music Mostly **pop**, **R&B** and **Broadway**. Deals with "all types of entertainers; no limitations." Current acts include Scott Evans and Company (variety song and dance), Dorit Zinger (female vocalist), Jeff Geist, Actors Repertory Theatre, Entertainment Express, Perfect Parties, Joy Deco (dance act), Flashback 2000 Revue (musical song and dance), Everybody Salsa (Latin song and dance) and Around the World (international song and dance).

Tips "Submit a neat, well put together, organized press kit."

☑ ◻ EXCLESISA BOOKING AGENCY

716 Windward Rd., Jackson MS 39206. (601)366-0220. E-mail: exclesis@bellsouth.net. Web site: www.exclesisa-booking.com. **Contact:** Roy and Esther Wooten, booking managers/owners. Booking agency. Estab. 1989. Represents groups from anywhere; currently handles 9 acts. Receives 15% commission. Reviews material for acts.

How to Contact *Call first and obtain permission to submit.* Submit demo by mail. Unsolicited submissions are OK. Prefers CD or videocassette. If seeking management, press kit should include CD or cassette, videocassette, pictures, address and telephone contact and bio. Does not return material. Responds in 2 months.

Music Gospel only. Current acts include The Canton Spirituals, Darrell McFadden & The Disciples, The Jackson Southernaires, Slim & The Supreme Angels, The Pilgrim Jubilees, Spencer Taylor & the Highway Q'cs, The Annointed Jackson Singers, The Southern Sons, Jewel & Converted, and Ms. B & Tha' Band.

Tips "Make sure your demo is clear with a good sound so the agent can make a good judgement."

☒ ◙ S.L. FELDMAN & ASSOCIATES

1505 W. Second Ave. #200, Vancouver BC V6H 3Y4 Canada. (604)734-5945. Fax: (604)732-0922. E-mail: feldman@slfa.com. Web site: www.slfa.com. Booking agency and artist management firm. Estab. 1970. Agency represents mostly Canadian artists and groups; currently handles over 200 acts.

How to Contact *Write or call first to obtain permission to submit a demo.* Prefers CD, photo and bio. If seeking management, contact Watchdog for consideration and include video in press kit. SAE and IRC. Responds in 2 months.

Music Current acts include Elvis Costello, The Chieftains, Joni Mitchell, Diana Krall, Norah Jones, Leonard Cohen, Anjani Thomas, Susan Tedeschi, Ry Cooder, Sissel, Sondre Lerche, Jesse Cook, Craig Northey, and Liam Titcomb.

◙ FRED T. FENCHEL ENTERTAINMENT AGENCY

2104 S. Jefferson Avenue, Mason City IA 50401. (641)423-4177. Fax: (641)423-8662. **Contact:** Fred T. Fenchel, president. Booking agency. Estab. 1964. Represents local and international individual artists and groups; currently handles up to 10 acts. Receives 20% commission.

How to Contact Submit demo by mail. Unsolicited submissions are OK. Prefers cassette or videocassette. Does not return material. Responds in 3 weeks.

Music Mostly **country**, **pop** and some **gospel**. Works primarily with dance bands and show groups; "artists we can use on club dates, fairs, etc." Current acts include New Odyssey (comedy & music), Nerness Family (family, variety music) and The Buck Hollow Band (duo, huge variety of music). "We deal primarily with established name acts with recording contracts, or those with a label and starting into popularity."

Tips "Be honest. Don't submit unless your act is exceptional rather than just starting out, amateurish and with lyrics that are written under the pretense of coming from qualified writers."

☒ ◙ B.C. FIEDLER MANAGEMENT

53 Seton Park Rd., Toronto ON M3C 3Z8 Canada. (416)421-4421. Fax: (416)421-0442. E-mail: info@bcfiedler.com. **Contact:** B.C. Fiedler/Alysha Main. Management firm, music publisher (B.C.

Fiedler Publishing) and record company (Sleeping Giant Music Inc.). Estab. 1964. Represents individual artists, groups and songwriters from anywhere; currently handles 3 acts. Receives 20-25% or consultant fees. Reviews material for acts.

How to Contact *Call first and obtain permission to submit.* Prefers CD or VHS videocassette with 3 songs and lyric sheet. If seeking management, press kit should include bio, list of concerts performed in past 2 years including name of venue, repertoire, reviews and photos. Does not return material. Responds in 2 months.

Music Mostly **classical/crossover**, **voice** and **pop**. Works primarily with classical/crossover ensembles, instrumental soloists, operatic voice and pop singer/songwriters. Current acts include Liona Boyd (classical guitar) and Pavlo (instrumental).

Tips "Invest in demo production using best quality voice and instrumentalists. If you write songs, hire the vocal talent to best represent your work. Submit CD and lyrics. Artists should follow up 6-8 weeks after submission."

FIRST TIME MANAGEMENT

Sovereign House, 12 Trewartha Rd., Praa Sands-Penzance, Cornwall TR20 9ST England (01736)762826. Fax: (01736)763328. E-mail: panamus@aol.com. Web site: www.songwriters-guild .co.uk. **Contact:** Roderick G. Jones, managing director. Management firm, record company (HepCat Records, Rainy Day Records, Mohock Records, Pure Gold Records) and music publisher (Panama Music Library, Melody First Music Library, Eventide Music Library, Musik' Image Music Library, Promo Sonor International Muisc Library, Caribbean Music Library, ADN Creation Music Library, Piano Bar Music Library, Corelia Music Library, PSI Music Library, First Time Music (Publishing) U.K.—registered members of The Mechanical Copyright Protection Society (MCPS) and The Performing Right Society (PRS). Estab. 1986. Represents local, regional and international individual aritsts, groups, composers and songwriters. Receives 15-25% commission. Reviews material for acts.

• Also see the listings for First Time Music (Publishing U.K.) in the Music Publishers section of this book.

How to Contact Submit demo by mail. Unsolicited submissions are OK. Prefers CD with 3 songs and lyric sheets. If seeking management, press kit should include cover letter, bio, photo, demo/CD, press clippings and anything relevant to make an impression. Does not return material. Responds in 1 month.

Music All styles. Works primarily with songwriters, composers, DJ remixers, rappers, vocalists, groups and choirs. Current acts include Willow (pop), Animal Cruelty (indie/heavy thrash), Bram Stoker (gothic rock group), Kevin Kendle (New Age), Peter Arnold (folk/roots), David Jones (urban/R&B), and Lisa Marie (extreme hardcore).

Tips "Become a member of the Guild of International Songwriters and Composers. Keep everything as professional as possible. Be patient and dedicated to your aims and objectives."

FREESTYLE ENTERTAINMENT

(formerly Biscuit Productions Inc.), 3315 E. Russell Rd., Suite A4-117, Las Vegas NV 89120. (888)271-0468. Web site: www.freestyleLLC.com. **President:** Steve Walker. Management firm. Estab. 1989. Represents individual artists and groups from anywhere; currently handles 3 acts. Receives 20% commission. Reviews material for acts.

How to Contact Submit demo by mail. Prefers cassette or VHS videocassette. Does not return material. Responds in 2 months.

Music Mostly **rap**, **R&B** and **dance**; also **pop** and **alternative**. Current acts include Jamariah, Biscuit and Brand X.

HALE ENTERPRISES

Rt. 1, Box 49, Worthington IN 47471-9310. (812)875-3664. E-mail: haleenterprises@epowerc.net. **Contact:** Rodger Hale, CEO. Management firm, record company (Projection Unlimited) and recording studio. Estab. 1976. Represents artists, groups, songwriters and studio musicians; currently handles 11 acts. Receives 15% commission for booking, 20% for management. Reviews material for acts.

How to Contact Submit demo by mail. Unsolicited submissions are OK. Prefers cassette or videocassette with 2-10 songs and lyric sheet. If seeking management include cover letter, résumé, lyric sheets, press clippings, current promo pack or photo, video-audio tape, clubs currently performing, short performance history and equipment list (if applicable). Does not return material. Responds in 1 week.

Music Mostly **country** and **top 40**; also **MOR**, **progressive**, **rock** and **pop**. Works primarily with show bands, dance bands and bar bands. Current acts include Indiana (country show band), Seventh Heaven (top 40 show) and Cotton (show band).

☑ BILL HALL ENTERTAINMENT & EVENTS
138 Frog Hollow Rd., Churchville PA 18966-1031. (215)357-5189. Fax: (215)357-0320. E-mail: Billha llevents@verizon.net. **Contact:** William B. Hall III, owner/president. Booking agency and production company. Represents individuals and groups; currently handles 20-25 acts. Receives 15% commission. Reviews material for acts.

How to Contact Submit demo by mail. Unsolicited submissions are OK. Prefers cassette or videocassette of performance with 2-3 songs "and photos, promo material and record or tape. We need quality material, preferably before a 'live' audience." Does not return material. Responds only if interested.

Music Marching band, **circus** and **novelty**. Works primarily with "unusual or novelty attractions in musical line, preferably those that appeal to family groups." Current acts include Fralinger and Polish-American Philadelphia Championship Mummers String Bands (marching and concert group), "Mr. Polynesian" Show Band and Hawaiian Revue (ethnic group), the "Phillies Whiz Kids Band" of Philadelphia Phillies Baseball team, Paul Richardson (Phillies' organist/entertainer), Mummermania Musical Quartet, Philadelphia German Brass Band (concert band), Vogelgesang Circus Calliope, Kromer's Carousel Band Organ, Reilly Raiders Drum & Bugle Corps, Hoebel Steam Calliope, Caesar Rodney Brass Band, Rohe Calliope, Philadelphia Police & Fire Pipes Band, Larry Rothbard's Circus Band and Tim Laushey Pep & Dance Band.

Tips "Please send whatever helps us to most effectively market the attraction and/or artist. Provide something that gives you a clear edge over others in your field!"

☑ ☑ HANSEN ENTERPRISES, LTD.
855 E. Twain #123411, Las Vegas NV 89109. (702)896-8115. Fax: (702)792-1363. **Contact:** J. Malcom Baird. Management firm. Estab. 1971. Represents individual artists, groups and songwriters from anywhere; currently handles 3 acts. Receives 15-25% commission "or contracted fee arrangement." Reviews material for acts.

How to Contact Submit demo by mail. Unsolicited submissions are OK. Prefers cassette. Include SASE. Responds in 3 weeks. We are looking for potential *hit songs*only: top 40, pop and Spanish. From time to time we need music for TV shows, commercials and films. Send SASE for requirements, which change from time to time depending upon the project(s).

Music Mostly **'50s & '60s rock** and **Spanish adult contemporary**. Current acts include The Ronettes, Pilita Corrales (top selling female Spanish recording star), and Mandrake.

☑ ☐ HARDISON INTERNATIONAL ENTERTAINMENT CORPORATION
P.O. Box 1732, Knoxville TN 37901-1732. (865)688-8680. Fax: (865)219-8094. E-mail: dennishardi son@bellsouth.net. Web site: www.hardisoninternational.netfirms.com. **Contact:** Dennis K. Hardison, CEO/founder. Management firm, booking agency, music publisher (Denlatrin Music), record company (Denlatrin Records) and record producer. Estab. 1984. Represents individual artists from anywhere; currently handles 3 acts. Receives 20% commission. Reviews material for acts.

• This company has promoted acts including New Edition, Freddie Jackson, M.C. Lyte and Kool Moe Dee.

How to Contact Submit demo by mail. Unsolicited submissions are OK. Prefers cassette or CD with 3 songs. If seeking management, press kit should include bio, promo picture and CD. Does not return material. Responds in 6 weeks to the best material.

Music Mostly **R&B**, **hip-hop** and **rap**. Current acts include Dynamo (hip-hop), Shorti (R&B singer/

former original member of female group Blaque) and Triniti (record producer, Public Enemy Dynamo, among others, current engineer for Chuck D).

Tips "We respond to the hottest material, so make it hot!"

⊘ M. HARRELL & ASSOCIATES

5444 Carolina, Merrillville IN 46410. (219)887-8814. Fax: (480)345-2255. E-mail: mhmkbmgs95@hotmail.com. **Contact:** Mary Harrell, owner. Management firm and booking agency. Estab. 1984. Represents individual artists, groups, songwriters, all talents—fashion, dancers, etc.; currently handles 30-40 acts. Receives 10-20% commission. Reviews material for acts.

How to Contact *Call first and obtain permission to submit.* Submit demo by mail. Prefers cassette or videocassette with 2-3 songs. Send résumé, bio, photo, demo/CD and press clippings. "Keep it brief and current." Does not return material. Responds in 1 month.

Music All types, **country**, **R&B**, **jazz**, **gospel**, **Big Band**, **light rock** and **reggae**. Current acts include Many B (showact), Michael Essany (celebrity talk show host), Bill Shelton & 11th Avenue ('50s rock & roll), Bang (R&B/jazz) and Retroactive.

Tips "The bands listed can and do tour in the U.S. and Europe (variety, mostly R&B, jazz and top 40) as well as the Chicagoland area. They get steady work and repeat business, because they are good and beat their competition. We also manage showbands."

☐ HOT STEAMING COFFEE FILMS

7522 Ave. T, #1, Brooklyn NY 11234. E-mail: enigpublus@aol.com. **Contact:** David K., personal manager. Management firm. Estab. 1997. Represents individual artists, groups and (rarely) songwriters; currently does not represent any act. Receives 12-25% commission.

How to Contact "E-mail for permission to submit, include a description of the type of material you have. Do not submit anything via mail, in person, or e-mail without WRITTEN PERMISSON via e-mail. If approved for submission, mail a CD with original songs and include lyric sheets. If mailing a press Kit, Press kit should include CD, cover letter, bio, photo, all lyrics with songs." **Does not return material and will not be held liable in any manner for any loss of submitted material. NO DROP OFFS.** Responds in 1 month. "We will contact artist if interested." Include e-mail address and phone number for reply. Do not mail MP3 files! Songs must be copyrighted to submit.

Music Commercial (Top 40) rock AND female Pop only. No other kinds of music. I am looking for a GREAT artist to work with exclusively. Someone with a commercial Look/Sound (i.e., Britney Spears, Jewel, Christina Aguilera) and/or great musical ability (i.e., Beck, Bob Dylan)" Works with original, solo artists and groups.

Tips "I am dedicated to artists I believe in. I act strictly as a personal manager which means I help them choose songs, submit songs, find a publisher, and/or a record company. Prefer artists who write and perform their own songs. I am currently seeking material. CDs accepted. NO cassette tapes. NO Mp3 files. Young male./female artists considered for development (ages 16-29) Do not contact me if you are beyond this age range. HINT: I am interested in poetic, melodic rock or a hot female pop artist with fresh hooks and commercial looks. Someone looking to express a social or political conscience in their music is a big PLUS."

Ⓝ Ⓥ ⊘ A HUGE PRODUCTION, INC.

138 Marston St., Lawrence MA 01841. (978)376-6952. E-mail: rippo@comcast.net. Web site: www.rippo.com. **Contact:** Richard M. Gordon, president. Management firm, music publisher (Cat Butt Musik/BMI) and record company (2 Funky International Records). Estab. 1996. Represents regional groups from the northeast; currently handles 2 acts. Receives negotiable commission.

• This company manages Rippopotamus, winner of 1996 Boston Music Award.

How to Contact *Write, e-mail, or call first and obtain permission to submit.* Prefers cassette with 3 songs and lyric sheet. If seeking management, press kit should include press, radio tracking, photo and CD. Include SASE. Responds in 1 month.

Music Mostly **pop/rock** and **funk**. Works with bands exclusively. Current acts include Rippopotamus (8 piece funk band—management), Dr. Akward (funk/rock—consulting) and Josh Cole (folk—consulting).

Tips "At this time we have restricted our activities to consulting and project management. Always call first. Promo packages are expensive, and you should always make sure we're actively seeking material, especially since most modern bands do their own songwriting. Being artists ourselves, we strongly recommend that you be very sure of people you work with and that they have same level of faith and confidence in the project that you do. Never give away the store and always make sure that you are aware of what is transpiring with your career, even if you have someone you trust handling it for you. Ultimately, no one has your interests as much at heart as you do, and thus you should always have your finger on your career's pulse."

⊘ INTERNATIONAL ENTERTAINMENT BUREAU

3612 N. Washington Blvd., Indianapolis IN 46205-3592. (317)926-7566. E-mail: ieb@prodigy.net. Booking agency. Estab. 1972. Represents individual artists and groups from anywhere; currently handles 157 acts. Receives 20% commission.

How to Contact *No unsolicited submissions.*

Music Mostly **rock**, **country** and **A/C**; also **jazz**, **nostalgia** and **ethnic**. Works primarily with bands, comedians and speakers. Current acts include Five Easy Pieces (A/C), Scott Greeson (country), and Cool City Swing Band (variety).

⊘ J & V MANAGEMENT

143 W. Elmwood, Caro MI 48723. (989)673-2889. **Manager/Publisher:** John Timko. Management firm, booking agency and music publisher. Represents local, regional or international individual artists, groups and songwriters. Receives 10% commission. Reviews material for acts.

How to Contact *Write first and obtain permission to submit.* Prefers CD or cassette with 3 songs maximum and lyric sheet. If seeking management, include short reference bio, cover letter and résumé in press kit. Include SASE. Responds in 2 months.

Music Mostly **country**. Works primarily with songwriters/vocalists and dance bands. Current acts include John Patrick (countr y) and Brandi Ewald (country).

⊡ ⊘ SHELDON KAGAN INTERNATIONAL

35 McConnell, Dorval QC H9S 5L9 Canada. (514)631-2160. Fax: (514)631-4430. E-mail: sheldon@s heldonkagan.com. Web site: www.sheldonkagan.com. **Contact:** Sheldon Kagan, president. Booking agency. Estab. 1965. Represents local individual artists and groups; currently handles 6 acts. Receives 10-20% commission. Reviews materials for acts.

How to Contact Submit demo by mail. Unsolicited submissions are OK. Prefers DVD, CD or VHS videocassette with 6 songs. Include SASE. Responds in 5 weeks.

Music Mostly **top 40**. Works primarily with vocalists and bands. Current acts include Quazz (jazz trio), City Lights (top 40 band), Jeux de Cordes (violin and guitar duo), The Soulmates (top 40) and Travelin' Band (top 40).

Ⓝ ⊘ KENDALL WEST AGENCY

P.O. Box 173776, Arlington TX 76003-3776. (817)468-7800. E-mail: kendallwestagency@adelphia. com. **Contact:** Michelle Vellucci. Booking agency and television producer. Estab. 1994. Represents individual artists and groups from anywhere. Receives 10% commission. Reviews material for acts.

How to Contact *Write first and obtain permission to submit or write to arrange personal interview.* Prefers CD or cassette with 5 songs and lead sheet. If seeking management, press kit should include bio, photo, cover letter, demo/CD and résumé. Include SASE. Responds in 1 month.

Music Mostly **country**, **blues/jazz** and **rock**; also **trios**, **dance** and **individuals**. Works primarily with bands. Current acts include Way Out West (country band), Breckenridge (variety band) and Jaz-Vil (jazz/blues).

⊕ ◯ KICKSTART MUSIC LTD.

12 Port House, Square Rigger Row, Plantation Wharf, London SW11 3TY England. (020)7223 8666. Fax: (020)7223 8777. E-mail: info@kickstart.uk.net. **Contact:** Frank Clark, director. Management/ publishing Company. Estab. 1994. Represents individual artists, groups or songwriters from any-

where; currently handles 7 acts. Receives 20-40% commission, "depends on contract." Reviews material for acts.

How to Contact Submit demo by mail. Unsolicited submissions are OK. Prefers CD, cassette or DAT with 3 songs and lyric and lead sheet. If seeking management, press kit should include photograph and bio. SAE and IRC. Responds in 2 weeks.

Music All genres including **pop**, **dance**, **rock**, **country** and **blues**. Works primarily with bands who perform a live set of original music and talented singer/songwriters who can cross over to all types of music. Current acts include Pal Joey (rock band), Simon Fox (songwriter) and The Electric Blues Anthology (blues band).

Tips "We prefer songwriters whose songs can cross over to all types of music, those who do not write in one style only."

N ☑ KITCHEN SYNC

8530 Holloway Dr. #208, West Hollywood CA 90069-2475. (310)855-1631. Fax: (310)657-7197. E-mail: ldg@hamptons.com. **Contact:** Laura Grover. Music production manager. Estab. 1990. Represents individual artists, groups and songwriters from anywhere. Reviews material for acts.

● Kitchen Sync primarily manages the production of music.

How to Contact *Write first and obtain permission to submit.* Prefers DVD with 3 songs and lyric sheet. If seeking management, press kit should include cover letter, résumé, bio, press clippings, discography and photo. Include SASE. Responds in 1 month.

Music Mostly **pop/rock**, **country** and **R&B**. Works primarily with producers and singer/songwriters.

Tips "Have a clear artistic mission statement and career goals. I'm mostly interested in overseeing/managing production of material, i.e., creating budgets and mapping out recording plan, booking studios, vendors, etc."

N ☑ JOANNE KLEIN

130 W. 28 St., New York NY 10001. **Contact:** Joanne Klein. Artist management firm and music publisher administration. Estab. 1982. Represents individual artists, songwriters and publishers from anywhere; currently handles 8 acts and 3 publishers. Receives 15-20% commission. Reviews material for acts.

How to Contact *Write first and obtain permission to submit.* Prefers CD. If seeking management/representation, press kit should include bio, photos, press/reviews, discography, information on compositions. Does not return material. Responds usually in 1 month.

Music Mostly **jazz**. Works primarily with instrumentalist/composers. Current acts include Kenny Barron (jazz), Victor Lewis (jazz), Horizon featuring Bobby Watson & Victor Lewis (jazz), Sylvia Cuenca (jazz),Terell Stafford (jazz), Eddie Henderson (jazz), Alex Blake (jazz), Dave Kikoski (jazz). Current publishing administration clients include Wazuri Publishing Company, Camille Music, and CKT Music.

N ☑ BOB KNIGHT AGENCY

185 Clinton Ave., Staten Island NY 10301. (718)448-8420. **Contact:** Bob Knight, president. Management firm, booking agency, music publisher and royalty collection firm. Estab. 1971. Represents artists, groups and songwriters; currently handles 4 acts. Receives 10-20% commission. Reviews material for acts and for submission to record companies and producers.

How to Contact Submit demo by mail. Unsolicited submissions are OK. Prefers cassette, CD, DVD, or videocassette (if available) with 5 songs and lead sheet "with bio and references." If seeking management, press kit should include bio, DVD, videocassette, CD, or audio cassette, as well as photo. Include SASE. Responds in 2 months.

Music Mostly **top 40/pop**; also **easy listening**, **MOR**, **R&B**, **soul**, **rock** (**nostalgia '50s and '60s**), **alternative**, **country**, and **country/pop**. Works primarily with recording and name groups and artists—'50s, '60s and '70s acts, high energy dance and show groups. Current acts include Delfonics (R&B nostalgia), B.T. Express, Brass Construction, Main Ingredient, Denny Carmella's Review, Denny Carmella's Booty Shack, Carl Thomas—Tribute to Bobby Darin, and Carl Thomas—A Night at the Copa.

Tips "We're seeking artists and groups with completed albums/demos. Also seeking male and female solo artists with powerful and dynamic voice—top 40, pop, R&B, and rock, country for recording and live performances."

◯ KUPER PERSONAL MANAGEMENT/RECOVERY RECORDINGS
P.O. Box 66274, Houston TX 77266. (713)520-5791. Fax: (713)520-5791. E-mail: recovery@wt.net. Web site: www.recoveryrecordings.com. **Contact:** Koop Kuper, owner. Management firm, music publisher (Kuper-Lam Music/BMI, Uvula Music/BMI, and Meauxtown Music/ASCAP) and record label (Recovery Recordings). Estab. 1979/2002. Represents individual artists, groups and songwriters from Texas; currently handles 5 acts. Receives 20% commission. Reviews material for acts.
How to Contact Submit demo by mail. Unsolicited submissions are OK. Prefers CD. If seeking management, press kit should include cover letter, press clippings, photo, bio (1 page) tearsheets (reviews, etc.) and demo CD. Does not return material. Responds in 2 months.
Music Mostly **singer/songwriters**, **triple AAA**, **roots rock** and **Americana**. Works primarily with self-contained and self-produced artists. Current acts include Philip Rodriguez (singer/songwriter), David Rodriguez (singer/songwriter), Def Squad (hip-hop), Texas (hip-hop) U.S. Representative for The Watchman (Dutch singer/songwriter), and The Very Girls (Dutch vocal duo).
Tips "Create a market value for yourself, produce your own master tapes, and create a cost-effective situation."

◗ LARI-JON PROMOTIONS
P.O. Box 216, Rising City NE 68658. (402)542-2336. **Contact:** Larry Good, owner. Management firm, music publisher (Lari-Jon Publishing Co./BMI) and record company (Lari-Jon Records). Represents individual artists, groups and songwriters; currently handles 3 acts. Receives 15% commission. Reviews material for acts.
How to Contact Submit demo by mail. Unsolicited submissions are OK. Prefers CD with 5 songs and lyric sheet. If seeking management, press kit should include 8×10 photos, cassette, videocassette and bio sheet. Include SASE. Responds in 2 months.
Music Mostly **country**, **gospel** and **'50s rock**. Works primarily with dance and show bands. Represents Kent Thompson (singer), Nebraskaland 'Opry (family type country show) and Brenda Allen (singer and comedienne).

◗ LEVINSON ENTERTAINMENT VENTURES INTERNATIONAL, INC.
1440 Veteran Ave., Suite 650, Los Angeles CA 90024. (323)663-6940. E-mail: leviinc@aol.com. President: Bob Levinson. **Contact:** Jed Leland, Jr. Management firm. Estab. 1978. Represents national individual artists, groups and songwriters; currently handles 4 acts. Receives 15-25% commission. Reviews material for acts.
How to Contact *Write first and obtain permission to submit.* Prefers CD, DVD, cassette, or VHS videocassette with 6 songs and lead sheet. If seeking management, press kit should include bio, pictures and press clips. Include SASE. Responds in 1 month.
Music Mostly **rock**, **MOR**, **R&B** and **country**. Works primarily with rock bands and vocalists.
Tips "Should be a working band, self-contained and, preferably, performing original material."

◖ RICK LEVY MANAGEMENT
4250 A1AS, D-11, St. Augustine FL 32080. (904)460-1225. Fax: (904)460-1226. E-mail: rick@ricklevy.com. Web site: www.ricklevy.com. **Contact:** Rick Levy, president. Management firm, music publisher (Flying Governor Music/BMI) and record company (Luxury Records). Estab. 1985. Represents local, regional or international individual artists and groups; currently handles 5 acts. Receives 15-20% commission. Reviews material for acts.
How to Contact *Write or call first and obtain permission to submit.* Prefers CD or videocassette with 3 songs and lyric sheet. If seeking management, press kit should include cover letter, bio, demo/CD, VHS video, photo and press clippings. Include SASE. Responds in 2 weeks.
Music Mostly **R&B** (no rap), **pop**, **country** and **oldies**; also **children's** and **educational videos** for schools. Current acts include Jay & the Techniques ('60s hit group), The Original Box Tops ('60s),

The Limits (pop), Freddy Cannon ('60s), The Fallin Bones (Blues/rock), Tommy Roe ('60s), and The Bushwhackers (country).

Tips "If you don't have 200% passion and committment, don't bother."

☑ ○ LOGGINS PROMOTION

26239 Senator Ave., Harbor City CA 90710. (310)325-2800. Fax: (310)427-7333. E-mail: promo@log ginspromotion.com. Web site: www.logginspromotion.com. **Contact:** Paul Loggins, CEO. Management firm and radio promotion. Represents individual artists, groups and songwriters from anywhere; currently handles 6 acts. Receives 20% commission. Reviews material for acts.

How to Contact If seeking management, press kit should include picture, short bio, cover letter, press clippings and CD (preferred). "Mark on CD which cut you, as the artist, feel is the strongest." Does not return material. Responds in 2 weeks.

Music Mostly **adult**, **top 40** and **AAA**; also **urban**, **rap**, **alternative**, **college**, **smooth jazz** and **Americana**. Works primarily with bands and solo artists.

◑ MANAGEMENT BY JAFFE

68 Ridgewood Ave., Glen Ridge, NJ 07028. (973)743-1075. Fax: (973)743-1075. E-mail: jerjaf@aol.c om. **President:** Jerry Jaffe. Management firm. Estab. 1987. Represents individual artists and groups from anywhere; currently handles 2 acts. Receives 20% commission. Reviews material for acts "rarely." Reviews for representation "sometimes."

How to Contact *Write or call first to arrange personal interview.* Prefers CD or cassette and videocassette with 3-4 songs and lyric sheet. Does not return material. Responds in 2 months.

Music Mostly **rock/alternative**, **pop** and **Hot AC**. Works primarily with groups and singers/songwriters. Current acts include Joe McIntrye (pop) and others.

Tips "If you are influenced by Jesus & Mary Chain, please e-mail. Create some kind of 'buzz' first."

☑ ◪ MANAGEMENT PLUS

1617 E. Commerce #4104, San Antonio TX 78205. (210)226-8450. Fax: (210)223-3251. E-mail: bill@bookyourevent.com. Web site: www.bookyourevent.com. **Contact:** Bill Angelini, owner. Management firm and booking agency. Estab. 1980. Represents individual artists and groups from anywhere; currently handles 6 acts. Receives 10-15% commission. Reviews material for acts.

How to Contact Submit demo by mail. Unsolicited submissions are OK. Prefers CD, VHS videocassette and bio. If seeking management, press kit should include pictures, bio, résumé and discography. Does not return material. Responds in 1 month.

Music Mostly **Latin American**, **Tejano** and **international**; also **Norteno** and **country**. Current acts include Jay Perez (Tejano), Ram Herrera (Tejano), Michael Salgado (Tejano), Flaco Jimenez (Tex-Mex), Rodeo (Tejano) and Grupo Vida (Tejano).

◪ ◪ THE MANAGEMENT TRUST LTD.

411 Queen St. W, 3rd Floor, Toronto ON M5V 2A5 Canada. (416)979-7070. Fax: (416)979-0505. E-mail: mail@mgmtrust.ca. Web site: www.mgmtrust.ca. Manager: Jake Gold. Manager: R.J. Guha. General Manager: Shelley Stertz. Management firm. Estab. 1986. Represents individual artists and/or groups; currently handles 8 acts.

How to Contact Submit demo by mail (Attn: A&R Dept.). Unsolicited submissions are OK. If seeking management, press kit should include CD or tape, bio, cover letter, photo and press clippings. Does not return material. Responds in 2 months.

Music All types . Current acts include Gord Downie (alternative rock), Doctor (rock band), Sass Jordan (rock), Brian Dyrne (folk rock), The Populars (rock), The Salads (rock), onlyforward (rock), Dearly Beloved (rock/alt), and Chris Koster (rock).

○ RICK MARTIN PRODUCTIONS

125 Fieldpoint Road, Greenwich CT 06830. E-mail: rick@easywaysystems.com. **Contact:** Rick Martin, president. Personal manager, music publisher, and independent producer. Held the Office of Secretary of the National Conference of Personal Managers for 22 years. Represents vocalists; cur-

rently produces pop music artists in private project studio and looking for a female pop vocalist in the general area of Greenwich, CT for production project. Receives 15% commission as a personal manager and/or customary production and publishing distributions.

How to Contact Please e-mail for initial contact or submit 2-3 songs and picture.

Music Top 40.

Tips ''Your demo does not have to be professionally produced to submit to producers, publishers, or managers. In other words, save your money. It's really not important what you've done. It's what you can do now that counts.''

☑ PHIL MAYO & COMPANY

P.O. Box 304, Bomoseen VT 05732. (802)468-2554. Fax: (802)468-2554. E-mail: pmcamgphil@aol.com. **Contact:** Phil Mayo, President. Management firm and record company (AMG Records). Estab. 1981. Represents individual artists, groups and songwriters from anywhere; currently handles 4 acts. Receives 15-20% commission. Reviews material for acts.

How to Contact *Contact first and obtain permission to submit.* Prefers CD with 3 songs (professinally recorded) and lyric or lead sheet. If seeking management, include bio, photo and lyric sheet in press kit. Does not return material. Responds in 2 months.

Music Mostly **Contemporary Christian pop**. Current and past acts have included John Hall, Guy Burlage, Jonell Mosser, Pam Buckland, Orleans, Gary Nicholson and Jon Pousette-Dart.

☑ ☑ MEDIA MANAGEMENT

P.O. Box 3773, San Rafael CA 94912-3773. (415)898-7474. Fax: (415)898-9191. E-mail: mediamanagement9@aol.com. **Contact:** Eugene, proprietor. Management firm. Estab. 1990. Represents international individual artists, groups and songwriters; currently handles 5 acts. Receives 15% commission. Reviews material for acts.

How to Contact Submit demo by mail. Unsolicited submissions are OK. Prefers CD or DVD with lyric sheet. If seeking management, include lyric sheets, demo, photo and bio. Does not return material.

Music Mostly **R&B**, **blues**, **rock** and **pop**. Works primarily with songwriting performers/bands. Current acts include Zakiya Hooker (r&b/blues/singer/songwriter), Greg Anton/The Anton Project (rock songwriter/group), John Lee Hooker Estate (blues), Ollan Christopher Bell (producer), and Peter Walker (acoustic guitar virtuoso—raga/flamenco).

Tips ''Write great radio-friendly songs with great musical and lyrical hooks.''

☑ ☑ MEGA MUSIC PRODUCTIONS

16950 North Bay Road, Suite 1706, Sunny Isle, FL 33160. (305)604-9666. E-mail: marco@megamusicevents.com. Web site: www.MegaMusicEvents.com. Contact: Marco Vinicio Carvajal, General Manager. Management firm, booking agency and record producer. Represents individual artists and groups from anywhere; currently handles 10 acts. Receives 25-35% commission. Reviews material for acts.

How to Contact Submit e-mail with Web site, mp3, and picture. Unsolicited submissions are OK. Prefers CD, DVD or VHS videocassette with 4 songs and lyric sheet. If seeking management, press kit should include cover letter, demo/CD, video, photos and bio. Does not return material. Responds in 1 month.

Music Mostly **rock**, **techno-dance** and **Latin rock**; also **Latin** and **pop**. Works primarily with bands and singers.

Tips ''Send us compact information and describe your goals.''

☐ MIDCOAST, INC.

1002 Jones Rd., Hendersonville TN 37075. (615)400-4664. E-mail: mid-co@ix.netcom.com. **Managing Director:** Bruce Andrew Bossert. Management firm and music publisher (MidCoast, Inc./BMI). Estab. 1984. Represents individual artists, groups and songwriters; currently handles 2 acts. Reviews material for acts.

How to Contact Submit demo by mail. Unsolicited submissions are OK. Prefers CD, cassette, VHS videocassette or DAT with 2-4 songs and lyric sheet. If seeking management, press kit should include cover letter, "short" bio, tape, video, photo, press clippings and announcements of any performances in Nashville area. Does not return material. Responds in 6 weeks if interested.

Music Mostly **rock**, **pop** and **country**. Works primarily with original rock and country bands and artists. Current acts include Room 101 (alternative rock).

◙ MONTEREY PENINSULA ARTISTS/PARADIGM

124 12th Ave. S., Suite 410, Nashville TN 37203. (615)251-4400. Fax: (615)251-4401. Web site: www.mpanashville.com. Booking agency. Represents individual artists, groups from anywhere; currently handles 37 acts. Receives 10% commission. Reviews material for acts.

How to Contact *Write or call first to arrange personal interview.*

Music Mostly **country**. Current acts include Lyle Lovett, Ricky Skaggs, Sawyer Brown, Junior Brown, Toby Keith, Travis Tritt, Montgomery Gentry, The Del McCoury Band, Grand Funk Railroad, Kasey Chambers, Robert Earl Keen, Shooter Jennings and Uncle Kracker.

◙ NIK ENTERTAINMENT CO.

274 N. Goodman St., Rochester NY 14607. (585)244-0331. Fax: (585)244-0356. E-mail: nikniceguy @aol.com. Web site: www.nikentertainment.com. **Contact:** General Manager/President: Gary Webb. Management firm and booking agency. Estab. 1986. Represents groups from anywhere; currently handles 10 acts. Reviews material for acts.

How to Contact Submit demo by mail. Unsolicited submissions are OK. Prefers cassette, VHS or CD with lyric or lead sheet. If seeking management, press kit should include photo, bio and demo. Does not return material.

Music Mostly **mainstream rock** and **pop**. Works primarily with bands. Current acts include Nik and the Nice Guys (pop show band), The Shag-adelics ('60s meets '90s), Fever—The Wrath of Polyester ('70s retro), Alpha Delta Nik (the world's only tribute to *Animal House*), The Blues Family (r&b review), Jazz Nik (basic jazz trio and more), The Bugzappers (swing band), Shamalama (oldies with an edge) and the Rochester Rat Pack (the cocktail culture revival).

◙ NOTEWORTHY PRODUCTIONS

124½ Archwood Ave., Annapolis MD 21401. (410)268-8232. Fax: (410)268-2167. E-mail: mcshane @mcnote.com. Web site: www.mcnote.com. **Contact:** McShane Glover, president. Management firm and booking agency. Estab. 1985. Represents individual artists, groups and songwriters from everywhere; currently handles 6 acts. Receives 15-20% commission. Reviews material for acts.

How to Contact *Write first and obtain permission to submit.* Prefers CD/CDR with lyric sheet. If seeking management, press kit should include cassette or CD, photo, bio, venues played and press clippings (preferably reviews). "Follow up with a phone call 3-5 weeks after submission." Does not return material. Responds in 2 months.

Music Mostly **Americana**, **folk**, and **Celtic**. Works primarily with performing singer/songwriters. Current acts include Seamus Kennedy (Celtic/contemporary), Dave's True Story (Jazz) and the Rev. Billy C. Wirty (blues).

◘ ON THE LEVEL MUSIC!

P.O. Box 508, Owego NY 13827. (607)222-4151. E-mail: fredny2020@yahoo.com. Contact: Fred Gage, CEO/president. Management firm, booking agency and music publisher (On The Level Music! Publishing). Estab. 1970. Represents individual artists, groups and songwriters from anywhere; currently handles 30 acts. Receives 15% commission. Reviews material for acts.

How to Contact Submit demo by mail. Unsolicited submissions are OK. Prefers CDs, DAT or VHS videocassette with 4 songs and lyric or lead sheet. If seeking management, press kit should include cover letter, bio, demo/CD, lyric sheets, press clippings, 8×10 photo and video. Does not return material. Responds in 1 month.

Music Mostly **rock**, **alternative** and **jazz**; also **blues**. Current acts include Ice River Blues and Summer Jam 2004.

ⓝ ☒ ◻ OUTLAW ENTERTAINMENT INTERNATIONAL

#101-1001 W. Broadway, Dept. 400, Vancouver BC V6H 4E4 Canada. (604)878-1494. Fax: (604)878-1495. E-mail: info@outlawentertainment.com. Web site: www.outlawentertainment.com. **CEO/President:** Tommy Floyd. Assistant President: Suzanne Marie. Management firm. Estab. 1995. Represents individual artists, groups and songwriters from anywhere; currently handles 3 acts. Receives 20% commission. Reviews material for acts.

How to Contact Submit demo CD by mail. Unsolicited submissions are OK. Prefers CD with 2-3 songs and lyric sheet. If seeking management, press kit should include 8×10 photo, bio and written statement of goals. SAE and IRC. Responds in 1 month.

Music Mostly **rock**, **metal** and **alt. country**. Works primarily with bands, "but welcomes dynamic singer/songwriters." Current acts include American Dog (hard rock act), Luba Dvorak (alt. country act) and Subsonic (heavy metal act).

Tips "Clearly define your target market. Write simple, emotional, primal songs."

◻ PRECISION MANAGEMENT

110 Coliseum Crossing, #158, Hampton VA 23666-5902. (800)275-5336, ext. 0381042. E-mail: precisionmanagement@netzero.com. Web site: www.pmmusicgroup.com. **Contact:** Cappriccieo Scates, operations director. Management firm and music publisher (Mytrell/BMI). Estab. 1990. Represents individual artists and/or groups and songwriters from anywhere; currently handles 3 acts. Receives 20% commission. Reviews material for acts.

How to Contact Submit demo by mail. Unsolicited submissions are OK. Prefers cassette or VHS videocassette with 3-4 songs and lyric sheet. If seeking management, press kit should include photo, bio, demo/CD, lyric sheets, press clippings and all relevant press information. Include SASE. Responds in 6 weeks.

Music Mostly **R&B**, **rap** and **gospel**; also **all types**.

ⓝ ◪ PRESTIGE MANAGEMENT

8600 Wilbur Ave., Northridge CA 91324. (818)993-3030. Fax: (818)993-4151. E-mail: prestige@gte.net. **Contact:** Waddell Solomon, vice president. Management firm. Estab. 1987. Represents individual artists, groups and songwriters from anywhere; currently handles 2 acts. Receives 15% commission. Reviews material for acts.

How to Contact Submit demo by mail. Unsolicited submissions are OK. Prefers CD with 3 songs, photo/bio and lyric sheet. If seeking management, press kit should include photos, bio, recent show dates and recent show reviews. Does not return material. Responds in 1 month.

Music Mostly **pop rock**, **hard rock**, **alternative rock**; also **R&B** and **AAA**. Works primarily with pop/rock bands with strong songs and live shows; also songwriters for film/TV projects. Current acts include Busted, McFly, and V.

◪ PRIME TIME ENTERTAINMENT

125 Ryan Industrial Court, Suite 310, San Ramon CA 94583. (408)289-9333. Fax: (415)532-2501. E-mail: artistmanager@aol.com. **Owner:** Jim Douglas. Management firm and booking agency. Estab. 1988. Represents individual artists, groups and songwriters from anywhere. Receives 10-20% commission. Reviews material for acts.

How to Contact Submit demo by mail. Unsolicited submissions are OK. Prefers cassette with 3-5 songs. If seeking management, press kit should include 8×10 photo, reviews and CDs/tapes. Include SASE. Responds in 1 month.

Music Mostly **jazz**, **country** and **alternative**; also **ethnic**. Artists include Craig Chaquico (jazz), Grant Geissman (fusion/jazz), Jody Watley (R&B), and Ray Parker, Jr. (jazz/R&B).

Tips "It's all about the song."

☑ ◻ PRO TALENT CONSULTANTS

P.O. Box 233, Nice CA 95464. (707)349-1809 or (310)367-5448 (Mar Vista/Beverly Hills, CA). E-mail: pro_talent_artists@yahoo.com. E-mail: pro_talent_artists@yahoo.com. **Contact:** John Eckert, coordinator. Management firm and booking agency. Estab. 1979. Represents individual artists and

groups; currently handles 12 acts. Receives 15% commission. Reviews material for acts.
How to Contact Submit demo by mail. Unsolicited submissions are OK. "We prefer CD (4 songs). Submit videocassette with live performance only." If seeking management, press kit should include an 8×10 photo, a cassette or CD of at least 4-6 songs, a bio on group/artist, references, cover letter, press clippings, video and business card or a phone number with address. Does not return material. Responds in 5 weeks.
Music Mostly **country, country/pop** and **rock**. Works primarily with vocalists, show bands, dance bands and bar bands. Current acts include Ronny and the Daytonas (pop/rock-top 40 band), Jimmy Torres (country singer), and Doug Stone (country vocalist).

❏ RAINBOW TALENT AGENCY
146 Round Pond Lane, Rochester NY 14626. (585)723-3334. Fax: (585)720-6172. E-mail: rtalent@frontiernet.net. **Contact:** Carl Labate, President. Management firm and booking agency. Represents artists and groups; currently handles 6 acts. Receives 15-20% commission.
How to Contact Submit demo by mail. Unsolicited submissions are OK. Prefers CD/CDR with minimum 3 songs. May send DVD if available; "a still photo and bio of the act; if you are a performer, it would be advantageous to show yourself or the group performing live. Theme videos are not helpful." If seeking management, include photos, bio, markets established, CD/DVD. Does not return material. Responds in 1 month.
Music Blues, rock and **R&B**. Works primarily with touring bands and recording artists. Current acts include Kristin Mainhart (alt light rock); Classic Albums Live (classic rock symphony); Hannah (original rock); The Buddhahood (jammin world beat) and Spanky Haschmann Swing Orchestra (high energy swing).
Tips "My main interest is with groups or performers that are currently touring and have some product. And are at least 50% percent original. Strictly songwriters should apply elsewhere."

❏ RASPBERRY JAM MUSIC
(formerly Endangered Species Artist Management), 4 Berachah Ave., South Nyack NY 10960-4202. (845)353-4001. Fax: (845)353-4332. E-mail: muzik@verizon.net. Web site: www.musicandamerica.com or www.anyamusic.com. **President:** Fred Porter. Vice President: Suzanne Buckley. Management firm. Estab. 1979. Represents individual artists, groups and songwriters from anywhere; currently handles 3 acts. Receives 20% commission. Reviews material for acts.
How to Contact *Call first and obtain permission to submit.* Prefers CD with 3 or more songs and lyric sheet. "Please include a demo of your music, a clear, recent photograph as well as any current press, if any. A cover letter indicating at what stage in your career you are and expectations for your future. Please label the cassette and/or CD with your name and address as well as the song titles." If seeking management, press kit should include cover letter, bio, photo, demo/CD, lyric sheet and press clippings. Include SASE. Responds in 6 weeks.
Music Mostly **pop, rock** and **world**; also **Latin/heavy metal, R&B, jazz** and **instrumental**. Current acts include Jason Wilson & Tabarruk (pop/reggae, nominated for Juno award 2001), and Anya (teen singer).
Tips "Listen to everything, classical to country, old to contemporary, to develop an understanding of many writing styles. Write with many other partners to keep the creativity fresh. Don't feel your style will be ruined by taking a class or a writing seminar. We all process moods and images differently. This leads to uniqueness in the music."

❏ DIANE RICHARDS WORLD MANAGEMENT, INC.
E-mail: drworldmgm@aol.com. **Contact:** Diane Richards, president. Management firm. Estab. 1994. Represents individual artists, groups, songwriters and producers from anywhere; currently handles 8 acts. Receives 20% commission. Reviews material for acts.
How to Contact *Write first (via e-mail) and obtain permission to submit.* If seeking management, press kit should include cover letter, photograph, biography, cassette tape, telephone number and address. Does not return material. Responds in 1 month.
Music Mostly **dance, pop** and **rap**; also **New Age, A/C** and **jazz**. Works primarily with pop and

dance acts, and songwriters who also are recording artists. Current acts include Sappho (songwriter/artist), Menace (songwriter/producer/artist) and Babygirl (R&B/rap artist).

◩ RIOHCAT MUSIC

P.O. Box 764, Hendersonville TN 37077-0764. (615)824-9313. Fax: (615)824-0797. E-mail: tachoir@bellsouth.net. Web site: www.tachoir.com. **Contact:** Robert Kayne, manager. Management firm, booking agency, record company (Avita Records) and music publisher. Estab. 1975. Represents individual artists and groups; currently handles 4 acts. Receives 15-20% commission.
   • Also see the listing for Avita Records in the Record Companies section of this book.

How to Contact *Contact first and obtain permission to submit.* Prefers CD and lead sheet. If seeking management, press kit should include cover letter, bio, photo, demo/CD and press clippings. Does not return material. Responds in 6 weeks.

Music Mostly **contemporary jazz** and **fusion**. Works primarily with jazz ensembles. Current acts include Group Tachoir (jazz), Tachoir/Manakas Duo (jazz) and Jerry Tachoir (jazz vibraphone artist).

◩ A.F. RISAVY, INC.

1312 Vandalia, Collinsville IL 62234. (618)345-6700. Fax: (618)345-2004. E-mail: swingcitymusic@ameritech.net. Web site: www.swingcitymusic.com. **Contact:** Art Risavy, president. Management firm and booking agency. Divisions include Artco Enterprises, Golden Eagle Records, Swing City Music and Swing City Sound. Estab. 1960. Represents artists, groups and songwriters; currently handles 35 acts. Receives 10% commission. Reviews material for acts.

How to Contact Submit demo by mail. Unsolicited submissions are OK. Prefers CD/CDR, cassette or VHS videocassette with 2-6 songs and lyric sheet. If seeking management, press kit should include pictures, bio and VHS videocassette. Include SASE. Responds in 3 weeks.

Music Mostly **rock**, **country**, **MOR** and **top 40**.

◩ CHARLES R. ROTHSCHILD PRODUCTIONS INC.

330 E. 48th St., New York NY 10017. (212)421-0592. **Contact:** Charles R. Rothschild, president. Booking agency. Estab. 1971. Represents individual artists, groups and songwriters from anywhere; currently handles 25 acts. Receives 25% commission. Reviews material for acts.

How to Contact *Call first and obtain permission to submit.* Prefers cassette, CD or VHS videocassette with 1 song and lyric and lead sheet. If seeking management, include cassette, photo, bio and reviews. Include SASE. Responds in 6 weeks.

Music Mostly **rock**, **pop**, **family** and **folk**; also **country** and **jazz**. Current acts include Richie Havens (folk singer), Leo Kottke (guitarist/composer), Emmylou Harris (country songwriter), Tom Chapin (kids' performer and folksinger) and John Forster (satirist).

◲ RUSTRON-WHIMSONG MUSIC PRODUCTIONS

Send all artist song submissions to: 1156 Park Lane, West Palm Beach FL 33417-5957. (561)686-1354. E-mail: RMP_WMP@bellsouth.net. **Contact:** Sheelah Adams, office administrator. Main Office in Connecticut. ("Main office does not review artist submissions—only South Florida Branch office does.") Executive Director: Rusty Gordon. Artist Consultants: Rusty Gordon and Davilyn Whims. Composition Management: Ron Caruso. Management firm, booking agency, music publisher (Rustron Music Publishers/BMI and Whimsong Publishing/ASCAP), record company and record producer. Estab. 1970. Represents individuals, groups and songwriters; currently handles 20 acts. Receives 10-30% commission. Reviews material for acts.
   • Also see listings for Rustron Music in the Music Publishers, Record Companies and Record Producers sections of this book.

How to Contact *Call to discuss submission.* Send CD or cassette with 10-15 songs (CD produced to sell at gigs with up to 15 songs on each CD preferred). Provide 8½×11 typed lyric sheets for every song in the submission. If seeking management, send press kit including: cover letter, bio, demo CD(s), typed lyric sheets and press clippings. "SASE or International Reply Coupons (IRC) required for all correspondence. No exceptions." Responds in 4 months.

Music Mostly **adult contemporary, electric acoustic, blues (country folk/urban, Southern), country (rock, blues, progressive), easy listening, Cabaret, soft rock & pop (ballads), women's music, R&B, folk/rock**; also **New Age instrumentals** and **New Age folk fusion**. Current acts include Jayne Margo-Reby (folk rock), Star Smiley (country), Robin Plitt (historical folk), Boomslang Swampsinger (Florida folk), Continental Divide (topical folk), Tracie Mitchell & Ivory Coast (folk rock/blues), Florida Rank & File (socio-political/folk/world music).

Tips "Carefully mix demo, don't drown the vocals, 10-15 songs in a submission. Prefer a for-sale CD made to sell at gigs with up to 15 songs on each. Send photo if artist is seeking marketing and/or production assistance. Very strong hooks, definitive verse melody, evolved concepts, unique and unpredictable themes. Flesh out a performing sound and style. The presentation should be unique to the artist. Stage presence a must!"

⊠ ◯ SA'MALL MANAGEMENT

P.O. Box 261488, Encino CA 91426. (310)317-0322. Fax: (818)506-8534. E-mail: samusa@aol.com. Web site: www.pplentertainmentgroup.com. **Contact:** Ted Steele, vice president of talent. Management firm, music publisher (Pollybyrd Publications) and record company (PPL Entertainment Group). Estab. 1990. Represents individual artists, groups and songwriters worldwide; currently handles 10 acts. Receives 10-25% commission. Reviews material for acts.

- ● Also see the listings for Pollybyrd Publications Limited and Zettitalia Music International in the Music Publishers section and PPL Entertainment Group in the Record Companies section of this book.

How to Contact *E-mail first and obtain permission to submit.* "Only professional full-time artists who tour and have a fan base need apply. No weekend warriors, please." Prefers CD or cassette. If seeking management, press kit should include picture, bio and tape. Include SASE. Responds in 2 months.

Music All types. Current acts include Riki Hendrix (rock), Buddy Wright (blues), Fhyne, Suzette Cuseo, The Band AKA, LeJenz, B.D. Fuoco, Juz-cuz and Donato.

◯ SAFFYRE MANAGEMENT

23401 Park Sorrento, #38, Calabasas CA 91302. (818)842-4368. E-mail: ebsaffyre@yahoo.com. **Contact:** Esta G. Bernstein, president. Management firm. Estab. 1990. Represents individual artists, groups and songwriters from anywhere; currently handles 2 acts. Receives 15% commission.

How to Contact *Call first and obtain permission to submit.* If seeking management, press kit should include cover letter, bio, photo, cassette with 3-4 songs and lyric sheets. Does not return material. Responds in 2 weeks only if interested.

Music Alternative/modern rock and **top 40.** "We work only with bands and solo artists who write their own material; our main objective is to obtain recording deals and contracts, while advising our artists on their careers and business relationships."

◻ SANDALPHON MANAGEMENT

P.O. Box 29110, Portland OR 97296. (503)957-3929. E-mail: jackrabbit01@sprintpcs.com. **Contact:** Ruth Otey, president. Management firm, music publisher (Sandalphon Music Publishing/BMI), and record company (Sandalphon Records). Estab. 2005. Represents individual artists, groups, songwriters; works with individual artists and groups from anywhere. Currently handles 0 acts. Receives negotiable commission. Reviews material for acts.

How to Contact Submit demo by mail. Unsolicited submissions are OK. Prefers cassette or CD with 1-5 songs and lyric sheet, cover letter. "Include name, address, and contact information." Include SASE or SAE and IRC for outside the United States. Responds in 1 month.

Music Mostly **rock, country,** and **alternative**; also **pop, gospel,** and **blues**. "We are looking for singers, bands, and singer/songwriters who are original but would be current in today's music markets. We help singers, bands, and singer-songwriters achieve their personal career goals."

Tips "Submit material you feel best represents you, your voice, your songs, or your band. Fresh and original songs and style are a plus. We are a West Coast management company looking for singers, bands, and singer-songwriters who are ready for the next level. We are looking for those with talent who are capable of being national and international contenders."

⊘ SENDYK, LEONARD & CO. INC.

532 Colorado Ave., Santa Monica CA 90401. (310)458-8860. Fax: (310)458-8862. **Contact:** Gerri Leonard, partner. Business management. Represents individual artists, groups and songwriters from anywhere; currently handles 25 acts. Receives 5% commission.

How to Contact "We do not solicit any songwriters for works to be submitted to artists, but are certainly interested in representing songwriters with respect to their financial affairs. We can also monitor their royalties; we have an extensive royalty administration department."

Music Current acts include Marilyn Manson (hard rock), Jonathon Butler (jazz/urban) and Kristy Swanson (actress/production).

⌨ ◔ SERGE ENTERTAINMENT GROUP

P.O. Box 2760, Acworth GA 30102. (678)445-0006. Fax: (678)494-9289. E-mail: sergeent@aol.com. Web site: www.serge.org. **Contact:** Sandy Serge, president. Management and PR firm and song publishers. Estab. 1987. Represents individual artists, groups, songwriters from anywhere; currently handles 20 acts. Receives 20% commission for management. Monthly fee required for PR acts.

How to Contact *E-mail first for permission to submit.* Submit demo or CD by mail. Unsolicited submissions are OK. Prefers CD with 4 songs and lyric sheet. If seeking management, press kit should include 8×10 photo, bio, cover letter, lyric sheets, max of 4 press clips, VHS videocassette, performance schedule and CD. "All information submitted must include name, address and phone number on each item." Does not return material. Responds in 6 weeks if interested.

Music Mostly **rock**, **pop** and **country**; also **New Age**. Works primarily with singer/songwriters and bands. Current acts include David McBee (rock), Moossa (jam band), and Mark Paul Smith (country).

☑ ◔ SIDDONS & ASSOCIATES

14724 Ventura Blvd., Penthouse Floor, Sherman Oaks CA 91403. (818)986-8040. Fax: (818)986-8041. E-mail: bill@coreentertainment.biz. **Contact:** Bill Siddons, president. Management firm. Estab. 1972. Represents individual artists and groups from anywhere; currently handles 6 acts. Receives 15-20% commission. Reviews material for acts.

How to Contact *Write first and obtain permission to submit.* Prefers CD or VHS videocassette with 3 songs and lyric sheet. If seeking management, press kit should include CD of 3 songs, lyric sheet, DVD if available, biography, past credits and discography. Does not return material. Responds in 3 months.

Music All styles. Current acts include Elayne Boosler (comedian), Jerry Cantrell (rock), D-SiSive (rapper/songwriter), Michael Glabicki (Rusted Root), and BSG (formerly Little River Band).

⬙ ☑ ◯ SILVER BOW MANAGEMENT

556 Amess St., New Westminster BC V3L 4A9 Canada. (604)523-9309. Fax: (604)523-9310. E-mail: saddlestone@shaw.ca. Web site: www.saddlestone.net. **President:** Grant Lucas. CEO: Candice James. Management firm, music publisher (Saddlestone Publishing, Silver Bow Publishing), record company (Saddlestone Records) and record producer (Silver Bow Productions, Krazy Cat Productions). Estab. 1988. Represents individual artists, groups, songwriters from anywhere; currently handles 8 acts. Receives standard commission. Reviews material for acts.

 • Also see the listings for Saddlestone Publishing in the Music Publishers section and Silver Bow Productions in the Record Producers section of this book.

How to Contact Submit demo by mail. Unsolicited submissions are OK. Prefers cassette with 3 songs and lyric sheet. If seeking management, press kit should include 8×10 photo, bio, cover letter, demo or CD with lyric sheets, press clippings, video, résumé and current itinerary. "Visuals are everything—submit accordingly." Does not return material. Responds in 2 months.

Music Mostly **country**, **pop** and **rock**; also **R&B**, **Christian** and **alternative**. Works primarily with bands, vocalists and singer/songwriters. Current acts include Darrell Meyers (country singer/songwriter), Nite Moves (variety band), Mark Vance (country/pop) and Stan Giles (country).

⊙ T. SKORMAN PRODUCTIONS, INC.

5156 S. Orange Ave., Orlando FL 32809. (407)895-3000. Fax: (407)895-1422. E-mail: ted@talentage ncy.com. Web site: www.talentagency.com. **Contact:** Ted Skorman, president. Management firm and booking agency. Estab. 1983. Represents groups; currently handles 40 acts. Receives 10-25% commission. Reviews material for acts.

How to Contact *E-mail first for permission to submit.* Prefers CD with 2 songs, or videocassette of no more than 6 minutes. "Live performance—no trick shots or editing tricks. We want to be able to view act as if we were there for a live show." If seeking management, press kit should include cover letter, bio, photo and demo CD or video. Does not return material. Responds only if interested.

Music Mostly **top 40**, **dance**, **pop** and **country**. Works primarily with high-energy dance acts, recording acts, and top 40 bands. Current acts include Steph Carse (pop).

Tips "We have many pop recording acts and are looking for commercial material for their next albums."

○ GARY SMELTZER PRODUCTIONS

603 W. 13th #2A, Austin TX 78701. (512)478-6020. Fax: (512)478-8979. E-mail: gsptalent@aol.com. **Contact:** Gary Smeltzer, president. Management firm and booking agency. Estab. 1967. Represents individual artists and groups from anywhere. Currently handles 20 acts. "We book about 100 different bands each year—none are exclusive." Receives 20% commission. Reviews material for acts.

How to Contact Submit demo by mail. Unsolicited submissions are OK. Prefers cassette, videocassette or CD. If seeking management, press kit should include cover letter, résumé, cassette or CD, bio, picture, lyric sheets, press clippings and video. Does not return material. Responds in 1 month.

Music Mostly **alternative**, **R&B** and **country**. Current acts include Ro Tel & the Hot Tomatoes (nostalgic '60s showband).

Tips "We prefer performing songwriters who can gig their music as a solo or group."

⊙ SOUND MANAGEMENT DIRECTION

10343 Jennifer Court, Seminole FL 33778. E-mail: sounddirection@aol.com. **Contact:** Bob Currie, president. Management firm, consultant, music publisher (Sun Face Music/ASCAP, Shaman Drum/ BMI) and record producer. Estab. 1986. Former music publisher, A&R with experience in US and UK. Representation for recording artists, songwriters and producers from anywhere. Payment options include fee-based, retainer or commission.

How to Contact Submit CD by mail. Unsolicited submissions are OK. Prefers CD or internet link with 2 songs and lyric sheet. If seeking management, press kit should include demo, photo and contact information including phone numbers. "If you want material returned, include SASE." Responds in 3 weeks.

Music Seeking commercial, contemporary and radio-oriented **rock**, **dance**, **jazz** and **urban**.

Tips "We only want your best, and be specific with style. Quality, not quantity."

Ⓝ ⊙ SOUTHEASTERN ATTRACTIONS

181 W. Valley Ave., Suite 105, Birmingham AL 35209. (205)942-6600. Fax: (205)942-7700. E-mail: staff@seattractions.com. Web site: www.seattractions.com. **Contact:** Agent. Booking agency. Estab. 1967. Represents groups from anywhere; currently handles 200 acts. Receives 20% commission.

How to Contact Submit demo by mail. Unsolicited submissions are OK. Prefers CD or DVD. Does not return material. Responds in 2 months.

Music Rock, alternative, oldies, country and dance. Works primarily with bands. Current acts include Leaderdog (rock), Undergrounders (variety to contemporary), Style Band (Motown/dance), The Connection (Motown/dance), Rollin in the Hay(bluegrass).

Ⓝ ○ SPHERE GROUP ONE

795 Waterside Drive, Marco Island FL 34145. (239)398-6800. Fax: (239)394-9881. E-mail: spheregro upone@att.net. **President:** Tony Zarrella. Talent Manager: Jon Zarrella. Management firm and

record producer. Estab. 1987. Represents individual artists and groups from anywhere; currently handles 5 acts. Receives commission.

How to Contact Submit demo by mail or e-mail. Unsolicited submissions are OK. Prefers CD or video with 3-5 songs. All submissions must include cover letter, lyric sheets, tape/CD, photo, bio and all press. "Due to large number of submissions we can only respond to those artists which we may consider working with." Does not return material

Music Mostly **pop/rock**, **pop/country** and **New Age**; also **R&B**. Works primarily with bands and solo singer/songwriters. Current acts include 4 of Hearts (pop/rock), Frontier 9 (pop/rock), Viewpoint (experimental) and Bombay Green (hybrid pop).

Tips "Develop and create your own style, focus on goals and work as a team and maintain good chemistry with all artists and business relationships."

ST. JOHN ARTISTS

P.O. Box 619, Neenah WI 54957-0619. (920)722-2222. Fax: (920)725-2405. E-mail: jon@stjohn-artists.com. Web site: www.stjohn-artists.com/. **Contact:** Jon St. John and Gary Coquoz, agents. Booking agency. Estab. 1968. Represents local and regional individual artists and groups; currently handles 20 acts. Receives 15-20% commission. Reviews material for acts.

How to Contact Call first and obtain permission to submit. Prefers CD or DVD. If seeking management, press kit should include cover letter, bio, photo, demo/CD, video and résumé. Include SASE.

Music Mostly **rock** and **MOR**. Current acts include Tribute (variety/pop/country), Boogie & the Yo-Yo's ('60s to 2000s), Vic Ferrari (Top 40 80's-2000's), Little Vito and the Torpedoes (variety 50's-2000's), Center Stage Variety Show Band (variety 60's-2000's) and Da Yoopers (musical comedy/novelty).

STAIRCASE PROMOTION

P.O. Box 211, East Prairie MO 63845. (573)649-2211. **Contact:** Tommy Loomas, president. Vice President: Joe Silver. Management firm, music publisher (Lineage Publishing) and record company (Capstan Record Production). Estab. 1975. Represents individual artists and groups from anywhere; currently handles 6 acts. Receives 25% commission. Reviews material for acts.

- Also see the listings for Lineage Publishing Co. in the Music Publishers section and Capstan Record Production in the Record Companies section of this book.

How to Contact Submit demo by mail. Unsolicited submissions are OK. Prefers cassette with 3 songs and lyric sheet. If seeking management, press kit should include bio, photo, audio cassette and/or video and press reviews, if any. "Be as professional as you can." Include SASE. Responds in 2 months.

Music Mostly **country**, **pop** and **easy listening**; also **rock**, **gospel** and **alternative**. Current acts include Skidrow Joe (country comedian, on Capstan Records), Vicarie Arcoleo (pop singer, on Treasure Coast Records) and Scarlett Britoni (pop singer on Octagon Records).

STANDER ENTERTAINMENT

11838 Hamlin St., #A, N. Hollywood CA 91606. (818)769-6365. E-mail: stander@earthlink.net. **Contact:** Jacqueline Stander, manager. Management firm, music publisher (DocRon Publishing), record company (Soaring Records) and consulting firm. Estab. 1970. Represents local individual artists, groups, film composers and songwriters; currently handles 6 acts. Receives 15% commission. Charges $50/hour consulting fee. Reviews material for acts. Places songs in film/TV.

How to Contact *Call first and obtain permission to submit.* Prefers cassette or VHS videocassette with 3-5 songs and lyric sheet. If seeking management, press kit should include photo, bio, press publicity, CD or cassette. Include SASE. Responds in 3 weeks.

Music Mostly **jazz**, **pop** and **R&B** (no rap); also **world music** and **Broadway**. Works primarily with national recording artists, film composers and singer/songwriters. Current and past acts include Bill Cunliffe (jazz pianist/producer), Freddie Ravel (contemporary Latin jazz keyboardist) and Lauren Wood (vocalist/songwriter).

Tips "Always looking for long term professionals who have worked to establish themselves in their market, yet want to go to the next level. For those who have something to offer and are just starting out, I am available for consulting by phone or in person. Please call for submission request."

☑ ◩ STARKRAVIN' MANAGEMENT

20501 Ventura Blvd., 217, Woodland Hills CA 91364. (818)587-6801. Fax: (818)587-6802. E-mail: bcmclane@aol.com. Web site: www.benmclane.com. **Contact:** B.C. McLane, Esq. Management and law firm. Estab. 1994. Represents individual artists, groups and songwriters. Receives 20% commission (management); $200/hour as attorney.

How to Contact Submit demo by mail. Unsolicited submissions are OK. Does not return material. Responds in 1 month if interested.

Music Mostly **rock**, **pop** and **R&B**. Works primarily with bands.

◩ T.L.C. BOOKING AGENCY

37311 N. Valley Rd., Chattaroy WA 99003. (509)292-2201. Fax: (509)292-2205. E-mail: tlcagent@ix. netcom.com. Web site: www.tlcagency.com. **Contact:** Tom or Carrie Lapsansky, agent/owners. Booking agency. Estab. 1970. Represents individual artists and groups from anywhere; currently handles 17 acts. Receives 10-15% commission. Reviews material for acts.

How to Contact *Call first and obtain permission to submit*. Prefers CD with 3-4 songs. Does not return material. Responds in 3 weeks.

Music Mostly **rock**, **country** and **variety**; also **comedians** and **magicians**. Works primarily with bands, singles and duos. Current acts include Nobody Famous (variety), Menagerie (variety-duo) and Soul Patrol (variety/top 40).

◩ TAS MUSIC CO./DAVE TASSE ENTERTAINMENT

N2467 Knollwood Dr., Lake Geneva WI 53147-9731. E-mail: david@baybreezerecords.com. Web site: www.baybreezerecords.com. **Contact:** David Tasse. Booking agency, record company and music publisher. Represents artists, groups and songwriters; currently handles 21 acts. Receives 10-20% commission. Reviews material for acts.

How to Contact Submit demo by mail. Unsolicited submissions are OK. Prefers cassette with 2-4 songs and lyric sheet. Include performance videocassette if available. If seeking management, press kit should include tape, bio and photo. Does not return material. Responds in 3 weeks.

Music Mostly **pop** and **jazz**; also **dance**, **MOR**, **rock**, **soul** and **top 40**. Works primarily with show and dance bands. Current acts include Max Kelly (philosophic rock) and L.J. Young (rap).

Ⓝ ◩ TEXAS SOUNDS ENTERTAINMENT

P.O. Box 1644, Dickinson TX 77539. (281)337-2473. Fax: (281)316-6958. E-mail: mikes@texas-sounds.com. Web site: www.texas-sounds.com. **Contact:** Mike Sandbergor George M. DeJesus, co-owners. Management firm, booking agency. Estab. 1980. Represents individual artists, groups and songwriters from anywhere. Currently handles 60 acts. Receives 10% commission.

How to Contact Write first and obtain permission to submit. Prefers CD or DVD with 3-4 songs and lyric and/or lead sheet. If seeking management, press kit should include bio, photo, accomplishments, demo. Does not return material.

Music Mostly **country**, **R&B** and **Latin pop**. Works primarily with bands, orchestras, singer/songwriters. Current acts include Johnny Lee (country singer), Chris Chitsey (country singer/songwriter), Patrick Murphy (country singer/songwriter), Hamilton Loomis (R&B singer/musician), Gene Kelton (R&B/rock), and Brian Black (country).

☑ ◩ TWENTIETH CENTURY PROMOTIONS

500 Zalley St., Providence RI 02908. Phone/fax: (401)467-1832. **Contact:** Gil Morse, president. Management firm, booking agency and record producer (20th Century). Estab. 1972. Represents individual artists and groups from anywhere; currently handles 9 acts. Receives 15% commission. Reviews material for acts.

How to Contact *Call first and obtain permission to submit or to arrange personal interview*. Prefers CD or cassette. If seeking management, press kit should include photo and bio. Does not return material. Responds in 3 weeks.

Music Mostly **country** and **blues**. Works primarily with individuals and groups. Current acts include Robbin Lynn, and Charlie Brown's Costars.

Tips ''Don't give up.''

☐ UNIVERSAL MUSIC MARKETING

P.O. Box 2297, Universal City TX 78148. (210)653-3989. E-mail: bswrl8@wmconnect.net. **Contact:** Frank Willson, president. Management firm, record company (BSW Records), booking agency, music publisher and record producer (Frank Wilson). Estab. 1987. Represents individual artists and groups from anywhere; currently handles 12 acts. Receives 15% commission. Reviews material for acts.

• Also see the listings for BSW Records in the Music Publishers and Record Companies sections and Frank Wilson in the Record Producers section of this book.

How to Contact Submit demo by mail. Unsolicited submissions are OK. Prefers CD or ¾'' videocassette with 3 songs and lyric sheet. If seeking management, include tape/CD, bio, photo and current activities. Include SASE. Responds in 6 weeks.

Music Mostly **country** and **light rock**; also **blues** and **jazz**. Works primarily with vocalists, singer/songwriters and bands. Current acts include Candee Land, Darlene Austin, Larry Butler, John Wayne, Sonny Marshall, Bobby Mountain, Crea Beal and Butch Martin (country).

ℕ ☐ RICHARD VARRASSO MANAGEMENT

P.O. Box 387, Fremont CA 94537. (510)792-8910. Fax: (510)792-0891. E-mail: richard@varasso.com. Web site: www.big7records.com. CEO: Richard Varrasso. A&R: Saul Vigil. Management firm. Estab. 1976. Represents individual artists, groups and songwriters from anywhere; currently handles several acts. Receives 10-20% commission. Reviews material for acts.

How to Contact Submit demo by mail. Unsolicited submissions are OK. Prefers cassette or CD. If seeking management, press kit should include photos, bios, cover letter, cassette, lyric sheets, press clippings, video, résumé and contact numbers. Good kits stand out. Does not return material. Responds in 2 months.

Music Mostly **rock**, **blues** and **young country**. Works primarily with concert headliners and singers. Current acts include Gary Cambra of the Tubes, Tim Murphy, Heat, Johnny Gunn, Famous Hits Band featuring Rich Varasso, Alameda Allstars (Greg Allman's backup band), Richie Barron of HWY2000, and Greg Douglass (songwriter).

☐ WILLIAM F. WAGNER AGENCY

14343 Addison St. #221, Sherman Oaks CA 91423. (818)905-1033. **Contact:** Bill Wagner, owner. Management firm and record producer (Bill Wagner). Estab. 1957. Represents individual artists and groups from anywhere; currently handles 2 acts. Receives 15% commission. Reviews materials for acts.

How to Contact Submit demo or CD by mail. Unsolicited submissions are OK. Prefers cassette or CD with 5 songs and lead sheet. If seeking management, press kit should include cover letter, bio, picture, tape or CD with 5 songs. "If SASE and/or return postage are included, I will reply in 30 days."

Music Mostly **jazz**, **contemporary pop** and **contemporary country**; also **classical**, **MOR** and **film and TV background**. Works primarily with singers, with or without band, big bands and smaller instrumental groups. Current acts include Page Cavanaugh (jazz/pop/contemporary/pianist), Sandy Graham (jazz singer), Brant Vogel (country singer and backing group), and Hector King (Spanish/English-language crossover artist/singer-songwriter).

Tips "Indicate in first submission what artists you are writing for, by name if possible. Don't send material blindly. Be sure all material is properly copyrighted. Be sure package shows 'all material herein copyrighted' on outside."

☐ CHERYL K. WARNER PRODUCTIONS

P.O. Box 2127, Pearland TX 77588-2127. Phone: (615)429-7849. E-mail: cherylkwarner@sbcglobal.net. Web site: www.cherylkwarner.com. **Contact:** Cheryl K. Warner and Associates. Recording and stage production, music consulting, music publisher, record label. Estab. 1988. Currently works with 2 acts. Reviews material for acts.

How to Contact Submit demo CD/DVD by mail. Unsolicited submissions are OK. Prefers CD or DVD, but will accept cassette with 3 best songs, lyric or lead sheet, bio and picture. Press kit should include CD, DVD, video/audio cassette with up-to-date bio, cover letter, lyric sheets, press clippings, and picture. Does not return material. Responds in 6 weeks if interested.

Music Mostly **country/traditional and contemporary**, **Christian/gospel** and **A/C/pop**. Works primarily with singer/songwriters and bands with original and versatile style. Current acts include Cheryl K. Warner (recording artist/entertainer) and Cheryl K. Warner Band (support/studio alt).

☑ ⌾ WEMUS ENTERTAINMENT

2006 Seaboard, Suite 400, Midland TX 79705. (432)689-3687. Fax: (432)687-0930. E-mail: wemus@ aol.com. Web site: www.wemus.com. **Contact:** Dennis Grubb, president. Management firm, booking agency and music publisher (Wemus Music, Inc.). Estab. 1983. Represents local and regional individual artists and groups; currently handles 4 acts. Receives 15-25% commission. Reviews material for acts.

How to Contact Submit demo by mail. Unsolicited submissions are OK. Prefers cassette, CD, DVD or VHS videocassette with 3-5 songs and lyric sheet. If seeking management, press kit should include glossy head and full body shots and extensive biography. "Make sure address, phone number and possible fax number is included in the packet, or a business card." Does not return material. Responds in 1 month if interested.

Music Mostly **country**. Current acts include The Image (variety), The Big Time (variety), The Pictures (variety) and Pryce Conner.

Tips "We preview and try to place good songs with national artists who are in need of good materials. We have a very tough qualification process and are very selective in forwarding materials to artists and their management."

☑ ⌾ WINTERLAND ENTERTAINMENT MANAGEMENT & PUBLISHING

(formerly T.J. Booker Ltd.), P.O. Box 969, Rossland BC V0G 1Y0 Canada. (250)362-7795. E-mail: winterland@netidea.com. **Contact:** Tom Jones, owner. Management firm, booking agency and music publisher. Estab. 1976. Represents individual artists, groups and songwriters from anywhere; currently handles 6 acts. Receives 15% commission. Reviews material for acts.

How to Contact Submit demo by mail. Unsolicited submissions are OK. Prefers CD, cassette or videocassette with 3 songs. If seeking management, include demo or CD, picture, cover letter and bio in press kit. Does not return material. Responds in 1 month.

Music Mostly **MOR**, **crossover**, **rock**, **pop** and **country**. Works primarily with vocalists, show bands, dance bands and bar bands. Current acts include Kirk Orr (folk/country), Mike Hamilton (rock/blues) and Larry Hayton (rock/blues).

⌾ RICHARD WOOD ARTIST MANAGEMENT

69 North Randall Ave., Staten Island NY 10301. (718)981-0641. Fax: (718)273-0797. **Contact:** Richard Wood. Management firm. Estab. 1974. Represents musical groups; currently handles 3 acts. Receives 20% commission. Reviews material for acts.

How to Contact Submit demo by mail. Unsolicited submissions are OK. Prefers cassette and lead sheet. If seeking management, press kit should include demo, photo, cover letter and résumé. Include SASE. Responds in 1 month.

Music Mostly **dance**, **R&B** and **top 40/pop**; also **MOR**. Works primarily with "high energy" show bands, bar bands and dance bands. Artists include Yami Bola (reggae), Truck (rap), and Haze (rap).

ⓝ ⊘ WORLD WIDE MANAGEMENT

P.O. Box 536, Bronxville NY 10708. Fax: (914)337-5309 **Contact:** David Reich, Marcy Drexler, directors. President: Steven Rosenfeld. Management firm and music publisher (Neighborhood Music/ASCAP). Estab. 1971. Represents artists, groups, songwriters and actors; currently handles 5 acts. Receives 15-20% commission. Reviews material for acts.

How to Contact *Write first and obtain permission to submit.* Prefers CD, cassette or videocassete of performance with 3-4 songs. If seeking management, press kit should include cover letter, bio, reviews, press clippings, CD or cassette with lyrics and photo. Does not return material. Responds in 1 month.

Music Mostly **contemporary pop**, **folk**, **folk/rock** and **New Age**; also **A/C**, **rock**, **jazz**, **bluegrass**, **blues**, **country** and **R&B**. Works primarily with self-contained bands and vocalists. Current acts include Gretchen Witt , Marshall Crenshaw, Oz Noy Trio featuring Anton Fig and Will Lee, The John Does, The Bradbury Press, Keith Reid, and Cliff Hillis and Forward Thinkers.

◢ WORLDSOUND, LLC

17837 1st Ave. South Suite 3, Seattle WA 98148. (206)444-0300. Fax: (206)244-0066. E-mail: music @worldsound.com. Web site: www.worldsound.com. **Contact:** Warren Wyatt, A&R manager. Management firm. Estab. 1976. Represents individual artists, groups and songwriters from any-where; currently handles 8 acts. Receives 20% commission. Reviews material for acts.

How to Contact "Online, send us an e-mail containing a link to your Web site where your songs can be heard and the lyrics are available—PLEASE DO NOT E-MAIL SONG FILES! By regular mail, unsolicited submissions are OK." Prefers CD with 2-10 songs and lyric sheet. "If seeking management, please send an e-mail with a link to your Web site—your site should contain song samples, band biography, photos, video (if available), press and demo reviews. By mail, please send the materials listed above and include SASE." Responds in 1 month.

Music Mostly **rock**, **pop** and **world**; also **heavy metal**, **hard rock** and **top 40**. Works primarily with pop/rock/world artists. Current acts include Makana (world music), Treble (pop), La Neo (contemporary/Hawaiian), and Keith Olsen (music producer).

Tips "Always submit new songs/material, even if you have sent material that was previously rejected; the music biz is always changing."

◢ ZANE MANAGEMENT, INC.

1650 Market St., One Liberty Place, 21st Floor, Philadelphia PA 19103. (215)575-3803. Fax: (215)575-3801. E-mail: lzr@braverlaw.com. Web site: www.zanemanagement.com. **Contact:** Lloyd Z. Remick, Esq., president. Entertainment/sports consultants and managers. Represents art-ists, songwriters, producers and athletes; currently handles 7 acts. Receives 10-15% commission.

How to Contact Submit demo by mail. Unsolicited submissions are OK. Prefers CD and lyric sheet. If seeking management, press kit should include cover letter, bio, photo, demo and video. Does not return material. Responds in 3 weeks.

Music Mostly **dance**, **easy listening**, **folk**, **jazz (fusion)**, **MOR**, **rock (hard and country)**, **soul** and **top 40/pop**. Current acts include Bunny Sigler (disco/funk), Peter Nero and Philly Pops (con-ductor), Cast in Bronze (rock group), Pieces of a Dream (jazz/crossover), Don't Look Down (rock/pop), Christian Josi (pop-swing), and Rosie Carlino (standards/pop).

◖ D. ZIRILLI MANAGEMENT

P.O. Box 255, Cupertino CA 95015-0255. (408)257-2533. Fax: (408)252-8938. E-mail: donzirilli@aol .com. Web site: www.zirilli.com. **Owner:** Don Zirilli. Management firm. Estab. 1965. Represents groups from anywhere; currently handles 1 act. Receives 20% commission. Reviews material for acts.

How to Contact Submit demo by mail. Unsolicited submissions are OK. Prefers CD, DAT, videocas-sette or DVD. If seeking management, press kit should include video. Does not return material. Responds in 2 weeks.

Music Mostly **rock**, **surf** and **MOR**. Current acts include Papa Doo Run Run (band).

Tips "Less is more."

ADDITIONAL MANAGERS & BOOKING AGENTS

The following companies are also managers/booking agents, but their listings are found in other sections of the book. Read the listings for submission information.

A

Audio-Visual Media Productions 145

C

Capstan Record Production 152

D

Deep South Entertainment 157
Diamond Entertainment, Joel 199

H

His Power Productions and Publishing 108

L

Lineage Publishing Co. 113
Lucifer Records, Inc. 167

M

Modal Music, Inc.™ 172

O

Orchid Publishing 119

P

Pollybyrd Publications Limited 121

S

Satkowski Recordings, Steve 209
Sphere Group One 210

T

Twin Towers Publishing Co. 131

Music Firms

Advertising, Audiovisual & Commercial

It's happened a million times—you hear a jingle on the radio or television and can't get it out of your head. That's the work of a successful jingle writer, writing songs to catch your attention and make you aware of the product being advertised. But the field of commercial music consists of more than just memorable jingles. It also includes background music that many companies use in videos for corporate and educational presentations, as well as films and TV shows.

SUBMITTING MATERIAL

More than any other market listed in this book, the commercial music market expects composers to have made an investment in the recording of their material before submitting. A sparse, piano/vocal demo won't work here; when dealing with commercial music firms, especially audiovisual firms and music libraries, high quality production is important. Your demo may be kept on file at one of these companies until a need for it arises, and it may be used or sold as you sent it. Therefore, your demo tape or reel must be as fully produced as possible.

The presentation package that goes along with your demo must be just as professional. A list of your credits should be a part of your submission, to give the company an idea of your experience in this field. If you have no experience, look to local television and radio stations to get your start. Don't expect to be paid for many of your first jobs in the commercial music field; it's more important to get the credits and exposure that can lead to higher-paying jobs.

Commercial music and jingle writing can be a lucrative field for the composer/songwriter with a gift for writing catchy melodies and the ability to write in many different music styles. It's a very competitive field, so it pays to have a professional presentation package that makes your work stand out.

Three different segments of the commercial music world are listed here: advertising agencies, audiovisual firms and commercial music houses/music libraries. Each looks for a different type of music, so read these descriptions carefully to see where the music you write fits in.

ADVERTISING AGENCIES

Ad agencies work on assignment as their clients' needs arise. Through consultation and input from the creative staff, ad agencies seek jingles and music to stimulate the consumer to identify with a product or service.

When contacting ad agencies, keep in mind they are searching for music that can capture and then hold an audience's attention. Most jingles are short, with a strong, memorable hook. When an ad agency listens to a demo, it is not necessarily looking for a finished product so much as for an indication of creativity and diversity. Many composers put together a reel of excerpts of work from previous projects, or short pieces of music that show they can write in a variety of styles.

AUDIOVISUAL FIRMS

Audiovisual firms create a variety of products, from film and video shows for sales meetings, corporate gatherings and educational markets, to motion pictures and TV shows. With the increase of home video use, how-to videos are a big market for audiovisual firms, as are spoken word educational videos. All of these products need music to accompany them. For your quick reference, companies working to place music in movies and TV shows (excluding commercials) have a ▨ preceding their listing (also see the Film & TV Index on page 390 for a complete list of these companies).

Like ad agencies, audiovisual firms look for versatile, well-rounded songwriters. When submitting demos to these firms, you need to demonstrate your versatility in writing specialized background music and themes. Listings for companies will tell what facet(s) of the audiovisual field they are involved in and what types of clients they serve. Your demo tape should also be as professional and fully produced as possible; audiovisual firms often seek demo tapes that can be put on file for future use when the need arises.

COMMERCIAL MUSIC HOUSES & MUSIC LIBRARIES

Commercial music houses are companies contracted (either by an ad agency or the advertiser) to compose custom jingles. Since they are neither an ad agency nor an audiovisual firm, their main concern is music. They use a lot of it, too—some composed by in-house songwriters and some contributed by outside, freelance writers.

Music libraries are different in that their music is not custom composed for a specific client. Their job is to provide a collection of instrumental music in many different styles that, for an annual fee or on a per-use basis, the customer can use however he chooses.

In the following listings, commercial music houses and music libraries, which are usually the most open to works by new composers, are identified as such by **bold** typeface.

The commercial music market is similar to most other businesses in one aspect: experience is important. Until you develop a list of credits, pay for your work may not be high. Don't pass up opportunities if a job is non- or low-paying. These assignments will add to your list of credits, make you contacts in the field, and improve your marketability.

Money and rights

Many of the companies listed in this section pay by the job, but there may be some situations where the company asks you to sign a contract that will specify royalty payments. If this happens, research the contract thoroughly, and know exactly what is expected of you and how much you'll be paid.

Depending on the particular job and the company, you may be asked to sell one-time rights or all rights. One-time rights involve using your material for one presentation only. All rights means the buyer can use your work any way he chooses, as many times as he likes. Be sure you know exactly what you're giving up, and how the company may use your music in the future.

In the commercial world, many of the big advertising agencies have their own publishing companies where writers assign their compositions. In these situations, writers sign contracts whereby they do receive performance and mechanical royalties when applicable.

ADDITIONAL LISTINGS

For additional names and addresses of ad agencies that may use jingles and/or commercial music, refer to the *Standard Directory of Advertising Agencies* (National Register Publishing).

For a list of audiovisual firms, check out the latest edition of *AV Marketplace* (R.R. Bowker). Both these books may be found at your local library. To contact companies in your area, see the Geographic Index at the back of this book.

Ⓝ THE AD AGENCY

P.O. Box 470572, San Francisco CA 94147. **Contact:** Michael Carden, creative director. Advertising agency and **jingle/commercial music production house**. Clients include business, industry and retail. Estab. 1971. Uses the services of music houses, independent songwriter/composers and lyricists for scoring of commercials, background music for video production, and jingles for commercials. Commissions 20 composers and 15 lyricists/year. Pays by the job or by the hour. Buys all or one-time rights.
How to Contact Submit demo tape of previous work. Prefers cassette with 5-8 songs and lyric sheet. Include SASE. Responds in 3 weeks.
Music Uses variety of musical styles for commercials, promotion, TV, video presentations.
Tips "Our clients and our needs change frequently."

ADVERTEL, INC.

P.O. Box 18053, Pittsburgh PA 15236-0053. (412)344-4700. Fax: (412)344-4712. E-mail: pberan@advertel.com. Web site: www.advertel.com. **Contact:** Paul Beran, president/CEO. **Telephonic/Internet production company**. Clients include small and multi-national companies. Estab. 1983. Uses the services of music houses and independent songwriters/composers for scoring of instrumentals (all varieties) and telephonic production. Commissions 3-4 composers/year. Pay varies. Buys all rights and phone exclusive rights.
How to Contact Submit demo of previous work. Prefers CD. "Most compositions are 2 minutes strung together in 6, 12, 18 minute length productions." Does not return material; prefers to keep on file. Responds "right away if submission fills an immediate need."
Music Uses all varieties, including unusual; mostly subdued music beds. Radio-type production used exclusively in telephone and Internet applications.
Tips "Go for volume. We have continuous need for all varieties of music in two minute lengths."

Ⓝ ◻ ANDERSON COMMUNICATIONS

Suite 202, 2245 Godby Rd., Atlanta GA 30349. (404)766-8000. **Contact:** Vanessa Vaughn, producer. **President:**Al Anderson. **Advertising agency and syndication operation**. Estab. 1971. Clients include major corporations, institutions and media. Uses the services of music houses, independent songwriters/composers and lyricists for background music for commercials and jingles for syndicated radio programs. Commissions 5-6 songwriters or composers and 6-7 lyricists/year. Pays by the job. Buys all rights.
How to Contact Write first to arrange personal interview or submit demo tape of previous work. Prefers cassette. Does not return material. Responds in 2 weeks or "when we have projects requiring your services."
Music Uses a variety of music for music beds for commercials and jingles for nationally syndicated radio programs and commercials targeted at the black consumer market.
Tips "Be sure the composition plays well in a 60-second format."

▣ CANTRAX RECORDERS

Dept. CM, 2119 Fidler Ave., Long Beach CA 90815. (562)498-4593. Fax: (562)498-4852. E-mail: cantrax@earthlink.net. **Contact:** Richard Cannata, owner. Recording studio. Clients include anyone needing recording services (i.e., industrial, radio, commercial). Estab. 1980. Uses the services of independent songwriters/composers and lyricists for scoring of independent features and films and background music for radio, industrials and promotions, commercials for radio and TV and jingles for radio. Commissions 10 composers/year. Pays fees set by the artist. "We take 15%."
How to Contact *"No phone calls, please."* Query with résumé of credits or submit demo CD of previous work. Prefers CD—no cassettes. Does not return material. Responds in 2 weeks if SASE is provided.

Music Uses jazz, New Age, rock, easy listening and classical for slide shows, jingles and soundtracks.
Tips "You must have a serious, professional attitude."

☑ CEDAR CREST STUDIO

#17 CR 830, Henderson AR 72544. Web site: www.cedarcreststudio.com. **Contact:** Bob Ketchum, owner. Audiovisual firm and **jingle/commercial music production house**. Clients include corporate, industrial, sales, music publishing, training, educational, legal, medical, music and Internet. Estab. 1973. Sometimes uses the services of independent songwriters/composers for background music for video productions, jingles for TV spots and commercials for radio and TV. Pays by the job or by royalties. Buys all rights or one-time rights.
How to Contact Query with résumé of credits or submit demo tape of previous work. Prefers CD, cassette, or DVD. Does not return material. "We keep it on file for future reference." Responds in 2 months.
Music Uses up-tempo pop (not too "rocky"), unobtrusive—no solos for commercials and background music for video presentations.
Tips "Hang, hang, hang. Be open to suggestions. Improvise, adapt, overcome."

COMMUNICATIONS FOR LEARNING

395 Massachusetts Ave., Arlington MA 02474. (781)641-2350. E-mail: comlearn@thecia.net. Web site: www.communicationsforlearning.com. **Contact:** Jonathan L. Barkan, executive producer/director. Video, multimedia, exhibit and graphic design firm. Clients include multi-nationals, industry, government, institutions, local, national and international nonprofits. Uses services of music houses and independent songwriters/composers as theme and background music for videos and multimedia. Commissions 1-2 composers/year. Pays $2,000-5,000/job and one-time fees. Rights purchased varies.
How to Contact Submit demo of previous work. Prefers CD. Does not return material; prefers to keep on file. "For each job we consider our entire collection." Responds in 3 months.
Music Uses all styles of music for all sorts of assignments.
Tips "Please don't call. Just send good material and when we're interested, we'll be in touch. Make certain your name and phone number are on all submitted work itself, not only on the cover letter."

ℕ ☑ D.S.M. PRODUCERS INC.

P.O. Box 1160, Marco Island FL 39146-1166. (212)245-0006. President, CEO: Suzan Bader. **Contact:** Elber Maldonado, Director A&R. Scoring service, **jingle/commercial music production house** and original stock library called "All American Composers Library (administered world wide except USA by Warner/Chappell Music, Inc.)" Clients include networks, corporate, advertising firms, film and video, book publishers (music only). Estab. 1979. Uses the services of independent songwriters/composers for scoring of TV and feature films, background music for feature films and TV, jingles for major products and commercials for radio and TV. Pays 50% royalty. Licenses all rights.
How to Contact *Write first and enclose SASE for return permission.* Prefers CD with 2 songs and lyric or lead sheet. "Use a large enough return envelope to put in a standard business reply letter." Responds in 3 months.
Music Uses **all styles** including **alternative**, **dance**, **New Age**, **country** and **rock** for adventure films and sports programs.
Tips "Carefully label your submissions. Include a short bio/résumé of your works. Lyric sheets are very helpful to A&R. Only send your best tapes and tunes. Invest in your profession and get a local professional to help you produce your works. A master quality tape is the standard today. This is your competition so if you really want to be a songwriter, act like the ones who are successful—get a good tape of your tune. This makes it easier to sell overall. Never use 'samples' or any other copyrighted material in your works without a license. D.S.M is a global publisher."

☑ DISK PRODUCTIONS

1100 Perkins Rd., Baton Rouge LA 70802. Fax: (225)343-0210. E-mail: disk_productions@yahoo.com. **Contact:** Joey Decker, director. **Jingle/production house.** Clients include advertising agencies and film companies. Estab. 1982. Uses the services of music houses, independent songwriters/composers and lyricists for scoring and background music for TV spots, films and jingles for radio and TV. Commissions 7 songwriters/composers and 7 lyricists/year. Pays by the job. Buys all rights.

How to Contact Submit demo of previous work. Prefers DVD, CD, cassette or DAT. Does not return material. Responds in 2 weeks.

Music Needs all types of music for jingles, music beds or background music for TV and radio, etc.

Tips "Advertising techniques change with time. Don't be locked in a certain style of writing. Give me music that I can't get from pay needle-drop."

ENTERTAINMENT PRODUCTIONS, INC.

2118 Wilshire Blvd. 744, Santa Monica CA 90403. (310)456-3143. Fax: (310)456-8950. **Contact:** Anne Bell, Music Director. Producer: Edward Coe. **Motion picture and television production company**. Clients include motion picture and TV distributors. Estab. 1972. Uses the services of music houses and songwriters for scores, production numbers, background and theme music for films and TV and jingles for promotion of films. Commissions/year vary. Pays by the job or by royalty. Buys motion picture, video and allied rights.

How to Contact Query with résumé of credits. Demo should show flexibility of composition skills. "Demo records/tapes sent at own risk—returned if SASE included." Responds by letter within 1 month, "but only if SASE is included."

Tips "Have résumé on file. Develop self-contained capability."

FINE ART PRODUCTIONS/RICHIE SURACI PICTURES, MULTIMEDIA, INTERACTIVE

67 Maple St., Newburgh NY 12550-4034. (914)527-9740. Fax: (845)561-5866. E-mail: rs7fap@bestw eb.net. Web site: www.idsi.net/~rs7fap/tentsales.htm. **Contact:** Richard Suraci, owner. Advertising agency, audiovisual firm, scoring service, **jingle/commercial music production house**, motion picture production company (Richie Suraci Pictures) and **music sound effect library**. Clients include corporate, industrial, motion picture and broadcast firms. Estab. 1987. Uses services of independent songwriters/composers for scoring, background music and jingles for various projects and commercials for radio and TV. Commissions 1-2 songwriters or composers and 1-2 lyricists/year. Pays by the job, royalty or by the hours. Buys all rights.

How to Contact Submit demo tape of previous work or tape demonstrating composition skills, query with résumé of credits or write or call first to arrange personal interview. Prefers CD, DVD, cassette (or ½″, ¾″, or 1″ videocassette) with as many songs as possible and lyric or lead sheets. Include SASE, but prefers to keep material on file. Responds in 1 year.

Music Uses all types of music for all types of assignments.

KEN-DEL PRODUCTIONS INC.

First State Production Center, 1500 First State Blvd., Wilmington DE 19804-3596. (302)999-1111. Estab. 1950. **Contact:** Edwin Kennedy, A&R manager. Clients include publishers, industrial firms and advertising agencies, how-to's and radio/TV. Uses services of songwriters for radio/TV commercials, jingles and multimedia. Pays by the job. Buys all rights.

How to Contact "Submit all inquiries and demos in any format to general manager." Does not return material. Will keep on file for 3 years. Generally responds in 1 month or less.

LAPRIORE VIDEOGRAPHY

67 Millbrook St. Ste. 114, Worcester MA 01606. (508)755-9010. E-mail: peter@lapriorevideo.com. Web site: www.lapriorevideo.com. **Contact:** Peter Lapriore, owner. Video production company. Clients include corporations, retail stores, educational and sports. Estab. 1985. Uses the services of music houses, independent songwriters/composers for background music for marketing, training, educational videos and TV commercials and for scoring video. "We also own several music libraries." Commissions 2 composers/year. Pays $150-1,000/job. Buys all or one-time rights.

How to Contact Submit demo tape of previous work. Prefers CD, or DVD with 5 songs and lyric sheet. Does not return material; prefers to keep on file. Responds in 3 weeks.

Music Uses slow, medium, up-tempo, jazz and classical for marketing, educational films and commercials.

Tips "Be very creative and willing to work on all size budgets."

PATRICK MOORE COMPOSITIONS

84 Harris Ave., Oshawa ON L1J 5K7 Canada. (905)576-9039. Web site: www.patrickmoore.ca. **Contact:** Patrick Moore, owner/president. **Scoring service and jingle/commercial music production house**. Clients include producers of documentaries/films (educational). Estab. 1988. Uses the services of orchestrators for scoring of orchestral scores.

How to Contact *Write first to arrange personal interview.* Prefers cassette. Does not return material. Prefers to keep submitted material on file. Responds in 1 month.

Music "I specialize in combining ethnic music with current music for educational films/documentaries."

Tips "My needs are very specific and must meet the requirements of the producer and music editor on each project. It is not unusual for me to work with film producers and music writers from all over the world. I do a great deal of work by mailing video tapes, cassette tapes and CDs of rough drafts to producers and other professionals involved in a film or video production."

QUALLY & COMPANY INC.

2 E. Oak, Suite 2903, Chicago IL 60611. (312)280-1898. **Contact:** Robert Qually, creative director. Advertising agency. Uses the services of music houses, independent songwriters/composers and lyricists for scoring, background music and jingles for radio and TV commercials. Commissions 2-4 composers and 2-4 lyricists/year. Pays by the job. Buys various rights depending on deal.

How to Contact Submit demo CD of previous work or query with résumé of credits. Include SASE, but prefers to keep material on file. Responds in 2 weeks.

Music Uses all kinds of music for commercials.

TRF PRODUCTION MUSIC LIBRARIES

Dept. SM, 747 Chestnut Ridge Rd., Chestnut Ridge NY 10977. (845)356-0800. Fax: (845)356-0895. E-mail: info@trfmusic.com. Web site: www.trfmusic.com. **Contact:** Anne Marie Russo. Music/ sound effect libraries. Estab. 1931. Uses the services of independent composers for all categories of production music for television, film and other media. Pays 50% royalty.

• Also see the listing for Alpha Music Inc. in the Music Publishers section of this book.

How to Contact Submit demo CD of new compositions. Prefers CD with 3-7 pieces. Can send audio cassette, DAT or CD with up to 12 tracks. Submissions are not returnable. Responds in 2 to 3 months after receipt.

Music Primarily interested in **acoustic instrumental** music suitable for use as production music, which is theme and background music for TV, film and AV/multimedia.

Play Producers & Publishers

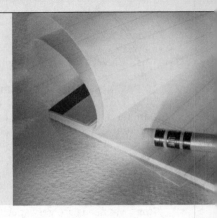

Finding a theater company willing to invest in a new production can be frustrating for an unknown playwright. But whether you write the plays, compose the music or pen the lyrics, it is important to remember not only where to start but how to start. Theater in the U.S. is a hierarchy, with Broadway, Off Broadway and Off Off Broadway being pretty much off limits to all but the Stephen Sondheims of the world.

Aspiring theater writers would do best to train their sights on nonprofit regional and community theaters to get started. The encouraging news is there is a great number of local theater companies throughout the U.S. with experimental artistic directors who are looking for new works to produce, and many are included in this section. This section covers two segments of the industry: theater companies and dinner theaters are listed under Play Producers (beginning on this page), and publishers of musical theater works are listed under the Play Publishers heading (beginning on page 260). All these markets are actively seeking new works of all types for their stages or publications.

BREAKING IN

Starting locally will allow you to research each company carefully and learn about their past performances, the type of musicals they present, and the kinds of material they're looking for. When you find theaters you think may be interested in your work, attend as many performances as possible, so you know exactly what type of material each theater presents. Or volunteer to work at a theater, whether it be moving sets or selling tickets. This will give you valuable insight into the day-to-day workings of a theater and the creation of a new show. On a national level, you will find prestigious organizations offering workshops and apprenticeships covering every subject from arts administration to directing to costuming. But it could be more helpful to look into professional internships at theaters and attend theater workshops in your area. The more knowledgeable you are about the workings of a particular company or theater, the easier it will be to tailor your work to fit its style and the more responsive they will be to you and your work. (See the Workshops & Conferences section on page 321 for more information.) As a composer for the stage, you need to know as much as possible about a theater and how it works, its history and the different roles played by the people involved in it. Flexibility is the key to successful productions, and knowing how a theater works will only help you in cooperating and collaborating with the director, producer, technical people and actors.

If you're a playwright looking to have his play published in book form or in theater publications, see the listings under the Play Publishers section (page 260). To find play producers and publishers in your area, consult the Geographic Index at the back of this book.

PLAY PRODUCERS

ARKANSAS REPERTORY THEATRE
601 Main, P.O. Box 110, Little Rock AR 72203. (501)378-0405. Fax: (501)378-0012. Web site: www.therep.org. **Contact:** Brad Mooy. Play producer. Estab. 1976. Produces 6-10 plays and musicals/year. "We perform in a 354-seat house and also have a 99-seat 2nd stage." Pays 5-10% royalty or $75-150 per performance.
How to Contact Query with synopsis, character breakdown and set description. Include SASE. Responds in 6 months.
Musical Theater "Small casts are preferred, comedy or drama and prefer shows to run 1:45 to 2 hours maximum. Simple is better; small is better, but we do produce complex shows. We aren't interested in children's pieces, puppet shows or mime. We always like to receive a tape of the music with the book."
Productions *Disney's Beauty & the Beast*, by Woolverton/Ashman/Rice/Menken (musical retelling of the myth); *Crowns*, by Taylor/Cunningham/Marberry (on the significance of African-American women's hats); and *A Chorus Line*, by Kirkwood/Hamlisch/Kleban (auditions).
Tips "Include a *good* cassette of your music, *sung well*, with the script."

☑ WILLIAM CAREY COLLEGE DINNER THEATRE
William Carey College, Hattiesburg MS 39401-5499. (601)318-6218. E-mail: thecom@wmcarey.edu. **Contact:** O.L. Quave, managing director. Play producer. Produces 2 musicals/year. "Our dinner theater operates only in summer and plays to family audiences." Payment negotiable.
How to Contact Query with synopsis, character breakdown and set description. Does not return material. Responds in 1 month.
Musical Theater "Plays should be simply-staged, have small casts (8-10 maximum), and be suitable for family viewing; two hours maximum length. Score should require piano only, or piano, synthesizer."
Productions *Smoke on the Mountain*; *Schoolhouse Rock Live*; and *Pump Boys and Dinettes*.

Ⓝ THE DIRECTORS COMPANY
311 W. 43rd St., Suite 307, New York NY 10036. (212)246-5877. Fax: (212)246-5882. Web site: http://mysite.verizon.net/directorscompany. **Contact:** Katherine Heberling, company manager. Artistic/Producing Director: Michael Parva. Play producer. Estab. 1980. Produces 1-2 new musicals/year. Performance space is a 99-seat theatre located in the heart of Manhattan's Theatre District. "It is beautifully equipped with dressing rooms, box office and reception area in the lobby." Pays negotiable rate.
How to Contact Query first. Include SASE. Responds in 1 year.
Musical Theater "The Harold Prince Musical Theatre Program develops new musicals by incorporating the director in the early stages of collaboration. The program seeks cutting edge material that works to break boundaries in music theatre. We produce workshops or developmental productions. The emphasis is on the material, not on production values, therefore, we do not limit cast sizes. However, there are limits on props and production values." No children's musicals or reviews.
Productions *Jubilee*, by Kelly Dupuis/Marc Smollin (an absurdly magical exploration of fate, family, and fish); *Tales of Tinseltown* (reading), by Michael Colby/Paul Katz (a sardonic parody of 1930s Hollywood); and *Nightmare Alley* (reading), by Jonathan Brielle (about a drifter in 1932 looking for a way to begin a life in hard times).

Ⓝ LOS ANGELES DESIGNERS' THEATRE
P.O. Box 1883, Studio City CA 91614-0883. (323)650-9600. Fax: (323)654-3210. E-mail: ladesigners@juno.com. **Contact:** Richard Niederberg, artistic director. Play producer. Estab. 1970. Produces 20-25 plays and 8-10 new musicals/year. Audience includes Hollywood production executives in film, TV, records and multimedia. Plays are produced at several locations, primarily Studio City, California. Pay is negotiable.

How to Contact Query first. Does not return material. Responds only if interested. *Send proposals only*.

Musical Theater ''We seek out controversial material. Street language OK, nudity is fine, religious themes, social themes, political themes are encouraged. Our audience is very 'jaded' as it consists of TV, motion picture and music publishing executives who have 'seen it all'.'' Does not wish to see bland, 'safe' material. We like first productions. In the cover letter state in great detail the proposed involvement of the songwriter, other than as a writer (i.e., director, actor, singer, publicist, designer, etc.). Also, state if there are any liens on the material or if anything has been promised.''

Productions *St. Tim*, by Fred Grab (historical '60s musical); *Slipper and the Rose* (gang musical); and *1593—The Devils Due* (historical musical).

Tips ''Make it very 'commercial' and inexpensive to produce. Allow for non-traditional casting. Be prepared with ideas as to how to transform your work to film or videotaped entertainment.''

THE OPEN EYE THEATER

P.O. Box 959, 1000 Main St., Margaretville NY 12455. E-mail: openeye@catskill.net. Web site: www.theopeneye.org. **Contact:** Amie Brockway, producing artistic director. Play producer. Estab. 1972. Produces approximately 3 full length or 3 new plays for multi-generational audiences. Pays on a fee basis.

How to Contact Query first. ''A manuscript will be accepted and read only if it is a play for all ages and is: 1) Submitted by a recognized literary agent; 2) Requested or recommended by a staff or company member; or 3) Recommended by a professional colleague with whose work we are familiar. Playwrights may submit a one-page letter of inquiry including a very brief plot synopsis. Please enclose a self-addressed (but not stamped) envelope. We will reply only if we want you to submit the script (within several months).''

Musical Theater ''The Open Eye Theater is a not-for-profit professional company working in a community context. Through the development, production and performance of plays for all ages, artists and audiences are challenged and given the opportunity to grow in the arts. In residence, on tour, and in the classroom, The Open Eye Theater strives to stimulate, educate, entertain, inspire and serve as a creative resource.''

Productions *Freddy, the King of Detectives*, by Sandra Fenichel Asher, music by Robert Cucinotta; *Twelfth Night or What You Will*, by William Shakespeare, music by Michael Anthony Worden; *The Wide Awake Princess*, adapted by David Paterson from the novel by Katherine Paterson, with music and lyrics by Steve Liebman; and *Pixies, Kings and Magical Things*, by Hans Christian Anderson, adapted by Ric Aver (four children's tales).

ⓝ PLAYHOUSE ON THE SQUARE

51 S. Cooper, Memphis TN 38104. (901)725-0776. Fax: (901)272-7530. **Contact:** Jackie Nichols, executive producer. Play producer. Produces 12 plays and 4 musicals/year. Plays are produced in a 260-seat proscenium resident theater. Pays $500 for outright purchase.

How to Contact Submit complete manuscript, score and tape of songs. Unsolicited submissions OK. Include SASE. Responds in 6 months.

Musical Theater Seeking ''any subject matter—adult and children's material. Small cast preferred. Stage is 26' deep by 43' wide with no fly system.''

Productions *Children of Eden*; and *Tommy*, by The Who.

PRIMARY STAGES

131 W. 45th St., 2nd Floor, New York NY 10036. (212)840-9705. Fax: (212)840-9725. E-mail: info@ primarystages.com. Web site: www.primarystages.com. **Contact:** Tyler Marchant, associate artistic director. Play producer. Estab. 1984. Produces 4-5 plays/year. ''New York theater-going audience representing a broad cross-section, in terms of age, ethnicity, and economic backgrounds. 199-seat, Off-Broadway theater.''

How to Contact Query first with synopsis, character breakdown, set description and tape. ''No unsolicited scripts accepted. Submissions by agents only.'' Include SASE. Responds in up to 8 months.

Musical Theater "We are looking for work of heightened theatricality, that challenges realism—musical plays that go beyond film and televisions standard fare. We are looking for small cast shows under 6 characters total, with limited sets. We are interested in original works, that have not been produced in New York."
Productions *I Sent a Letter to My Love*, by Melissa Manchester/Jeffrey Sweet; *Nightmare Alley*, by Jonathan Brielle, and *Call the Children Home*, by Mildred Kryden and Thomas Babe.

⃠ PRINCE MUSIC THEATER

100 S. Broad St., Suite 650, Philadelphia PA 19110. Phone/fax: (215)972-1000. E-mail: info@prince musictheater.org. Web site: www.princemusictheater.org. **Contact:** Marjorie Samoff, president and producing director. Play producer. Estab. 1984. Produces 4-5 musicals/year. "Our average audience member is in their mid-40s. We perform to ethnically diverse houses."
How to Contact Submit two-page synopsis with tape or CD of 4 songs. Include SASE. "May include complete script, but be aware that response is at least 10 months."
Music "We seek musicals ranging from the traditional to the experimental. Topics can range. Musical styles can vary from folk pop through opera. Orchestra generally limited to a maximum of 9 pieces; cast size maximum of 10-12."
Musical Theater 2006-2007 Season: *The Musical of Musicals*, by Eric Rockwell/Jean Bogart; *Dreamgirls*, by Tom Eyen/Harry Kreiger; *Cole Porter's The Pirate*, by Zack Manna/David Levy.
Tips "We only produce pieces that are music/lyric driven, not merely plays with music."

☑ SHAKESPEARE SANTA CRUZ

Theater Arts Center, U.C.S.C., 1156 High Street, Santa Cruz CA 95064. (831)459-3928. E-mail: iago@cats.ucsc.edu. Web site: www.shakespearesantacruz.org. **Contact:** Paul Whitworth, artistic director. Play producer. Estab. 1982. Produces 4 plays/year. Performance spaces are an outdoor redwood grove; and an indoor 540-seat thrust. Pay is negotiable.
How to Contact Query first. Include SASE. Responds in 2 months.
Musical Theater "Shakespeare Santa Cruz produces musicals in its Winter Holiday Season (Oct-Dec). We are also interested in composers' original music for pre-existing plays—including songs, for example, for Shakespeare's plays."
Productions *Cinderella*, by Kate Hawley (book and lyrics) and Gregg Coffin (composer); *Gretel and Hansel*, by Kate Hawley (book and lyrics) and composer Craig Bohmler; and *The Princess and the Pea*, by Kate Hawley (book and lyrics) and composer Adam Wernick.
Tips "Always contact us before sending material."

THE TEN-MINUTE MUSICALS PROJECT

P.O. Box 461194, West Hollywood CA 90046. E-mail: info@tenminutemusicals.org. Web site: www .tenminutemusicals.org. **Contact:** Michael Koppy, producer. Play producer. Estab. 1987. All pieces are new musicals. Pays $250 advance.
How to Contact Submit complete manuscript, score and tape of songs. Include SASE. Responds in 3 months.
Musical Theater Seeks complete short stage musicals of 8-15 minutes in length. Maximum cast: 9. "No parodies—original music only."
Productions *Away to Pago Pago*, by Jack Feldman/Barry Manilow/John PiRoman/Bruce Sussman; *The Bottle Imp*, by Kenneth Vega (from the story of the same title by Robert Louis Stevenson); and *The Furnished Room*, by Saragail Katzman (from the story of the same title by O. Henry), and many others.
Tips "Start with a *solid* story—either an adaptation or an original idea—but with a solid beginning, middle and end (probably with a plot twist at the climax). We caution that it will surely take much time and effort to create a quality work. (Occasionally a clearly talented and capable writer and composer seem to have almost 'dashed' something off, under the misperception that inspiration can carry the day in this format. Works selected in previous rounds all clearly evince that considerable deliberation and craft were invested.) We're seeking short contemporary musical theater material, in the style of what might be found on Broadway, Off-Broadway or the West End. Think of shows

like *Candide* or *Little Shop of Horrors*, pop operas like *Sweeney Todd* or *Chess*, or chamber musicals like *Once on this Island* or *Falsettos*. (Even small accessible operas like *The Telephone* or *Trouble in Tahiti* are possible models.) All have solid plots, and all rely on sung material to advance them. Of primary importance is to start with a strong story, even if it means postponing work on music and lyrics until the dramatic foundation is complete.''

N THUNDER BAY THEATRE

400 N. Second Ave., Alpena MI 49707. (989)354-2267. E-mail: tbt@deepnet.com. Web site: www.tb t.deepnet.com. Artistic Director: Tim Bennett. Play producer. Estab. 1967. Produces 12 plays and 6 musicals (1 new musical)/year. Performance space is thrust/proscenium stage. Pays variable royalty or per performance.
How to Contact Submit complete manuscript, score and tape of songs. Include SASE. Responds in 3 months.
Musical Theater Small cast. Not equipped for large sets. Considers original background music for use in a play being developed or for use in a pre-existing play.
Productions 2006 Musicals: *Nunsense*; *Stand By Your Man: The Tammy Wynette Story*; *Grease*; *You're a Good Man, Charlie Brown*.

WEST END ARTISTS

18034 Ventura Blvd. #291, Encino CA 91316. (818)623-0040. Fax: (818)623-0202. E-mail: egaynes@ aol.com. **Contact:** Pamela Hall, associate artistic director. Artistic Director: Edmund Gaynes. Play producer. Estab. 1983. Produces 5 plays and 3 new musicals/year. Audience ''covers a broad spectrum, from general public to heavy theater/film/TV industry crowds. Pays 6% royalty.
How to Contact Submit complete manuscript, score and tape of songs. Include SASE. Responds in 3 months.
Musical Theater ''Prefer small-cast musicals and revues. Full length preferred. Interested in children's shows also.'' Cast size: ''Maximum 12; exceptional material with larger casts will be considered.''
Productions *The Taffetas*, by Rick Lewis ('50s nostalgia, received 3 Ovation Award nominations); *Songs the Girls Sang*, by Alan Palmer (songs written for women now sung by men, received 1 Ovation Award nomination); *Crazy Words, Crazy Tunes* (played 2 years to Los Angeles and nationwide).
Tips ''If you feel every word or note you have written is sacred and chiseled in stone and are unwilling to work collaboratively with a professional director, don't bother to submit.''

PLAY PUBLISHERS

ARAN PRESS

1036 S. Fifth St., Louisville KY 40203. (502)568-6622. Fax: (502)561-1124. E-mail: aranpres@aye.n et. Web site: http://members.aye.net/ ~ aranpres. **Contact:** Tom Eagan, editor/publisher. Play publisher. Estab. 1983. Publishes 5-10 plays and 1-2 musicals/year. Professional, college/university, community, summer stock and dinner theater audience. Pays 50% production royalty or 10% book royalty.
How to Contact Submit manuscript, score and tape of songs. Include SASE. Responds in 2 weeks.
Musical Theater ''The musical should include a small cast, simple set for professional, community, college, university, summer stock and dinner theater production.''
Publications *Whiskey & Wheaties*, by Bruce Feld; *Who Says Life is Fair*, by Mike Willis; and *Burning Bridges*, by Stephen Avery.

BAKER'S PLAYS

P.O. Box 699222, Quincy MA 02269-9222. (617)745-0805. Fax: (617)745-9891. E-mail: info@bakers plays.com. Web site: www.bakersplays.com. **Contact:** Associate Editor. Play publisher. Estab. 1845. Publishes 15-22 plays and 0-3 new musicals/year. Plays are used by children's theaters, junior and senior high schools, colleges and community theaters. Pays negotiated book and production royalty.

• See the listing for Baker's Plays High School Playwriting Contest in the Contests & Awards section.

How to Contact Submit complete manuscript, score and cassette tape of songs. Include SASE. Responds in 4 months.

Musical Theater "Seeking musicals for teen production and children's theater production. We prefer large cast, contemporary musicals which are easy to stage and produce. Plot your shows strongly, keep your scenery and staging simple, your musical numbers and choreography easily explained and blocked out. Music must be camera-ready." Would consider original music for use in a play being developed or in a pre-existing play.

Productions *Oedipus/A New Magical Comedy*, by Bob Johnson.

Tips "As we publish musicals that can be produced by high school theater departments with high school talent, the writer should know if their play can be done on the high school stage. I recommend that the writer go to performances of original high school musicals whenever possible."

CONTEMPORARY DRAMA SERVICE

885 Elkton Dr., Colorado Springs CO 80907. (719)594-4422. E-mail: merpcds@aol.com. Web site: www.contemporarydrama.com. **Contact:** Arthur Zapel, associate editor. Play publisher. Estab. 1979. Publishes 40-50 plays and 4-6 new musicals/year. "We publish for young children and teens in mainstream Christian churches and for teens and college level in the secular market. Our musicals are performed in churches, schools and colleges." Pays 10-50% book and performance royalty.

How to Contact *Query first* then submit complete manuscript, score and tape of songs. Include SASE. Responds in 1 month.

Musical Theater "For churches we publish musical programs for children and teens to perform at Easter, Christmas or some special occasion. Our school musicals are for teens to perform as class plays or special entertainments. Cast size may vary from 15-25 depending on use. We prefer more parts for girls than boys. Music must be written in the vocal range of teens. Staging should be relatively simple but may vary as needed. We are not interested in elementary school material. Elementary level is OK for church music but not public school elementary. Music must have full piano accompaniment and be professionally scored for camera-ready publication."

Publications *Lucky, Lucky Hudson and the 12th Street Gang*, by Tim Kelly, book, and Bill Francoeur, music and lyrics (spoof of old time gangster movies); *Is There A Doctor in the House?*, by Tim Kelly, book, and Bill Francoeur, music and lyrics (adapted from Moliere comedy); and *Jitterbug Juliet*, by Mark Dissette, book, and Bill Francoeur, music and lyrics (spoof of *Romeo and Juliet*).

Tips "Familiarize yourself with our market. Send $1 postage for catalog. Try to determine what would fit in, yet still be unique."

THE DRAMATIC PUBLISHING COMPANY

311 Washington St., Woodstock IL 60098. (815)338-7170. E-mail: plays@dramaticpublishing.com. Web site: dramaticpublishing.com. **Contact:** Music Editor. Play publisher. Publishes 35 plays and 3-5 musicals/year. Estab. 1885. Plays used by professional and community theaters, schools and colleges. Pays negotiable royalty.

How to Contact Submit complete manuscript, score and tape of songs. Include SASE. Responds in 3 months.

Musical Theater Seeking "children's musicals not over 1¼ hours, and adult musicals with 2 act format. No adaptations for which the rights to use the original work have not been cleared. If directed toward high school market, large casts with many female roles are preferred. For professional, stock and community theater small casts are better. Cost of producing a play is always a factor to consider in regard to costumes, scenery and special effects." Would also consider original music for use in a pre-existing play, "if we or the composer hold the rights to the non-musical work."

Publications *The Little Prince*, by Rick Cummins/John Scoullar; *Hans Brinker*, by Gayle Hudson/Bobbe Bramson; and *Bubbe Meises, Bubbe Stories*, by Ellen Gould/Holly Gewandter (all are full-length family musicals).

Tips "A complete score, ready to go is highly recommended. Tuneful songs which stand on their own are a must. Good subject matter which has wide appeal is always best but not required."

ELDRIDGE PUBLISHING CO., INC.

P.O. Box 14367, Tallahassee FL 32317. (800)HI-STAGE. E-mail: info@histage.com. Web site: www. histage.com. **Contact:** Susan Shore, musical editor. Play publisher. Estab. 1906. Publishes 50 plays and 1-2 musicals/year. Seeking "large cast musicals which appeal to students. We like variety and originality in the music, easy staging and costuming. Also looking for children's theater musicals which have smaller casts and are easy to tour. We serve the school market (6th grade through 12th); and church market (Christmas musicals)." Pays 50% royalty and 10% copy sales in school market.

How to Contact Submit manuscript, score or lead sheets and CD of songs. Include SASE. Responds in 1 month.

Publications *The Bard is Back*, by Stephen Murray ("a high school's production of Romeo & Juliet is a disaster!"); and *Boogie-Woogie Bugle Girls*, book by Craig Sodaro, music and lyrics by Stephen Murray (WWII themed musical).

Tips "We're always looking for talented composers but not through individual songs. We're only interested in complete school or church musicals. Lead sheets, CDs tape and script are best way to submit. Let us see your work!"

THE FREELANCE PRESS

P.O. Box 548, Dover MA 02030. (508)785-8250. E-mail: info@freelancepress.org. Web site: www.fr eelancepress.org. Managing Editor: Narcissa Campion. Play publisher. Estab. 1979. Publishes up to 3 new musicals/year. "Pieces are primarily to be acted by elementary/middle school to high school students (9th and 10th grades); large casts (approximately 30); plays are produced by schools and children's theaters." Pays 10% of purchase price of script or score, 50% of collected royalty.

How to Contact Query first. Include SASE. Responds in 6 months.

Musical Theater "We publish previously produced musicals and plays to be acted by children in the primary grades through high school. Plays are for large casts (approximately 30 actors and speaking parts) and run between 45 minutes to 1 hour and 15 minutes. Subject matter should be contemporary issues (sibling rivalry, friendship, etc.) or adaptations of classic literature for children (*Syrano de Bergerac*, *Rip Van Winkle*, *Pied Piper*, *Treasure Island*, etc.). We do not accept any plays written for adults to perform for children."

Publications *Tortoise vs. Hare*, by Stephen Murray (modern version of classic); *Tumbleweed*, by Sebastian Stuart (sleepy time western town turned upside down); and *Mything Links*, by Sam Abel (interweaving of Greek myths with a great pop score).

Tips "We enjoy receiving material that does not condescend to children. They are capable of understanding many current issues, playing complex characters, handling unconventional material, and singing difficult music."

SAMUEL FRENCH, INC.

45 W. 25th St., New York NY 10010. (212)206-8990. Fax: (212)206-1429. Web site: www.samuelfre nch.com. Hollywood office: 7623 Sunset Blvd., Hollywood CA 90046. (323)876-0570. Fax: (323)876-6822. President: Charles R. Van Nostrand. **Contact:** Lawrence Harbinson, editor. Play publisher. Estab. 1830. Publishes 40-50 plays and 2-4 new musicals/year. Amateur and professional theaters.

How to Contact Query first. Include SASE. Responds in 10 weeks.

Musical Theater "We publish primarily successful musicals from the NYC, London and regional stage."

Publications *Spin*, by M. Kilburg Reedy (Greek myth); *Johnny Guitar*, by Joel Higgins—music, and Nicholas Van Hoogstraten—book (Western); and *The Musical of Musicals*, by Eric Rockwell—music, Joanne Bogart—lyrics/book, and Eric Rockwell—book (spoof of musical theater).

☑ HEUER PUBLISHING CO.

P.O. Box 248, Cedar Rapids IA 52406. Main Office: 211 First Ave., SE Suite 200, Cedar Rapids IA 52401. 1-800-950-7529. E-mail: editor@hitplays.com. Web site: www.hitplays.com. Publisher: C. Emmett McMullen. Play publisher. Estab. 1928. Publishes plays, musicals, operas/operettas and guides (choreography, costume, production/staging) for amateur and professional markets, including junior and senior high schools, college/university and community theatres. Focus includes comedy, drama, fantasy, mystery and holiday. Pays by percentage royalty or outright purchase. Pays by outright purchase or percentage royalty.

How to Contact Query with musical CD/tape or submit complete manuscript and score. Include SASE. Responds in 2 months.

Musical Theater "We prefer one, two or three act comedies or mystery-comedies with a large number of characters."

Publications *Happily Ever After*, by Allen Koepke (musical fairytale); *Brave Buckaroo*, by Renee J. Clark (musical melodrama); and *Pirate Island*, by Martin Follose (musical comedy).

Tips "We are willing to review single-song submissions as cornerstone piece for commissioned works. Special interest focus in multicultural, historic, classic literature, teen issues, and biographies."

☑ PIONEER DRAMA SERVICE

P.O. Box 4267, Englewood CO 80155. 1-800-333-7262. Fax: (303)779-4315. Web site: www.pioneer drama.com. **Contact:** Lori Conary, assistant editor. Play publisher. Estab. 1963. "Plays are performed by junior high and high school drama departments, church youth groups, college and university theaters, semi-professional and professional children's theaters, parks and recreation departments." Playwrights paid 50% royalty (10% sales).

How to Contact Query with character breakdown, synopsis and set description. Include SASE. Responds in 6 months.

Musical Theater "We seek full length children's musicals, high school musicals and one act children's musicals to be performed by children, secondary school students, and/or adults. We want musicals easy to perform, simple sets, many female roles and very few solos. Must be appropriate for educational market. We are not interested in profanity, themes with exclusively adult interest, sex, drinking, smoking, etc. Several of our full-length plays are being converted to musicals. We edit them, then contract with someone to write the music and lyrics."

Publications *The Stories of Scheherazade*, book by Susan Pargmon, music and lyrics by Bill Francoeur (musical *Arabian Nights*); *Hubba Hubba: The 1940s Hollywood Movie Musical*, by Gene Casey and Jan Casey (tribute to the 1940s Hollywood movie musical); and *Cinderella's Glass Slipper*, book by Vera Morris, music and lyrics by Bill Francoeur (musical fairy tale).

Tips "Research and learn about our company. Our Web site and catalog provide an incredible amount of information."

PLAYERS PRESS, INC.

P.O. Box 1132, Studio City CA 91614. (818)789-4980. Associate Editor: Karen Flathers. Vice President: Robert W. Gordon. Play publisher, music book publisher, educational publisher. Estab. 1965. Publishes 20-70 plays and 1-3 new musicals/year. Plays are used primarily by general audience and children. Pays variable royalty and variable amount/performance.

How to Contact Query first. Include SASE. Responds in 3-6 months (3 weeks on queries).

Musical Theater "We will consider all submitted works. Presently musicals for adults and high schools are in demand. When cast size can be flexible (describe how it can be done in your work) it sells better."

Publications *Silly Soup*, by Carol Korty (children's plays with music and songs); *Everybody Sing and Dance*, by Esther Nelson (book for teaching song and dance to children); and *Lady Godiva*, by Judith Prior (cabaret/dinner theater musical).

Tips "For plays and musicals, have your work produced at least twice. Be present for rehearsals and work with competent people. Then submit material asked for in good clear copy with good audio tapes."

Classical Performing Arts

F inding an audience is critical to the composer of orchestral music. Fortunately, baby boomers are swelling the ranks of classical music audiences and bringing with them a taste for fresh, innovative music. So the climate is fair for composers seeking their first performance.

Finding a performance venue is particularly important because once a composer has his work performed for an audience and establishes himself as a talented newcomer, it can lead to more performances and commissions for new works.

BEFORE YOU SUBMIT

Be aware that most classical music organizations are nonprofit groups, and don't have a large budget for acquiring new works. It takes a lot of time and money to put together an orchestral performance of a new composition, therefore these groups are quite selective when choosing new works to perform. Don't be disappointed if the payment offered by these groups is small or even non-existent. What you gain is the chance to have your music performed for an appreciative audience. Also realize that many classical groups are understaffed, so it may take longer than expected to hear back on your submission. It pays to be patient, and employ diplomacy, tact and timing in your follow-up.

In this section you will find listings for classical performing arts organizations throughout the U.S. But if you have no prior performances to your credit, it's a good idea to begin with a small chamber orchestra, for example. Smaller symphony and chamber orchestras are usually more inclined to experiment with new works. A local university or conservatory of music, where you may already have contacts, is a great place to start.

All of the groups listed in this section are interested in hearing new works from contemporary classical composers. Pay close attention to the music needs of each group, and when you find one you feel might be interested in your music, follow submission guidelines carefully. To locate classical performing arts groups in your area, consult the Geographic Index at the back of this book.

ACADIANA SYMPHONY ORCHESTRA

P.O. Box 53632, Lafayette LA 70505. (337)232-4277. Fax: (337)237-4712. E-mail: information@acad ianasymphony.org. Web site: www.acadianasymphony.org. **Contact:** Geraldine Hubbel, executive director. Symphony orchestra. Estab. 1984. Members are amateurs and professionals. Performs 20 concerts/year, including 1 new work. Commissions 1 new work/year. Performs in 2,230-seat hall with "wonderful acoustics." Pays "according to the type of composition."

How to Contact Call first. Does not return material. Responds in 2 months.

Music Full orchestra: 10 minutes at most. Reduced orchestra, educational pieces: short, up to 5 minutes.

Performances Quincy Hilliard's *Universal Covenant* (orchestral suite); James Hanna's *In Memoriam* (strings/elegy); and Gregory Danner's *A New Beginning* (full orchestra fanfare).

Ⓝ ADRIAN SYMPHONY ORCHESTRA

110 S. Madison St., Adrian MI 49221. (517)264-3121. Fax: (517)264-3833. E-mail: aso@lni.net. Web site: www.aso.org. **Contact:** John Dodson, music director. Symphony orchestra and chamber music ensemble. Estab. 1981. Members are professionals. Performs 25 concerts/year including new works. 1,200 seat hall—"Rural city with remarkably active cultural life." Pays $200-1,000 for performance.

How to Contact Query first. Does not return material. Responds in 6 months.

Music Chamber ensemble to full orchestra. "Limited rehearsal time dictates difficulty of pieces selected." Does not wish to see "rock music or country—not at this time."

Performances Michael Pratt's *Dancing on the Wall* (orchestral—some aleatoric); Sir Peter Maxwell Davies' *Orkney Wedding* (orchestral); and Gwyneth Walker's *Fanfare, Interlude, Finale* (orchestral).

☑ THE AMERICAN BOYCHOIR

19 Lambert Dr., Princeton NJ 08540. (609)924-5858. Fax: (609)924-5812. E-mail: jkaltenbach@ame ricanboychoir.org. Web site: www.americanboychoir.org. **General Manager:** Janet B. Kaltenbach. Music Director: Fernando Malvar-Ruíz. Professional boychoir. Estab. 1937. Members are musically talented boys in grades 5-8. Performs 200 concerts/year, including 10-25 new works. Commissions 1 new work approximately every 3 years. Actively seeks high quality arrangements. Performs national and international tours, orchestral engagements, church services, workshops, school programs, local concerts, and at corporate and social functions.

How to Contact Submit complete score. Include SASE. Responds in 1 year.

Music Choral works in unison, SA, SSA, SSAA or SATB division; unaccompanied and with piano or organ; occasional chamber orchestra or brass ensemble. Works are usually sung by 28 to 60 boys. Composers must know boychoir sonority.

Performances *Four Seasons*, by Michael Torke (orchestral-choral); *Garden of Light*, by Aaron Kernis (orchestral-choral); *Reasons for Loving the Harmonica*, by Libby Larsen (piano); and *Songs Eternity*, by Steven Paulus (piano).

AMHERST SAXOPHONE QUARTET

64 Roycroft Blvd., Amherst NY 14226. (716)839-9716. E-mail: steve@caramaxstudio.com. Web site: www.amherstsaxophonequartet.buffalo.edu. **Contact:** Steve Rosenthal, director. Chamber music ensemble. Estab. 1978. Performs 80 concerts/year including 10-20 new works. Commissions 1-2 composers or new works/year. "We are a touring ensemble." Payment varies.

How to Contact Query first. Include SASE. Responds in 1 month.

Music "Music for soprano, alto, tenor and baritone (low A) saxophone. We are interested in great music of many styles. Level of difficulty is commensurate with full-time touring ensembles."

Performances Lukas Foss's *Saxophone Quartet* (new music); David Stock's *Sax Appeal* (new music); and Chan Ka Nin's *Saxophone Quartet* (new music).

Tips "Professionally copied parts help! Write what you truly want to write."

▣ ANDERSON SYMPHONY ORCHESTRA

P.O. Box 741, Anderson IN 46015. (765)644-2111. Fax: (765)644-7703. E-mail: aso@andersonsymp hony.org. Web site: www.andersonsymphony.org. **Contact:** Dr. Richard Sowers, conductor. Executive Director: George W. Vinson. Symphony orchestra. Estab. 1967. Members are professionals. Performs 7 concerts/year. Performs for typical mid-western audience in a 1,500-seat restored Paramount Theatre. Pay negotiable.

How to Contact Query first. Include SASE. Responds in several months.

Music "Shorter lengths better; concerti OK; difficulty level: mod high; limited by typically 3 full service rehearsals."

▣ ARCADY

P.O. Box 955, Simcoe ON N3Y 5B3 Canada. (519)428-3185. E-mail: info@arcady.ca. Web site: www.arcady.ca. **Contact:** Ronald Beckett, director. Professional chorus and orchestra. Members are professionals, university music majors and recent graduates from throughout Ontario. "Arcady forms the bridge between the student and the professional performing career." Performs 12 concerts/year including 1 new work. Pay negotiable.

How to Contact Submit complete score and tape of piece(s). Does not return material. Responds in 3 months.

Music "Compositions appropriate for ensemble accustomed to performance of chamber works, accompanied or unaccompanied, with independence of parts. Specialize in repertoire of 17th, 18th and 20th centuries. Number of singers does not exceed 30. Orchestra is limited to strings, supported by a professional quartet. No popular, commercial or show music."

Performances Ronald Beckett's *I Am . . .* (opera); Ronald Beckett's *John* (opera); and David Lenson's *Prologue to Dido and Aeneas* (masque).

Tips "Arcady is a touring ensemble experienced with both concert and stage performance."

ATLANTA POPS ORCHESTRA

P.O. Box 15037, Atlanta GA 30333. (404)636-0020. E-mail: ladkmusic@aol.com. Web site: www.atl antapops.com. **Contact:** Leonard Altieri, general manager. Pops orchestra. Estab. 1945. Members are professionals. Performs 5-10 concerts/year. Concerts are performed for audiences of 5,000-10,000, "all ages, all types." Composers are not paid; concerts are free to the public.

How to Contact Call to request permission to submit. Then send cassette, and score or music, if requested. Include SASE. Responds "as soon as possible."

Performances Vincent Montana, Jr.'s *Magic Bird of Fire*; Louis Alter's *Manhattan Serenade*; and Nelson Riddle's *It's Alright With Me*.

Tips "My concerts are pops concerts—no deep classics."

▣ AUREUS QUARTET

22 Lois Ave., Demarest NJ 07627-2220. (201)767-8704. E-mail: AureusQuartet@aol.com. **Contact:** James J. Seiler, artistic director. Vocal ensemble (a cappella). Estab. 1979. Members are professionals. Performs 75 concerts/year, including 12 new works. Commissions 5 composers or new works/ year. Pay varies for outright purchase.

How to Contact Query first. Include SASE. Responds in 2 months.

Music "We perform anything from pop to classic—mixed repertoire so anything goes. Some pieces can be scored for orchestras as we do pops concerts. Up to now, we've only worked with a quartet. Could be expanded if the right piece came along. Level of difficulty—no piece has ever been too hard." Does not wish to see electronic or sacred pieces. "Electronic pieces would be hard to program. Sacred pieces not performed much. Classical/jazz arrangements of old standards are great! Unusual Christmas arrangements are most welcome!"

Tips "We perform for a very diverse audience. Luscious, four part writing that can showcase well-trained voices is a must. Also, clever arrangements of old hits from '50s through '60s are sure bets. (Some pieces could take optional accompaniment)."

BILLINGS SYMPHONY

201 N. Broadway., Suite 350, Billings MT 59101-1936. (406)252-3610. Fax: (406)252-3353. E-mail: symphony@billingssymphony.org. Web site: www.billingssymphony.org. **Contact:** Dr. Uri Barnea, music director. Symphony orchestra, orchestra and chorale. Estab. 1950. Members are professionals and amateurs. Performs 12-15 concerts/year, including 6-7 new works. Traditional audience. Performs at Alberta Bair Theater (capacity 1,416). Pays by outright purchase (or rental).
How to Contact Query first. Include SASE. Responds in 2 weeks.
Music Any style. Traditional notation preferred.
Performances Jim Cockey's *Symphony No. 2 (Parmly's Dream)* (symphony orchestra with chorus and soloists); Ilse-Mari Lee's *Cello Concerto* (concerto for cello solo and orchestra); and Jim Beckel's *Christmas Fanfare* (brass and percussion).
Tips "Write what you feel (be honest) and sharpen your compositional and craftsmanship skills."

BIRMINGHAM-BLOOMFIELD SYMPHONY ORCHESTRA

1592 Buckingham, Birmingham MI 48009. (248)645-2276. Fax: (248)645-2276, *51. Web site: www .bbso.org. **Contact:** Charles Greenwell, music director and conductor. Conductor Laureate: Felix Resnick. President and Executive Director: Carla Lamphere. Symphony orchestra. Estab. 1975. Members are professionals. Performs 5 concerts including 1 new work/year. Commissions 1 composer or new work/year "with grants." Performs for middle-to-upper class audience at Temple Beth El's Sanctuary. Pays per performance "depending upon grant received."
How to Contact *Query first.* Does not return material. Responds in 6 months.
Music "We are a symphony orchestra but also play pops. Usually 3 works on program (2 hrs.) Orchestra size 65-75. If pianist is involved, they must rent piano."
Performances Brian Belanger's *Tuskegee Airmen Suite* (symphonic full orchestra); Larry Nazer & Friend's *Music from "Warm" CD* (jazz with full orchestra) ; and Mark Gottlieb's *Violin Concerto for Orchestra* (new world premiere, 2006).

THE BOSTON PHILHARMONIC

295 Huntington Ave., #210, Boston MA 02115. (617)236-0999. Fax: (617)236-8613. E-mail: office@ bostonphil.org. Web site: www.bostonphil.org. **Music Director:** Benjamin Zander. Symphony orchestra. Estab. 1979. Members are professionals, amateurs and students. Performs 2 concerts/year. Audience is ages 30-70. Performs at New England Conservatory's Jordan Hall, Boston's Symphony Hall and Sanders Theatre in Cambridge. Both Jordan Hall and Sanders Theatre are small (approximately 1,100 seats) and very intimate.
How to Contact *Does not accept new music at this time.*
Music Full orchestra only.
Performances Dutilleuxs' *Tout un monde lointain* for cello and orchestra (symphonic); Bernstein's *Fancy Free* (symphonic/jazzy); Copland's *El Salon Mexico* (symphonic); Gershwin's *Rhapsody in Blue*; Shostakovitch's *Symphony No. 10*; Harbison's *Concerto for Oboe*; Holst's *The Planet Suite*; Schwantner's *New Morning for the World*; Berg's *Seven Early Songs*; and Ive's *The Unanswered Question*.

BRAVO! L.A.

16823 Liggett St., North Hills CA 91343. (818)892-8737. Fax: (818)892-1227. E-mail: info@bravo-la.com. Web site: www.bravo-la.com. **Contact:** Dr. Janice Foy, director. An umbrella organization of recording/touring musicians, formed in 1994. Includes the following musical ensembles: Celllissimo! L.A. (cello ensemble); Interstellar Strings (expandable string group with optional piano); Mesto Chamber Players; the New American Quartet (string quartet); The Ascending Wave (harp, soprano, cello or harp/cello duo); Cellissimo! L.A. (cello ensemble); Musical Combustion (harp, flute, cello); I Musicanti (singer, piano and cello); and the Sierra Chamber Players (piano with strings or mixed ensemble). Performs 4 concerts/year, including 1 new work. "We take care of PR. There is also grant money the composer can apply for."
How to Contact Submit complete score and tape of piece(s). Include SASE. Responds in a few months.

Music "Classical, Romantic, Baroque, Popular (including new arrangements done by Shelly Cohen, from the 'Tonight Show Band'), ethnic (including gypsy) and contemporary works (commissioned as well). The New American Quartet has a recording project which features music of Mozart's *Eine Kleine Nachtmusik*, Borodin's *Nocturne*, a Puccini Opera Suite (S. Cohen), Strauss' *Blue Danube Waltz*, *Trepak* of Tschaikovsky, *'El Choclo'* (Argentinian tango), *Csardas!* and arrangements of Cole Porter, Broadway show tunes and popular classics."

Performances Joe Giarrusso's *Rhapsody for Cello and Piano* (concert piece modern romantic); Joe Giarrusso's *Cello Sonata* (concert piece); and Dan Bogley's *Foybles* (contemporary solo cello).

Tips "Please be open to criticism/suggestions about your music and try to appeal to mixed audiences. We also look for innovative techniques, mixed styles or entertaining approaches, such as classical jazz or Bach and pop, or ethnic mixes. There are four CD's currently available for purchase online for $20 each. There are also sound clips on the Web site."

☒ CANADIAN OPERA COMPANY

227 Front St. E., Toronto ON M5A 1E8 Canada. (416)363-6671. Fax: (416)363-5584. E-mail: ensembl e@coc.ca. Web site: www.coc.ca. **Contact:** Sandra J. Gavinchuk, music administrator. Opera company. Estab. 1950. Members are professionals. 50-55 performances, including a minimum of 1 new work/year. Pays by contract.

How to Contact Submit complete score and tapes of vocal and/or operatic works. "Vocal works please." Include SASE. Responds in 5 weeks.

Music Vocal works, operatic in nature. "Do not submit works which are not for voice. Ask for requirements for the Composers-In-Residence program."

Performances Dean Burry's *Brothers Grimm* (children's opera, 50 minutes long); Paul Ruders' *Handmaid's Tale* (full length opera, 2 acts, epilogue); Dean Burry's *Isis and the Seven Scorpions* (45-minute opera for children); Berg's *Wozzeck*; James Rolfe's *Swoon* (work title for forthcoming work).

Tips "We have a Composers-In-Residence program which is open to Canadian composers or landed immigrants."

☒ CANTATA ACADEMY

2441 Pinecrest Dr., Ferndale MI 48220. (248)358-9868. **Contact:** Phillip O'Jibway, business manager. Music Director: Dr. Michael Mitchell, music director. Vocal ensemble. Estab. 1961. Members are professionals. Performs 10-12 concerts/year including 1-3 new works. "We perform in churches and small auditoriums throughout the Metro Detroit area for audiences of about 500 people." Pays variable rate for outright purchase.

How to Contact Submit complete score. Include SASE. Responds in 3 months.

Music Four-part a cappella and keyboard accompanied works, two and three-part works for men's or women's voices. Some small instrumental ensemble accompaniments acceptable. Work must be suitable for forty voice choir. No works requiring orchestra or large ensemble accompaniment. No pop.

Performances Libby Larsen's *Missa Gaia: Mass for the Earth* (SATB, string quartet, oboe, percussion, 4-hand piano); Dede Duson's *To Those Who See* (SATB, SSA); and Sarah Hopkins' *Past Life Melodies* (SATB with Harmonic Overtone Singing).

Tips "Be patient. Would prefer to look at several different samples of work at one time."

☒ CARMEL SYMPHONY ORCHESTRA

P.O. Box 761, Carmel IN 46082-0761. (317)844-9717. Fax: (317)844-9916. E-mail: cso@carmelsymp hony.org. Web site: www.carmelsymphony.org. **Contact:** Allen Davis, executive director. Symphony orchestra. Estab. 1976. Members are professionals and amateurs. Performs 15 concerts/year, including 1-2 new works. Audience is "40% senior citizens, 85% white." Performs in a 1,500-seat high school performing arts center. Pay is negotiable.

How to Contact Query first. Include SASE. Responds in 3 months.

Music "Full orchestra works, 10-20 minutes in length. Can be geared toward 'children's' or 'Masterworks' programs. 65-70 piece orchestra, medium difficulty."
Performances Jim Beckel's *Glass Bead Game* (full orchestra); Percy Grainger's *Molly on the Shore* (full orchestra); and Frank Glover's *Impressions of New England* (full orchestra and jazz quartet).

▨ CHAMBER ORCHESTRA OF SOUTH BAY/CARSON-DOMINIQUEZ HILLS SYMPHONY
21 La Vista Verde, Rancho Palos Verdes CA 90275. (310)243-3947. E-mail: FSteiner@csudh.edu. **Contact:** Dr. Frances Steiner, music director. Symphony orchestra. Estab. 1972. Members are professionals (chamber orchestra); professionals and amatuers (symphony). Performs 10-11 concerts/year including 3-4 new works. Commissions 0-1 new works/year. Chamber orchestra audience is conservative in musical taste; symphony has an ethnically diverse and new student audience. Performance spaces seat 450-480. Pays ASCAP/BMI royalty or rental fee to publisher.
How to Contact Query first. Include SASE. Responds in 3 months.
Music Prefers 10-15 minute works for chamber orchestra, string orchestra and symphony orchestra (winds in pairs). Works should have "audience appeal" and not be too difficult to learn; there is special interest in works by women composers of diverse ethnicity.
Performances Michael Abels's *Global Warming* (ethinic, melodic ideas); Augusta Reid Thomas's *Flute Concerto #1* (contemporary); and Kevin O'Neal's *Japanese Sketches* (jazz and orchestra).

CONNECTICUT CHORAL ARTISTS/CONCORA
52 Main St., New Britain CT 06051. (860)224-7500. Web site: www.concora.org. **Contact:** Jane Penfield, executive director. Richard Coffey, artistic director. Professional concert choir, also an 18-voice ensemble dedicated to contemporary a cappella works. Estab. 1974. Members are professionals. Performs 15 concerts/year, including 3-5 new works. "Mixed audience in terms of age and background; performs in various halls and churches in the region." Payment "depends upon underwriting we can obtain for the project."
How to Contact Query first. "No unsolicited submissions accepted." Include SASE. Responds in 1 year.
Music Seeking "works for mixed chorus of 36 singers; unaccompanied or with keyboard and/or small instrumental ensemble; text sacred or secular/any language; prefers suites or cyclical works, total time not exceeding 15 minutes. Performance spaces and budgets prohibit large instrumental ensembles. Works suited for 750-seat halls are preferable. Substantial organ or piano parts acceptable. Scores should be very legible in every way."
Performances Wm. Schuman's *Carols of Death* (choral SATB); Robert Cohen's *Peter Quince as the Clavier* (choral, a cappella); Chen Yi's *The Flowing Station* (choral, a cappella); Charles Ives' *Psalm 90* (choral SATB); and Frank Martin's *Mass for Double Chorus* (regional premiere).
Tips "Use conventional notation and be sure manuscript is legible in every way. Recognize and respect the vocal range of each vocal part. Work should have an identifiable *rhythmic* structure."

▨ DUO CLASICO
4 Essex St., Clifton NJ 07014. (973)655-4379. E-mail: wittend@mail.montclair.edu. Web site: www.davidwitten.com. **Contact:** David Witten. Chamber music ensemble. Estab. 1986. Members are professionals. Performs 16 concerts/year including 4 new works. Commissions 1 composer or new work/year. Performs in small recital halls. Pays 10% royalty.
How to Contact Query first. Include SASE. Responds in 6 weeks.
Music "We welcome scores for flute solo, piano solo or duo. Particular interest in Latin American composers."
Performances Diego Luzuriaga's *La Muchica* (modern, with extended techniques); Robert Starer's *Yizkor & Anima Aeterna* (rhythmic); and Piazzolla's *Etudes Tanguistiques* (solo flute).
Tips "Extended techniques, or with tape, are fine!"

HEARTLAND MEN'S CHORUS
P.O. Box 32374, Kansas City MO 64171-5374. (816)931-3338. Fax: (816)531-1367. E-mail: hmc@hmckc.org. Web site: www.hmckc.org. **Contact:** Joseph Nadeau, artistic director. Men's chorus. Estab.

1986. Members are professionals and amateurs. Performs 3 concerts/year; 9-10 are new works. Commissions 1 composer or new works/year. Performs for a diverse audience at the Folly Theater (1,100 seats). Pay is negotiable.

How to Contact Query first. Include SASE. Responds in 2 months.

Music "Interested in works for male chorus (ttbb). Must be suitable for performance by a gay male chorus. We will consider any orchestration, or a cappella."

Performances Mark Hayes' "Two Flutes Playing" (commissioned song cycle); Alan Shorter's "Country Angel Christmas" (commissioned chidren's musical); Kevin Robinson's "Life is a Cabaret: The Music of Kander and Ebb" (commissioned musical).

Tips "Find a text that relates to the contemporary gay experience, something that will touch peoples' lives."

HERMANN SONS GERMAN BAND

P.O. Box 162, Medina TX 78055. (830)589-2268. E-mail: herbert@festmusik.com. Web site: www.festmusik.com. **Contact:** Herbert Bilhartz, music director. Community band with German instrumentation. Estab. 1990. Members are both professionals and amateurs. Performs 4 concerts/year including 2 new works. Commissions no new composers or new works/year. Performs for "mostly older people who like German polkas, waltzes and marches. We normally play only published arrangements from Germany."

How to Contact Query first; then submit full set of parts and score, condensed or full. Include SASE. Responds in 6 weeks.

Music "We like European-style polkas or waltzes (Viennese or Missouri tempo), either original or arrangements of public domain tunes. Arrangements of traditional American folk tunes in this genre would be especially welcome. Also, polkas or waltzes featuring one or two solo instruments (from instrumentation below) would be great. OK for solo parts to be technically demanding. Although we have no funds to commission works, we will provide you with a cassette recording of our performance. Also, we would assist composers in submitting works to band music publishers in Germany for possible publication. Polkas and waltzes generally follow this format: Intro; 1st strain repeated; 2nd strain repeated; DS to 1 strain; Trio: Intro; 32 bar strain; 'break-up' strain; Trio DS. Much like military march form. Instrumentation: Fl/Picc, 3 clars in Bb, 2 Fluegelhorns in Bb; 3 Tpts in Bb, 2 or 4 Hns in F or Eb, 2 Baritones (melody/countermelody parts; 1 in Bb TC, 1 in BC), 2 Baritones in Bb TC (rhythm parts), 3 Trombones, 2 Tubas (in octaves, mostly), Drum set, Timpani optional. We don't use saxes, but a German publisher would want 4-5 sax parts. Parts should be medium to medium difficult. All brass parts should be considered one player to the part; woodwinds, two to the part. No concert type pieces; no modern popular or rock styles. However, a 'theme and variations' form with contrasting jazz, rock, country, modern variations would be clever, and our fans might go for such a piece (as might a German publisher)."

Performances New music performed in 2005: Stefan Rundel's *Mein Gluecksstern* ("*My Lucky Star*").

Tips "German town bands love to play American tunes. There are many thousands of these bands over there and competition among band music publishers in Germany is keen. Few Americans are aware of this potential market, so few American arrangers get published over there. Simple harmony is best for this style, but good counterpoint helps a lot. Make use of the dark quality of the Fluegelhorns and the bright, fanfare quality of the trumpets. Give the two baritones (one in TC and one in BC) plenty of exposed melodic material. Keep them in harmony with each other (3rds and 6ths), unlike American band arrangements, which have only one Baritone line. If you want to write a piece in this style, give me a call, and I will send you some sample scores to give you a better idea."

ⓃHERSHEY SYMPHONY ORCHESTRA

P.O. Box 93, Hershey PA 17033. (800)533-3088. E-mail: drdackow@aol.com. **Contact:** Dr. Sandra Dackow, music director. Symphony orchestra. Estab. 1969. Members are professionals and amateurs. Performs 8 concerts/year, including 1-3 new works. Commissions "possibly 1-2" composers or new works/year. Audience is family and friends of community theater. Performance space is a 1,900 seat grand old movie theater. Pays commission fee.

How to Contact Submit complete score and tape of piece(s). Include SASE. Responds in 3 months.
Music "Symphonic works of various lengths and types which can be performed by a non-professional orchestra. We are flexible but like to involve all our players."
Performances Paul W. Whear's *Celtic Christmas Carol* (orchestra/bell choir) and Linda Robbins Coleman's *In Good King Charlie's Golden Days* (overture).
Tips "Please lay out rehearsal numbers/letter and rests according to phrases and other logical musical divisions rather than in groups of ten measures, etc., which is very unmusical and wastes time and causes a surprising number of problems. Also, please do not send a score written in concert pitch; use the usual transpositions so that the conductor sees what the players see; rehearsal is much more effective this way. Cross cue all important solos; this helps in rehearsal where instruments may be missing."

LAMARCA AMERICAN VARIETY SINGERS
2655 W. 230th Place, Torrance CA 90505. (310)325-8708. E-mail: lamarcamusic@lycos.com. **Contact:** Priscilla LaMarca/Kandell, director. Youth to adult show choirs. Estab. 1979. Members are professionals and amateurs. Performs 10 concerts/year including 3 new works. Performs at major hotels, conventions, community theaters, fund raising events, cable TV, holiday events, community fairs and Disneyland. Pays showcase only.
How to Contact Query first. Include SASE. Responds in 2 weeks.
Music "Seeks 3-10 or 15 minute medleys; a variety of musical styles from Broadway—pop styles to humorous specialty songs. Top 40 dance music, light rock and patriotic themes. No rap or anything not suitable for family audiences."
Performances *Disney Movie Music* (uplifting); *Children's Music* (educational/positive); and *Beatles Medley* (love songs).

LITHOPOLIS AREA FINE ARTS ASSOCIATION
3825 Cedar Hill Rd., Canal Winchester OH 43110-8929. (614)837-8925. Web site: www.cwda.net/LAFAA/. **Contact:** Virginia E. Heffner, assistant series director. Performing Arts Series. Estab. 1973. Members are professionals and amateurs. Performs 6-7 concerts/year including 2-3 new works. "Our audience consists of couples and families 30-80 in age. Their tastes run from classical, folk, ethnic, big band, pop and jazz. Our hall is acoustically excellent and seats 400. It was designed as a lecture-recital hall in 1925." Composers "may apply for Ohio Arts Council Grant under the New Works category." Pays straight fee to ASCAP.
How to Contact *Query first.* Include SASE. Responds in 3 weeks.
Music "We prefer that a composer is also the performer and works in conjunction with another artist, so they could be one of the performers on our series. Piece should be musically pleasant and not too dissonant. It should be scored for small vocal or instrumental ensemble. Dance ensembles have difficulty with 15′ high 15′ deep and 27′ wide stage. We do not want avant-garde or obscene dance routines. No ballet (space problem). We're interested in something historical—national or Ohio emphasis would be nice. Small ensembles or solo format is fine."
Performances Patsy Ford Simms' *Holiday Gloria* (Christmas SSA vocal); Andrew Carter's *A Maiden Most Gentle* (Christmas SSA vocal); and Luigi Zaninelli's *Alleluia, Silent Night* (Christmas SSA vocal).
Tips "Call in December of 2006 or January 2007 for queries about our 2006-2007 season. We do a varied program. We don't commission artists. Contemporary music is used by some of our artist or groups. By contacting these artists, you could offer your work for inclusion in their program."

HENRY MANCINI INSTITUTE ORCHESTRA
(formerly American Jazz Philharmonic), 10811 Washington Blvd., Suite 250, Culver City CA 90232. (310)HMI-1903. Web site: www.manciniinstitute.org. **Contact:** Patrick Williams, artistic director. Symphonic jazz orchestra (72 piece). Estab. 1979. Members are professionals. Performs 8 concerts/year, including 10 new works. Commissions 2-5 composers or new works/year. Performs in major concert halls nationwide: Avery Fisher (New York), Karen & Richard Carpenter Performing Arts Center (Long Beach), Royce Hall (Los Angeles), Pick-Staiger (Chicago). Pays $2,500-5,000 for commission.

How to Contact Query first then submit complete score and tape of piece(s) with résumé. Include SASE. "Newly commissioned composers are chosen each July. Submissions should be sent by June 15th, returned by August 15th."

Music "The AJP commissions 1-2 new symphonic jazz works annually. Decisions to commission are based on composer's previous work in the symphonic jazz genre. The AJP is a 72-piece symphonic jazz ensemble that includes a rhythm section and woodwinds who double on saxophones, plus traditional symphonic orchestra."

Performances John Clayton's *Three Shades of Blue* (solo tenor sax and orchestra); Lennie Niehaus' *Tribute to Bird* (solo alto sax and orchestra); and Eddie Karam's *Stay 'N See* (symphonic jazz overture).

Tips "The AJP has been a recipient of a Reader's Digest/Meet the Composer grant and has received awards from ASCAP and the American Symphony Orchestra League for its programming. The ensemble has also received a Grammy Award nomination for its debut album on GRP Records featuring Ray Brown and Phil Woods. The AJP has recently established the Henry Mancini Institute—a four week summer educational music program for talented young musicians and composer/arrangers chosen from auditions held nationally. Participants study and perform with the principal players of the AJP and guest artists and composers/conductors. Program includes private lessons, ensemble rehearsals, panel discussions/clinics, master classes, soloist opportunities and performances in orchestra, big band, chamber ensembles and combos."

MASTER CHORALE OF WASHINGTON

1200 29th St. NW, Suite LL2, Washington DC 20007. (202)471-4050. Fax: (202)471-4051. E-mail: singing@masterchorale.org. Web site: www.masterchorale.org. **Contact:** Donald McCullough, music director. Vocal ensemble. Estab. 1967. Members are professionals and amateurs. Performs 8 concerts/year including 1-3 new works. Commissions one new composer or work every 2 years. "Audience covers a wide range of ages and economic levels drawn from the greater Washington DC metropolitan area. Kennedy Center Concert Hall seats 2,400." Pays by outright purchase.

How to Contact Submit complete score and tape of piece(s). Include SASE. Responds in 9 months.

Music Seeks new works for: 1) large chorus with or without symphony orchestras; 2) chamber choir and small ensemble.

Performances Stephen Paulus' *Mass*; Joonas Kokkonen's *Requiem* (symphonic choral with orchestra); Morten Lauridsen's *Lux Aeterna*; Donald McCullough's *Let My People Go!: A Spiritual Journey*; Daniel E. Gawthrop's *In Quiet Resting Places*; and Adolphus Hailstork's *Whitman's Journey*.

ORCHESTRA SEATTLE/SEATTLE CHAMBER SINGERS

P.O. Box 15825, Seattle WA 98115. (206)682-5208. E-mail: osscs@osscs.org. Web site: www.osscs.org. **Contact:** Andrew Danilchik, librarian. Symphony orchestra, chamber music ensemble and community chorus. Estab. 1969. Members are amateurs and professionals. Performs 8 concerts/year including 2-3 new works. Commissions 1-2 composers or new works/year. "Our audience is made up of both experienced and novice classical music patrons. The median age is 45 with an equal number of males and females in the upper income range. Most concerts now held in Benaroya Hall."

How to Contact Query first. Include SASE. Responds in 1 year.

Performances Robert Kechley's *Trumpet Concerto* (classical concerto); Carol Sams's *Earthmakers* (oratorio); and Murl Allen Sanders's *Accordion Concerto* (classical concerto).

Ⓝ PICCOLO OPERA COMPANY INC.

24 Del Rio Blvd., Boca Raton FL 33432-4734. (800)282-3161. Fax: (561)394-0520. E-mail: leejon51@msn.com. **Contact:** Lee Merrill, executive assistant. Traveling opera company. Estab. 1962. Members are professionals. Performs 1-50 concerts/year including 1-2 new works. Commissions 0-1 composer or new work/year. Operas are performed for a mixed audience of children and adults. Pays by performance or outright purchase. Operas in English.

How to Contact Query first. Include SASE.

Music "Musical theater pieces, lasting about one hour, for adults to perform for adults and/or youngsters. Performers are mature singers with experience. The cast should have few performers (up to 10), no chorus or ballet, accompanied by piano or local orchestra. Skeletal scenery. All in English.''

Performances Menotti's *The Telephone*; Mozart's *Cosi Fan Tutte*; and Puccini's *La Boheme* (repertoire of more than 22 productions).

☑ SAN FRANCISCO GIRLS CHORUS

44 Page Street, Suite 200, San Francisco CA 94102. (415)863-1752. E-mail: info@sfgirlschorus.org. Web site: www.sfgirlschorus.org. **Contact:** Susan McMane, artistic director. Choral ensemble. Estab. 1978. Advanced choral ensemble of young women's voices. Performs 8-10 concerts/year including 3-4 new works. Commissions 2 composers or new works/year. Concerts are performed for ''choral/classical music lovers, plus family audiences and audiences interested in international repertoire. Season concerts are performed in a 800-seat church with excellent acoustics and in San Francisco's Davies Symphony Hall, a 2,800-seat state-of-the-art auditorium.'' Pay negotiable for outright purchase.

• The San Francisco Girls Chorus has won three Grammy Awards as guest performers on the San Francisco Symphony's recordings.

How to Contact Submit complete score and CD recording, if possible. Does not return material. Responds in 6 months.

Music ''Music for treble voices (SSAA); a cappella, piano accompaniment, or small orchestration; 3-10 minutes in length. Wide variety of styles; 45 singers; challenging music is encouraged.''

Performances See Web site under ''Music/Commissions'' for a listing of SFGC commissions. Examples: Jake Heggie's *Patterns* (piano, mezzo-soprano soloist, chorus); and Chen Yi's *Chinese Poems* (a cappella).

Tips ''Choose excellent texts and write challenging music. The San Francisco Girls Chorus has pioneered in establishing girls choral music as an art form in the United States. The Girls Chorus is praised for its 'stunning musical standard' (*San Francisco Chronicle*) in performances in the San Francisco Bay Area and on tour. SFGC's annual concert season showcases the organization's concert/touring ensembles, Chorissima and Virtuose, in performances of choral masterworks from around the world, commissioned works by contemporary composers, and 18th-century music from the Venetian Ospedali and Mexican Baroque which SFGC has brought out of the archives and onto the concert stage. Chorissima and Virtuose tour through California with partial support provided by the California Arts Council Touring Program and have represented the U.S. and the City of San Francisco nationally and abroad. The choruses provide ensemble and solo singers for performances and recordings with the San Francisco Symphony and San Francisco Opera, Women's Philharmonic, and many other music ensembles. SFGC's discography includes four CD recordings, *I Never Saw Another Butterfly* (20th Century music); *A San Francisco Christmas*; Benjamin Britten's *A Ceremony of Carols* and other holiday music; a 1998 release, *Music from the Venetian Ospedali* (18th-century works for girls chorus) (called ''fresh'' by *The New Yorker*); and a 2000 release, *Crossroads* (a collection of international music).''

☑ SINGING BOYS OF PENNSYLVANIA

P.O. Box 206, Wind Gap PA 18091. (610)759-6002. Fax: (570)223-2748. **Contact:** K. Bernard Schade, Ed. D., director. Vocal ensemble. Estab. 1970. Members are professional children. Performs 100 concerts/year including 3-5 new works. ''We attract general audiences: family, senior citizens, churches, concert associations, university concert series and schools.'' Pays $300-3,000 for outright purchase.

How to Contact Query first. Does not return material. Responds in 3 weeks.

Music ''We want music for commercials, voices in the SSA or SSAA ranges, sacred works or arrangements of American folk music with accompaniment. Our range of voices are from G below middle C to A (13th above middle C). Reading ability of choir is good but works which require a lot of work with little possibility of more than one performance are of little value. We sing very few popular songs except for special events. We perform music by composers who are well-known and works by living composers who are writing in traditional choral forms. Works which have a full orchestral score are of interest. The orchestration should be fairly light, so as not to cover the voices. Works for Christmas have more value than some other, since we perform with orchestras on an annual basis."

Performances Don Locklair's *The Columbus Madrigals* (opera).

Tips "It must be appropriate music and words for children. We do not deal in pop music. Folk music, classics and sacred are acceptable."

SOLI DEO GLORIA CANTORUM

3402 Woolworth Ave., Omaha NE 68105. (402)341-4111. E-mail: cantorum@berkey.com. Web site: www.berkey.com. **Contact:** Almeda Berkey, music director. Professional choir. Estab. 1988. Members are professionals. Performs 5-7 concerts/year; several are new works. Commissions 1-2 new works/year. Performance space: "cathedral, symphony hall, smaller intimate recital halls as well." Payment is "dependent upon composition and composer."

How to Contact Submit complete score and tape of piece(s). Include SASE. Responds in 2 months.

Music "Chamber music mixed with topical programming (e.g., all Celtic or all Hispanic programs, etc.). Generally a cappella compositions from very short to extended range (6-18 minutes) or multi-movements. Concerts are of a formal length (approx. 75 minutes) with 5 rehearsals. Difficulty must be balanced within program in order to adequately prepare in a limited rehearsal time. 28 singers. Not seeking orchestral pieces, due to limited budget."

Performances Jackson Berkey's *Native Am Ambience* (eclectic/classical); John Rutter's *Hymn to the Creator of Light* (classical); and Arvo Part's *Te Deum* (multi-choir/chant-based classical).

Performances 1999-2000 season included world premiere of James Barnes' *Autumn Soliloquy*. Other performances include Richard Arnell's *Symphony No. 6*, and Malcolm Arnold's *Clarinet Concerto No. 2*.

Tips "Send a nice clean score. Don't get discouraged as we only have limited performance options. We appreciate knowing if you have orchestral parts available. We are especially excited by the possibility of discovering talented, unknown composers who have not had the opportunities available to those who are well-connected."

SUSQUEHANNA SYMPHONY ORCHESTRA

P.O. Box 485, Forest Hill MD 21050. (410)838-6465. E-mail: sheldon.bair@ssorchestra.org. Web site: www.ssorchestra.org. **Contact:** Sheldon Bair, music director. Symphony orchestra. Estab. 1978. Members are amateurs. Performs 6 concerts/year including 1-2 new works. Composers paid depending on the circumstances. "We perform in 1 hall, 600 seats with fine acoustics. Our audience encompasses all ages."

How to Contact Query first. Include SASE. Responds in 3 or more months.

Music "We desire works for large orchestra, any length, in a 'conservative 20th and 21st century' style. Seek fine music for large orchestra. We are a community orchestra, so the music must be within our grasp. Violin I to 7th position by step only; Violin II—stay within 5th position; English horn and harp are OK. Full orchestra pieces preferred."

Performances Derek Bourgeois' *Trombone Concerto*; Gwyneth Walker's *The Magic Oboe*; and Johan de Meij's *Symphony No. 1 "Lord of the Rings"*.

TOURING CONCERT OPERA CO. INC.

228 E. 80th, New York NY 10021. (212)988-2542. Fax: (518)851-6778. E-mail: tcoc@mhonline.net. **Contact:** Anne DeFigols, director. Opera company. Estab. 1971. Members are professionals. Performs 30 concerts/year including 1 new work. Payment varies.

How to Contact Submit complete score and tape of piece(s). Does not return material. Response time varies.

Music "Operas or similar with small casts."

Tips "We are a touring company which travels all over the world. Therefore, operas with casts that are not large and simple but effective sets are the most practical."

VANCOUVER CHAMBER CHOIR

1254 W. Seventh Ave., Vancouver BC V6H 1B6 Canada. E-mail: info@vancouverchamberchoir.com. Web site: www.vancouverchamberchoir.com. **Contact:** Jon Washburn, artistic director. Vocal ensemble. Members are professionals. Performs 40 concerts/year including 5-8 new works. Commissions 2-4 composers or new works/year. Pays SOCAN royalty or negotiated fee for commissions.

How to Contact Submit complete score and tape of piece(s). Does not return material. Responds in 6 months if possible.

Music Seeks "choral works of all types for small chorus, with or without accompaniment and/or soloists. Concert music only. Choir made up of 20 singers. Large or unusual instrumental accompaniments are less likely to be appropriate. No pop music."

Performances The VCC has commissioned and premiered over 180 new works by Canadian and international composers, including Alice Parker's *That Sturdy Vine* (cantata for chorus, soloists and orchestra); R. Murray Schafer's *Magic Songs* (SATB a cappella); and Jon Washburn's *A Stephen Foster Medley* (SSAATTBB/piano).

Tips "We are looking for choral music that is performable yet innovative, and which has the potential to become 'standard repertoire.' Although we perform much new music, only a small portion of the many scores which are submitted can be utilized."

WHEATON SYMPHONY ORCHESTRA

(formerly City Symphony of Chicago), 344 Spring Ave., Glen Ellyn IL 60137. (630)858-5552. Fax: (630)790-9703. E-mail: dmattob@aol.com. **Contact:** Don Mattison, manager. Symphony orchestra. Estab. 1959. Members are professionals and amateurs. Performs 6 concerts/year including a varying number of new works. "No pay for performance but can probably record your piece."

How to Contact Query first. Include SASE. Responds in 1 month.

Music "This is a *good* amateur orchestra that wants pieces in a traditional idiom. Large scale works for orchestra only. No avant garde, 12-tone or atonal material. Pieces should be 20 minutes or less and must be prepared in 3 rehearsals. Instrumentation needed for woodwinds in 3s, full brass 4-3-3-1, 4 percussion and strings—full-instrumentation only. Selections for full orchestra only. No pay for reading your piece, but we will record it at our expense."

Performances Richard Williams's *Symphony in G Minor* (4 movement symphony); Dennis Johnson's *Must Jesus Bear the Cross Alone, Azon* (traditional); and Michael Diemer's *Skating* (traditional style).

Contests & Awards

Participating in contests is a great way to gain exposure for your music. Prizes vary from contest to contest, from cash to musical merchandise to studio time, and even publishing and recording deals. For musical theater and classical composers, the prize may be a performance of your work. Even if you don't win, valuable contacts can be made through contests. Many times, contests are judged by music publishers and other industry professionals, so your music may find its way into the hands of key industry people who can help further your career.

HOW TO SELECT A CONTEST

It's important to remember when entering any contest to do proper research before signing anything or sending any money. We have confidence in the contests listed in *Songwriter's Market*, but it pays to read the fine print. First, be sure you understand the contest rules and stipulations once you receive the entry forms and guidelines. Then you need to weigh what you will gain against what they're asking you to give up. If a publishing or recording contract is the only prize a contest is offering, you may want to think twice before entering. Basically, the company sponsoring the contest is asking you to pay a fee for them to listen to your song under the guise of a contest, something a legitimate publisher or record company would not do. For those contests offering studio time, musical equipment or cash prizes, you need to decide if the entry fee you're paying is worth the chance to win such prizes.

Be wary of exorbitant entry fees, and if you have any doubts whatsoever as to the legitimacy of a contest, it's best to stay away. Songwriters need to approach a contest, award or grant in the same manner as they would a record or publishing company. Make your submission as professional as possible; follow directions and submit material exactly as stated on the entry form.

Contests in this section encompass all types of music and levels of competition. Read each listing carefully and contact them if the contest interests you. Many contests now have websites that offer additional information and even entry forms you can print. Be sure to read the rules carefully and be sure you understand exactly what a contest is offering before entering.

AGO/ECS PUBLISHING AWARD IN CHORAL COMPOSITION

American Guild of Organists, 475 Riverside Dr., Suite 1260, New York NY 10115. (212)870-2310. Fax: (212)870-2163. E-mail: info@agohq.org. Web site: www.agohq.org. **Contact:** Karen A. Rich, competitions coordinator. Biannual award.

Requirements Composers are invited to submit a work for SATB choir and organ in which the organ plays a significant and independent role. Work submitted must be unpublished and approximately 3.5 to 5 minutes in length. There is no age restriction. Deadline: TBA, ''but usually late fall in even numbered years.'' Application information on the Web site.

Awards $2,000 cash prize, publication by ECS Publishing and premier performance at the AGO National Convention.

ALEA III INTERNATIONAL COMPOSITION PRIZE

855 Commonwealth Ave., Boston MA 02215. (617)353-3340. E-mail: kalogeras@earthlink.com. Web site: www.aleaiii.com. For composers. Annual award.

Purpose To promote and encourage young composers in the composition of new music.

Requirements Composers born after January 1, 1977 may participate; 1 composition per composer. Works may be for solo voice or instrument or for chamber ensemble up to 15 members lasting between 6 and 15 minutes. Available instruments are: one flute (doubling piccolo or alto), one oboe (doubling English horn), one clarinet (doubling bass clarinet), one bassoon, one horn, one trumpet, one trombone, one tuba, two percussion players, one harp, one keyboard player, one guitar, two violins, one viola, one cello, one bass, tape and one voice. All works must be unpublished and must not have been publicly performed or broadcast, in whole or in part or in any other version before the announcement of the prize in late September or early October of 2007. Works that have won other awards are not eligible. Deadline: March 15 2007. Send for application. Submitted work required with application. ''Real name should not appear on score; a nom de plume should be signed instead. Sealed envelope with entry form should be attached to each score.''

Awards ALEA III International Composition Prize: $2,500. Awarded once annually. Between 6-8 finalists are chosen and their works are performed in a competition concert by the ALEA III contemporary music ensemble. At the end of the concert, one piece will be selected to receive the prize. One grand prize winner is selected by a panel of judges.

Tips ''Emphasis placed on works written in 20th century compositional idioms.''

☑ AMERICAN SONGWRITER LYRIC CONTEST

1303 16th Avenue S., 2nd Floor, Nashville TN 37212. (615)321-6096. Fax: (615)321-6097. E-mail: info@americansongwriter.com. Web site: www.americansongwriter.com. **Contact:** Matt Shearon. Estab. 1984. For songwriters and composers. Award for each bimonthly issue of *American Songwriter* magazine, plus grand prize winner at year-end.

Purpose To promote the art of songwriting.

Requirements Lyrics must be typed and a check for $10 (per entry) must be enclosed. Deadlines: January 18, March 21, May 18, July 20, September 20, November 15. Send along with official entry form found on our Web site, or submit online through sonicbids.com. Lyrics only, no cassettes.

Awards A DX1 Martin guitar valued at $700 to bi-monthly contest winner. Grand prize winner receives airfare to Nashville and a demo session; and top 5 winning lyrics reprinted in each magazine. Lyrics judged by independent A&R, PRO representatives, songwriters, publishers, and *American Songwriter* staff.

Tips ''You do not have to be a subscriber to enter or win. You may submit as many entries as you like. All genres of music accepted.''

Ⓝ ARTISTS' FELLOWSHIPS

New York Foundation for the Arts, 155 Avenue of Americas, 14th Floor, New York NY 10013. (212)366-6900. Fax: (212)366-1778. E-mail: nyfaafp@nyfa.org. Web site: www.nyfa.org. To receive an application, or contact the fellowship's department, call: (212)366-6900, ext. 217. **Contact:** Penelope Dannenberg, director of programs. For songwriters, composers and musical playwrights. Annual award, but each category funded biennially. Estab. 1984.

Purpose "Artists' Fellowships are $7,000 grants awarded by the New York Foundation for the Arts to individual originating artists living in New York State. The Foundation is committed to supporting artists from all over New York State at all stages of their professional careers. Fellows may use the grant according to their own needs; it should not be confused with project support."

Requirements Must be 18 years of age or older; resident of New York State for 2 years prior to application; and cannot be enrolled in any graduate or undergraduate degree program. Applications will be available in July. Deadline: October. Samples of work are required with application. 1 or 2 original compositions on separate audiotapes or audio CDs and at least 2 copies of corresponding scores or fully harmonized lead sheets.

Awards All Artists' Fellowships awards are for $7,000. Payment of $6,300 upon verification of NY State residency, and remainder upon completion of a mutually agreed upon public service activity. Nonrenewable. "Fellowships are awarded on the basis of the quality of work submitted. Applications are reviewed by a panel of 5 composers representing the aesthetic, ethnic, sexual and geographic diversity within New York State. The panelists change each year and review all allowable material submitted."

Tips "Please note that musical playwrights may submit only if they write the music for their plays—librettists must submit in our playwriting category."

BILLBOARD SONG CONTEST

P.O. Box 470306, Tulsa OK 74147. (918)827-6529. Fax: (918)827-6533. E-mail: mark@jimhalsey.com. Web site: www.billboardsongcontest.com. **Contact:** Mark Furnas, Director. Estab. 1988. For songwriters, composers and performing artists. Annual international contest.

Purpose "To reward deserving songwriters and performers for their talent."

Requirements Entry fee: $30.

Awards To be announced. For entry forms and additional information send SASE to the above address or visit Web site.

Tips "Participants should understand popular music structure."

ⓝ THE BLANK THEATRE COMPANY YOUNG PLAYWRIGHTS FESTIVAL

1301 Lucile Ave., Los Angeles CA 90026. (323)662-7734. Fax: (323)661-3903. E-mail: info@theblank.com. Web site: www.youngplaywrights.com. Estab. 1993. For both musical and non-musical playwrights. Annual award.

Purpose "To give young playwrights an opportunity to learn more about playwriting and to give them a chance to have their work mentored, developed, and presented by professional artists."

Requirements Playwrights must be 19 years old or younger on March 15, 2005. Send legible, original plays of any length and on any subject (co-written plays are acceptable provided all co-writers meet eligibility requirements). Submissions must be postmarked by March 15 and must include a cover sheet with the playwright's name, date of birth, school (if any), home address, home phone number, e-mail address and production history. Pages must be numbered and submitted unbound (unstapled). For musicals, a tape or CD of a selection from the score should be submitted with the script. Manuscripts will not be returned. Please do not send originals. Semifinalists and winners will be contacted in May.

Awards Winning playwrights receive a workshop presentation of their work.

BUSH ARTIST FELLOWS PROGRAM

E-900 First National Bank Bldg., 332 Minnesota St., St. Paul MN 55101. (651)227-5222. E-mail: kpolley@bushfound.org. Web site: www.bushfoundation.org. **Contact:** Kathi Polley, program assistant. Estab. 1976. For songwriters, composers and musical playwrights. Applications in music composition are accepted in even-numbered years.

Purpose "To provide artists with significant financial support that enables them to further their work and their contribution to their communities."

Requirements Applicant must be U.S. Citizens or permanent Residents AND a Minnesota, North

Dakota, South Dakota or western Wisconsin resident for 12 of preceeding 36 months, 25 years or older, not a student. Deadline: late October. Send for application. Audio work samples required with application. "Music composition applications will not be taken again until the fall of 2006. Applications will be taken in the fall of 2006 in the following areas: music composition, scriptworks (screenwriting and playwriting), literature (creative non-fiction, fiction, poetry) and film/video. **Awards** Fellowships: $48,000 stipend for a period of 12-24 months. "Five years after completion of preceding fellowship, one may apply again." Applications are judged by peer review panels.

☑ THE CLW MUSIC AWARD

"E-mail for entry." E-mail: bej@india.com. Web site: www.clwma.5u.com. **Contact:** Holly Nigelson or Brenda Jackson, owners/partners (for information and an application). Estab. 2002. For Songwriters and Composers.

Purpose "To aid or further the careers of independent musicians, eligible enrolled music students and certain Native/African/Asian/American Organizations musically.

Requirements "Each song entered must be an original work. The songs may have multiple writers, but only one name need be on the application. The performer or performers must be the writers of the material submitted and must be the same individuals who are attend the Awards. Division of the prizes to any co-writers shall be the responsibility of the person named on the entry form as the leader of the Band or Group. No song previously recorded and released through national or any other type of distribution in any country will be eligible to win. Each entry must consist of: 1) A CD or audiocassette containing 1 song, which shall be 5 minutes in length or less. The side with the entry shall be cued to the beginning of the song and it shall be named or marked so. Failure to maintain this regulation shall result in disqualification; 2) The entry form must be signed in ink, in any color, no roller balls, felt tips, Magic Markers, or anything similar shall be accepted. Any non-legible entry forms shall be disqualified. All signatures must be the originals, and shall be verified; 3) If there are any lyrics included with a song, a lyric sheet must be typed or laser printed, no hand written or ink jet printed lyric sheets shall be accepted. Lyrics must have an English translation lyric sheet also, if applicable. Instrumental music shall not require either; 4) The entry fee of $30, payable by money order, Personal or Business check or Credit Card. Entry fees are not refundable. No solo entries or a-cappella entries shall be accepted. *Employees Family, friends, Affiliates and Associates of this contest are not eligible to win the Contest. Do not send Cash and if you use a major Credit Card, an additional $1.50 will be charged to your account!* There are 5 preliminary rounds of Judging and the Contest Final rounds. 1 Finalist from each category will be selected as a Finalist and 5 Finalists with the highest point totals from the rest of the field will be chosen as Finalists also. After Judging, the 15 Finalists shall be notified by mail and will be sent the proper affidavits, which must be returned not more than 40 Business Days after the date on the Congratulatory letter each shall receive. Any fraudulent or inaccurate information shall result in disqualification and an alternate winner shall be selected. Any printed or recorded submissions shall not be returned. Each contestant must be age 15 or older. Any Winners under the age of 21 shall require a parent or guardian present for the administering of prizes. In the instances where any entrants are younger than age 21, the parent or guardian must also sign the entry form. Winners shall be determined 3 months after the close of submissions for the current contest. The odds for winning the overall CLW Music Award are, at maximum, 12,000 to 1 based upon a person making 1 entry, of the 12,000 required to start the Judging round. The format of this contest does not allow these odds to be greater. If a person enters more than 1 recording, the odds for winning increase accordingly, if the entries are in the same contest. A person can enter more than once in any category but a separate fee is required for each entry. If a contestant does not make the finals they may enter a future contest if they choose to. If a contestant finishes in Third Place or lower and finishes no higher by replacing any finalists that may be disqualified by some means, that contestant may enter a future contest if they choose to. The CLW Music Award and Aubusson Music Publishing are not responsible for any late, lost, damaged or mishandled entries. The contest is open to all Amateur persons in the world who have not earned more than $5,000 from music royalties in the last 2 years. This rule shall apply to an individual or all members of a group or band collectively. If it is found that an entrant violates these requirements, the entrant shall be prosecuted for fraud, and in addition, any amount of winnings shall be returned and the contestant will be disqualified, with another winner being selected in place of the fraudulent one. 15 finalists will perform their entry song, or songs at the finals and be Judged. Those entrants who finish 3rd Place or lower and no higher, are eligible to enter again in the next contest. There are a total of 15 rounds of judging and the results remain unknown to everyone until the presentations. The Awards ceremony will be taped for Broadcast at a later date.

Awards Prizes: 1 CLW Music Award Winner, who will receive $30,000 cash and a Publishing Award; 1 Grand Prize Winner, who will receive $15,000 in cash and a Publishing Award; 1 First Prize Winner, who will receive $7,500 cash and a Publishing Award; 1 Second Prize Winner, who will receive $5,000 cash and a Publishing Award; 1 Third Prize Winner, who will receive $2,500 in cash only; 1 Fourth Prize Winner, who will receive $1,500 cash; 1 Honorary Native American Music Award; 1 Honorary Asian American Music Award; and 1 Honorary African-American Music Award. There will also be 5 Runners Up with the Runners Up each receiving $1,000 cash. No substitutions for any prizes can, or will be, made.

Tips "DO NOT PHOTOCOPY YOUR ENTRY FORM FOR SOMEONE ELSE, they must have their own contestant serial number on their application. Photocopies are only for you in other categories. Make sure you read the rules and prepare your recording properly. Judging has been configured so that all types of music DO have the same chance of winning this contest. Make sure that you can perform your song live and be prepared to come to do so."

COLUMBIA ENTERTAINMENT COMPANY'S JACKIE WHITE MEMORIAL PLAYWRITING CONTEST

309 Parkade Blvd., Columbia MO 65202. (573)874-5628. **Contact:** Betsy Phillips, contest director, CEC contest. For musical playwrights. Annual award.

Purpose "We are looking for top-notch scripts suitable for family audiences with 7 or more fully-developed roles."

Requirements "May be adaptations or plays with original story lines and cannot have been previously published. Please write or call for complete rules." Send SASE for application; then send scripts to address above. Full-length play, neatly typed. No name on title page, but name, address and name of play on a 3×5 index card and lead sheets, as well as tape of musical numbers. $20 entry fee.

Awards $500 1st Prize. Play may or may not be produced at discretion of CEC. "The judging committee is taken from members of Columbia Entertainment Company's Executive and Advisory boards, and from theater school parents. Readings by up to eight members, with at least three readings of all entries, and winning entries being read by entire committee. All plays will receive a written evaluation."

Tips "We especially like plays that deal with current day problems and concerns. However, if the play is good enough, any suitable subject matter is fine."

☑ CRS NATIONAL COMPOSERS COMPETITION

724 Winchester Rd., Broomall PA 19008. (610)544-5920. E-mail: crsnews@verizon.net. Web site: www.crsnews.org. **Contact:** Caroline Hunt, administrative assistant. Senior Representative: Jack Shusterman. Estab. 1981. For songwriters, composers and performing artists. College faculty and gifted artists. Annual award.

Requirements For composers, songwriters, performing artists and ensembles. The work submitted must be non-published (prior to acceptance) and not commercially recorded on any label. The work submitted must not exceed nine performers. Each composer may submit one work for each application submitted. (Taped performances are additionally encouraged.) Composition must not exceed twenty-five minutes in length. CRS reserves the right not to accept a First Prize Winner. Write with SASE for application or visit Web site. Add $3.50 for postage and handling. Deadline: December 10. Send a detailed résumé with application form available on our Web page. Samples of work required with application. Send score and parts with optional CD or DAT. Application fee: $50.

Awards 1st Prize: Commercial recording grant. Applications are judged by panel of judges determined each year.

CUNNINGHAM COMMISSION FOR YOUTH THEATRE

(formerly Cunningham Prize for Playwriting), The Theatre School at DePaul University, 2135 N. Kenmore Ave., Chicago IL 60614. (773)325-7938. Fax: (773)325-7920. E-mail: lgoetsch@depaul.e du. Web site: http://theatreschool.depaul.edu. **Contact:** Lara Goetsch, director of marketing/public relations. Estab. 1990. For playwrights. Annual award.

Purpose "The purpose of the Commission is to encourage the writing of dramatic works for young audiences that affirm the centrality of religion, broadly defined, and the human quest for meaning, truth, and community. The Theatre School intends to produce the plays created through this commission in its award-winning Chicago Playworks for Families and Young Audiences series at the historic Merle Reskin Theatre. Each year Chicago Playworks productions are seen by 35,000 students and families from throughout the Chicago area."

Requirements "Candidates for the commission must be writers whose residence is in the Chicago area, defined as within 100 miles of the Loop. Playwrights who have won the award within the last five years are not eligible. Deadline: annually by December 1. Candidates should submit a résumé, a 20 page sample of their work, and a brief statement about their interest in the commission. The submission should not include a proposal for a project the playwright would complete if awarded the commission. The writing sample may be from a play of any genre for any audience."

Awards $5,000. "Winners will be notified by May 1. The Selection Committee is chaired by the Dean of The Theatre School and is composed of members of the Cunningham Commission advisory committee and faculty of The Theatre School."

N DELTA OMICRON INTERNATIONAL COMPOSITION COMPETITION

12297 W. Tennessee Place, Lakewood CO 80228. (303)989-2871. E-mail: rbzdx@webtv.net. Web site: www.delta-omicron.org. **Composition Competition Chair:** Judith L. Eidson. For composers. Triennial award.

Purpose "To encourage composers worldwide to continually add to our wonderful heritage of musical creativity instrumentally and/or vocally."

Requirements People from college age on (or someone younger who is enrolled in college). Work must be unpublished and unperformed in public. "View our Web site (www.delta-omicron.org) for specific submission guidelines such as instrument selection and deadline Click on 'Composition Competition' on homepage." Manuscripts should be legibly written in ink or processed, signed with *nom de plume*, and free from any marks that would identify the composer to the judges. Entry fee: $25 per composition. Send for application. Composition is required with application. A total of three copies of composition are required, one for each judge. Music copies should *not* be spiral bound.

Awards 1st Place: $1,000 and world premiere at Delta Omicron Triennial Conference. Judged by 2-3 judges (performers, conductors, and/or composers).

N EUROPEAN INTERNATIONAL COMPETITION FOR COMPOSERS/IBLA FOUNDATION

226 E. 2nd St., Penthouse 6C, New York NY 10009. (212)387-0111. E-mail: iblanyc@aol.com. Web site: www.ibla.org. **Contact:** Mr. Gregory Naber, assistant director. Chairman: Dr. S. Moltisanti. Estab. 1995. For songwriters and composers. Annual award.

Purpose "To promote the winners' career through exposure, publicity, recordings with Athena Records and nationwide distribution with the Empire Group."

Requirements Deadline: April 30. Send for application. Samples of work are required with application.

Awards Winners are presented in concerts in Europe-Japan, USA.

N FULBRIGHT SCHOLAR PROGRAM, COUNCIL FOR INTERNATIONAL EXCHANGE OF SCHOLARS

3007 Tilden St. NW, Suite 5L, Washington DC 20008-3009. (202)686-7877. E-mail: scholars@cies.ii e.org. Web site: www.cies.org. Estab. 1946. For composers and academics. Annual award.

Purpose "Awards for university lecturing and advanced research abroad are offered annually in virtually all academic disciplines including musical composition."

Requirements "U.S. citizenship at time of application; M.F.A., Ph.D. or equivalent professional qualifications; for lecturing awards, university teaching experience (some awards are for professionals non-academic)." Applications become available in March each year, for grants to be taken up 1½ years later. Application deadlines: August 1, all world areas. Write or call for application. Samples of work are required with application.

Awards "Benefits vary by country, but generally include round-trip travel for the grantee and for most full academic-year awards, one dependent; stipend in U.S. dollars and/or local currency; in many countries, tuition allowance for school age children; and book and baggage allowance. Grant duration ranges from 3 months-1 academic year."

HARVEY GAUL COMPOSITION CONTEST

The Pittsburgh New Music Ensemble, Inc., P.O. Box 99476, Pittsburgh PA 15233. E-mail: pnme@pnme.org. Web site: www.pnme.org. **Contact:** Jeffrey Nytch, DMA, managing director. For composers. Biennial.

Purpose Objective is to encourage composition of new music.

Requirements "Must be citizen of the US. Please submit score and recording, if available (CDs only) of a representative instrumental score." Deadline: September 30, 2008. Send SASE for application or download from www.pnme.org. Samples of work are required with application. Entry fee: $20.

Awards Harvey Gaul Composition Contest: $6,000. Winner will receive commission for new work to be premiered by the PNME.

GRASSY HILL KERRVILLE NEW FOLK COMPETITION

(formerly New Folk Concerts For Emerging Songwriters), P.O. Box 291466, Kerrville TX 78029. (830)257-3600. Fax: (830)257-8680. E-mail: info@kerrville-music.com. Web site: www.kerrvillefolkfestival.com. **Contact:** Dalis Allen, producer. For songwriters. Annual award.

• Also see the listing for Kerrville Folk Festival in the Workshops section of this book.

Purpose "To provide an opportunity for unknown songwriters to be heard and rewarded for excellence."

Requirements Songwriter enters 2 original previously unrecorded songs on same side of rewound cassette tape, burned CD, or SonicBids, with entry fee; no more than one tape may be entered; 6-8 minutes total for 2 songs. No written application necessary; no lyric sheets or press material needed. Submissions accepted between December 1-March 15 or first 600 entries received prior to that date. Call or e-mail to request rules. Entry fee: $20.

Awards New Folk Award Winner. 32 finalists invited to sing the 2 songs entered during The Kerrville Folk Festival in May. 6 writers are chosen as award winners. Each of the 6 receives a cash award of $450 or more and performs at a winner's concert during the Kerrville Folk Festival i n June. Initial round of entries judged by the Festival Producer. 32 finalists judged by panel of 3 performer/songwriters.

Tips "Make certain cassette is rewound and ready to play. Do not allow instrumental accompaniment to drown out lyric content. Don't enter without complete copy of the rules. Former winners and finalists include Lyle Lovett, Nanci Griffith, Hal Ketchum, John Gorka, David Wilcox, Lucinda Williams and Robert Earl Keen, Tish Hinojosa, Carrie Newcomer, Jimmy Lafave, etc."

GREAT AMERICAN SONG CONTEST

PMB 135, 6327-C SW Capitol Hill Hwy., Portland OR 97239-1937. E-mail: info@GreatAmericanSong.com. Web site: www.GreatAmericanSong.com. **Contact:** Carla Starrett, event coordinator. Estab. 1998. For songwriters, composers and lyricists. Annual award.

• Also see the listing for Songwriters Resource Network in the Organizations section of this book.

Purpose To help songwriters get their songs heard by music-industry professionals; to generate educational and networking opportunities for participating songwriters; to help songwriters open doors in the music business.

Requirements Entry fee: $25. "Annual deadline. Check our Web site for details or send SASE along with your mailed request for information."

Awards Winners receive a mix of cash awards and prizes. The focus of the contest is on networking and educational opportunities. (All participants receive detailed evaluations of their songs by industry professionals.) Songs are judged by knowledgeable music-industry professionals, including prominent hit songwriters, producers and publishers.

Tips "Focus should be on the song. The quality of the demo isn't important. Judges will be looking for good songwriting talent. They will base their evaluations on the song—not the quality of the recording or the voice performance."

HENRICO THEATRE COMPANY ONE-ACT PLAYWRITING COMPETITION

P.O. Box 27032, Richmond VA 23273. (804)501-5115. Fax: (804)501-5284. E-mail: per22@co.henric o.va.us. **Contact:** Amy A. Perdue, cultural arts coordinator. Cultural Arts Assistant: Elaome Payne. For musical playwrights, songwriters, composers and performing artists. Annual award.

Purpose Original one-act musicals for a community theater organization.

Requirements "Only one-act plays or musicals will be considered. The manuscript should be a one-act original (not an adaptation), unpublished, and unproduced, free of royalty and copyright restrictions. Scripts with smaller casts and simpler sets may be given preference. Controversial themes and excessive language should be avoided. Standard play script form should be used. All plays will be judged anonymously; therefore, there should be two title pages; the first must contain the play's title and the author's complete address and telephone number. The second title page must contain only the play's title. The playwright must submit two excellent quality copies. Receipt of all scripts will be acknowledged by mail. Scripts will be returned if SASE is included. No scripts will be returned until after the winner is announced. The HTC does not assume responsibility for loss, damage or return of scripts. All reasonable care will be taken." Deadline: July 1st. Send for application first.

Awards 1st Prize $300; 2nd Prize $200; 3rd Prize $200.

☑ HOLTKAMP-AGO AWARD IN ORGAN COMPOSITION

American Guild of Organists, 475 Riverside Dr., Suite 1260, New York NY 10115. (212)870-2310. Fax: (212)870-2163. E-mail: info@agohq.org. Web site: www.agohq.org. **Contact:** Karen A. Rich, competitions coordinator. For composers and performing artists. Biennial award.

Requirements Organ solo, no longer than 8 minutes in duration. Specifics vary from year to year. Deadline: TBA, but usually early spring of odd-numbered year. Go to the Web site for application.

Award $2,000 provided by the Holtkamp Organ Company; publication by Hinshaw Music Inc.; performance at the biennial National Convention of the American Guild of Organists.

Ⓝ KATE NEAL KINLEY MEMORIAL FELLOWSHIP

University of Illinois, College of Fine and Applied Arts, 608 E. Lorado Taft Dr. #100, Champaign IL 61820. (217)333-1661. Web site: www.faa.uiuc.edu. **Contact:** Dr. Kathleen F. Conlin, chair. Estab. 1931. For students of architecture, art or music. Annual award.

Purpose The advancement of study in the fine arts.

Requirements "The Fellowship will be awarded upon the basis of unusual promise in the fine arts. Open to college graduates whose principal or major studies have been in the fields of architecture, art or music." Write or call for fall deadline. Send for application or call. Samples of work are required with application.

Awards "Two or three major Fellowships which yield the sum of $7,500 each which is to be used by the recipients toward defraying the expenses of advanced study of the fine arts in America or abroad." Good for 1 year. Grant is nonrenewable.

Ⓝ L.A. DESIGNERS' THEATRE MUSIC AWARDS

P.O. Box 1883, Studio City CA 91614-0883. (323)650-9600. Fax: (323)654-3210. E-mail: ladesigners @juno.com. Artistic Director: Richard Niederberg. For songwriters, composers, performing artists, musical playwrights and rights holders of music.

Purpose To produce new musicals, operettas, opera-boufes and plays with music, as well as new dance pieces with new music scores.

Requirements Submit nonreturnable cassette, tape, CD or any other medium by first or 4th class mail. *"We prefer proposals to scripts."* Acceptance: continuous. Submit nonreturnable materials with cover letter. No application form or fee is necessary.

Awards Music is commissioned for a particular project. Amounts are negotiable. Applications judged by our artistic staff.

☑ THE JOHN LENNON SONGWRITING CONTEST

180 Brighton Rd., Suite 801, Clifton NJ 07012. E-mail: info@jlsc.com. Web site: www.jlsc.com. Estab. 1996. For songwriters. Open year-round.

Purpose "The purpose of the John Lennon Songwriting Contest is to promote the art of songwriting by assisting in the discovery of new talent as well as providing more established songwriters with an opportunity to advance their careers."

Requirements Each entry must consist of the following: completed and signed application; audio cassette, CD or mp3 containing one song only, 5 minutes or less in length; lyric sheet typed or printed legibly (English translation is required when applicable); $30 entry fee. Deadline: December 15, 2006. Applications can be found in various music-oriented magazines and on our Web site. Prospective entrants can send for an application or contact the contest via e-mail at info@jlsc.com.

Awards Entries are accepted in the following 12 categories: rock, country, jazz, pop, world, gospel/inspirational, R&B, hip-hop, Latin, electronic, folk and children's music. Winners will receive EMI Publishing Contracts, Studio Equipment from Brian Moore Guitars, Roland, Edirol and Audio Technica, 1,000 CDs in full color with premium 6-panel Digipaks courtesy of Discmakers, and gift certificates from Musiciansfriend.com. One entrant wil be chosen to TOUR and PERFORM for one week on Warped Tour '06. One Lennon Award winning song will be named "Maxell Song of the Year" and take home an additional $20,000 in cash courtesy of the Maxell Corporation.

MAXIM MAZUMDAR NEW PLAY COMPETITION

One Curtain Up Alley, Buffalo NY 14202-1911. (716)852-2600. Fax: (716)852-2266. E-mail: newplays@alleyway.com. Web site: www.alleyway.com. **Contact:** Literary Manager. For musical playwrights. Annual award.

Purpose Alleyway Theatre is dedicated to the development and production of new works. Winners of the competition will receive production and royalties.

Requirements Unproduced full-length work not less than 90 minutes long with cast limit of 10 and unit or simple set, or unproduced one-act work less than 15 minutes long with cast limit of 6 and simple set; prefers work with unconventional setting that explores the boundaries of theatricality; limit of 1 submission in each category; guidelines available, no entry form. $25 playwright entry fee. Script, résumé, SASE optional. Cassette mandatory. Deadline: July 1.

Awards Production for full-length play or musical with royalty and travel and housing determined on a yearly basis; and production for one-act play or musical.

Tips "Entries may be of any style, but preference will be given to those scripts which take place in unconventional settings and explore the boundaries of theatricality. No more than ten performers is a definite, unchangeable requirement."

MID-ATLANTIC SONG CONTEST

Songwriters' Association of Washington, PMB 106-137, 4200 Wisconsin Ave., NW, Washington DC 20016. (301)654-8434. E-mail: masc@saw.org. Web site: www.saw.org. For songwriters and composers. Estab. 1982. Annual award.

● Also see the listing for Songwriters Association of Washington in the Organizations section.

Purpose This is one of the longest-running contests in the nation; SAW has organized twenty contests since 1982. The competition is designed to afford rising songwriters in a wide variety of genres the opportunity to receive awards and exposure in an environment of peer competition.

Requirements Amateur status is important. Applicants should request a brochure/application using the contact information above. Rules and procedures are clearly explained in that brochure. Cassette or CD and 3 copies of the lyrics are to be submitted with an application form and fee for each entry. Beginning this year, online enteries will also be accepted. Reduced entry fees are offered to members of Songwriters' Association of Washington; membership can be arranged simultaneously with entering. Multie-song discounts are also offered. Applications are mailed out and posted on their Web site around June 1; the submission deadline is usually sometime in mid-August; awards are typically announced late in the fall.

Awards The two best songs in each of ten categories win prize packages donated by the contest's corporate sponsors: Writer's Digest Books, BMI, Oasis CD Manufacturing, Omega Recording Studios, TAXI, Mary Cliff and Sonic Bids. Winning songwriters are invited to perform in Washington, DC at the Awards Ceremony Gala, and the twenty winning songs are included on a compilation CD. The best song in each category is eligible for three grand cash prizes. Certificates are awarded to other entries meriting honorable mention.

Tips "Enter the song in the most appropriate category. Make the sound recording the best it can be (even though judges are asked to focus on melody and lyric and not on production.) Avoid clichés, extended introductions, and long instrumental solos."

THELONIOUS MONK INTERNATIONAL JAZZ COMPOSERS COMPETITION

(Sponsored by BMI) Thelonious Monk Institute of Jazz, 5225 Wisconsin Ave. NW, #605, Washington DC 20015. (202)364-7272. Fax: (202)364-0176. E-mail: lebrown@tmonkinst.org. Web site: www.monkinstitute.org. **Contact:** Leonard Brown, program director. Estab. 1993. For songwriters and composers. Annual award.

Purpose The award is given to an aspiring jazz composer who best demonstrates originality, creativity and excellence in jazz composition.

Requirements Deadline: July 17. Send for application. Submission must include application form, résumé of musical experience, CD or cassette, entry, four copies of the full score, and a photo. The composition features a different instrument each year. Entry fee: $35.

Awards $10,000. Applications are judged by panel of jazz musicians. "The Institute will provide piano, bass, guitar, drum set, tenor saxophone, and trumpet for the final performance. The winner will be responsible for the costs of any different instrumentation included in the composition."

☑ NACUSA YOUNG COMPOSERS' COMPETITION

Box 49256 Barrington Station, Los Angeles CA 90049. (310)838-4465. E-mail: nacusa@music-usa.org. Web site: www.music-usa.org/nacusa. **Contact:** Daniel Kessner, president, NACUSA. Estab. 1978. For composers. Annual award.

- Also see the National Association of Composers/USA (NACUSA) listing in the Organization section.

Purpose To encourage the composition of new American concert hall music.

Requirements Entry fee: $20 (membership fee). Deadline: October 30. Send for application. Samples are not required.

Awards 1st Prize: $400; 2nd Prize: $100; and possible Los Angeles performances. Applications are judged by a committee of experienced NACUSA composer members.

SAMMY NESTICO AWARD/USAF BAND AIRMEN OF NOTE

201 McChord St., Bolling AFB, Washington DC 20032-0202. (202)767-1756. Fax: (202)767-0686. E-mail: alan.baylock@bolling.af.mil. **Contact:** Alan Baylock, master sergeant. Estab. 1995. For composers. Annual award.

Purpose To carry on the tradition of excellence of Sammy Nestico's writing through jazz composition. The winner will have their composition performed by the USAF Airmen of Note, have it professionally recorded and receive a $1,000 follow up commission for a second work.

Requirements Unpublished work for jazz ensemble instrumentation (5,4,4,4) style, form and length are unrestricted. Deadline: October 2, 2006. Send for application. Samples of work are required with full score and set of parts (or CD recording).

Awards Performance by the USAF Band Airmen of Note; expense paid travel to Washington, DC for the performance; professionally produced recording of the winning composition; and $1,000 follow up commission for second work. Applications are judged by panel of musicians.

☑ NSAI/CMT ANNUAL SONG CONTEST

1710 Roy Acuff Place, Nashville TN 37203. (615)256-3354. Fax: (615)256-0034. E-mail: songcontest@nashvillesongwriters.com. Web site: www.nashvillesongwriters.com. **Contact:** Deanie Williams, director. Annual award for songwriters.

Purpose "A chance for aspiring songwriters to be heard by music industry decision makers. Winners are flown to Nashville for a recording session and an appointment with Music Row executives."

Susan Greenbaum

*Singer-songwriter scores
double contest win*

Singer-songwriter Susan Greenbaum, from Richmond, Virginia, scored a double win in the 2006 Mid-Atlantic Song Contest (sponsored by Songwriter's Association of Washington), winning both First and Second Place Overall for two radically different songs—"Spin Like A Top," a driving pop song dedicated to a series of unscrupulous club owners, and "You Are My Holiday," a non-denominational holiday song (winners of First and Second Place, respectively). But this success is just her latest accomplishment.

Following the loss of one of her three brothers to cancer, Greenbaum decided life was too short and gave up her job as an executive at a Fortune 500 company to pursue music as an independent singer-songwriter. By 2000, she had achieved enough success as an independent artist to forgo any day job at all, and she now has three independently-released albums to her credit (with a fourth on the way), each selling well enough by her own efforts to be profitable.

She has won Finalist awards in the John Lennon Songwriting Contest and the U.S.A. Songwriting Contest, and also won a slot opening 10 concerts for singer-songwriter Jewel through an online contest sponsored by Jewel's management (judged by music industry professionals and online voters). "Spin Like A Top" has also received positive reviews in the "Singles" column of *Billboard* magazine. (Visit her Web site at www.susangreenbaum.com.)

Here she reflects on her Mid-Atlantic Song Contest win and offers advice on developing a wide-ranging level of songwriting craft.

The world of professional songwriting is extremely competitive, so what kind of steps have you taken to enhance your craft and find such success?
I basically just try to let my work and my performances speak for themselves, and I've been very fortunate to do well enough in a couple of contests. When I very first started to try this out, I entered the John Lennon Songwriting Contest and was a finalist in the Folk category, and that was exciting because I had never entered any contests like that before. I've never taken a songwriting class. I've never done anything like that or gone to any seminars or anything. I've always been a writer and majored in English in college, but I really came to songwriting pretty late, and I think the best I've done is just to always listen to really good songwriters.

At the song contest awards gala you performed your winning songs on acoustic guitar, and the songs still came across even without the additional production on the demos, which in the case of "Spin Like A Top" was quite elaborate. How do you get a song to transfer credibly from an acoustic guitar presentation

to an aggressive pop arrangement? Should a songwriter be able to perform the lyrics and melody of a song *a capella* and still have it work?

I think you should be able to do that with a song. *A capella* is a little extreme, just because it's nice to have the chordal framework of a guitar or piano or whatever, just to give a context to some degree melodically, but I think it's much more important that a song have good melody and lyrics than they have a fabulous arrangement. Because as long as you have a great foundation of a good lyric and a good melody, you can come up with a whole bunch of different arrangements that will really show off the song—as long as it's worth being shown off!

How did it feel to win both the First and Second Place Overall awards, considering each of the winning songs were so different? Has it always been your aspiration to write for multiple styles and genres?

According to the [contest director Jean Bayou], there was quite a struggle among the judges, because they were having a hard time choosing between the Second and First Place songs. It was quite a shock to me when it turned out I had won First Place as well, and she said that it was an even bigger shock to the judges, because they didn't have any idea it was the same person who sang both songs! It was the wildest thing, and I think it was because the songs are so dramatically different in style and tone. Everything about the two songs is different from one another. One of the things I feel is not good about some of the music the big companies play on the radio, is that they all sound the same, and I pride myself on being able to write across a variety of styles and across a variety of emotions.

Was it unusual for you to perform in an acoustic format? Do you usually have a backup band?

I perform in all ways. I have a band, but I also perform solo. I perform in a duo with my husband who plays percussion and also plays drums in the band. So, it's nice to be flexible, and that's another great way if you're talking about being competitive. If you can provide a potential customer, not necessarily a songwriting customer, but a person who needs a performer, you can say, well, if you're budget is only this much, I can play solo. If your budget is this much, I can bring a band. To have that flexibility in format is really helpful.

Were these the only two songs you submitted to the contest?

I submitted several others and wound up winning seven awards overall, two of which were Gold Awards that resulted in the two First and Second Place Overall winners. I think I had two songs that were Honorable Mentions, and three songs that were Finalists, as well as the two songs that won Gold [in their categories].

How did you go about choosing which songs to send in?

I looked at how much it was going to cost! [laughs] That was honestly a big part of it. I think that's the only thing that limits a songwriter in selecting songs, is that generally songwriters generally don't have a lot of spare cash lying around, so they can't necessarily enter everything that they like. I also went with songs that have been particularly well received by my audiences, and also just songs that I feel really good about. As far as the holiday song goes, I had never entered that one in a contest before, partly because it's pretty new, and partly because it struck me when I was reading the rules for this contest, that they dictated the Open category included holiday songs. I thought, "Oh, I have a holiday song!" And so that was what motivated me to do that, and that was very fun. I thought, "Well, that's a neat category to have, because not every song fits snugly into these categories."

What was the inspiration behind "You Are My Holiday"?

We have a wonderful radio DJ here in Richmond named Bill Bevins, who is the morning show guy on a Clear Channel station. He has the number one morning drive show here in the city, and he has been remarkably good to us. He had us come in a couple years ago in 2001, and I wrote a special song because it was the first holiday season following 9/11. And then last year, he asked us to come back and this was my first holiday season as a married person. My husband is Methodist and I'm Jewish, and so sometimes that can be troublesome for people, but certainly isn't for us. What we choose to do is merge our traditions and teach other about our respective religions. And so I wrote the song as kind of a holiday present to my husband, where I'm saying, "You are my holiday, and this is how we'll celebrate." And a lot of people have contacted me about it because either they have interfaith marriages, or they have family members who are married to someone of another faith, and they really love it because it gives them a context for their own celebration.

Tell me about the writing of "Spin Like A Top" and what led to the decision to produce it in that aggressive pop style rather than acoustic.

I wrote that song actually a long time ago and let it sit around for a while. I wrote it when I first started playing in Richmond, and had been playing solo for maybe six or seven months. It's very hard when you first start out to get people to give you a chance. There are amazing, wonderful club owners, and then there are less wonderful club owners [laughs], and I had mostly good experiences, but also some experiences with two club owners in particular who cheated me. And I immortalized my anger in song, changed their names enough so nobody would know who it was, and turned them into much more diabolical characters than they are in real life, just to make it a more powerful song. And I wasn't necessarily trying to send a message to them or anything, because they wouldn't even know it was about them.

But, I knew it was going to have two different tempos, because of the way the song was structured in my head, the rhythmic feel of the verse versus the rhythmic feel of the chorus. After several years of having the song sitting around and occasionally performing it, it was time to record our next disc. I work with a guy who is absolutely a brilliant producer and engineer, named John Morand, and he co-owns a studio called Sound of Music Studios here in Richmond with David Lowery of Cracker. He really has a knack for knowing how to translate what I'm thinking in terms of a song style into what it actually has the potential to become. Neither one of us wanted it to be an acoustic kind of number, but I think he took it to the ultimate level.

Would you say your win validated the level of craft you have developed?

Without question. I was just going to say I was overjoyed to win because it is this incredible validation, not only publicly and in front of a whole bunch of people who clearly have a respect for songwriting. But also, to get money and a really tangible prize for writing a good song is tremendous. I'm fortunate to make money selling my CDs, which of course is a way of making money from songwriting, but to just unabashedly win a big pile of money for a song that people thought was a really good song—holy guacamole! It's the greatest feeling. It was a huge honor. It was a great night.

—*Ian Bessler*

Requirements Entry fee: $45 for one entry; $60 for 2. In order to be eligible contestants must not be receiving income from any work submitted—original material only. Submissions must include both lyrics and melody. Deadline is different each year; check Web site or send for application. Samples are required with application in the format of cassette or CD.

Awards Varies from year to year; check Web site.

PLAYHOUSE ON THE SQUARE NEW PLAY COMPETITION

51 S. Cooper, Memphis TN 38104. (901)725-0776. **Contact:** Jackie Nichols, executive director. For musical playwrights. Annual award. Estab. 1983.

Requirements Send script, tape and SASE. "Playwrights from the South will be given preference." Open to full-length, unproduced plays. Musicals must be fully arranged for piano when received. Deadline: April 1.

Awards Grants may be renewed. Applications judged by 3 readers.

✓ PORTLAND SONGWRITERS ASSOCIATION ANNUAL SONGWRITING COMPETITION

P.O. Box 42389, Portland OR 97242. (503)914-1000. E-mail: info@portlandsongwriters.org. Web site: www.portlandsongwriters.org. Estab. 1991. For songwriters and composers. Annual award.

Purpose To provide opportunities for songwriters to improve their skills in the art and craft of songwriting, to connect our performing songwriters with the public through PSA sponsored venues and to create a presence and an avenue of approach for members' songs to be heard by industry professionals.

Requirements For information, send SASE. All amateur songwriters may enter. Deadline: September 30 postmark. Entry fee: $15 members; $20 nonmembers.

Awards Multiple awards totaling $1,000 in prizes. All songs will be reviewed by at least three qualified judges, including industry pros. Finalists may have their songs reviewed by celebrity judges.

PULITZER PRIZE IN MUSIC

709 Journalism Building, Columbia University, New York NY 10027. (212)854-3841. Fax: (212)854-3342. E-mail: pulitzer@www.pulitzer.org. Web site: www.pulitzer.org. **Contact:** Music Secretary. For composers and musical playwrights. Annual award.

Requirements "For distinguished musical composition by an American that has had its first performance or recording in the United States during the year." Entries should reflect current creative activity. Works that receive their American premiere between January 16, 2006 and January 15, 2007 are eligible. A public performance or the public release of a recording shall constitute a premiere. Deadline: January 15. Samples of work are required with application, biography and photograph of composer, date and place of performance, score or manuscript and recording of the work, entry form and $50 entry fee.

Awards "One award: $10,000. Applications are judged first by a nominating jury, then by the Pulitzer Prize Board."

✓ ROCKY MOUNTAIN FOLKS FESTIVAL SONGWRITER SHOWCASE

Planet Bluegrass, ATTN: Songwriter Showcase, P.O. Box 769, Lyons CO 80540. (800)624-2422 or (303)823-0848. Fax: (303)823-0849. E-mail: emily@bluegrass.com. Web site: www.bluegrass.com. **Contact:** Steve Szymanski, director. Estab. 1993. For songwriters, composers and performers. Annual award.

Purpose Award based on having the best song and performance.

Requirements Deadline: June 30. Finalists notified by July 14. Rules available on Web site. Samples of work are required with application. Send CD or cassette with $10/song entry fee. Can now submit online: www.sonicbids.com/rockymountainfolk06. Contestants cannot be signed to a major label or publishing deal. No backup musicians allowed.

Awards 1st Place is a 2006 Festival Main Stage set, custom Hayes Guitar, $100, and a free one song drumoverdubs (http://www.drumoverdubs.com) certificate (valued at $300); 2nd Place is

Contests & Awards

$500 and a Baby Taylor Guitar; 3rd Place is $400 and a Baby Taylor Guitar; 4th Place is $300; 5th Place is $200; 6th to 10th Place is $100 each. Each finalist will also receive a complimentary three-day Folks Festival pass that includes onsite camping, and a Songwriter In The Round slot during the Festival on our workshop stage.

☑ RICHARD RODGERS AWARDS

American Academy of Arts and Letters, 633 W. 155th St., New York NY 10032. (212)368-5900. **Contact:** Jane Bolster, coordinator. Estab. 1978. Deadline: November 1, 2006. "The Richard Rodgers Awards subsidize staged reading, studio productions, and full productions by nonprofit theaters in New York City of works by composers and writers who are not already established in the field of musical theater. The awards are only for musicals—songs by themselves are not eligible. The authors must be citizens or permanent residents of the United States." Guidelines for this award may be obtained by sending a SASE to above address or download from www.arts andletters.org.

ROME PRIZE COMPETITION FELLOWSHIP

American Academy in Rome, 7 E. 60th St., New York NY 10022-1001. (212)751-7200. Fax: (212)751-7220. E-mail: info@aarome.org. Web site: www.aarome.org. **Contact:** Programs Department. For composers. Annual award.

Purpose "Rome Prize Competition winners pursue independent projects."

Requirements "Applicants for 11-month fellowships must hold a bachelor's degree in music, musical composition or its equivalent." Deadline: November 1. Entry fee: $25. Application guidelines are available to download through the Academy's Web site.

Awards "Up to two fellowships are awarded annually. Fellowship stipend is $21,000 for 11-months, and includes room and board, and a study or studio at Academy facilities in Rome. In all cases, excellence is the primary criterion for selection, based on the quality of the materials submitted. Winners are announced in mid-April."

☑ TELLURIDE TROUBADOUR CONTEST

Planet Bluegrass, ATTN: Troubadour Competition, P.O. Box 769, Lyons CO 80540. (303)823-0848 or (800)624-2422. Fax: (303)823-0849. E-mail: emily@bluegrass.com. Web site: www.bluegrass.com. **Contact:** Steve Szymanski, director. Estab. 1991. For songwriters, composers and performers. Annual award.

Purpose Award based on having best song and performance.

Requirements Deadline: must be postmarked by April 28; notified May 12, if selected. Rules available on Web site. Send cassette or CD and $10/song entry fee (limit of 2 songs). Can now submit music online at www.sonicbids.com/telluride2006. Contestants cannot be signed to a major label or publishing deal. No backup musicians allowed.

Awards 1st: custom Shanti Guitar, $200 and Festival Main Stage Set; 2nd: $400, "Limo" portable amplifier, and Little Martin guitar; 3rd: $300 and Little Martin guitar; 4th: $200 and Little Martin guitar; 5th: $100 and Baby Taylor guitar. Applications judged by panel of judges.

THE TEN-MINUTE MUSICALS PROJECT

P.O. Box 461194, West Hollywood CA 90046. Web site: www.tenminutemusicals.org. **Contact:** Michael Koppy, producer. For songwriters, composers and musical playwrights. Annual award.

Purpose "We are building a full-length stage musical comprised of complete short musicals, each of which play for between 8-14 minutes. Award is $250 for each work chosen for development towards inclusion in the project, plus a share of royalties when produced."

Requirements Deadline: August 31. Write for guidelines. Final submission should include script, cassette or CD, and lead sheets.

Awards $250 for each work selected. "Works should have complete stories, with a definite beginning, middle and end."

U.S.-JAPAN CREATIVE ARTISTS EXCHANGE FELLOWSHIP PROGRAM

Japan-U.S. Friendship Commission, 1201 15th St. NW, Suite 330, Washington DC 20005. (202)653-9800. Fax: (202)653-9802. E-mail: jusfc@jusfc.gov. Web site: www.jusfc.gov. **Contact:** Margaret Mihozi, assistant executive director. Estab. 1980. For all creative artists. Annual award.

Purpose "For artists to go as seekers, as cultural visionaries, and as living liaisons to the traditional and contemporary life of Japan."

Requirements "Artists' works must exemplify the best in U.S. arts." Deadline: Feb. 1, 2007. Send for application and guidelines. Applications available via Internet. Samples of work are required with application. Requires 2 pieces on CD, DVD, or videotape, cued to the 3-5 minute section to be reviewed.

Awards Five artists are awarded a 5 month residency anywhere in Japan. Awards monthly stipend for living expenses, housing and professional support services; up to $6,000 for pre-departure costs, including such items as language training and economy class roundtrip airfare, plus . Residency is good for 1 year. Applications are judged by a panel of previous recipients of the awards plus 600,000 yen for monthly living expenses, housing allowance, and professional support services, as well as other arts professionals with expertise in Japanese culture.

Tips "Applicants should anticipate a highly rigorous review of their artistry and should have compelling reasons for wanting to work in Japan."

U.S.A. SONGWRITING COMPETITION

4331 N. Federal Hwy., Suite 403A, Ft. Lauderdale FL 33308. (954)776-1577. Fax: (954)776-1132. E-mail: info@songwriting.net. Web site: www.songwriting.net. **Contact:** Contest Manager. Estab. 1994. For songwriters, composers, performing artists and lyricists. Annual award.

Purpose "To honor good songwriters/composers all over the world, especially the unknown ones."

Requirements Open to professional and beginner songwriters. No limit on entries. Each entry must include an entry fee, a cassette tape of song(s) and lyric sheet(s). Judged by music industry representatives. Past judges have included record label representatives and publishers from Arista Records, EMI and Warner/Chappell. Deadline: To be announced. Entry fee: To be announced. Send SASE with request or e-mail for entry forms at any time. Samples of work are not required.

Awards Prizes include cash and merchandise in 15 different categories: pop, rock, country, Latin, R&B, gospel, folk, jazz, "lyrics only" category, instrumental and many others.

Tips "Judging is based on lyrics, originality, melody and overall composition. CD quality production is great but not a consideration in judging."

UNISONG INTERNATIONAL SONG CONTEST

5198 Arlington Ave., PMB 513, Riverside CA 92504. (213)673-4067. E-mail: entry@unisong.com. Web site: www.unisong.com. Founders: Alan Roy Scott and David Stark. London office: P.O. Box 13383, London, NW3 5ZR United Kingdom. (44)(0208)387-9293. Estab. 1997. For songwriters, composers and lyricists. Annual songwriting contest.

Purpose "Unisong was created by songwriters for songwriters."

Requirements Send for an entry form or request one by phone or e-mail. Download entry form from Web site or enter online. Send cassette or CD only. No DATs. Entries also accepted via MP3.

Awards Over $50,000 in cash and prizes. Grand Prize winner to write with professional writers and artists through Music Bridges Around The World. Songs judged on song quality only, not demo.

Tips "Please make sure your song is professionally presented. Make sure lyrics are typed or printed clearly. Print your personal information clearly. Enter your song in the most appropriate categories."

Y.E.S. FESTIVAL OF NEW PLAYS

Northern Kentucky University Dept. of Theatre, FA-205, Highland Heights KY 41099-1007. (859)572-6303. Fax: (859)572-6057. E-mail: forman@nku.edu. **Contact:** Sandra Forman, project director. Estab. 1983. For musical playwrights. Biennial award (odd numbered years).

Purpose "The festival seeks to encourage new playwrights and develop new plays and musicals. Three plays or musicals are given full productions."

Requirements "No entry fee. Submit a script with a completed entry form. Musicals should be submitted with a piano/conductor's score and a vocal parts score. Scripts may be submitted May 1 through Sept. 30, 2006, for the New Play Festival occuring April 2007. Send for application."

Awards Three awards of $500. "The winners are brought to NKU at our expense to view late rehearsals and opening night." Submissions are judged by a panel of readers.

Tips "Plays/musicals which have heavy demands for mature actors are not as likely to be selected as an equally good script with roles for 18-30 year olds."

Organizations

O ne of the first places a beginning songwriter should look for guidance and support is a songwriting organization. Offering encouragement, instruction, contacts and feedback, these groups of professional and amateur songwriters can help an aspiring songwriter hone the skills needed to compete in the ever-changing music industry.

The type of organization you choose to join depends on what you want to get out of it. Local groups can offer a friendly, supportive environment where you can work on your songs and have them critiqued in a constructive way by other songwriters. They're also great places to meet collaborators. Larger, national organizations can give you access to music business professionals and other songwriters across the country.

Most of the organizations listed in this book are non-profit groups with membership open to specific groups of people—songwriters, musicians, classical composers, etc. They can be local groups with a membership of less than 100 people, or large national organizations with thousands of members from all over the country. In addition to regular meetings, most organizations occasionally sponsor events such as seminars and workshops to which music industry personnel are invited to talk about the business, and perhaps listen to and critique demo tapes.

Check the following listings, bulletin boards at local music stores and your local newspapers for area organizations. If you are unable to locate an organization within an easy distance of your home, you may want to consider joining one of the national groups. These groups, based in New York, Los Angeles and Nashville, keep their members involved and informed through newsletters, regional workshops and large yearly conferences. They can help a writer who feels isolated in his hometown get his music heard by professionals in the major music centers.

In the following listings, organizations describe their purpose and activities, as well as how much it costs to join. Before joining any organization, consider what they have to offer and how becoming a member will benefit you. To locate organizations close to home, see the Geographic Index at the back of this book.

N AARON ENTERPRISES SONGWRITERS GROUP

4411 Red Gate Dr., Disputanta VA 23842. (804)733-5908. **Contact:** Cham Laughlin, founder. Estab. 1997. ''Songwriters of all ages, all styles and all skill levels are welcome to join. Applicants must have an interest in songwriting—music writing, lyric writing or co-writing. The main purpose of this organization is to educate songwriters about the business of songwriting, the art and craft of songwriting, lyric writing and structure, musical composition, song structure or arranging and professional presentation of your songs.'' Offers newsletter, evaluation services, seminars, discounts on demos and leads to publishers. Applications accepted year-round. Membership fee: $25/ year with discounts for multiple years.

Tips ''Networking is a very important part of this business. Members are offered a large amount of information and that information is explained to them through free seminars, the newsletter or one-on-one phone consultations to ensure the best possible support network for their songwriting careers.''

ACADEMY OF COUNTRY MUSIC

4100 W. Alameda Ave., Suite 208, Burbank CA 91505. (818)842-8400. Fax: (818)842-8535. E-mail: info@acmcountry.com. Web site: www.acmcountry.com. **Contact:** Bob Romeo, executive director. Estab. 1964. Serves country music industry professionals. Eligibility for professional members is limited to those individuals who derive some portion of their income directly from country music. Each member is classified by one of the following categories: artist/entertainer, club/venue operator, musician, on-air personality, manager, talent agent, composer, music publisher, public relations, publications, radio, TV/motion picture, record company, talent buyer or affiliated (general). The purpose of ACM is to promote and enhance the image of country music. The Academy is involved year-round in activities important to the country music community. Some of these activities include charity fund-raisers, participation in country music seminars, talent contests, artist showcases, assistance to producers in placing country music on television and in motion pictures and backing legislation that benefits the interests of the country music community. The ACM is governed by directors and run by officers elected annually. Applications are accepted throughout the year. Membership is $75/year.

N ALABAMA SONGWRITER'S GUILD

201 Bangor Cemetery Rd., Hayden AL 35079. (256)352-4873. **''Please restrict phone calls to between 9:00 a.m. and 5:00 p.m. Central Standard Time!''** E-mail: lithics@localnet.com. **Contact:** Dennis N. Kahler. Estab. 1992. ''The Alabama Songwriter's Guild is comprised of songwriters and their supporters, with no restrictions. We have members who are just beginning to write, and others who have number one hits under their belts on the Billboard charts. We welcome all genres of songwriting, and count several non-writers as members of our network efforts. The main purpose of the ASG is to help link Alabama and outside songwriters to information on seminars, showcases, publishing and song-plugging opportunities, local associations, workshops, and other events from one end of the state to the other. We help spread word of the induction ceremonies and other events at the Alabama Music Hall of Fame, report on the annual Frank Brown International Songwriter's Festival in Gulf Shores/Orange Beach every November, and help link writers together with like-minded individuals for co-writes. Any purpose that serves the songwriter is of interest to us.'' Queries welcomed anytime.

Tips ''Networking is crucial! Wherever you live, develop your network. If you need songwriting contacts in Alabama, contact us.''

ALL SONGWRITERS NETWORK (ASN)

(formerly American Songwriters Network), Dept A95, Box 23912, Ft. Lauderdale FL 33307. (954)537-3463. E-mail: asn@tiac.net. Web site: http://home.tiac.net/~asn. **Contact:** Network Manager. Estab. 1995. Serves ''professional level songwriters/composers with monthly music industry leads tipsheet. The tipsheet includes the most current listing of producers, A&R managers, record labels, entertainment attorneys, agents and publishing companies looking for specific ma-

terial for their projects/albums. Any songwriter from any part of the country or world can be a member of this organization. The purpose of this organization is to foster a better professional community by helping members to place their songs." Membership fee: $140/year.
Tips "Please send SASE or e-mail for application form."

✓ ☐ AMERICAN COMPOSERS FORUM

332 Minnesota St., Suite E-145, St. Paul MN 55101. (651)251-2824. Fax: (651)291-7978. Web site: www.composersforum.org. **Contact:** Wendy Collins, member services manager. Estab. 1973. "The American Composers Forum links communities with composers and performers, encouraging the making, playing and enjoyment of new music. Building two-way relationships between artists and the public, the Forum develops programs that educate today's and tomorrow's audiences, energize composers' and performers' careers, stimulate entrepreneurship and collaboration, promote musical creativity, and serve as models of effective support for the arts. Programs include residencies, fellowships, commissions, producing and performance opportunities, a recording assistance program and a widely-distributed recording label. The Forum's members, more than 1,200 strong, live in 49 states and 16 countries; membership is open to all." Membership dues: Regular (U.S.): $55; Student/Senior (U.S.): $35; Regular (Outside U.S.): $65; Student/Senior (Outside U.S.): $45.

AMERICAN MUSIC CENTER, INC.

30 W. 26th St., Suite 1001, New York NY 10010-2011. (212)366-5260. Fax: (212)366-5265. E-mail: center@amc.net. Web site: www.amc.net. **Contact:** Membership Department. The American Music Center, founded by a consortium led by Aaron Copland in 1939, is the first-ever national service and information center for new classical music and jazz by American composers. The Center has a variety of innovative new programs and services, including a montly Internet magazine (www.newmusicbox.org) for new American music, online databases of contemporary ensembles and ongoing opportunities for composers, an online catalog of new music for educators specifically targeted to young audiences, a series of professional development workshops, and an online library (www.newmusicjukebox.org). Each month, AMC provides its over 2,500 members with a listing of opportunities including calls for scores, competitions, and other new music performance information. Each year, AMC's Information Services Department fields thousands of requests concerning composers, performers, data, funding, and support programs. The AMC Collection at the New York Public Library for the Performing Arts presently includes over 60,000 scores and recordings, many unavailable elsewhere. "AMC also continues to administer several grant programs: the Aaron Copland Fund for Music; the Henry Cowell Performance Incentive Fund; and its own programs Live Music for Dance and the Composer Assistance Program." Members also receive a link their Web sites on www.amc.net. The American Music Center is not-for-profit and has an annual membership fee.

AMERICAN SOCIETY OF COMPOSERS, AUTHORS AND PUBLISHERS (ASCAP)

One Lincoln Plaza, New York NY 10023. (212)621-6000 (administration); (212)621-6240 (membership). E-mail: info@ascap.com. Web site: www.ascap.com. President and Chairman of the Board: Marilyn Bergman. CEO: John LoFrumento. Executive Vice President/Membership: Todd Brabec. **Contact:** Member Services at (800)95-ASCAP. **Regional offices—West Coast:** 7920 Sunset Blvd., 3rd Floor, Los Angeles CA 90046, (323)883-1000; **Nashville:** 2 Music Square W., Nashville TN 37203, (615)742-5000; **Chicago:** 1608 N. Milwaukee Ave., Suite 1007, Chicago IL 60647, (773)394-4286; **Atlanta:** PMB 400-541 10th St. NW, Atlanta GA 30318, (404)351-1224; **Florida:** 420 Lincoln Rd., Suite 385, Miami Beach FL 33139, (305)673-3446; **United Kingdom:** 8 Cork St., London W1S 3LJ England, 011-44-207-439-0909; **Puerto Rico:** 654 Ave. Munoz Rivera, IBM Plaza Suite 1101 B, Hato Rey, Puerto Rico 00918, (787)281-0782. ASCAP is a membership association of over 240,000 composers, lyricists, songwriters, and music publishers, whose function is to protect the rights of its members by licensing and collecting royalties for the nondramatic public performance of their copyrighted works. ASCAP licensees include radio, television, cable, live concert promoters, bars, restaurants, symphony orchestras, new media, and other users of music. ASCAP is the leading performing rights society in the world. All revenues, less operating expenses, are distributed to members (about 86 cents of each dollar). ASCAP was the first US performing rights organization

Shawn Murphy

ASCAP Helps Build Music Careers

Y ou've heard the acronyms bandied about in musical circles—ASCAP, BMI, SESAC. You know they have something to do with songs and music but may not be sure how they fit in to your quest to become a successful songwriter. Don't let those confusing acronyms intimidate you—these organizations exist to help you, as a songwriter, composer, or lyricist, receive the royalties you deserve.

ASCAP, which stands for "American Society of Composers, Authors and Publishers," has over 240,000 members in the United States. It's been around since 1914 and is home to some of the biggest names in songwriting history—Duke Ellington, George Gershwin, Bruce Springsteen, Madonna, Dr. Dre, and Wynton Marsalis are just a few of ASCAP's many members. ASCAP works as an advocate for its members by licensing and distributing royalties for public performances of their work. Was your song played on the radio or in another public forum? If you're a member, ASCAP will make sure you get paid.

But ASCAP does more than just collect royalties. They keep on top of copyright laws to ensure that songwriters are fairly represented when new laws are introduced. They provide educational opportunities as well as workshops and showcases for members throughout the country. And the folks at ASCAP actively work with songwriters and artists to help them set up the necessary foundations needed for a successful career.

One such person is Shawn Murphy, director of membership in ASCAP's Chicago office. He is instrumental in discovering new songwriters and artists and helping them get their careers off the ground. Shawn comes from a musical family—his father, Ralph Murphy, was the largest independent music publisher in Nashville for about 10 years, and his mother, Anne, worked in music publishing as well. So it's only natural that Murphy ended up on the publishing end of the music business.

Murphy's main function at ASCAP is to find songwriters who have the potential for commercial success and help them get their publishing and copyrights in order. "I also help to facilitate the careers of the writers that I work with through our showcases and workshops and by plugging them into opportunities in our other offices," he says. "ASCAP can be a very powerful organization when it comes to getting a writer's or artist's career off the ground.

"The most basic way I can describe what ASCAP does is that we make sure a songwriter gets paid when his or her song is played on radio or television," he continues. "That description leaves out so many of the vital functions that ASCAP performs, but it at least gives writers an idea of what the society is all about. The entire music business is based on the idea of 'publishing' or putting out music for public consumption. Every aspect of the industry, from putting out records to playing live shows to getting placements in film and television, is about publishing music. What writers must understand is how they are paid for all those different usages."

The first thing Murphy looks for when asked for help from a writer is to ask if the writer has been "published," which basically means that he or she has to have a song that is out for public consumption. "That means it has been performed live in a venue, put out on record, played on the radio or TV, published as sheet music, or posted somewhere on the Internet," he says.

One of the most important things that bands and singer/songwriters need to understand about music publishing in relation to recording contracts is that *publishing and record deals are and should be two completely separate things.* "I'm seeing more and more indies taking publishing automatically as part of the record deal," Murphy says, "and I don't think it makes them work the record any harder. What it does do is tie up the composition with a company that probably won't be around in another 10 years and that probably won't have the necessary expertise to exploit the songs it owns while it does exist. If a company really wants the publishing that badly, make them negotiate a contract with you as the songwriter that is separate from your artist contract. They are two separate jobs. Think of it as if they hired someone to produce records for them and that person also did some plumbing work. They wouldn't address both of those functions in the same contract.

"The songwriter/artist is following a completely different track from a straight song-writer," Murphy says. "The writer who is also an artist is trying to create a persona that is unique and should write songs that play to his or her own strengths. Professional writers, unless they have been commissioned to write with or for a particular artist, often don't know who will be singing their songs. They need to keep their themes universal and genre-appropriate to increase the chance that the song will be cut."

The songwriter/artist will also face different contract issues than a "straight" song-writer. "The controlled composition clause is something that a writer/artist will inevitably have to deal with if he or she gets a recording contract," Murphy says. "It basically states that since the artist is signed to a label, and since the artist owns his or her own songs, the artist should agree to license the songs to the record label for a reduced royalty rate. It is a particularly onerous part of current recording agreements, and it is worth trying to negotiate that section out of the contract."

If it's important to keep publishing and recording contracts separate, what about record labels that have "sister" publishing companies? "As long as it is a separate negotiation from the recording contract, there is no reason why, on principle, a songwriter shouldn't sign a publishing deal with the label's affiliated publishing company," Murphy says. "In some cases it may even be a good thing that your publishing company doesn't have to wrangle with your record label to get clearance to use the master recording in a film or TV show. It is something that should be analyzed on a case-by-case basis."

This subject was a hot one at a recent MIDEM conference, which brings together industry professionals to discuss international licensing concerns. "There were several companies that were going around with hundreds of millions of dollars in venture capital money and buying up [song] catalogs," Murphy says. "These companies anticipate an explosion in the value of copyrights over the next five to ten years. They see China and India coming online as vast consumer markets and the Internet and wireless networks giving American creators the means to sell to them directly. Anyone who owns copyrights at this point should seriously consider their long-term potential value when negotiating a publishing deal."

With three different performance rights organizations to choose from—ASCAP, BMI, and SESAC—how does a songwriter choose which one to work with? "When anyone makes a deal with any company, a primary question to ask should be, 'Does this company have the same goals and priorities as I do?'" Murphy says. "In the case of ASCAP, a songwriter can take comfort in the fact that we are owned and operated by our writer and publisher members. If you Google our board of directors you'll see that the board consists of writers like Jimmy Jam and Paul Williams, as well as publishers like Leeds Levy and David Renzer. These are people who want to make as much money as possible from their music."

"BMI is run by broadcasters. Some of the people that work over there are very nice, but the people who run the company are folks like Catherine Hughes of Radio One and Jerome Kersting, executive vice president and CFO of Clear Channel Radio. I have nothing personally against Clear Channel, but they are a company with whom songwriters have to negotiate licensing fees. I don't understand how a company that is run by Clear Channel can negotiate effectively with Clear Channel on behalf of its songwriter affiliates."

"SESAC, a for-profit company, really doesn't make any sense to me when you have the option to join a not-for-profit company like ASCAP."

To become a member of ASCAP, all one has to do is apply, and ASCAP has made that easy through their Web site, www.ascap.com. Writers can access ASCAP applications online as PDF documents and should join ASCAP both as a songwriter *and* a music publisher. Applying for ASCAP membership is free and only takes about 15 minutes. Writers who have questions about the application process can call any of the ASCAP offices for assistance.

Along with becoming ASCAP members to protect their copyrights and further their careers, Murphy feels that songwriters should also become politically involved. "It is vital," he says. "ASCAP has a political action committee (PAC) that is very active, and songwriters can look to us to champion their cause in Washington, but there needs to be more of a grassroots push by writers to ensure that some of the anti-copyright legislation that is introduced in Congress does not get signed into law. This is a critical moment in the evolution of the music industry, and songwriters can either be masters of their music and their business or wind up as employees of a new, bigger, even less sympathetic boss."

—*Cynthia Laufenberg*

to distribute royalties from the Internet. Founded in 1914, ASCAP is the only society created and owned by writers and publishers. The ASCAP Board of Directors consists of 12 writers and 12 publishers, elected by the membership. ASCAP's Member Card provides exclusive benefits geared towards working music professionals. Among the benefits are health, musical instrument and equipment, tour and studio liability, term life and long term care insurance, discounts on musical instruments, equipment and supplies, access to a credit union, and much more. ASCAP hosts a wide array of showcases and workshops throughout the year, and offers grants, special awards, and networking opportunities in a variety of genres. Visit their Web site listed above for more information.

ARIZONA SONGWRITERS ASSOCIATION

P.O. Box 678, Phoenix AZ 85001-0678. (602)973-1988. E-mail: azsongwriters@cox.net. **Contact:**John Iger, membership director. Estab. 1977. Members are all ages with wide variety of interests; beginners and those who make money from their songs. Most members are residents of Arizona. Purpose is to educate about the craft and business of songwriting and to facilitate networking with business professionals and other local songwriters. Offers instruction, newsletter, lectures, workshops and performance opportunities. Applications accepted year-round. Membership fee: $25/year.

ASSOCIATION DES PROFESSIONEL.LE.S DE LA CHANSON ET DE LA MUSIQUE

292 Montreal Rd, Suite 200, ON K1L 6B7 Canada. (613)745-5642. Fax: (613)745-9715. E-mail: info-apcm@rogers.com. Web site: www.apcm.ca. **Contact:** Jean-Emmanuel Simiand, agent de communication. Director: Lucie Mailloux. Estab. 1989. Members are French Canadian singers and musicians. Members must be French singing and may have a CD to be distributed. Purpose is to gather French speaking artists (outside of Quebec, mainly in Ontario) to distribute their material, other workshops, instructions, lectures, etc. Offers instruction, newsletter, lectures, workshops, and distribution. Applications accepted year-round. Membership fee: $60 (Canadian).

ASSOCIATION OF INDEPENDENT MUSIC PUBLISHERS

Los Angeles Chapter: P.O. Box 69473, Los Angeles CA 90069. (818)771-7301. New York line: (212)391-2532. E-mail: LAinfo@aimp.org or NYinfo@aimp.org. Web site: www.aimp.org. Estab. 1977. Purpose is to educate members on new developments in the music publishing industry and to provide networking opportunities. Offers monthly panels and networking events. Applications accepted year-round. Membership fee: NY: $75/year; LA: $65/year.

AUSTIN SONGWRITERS GROUP

P.O. Box 2578, Austin TX 78768. (512)442-TUNE. E-mail: info@austinsongwritersgroup.com. Web site: www.austinsongwritersgroup.com. **Contact:** Lee Duffy, president. Vice President: Brent Allen. Estab. 1986. Serves all ages and all levels, from just beginning to advanced. Perspective members should have an interest in the field of songwriting, whether it be for profit or hobby. The main purpose of this organization is "to educate members in the craft and business of songwriting; to provide resources for growth and advancement in the area of songwriting; and to provide opportunities for performance and contact with the music industry." The primary benefit of membership to a songwriter is "exposure to music industry professionals, which increases contacts and furthers the songwriter's education in both craft and business aspects." Offers competitions, instruction, lectures, library, newsletter, performance opportunities, evaluation services, workshops and "contact with music industry professionals through special guest speakers at meetings, plus our yearly 'Austin Songwriters Conference,' which includes instruction, song evaluations, and song pitching direct to those pros currently seeking material for their artists, publishing companies, etc." Applications accepted year-round. Membership fee: $40/year.
Tips "Our newsletter is top-quality—packed with helpful information on all aspects of songwriting—craft, business, recording and producing tips, and industry networking opportunities."

BALTIMORE SONGWRITERS ASSOCIATION

P.O. Box 22496, Baltimore MD 21203. (410)813-4039. E-mail: info@baltimoresongwriters.org. Web site: www.baltimoresongwriters.org. **Contact:** Karyn Oliver, president. Estab. 1997. "The BSA is an inclusive organization with all ages, skill levels and genres of music welcome." Offers instruction, newsletter, lectures, workshops, performance opportunities, music publishing. Applications accepted year-round; membership not limited to location or musical status. Membership fee: $25.
Tips "We are trying to build a musical community that is more supportive and less competitive We are dedicated to helping songwriters grow and become better in their craft."

THE BLACK ROCK COALITION

P.O. Box 1054, Cooper Station, New York NY 10276. (212)713-5097. E-mail: ldavise@blackrockcoalition.org. Web site: www.blackrockcoalition.org. **Contact:** LaRonda Davis, president. Estab. 1985. Serves musicians, songwriters—male and female ages 18-40 (average). Also engineers, entertainment attorneys and producers. Looking for members who are "mature and serious about music as an artist or activist willing to help fellow musicians. The BRC independently produces, promotes and distributes Black alternative music acts as a collective and supportive voice for such musicians within the music and record business. The main purpose of this organization is to produce, promote and distribute the full spectrum of black music along with educating the public on what black music is. The BRC is now soliciting recorded music by bands and individuals for Black Rock Coalition Records. Please send copyrighted and original material only." Offers instruction, newsletter, lectures, free seminars and workshops, monthly membership meeting, quarterly magazine, performing opportunities, evaluation services, business advice, full roster of all members. Applications accepted year-round. Bands must submit a tape, bio with picture and a self-addressed, stamped envelope before sending their membership fee. Membership fee: $25 per individual/$100 per band.

ℕ THE BOSTON SONGWRITERS WORKSHOP

(617)499-6932. Web site: www.bostonsongwriters.org. Estab. 1988. "The Boston Songwriters Workshop is made up of a very diverse group of people, ranging in age from late teens to people in their sixties, and even older. The interest areas are also diverse, running the gamut from folk, pop and rock to musical theater, jazz, R&B, dance, rap and classical. Skill levels within the group range from relative newcomers to established veterans that have had cuts and/or songs published. By virtue of group consensus, there are no eligibility requirements other than a serious desire to pursue one's songwriting ventures, and availability and interest in volunteering for the various activities required to run the organization. The purpose of the BSW is to establish a community of songwriters and composers within the greater Boston area, so that its members may better help each other to make further gains in their respective musical careers." Offers performance opportunities, instruction, newsletter, workshops and bi-weekly critique sessions. Applications accepted year-round. Membership: $35/year; newsletter subscription only: $10/year; guest (nonmember) fees: free, limited to two meetings.

✓ BROADCAST MUSIC, INC. (BMI)

320 W. 57th St., New York NY 10019. (212)586-2000. E-mail: newyork@bmi.com. Web site: www.b mi.com. **Los Angeles:** 8730 Sunset Blvd., Los Angeles CA 90069. (310)659-9109. E-mail: losangeles @bmi.com. **Nashville:** 10 Music Square East, Nashville TN 37203. (615)401-2000. E-mail: nashville @bmi.com. **Miami:** 5201 Blue Lagoon Dr., Suite 310, Miami FL 33126. (305)266-3636. E-mail: miami@bmi.com. **Atlanta:** Tower Place 100, 3340 Peachtree Rd., NE, Suite 570, Atlanta GA 30326. (404)261-5151. E-mail: atlanta@bmi.com. **Puerto Rico:** MCS Plaza, Suite 206, 255 Ponce De Leon Ave., San Juan PR 00917. (787)754-6490. **United Kingdom:** 84 Harley House, Marylebone Rd., London NW1 5HN United Kingdom. 011-44-207-486-2036. E-mail: london@bmi.com. President and CEO: Del R. Bryant. Senior Vice Presidents, New York: Phillip Graham, Writer/Publisher Relations; Alison Smith, Performing Rights. Vice Presidents: New York: Charlie Feldman; Los Angeles: Barbara Cane and Doreen Ringer Ross; Nashville: Paul Corbin; Miami: Diane J. Almodovar; Atlanta: Catherine Brewton. Senior Executive, London: Brandon Bakshi. BMI is a performing rights organization representing approximately 300,000 songwriters, composers and music publishers in all genres of music, including pop, rock, country, R&B, rap, jazz, Latin, gospel and contemporary classical. "Applicants must have written a musical composition, alone or in collaboration with other writers, which is commercially published, recorded or otherwise likely to be performed." Purpose: BMI acts on behalf of its songwriters, composers and music publishers by insuring payment for performance of their works through the collection of licensing fees from radio stations, Internet outlets, broadcast and cable TV stations, hotels, nightclubs, aerobics centers and other users of music. This income is distributed to the writers and publishers in the form of royalty payments, based on how the music is used. BMI also undertakes intensive lobbying efforts in Washington D.C. on behalf of its affiliates, seeking to protect their performing rights through the enactment of new legislation and enforcement of current copyright law. In addition, BMI helps aspiring songwriters develop their skills through various workshops, seminars and competitions it sponsors throughout the country. Applications accepted year-round. There is no membership fee for songwriters; a one-time fee of $150 is required to affiliate an individually-owned publishing company; $250 for partnerships, corporations and limited-liability companies. "Visit our Web site for specific contacts, e-mail addresses and additional membership information."

CALIFORNIA LAWYERS FOR THE ARTS

Fort Mason Center, Building C, Room 255, San Francisco CA 94123. (415)775-7200. Fax: (415)775-1143. E-mail: cla@calawyersforthearts.org. Web site: www.calawyersforthearts.org. **Southern California:** 1641 18th St., Santa Monica CA 90404. (310)998-5590. Fax: (310)998-5594. E-mail: usercla

@aol.com. **Sacramento Office:** 1127 11th St., Suite 214, Sacramento CA 95814. (916)442-6210. Fax: (916)442-6281. E-mail: clasacto@aol.com. **Oakland Office:** 1212 Broadway St., Suite 834, Oakland CA 94612. (510)444-6351. Fax: (510)444-6352. E-mail: oakcla@there.net. **Contact:** Alma Robinson, executive director. Systems Coordinator: Josie Porter. Estab. 1974. "For artists of all disciplines, skill levels, and ages, supporting individuals and organizations, and arts organizations. Artists of all disciplines are welcome, whether professionals or amateurs. We also welcome groups and individuals who support the arts. We work most closely with the California arts community. Our mission is to establish a bridge between the legal and arts communities so that artists and art groups may handle their creative activities with greater business and legal competence; the legal profession will be more aware of issues affecting the arts community; and the law will become more responsive to the arts community." Offers newsletter, lectures, library, workshops, mediation service, attorney referral service, housing referrals, publications and advocacy. Membership fee: $20 for senior citizens and full-time students; $25 for working artists; $40 for general individual; $60 for panel attorney; $100 to $1,000 for patrons. Organizations: $50 for small organizations (budget under $100,000); $90 for large organizations (budget of $100,000 or more); $100 to $1,000 for corporate sponsors.

▨ ☷ CANADA COUNCIL FOR THE ARTS/CONSEIL DES ARTS DU CANADA

350 Albert St., P.O. Box 1047, Ottawa ON K1P 5V8 Canada. (613)566-4414, ext. 5060. E-mail: info@canadacouncil.ca. Web site: www.canadacouncil.ca. **Contact:** Lise Rochon, information officers. Estab. 1957. An independent agency that fosters and promotes the arts in Canada by providing grants and services to professional artists including songwriters and musicians. "Individual artists must be Canadian citizens or permanent residents of Canada, and must have completed basic training and/or have the recognition as professionals within their fields. The Canada Council offers grants to professional musicians to pursue their individual artistic development and creation. There are specific deadline dates for the various programs of assistance. Visit our Web site at www.canadacouncil.ca/music for more details."

☷ CANADIAN ACADEMY OF RECORDING ARTS & SCIENCES (CARAS)

355 King St. W, Suite 501, Toronto ON M5V 1J6 Canada. (416)485-3135. Fax: (416)485-4978. E-mail: info@carasonline.ca. Web site: www.juno-awards.ca. **Contact:** Brenna Knought, project coordinator. President: Melanie Berry. Manager, Awards and Events: Leisa Peacock. Manager, Marketing and Communications: Tammy Watson. Membership is open to all employees (including support staff) in broadcasting and record companies, as well as producers, personal managers, recording artists, recording engineers, arrangers, composers, music publishers, album designers, promoters, talent and booking agents, record retailers, rack jobbers, distributors, recording studios and other music industry related professions (on approval). Applicants must be affliliated with the Canadian recording industry. Offers newsletter, nomination and voting privileges for Juno Awards and discount tickets to Juno awards show. "CARAS strives to foster the development of the Canadian music and recording industries and to contribute toward higher artistic standards." Applications accepted year-round. Membership fee is $50/year (Canadian) + GST=$53.50. Applications accepted from individuals only, not from companies or organizations.

☑ ☷ CANADIAN COUNTRY MUSIC ASSOCIATION (CCMA)

626 King Street West, Suite 203, Toronto ON MV5 1M7 Canada. (416)947-1331. Fax: (416)947-5924. E-mail: country@ccma.org. Web site: www.ccma.org. **Contact:** Brandi Mills, communications & marketing. Estab. 1976. Members are artists, songwriters, producers, radio station personnel, managers, booking agents and others. Offers newsletter, workshops, performance opportunities and the CCMA awards every September. "Through our newsletters and conventions we offer a means of meeting and associating with artists and others in the industry. The CCMA is a federally chartered, nonprofit organization, dedicated to the promotion and development of Canadian country music throughout Canada and the world and to providing a unity of purpose for the Canadian country music industry." See Web site for membership information and benefits.

▣ CANADIAN MUSICAL REPRODUCTION RIGHTS AGENCY LTD.

56 Wellesley St. W, #320, Toronto ON M5S 2S3 Canada. (416)926-1966. Fax: (416)926-7521. E-mail: inquiries@cmrra.ca. Web site: www.cmrra.ca. **Contact:** Michael Mackie, membership services. Estab. 1975. Members are music copyright owners, music publishers, sub-publishers and administrators. Representation by CMRRA is open to any person, firm or corporation anywhere in the world, which owns and/or administers one or more copyrighted musical works. CMRRA is a music licensing agency—Canada's largest—which represents music copyright owners, publishers and administrators for the purpose of mechanical and synchronization licensing in Canada. Offers mechanical and synchronization licensing. Applications accepted year-round.

▣ CENTRAL CAROLINA SONGWRITERS ASSOCIATION (CCSA)

6016 Silkwater Court, Raleigh NC 27610. (919)662-7176. E-mail: ccsa_raleigh@yahoo.com. Web site: www.ccsa-raleigh.com. **Contact:** Dawn Williams, president. Founder: Shantel R. Davis. Estab. 1995. "CCSA welcomes both beginner and published songwriters from North Carolina to join our group. Our members' musical background varies covering a wide array of musical genres. All songwriters and musicians can find benefit in joining CCSA. We meet monthly in Raleigh, NC. We are open to songwriters in the state of North Carolina (sorry, applications cannot be accepted from incarcerated persons or those who do not reside in the state of North Carolina). Our group's primary focus is on songwriters who are able to attend meetings, workshops, and other functions—to ensure members get the best value for their yearly dues. CCSA strives to provide each songwriter and musician a resourceful organization where members are able to grow musically by networking and sharing with one another. We want to reach every interested songwriter we can and attend to his/her musical needs. For those members who are unable to attend the monthly meetings in Raleigh, CCSA does offer a Critique-By-Mail service. Offers instruction, newsletter, workshops, evaluation services, and musicians/collaborators network. Applications are accepted year round. Dues are $12/year, with annual renewal each January. For new members, dues are pro-rated for the first year at $1/month by date of application.

▣ CENTRAL OREGON SONGWRITERS ASSOCIATION

782 SW Rimrock Way, Redmond OR 97756. (541)548-2495. E-mail: cosapresident@lycos.com. Web site: www.centraloregonmusic.com. President: Matt Engle. Estab. 1993. "Our members range in age from their 20s into their 80s. Membership includes aspiring beginners, accomplished singer/songwriter performing artists and all in between. Anyone with an interest in songwriting (any style) is invited to and welcome at COSA. COSA is a nonprofit organization to promote, educate and motivate members in the skills of writing, marketing and improving their craft." Offers competitions, instruction, newsletter, lectures, library, workshops, performance opportunities, songwriters round, awards, evaluation services and collaboration. Applications accepted year-round. Membership fee is $25.

CHICAGO DANCE AND MUSIC ALLIANCE

(formerly Chicago Music Alliance), 410 S. Michigan Ave., Suite 819, Chicago IL 60605. (312)987-9296. Fax: (312)987-1127. E-mail: info@chicagoperformances.org. Web site: www.chicagoperformances.org. Executive Director: Molly Rosen. Estab. 1984. "Chicago Dance and Music Alliance provides direct services to members engaged in all genres of dance and music in the Chicago area, acts as an advocate on their behalf, and disseminates information about their activities to the general public. The alliance includes administrators, composers, choreographers, students, performers, educators and others, as well as groups from the smallest ensemble to full symphony orchestras and major dance companies. Members generally have a direct connection to Chicago, with most organizational members based in the Chicago metropolitan area. As a service organization the Alliance is committed to meeting the needs of members. Services for individual members include ticket and merchandise discounts, credit union membership and résumé/career counseling. The Alliance also publishes a monthly Newsletter, and offers occasional workshops or topical meetings. The Newsletter includes audition and employment notices. The Web site includes a searchable performance directory and a teaching directory. The teaching directory is available to members as well as to for-profit schools. Applications accepted year-round. All memberships expire December 31. Individual dues are $40 per year. Fees for ensembles vary by budget size.

THE COLLEGE MUSIC SOCIETY

312 E. Pine St., Missoula MT 59802. (406)721-9616. Fax: (406)721-9419. E-mail: cms@music.org. Web site: www.music.org. Estab. 1959. Serves college, university and conservatory professors, as well as independent musicians. "The College Music Society is a consortium of college, conservatory, university and independent musicians and scholars interested in all disciplines of music. Its mission is to promote music teaching and learning, musical creativity and expression, research and dialogue, and diversity and interdisciplinary interaction." Offers journal, newsletter, lectures, workshops, performance opportunities, job listing service, databases of organizations and institutions, music faculty and mailing lists. Applications accepted year-round. Membership fee: $60 (regular dues), $30 (student dues).

☑ CONNECTICUT SONGWRITERS ASSOCIATION

P.O. Box 511, Mystic CT 06355. (860)945-1272. E-mail: info@ctsongs.com. Web site: www.ctsongs. com. **Contact:** Bill Pere, Executive Director. Associate Director: Kay Pere. "We are an educational, nonprofit organization dedicated to improving the art and craft of original music. Founded in 1979, CSA had almost 2,000 active members and has become one of the best known and respected songwriters' associations in the country. Membership in the CSA admits you to 12-18 seminars/workshops/song critique sessions per year at 3-5 locations in Connecticut. Out-of-state members may mail in songs for free critiques at our meetings. Noted professionals deal with all aspects of the craft and business of music including lyric writing, music theory, music technology, arrangement and production, legal and business aspects, performance techniques, song analysis and recording techniques. CSA offers song screening sessions for members (songs which are voted on by the panel). Songs that 'pass' are then eligible for inclusion on the CSA sampler anthology CD series. Fifteen compilation recordings have been released so far are for sale at local retail outlets and are given to speakers and prospective buyers. CSA is well connected in both the independent music scene, and the traditional music industry. CSA also offers showcases and concerts which are open to the public and designed to give artists a venue for performing their original material for an attentive, listening audience. CSA benefits help local soup kitchens, group homes, hospice, world hunger, libraries, nature centers, community centers and more. CSA shows encompass ballads to bluegrass and Bach to rock. Our monthly newsletter, *Connecticut Songsmith*, offers free classified advertising for members, and has been edited and published by Bill Pere since 1980. Annual dues: $40; senior citizen and full time students $30; organizations $80. Memberships are tax-deductible as business expenses or as charitable contributions to the extent allowed by law."

Ⓝ COUNTRY MUSIC ASSOCIATION OF TEXAS

P.O. Box 549, Troy TX 76579. (254)938-2454. Fax: (254)938-2049. **Contact:** Bud Fisher, founder/executive director. Estab. 1989. Open to songwriters, singers, pickers, fans and other professionals of all ages from all over the world. Members are interested in country music, especially traditional, classics. Purpose is to promote traditional and independent country music. Offers performance opportunities and evaluation services. Applications accepted year-round. Membership fee: $35.00/year.

Tips "Membership has grown to over 4,000 fans, musicians and songwriters, making it one of the largest state organizations in America. We hold numerous functions throughout the year and we have helped many local recording artists chart their releases nationwide and in Europe. Texas country music is hot!"

☑ DALLAS SONGWRITERS ASSOCIATION

Sammons Center for the Arts, 3630 Harry Hines, Box 20, Dallas TX 75219. (214)750-0916. Fax: (214)692-1392. E-mail: info@dallassongwriters.org. Web site: www.dallassongwriters.org. **Contact:** Jose Volante, membership director. President: Alex Townes. Founding President Emeritis: Barbara McMillen. Estab. 1986. Serves songwriters and lyricists of Dallas/Ft. Worth metroplex.

Members are adults ages 18-65, Dallas/Ft. Worth area songwriters/lyricists who are or aspire to be professionals. Purpose is to provide songwriters an opportunity to meet other songwriters, share information, find co-writers and support each other through group discussions at monthly meetings; to provide songwriters an opportunity to have their songs heard and critiqued by peers and professionals by playing cassettes and providing an open mike at monthly meetings and by offering contests judged by publishers; to provide songwriters opportunities to meet other music business professionals by inviting guest speakers to monthly meetings and the Dallas Songwriters Seminar; and to provide songwriters opportunities to learn more about the craft of songwriting and the business of music by presenting mini-workshops at each monthly meeting. "We offer a chance for the songwriter to learn from peers and industry professionals and an opportunity to belong to a supportive group environment to encourage the individual to continue his/her songwriting endeavors." Offers competitions (including the Annual Song Contest with over $5,000 in prizes, and the Quarterly Lyric Contest), field trips, instruction, lectures, newsletter, performance opportunities, social outings, workshops and seminars. "Our members are eligible for discounts at several local music stores and seminars." Applications accepted year-round. Membership fee: $45. "When inquiring by phone, please leave complete mailing address and phone number where you can be reached day and night."

THE DRAMATISTS GUILD OF AMERICA, INC.

(formerly The Dramatists Guild, Inc.), 1501 Broadway, Suite 701, New York NY 10036. (212)398-9366. Fax: (212)944-0420. E-mail: membership@dramatistsguild.com. Web site: www.dramatistsguild. com. **Contact:** Tom Epstein, membership director. "For over three-quarters of a century, The Dramatists Guild has been the professional association of playwrights, composers and lyricists, with more than 6,000 members across the country. All theater writers, whether produced or not, are eligible for Associate membership ($95/year); those who are engaged in a drama-related field but are not a playwright are eligible for Subscribing membership ($25/year); students enrolled in writing degree programs at colleges or universities are eligible for Student membership ($35/year); writers who have been produced on Broadway, Off-Broadway or on the main stage of a LORT theater are eligible for Active membership ($150/year). The Guild offers its members the following activities and services: use of the Guild's contracts (including the Approved Production Contract for Broadway, the Off-Broadway contract, the LORT contract, the collaboration agreements for both musicals and drama, the 99 Seat Theatre Plan contract, the Small Theatre contract, commissioning agreements, and the Underlying Rights Agreements contract; advice on all theatrical contracts including Broadway, Off-Broadway, regional, showcase, Equity-waiver, dinner theater and collaboration contracts); a nationwide toll-free number for all members with business or contract questions or problems; advice and information on a wide spectrum of issues affecting writers; free and/or discounted ticket service; symposia led by experienced professionals in major cities nationwide; access to health insurance programs; and a spacious meeting room which can accommodate up to 50 people for readings and auditions on a rental basis. The Guild's publications are: *The Dramatist*, a bimonthly journal containing articles on all aspects of the theater (which includes *The Dramatists Guild Newsletter*, with announcements of all Guild activities and current information of interest to dramatists); and an annual resource directory with up-to-date information on agents, publishers, grants, producers, playwriting contests, conferences and workshops.

THE FIELD

161 Sixth Ave., New York NY 10013. (212)691-6969. Fax: (212)255-2053. E-mail: info@thefield.org. Web site: www.thefield.org. **Contact:** Program Manager, programs & outreach. Estab. 1986. "The Field gives independent performing artists the tools to develop and sustain their creative and professional lives, while allowing the public to have immediate, direct access to a remarkable range of contemporary artwork. The organization was started by eight emerging artists who shared common roots in contemporary dance and theater. Meeting regularly, these artists created a structure to help each other improve their artwork, and counter the isolation that often comes with the territory of an artistic career. The Field offers a comprehensive program structure similar to an urban artists' residency or graduate program. Participants select from a broad array of programs and services

including art development workshops, performance opportunities, career management training and development, fundraising consultations, fiscal sponsorship, informational publications, and artist residencies. The Field's goal is to help artists develop their best artwork by deepening the artistic process and finding effective ways to bring that art into the marketplace. Most Field programs cost under $100, and tickets to our performance events are $10. In addition, since 1992, The Field has coordinated a network of satellite sites in Atlanta, Chicago, Houston, Miami, North Adams (MA), Philadelphia, Plainfield (MA), Phoenix, Rochester (NY), Salt Lake City, San Francisco, Seattle, Tucson, Richmond (VA), Washington, DC and Tokyo, Japan. The Field is the only organization in New York that provides comprehensive programming for independent performing artists on a completely non-exclusive basis. Programs are open to artists from all disciplines, aesthetic viewpoints, and levels of development.'' Offers workshops and performance opportunities on a seasonal basis. Applications accepted year-round. Membership fee: $100/year.

Tips ''There are two new additions to the field: IPARC (Independent Artists Resource Center) and GoTour. Located at The Field's office, IPARC offers fund-raising resources and hands-on assistance, including databases such as the Foundation Directory Online, computer workstations, and a library of books, journals, and information directories. One-on-one assistance and consultations are also available to guide users through grant writing and other fund-raising endeavors. GoTour (www.go-tour.org) is a free Web site offering independent artists the resources they need to take their show on the road. Visitors log on for free and access a national arts network where they can search for venues, network with artists nationwide, find media contacts, read advice from other artists and arts professionals, add information on their local arts community, post tour anecdotes, and list concert informaton and classified ads.''

☑ 🖼 FILM MUSIC NETWORK

5777 West Century Blvd., Suite 1550, Los Angeles CA 90045. 1-800-774-3700. E-mail: info@filmmusic.net. Web site: www.filmmusicworld.com or www.filmmusic.net. President/Founder: Mark Northam. NY Chapter Manager: Beth Krakower.

🆕 FORT WORTH SONGWRITERS ASSOCIATION

P.O. Box 162443, Fort Worth TX 76161. (817)654-5400. E-mail: info@fwsa.com. Web site: www.fwsa.com. President: John Terry. Secretary: James Michael Taylor. Treasurer: Rick Tate. Estab. 1992. Members are ages 18-83, beginners up to and including published writers. Interests cover gospel, country, western swing, rock, pop, bluegrass and blues. Purpose is to allow songwriters to become more proficient at songwriting; to provide an opportunity for their efforts to be performed before a live audience; to provide songwriters an opportunity to meet co-writers. ''We provide our members free critiques of their efforts. We provide a monthly newsletter outlining current happenings in the business of songwriting. We offer competitions and mini workshops with guest speakers from the music industry. We promote a weekly open 'mic' for singers of original material, and hold invitational songwriter showcase events a various times throughout the year. Each year, we hold a Christmas Song Contest, judged by independent music industry professionals. We also offer free web pages for members or links to member Web sites.'' Applications accepted year-round. Membership fee: $35.

GOSPEL MUSIC ASSOCIATION

1205 Division St., Nashville TN 37203. (615)242-0303. E-mail: megan@gospelmusic.org. Web site: www.gospelmusic.org. **Contact:** Megan Ledford, member and customer service representative. Estab. 1964. Serves songwriters, musicians and anyone directly involved in or who supports gospel music. Professional members include advertising agencies, musicians, agents/managers, composers, retailers, music publishers, print and broadcast media, and other members of the recording industry. Associate members include supporters of gospel music and those whose involvement in the industry does not provide them with income. The primary purpose of the GMA is to expose, promote, and celebrate the Gospel through music. A GMA membership offers newsletters, performance experiences and workshops, as well as networking opportunities. Applications accepted year-round. Membership fee: $85/year (professional); $60/year (associate); and $25/year (college student).

🌐 THE GUILD OF INTERNATIONAL SONGWRITERS & COMPOSERS

Sovereign House, 12 Trewartha Rd., Praa Sands, Penzance, Cornwall TR20 9ST England. (01736)762826. Fax: (01736)763328. E-mail: songmag@aol.com. Web site: www.songwriters-guild .com. **Contact:** C.A. Jones, secretary. Serves songwriters, musicians, record companies, music publishers, etc. "Our members are amateur and professional songwriters and composers, musicians, publishers, studio owners and producers. Membership is open to all persons throughout the world of any age and ability. The Guild gives advice and services relating to the music industry. A free magazine is available upon request with an SAE or 3 IRCs or visit our Web site. We provide contact information for artists, record companies, music publishers, industry organizations; free copyright service; *Songwriting & Composing Magazine*; and many additional free services." Applications accepted year-round. Annual dues: £45 in the U.K.; £50 in E.E.C. countries; 50 overseas (subscriptions in pounds sterling only).

HAWAI'I SONGWRITERS ASSOCIATION

P.O. Box 10248, Honolulu HI 96816. (808)988-6878. Fax: (808)988-6236. E-mail: stanrubens@aol.c om. Web site: www.stanrubens.com. **Contact:** Stan Rubens, secretary. Estab. 1972. "We have two classes of membership: Professional (must have had at least one song commercially published and for sale to general public) and Regular (any one who wants to join and share in our activities). Both classes can vote equally, but only Professional members can hold office. Must be 18 years old to join. Our members include musicians, entertainers and record producers. Membership is world-wide and open to all varieties of music, not just ethnic Hawaiian. President, Stan Rubens, has published 4 albums." Offers competitions, instruction, monthly newsletter, lectures, workshops, performance opportunities and evaluation services. Applications accepted year-round. Membership fee: $24. Stan Rubens teaches Songwriting at McKinley High, Adult education.

🆕 HOUSTON FORT BEND SONGWRITERS ASSOCIATION

P.O. Box 1273, Richmond TX 77406. (281)573-5318. E-mail: gtaylor1@pdq.net. Web site: www.hfb sa.org. President: Gary Taylor. Estab. 1991. Serves "any person, amateur or professional, interested in songwriting or music. Our members write pop, rock, country, rockabilly, gospel, R&B, children's music and musical plays." Open to all, regardless of geographic location or professional status. The FBSA provides its membership with help to perfect their songwriting crafts. The FBSA provides instruction for beginning writers and publishing and artist tips for the more accomplished writer. The FBSA networks with producers, publishers, music industry professionals and other songwriting groups to help members place songs. Offers competitions, field trips, instruction, lectures, newsletter, performance opportunities, workshops, mail-in critiques and collaboration opportunities. Applications accepted year-round. Membership fees are: Regular: $35; Renewals; $25; Band: $45; Associate: $20; and Lifetime: $250. For more information send SASE.

✅ INTERNATIONAL BLUEGRASS MUSIC ASSOCIATION (IBMA)

2 Music Circle South, Suite 100, Nashville TN 37203. 1(888)GET-IBMA. Fax: (615)256-0450. E-mail: info@ibma.org. Web site: www.ibma.org. Member Services: Jill Snider. Estab. 1985. Serves songwriters, musicians and professionals in bluegrass music. "IBMA is a trade association composed of people and organizations involved professionally and semi-professionally in the bluegrass music industry, including performers, agents, songwriters, music publishers, promoters, print and broadcast media, local associations, recording manufacturers and distributors. Voting members must be currently or formerly involved in the bluegrass industry as full or part-time professionals. A songwriter attempting to become professionally involved in our field would be eligible. Our mission statement reads: "IBMA: Working together for high standards of professionalism, a greater appreciation for our music, and the success of the world-wide bluegrass music community." IBMA publishes a bimonthly *International Bluegrass*, holds an annual trade show/convention with a songwriters showcase in the fall, represents our field outside the bluegrass music community, and compiles and disseminates databases of bluegrass related resources and organizations. Market research on the bluegrass consumer is available and we offer Bluegrass in the Schools information and matching grants. The primary value in this organization for a songwriter is having current

information about the bluegrass music field and contacts with other songwriters, publishers, musicians and record companies." Offers workshops, liability insurance, rental car discounts, consultation and databases of record companies, radio stations, press, organizations and gigs. Applications accepted year-round. Membership fee: for a non-voting patron \$40/year; for an individual voting professional \$65/year; for an organizational voting professional \$150/year.

⊞ INTERNATIONAL SONGWRITERS ASSOCIATION LTD.

P.O. Box 46, Limerick City, Ireland. E-mail: jliddane@songwriter.iol.ie. Web site: www.songwriter.co.uk. **Contact:** Anna M. Sinden, membership department. Serves songwriters and music publishers. "The ISA headquarters is in Limerick City, Ireland, and from there it provides its members with assessment services, copyright services, legal and other advisory services and an investigations service, plus a magazine for one yearly fee. Our members are songwriters in more than 50 countries worldwide, of all ages. There are no qualifications, but applicants under 18 are not accepted. We provide information and assistance to professional or semi-professional songwriters. Our publication, *Songwriter*, which was founded in 1967, features detailed exclusive interviews with songwriters and music publishers, as well as directory information of value to writers." Offers competitions, instruction, library, newsletter and a weekly e-mail newsletter *Songwriter Newswire*. Applications accepted year-round. Membership fee for European writers is £19.95; for non-European writers, US \$30.

Ⓝ INTERNATIONAL SONGWRITERS GUILD

5108 Louvre Ave., Orlando FL 31028. (407)851-5328. E-mail isg2000@yahoo.com. **Contact:** Russ Robinson, president. Estab. 1977. Members are lyricists, composers, performers, arrangers, publishers, songwriters of all ages, backgrounds and skill levels. Open to anyone interested in songwriting and in improving their songwriting skills. The main purpose of the organization is to guide and educate those people wanting to write commercial music successfully. We use monthly critiquing sessions of approximately 10 songs, where the top 5 winners are announced in the next monthly newsletter, "Guild Tidings." Offers competitions, lectures, performance opportunities, instruction, evaluation services, newsletters, workshops and industry contacts. Applications accepted year-round. Membership fee: \$35 annually.

- • Russ Robinson, President of the Guild, played piano for Judy Garland and Frank Sinatra, among others, and was a member of "The Modernairs" (five-part harmony vocals). He is a writer of national commercials, and is well-known in the music and film industry.

✅ JUST PLAIN FOLKS MUSIC ORGANIZATION

5327 Kit Dr., Indianapolis IN 46237. (317)513-6557. E-mail: info@jpfolks.com. Web site: www.jpfolks.com. **Contact:** Brian Austin Whitney(brian@jpfolks.com), founder or Linda Berger (linda@jpfolks.com), projects director. Estab. 1998. "Just Plain Folks is among the world's largest Music Organizations. Our members cover nearly every musical style and professional field, from songwriters, artists, publishers, producers, record labels, entertainment attorneys, publicists and PR experts, performing rights organization staffers, live and recording engineers, educators, music students, musical instrument manufacturers, TV, Radio and Print Media and almost every major Internet Music entity. Representing all 50 US States and over 100 countries worldwide, we have members of all ages, musical styles and levels of success, including winners and nominees of every major music industry award, as well as those just starting out. A complete demographics listing of our group is available on our Web site. Whether you are a #1 hit songwriter or artist, or the newest kid on the block, you are welcome to join. Membership does require an active e-mail account." The purpose of this organization is "to share wisdom, ideas and experiences with others who have been there, and to help educate those who have yet to make the journey. Just Plain Folks provides its members with a friendly networking and support community that uses the power of the Internet and combines it with good old-fashioned human interaction. We help promote our members ready for success and educate those still learning." Offers special programs to members, including:

● *Just Plain Notes Newsletter:* Members receive our frequent e-mail newsletters full of expert info on how to succeed in the music business, profiles of members successes and advice, opportunities to develop your career and tons of first-person networking contacts to help you along the way. (Note: we send this out 2-3 times/month via e-mail only.)

● *Just Plain Mentors:* We have some of the friendliest expert educators, writers, artists and industry folks in the business who volunteer their time as part of our Mentor Staff. Included are John and JoAnn Braheny, Jason Blume, Harriet Schock, Pat and Pete Luboff, Derek Sivers, Jodi Krangle, Steve Seskin, Alan O'Day, Walter Egan, Sara Light, Danny Arena, Barbara Cloyd, Michael Laskow, Anne Leighton, Mark Keefner, Valerie DeLaCruz, Karen Angela Moore, Ben McLane, Jack Perricone, Pat Pattison, Mark Baxter, Harold Payne, Joey Arreguin, John Beland, Susan Gibson, Art Twain, Diane Rapaport, Nancy Moran, Fett, Mike Dunbar, R. Chris Murphy, Bobby Borg, Paul Reisler, and many others.

● *JPFolks.com Web site:* Our home page serves as your pathway to the resources and members of the group worldwide. With message boards, lyric feedback forums, featured members music, member profiles, member contact listings, member links pages, chapter homepages, demographics information, our Internet radio station and all the back issues of our newsletter, "Just Plain Notes."

● *Roadtrips:* We regularly tour the US and Canada, hosting showcases, workshops and friendly member gatherings in each city we visit. We provide opportunities for all our members, at all levels and welcome everyone to our events. Most events are free of charge.

● *Chapters:* Just Plain Folks has over 100 active local chapters around the world run by local member volunteer coordinators. Each chapter is unique but many host monthly networking gatherings, showcases, educational workshops and community service events. To join a chapter, or start one in your city, please visit the chapter section of the jpfolks.com Web site for a current list of chapters and guidelines.

● *Music Awards:* Just Plain Folks has one of the largest and most diverse Member Music Awards programs in the world. The most recent awards involved over 25,000 albums and 350,000 songs in over 50 genres. Music Award nominees and winners receive featured performance slots at showcases around the world throughout the year. Current submission instructions can be found on the Web site in the Awards section.

Membership requests are accepted year-round. "To become a member, simply send an e-mail to join@jpfolks.com with the words 'I Want To Join Just Plain Folks.' In the e-mail, include your name, address, Web site (if applicable) and phone number for our files." There are currently no membership fees.

Tips "Our motto is 'We're All In This Together!'"

ⓝ KNOXVILLE SONGWRITERS ASSOCIATION

P.O. Box 603, Knoxville TN 37901. (865)573-1025. E-mail: composerr@aol. com. **Contact:** John Morris, Newsletter Editor. President: Richard Ratledge. Estab. 1982. Serves songwriters of all ages. "Some have been members since 1982, others are beginners. Members must be interested in learning the craft of songwriting. Not only a learning organization but a support group of songwriters who wants to learn what to do with their song after it has been written. We open doors for aspiring writers. The primary benefit of membership is to supply information to the writer on how to write a song. Many members have received major cuts." Offers showcases, instruction, lectures, library, newsletter, performance opportunities, evaluation services and workshops. Applications accepted year-round. Membership fee: $30/year.

THE LAS VEGAS SONGWRITERS ASSOCIATION

P.O. Box 42683, Las Vegas NV 89116-0683. (702)223-7255. E-mail: Betty_Miller@McGraw-Hill.c om. Web site: www.lasvegassongwriters.com. **Contact:** Betty Kay Miller, president. Secretary: Barbara Jean Smith. Estab. 1980. "We are an educational, nonprofit organization dedicated to improving the art and craft of the songwriter. We want members who are serious about their craft. We want our members to respect their craft and to treat it as a business. Members must be at least 18 years of age. We offer quarterly newsletters, monthly information meetings, workshops three times a month and quarterly seminars with professionals in the music business. We provide support and encouragement to both new and more experienced songwriters. We critique each song or lyric that's presented during workshops, we make suggestions on changes—if needed. We help turn amateur writers into professionals. Several of our songwriters have had their songs recorded on both independent and major labels." Dues: $30/year.

☑ LOS ANGELES MUSIC NETWORK

P.O. Box 2446, Toluca Lake CA 91610-2446. (818)769-6095. E-mail: info@lamn.com. Web site: www.lamn.com. **Contact:** Tess Taylor, president. Estab. 1988. "Connections. Facts. Career advancement. All that is available with your membership in the Los Angeles Music Network (LAMN). Our emphasis is on sharing knowledge and information, giving you access to top professionals and promoting career development. LAMN is an association of music industry professionals, i.e., artists, singers, songwriters, and people who work in various aspects of the music industry with an emphasis on the creative. Members are ambitious and interested in advancing their careers. LAMN promotes career advancement, communication and continuing education among music industry professionals and top executives. LAMN sponsors industry events and educational panels held bimonthly at venues in the Los Angeles area, and now in other major music hubs around the country (New York, Las Vegas, Chicago).Monthly LAMN Jams are extremely popular among our members: the 'anti-American Idol' singer-songwriter contest gives artists an opportunity to perform in front of industry experts and receive instant feedback to their music, lyrics and performance. As a result of the exposure, Tim agan won the Esquire songwriting contest. This paired him with multi-platinum songwriter and recording artist John Mayer, with whom Fagan co-wrote 'Deeper.' Publisher Robert Walls has pitched music from LAMN performers to hit TV shows like *The OC* and *Gray' s Anatomy*, and the upcoming flick *The Devil Wears Prada*. Other performers have received offers including publishing deals and studio gigs." Offers instruction, newsletter, lectures, seminars, music industry job listings, career counseling, résumé publishing, mentor network, résumé resource guide and many professional networking opportunities. See our Web site for current job listings and a calendar of upcoming events. Applications accepted year-round. Annual membership fee is $110 (subject to change without notice).

LOUISIANA SONGWRITERS ASSOCIATION

P.O. Box 80425, Baton Rouge LA 70898-0425. (504)443-5390. E-mail: zimshah@aol.com. Web site: www.lasongwriters.org. **Contact:** Connie Zimmerman, membership coordinator. Serves songwriters. "LSA was organized to educate songwriters in all areas of their trade, and promote the art of songwriting in Louisiana. LSA is honored to have a growing number of songwriters from other states join LSA and fellowship with us. LSA membership is open to people interested in songwriting, regardless of age, musical ability, musical preference, ethnic background, etc. At the time we are operating as an Internet-only Yahoo Group where we share info, gigs, opportunities, etc. At this time we are not holding regular meetings, although we do meet for various functions periodically. Please visit our group at http://launch.groups.yahoo.com/group/louisianasongwriters/. We do not at this time require any dues for membership participation."

☑ MANITOBA AUDIO RECORDING INDUSTRY ASSOCIATION (MARIA)

1-376 Donald St., Winnipeg MB R3B 2J2 Canada. (204)942-8650. Fax: (204)942-6083. E-mail: info@ manitobamusic.com. Web site: www.manitobamusic.com. **Contact:** Rachel Stone, associate coordinator. Estab. 1987. Organization consists of "songwriters, producers, agents, musicians, managers, retailers, publicists, radio, talent buyers, media, record labels, etc. (no age limit, no skill level minimum). Must have interest in the future of Manitoba's sound recording industry." The main purpose of MARIA is to foster growth in all areas of the Manitoba music industry primarily through education, promotion and lobbying. Offers newsletter, lectures, directory of Manitoba's music industry, workshops and performance opportunities; also presents demo critiquing sessions and comprehensive member discount program featuring a host of participating Manitoba businesses. MARIA is also involved with the Prairie Music Weekend festival, conference and awards show. Applications accepted year-round. Membership fee: $50 (Canadian funds).

MEET THE COMPOSER

75 Ninth Ave, 3R Suite C, New York NY 10011. (212)645-6949. Fax: (212)645-9669. E-mail: mtc@m eetthecomposer.org. Web site: www.meetthecomposer.org. Estab. 1974. "Meet The Composer serves composers working in all styles of music, at every career stage, through a variety of grant programs and information resources. A nonprofit organization, Meet The Composer raises money from foundations, corporations, individual patrons and government sources and designs programs that support all genres of music—from folk, ethnic, jazz, electronic, symphonic, and chamber to choral, music theater, opera and dance. Meet The Composer awards grants for composer fees to non-profit organizations that perform, present, or commission original works. This is not a membership organization; all composers are eligible for support. Meet The Composer was founded in 1974 to increase artistic and financial opportunities for composers by fostering the creation, performance, dissemination, and appreciation of their music." Offers grant programs and information services. Deadlines vary for each grant program.

☑ MEMPHIS SONGWRITERS' ASSOCIATION

4728 Spottswood, #191, Memphis TN 38117-4815. (901)577-0906. E-mail: admin@memphissongwr iters.org. Web site: www.memphissongwriters.org. **Contact:** Jon Dillard, president. Estab. 1973. "MSA is a nonprofit songwriters organization serving songwriters nationally. Our mission is to dedicate our services to promote, advance, and help songwriters in the composition of music, lyrics and songs; to work for better conditions in our profession; and to secure and protect the rights of MSA songwriters. We also supply copyright forms. We offer critique sessions for writers at our monthly meetings. We also have monthly open mic songwriters night to encourage creativity, networking and co-writing. We host an annual songwriter's seminar and an annual songwriter's showcase, as well as a bi-monthly guest speaker series, which provide education, competition and entertainment for the songwriter. In addition, our members receive a bimonthly newsletter to keep them informed of MSA activities, demo services and opportunities in the songwriting field." Annual fee: $50; Student/Senior: $35.

MINNESOTA ASSOCIATION OF SONGWRITERS

P.O. Box 333, Chicago City MN 55013. (651)254-9779. E-mail: info@mnsongwriters.org. Web site: www.mnsongwriters.org. "Includes a wide variety of members, ranging in age from 18 to 80; type of music is very diverse ranging from alternative rock to contemporary Christian; skill levels range from beginning songwriters to writers with recorded and published material. Main requirement is an interest in songwriting. Although most members come from the Minneapolis-St. Paul area, others come in from surrounding cities, nearby Wisconsin, and other parts of the country. Some members are fulltime musicians, but most represent a wide variety of occupations. MAS is a nonprofit community of songwriters which informs, educates, inspires and assists its members in the art and business of songwriting." Offers instruction, newsletter, lectures, workshops, performance opportunities and evaluation services. Applications accepted year-round. Membership fee: Individual: $25; Business: $65.

Tips "Members are kept current on resources and opportunities. Original works are played at meetings and are critiqued by involved members. Through this process, writers hone their skills and gain experience and confidence in submitting their works to others."

Ⓝ MUSICIANS CONTACT

P.O. Box 788, Woodland Hills CA 91365. (818)888-7879. Fax: (818)340-1446. E-mail: muscontact@ aol.com. Web site: www.musicianscontact.com. **Contact:** Stirling Howard, president. Estab. 1969. "The primary source of paying jobs for musicians and vocalists nationwide. Job opportunities are posted daily on the Internet. Also offers exposure to the music industry for solo artists and complete acts seeking representation."

NASHVILLE SONGWRITERS ASSOCIATION INTERNATIONAL (NSAI)

1710 Roy Acuff Place, Nashville TN 37203. (615)256-3354 or (800)321-6008. Fax: (615)256-0034. E-mail: nsai@nashvillesongwriters.com. Web site: www.nashvillesongwriters.com. Executive Director: Barton Herbison. Purpose: a not-for-profit service organization for both aspiring and professional songwriters in all fields of music. Membership: Spans the United States and several foreign countries. Songwriters may apply in one of four annual categories: Active ($150 U.S/$100 International—for songwriters who have at least one song contractually signed to a publisher affiliated with ASCAP, BMI or SESAC); Associate ($150 U.S/$100 International—for songwriters who are not yet published or for anyone wishing to support songwriters); Student ($100 U.S/$100 International—for full-time college students or for students of an accredited senior high school); Professional ($100—for songwriters who derive their primary source of income from songwriting or who are generally recognized as such by the professional songwriting community). Membership benefits: music industry information and advice, song evaluations by mail, quarterly newsletter, access to industry professionals through weekly Nashville workshop and several annual events, regional workshops, use of office facilities, discounts on books and discounts on NSAI's three annual events. There are also "branch" workshops of NSAI. Workshops must meet certain standards and are accountable to NSAI. Interested coordinators may apply to NSAI.

- Also see the listing for NSAI Songwriters Symposium (formerly NSAI Spring Symposium) in the Workshops section of this book.

N: NATIONAL ACADEMY OF POPULAR MUSIC (NAPM)
330 W. 58th St., Suite 411, New York NY 10019-1827. (212)957-9230. Fax: (212)957-9227. E-mail: info@songwritershalloffame.org. Web site: www.shof.org. **Contact:** Bob Leone, projects director. Managing Director: April Anderson. Estab. 1969. "The majority of our members are songwriters, but also on NAPM's rolls are music publishers, producers, record company executives, music attorneys, and lovers of popular music of all ages. Professional members are affiliated with ASCAP, BMI and/or SESAC; or are employed by music industry firms. Associate membership, however, merely requires a completed application and $25 dues. NAPM was formed to determine a variety of ways to celebrate the songwriter (e.g., induction into the Songwriters Hall of Fame). We also provide educational and networking opportunities to our members through our workshop and showcase programs." Offers newsletter, workshops, performance opportunities, networking meetings with industry pros and scholarships for excellence in songwriting. Applications accepted year-round. Membership fee: $25 and up.

☑ THE NATIONAL ASSOCIATION OF COMPOSERS/USA (NACUSA)
P.O. Box 49256, Barrington Station, Los Angeles CA 90049. E-mail: nacusa@music-usa.org. Web site: www.music-usa.org/nacusa. **Contact:** Daniel Kessner, president. Estab. 1932. Serves songwriters, musicians and classical composers. "We are of most value to the concert hall composer. Members are serious music composers of all ages and from all parts of the country, who have a real interest in composing, performing, and listening to modern concert hall music. The main purpose of our organization is to perform, publish, broadcast and write news about composers of serious concert hall music— mostly chamber and solo pieces. Composers may achieve national notice of their work through our newsletter and concerts, and the fairly rare feeling of supporting a non-commercial music enterprise dedicated to raising the musical and social position of the serious composer." Offers competitions, lectures, performance opportunities, library and newsletter. Applications accepted year-round. Membership fee: National (regular): $25; National (students/seniors): $15.

- Also see the listing for NACUSA Young Composers' Competition in the Contests section of this book.

Tips "99% of the money earned in music is earned, or so it seems, by popular songwriters who might feel they owe the art of music something, and this is one way they might help support that art. It's a chance to foster fraternal solidarity with their less prosperous, but wonderfully interesting classical colleagues at a time when the very existence of serious art seems to be questioned by the general populace."

N: NORTH AMERICAN FOLK MUSIC AND DANCE ALLIANCE
510 South Main St., Memphis TN 38103. (901)522-1170. Fax: (901)522-1172. E-mail: fa@folk.org. Web site: www.folk.org. Executive Director: Louis Jay Meyers. Estab. 1989.

Members are organizations and individuals involved in traditional and contemporary folk music and dance in the US and Canada (in any genre—blues, bluegrass, Celtic, Latino, old-time, singer/songwriter, etc.). The Folk Alliance hosts its annual conference (which includes performance showcases) in late February at different locations throughout US and Canada. The conferences include workshops, panel discussions, the largest all folk exhibit hall and showcases. The Folk Alliance also serves members with their newsletter and through education, advocacy and field development. Memberships accepted year-round. Membership fee: $70 ($90 Canadian)/year for individual (voting); $150-505 ($230-700 Canadian)/year for organizational. "We do not offer songwriting contests, but do host performance showcases."

NORTH FLORIDA CHRISTIAN MUSIC WRITERS ASSOCIATION

P.O. Box 61113, Jacksonville FL 32236. (904)786-2372. E-mail: justsongs@aol.com. Web site: www.christiansongwriter.com. **Contact:** Jackie Hand, president. Estab. 1974. "Members are people from all walks of life who promote Christian music—not just composers or performers, but anyone who wants to share today's message in song with the world. No age limit. Anyone interested in promoting Christian music is invited to join. If you are talented in several areas you might be asked to conduct a training session or workshop. Your expertise is wanted and needed by our group. The group's purpose is to serve God by using our God-given talents and abilities and to assist our fellow songwriters, getting their music in the best possible form to be ready for whatever door God chooses to open for them concerning their music. Members' works are included in songbooks published by our organization— also biographies." Offers competitions, performance opportunities, field trips, instruction, newsletter, workshops and critiques. This year we offer a new Web site featuring song clips by members as well as a short bio. Also featured is a special "Memorial Members" list honoring deceased members by keeping their music alive. The one time fee of $100 to place loved ones on the list includes a song clip on our Web site and entry privileges in our songwriting contest. Applications accepted year-round. Membership fee: $25/year ($35 for outside US), $35 for husband/wife team ($45 for outside US). "The 25th Anniversary Edition songbook of our members music (plus our 25 years as a songwriting organization) is $10 plus $3.00 S&H. White Tee Shirt with black graphic and message, "North Florida Christian Music Writers Association" and a graphic of a beautiful piano and other instruments on front is also $10 plus $3.00 S&H." Make checks payable to Jackie Hand.

Tips "If you are serious about your craft, you need fellowship with others who feel the same. A Christian songwriting organization is where you belong if you write Christian songs."

N OKLAHOMA SONGWRITERS & COMPOSERS ASSOCIATION

105 S. Glenn English, Cordell OK 73632. Web site: www.oksongwriters.com. **Contact:** Ann Wilson Hardin, treasurer/membership. Estab. 1983. Serves songwriters, musicians, professional writers and amateur writers. "A nonprofit, all-volunteer organization providing educational and networking opportunities for songwriters, lyricists, composers and performing musicians. All styles of music. We sponsor major workshops, open-mic nights, demo critiques and the OSCA News. Throughout the year we sponsor contests and original music showcases." Applications accepted year-round. Membership fee: $20 for new members, $10 for renewal, $15 for out-of-state newsletter only.

✓ OPERA AMERICA

330 Seventh Ave., 16th Floor, New York NY 10001. (212)796-8620. Fax: (212)796-8636. E-mail: frontdesk@operaamerica.org. Web site: www.operaamerica.org. **Contact:** Sabrina Neilson, membership operations coordinator. Estab. 1970. Members are composers, librettists, musicians, singers, and opera/music theater producers. "OPERA America maintains an extensive library of reference books and domestic and foreign music periodicals, and the most comprehensive operatic archive in the United States. OPERA America draws on these unique resources to supply information to its members." Offers conferences. Publishes online database of opera/music theater companies in the US and Canada, online directory of opera and musical performances world-wide and US, and an online directory of new works created and being developed by current-day composers and librettists, to encourage the performance of new works. Applications accepted year-round. Publishes 40-page magazine 10 times/year. Membership fee is on a sliding scale by membership level.

OUTMUSIC

P.O. Box 376, Old Chelsea Station, New York NY 10113-0376. (212)330-9197. E-mail: info@outmusi c.com. Web site: www.outmusic.com. **Contact:** Ed Mannix, communications director. Estab. 1990. "OUTMUSIC is comprised of gay men, lesbians, bisexuals and transgenders. They represent all different musical styles from rock to classical. Many are writers of original material. We are open to all levels of accomplishment—professional, amateur, and interested industry people. The only requirement for membership is an interest in the growth and visibility of music and lyrics created by the LGBT community. We supply our members with support and networking opportunities. In addition, we help to encourage artists to bring their work 'OUT' into the world." Offers newsletter, lectures, workshops, performance opportunities, networking, industry leads and monthly open mics. Sponsors Outmusic Awards. Applications accepted year-round. For membership information go to www.outmusic.com.

Tips "OUTMUSIC has spawned *The Gay Music Guide*, The Gay and Lesbian American Music Awards (GLAMA), several compilation albums and many independent recording projects."

⚡ ✅ PACIFIC MUSIC INDUSTRY ASSOCIATION

#501-425 Carrall St., Vancouver BC V6B 6E3 Canada. (604)873-1914. Fax: (604)873-9686. E-mail: info@musicbc.org. Web site: www.musicbc.org. Estab. 1990. Music BC is a non-profit society that supports and promotes the spirit, development, and growth of the BC music community provincially, nationally, and internationally. Music BC provides education, resources, advocacy, funding opportunities, and a forum for communication. Applications accepted year-round. E-mail for info about the different levels of Memberships.

🄽 PACIFIC NORTHWEST SONGWRITERS ASSOCIATION

P.O. Box 98564, Seattle WA 98198. (206)824-1568. E-mail: pnsapals@hotmail.com. "PNSA is a nonprofit organization, serving the songwriters of the Puget Sound area since 1977. Members have had songs recorded by national artists on singles, albums, videos and network television specials. Several have released their own albums and the group has done an album together. For only $45 per year, PNSA offers monthly workshops, a quarterly newsletter and direct contact with national artists, publishers, producers and record companies. New members are welcome and good times are guaranteed. And remember, the world always needs another great song!"

🄽 PITTSBURGH SONGWRITERS ASSOCIATION

523 Scenery Dr., Elizabeth PA 15037. (412)751-9584. E-mail: vstragand@aol.com. Web site: www.p ittsburghsongwritersassociation.com. **Contact:** Van Stragand, president. Estab. 1983. "We are a non-profit organization dedicated to helping its members develop and market their songs. Writers of any age and experience level welcome. Current members are from 20s to 50s. All musical styles and interests are welcome. Our organization wants to serve as a source of quality material for publishers and other industry professionals. We assist members in developing their songs and their professional approach. We provide meetings, showcases, collaboration opportunities, instruction, industry guests, library and social outings. Annual dues: $25. We have no initiation fee. Prospective members are invited to attend two free meetings. Interested parties please call Van Stragand at (412)751-9584."

POP RECORD RESEARCH

10 Glen Ave., Norwalk CT 06850. E-mail: horar@earthlink.net. **Director:** Gary Theroux. Estab. 1962. Serves songwriters, musicians, writers, researchers and media. "We maintain archives of materials relating to music, TV and film, with special emphasis on recorded music (the hits and hitmakers 1877-present): bios, photos, reviews, interviews, discographies, chart data, clippings, films, videos, etc." Offers library and clearinghouse for accurate promotion/publicity to biographers, writers, reviewers, the media. Offers programming, annotation and photo source for reissues or retrospective album collections on any artist (singers, songwriters, musicians, etc.), also music consultation services for film or television projects. "There is no charge to include publicity, promotional or biographical materials in our archives. Artists, writers, composers, performers, producers,

labels and publicists are always invited to add or keep us on their publicity/promotion mailing list with career data, updates, new releases and reissues of recorded performances, etc. Fees are assessed only for reference use by researchers, writers, biographers, reviewers, etc. Songwriters and composers (or their publicists) should keep or put us on their publicity mailing lists to ensure that the information we supply others on their careers, accomplishments, etc. is accurate and up-to-date."

N PORTLAND SONGWRITERS ASSOCIATION

P.O. Box 42389, Portland OR 97242. E-mail: membership@portlandongwriters.org. Web site: www. portlandsongwriters.org. Estab. 1991. "The PSA is a nonprofit organization providing education and opportunities that will assist writers in creating and marketing their songs. The PSA offers an annual National Songwriting Contest, monthly workshops, songwriter showcases, special performance venues, quarterly newsletter, mail-in critique service, discounted seminars by music industry pros." Annual dues: $35 (no eligibility requirements).

Tips "Although most of our members are from the Pacific Northwest, we offer services that can assist songwriters anywhere. Our goal is to provide information and contacts to help songwriters grow artistically and gain access to publishing, recording and related music markets. For more information, please call, write or e-mail."

☑ RHODE ISLAND SONGWRITERS' ASSOCIATION (RISA)

P.O. Box 367, Harmony RI 02829. E-mail: hearingri@ids.net or risongwriters@yahoo.com. Web site: www.risongwriters.com. **Co-Chairs:** John Fuzek and Bill Furney. Estab. 1993. "Membership consists of novice and professional songwriters. RISA provides opportunities to the aspiring writer or performer as well as the established regional artists who have recordings, are published and perform regularly. The only eligibility requirement is an interest in the group and the group's goals. Non-writers are welcome as well." The main purpose is to "encourage, foster and conduct the art and craft of original musical and/or lyrical composition through education, information, collaboration and performance." Offers instruction, newsletter, lectures, workshops, performance opportunities and evaluation services. Applications accepted year-round. Membership fees: $25/year (individual); $40/year (family/band). "The group holds twice monthly critique sessions; twice monthly performer showcases (one performer featured) at a local coffeehouse; songwriter showcases (usually 6-8 performers); weekly open mikes; and a yearly songwriter festival called 'Hear In Rhode Island,' featuring approximately 50 Rhode Island acts, over two days."

N SAN DIEGO SONGWRITERS GUILD

3368 Governor Dr., Suite F-326, San Diego CA 92122. E-mail: sdsongwriters@hotmail.com. Web site: www.sdsongwriters.org. **Contact:** Joseph Carmel, membership/correspondence. Estab. 1982. "Members range from their early 20s to senior citizens with a variety of skill levels. Several members perform and work full time in music. Many are published and have songs recorded. Some are getting major artist record cuts. Most members are from San Diego county. New writers are encouraged to participate and meet others. All musical styles are represented." The purpose of this organization is to "serve the needs of songwriters and artists, especially helping them in the business and craft of songwriting through industry guest appearances." Offers competitions, newsletter, workshops, performance opportunities, discounts on services offered by fellow members, in-person song pitches and evaluations by publishers, producers and A&R executives. Applications accepted year-round. Membership dues: $55 full; $30 student; $125 corporate sponsorship. Meeting admission for non-members: $20 (may be applied toward membership if joining within 30 days).

Tips "Members benefit most from participation in meetings and concerts. Generally, one major meeting held monthly on a Monday evening, at the Doubletree Hotel, Hazard Center, San Diego. E-mail for meeting details. Can join at meetings."

☑ SAN FRANCISCO FOLK MUSIC CLUB

885 Clayton, San Francisco CA 94117. (415)661-2217. E-mail: sffolk@aol.com. Web site: www.sffm c.org. **Contact:** Membership Coordinator. Serves songwriters, musicians and anyone who enjoys

folk music. "Our members range from ages 2 to 80. The only requirement is that members enjoy, appreciate and be interested in sharing folk music. As a focal point for the San Francisco Bay Area folk music community, the SFFMC provides opportunities for people to get together to share folk music, and the newsletter *The Folknik* disseminates information. We publish two songs an issue (six times a year) in our newsletter, our meetings provide an opportunity to share new songs, and at our camp-outs there are almost always songwriter workshops." Offers library, newsletter, informal performance opportunities, annual free folk festival, social outings and workshops. Applications accepted year-round. Membership fee: $10/year.

SESAC INC.

152 W. 57th St., 57th Floor, New York NY 10019. (212)586-3450. Fax: (212)489-5699. Web site: www.sesac.com. **Nashville:** 55 Music Square East, Nashville TN 37203. (615)320-0055. Fax: (615)329-9627; **Los Angeles:** 501 Santa Monica Blvd., Suite 450, Santa Monica CA 90401. (310)393-9671. Fax: (310)393-6497; **London:** 67 Upper Berkeley St., London WIH 7QX United Kingdom. (020)76169284. **Contact:** Tim Fink, associate vice president writer/publisher relations. Chief Operating Officer: Pat Collins. Coordinator-Writer/Publisher Relations: Mandy Reilly. SESAC is a selective organization taking pride in having a repertory based on quality rather than quantity. Serves writers and publishers in all types of music who have their works performed by radio, television, nightclubs, cable TV, etc. Purpose of organization is to collect and distribute performance royalties to all active affiliates. As a SESAC affiliate, the individual may obtain equipment insurance at competitive rates. Tapes are reviewed upon invitation by the Writer/Publisher Relations dept.

SOCAN (SOCIETY OF COMPOSERS, AUTHORS, AND MUSIC PUBLISHERS OF CANADA)

Head Office: 41 Valleybrook Dr., Toronto ON M3B 2S6 Canada. English Information Center: (866)(307)6226. French Information Center: (866) (800)55-SOCAN. Fax: (416)445-7108. Web site: www.socan.ca. CEO: Andre LeBel. Vice President Member Relations & General Manager, West Coast Division: Kent Sturgeon. Vice President Member Services: Jeff King. Director, Member Relations: Lynne Foster. " SOCAN is the Canadian copyright collective for the communication and performance of musical works. We administer these rights on behalf of our members (composers, lyricists, songwriters, and their publishers) and those of affiliated international organizations by licensing this use of their music in Canada. The fees collected are distributed as royalties to our members and to affiliated organizations throughout the world. We also distribute royalties received from those organizations to our members for the use of their music worldwide. SOCAN has offices in Toronto, Montreal, Vancouver, Edmonton, and Dartmouth."

SOCIETY OF COMPOSERS & LYRICISTS

400 S. Beverly Dr., Suite 214, Beverly Hills CA 90212. (310)281-2812. Fax: (310)284-4861. E-mail: execdir@thescl.com. Web site: www.thescl.com. The professional nonprofit trade organization for members actively engaged in writing music/lyrics for films, TV, and/or video games, or are students of film composition or songwriting for film. Primary mission is to advance the interests of the film and TV music community. Offers an award-winning quarterly publication, educational seminars, screenings, special member-only events, and other member benefits. Applications accepted year-round. Membership fee: $135 Full Membership (composers, lyricists, songwriters—film/TV music credits must be submitted); $85 Associate/Student Membership for composers, lyricists, songwriters without credits only; $135 Sponsor/Special Friend Membership (music editors, music supervisors, music attorneys, agents, etc.).

SODRAC INC.

759 Victoria Square, Suite 420, Montreal QC H2Y 2J7 Canada. (514)845-3268. Fax: (514)845-3401. E-mail: sodrac@sodrac.ca. Web site: www.sodrac.ca. **Contact:** Chantal Beaudoin, membership and licensing department (author, composer and publisher) or Diane Lamarre, visual arts and crafts department (visual artist and rights owner). Estab. 1985. "SODRAC is a reproduction rights collective society facilitating since 1985 the clearing of rights on musical and artistic works through collective or individual agreements concluded with any users and is responsible for the distribution

of royalties to its national and international members. The Society counts over 5,000 Canadian members and represents musical repertoire originating from nearly 100 foreign countries and manages the right of over 25,000 Canadian and foreign visual artists. SODRAC is the only Reproduction Rights Society in Canada where both songwriters and music publishers are represented, equally and directly.'' Serves those with an interest in songwriting and music publishing no matter what their age or skill level is. ''Members must have written or published at least one musical work that has been reproduced on an audio (CD, cassettte, LP) or audio-visual support (TV, DVD, video). The new member will benefit of a society working to secure his reproduction rights (mechanicals) and broadcast mechanicals.'' Applications accepted year-round.

☑ SONGWRITERS AND POETS CRITIQUE
P.O. Box 21065, Columbus OH 43221. E-mail: leeann@SongwritersCritique.com. Web site: www.so ngwriterscritique.com. **Contact:** LeeAnn Pretzman, secretary. Estab. 1985. Serves songwriters, musicians, poets, lyricists and performers. Meets second and fourth Friday of every month to discuss club events and critique one another's work. Offers seminars and workshops with professionals in the music industry. ''We critique mail-in submissions from long-distance members. Our goal is to provide support and opportunity to anyone interested in creating songs or poetry.'' Applications are accepted year-round. Annual dues: $30.

SONGWRITERS ASSOCIATION OF WASHINGTON
PMB 106-137, 4200 Wisconsin Ave. NW, Washington DC 20016. (301)654-8434. E-mail: membershi p@SAW.org. Web site: www.SAW.org. Estab. 1979. ''SAW is a nonprofit organization operated by a volunteer board of directors. It is committed to providing its members opportunities to learn more about the art of songwriting, to learn more about the music business, to perform in public, and to connect with fellow songwriters. SAW sponsors various events to achieve these goals: workshops, open mics, songwriter exchanges, and showcases. In addition, SAW organizes the Mid-Atlantic Song Contest open to entrants nationwide each year; ''the competition in 2003 was the twentieth contest SAW has adjudicated since 1982.'' (Contest information masc@saw.org). As well as maintaining a Web site, SAW publishes *SAW Notes*, a bimonthly newsletter for members containing information on upcoming local events, member news, contest information, and articles of interest. Joint introductory membership with the Washington Area Music Association is available at a savings. Use the contact information above for membership inquiries.

THE SONGWRITERS GUILD OF AMERICA (SGA)
1560 Broadway, Suite #1306, New York NY 10036. (212)768-7902. Fax: (212)768-9048. E-mail: ny@songwritersguild.com. Web site: www.songwritersguild.com. **New York Office:** 1560 Broadway, Suite #408, New York, NY 10036; **Los Angeles Office:** 6430 Sunset Blvd., Suite 705, Hollywood CA 90028, (323)462-1108. Fax: (323)462-5430. E-mail: la@songwritersguild.com. **Nashville Office:** 209 10th Ave. S., Suite 534, Nashville TN 37203. (615)742-9945. Fax: (615)742-9948. E-mail: nash@ songwritersguild.com. **SGA Administration:** 1500 Harbor Blvd., Wechawken NJ 07086. (201)867-7603. Fax:(201)867-7535. E-mail: corporate@songwritersguild.com.
   ● Also see the listings for The Songwriters Guild Foundation in the Workshops & Conferences section.
President: Rick Carnes. Executive Director: Lewis M. Bachman. East Coast Project Manager: Mark Saxon. West Coast Project Manager: Aaron Lynn. Central Project Manager: Evan Shoemke. Estab. 1931. ''The Songwriters Guild of America (SGA) is a voluntary songwriter association run by and for songwriters. It is devoted exclusively to providing songwriters with the services and activities they need to succeed in the business of music. The preamble to the SGA constitution charges the board to take such lawful actions as will advance, promote and benefit the profession. Services of SGA cover every aspect of songwriting including the creative, administrative and financial.'' A full member must be a published songwriter. An associate member is any unpublished songwriter with a desire to learn more about the business and craft of songwriting. The third class of membership comprises estates of deceased writers. The Guild contract is considered to be the best available in the industry, having the greatest number of built-in protections for the songwriter. The Guild's

Royalty Collection Plan makes certain that prompt and accurate payments are made to writers. The ongoing Audit Program makes periodic checks of publishers' books. For the self-publisher, the Catalogue Administration Program (CAP) relieves a writer of the paperwork of publishing for a fee lower than the prevailing industry rates. The Copyright Renewal Service informs members a year in advance of a song's renewal date. Other services include workshops in New York and Los Angeles, free Ask-A-Pro sessions with industry pros, critique sessions, collaborator service and newsletters. In addition, the Guild reviews your songwriter contract on request (Guild or otherwise); fights to strengthen songwriters' rights and to increase writers' royalties by supporting legislation which directly affects copyright; offers a group medical and life insurance plan; issues news bulletins with essential information for songwriters; provides a songwriter collaboration service for younger writers; financially evaluates catalogues of copyrights in connection with possible sale and estate planning; operates an estates administration service; and maintains a nonprofit educational foundation (The Songwriters Guild Foundation)."

SONGWRITERS OF OKLAHOMA

P.O. Box 4121, Edmond OK 73083-4121. E-mail: furrowmusic@sbcglobal.net. **Contact:** Harvey Derrick, president. Offers information on the music industry: reviews publishing/artist contracts, where and how to get demo tapes produced, presentation of material to publishers or record companies, royalties and copyrights. Also offers information on the craft of songwriting: co-writers, local songwriting organizations, a written critique of lyrics, songs and compositions on tapes/CDs as long as a SASE is provided for return of critique. No more than 1 song per tape and 3 per CD. All of these services are free to current members. Membership dues: $25/year. A SASE must be included with all submissions/inquiries.

☑ SONGWRITERS OF WISCONSIN INTERNATIONAL

P.O. Box 1027, Neenah WI 54957-1027. (920)725-5129. E-mail: sowi@new.rr.com. Web site: www.songwritersofwisconsin.org. **Contact:** Tony Ansems, president. Workshops Coordinator: Mike Heath. Estab. 1983. Serves songwriters. "Membership is open to songwriters writing all styles of music. Residency in Wisconsin is recommended but not required. Members are encouraged to bring tapes and lyric sheets of their songs to the meetings, but it is not required. We are striving to improve the craft of songwriting in Wisconsin. Living in Wisconsin, a songwriter would be close to any of the workshops and showcases offered each month at different towns. The primary value of membership for a songwriter is in sharing ideas with other songwriters, being critiqued and helping other songwriters." Offers competitions (contest entry deadline: May 15), field trips, instruction, lectures, newsletter, performance opportunities, social outings, workshops and critique sessions. Applications accepted year-round. Membership dues: $30/year.

Tips "Critique meetings every last Thursday of each month, January through October, 7 p.m.-10 p.m. at The Hampton Inn, 350 N. Fox River Dr., Appleton WI."

N SONGWRITERS RESOURCE NETWORK

PMB 135, 6327-C SW Capitol Hill, Portland OR 97239-1937. E-mail: info@SongwritersResourceNetwork.com. Web site: www.SongwritersResourceNetwork.com. **Contact:** Steve Cahill, president. Estab. 1998. "For songwriters and lyricists of every kind, from beginners to advanced." No eligibility requirements. "Purpose is to provide free information to help songwriters develop their craft, market their songs, and learn about songwriting opportunities." Sponsors the annual Great American Song Contest, offers marketing tips and Web site access to music industry contacts. "We provide leads to publishers, producers and other music industry professionals." Visit Web site or send SASE for more information.

- Also see the listing for Great American Song Contest in the Contests and Awards section of this book.

SOUTHWEST VIRGINIA SONGWRITERS ASSOCIATION

P.O. Box 698, Salem VA 24153. Web site: www.svsa.info. **Contact:** Britt Mistele. Estab. 1981. 80 members of all ages and skill all levels, mainly country, folk, gospel, contemporary and rock but

other musical interests too. "The purpose of SVSA is to increase, broaden and expand the knowledge of each member and to support, better and further the progress and success of each member in
songwriting and related fields of endeavor." Offers performance opportunities, evaluation services,
instruction, newsletter, workshops, monthly meetings and monthly newsletter. Application accepted year-round. Membership fee: $18/year.

☑ 🌐 SPNM—PROMOTING NEW MUSIC

(Society for the Promotion of New Music (SPNM)), St. Margarets House, 4th Floor, 18-20 Southwark
St., London SE1 1TJ United Kingdom. 020 7407 1640. Fax: 020 7403 7652. E-mail: spnm@spnm.org.
uk. Web site: www.spnm.org.uk. Executive Director: Abigail Pogson. Administrator: Katy Kirk.
Estab. 1943. "All ages and backgrounds are welcome, with a common interest in the innovative and
unexplored. We enable new composers to hear their works performed by top-class professionals in
quality venues." Offers magazine, lectures, workshops, special offers and concerts. Annual selection procedure, deadline September 30. "From contemporary jazz, classical and popular music to
that written for film, dance and other creative media, spnm is one of the main advocates of new
music in Britain today. Through its eclectic program of concerts, workshops, education projects
and collaborations and through its publications, *new notes*, spnm brings new music in all guises
to many, many people." Other calls for specific events throughout year. Membership fee: Ordinary:
£25; Concessions: £10; Friend: £35.
Tips "Most calls for pieces are restricted to those living and/or studying in UK/Ireland, or to British
composers living overseas."

THE TENNESSEE SONGWRITERS INTERNATIONAL

P.O. Box 2664, Hendersonville TN 37077-2664. (615)969-5967. E-mail: asktsai@aol.com. Web site:
www.clubnashville.com/tsai.htm. **Contact:** Margie Reeves, membership director. Executive Director: Jim Sylvis. Serves songwriters. "Our membership is open to all ages and consists of both
novice and experienced professional songwriters. The only requirement for membership is a serious
interest in the craft and business of songwriting. Our main purpose and function is to educate and
assist the songwriter, both in the art/craft of songwriting and in the business of songwriting. In
addition to education, we also provide an opportunity for camaraderie, support and encouragement,
as well a chance to meet co-writers. We also critique each others' material and offer suggestions
for improvement, if needed. We offer the following to our members: Informative monthly newsletters; 'Pro-Rap'—once a month a key person from the music industry addresses our membership
on their field of specialty. They may be writers, publishers, producers and sometimes even the
recording artists themselves; 'Pitch-A-Pro'—we schedule a publisher, producer or artist who is
currently looking for material to come to our meeting and listen to songs pitched by our members;
'Legends Night'—several times a year, a 'legend' in the music business will be our guest speaker.
Annual Awards Dinner—honoring the most accomplished of our TSAI membership during the past
year; Tips—letting our members know who is recording and how to get their songs to the right
people. Workshops are held at Belmont University, Wedgewood Ave., Nashville TN in the Massey
Business Center Building, Room 200-B on Wednesday evenings from 7-9 p.m." Applications accepted year-round. Membership runs for one year from the date you join. Membership fee is $50/
year in the U.S. and $65 in all foreign countries.

☑ TEXAS ACCOUNTANTS & LAWYERS FOR THE ARTS

1540 Sul Ross, Houston TX 77006-4730. (713)526-4876 ext. 201 or (800)526-TALA ext. 201. Fax:
(713)526-1299. E-mail: info@talarts.org. Web site: www.talarts.org. **Contact:** Jane Lowery, Esq.,
executive director. Estab. 1979. TALA's members include accountants, attorneys, museums, theatre
groups, dance groups, actors, artists, musicians and filmmakers. Our members are of all age groups
and represent all facets of their respective fields. TALA is a nonprofit organization that provides
pro bono legal and accounting services to income-eligible artists from all disciplines and to nonprofit
arts organizations. TALA also provides mediation services for resolving disputes as a low cost-
nonadversarial alternative to litigation. Offers newsletter, lectures, library and workshops. Applications accepted year-round. Membership fee for artists: $30; bands: $75.

Tips TALA's speakers program presents low-cost seminars on topics such as The Music Business, Copyright and Trademark, and The Business of Writing. These seminars are held annually at a location in Houston. TALA's speaker's program also provides speakers for seminars by other organizations.

TEXAS MUSIC OFFICE
P.O. Box 13246, Austin TX 78711. (512)463-6666. Fax: (512)463-4114. E-mail: music@governor.sta te.tx.us. Web site: www.governor.state.tx.us/music. **Contact:** Casey Monahan, director. Estab. 1990. ''The main purpose of the Texas Music Office is to promote the Texas music industry and Texas music, and to assist music professionals around the world with information about the Texas market. The Texas Music Office serves as a clearinghouse for Texas music industry information using their seven databases: Texas Music Industry (7,150 Texas music businesses in 94 music business categories); Texas Music Events (915 Texas music events); Texas Talent Register (7,050 Texas recording artists); Texas Radio Stations (837 Texas stations); U.S. Record Labels; Classical Texas (detailed information for all classical music organizations in Texas); and International (450 foreign businesses interested in Texas music). Provides referrals to Texas music businesses, talent and events in order to attract new business to Texas and/or to encourage Texas businesses and individuals to keep music business in-state. Serves as a liaison between music businesses and other government offices and agencies. Publicizes significant developments within the Texas music industry.'' Publishes the *Texas Music Industry Directory* (see the Publications of Interest section for more information).

TORONTO MUSICIANS' ASSOCIATION
15 Gervais Dr., Suite 500, Toronto ON M3C 1Y8 Canada. (416)421-1020. Fax: (416)421-7011. E-mail: info@torontomusicians.org. Web site: www.torontomusicians.org. Executive Director: Bill Skolnick. Estab. 1887. Serves musicians—*All* musical styles, background, areas of the industry. ''Must be a Canadian citizen, show proof of immigration status, or have a valid work permit for an extended period of time.'' The purpose of this organization is ''to unite musicians into one organization, in order that they may, individually and collectively, secure, maintain and profit from improved economic, working and artistic conditions.'' Offers newsletter. Applications accepted year-round. Joining fee: $225 (Canadian); student fee: $100 (Canadian). Student must have proof of school enrollment.

VOLUNTEER LAWYERS FOR THE ARTS
1 E. 53rd St., 6th Floor, New York NY 10022. (212)319-ARTS (2787), ext. 1 (Monday-Friday 9:30-12 and 1-4 EST). Fax: (212)752-6575. E-mail: vlany@vlany.org. Web site: www.vlany.org. **Contact:** Elena M. Paul, esq., executive director. Estab. 1969. Serves songwriters, musicians and all performing, visual, literary and fine arts artists and groups. Offers legal assistance and representation to eligible individual artists and arts organizations who cannot afford private counsel and a mediation service. VLA sells publications on arts-related issues and offers educational conferences, lectures, seminars and workshops. In addition, there are affiliates nationwide who assist local arts organizations and artists. Call for information.

WASHINGTON AREA MUSIC ASSOCIATION
6263 Occoquan Forest Drive, Manassas VA 20112. (202)338-1134. Fax: (703)393-1028. E-mail: dcmusic@wamadc.com. Web site: www.wamadc.com. **Contact:** Mike Schreibman, president. Estab. 1985. Serves songwriters, musicians and performers, managers, club owners and entertainment lawyers; ''all those with an interest in the Washington music scene.'' The organization is designed to promote the Washington music scene and increase its visibility. Its primary value to members is its seminars and networking opportunities. Offers lectures, newsletter, performance opportunities and workshops. WAMA sponsors the annual Washington Music Awards (The Wammies) and The Crosstown Jam or annual showcase of more than 300 artists at 60 venues in the DC area. Applications accepted year-round. Annual dues: $30.

WEST COAST SONGWRITERS

(formerly Northern California Songwriters Association), 1724 Laurel St., Suite 120, San Carlos CA 94070. (650)654-3966. E-mail: ian@westcoastsongwriters.org. Web site: www.westcoastsongwrite rs.org. **Contact:** Ian Crombie, executive director. Serves songwriters and musicians. Estab. 1979. "Our 1,200 members are lyricists and composers from ages 16-80, from beginners to professional songwriters. No eligibility requirements. Our purpose is to provide the education and opportunities that will support our writers in creating and marketing outstanding songs. WCS provides support and direction through local networking and input from Los Angeles and Nashville music industry leaders, as well as valuable marketing opportunities. Most songwriters need some form of collaboration, and by being a member they are exposed to other writers, ideas, critiquing, etc." Offers annual West Coast Songwriters Conference, "the largest event of its kind in northern California. This 2-day event held the second hand in September features 16 seminars, 50 screening sessions (over 1,200 songs listened to by industry professionals) and a sunset concert with hit songwriters performing their songs." Also offers monthly visits from major publishers, songwriting classes, competitions, seminars conducted by hit songwriters ("we sell audio tapes of our seminars—list of tapes available on request"), mail-in song-screening service for members who cannot attend due to time or location, a monthly e-newsletter, monthly performance opportunities and workshops. Applications accepted year-round. Dues: $40/year, student; $75/year, regular membership; $150/year, pro-membership; $250/year, contributing membership.

Tips "WCS's functions draw local talent and nationally recognized names together. This is of a tremendous value to writers outside a major music center. We are developing a strong songwriting community in Northern and Southern California. We serve the San Jose, Monterey Bay, East Bay, San Francisco, Los Angeles, and Sacramento areas and we have the support of some outstanding writers and publishers from both Los Angeles and Nashville. They provide us with invaluable direction and inspiration."

WOMEN IN MUSIC

P.O. Box 1215, Chelsea Station, New York NY 10113. (212)459-4580. E-mail: wim@womeninmusic. org. Web site: www.womeninmusic.org. Estab. 1985. Members are professionals in the business and creative areas: record company executives, managers, songwriters, musicians, vocalists, attorneys, recording engineers, agents, publicists, studio owners, music publishers and more. Purpose is to support, encourage and educate as well as provide networking opportunities. Offers newsletter, lectures, workshops, performance opportunities and business discounts. Presents annual "Touchstone Award" luncheon helping to raise money to support other organizations and individuals through WIM donations and scholarships. Applications accepted year-round. Membership fee: Professional: $75; Student: $35.

Workshops & Conferences

For a songwriter just starting out, conferences and workshops can provide valuable learning opportunities. At conferences, songwriters can have their songs evaluated, hear suggestions for further improvement and receive feedback from music business experts. They are also excellent places to make valuable industry contacts. Workshops can help a songwriter improve his craft and learn more about the business of songwriting. They may involve classes on songwriting and the business, as well as lectures and seminars by industry professionals.

Each year, hundreds of workshops and conferences take place all over the country. Songwriters can choose from small regional workshops held in someone's living room to large national conferences such as South by Southwest in Austin, Texas, which hosts more than 6,000 industry people, songwriters and performers. Many songwriting organizations—national and local—host workshops that offer instruction on just about every songwriting topic imaginable, from lyric writing and marketing strategy to contract negotiation. Conferences provide songwriters the chance to meet one on one with publishing and record company professionals and give performers the chance to showcase their work for a live audience (usually consisting of industry people) during the conference. There are conferences and workshops that address almost every type of music, offering programs for songwriters, performers, musical playwrights and much more.

This section includes national and local workshops and conferences with a brief description of what they offer, when they are held and how much they cost to attend. Write or call any that interest you for further information. To find out what workshops or conferences take place in specific parts of the country, see the Geographic Index at the end of this book.

Get the Most From a Conference

BEFORE YOU GO:

- **Save money.** Sign up early for a conference and take advantage of the early registration fee. Don't put off making hotel reservations either—the conference will usually have a block of rooms reserved at a discounted price.

- **Become familiar with all the pre-conference literature.** Study the maps of the area, especially the locations of the rooms in which your meetings/events are scheduled.

- **Make a list of three to five objectives you'd like to obtain,** e.g., what you want to learn more about, what you want to improve on, how many new contacts you want to make.

AT THE CONFERENCE:

- **Budget your time.** Label a map so you know where, when and how to get to each session. Note what you want to do most. Then, schedule time for demo critiques if they are offered.

- **Don't be afraid to explore new areas.** You are there to learn. Pick one or two sessions you wouldn't typically attend. Keep your mind open to new ideas and advice.

- **Allow time for mingling.** Some of the best information is given after the sessions. Find out "frank truths" and inside scoops. Asking people what they've learned at the conference will trigger a conversation that may branch into areas you want to know more about, but won't hear from the speakers.

- **Attend panels.** Panels consist of a group of industry professionals who have the capability to further your career. If you're new to the business you can learn so much straight from the horse's mouth. Even if you're a veteran, you can brush up on your knowledge or even learn something new. Whatever your experience, the panelist's presence is an open invitation to approach him with a question during the panel or with a handshake afterwards.

- **Collect everything:** especially informational materials and business cards. Make notes about the personalities of the people you meet to later remind you who to contact and who to avoid.

AFTER THE CONFERENCE:

- **Evaluate.** Write down the answers to these questions: Would I attend again? What were the pluses and minuses, e.g., speakers, location, food, topics, cost, lodging? What do I want to remember for next year? What should I try to do next time? Who would I like to meet?

- **Write a thank-you letter** to someone who has been particularly helpful. They'll remember you when you later solicit a submission.

Resources

☑ APPEL FARM ARTS AND MUSIC FESTIVAL

P.O. Box 888, Elmer NJ 08318. (856)358-2472. Fax: (856)358-6513. E-mail: perform@appelfarm.org. Web site: www.appelfarm.org. **Contact:** Sean Timmons, artistic director. Estab Festival: 1989; Series: 1970. "Our annual open air festival is the highlight of our year-round Performing Arts Series which was established to bring high quality arts programs to the people of South Jersey. Festival includes acoustic and folk music, blues, etc." Past performers have included Indigo Girls, John Prine, Ani DiFranco, Randy Newman, Jackson Browne, Mary Chapin Carpenter, David Gray, Nanci Griffith and Shawn Colvin. In addition, our Country Music concerts have featured Toby Keith, Joe Diffie, Ricky Van Shelton, Doug Stone and others. Programs for songwriters and musicians include performance opportunities as part of Festival and Performing Arts Series. Programs for musical playwrights also include performance opportunities as part of Performing Arts Series. Festival is a one-day event held in June, and Performing Arts Series is held year-round. Both are held at the Appel Farm Arts and Music Center, a 176-acre farm in Southern New Jersey. Up to 20 songwriters/musicians participate in each event. Participants are songwriters, individual vocalists, bands, ensembles, vocal groups, composers, individual instrumentalists and dance/mime/movement. Participants are selected by CD submissions. Applicants should send a press packet, CD and biographical information. Application materials accepted year round. Faculty opportunities are available as part of residential Summer Arts Program for children, July/August.

ASCAP MUSICAL THEATRE WORKSHOP

1 Lincoln Plaza, New York NY 10023. (212)621-6234. Fax: (212)621-6558. E-mail: mkerker@ascap.com. Web site: www.ascap.com. **Contact:** Michael A. Kerker, director of musical theatre. Estab. 1981. Workshop is for musical theatre composers and lyricists only. Its purpose is to nurture and develop new musicals for the theatre. Offers programs for songwriters. Offers programs annually, usually April through May. Event took place in New York City. Four musical works are selected. Others are invited to audit the workshop. Participants are amateur and professional songwriters, composers and musical playwrights. Participants are selected by demo tape submission. Send for application. Deadline: mid-March. Also available: the annual ASCAP/Disney Musical Theatre Workshop in Los Angeles. It takes place in January and February. Deadline is late November. Details similar to New York workshop as above.

ASCAP WEST COAST/LESTER SILL SONGWRITER'S WORKSHOP

7920 Sunset Blvd., 3rd Floor, Los Angeles CA 90046. (323)883-1000. Fax: (323)883-1049. E-mail: info@ascap.com. Web site: www.ascap.com. Estab. 1963. Offers programs for songwriters. Offers programs annually. Event takes place mid-January through mid-February. 14 songwriters/musicians participate in each event. Participants are amateur and professional songwriters. Participants are selected by demo tape submission or by invitation. "Send in two songs with lyrics, bio and brief explanation why you'd like to participate." Deadline: TBA.

☑ BMI-LEHMAN ENGEL MUSICAL THEATRE WORKSHOP

320 W. 57th St., New York NY 10019. (212)586-2000. E-mail: musicaltheatre@bmi.com. Web site: www.bmi.com. **Contact:** Jean Banks, senior director of musical theatre. Estab. 1961. "BMI is a music licensing company which collects royalties for affiliated writers. We have departments to help writers in jazz, concert, Latin, pop and musical theater writing." Offers programs "to musical theater composers, lyricists and librettists. The BMI-Lehman Engel Musical Theatre Workshops were formed in an effort to refresh and stimulate professional writers, as well as to encourage and develop new creative talent for the musical theater." Each workshop meets 1 afternoon a week for 2 hours at BMI, New York. Participants are professional songwriters, composers and playwrights. "BMI-Lehman Engel Musical Theatre Workshop Showcase presents the best of the workshop to producers, agents, record and publishing company execs, press and directors for possible option and production." Call for application. Tape and lyrics of 3 compositions required with application. "BMI also sponsors a jazz composers workshop. For more information call David Sanjek at (212)586-2000."

☑ BONK FESTIVAL OF NEW MUSIC

% Bonk Inc., 407 W. Frances Ave., Tampa FL 33602. E-mail: bonk@music.org. Web site: www.bon kfest.org. **Contact:** Festival Director. Estab. 1994. Offers programs for composers and performers. Offers programs annually. Event takes place in March. Participants are amateur and professional composers and instrumentalists. Participants are selected by demo tape audition. Demo tape criteria available on Web site. Include SASE. Deadline: September 30.

☑ ▣ CANADIAN MUSIC WEEK

5355 Vail Court, Mississauga ON L5M 6G9 Canada. E-mail: festival@cmw.net. Web site: www.cmw .net. **Contact:** Phil Klygo, festival coordinator. Estab. 1985. Offers annual programs for songwriters, composers and performers. Event takes place mid-March in Toronto. 100,000 public, 300 bands and 1,200 delegates participate in each event. Participants are amateur and professional songwriters, vocalists, composers, bands and instrumentalists. Participants are selected by submitting demonstration tape. Send for application and more information. Concerts take place in 25 clubs and 5 concert halls, and 3 days of seminars and exhibits are provided. Fee: $375 (Canadian).

CMJ MUSIC MARATHON, MUSICFEST & FILMFEST

151 W. 25th St., 12th Floor, New York NY 10001. (917)606-1908. Fax: (917)606-1914. Web site: www.cmj.com/Marathon. **Contact:** Operations Manager. Estab. 1981. Premier annual alternative music gathering of more than 9,000 music business and film professionals. Fall, NYC. Features 4 days and nights of more than 50 panels and workshops focusing on every facet of the industry; exclusive film screenings; keynote speeches by the world's most intriguing and controversial voices; exhibition area featuring live performance stage; over 1,000 of music's brightest and most visionary talents (from the unsigned to the legendary) performing over 4 evenings at more than 50 of NYC's most important music venues. Participants are selected by submitting demonstration tape. Go to Web site for application.

CUTTING EDGE MUSIC BUSINESS CONFERENCE

1524 N. Claiborne Ave., New Orleans LA 70116. (504)945-1800. Fax: (504)945-1873. E-mail: cut_ed ge@bellsouth.net. Web site: www.jass.com/cuttingedge. Executive Producer: Eric L. Cager. Showcase Producer: Nathaniel Franklin. Estab. 1993. "The conference is a five-day international conference which covers the business and educational aspects of the music industry. As part of the conference, the New Works showcase features over 200 bands and artists from around the country and Canada in showcases of original music. All music genres are represented." Offers programs for songwriters and performers. "Bands and artists should submit material for consideration of entry into the New Works showcase." Event takes place during August in New Orleans. 1,000 songwriters/musicians participate in each event. Participants are songwriters, vocalists and bands. Send for application. Deadline: June 1. "The Music Business Institute offers a month-long series of free educational workshops for those involved in the music industry. The workshops take place each October. Further information is available via our Web site."

PETER DAVIDSON'S WRITER'S SEMINAR

P.O. Box 497, Arnolds Park IA 51331. (712)332-9329. E-mail: peterdavidson@mchsi.com. **Contact:** Peter Davidson, seminar presenter. Estab. 1985. "Peter Davidson's Writer's Seminar is for persons interested in writing all sorts of materials, including songs. Emphasis is placed on developing salable ideas, locating potential markets for your work, copyrighting, etc. The seminar is not specifically for writers of songs, but is very valuable to them, nevertheless." Offers programs year-round. One-day seminar, 9:00 a.m.-4:00 p.m. Event takes place on various college campuses. In even-numbered years offers seminars in Minnesota, Iowa, Nebraska, South Dakota, Kansas, Colorado and Wyoming. In odd-numbered years offers seminars in Minnesota, Iowa, Nebraska, South Dakota, Missouri, Illinois, Arkansas and Tennessee. Anyone can participate. Send SASE for schedule. Deadline: day of the seminar. Fee: $45 to $59. "All seminars are held on college campuses in college facilities—various colleges sponsor and promote the seminars."

FOLK ALLIANCE ANNUAL CONFERENCE

962 Wayne Ave., Suite 902, Silver Spring MD 20910. (301)588-8185. Fax: (301)588-8186. E-mail: fa@folk.org. Web site: www.folk.org. **Contact:** Tony Ziselberger, membership services director. Estab. 1989. Conference/workshop topics change each year. Conference takes place mid-February and lasts 4 days at a different location each year. 2,000 attendees include artists, agents, arts administrators, print/broadcast media, folklorists, folk societies, merchandisers, presenters, festivals, recording companies, etc. Artists wishing to showcase should contact the office for a showcase application form. Closing date for application is May 31. Application fee is $20 for 2005 conference. Additional costs vary from year to year. Housing is separate for the event, scheduled for Feb. 16-19, 2006 in Austin, TX.
- Also see the listing for The Folk Alliance in the Organizations section of this book.

N GENESIUS THEATRE GROUP

(formerly Genesius Theatre Guild), 520 Eighth Ave., 3rd Floor, Suite 320, New York NY 10018. (212)244-5404. E-mail: gtgnyc.org. Web site: www.gtgnyc.org. **Contact:** Dana Harrel, co-artistic director. Estab. 1994. "The company mission is to produce writers who have not been produced in New York City, including musical theater, opera, dance and other musical performance art. GTG also conducts readings and workshops for development towards production. Please send CD of music, script, synopsis, résumé/bio and letter. Productions, workshops and readings in venues with 99 or fewer seats."

N HOLLYWOOD REPORTER/BILLBOARD FILM & TV MUSIC CONFERENCE

% The Hollywood Reporter, 5055 Wilshire Blvd., Los Angeles CA 90036- 4396. (646)654-4643. E-mail: eparker@billboard.com. Web site: www.billboardevents.com/. **Contact:** Special Events Coordinator. Estab. 1995. Promotes all music for film and television. Offers programs for songwriters and composers. Offers programs annually in April. Held at the Directors Guild of America. More than 350 songwriters/musicians participate in each event. Participants are professional songwriters, composers, plus producers, directors, etc. Conference panelists are selected by invitation. For registration information, call the Special Events Dept. at Hollywood Reporter. Fee: $425/person.

☑ I WRITE THE SONGS

2221 Justin Rd., Suite 119-142, Highland Village TX 75028. (972)317-2760. Fax: (972)317-4737. E-mail: info@iwritethesongs.com. Web site: www.iwritethesongs.com. **Contact:** Sarah Marshall, administrative director. Estab. 1996. "I Write the Songs is an on-the-air songwriting seminar. It is a syndicated radio talk show available both on the radio and on the Internet. A detailed description of the program and its hosts, Mary Dawson and Sharon Braxton, can be found on the Web site. The Web site address will also link you to the Internet broadcasts and list the radio stations that carry the program. You can also hear current and archived shows covering INSTRUCTION on the craft and business of songwriting; INTERVIEWS with famous and 'soon-to-be-famous' songwriters; and CRITIQUES of original songs submitted by our listeners. I Write the Songs has been created to inspire and instruct aspiring songwriters of all genres of music." Offers programs, including weekly programs on radio and the Internet, for songwriters, composers and performers. "We hold regular contests and competitions. All aspiring songwriters earning less than $5,000 annually from song royalties are eligible." I Write the Songs features "Critique Shows" every 4-6 weeks. Songwriters can submit demos on cassette or CD with typed lyric sheet. Does not return material. Featured songs are selected at random. Writers whose songs are selected for a show will receive a taped copy of the program on which their song is critiqued. Mary Dawson conducts songwriting seminars across the country and internationally. For a list of upcoming seminars, check the Web site.

☑ INDEPENDENT MUSIC CONFERENCE

InterMixx.com, Inc., 304 Main Ave., PMB 287, Norwalk CT 06851. 1-800-MIXX-MAG. Fax: (215)483-3151. E-mail: info@gopmc.com. Web site: www.gopmc.com. Executive Director: Noel Ramos. Estab. 1992. "The purpose of the IMC is to bring together rock, hip hop and acoustic music for of panels and showcases. Offers programs for songwriters, composers and performers. 250

showcases at 20 clubs around the city. Also offer a DJ cutting contest." Held annually at the Sheraton Society Hill Hotel in Philadelphia in September. 3,000 amateur and professional songwriters, composers, individual vocalists, bands, individual instrumentalists, attorneys, managers, agents, publishers, A&R, promotions, club owners, etc. participate each year. Send for application.

KERRVILLE FOLK FESTIVAL

Kerrville Festivals, Inc., P.O. Box 291466, Kerrville TX 78029. (830)257-3600. E-mail: info@kerrville-music.com. Web site: www.kerrvillefolkfestival.com. **Contact:** Dalis Allen, producer. Estab. 1972. Hosts 3-day songwriters' school, a 4-day music business school and New Folk concert competition sponsored by *Performing Songwriter* magazine. Festival produced in late spring and late summer. Spring festival lasts 18 days and is held outdoors at Quiet Valley Ranch. 110 or more songwriters participate. Performers are professional songwriters and bands. Participants selected by submitting demo, by invitation only. Send cassette, or CD, promotional material and list of upcoming appearances. "Songwriter and music schools include lunch, experienced professional instructors, camping on ranch and concerts. Rustic facilities. Food available at reasonable cost. Audition materials accepted at above address. These three-day and four-day seminars include noon meals, handouts and camping on the ranch. Usually held during Kerrville Folk Festival, first and second week in June. Write or check the Web site for contest rules, schools and seminars information, and festival schedules. Also establishing a Phoenix Fund to provide assistance to ill or injured singer/songwriters who find themselves in distress."

• Also see the listing for New Folk Concerts For Emerging Songwriters in the Contests & Awards section of this book.

LAMB'S RETREAT FOR SONGWRITERS

Presented by SPRINGFED ARTS, a nonprofit organization, P.O. Box 304, Royal Oak MI 48068-0304. (248)589-1594. Fax: (248)589-3913. E-mail: johndlamb@ameritech.net. Web site: www.springfed.org. **Contact:** John D. Lamb, director. Estab. 1995. Offers programs for songwriters on annual basis; November 2-5, 2006 and November 9-12, 2006 at The Birchwood Inn, Harbor Springs, MI. 60 songwriters/musicians participate in each event. Participants are amateur and professional songwriters. Anyone can participate. Send for registration or e-mail. Deadline: two weeks before event begins. Fee: $275-495, includes all meals. Facilities are single/double occupancy lodging with private baths; 2 conference rooms and hospitality lodge. Offers song assignments, songwriting workshops, song swaps, open mic and one-on-one mentoring. Faculty are noted songwriters, such as Jack Williams, Dana Cooper, Chuck Brodsley, and Amy Rigby. Partial scholarships may be available by writing: Blissfest Music Organization, % Jim Gillespie, P.O. Box 441, Harbor Springs, MI 49740. Deadline: 2 weeks before event.

MANCHESTER MUSIC FESTIVAL

P.O. Box 33, Manchester VT 05254. (802)362-1956 or (800)639-5868. Fax: (802)362-0711. E-mail: info@ManchesterMusicFestival.org. Web site: www.mmfvt.org. **Contact:** Robyn Madison, managing director. Estab. 1974. Offers classical music education and performances. Summer program for young professional musicians offered in tandem with a professional concert series in the mountains of Manchester VT. Up to 23 young professionals, age 18 and up, are selected by audition for the Young Artists Program, which provides instruction, performance and teaching opportunities, with full scholarship for all participants. Printable application available on Web site. Application fee: $40. Commissioning opportunities for new music, and performance opportunities for professional chamber ensembles and soloists for both summer and fall/winter concert series. "Celebrating 28 years of fine music."

MUSIC BUSINESS SOLUTIONS/CAREER BUILDING WORKSHOPS

P.O. Box 230266, Boston MA 02123-0266. (888)655-8335. E-mail: peter@mbsolutions.com. Web site: www.mbsolutions.com. **Contact:** Peter Spellman, director. Estab. 1991. Workshop titles include "Discovering Your Music Career Niche," "How to Release an Independent Record" and "Promoting and Marketing Music in the 21st Century." Offers programs for music entrepreneurs, songwriters, musical playwrights, composers and performers. Offers programs year-round, annually and bi-annually. Event takes place at various colleges, recording studios, hotels, conferences. 10-100 songwriters/musicians participate in each event. Participants are both amateur and professional songwriters, vocalists, music business professionals, composers, bands, musical playwrights and instrumentalists. Anyone can participate. Fee: varies. "Music Business Solutions offers a number of other services and programs for both songwriters and musicians including: private music career counseling, business plan development and internet marketing; publication of *Music Biz Insight: Power Reading for Busy Music Professionals*, a bimonthly e-zine chock full of music management and marketing tips and resources. Free subscription with e-mail address."

NASHVILLE MUSIC FESTIVAL

P.O. Box 291827, Nashville TN 37229-1827. (615)252-8202. Fax: (615)321-0384. E-mail: c4promo@aol.com. Web site: www.radiocountry.org. (festivals). **Contact:** Ambassador Charlie Ray, director. Estab. 2000. Offers 100 booth spaces for makers of instruments, craftspeople, independent record companies, and unsigned artists; seminars by successful music industry professionals; contests; and stages on which to perform. "Nashville record companies big and small are looking for new talent. A lot of them will have talent scouts at the festival. If they see you on stage and like what they see, you could be signed to a recording contract. There will also be a songwriter's stage each year. This is an annual event. It takes place Memorial Day weekend each year. It has been expanded to 4 days. It always starts on Friday and ends about 10 p.m. the last Monday in May. Complete directions to festival location will be mailed with your tickets and posted on our Web page."

N NATIONAL ACADEMY OF POPULAR MUSIC SONGWRITING WORKSHOP PROGRAM

330 W. 58th St. Suite 411, New York NY 10019. (212)957-9230. Fax: (212)957-9227. E-mail: 73751.1142@compuserve.com. Web site: www.shof.org. **Contact:** Bob Leone, projects director. Estab. 1969. "For all forms of pop music, from rock to R&B to dance." Offers programs for member lyricists and composers including songwriting workshops (beginning to master levels) and songwriter showcases. "The Abe Olman Scholarship for excellence in songwriting is awarded ($1,200) to a student who has been in our program for at least 4 quarters." Offers programs 3 times/year: fall, winter and spring. Event takes place mid-September to December, mid-January to April, mid-April to July (10 2-3 hour weekly sessions) at New York Spaces, 131 W. 72nd St., New York. Also offers networking meetings with industry pros and open mics. 50 students involved in 4 different classes. Participants are amateur and professional lyricists and composers. Some participants are selected by submitting demonstration tape, and by invitation. Send for application. Deadline: first week of classes. Annual dues: $25 and up. Sponsors songwriter showcases in March, June, September and December.

NEMO MUSIC SHOWCASE & CONFERENCE

312 Stuart St. 4th Floor, Boston MA 02116. (617)348-2899. E-mail: kristin@nemoboston.com. Web site: www.nemoboston.com. **Contact:** Kristin Bredimus, conference &festival director. Estab. 1996. Music showcase and conference, featuring the Boston Music Awards and 3 days/nights of a conference with trade show and more than 200 nightly showcases in Boston. Offers showcases for songwriters. Offers programs annually. Event takes place in October. 1,500 songwriters/musicians participate at conference; 3,000 at awards show; 20,000 at showcases. Participants are professional songwriters, vocalists, composers, bands and instrumentalists. Participants are selected by invitation. Send for application or visit Web site.

N NORTH BY NORTHEAST MUSIC FESTIVAL AND CONFERENCE (NXNE)

189 Church St., Lower Level, Toronto ON M5B 1Y7 Canada. (416)863-6963. Fax: (416)863-0828. E-mail: info@nxne.com. Web site: www.nxne.com. **Contact:** Travis Bird, festival manager or Gillian Zulauf, conference registrar. Estab. 1995. "Our festival takes place mid-June at over 30 venues across downtown Toronto, drawing over 2,000 conference delegates, 400 bands and 50,000 music fans. Musical genres include everything from folk to funk, roots to rock, polka to punk and all points in between, bringing exceptional new talent, media front-runners, music business heavies

and music fans from all over the world to Toronto.'' Participants include emerging and established songwriters, vocalists, composers, bands and instrumentalists. Festival performers are selected by submitting a CD and accompanying press kit or applying through sonicbids.com. Application forms are available by Web site or by calling the office. Submission period each year is from November 1 to the third weekend in January. Submissions ''early bird'' fee: $20. Conference registration fee: $175-300. ''Our conference is held at the deluxe Holiday Inn on King and the program includes mentor sessions—15-minute one-on-one opportunities for songwriters and composers to ask questions of industry experts, roundtables, panel discussions, keynote speakers, etc. North By Northeast 2006 will be held June 8-10.''

☑ NSAI SONG CAMPS
1710 Roy Acuff Place, Nashville TN 37023. 1-800-321-6008 or (615)256-3354. Fax: (615)256-0034. E-mail: songcamps@nashvillesongwriters.com. Web site: www.nashvillesongwriters.com. **Contact:** Jeanie Williams, NSAI Events Director. Estab. 1992. Offers programs strictly for songwriters. Event held 4 times/year in Nashville. ''We provide most meals and lodging is available. We also present an amazing evening of music presented by the faculty.'' Camps are 3 days long, with 36-112 participants, depending on the camp. ''There are different levels of camps, some having preferred prerequisites. Each camp varies. Please call, e-mail or refer to Web site. It really isn't about the genre of music, but the quality of the song itself. Song Camp strives to strengthen the writer's vision and skills, therefore producing the better song. Song Camp is known as 'boot camp' for songwriters. It is guaranteed to catapult you forward in your writing! Participants are all aspiring songwriters led by a pro faculty. We do accept lyricists only and composers only with the hopes of expanding their scope.'' Participants are selected through submission of 2 songs with lyric sheet. Song Camp is open to NSAI members, although anyone can apply and upon acceptance join the organization. There is no formal application form. See Web site for membership and event information.

• Also see the listing for Nashville Songwriters Association International (NSAI) in the Organizations section of this book.

☑ NSAI SONGWRITERS SONGPOSIUM
1710 Roy Acuff Place, Nashville TN 37203. (615)256-3354 OR 1-800-321-6008. Fax: (615)256-0034. E-mail: events@NashvilleSongwriters.com. Web site: www.nashvillesongwriters.com. Covers ''all types of music. Participants take part in publisher evaluations, as well as large group sessions with different guest speakers.'' Offers annual programs for songwriters. Event takes place in April in downtown Nashville. 300 amateur songwriters/musicians participate in each event. Send for application.

▣ ORFORD FESTIVAL
Orford Arts Centre, 3165 Chemim DuParc, Orford QC J1X 7A2 Canada. (819)843-9871 or 1-800-567-6155. Fax: (819)843-7274. E-mail: centre@arts-orford.org. Web site: www.arts-orford.org. **Contact:** Anne-Marie Dubois, registrar/information manager. Artistic Coordinator: Nicolas Bélanger. Estab. 1951. ''Each year, the Orford Arts Centre produces up to 35 concerts in the context of its Music Festival. It receives artists from all over the world in classical and chamber music.'' Offers master classes for music students, young professional classical musicians and chamber music ensembles. New offerings include master classes for all instruments,voice, and opera. Master classes last 2 months and take place at Orford Arts Centre from the end of June to the middle of August. 350 students participate each year. Participants are selected by demo tape submissions. Send for application. Closing date for application is mid to late March. Check our Web site for specific dates and deadlines. Scholarships for qualified students.

▣ THE SHIZNIT MUSIC CONFERENCE
P.O. Box 1881, Baton Rouge LA 70821. (225)248-9526. Fax: (225)927-8705. E-mail: staffers@bellso uth.net. Web site: www.theshiznit.com. Public Relations: Lee Williams. Vice President: Sedrick Hills. Purpose is to provide performance and networking opportunities for a wide variety of music

and music related businesses, from urban to country, from blues to zydeco. Showcases, networking, trade shows and seminars offer information about the music industry. Offers programs annually for songwriters and performers. Event takes place June at over 40 venues in Baton Rouge and New Orleans. 400 songwriters/musicians participate in each event. Participants are amateur and professional songwriters, vocalists and bands. Participants are selected by demo tape audition. Fee: $185. Send for application.

☑ THE SONGWRITERS GUILD FOUNDATION

6430 Sunset Blvd., Suite 705, Hollywood CA 90028. (323)462-1108. Fax: (323)462-5430. E-mail: la@songwritersguild.com. Web site: www.songwritersguild.com. West Coast Regional Director: B. Aaron Meza. Assistant West Coast Regional Director: Eric Moromisato. Nashville office: 1222 16th Ave., S, Nashville TN 37212. (615)329-1782. Fax: (615)329-2623. Southern Regional Director: Rundi Ream. Assistant Southern Regional Director: Evan Shoemake. E-mail: sganash@aol.com. New York office: 200 W. 72nd Street, New York NY 10023. (212)768-7902. Fax: (212)768-9048. National Projects Director: George Wurzbach. Offers a series of workshops with discounts to members. "There is a charge for each songwriting class. Charges vary depending on the class. SGA members receive discounts! Also, the Re-write workshop and Ask-A-Pro/Song Critique are free!"

• Also see the Songwriters Guild of America listing in the Organizations section.

Ask-a-Pro/Song Critique (Hollywoood and Nashville offices) SGA members are given the opportunity to present their songs and receive constructive feedback from industry professionals. A great chance to meet industry people, make contacts, ask questions and get your song heard! Free to SGA members. Reservations required. Call for schedule. Free.

Phil Swan Song Styles/Songwriting Workshops (Hollywood and Nashville offices) This 8-week workshop taught by Phil Swann, Dreamworks SKG staff writer is perfect for those writers who want to become better songwriters in the country, pop, and rock genres as well as more savvy the changing marketplaces. Fee.

Special Seminars and Workshops Other special seminars have been presented by such industry professionals as Dale Kawashima, John Braheny and Dr. George Gamez. Fee.

Building a Songwriting Career A 3-day workshop for songwriters, musicians and recording artists, etc. to help them discover how they can establish a career in the exciting world of songwriting. Features SGA professional songwriters and music business executives in panel discussions about intellectual property, creativity, the craft and business of songwriting and more. Fee.

Re-Write Workshops (Hollywood office) Conducted by Michael Allen. Songwriters will have the chance to have their songs critiqued by their peers with an occasional guest critique. Free.

Harriet Schock Songwriting Workshops (Hollywood office) A 10-week course consisting of nine lessons which help create a solid foundation for writing songs effortlessly. Fee.

Jai Josefs Writing Music for Hit Songs (Hollywood office) This 10-week course will show songwriters how to integrate the latest chord progressions, melodies, and grooves from all styles of music into their writing.

Song Critique New York's oldest ongoing song critique. Guild songwriters are invited to either perform their song live or present a cassette demo for feedback. A Guild moderator is on hand to direct comments. Nonmembers may attend and offer comments. Free.

Street Smarts (New York office) Street Smarts is a 3-hour orientation session for new SGA members. It introduces the basics in areas such as: contracts, copyrights, royalties, song marketing and more. The session is free to members and is scheduled whenever there is a minimum of 8 participants.

Pro-Shop For each of 6 sessions an active publisher, producer or A&R person is invited to personally screen material from professional Guild writers. Participation is limited to 10 writers, and audit of 1 session. Audition of material is required. Coordinator is producer/musician/award winning singer, Ann Johns Ruckert. Fee; $75 (SGA members only).

SGA Week Held in spring/summer of each year, this is a week of scheduled events and seminars of interest to songwriters at each of SGA's regional offices. Events include workshops, seminars and showcases. For schedule and details contact the SGA office beginning several weeks prior to SGA Week.

SOUTH BY SOUTHWEST MUSIC CONFERENCE (SXSW)

SXSW Headquarters, P.O. Box 4999, Austin TX 78765. (512)467-7979. Fax: (512)451-0754. E-mail: sxsw@sxsw.com. Web site: www.sxsw.com. **Contact:** Conference Organizer. **Europe:** Cill Ruan, 7 Ard na Croise, Thurles, Co. Tipperary Ireland. Phone: 353-504-26488. Fax: 353-504-26787. E-mail: una@sxsw.com. **Contact:** Una Johnston. **Asia:** Meijidori Bldg. 403, 2-3-21 Kabuki-cho Shinjuku-ku, Tokyo 160-0021 Japan. Phone: +82 3-5292-5551. Fax: +82 3-5292-5552. E-mail: info@sxsw-asia.com. **Contact:** Hiroshi Asada. **Australia/New Zealand/Hawaii:** 20 Hordern St., Newtown NSW 2042 Australia. Phone: 61-2-9557-7766. Fax: 61-2-9557-7788. E-mail: tripp@sxsw.om. **Contact:** Phil Tripp. Estab. 1987. South by Southwest (SXSW) is a private company based in Austin, Texas, with a year-round staff of professionals dedicated to building and delivering conference and festival events for entertainment and related media industry professionals. Since 1987, SXSW has produced the internationally-recognized music and media conference and festival (SXSW). As the entertainment business adjusted to issues of future growth and development, in 1993, SXSW added conferences and festivals for the film industry (SXSW Film) as well as for the blossoming interactive media (SXSW Interactive Festival). Now three industry events converge in Austin during a Texas-sized week, mirroring the ever increasing convergence of entertainment/media outlets. The next SXSW Music Conference and Festival will be held March 15-19, 2006 at the Austin Convention Center in Austin, TX. Offers panel discussions, "Crash Course" educational seminars and nighttime showcases. The 2005 Keynote speaker was Robert Plant. SXSW Music seeks out speakers who have developed unique ways to create and sell music. With our Wednesday Crash Courses and introductory panels, the basics will be covered in plain English. From Thursday through Saturday, the conference includes over fifty sessions including a panel of label heads discussing strategy, interviews with notable artists, topical discussions, demo listening sessions and the mentor program. And when the sun goes down, a multitude of performances by musicians and songwriters from across the country and around the world populate the SXSW Music Festival, held in venues in central Austin." Write, e-mail or visit Web site for dates and registration instructions.
Tips "Go to the Web site in early-September to apply for showcase consideraton. SXSW is also involved in North by Northeast (NXNE), held in Toronto, Canada in late Spring."

THE SWANNANOA GATHERING—CONTEMPORARY FOLK WEEK

Warren Wilson College, P.O. Box 9000, Asheville NC 28815-9000. E-mail: gathering@warren-wilson.edu. Web site: www.swangathering.com. Director: Jim Magill. "For anyone who ever wanted to make music for an audience, we offer a comprehensive week in artist development, divided into four major subject areas: Songwriting, Performance, Sound & Recording and Vocal Coaching, along with daily panel discussions of other business matters such as promotion, agents and managers, logistics of touring, etc." 2005 staff includes Brooks Williams, Tom Kimmel, Deidre McCalla, Kate Campbell, Tom Prasada-Rao, Bernice Lewis, Amy Fradon, Cindy Novelo, Rachel Cross, Greg Trafidlo, Mae Robertson, Stobhan Quinn, Ray Chesna, and Doc & Jean Russell. For a brochure or other info contact Jim Magill, Director, The Swannanoa Gathering, at the phone number/address above. Tuition: $405. Takes place July 30 to August 5. Housing (including all meals): $305. Annual program of The Swannanoa Gathering Folk Arts Workshops.

THE TEN-MINUTE MUSICALS PROJECT

P.O. Box 461194, West Hollywood CA 90046. E-mail: info@tenminutemusicals.org. Web site: www.tenminutemusicals.org. **Contact:** Michael Koppy, producer. Estab. 1986. Promotes short complete stage musicals. Offers programs for songwriters, composers and musical playwrights. "Works selected are generally included in full-length 'anthology musical'—11 of the first 16 selected works are now in the show *Stories 1.0*, for instance." Awards a $250 royalty advance for each work selected. Participants are amateur and professional songwriters, composers and musical playwrights. Participants are selected by demonstration tape or CD, script, lead sheets. Send for application or visit Web site. Deadline: August 31st annually.

[N] TUNESMITH SUMMER & WINTER SEMINARS

E-mail: info@tunesmith.net. Web site: www.tunesmith.net. **Contact:** Nancy Cassidy, Tunesmith owner and seminar organizer. Estab. 2001. Offers programs twice a year. "The event is open to all songwriters, from hobbyist to more advanced. Learn how to impress publishers with your songs and yourself. Learn about the craft of commercial songwriting from professional hit songwriters. Learn the art of networking as it pertains to the music business and how to make connections down on Music Row.'' At our seminars you will write a song during the seminar and the winning song will be pitched to Nashville publishers. E-mail or visit Web site for dates and fees.

UNDERCURRENTS

P.O. Box 94040, Cleveland OH 44101-6040. (440)331-0700. E-mail: music@undercurrents.com. Web site: www.undercurrents.com. **Contact:** John Latimer, president. Estab. 1989. A music, event and art marketing and promotion network with online and offline exposure featuring music showcases, seminars, trade shows, networking forums. Ongoing programs and performances for songwriters, composers, and performers. Participants are selected by EPK, demo, biography and photo. Register at www.undercurrents.com.

WEST COAST SONGWRITERS CONFERENCE

(formerly Northern California Songwriters Association Conference), 1724 Laurel St., Suite 120, San Carlos CA 94070. (650)654-3966 or (800)FOR-SONG. Fax: (650)654-2156. E-mail: info@westcoasts ongwriters.org. Web site: www.westcoastsongwriters.org. **Contact:** Ian Crombie, executive director. Estab. 1980. ''Conference offers opportunity and education. 16 seminars, 50 song screening sessions (1,500 songs reviewed), performance showcases, one on one sessions and concerts.'' Offers programs for lyricists, songwriters, composers and performers. ''During the year we have competitive open mics. Winners go into the playoffs. Winners of the playoffs perform at the sunset concert at the conference.'' Event takes place second weekend in September at Foothill College, Los Altos Hills CA. Over 500 songwriters/musicians participate in this event. Participants are songwriters, composers, musical playwrights, vocalists, bands, instrumentalists and those interested in a career in the music business. Send for application. Deadline: September 1. Fee: $110-315. ''See our listing in the Organizations section.''

WINTER MUSIC CONFERENCE INC.

3450 NE 12 Terrace, Ft. Lauderdale FL 33334. (954)563-4444. Fax: (954)563-1599. E-mail: info@win termusicconference.com. Web site: www.wintermusicconference.com. President: Margo Possenti. Estab. 1985. Features educational seminars and showcases for dance, hip hop, alternative and rap. Offers programs for songwriters and performers. Offers programs annually. Event takes place March of each year in Miami FL. 3,000 songwriters/musicians participate in each event. Participants are amateur and professional songwriters, composers, musical playwrights, vocalists, bands and instrumentalists. Participants are selected by submitting demo tape. Send SASE, visit Web site or call for application. Deadline: February. Event held at either nightclubs or hotel with complete staging, lights and sound.

Retreats & Colonies

This section provides information on retreats and artists' colonies. These are places for creatives, including songwriters, to find solitude and spend concentrated time focusing on their work. While a residency at a colony may offer participation in seminars, critiques or performances, the atmosphere of a colony or retreat is much more relaxed than that of a conference or workshop. Also, a songwriter's stay at a colony is typically anywhere from one to twelve weeks (sometimes longer), while time spent at a conference may only run from one to fourteen days.

Like conferences and workshops, however, artists' colonies and retreats span a wide range. Yaddo, perhaps the most well-known colony, limits its residencies to artists "working at a professional level in their field, as determined by a judging panel of professionals in the field." The Brevard Music Center offers residencies only to those involved in classical music. Despite different focuses, all artists' colonies and retreats have one thing in common: They are places where you may work undisturbed, usually in nature-oriented, secluded settings.

SELECTING A COLONY OR RETREAT

When selecting a colony or retreat, the primary consideration for many songwriters is cost, and you'll discover that arrangements vary greatly. Some colonies provide residencies as well as stipends for personal expenses. Some suggest donations of a certain amount. Still others offer residencies for substantial sums but have financial assistance available.

When investigating the various options, consider meal and housing arrangements and your family obligations. Some colonies provide meals for residents, while others require residents to pay for meals. Some colonies house artists in one main building; others provide separate cottages. A few have provisions for spouses and families. Others prohibit families altogether.

Overall, residencies at colonies and retreats are competitive. Since only a handful of spots are available at each place, you often must apply months in advance for the time period you desire. A number of locations are open year-round, and you may find planning to go during the "off-season" lessens your competition. Other colonies, however, are only available during certain months. In any case, be prepared to include a sample of your best work with your application. Also, know what project you'll work on while in residence and have alternative projects in mind in case the first one doesn't work out once you're there.

Each listing in this section details fee requirements, meal and housing arrangements, and space and time availability, as well as the retreat's surroundings, facilities and special activities. Of course, before making a final decision, send a SASE to the colonies or retreats that interest you to receive their most up-to-date details. Costs, application requirements and deadlines are particularly subject to change.

MUSICIAN'S RESOURCE

For other listings of songwriter-friendly colonies, see *Musician's Resource* (available from Watson-Guptill Publications, 770 Broadway, New York NY 10003, 1-800-278-8477, info@watsonguptill.com), which not only provides information about conferences, workshops and academic programs but also residencies and retreats. Also check the Publications of Interest section in this book for newsletters and other periodicals providing this information.

BREVARD MUSIC CENTER

P.O. Box 312, 349 Andante Ln., Brevard NC 28712. (828)862-2140. Fax: (828)884-2036. E-mail: bmc@brevardmusic.org. Web site: www.brevardmusic.org. **Contact:** Dorothy Knowles, admissions coordinator. Estab. 1936. Offers 6-week residencies from June through the first week of August. Open to professional and student composers, pianists, vocalists, collaborative pianists and instrumentalists of classical music. A 2-week jazz workshop is offered in June. Accommodates 400 at one time. Personal living quarters include cabins. Offers rehearsal, teaching and practice cabins. **Costs** $4,100 for tuition, room and board. Scholarships are available.
Requirements Call for application forms and guidelines. $50 application fee. Participants are selected by audition or demonstration tape and then by invitation. There are 80 different audition sites throughout the US.

DORSET COLONY HOUSE

P.O. Box 510, Dorset VT 05251-0510. (802)867-2223. Fax: (802)867-0144. E-mail: dorsetcolony@hotmail.com. Web site: www.dorsetcolony.org. **Contact:** John Nassivera, executive director. Estab. 1980. Offers up to 1-month residencies September-November and April-May. Open to writers, composers, directors, designers and collaborators of the theatre. Accommodates 9 at one time. Personal living quarters include single rooms with desks with shared bath and shared kitchen facilities. **Costs** $800/week. Meals not included. Transportation is residents' responsibility.
Requirements Send SASE for application forms and guidelines. Accepts inquiries via fax or e-mail. Submit letter with requested dates, description of project and résumé of productions.

⊕ THE TYRONE GUTHRIE CENTRE

Annaghmakerrig, Newbliss, County Monaghan, Ireland. (353)(047)54003. Fax: (353)(047)54380. E-mail: info@tyroneguthrie.ie. Web site: www.tyroneguthrie.ie. **Contact:** Program Director. Estab. 1981. Offers year-round residencies. Artists may stay for anything from 1 week to 3 months in the Big House, or for up to 6 months at a time in one of the 5 self-catering houses in the old farmyard. Open to artists of all disciplines. Accommodates 15 at one time. Personal living quarters include bedroom with bathroom en suite. Offers a variety of workspaces. There is a music room for composers and musicians, a photographic darkroom and a number of studios for visual artists. At certain times of the year it is possible, by special arrangement, to accommodate groups of artists, symposiums, master classes, workshops and other collaborations. **Costs** Artists who are not Irish residents must pay €650 per week, all found, for a residency in the Big House and €325 per week (plus gas and electricity costs) for one of the self-catering farmyard houses. To qualify for a residency, it is necessary to show evidence of a significant level of achievement in the relevant field.
Requirements Send SAE and IRC for application forms and guidelines. Accepts inquiries via fax or e-mail. Fill in application form with cv to be reviewed by the board members at regular meetings.

THE HAMBIDGE CENTER

Attn: Residency Director, P.O. Box 339, Rabun Gap GA 30568. (706)746-5718. Fax: (706)746-9933 E-mail: residents@hambidge.org. Web site: www.hambidge.org. **Contact:** Rosemary Magee, residency chair. Estab. 1934 (Center); 1988 (residency). Offers 2-week to 2-month residencies year round. Open to all artists. Accommodates 8 at one time. Personal living quarters include a private cottage with kitchen, bath, and living/studio space. Offers composer/musical studio equipped with piano. Activities include communal dinners February through December and nightly or periodic sharing of works-in-progress.

Costs $150/week.

Requirements Send SASE for application forms and guidelines, or available on Web site. Accepts inquiries via fax and e-mail. Application fee: $30. Deadlines: January 15, April 15, and September 15.

ISLE ROYALE NATIONAL PARK ARTIST-IN-RESIDENCE PROGRAM

800 E. Lakeshore Dr., Houghton MI 49931. (906)482-0984. Fax: (906)482-8753. E-mail: ISRO_Parkin fo@nps.gov. Web site: www.nps.gov/ISRO/. **Contact:** Greg Blust, coordinator. Estab. 1991. Offers 2-3 week residencies from mid-June to mid-September. Open to all art forms. Accommodates 1 artist with 1 companion at one time. Personal living quarters include cabin with shared outhouse. A canoe is provided for transportation. Offers a guest house at the site that can be used as a workroom. The artist is asked to contribute a piece of work representative of their stay at Isle Royale, to be used by the park in an appropriate manner. During their residency, artists will be asked to share their experience (1 presentation per week of residency, about 1 hour/week) with the public by demonstration, talk, or other means.

Requirements Send for application forms and guidelines. Accepts inquiries via fax or e-mail. A panel of professionals from various disciplines, and park representatives will choose the finalists. The selection is based on artistic integrity, ability to reside in a wilderness environment, a willingness to donate a finished piece of work inspired on the island, and the artist's ability to relate and interpret the park through their work.

THE MACDOWELL COLONY

100 High St., Peterborough NH 03458. (603)924-3886. Fax: (603)924-9142. E-mail: admissions@ma cdowellcolony.org. Web site: www.macdowellcolony.org. **Contact:** Admissions Director. Estab. 1907. Offers year-round residencies of up to 8 weeks. Open to writers, playwrights, composers, film/video makers, visual artists, architects and interdisciplinary artists. Personal living quarters include single rooms with shared baths. Offers private studios on 450-acre grounds.

Cost None (contributions accepted).

Requirements Visit Web site for residency periods, application forms and guidelines which include work sample requirements. Application deadline: January 15, April 15 and September 15.

NORTHWOOD UNIVERSITY ALDEN B. DOW CREATIVITY CENTER

4000 Whiting Dr., Midland MI 48640. (989)837-4478. E-mail: creativity@northwood.edu. Web site: www.northwood.edu/abd. **Contact:** Dr. Grover B. Proctor, Jr., executive director. Estab. 1979. Offers 10-week summer residencies (mid-June through mid-August). Fellowship Residency is open to individuals in all fields (the arts, humanities or sciences) who have innovative, creative projects to pursue. Accommodates 4 at one time. Each Fellow is given a furnished apartment on campus, complete with 2 bedrooms, kitchen, bath and large living room. Fellows' apartments serve as their work space as well as their living quarters unless special needs are requested.

Cost $10 application fee. Room and board is provided plus a $750 stipend to be used toward project costs or personal needs. "We look for projects which are innovative, creative, unique. We ask the applicant to set accomplishable goals for the 10-week residency."

Requirements Send for application information and guidelines. Accepts inquiries via fax or e-mail. Applicants submit 2-page typed description of their project; cover page with name, address, phone numbers plus summary (30 words or less) of project; support materials such as tapes, CDs; personal résumé; facilities or equipment needed; and $10 application fee. Application deadline: December 31 (postmarked).

VIRGINIA CENTER FOR THE CREATIVE ARTS

154 San Angelo Dr., Amherst VA 24521. (434)946-7236. Fax: (434)946-7239. E-mail: vcca@vcca.c om. Web site: www.vcca.com. **Contact:** Sheila Gulley Pleasants, director of artists' services. Estab. 1971. Offers residencies year-round, typical residency lasts 2 weeks to 2 months. Open to originating

artists: composers, writers and visual artists. Accommodates 22 at one time. Personal living quarters include 20 single rooms, 2 double rooms, bathrooms shared with one other person. All meals are served. Kitchens for fellows' use available at studios and residence. Activities include trips in the VCCA van twice a week into town. Fellows share their work regularly. Four studios have pianos.

Cost No transportation costs are covered. Artists are accepted at the VCCA without consideration for their financial situation. The actual cost of a residency at the Virginia Center is $120 per day per Fellow. "We ask Fellows to contribute according to their ability. Suggested daily contribution is $30."

Requirements Send SASE for application forms or call the above number. Applications are reviewed by a panel of judges. Application fee: $25. Deadline: May 15 for October-January residency; September 15 for February-May residency; January 15 for June-September residency.

State & Provincial Grants

A rts councils in the United States and Canada provide assistance to artists (including poets) in the form of fellowships or grants. These grants can be substantial and confer prestige upon recipients; however, **only state or province residents are eligible**. Because deadlines and available support vary annually, query first (with a SASE).

UNITED STATES ARTS AGENCIES

Alabama State Council on the Arts, 201 Monroe St., Montgomery AL 36130-1800. (334)242-4076. E-mail: staff@arts.alabama.gov. Website: www.arts.state.al.us.

Alaska State Council on the Arts, 411 W. Fourth Ave., Suite 1-E, Anchorage AK 99501-2343. (907)269-6610 or (888)278-7424. E-mail: aksca_info@eed.state.ak.us. Website: www.educ.state.ak.us/aksca.

Arizona Commission on the Arts, 417 W. Roosevelt, Phoenix AZ 85003-1326. (602)255-5882. E-mail: info@azarts.org. Website: www.azarts.org.

Arkansas Arts Council, 1500 Tower Bldg., 323 Center St., Little Rock AR 72201. (501)324-9766. E-mail: info@arkansasarts.com. Website: www.arkansasarts.com.

California Arts Council, 1300 I St., Suite 930, Sacramento CA 95814. (916)322-6555 or (800)201-6201. E-mail: info@cqartscouncil.com. Website: www.cac.ca.gov.

Colorado Council on the Arts, 1625 Broadway, Suite 2700, Denver CO 80202. (303)892-3802. Website: www.coloarts.state.co.us.

Connecticut Commission on Culture & Tourism, 755 Main St., 1 Financial Plaza, Hartford CT 06103. (860)256-2800. Website: www.cultureandtourism.org.

Delaware Division of the Arts, Carvel State Office Building, 820 N. French St., Wilmington DE 19801. (302)577-8278. E-mail: delarts@state.de.us. Website: www.artsdel.org.

District of Columbia Commission on the Arts & Humanities, 410 Eighth St. NW, 5th Floor, Washington DC 20004. (202)724-5613. E-mail: cah@dc.gov. Website: http://dcarts.dc.gov.

Florida Arts Council, Division of Cultural Affairs, R.A. Gray Building, 3rd Floor, 500 S. Bronough St., Tallahassee FL 32399-0250. (850)245-6470. Website: www.florida-arts.org.

Georgia Council for the Arts, 260 14th St. NW, Suite 401, Atlanta GA 30318-5793. (404)685-2787. E-mail: gaarts@gaarts.org. Website: www.gaarts.org.

Hawaii State Foundation on Culture & Arts, 250 S. Hotel St., 2nd Floor, Honolulu HI 96813. (808)586-0300. E-mail: ken.hamilton@hawaii.gov. Website: www.state.hi.us/sfca.

Idaho Commission on the Arts, P.O. Box 83720, Boise ID 83720-0008. (208)334-2119 or (800)278-3863. E-mail: info@arts.idaho.gov. Website: www2.state.id.us/arts.

Illinois Arts Council, 100 W. Randolph, Suite 10-500, Chicago IL 60601. (312)814-6750. E-mail: info@arts.state.il.us. Website: www.state.il.us/agency/iac.

Indiana Arts Commission, 150 W. Market St., Suite 618, Indianapolis IN 46204. (317)232-1268. E-mail: IndianaArtsCommission@iac.in.gov. Website: www.state.in.us/iac.

Iowa Arts Council, 600 E. Locust, Capitol Complex, Des Moines IA 50319-0290. (515)281-6412. Website: www.iowaartscouncil.org.

Kansas Arts Commission, 700 SW Jackson, Suite 1004, Topeka KS 66603. (785)296-3335. E-mail: KAC@arts.state.ks.us. Website: http://arts.state.ks.us.

Kentucky Arts Council, Capital Plaza Tower, 500 Mero St., Frankfort KY 40601-1987. (502)564-3757. E-mail: kyarts@ky.gov. Website: http://artscouncil.ky.gov.

Louisiana State Arts Council, P.O. Box 44247, Baton Rouge LA 70804. (225)342-8180. E-mail: arts@crt.state.la.us. Website: www.crt.state.la.us/arts.

Maine Arts Commission, 193 State St., 25 State House Station, Augusta ME 04333-0025. (207)287-2724. E-mail: mainearts.info@maine.gov. Website: www.mainearts.com.

Maryland State Arts Council, 175 West Ostend Street, Suite E, Baltimore MD 21230. (410)767-6555. E-mail: msac@msac.org. Website: www.msac.org.

Massachusetts Cultural Council, 10 St. James Ave., 3rd Floor, Boston MA 02116-3803. (617)727-3668. E-mail: mcc@art.state.ma.us. Website: www.massculturalcouncil.org.

Michigan Council for Arts & Cultural Affairs, 722 West Kalamazoo Street, P.O. Box 30705, Lansing, MI 48909-8205. (517)373-1592. E-mail: artsinfo@michigan.gov. Website: www. michigan.gov/hal/.

Minnesota State Arts Board, Park Square Court, 400 Sibley St., Suite 200, St. Paul MN 55101-1928. (651)215-1600. E-mail: msab@state.mn.us. Website: www.arts.state.mn.us.

Mississippi Arts Commission, 501 N. West St., Suite 701B, Woolfolk Building, Jackson MS 39201. (601)359-6030. E-mail: jcleary@arts.state.ms.us. Website: www.arts.state.ms.us.

Missouri Arts Council, 111 N. Seventh St., Suite 105, St. Louis MO 63101-2188. (314)340-6845. E-mail: moarts@ded.mo.gov. Website: www.missouriartscouncil.org.

Montana Arts Council, P.O. Box 202201, Helena MT 59620-2201. (406)444-6430. E-mail: mac@mt.gov. Website: www.art.state.mt.us.

National Endowment for the Arts, 1100 Pennsylvania Ave. NW, Washington DC 20506. (202)682-5400. E-mail: webmgr@arts.endow.gov. Website: www.arts.endow.gov.

Nebraska Arts Council, 1004 Farnam St., Plaza Level, Omaha NE 68102. (402)595-2122. E-mail: khardin@nebraskaartscouncil.org. Website: www.nebraskaartscouncil.org.

Nevada State Council on the Arts, 716 N. Carson St., Suite A, Carson City NV 89701. (775)687-6680. Website: dmla.clan.lib.nv.us/docs/arts/

New Hampshire State Council on the Arts, 2½ Beacon St., 2nd Floor, Concord NH 03301-4974. (603)271-2789. E-mail: ystahr@nharts.state.nh.us. Website: www.state.nh.us/nharts.

New Jersey State Council on the Arts, P.O. Box 306, 225 W. State St., Trenton NJ 08625. (609)292-6130. E-mail: njsca@arts.sos.state.nj.us. Website: www.njartscouncil.org.

New Mexico Arts Division, P.O. Box 1450, Santa Fe NM 87504. (505)827-6490. E-mail: virginia.castellano@state.nm.us. Website: www.nmarts.org.

New York State Council on the Arts, 175 Varick St., 3rd Floor, New York NY 10014. (212)627-4455. E-mail: ljohnson@nysca.org. Website: www.nysca.org.

North Carolina Arts Council, Department of Cultural Resources, MSC #4632, Raleigh NC 27699-4632. (919)733-2111. E-mail: ncarts@ncmail.net. Website: www.ncarts.org.

North Dakota Council on the Arts, 1600 East Century Avenue, Suite 6, Bismarck ND 58503. (701)328-7590. E-mail: comserv@state.nd.us. Website: www.state.nd.us/arts.

Ohio Arts Council, 727 E. Main St., Columbus OH 43205-1796. (614)466-2613. E-mail: webm aster@oac.state.oh.us. Website: www.oac.state.oh.us.

Oklahoma Arts Council, P.O. Box 52001-2001, Oklahoma City OK 73152-2001. (405)521-2931. E-mail: okarts@arts.state.ok.us. Website: www.state.ok.us/~arts.

Oregon Arts Commission, 775 Summer St. NE, Suite 200, Salem OR 97301-1284. (503)986-0082. E-mail: oregon.artscomm@state.or.us. Website: www.oregonartscommission.org.

Pennsylvania Council on the Arts, Room 216, Finance Bldg., Harrisburg PA 17120. (717)787-6883. E-mail: kcswartz@state.pa.us. Website: www.artsnet.org/pca.

Institute of Puerto Rican Culture, P.O. Box 9024184, San Juan PR 00902-4184. (787)725-5137. E-mail: IPRAC@aspira.org. Website: http://iprac.aspira.org.

Rhode Island State Council on the Arts, One Capitol Hill, 3rd Floor, Providence RI 02908. (401)222-3880. E-mail: info@risca.state.ri.us. Website: www.risca.state.ri.us.

South Carolina Arts Commission, 1800 Gervais St., Columbia SC 29201. (803)734-8696. E-mail: jguinn@arts.state.sc.us. Website: www.state.sc.us/arts.

South Dakota Arts Council, 800 Governors Dr., Pierre SD 57501-2294. (605)773-3131. E-mail: sdac@state.sd.us. Website: www.artscouncil.sd.gov.

Tennessee Arts Commission, 401 Charlotte Ave., Nashville TN 37243-0780. (615)741-1701. Website: www.arts.state.tn.us.

Texas Commission on the Arts, P.O. Box 13406, Austin TX 78711-3406. (512)463-5535. E-mail: front.desk@arts.state.tx.us. Website: www.arts.state.tx.us.

Utah Arts Council, 617 E. South Temple, Salt Lake City UT 84102-1177. (801)236-7555. E-mail: artistgrant@utah.gov. Website: http://arts.utah.gov/.

Vermont Arts Council, 136 State St., Drawer 33, Montpelier VT 05633-6001. (802)828-3291. E-mail: info@vermontartscouncil.org. Website: www.vermontartscouncil.org.

Virgin Islands Council on the Arts, 5070 Norre Gada, St. Thomas VI 00802-6876. (340)774-5984. E-mail: adagio@islands.vi. Website: www.vicouncilonarts.org/.

Virginia Commission for the Arts, Lewis House, 2nd Floor, 223 Governor St., Richmond VA 23219-2010. (804)225-3132. E-mail: arts@artsvirginia.gov. Website: www.arts.state.va.us/.

Washington State Arts Commission, P.O. Box 42675, Olympia WA 98504-2675. (360)753-3860. E-mail: info@arts.wa.gov. Website: www.arts.wa.gov.

Resources

West Virginia Arts Commission, Cultural Center, 1900 Kanawha Blvd. E., Charleston WV 25305-0300. (304)558-0220. Website: www.wvculture.org.

Wisconsin Arts Board, 101 E. Wilson St., 1st Floor, Madison WI 53702. (608)266-0190. E-mail: artsboard@arts.state.wi.us. Website: www.arts.state.wi.us.

Wyoming Arts Council, 2320 Capitol Ave., Cheyenne WY 82002. (307)777-7742. E-mail: ebratt@state.wy.us. Website: http://wyoarts.state.wy.us.

CANADIAN PROVINCES ARTS AGENCIES

Alberta Foundation for the Arts, 10708-105 Ave., Edmonton, Alberta T5M 2X2. (780)427-6315. Website: www.cd.gov.ab.ca/affta.

British Columbia Arts Council, P.O. Box 9819, Stn Prov Govt, Victoria, British Columbia V8W 9W3. (250)356-1718. E-mail: bcartscouncil@gov.bc.ca. Website: www.bcartscouncil.ca.

Manitoba Arts Council, 525 - 93 Lombard Ave., Winnipeg, Manitoba R3B 3B1. (204)945-2237. E-mail: info@artscouncil.mb.ca. Website: www.artscouncil.mb.ca.

New Brunswick Arts Board, 634 Queen St., Suite 300, Fredericton, New Brunswick E3B 1C2. (866)460-2787. E-mail: ldugas@artsnb.ca. Website: www.artsnb.ca.

Newfoundland & Labrador Arts Council, P.O. Box 98, St. John's, Newfoundland A1C 5H5. (709)726-2212. E-mail: nlacmail@nfld.net. Website: www.nlac.nf.ca.

Nova Scotia Arts Council, Suite 601, 1800 Argyle St., P.O. Box 456, Halifax, Nova Scotia B3J 2R5. (902)424-6471. E-mail: nsacpc@gov.ns.ca. Website: www.nsapc.com.

The Canada Council for the Arts, 350 Albert St., P.O. Box 1047, Ottawa, Ontario K1P 5V8. (613)566-4414. Website: www.canadacouncil.ca.

Ontario Arts Council, 151 Bloor St. W., 5th Floor, Toronto, Ontario M5S 1T6. (416)961-1660. E-mail: info@arts.on.ca. Website: www.arts.on.ca/.

Prince Edward Island Council of the Arts, 115 Richmond, Charlottetown, Prince Edward Island C1E 1H7. (902)368-4410. E-mail: info@peiartscouncil.com. Website: www.peiartscouncil.com.

Saskatchewan Arts Board, 2135 Broad St., Regina, Saskatchewan S4P 1Y6. (306)787-4056. E-mail: sab@artsboard.sk.ca. Website: ww.artsboard.sk.ca.

Yukon Arts Branch, Box 2703, Whitehorse, Yukon Y1A 2C6. (867)667-8589. E-mail: arts@gov.yk.ca. Website: www.btc.gov.yk.ca/cultural/arts.

Resources

Publications of Interest

Knowledge about the music industry is essential for both creative and business success. Staying informed requires keeping up with constantly changing information. Updates on the evolving trends in the music business are available to you in the form of music magazines, music trade papers and books. There is a publication aimed at almost every type of musician, songwriter and music fan, from the most technical knowledge of amplification systems to gossip about your favorite singer. These publications can enlighten and inspire you and provide information vital in helping you become a more well-rounded, educated, and, ultimately, successful musical artist.

This section lists all types of magazines and books you may find interesting. From songwriters' newsletters and glossy music magazines to tip sheets and how-to books, there should be something listed here that you'll enjoy and benefit from.

PERIODICALS

The Album Network, 110 West Spazier, Burbank CA 91502. (818)842-2600. Website: www. musicbiz.com. *Weekly music industry trade magazine.*

American Songwriter Magazine, 50 Music Square W., Suite 604, Nashville TN 37203-3227. (615)321-6096. E-mail: info@americansongwriter.com. Website: www.americansongwrit er.com. *Bimonthly publication for and about songwriters.*

Back Stage East, 770 Broadway, 4th Floor, New York NY 10003. (646)654-5700.

Back Stage West, 5055 Wilshire Blvd., Los Angeles CA 90036. (323)525-2358 or (800)745-8922. Website: www.backstage.com. *Weekly East and West Coast performing artist trade papers.*

Bass Player, P.O. Box 57324, Boulder CO 80323-7324. (800)234-1831. E-mail: bassplayer@n eodata.com. Website: www.bassplayer.com. *Monthly magazine for bass players with lessons, interviews, articles, and transcriptions.*

Billboard, 1515 Broadway, New York NY 10036. (800)745-8922. E-mail: bbstore@billboard.c om. Website: www.billboard.com. *Weekly industry trade magazine.*

Canadian Musician, 23 Hannover Dr., Suite 7, St. Catharines, Ontario L2W 1A3 Canada. (877)746-4692. Website: www.canadianmusician.com. *Bimonthly publication for amateur and professional Canadian musicians.*

Chart, 200-41 Britain St., Toronto, Ontario M5A 1R7 Canada. (416)363-3101. E-mail: chart@c hartnet.com. Website: www.chartattack.com. *Monthly magazine covering the Canadian and international music scenes.*

CMJ New Music Report, 151 W. 25th St., 12 Floor, New York NY 10001. (917)606-1908. E-mail: subscriptions@cmj.com. Website: www.cmjmusic.com. *Weekly college radio and alternative music tip sheet.*

Country Line Magazine, 16150 S. IH-35, Buda TX 78610. (512)295-8400. E-mail: editor@cou ntrylinemagazine.com. Website: http://countrylinemagazine.com. *Monthly Texas-only country music cowboy and lifestyle magazine.*

Daily Variety, 5700 Wilshire Blvd., Suite 120, Los Angeles CA 90036. (323)857-6600. Website: www.variety.com. *Daily entertainment trade newspaper.*

Dramalogue, 1456 N. Gordon, Hollywood CA 90028. Website: www.dramalogue.com. *L.A.-based entertainment newspaper with an emphasis on theatre and cabaret.*

The Dramatist, 1501 Broadway, Suite 701, New York NY 10036. (212)398-9366. Fax: (212)944-0420. Website: www.dramaguild.com. *The quarterly journal of the Dramatists Guild, the professional association of playwrights, composers and lyricists.*

Entertainment Law & Finance, New York Law Publishing Co., 345 Park Ave. S., 8th Floor, New York NY 10010. (212)545-6174. E-mail: leader@ljextra.com. *Monthly newsletter covering music industry contracts, lawsuit filings, court rulings and legislation.*

Exclaim!, 7-B Pleasant Blvd., Suite 966, Toronto, Ontario M4T 1K2 Canada. (416)535-9735. E-mail: exclaim@exclaim.ca. Website: http://exclaim.ca. *Canadian music monthly covering all genres of non-mainstream music.*

Fast Forward, Disc Makers, 7905 N. Rt. 130, Pennsauken NJ 08110-1402. (800)468-9353. Website: www.discmakers.com/music/ffwd. *Quarterly newsletter featuring companies and products for performing and recording artists in the independent music industry.*

Guitar Player, 1601 W. 23rd St., Suite 200, Lawrence KS 60046-0127. (800)289-9839. Website: www.guitarplayer.com. Monthly guitar magazine with transcriptions, columns, and interviews, including occasional articles on songwriting.

Hits Magazine, 14958 Ventura Blvd., Sherman Oaks CA 91403. (818)501-7900. Website: www.hitsmagazine.com. *Weekly music industry trade publication.*

Jazztimes, 8737 Colesville Rd., 9th Floor, Silver Spring MD 20910-3921. (301)588-4114. Website: http://jazztimes.com. 10 issues/year magazine covering the American jazz scene.

The Leads Sheet, Allegheny Music Works, 1611 Menoher Blvd., Johnstown PA 15905. (814)255-4007. Website: www.alleghenymusicworks.com. Monthly tip sheet.

Lyricist Review, 4535 W. Sahara Ave., Suite 100A-638, Las Vegas NV 89102. 1-888-732-1176. E-mail: info@virtualstudiosystems.com. Website: www.virtualstudiosystems.com. Quarterly commentaries on song lyrics and previously unpublished lyrics available to performing musicians.

Music Books Plus, P.O. Box 670, 240 Portage Rd., Lewiston NY 14092. (800)265-8481. E-mail: mail@nor.com. Website: www.musicbooksplus.com.

Music Business International Magazine, 460 Park Ave., S. of 9th, New York NY 10116. (212)378-0406. *Bimonthly magazine for senior executives in the music industry.*

Music Connection Magazine, 16130 Ventura Blvd., Suite 540, Encino CA 91436. (818)795-0101. E-mail: contactMC@musicconnection.com. Website: www.musicconnection.com. *Biweekly music industry trade publication.*

Music Morsels, P.O. Box 2760, Acworth GA 30102. (678)445-0006. Fax: (678)494-9269. E-mail: SergeEnt@aol.com. Website: www.serge.org/musicmorsels.htm. *Monthly songwriting publication.*

Music Row Magazine, 1231 17th Ave. S, Nashville TN 37212. (615)321-3617. E-mail: info@musicrow.com. Website: www.musicrow.com. *Biweekly Nashville industry publication.*

Offbeat Magazine, OffBeat Publications, 421 Frenchman St., Suite 200, New Orleans LA 70116. (504)944-4300. E-mail: offbeat@offbeat.com. Website: www.offbeat.com. *Monthly magazine covering Louisiana music and artists.*

Performance Magazine, 1203 Lake St., Suite 200, Fort Worth TX 76102-4504. (817)338-9444. E-mail: sales@performancemagazine.com. Website: www.performancemagazine.com. *Weekly publication on touring itineraries, artist availability, upcoming tours, and production and venue news.*

The Performing Songwriter, P.O. Box 40931, Nashville TN 37204. (800)883-7664. E-mail: order@performingsongwriter.com. Website: www.performingsongwriter.com. *Bimonthly songwriters' magazine.*

Producer Report, 415 S. Topanga Canyon Blvd., Suite 114, Topanga CA 90290. (310)455-0888. Fax: (310)455-0894. E-mail: encyclopedia@mojavemusic.com. Website: www.mojavemusic.com. *Semimonthly newsletter covering which producers are working on which acts, and upcoming, current and recently completed projects.*

Public Domain Report, P.O. Box 3102, Margate NJ 08402. (609)822-9401. Website: www.pubdomain.com. *Monthly guide to significant titles entering the public domain.*

Radio and Records, 2049 Century Park East, 41st Floor, Los Angeles CA 90067. (310)553-4330. Fax: (310)203-9763. E-mail: subscribe@radioandrecords.com. Website: www.radioandrecords.com. *Weekly newspaper covering the radio and record industries.*

Radir, Radio Mall, 2412 Unity Ave. N., Dept. WEB, Minneapolis MN 55422. (800)759-4561. E-mail: info@bbhsoftware.com. Website: www.bbhsoftware.com. *Quarterly radio station database on disk.*

Sing Out!, P.O. Box 5460, Bethlehem PA 18015. (888)SING-OUT. Fax: (610)865-5129. E-mail: info@singout.org. Website: www.singout.org. *Quarterly folk music magazine.*

Songcasting, 15445 Ventura Blvd. #260, Sherman Oaks CA 91403. (818)377-4084. *Monthly tip sheet.*

Songlink International, 23 Belsize Crescent, London NW3 5QY England. Website: www.songlink.com. *10 issues/year newsletter including details of recording artists looking for songs; contact details for industry sources; also news and features on the music business.*

Variety, 5700 Wilshire Blvd., Suite 120, Los Angeles CA 90036. (323)857-6600. Fax: (323)857-0494. Website: www.variety.com. *Weekly entertainment trade newspaper.*

Words and Music, 41 Valleybrook Dr., Don Mills, Ontario M3B 2S6 Canada. (416)445-8700. Website: www.socan.ca. *Monthly songwriters' magazine.*

BOOKS & DIRECTORIES

88 Songwriting Wrongs & How to Right Them, by Pat & Pete Luboff, Writer's Digest Books, 4700 E. Galbraith Rd., Cincinnati OH 45236. (800)448-0915. Website: www.writers digest.com.

The A&R Registry, by Ritch Esra, SRS Publishing, 7510 Sunset Blvd. #1041, Los Angeles CA 90046-3418. (800)377-7411 or (800)552-7411. E-mail: musicregistry@compuserve.com.

Attention: A&R, by Teri Muench and Susan Pomerantz, Alfred Publishing Co. Inc., P.O. Box 10003, Van Nuys CA 91410-0003. (818)892-2452. Website: www.alfredpub.com.

The Billboard Guide to Music Publicity, revised edition, by Jim Pettigrew, Jr., Billboard Books, 1695 Oak St., Lakewood NJ 08701. (800)344-7119.

Breakin' Into Nashville, by Jennifer Ember Pierce, Madison Books, University Press of America, 4501 Forbes Rd., Suite 200, Lanham MD 20706. (800)462-6420.

CMJ Directory, 151 W. 25th St., 12th Floor, New York NY 10001. (917)606-1908. Website: www.cmj.com.

Contracts for the Music industry, P.O. Box 952063, Lake Mary FL 32795-2063. (407)834-8555. E-mail: info@songwriterproducts.com. Website: www.songwriterproducts.com. *Book and computer software of a variety of music contracts.*

The Craft and Business of Songwriting, by John Braheny, Writer's Digest Books, 4700 E. Galbraith Rd., Cincinnati OH 45236. (800)448-0915. Website: www.writersdigest.com.

The Craft of Lyric Writing, by Sheila Davis, Writer's Digest Books, 4700 E. Galbraith Rd., Cincinnati OH 45236. (800)448-0915. Website: www.writersdigest.com.

Creating Melodies, by Dick Weissman, Writer's Digest Books, 4700 E. Galbraith Rd., Cincinnati OH 45236. (800)448-0915. Website: www.writersdigest.com.

Directory of Independent Music Distributors, by Jason Ojalvo, Disc Makers, 7905 N. Rt. 130, Pennsauken NJ 08110. (800)468-9353. E-mail: discman@discmakers.com. Website: www.discmakers.com.

Easy Tools for Composing, by Charles Segal, Segal's Publications, 16 Grace Rd., Newton MA 02159. (617)969-6196.

FILM/TV MUSIC GUIDE, by Ritch Esra, SRS Publishing, 7510 Sunset Blvd. #1041, Los Angeles CA 90046-3418. (800)552-7411. E-mail: musicregistry@compuserve.com or srspu bl@aol.com. Website: www.musicregistry.com.

Finding Fans & Selling CDs, by Veronique Berry and Jason Ojalvo, Disk Makers, 7905 N. Rt. 130, Pennsauken NJ 08110-1402. (800)468-9353. E-mail: discman@diskmakers.com. Website: www.discmakers.com.

Guide to Independent Music Publicity, by Veronique Berry, Disc Makers, 7905 N. Rt. 130, Pennsauken NJ 08110-1402. (800)468-9353. E-mail: discman@discmakers.com.

Guide to Master Tape Preparation, by Dave Moyssiadis, Disk Makers, 7905 N. Rt. 130, Pennsauken NJ 08110-1402. (800)468-9353. E-mail: discman@discmakers.com.

Hollywood Creative Directory, 3000 W. Olympic Blvd. #2525, Santa Monica CA 90404. (800)815-0503. Website: www.hcdonline.com. *Lists producers in film and TV.*

The Hollywood Reporter Blu-Book Production Directory, 5055 Wilshire Blvd., Los Angeles CA 90036. (323)525-2150. Website: www.hollywoodreporter.com.

Hot Tips for the Home Recording Studio, by Hank Linderman, Writer's Digest Books, 4700 E. Galbraith Rd., Cincinnati OH 45236. (800)448-0915. Website: www.writersdigest.com.

How to Promote Your Music Successfully on the Internet, by David Nevue, Midnight Rain Productions, P.O. Box 21831, Eugene OR 97402. Website: www.rainmusic.com.

How to Write Songs on Guitar: A Guitar-Playing and Songwriting Course, by Rikky Rooksby, Backbeat Books, 600 Harrison St., San Francisco CA 94107. (415)947-6615. E-mail: books@musicplayer.com. Website: www.backbeatbooks.com.

How You Can Break Into the Music Business, by Marty Garrett, Lonesome Wind Corporation, P.O. Box 2143, Broken Arrow OK 74013-2143. (800)210-4416.

Louisiana Music Directory, OffBeat, Inc., 421 Frenchmen St., Suite 200, New Orleans LA 70116. (504)944-4300. Website: www.offbeat.com.

Melody in Songwriting, by Jack Perricone, Berklee Press, 1140 Boylston St., Boston MA 02215. (617)747-2146. E-mail: info@berkleepress.com. Website: www.berkleepress.com.

Melody: How to Write Great Tunes, by Rikky Rooksby, Backbeat Books, 600 Harrison St., San Francisco CA 94107. (415)947-6115. E-mail: books@musicplayer.com. Website: www.backbeatbooks.com.

Music Attorney Legal & Business Affairs Registry, by Ritch Esra and Steve Trumbull, SRS Publishing, 7510 Sunset Blvd. #1041, Los Angeles CA 90046-3418. (800)552-7411. E-mail: musicregistry@compuserve.com or srspubl@aol.com.

Music Directory Canada, seventh edition, Norris-Whitney Communications Inc., 23 Hannover Dr., Suite 7, St. Catherines, Ontario L2W 1A3 Canada. (877)RING-NWC. E-mail: mail@nor.com. Website: http://nor.com.

Music Law: How to Run Your Band's Business, by Richard Stin, Nolo Press, 950 Parker St., Berkeley CA 94710-9867. (510)549-1976. Website: www.nolo.com.

Music, Money and Success: The Insider's Guide to the Music Industry, by Jeffrey Brabec and Todd Brabec, Schirmer Books, 1633 Broadway, New York NY 10019.

The Music Publisher Registry, by Ritch Esra, SRS Publishing, 7510 Sunset Blvd. #1041, Los Angeles CA 90046-3418. (800)552-7411. E-mail: musicregistry@compuserve.com or srspubl@aol.com.

Music Publishing: A Songwriter's Guide, revised edition, by Randy Poe, Writer's Digest Books, 4700 E. Galbraith Rd., Cincinnati OH 45236. (800)448-0915. Website: www.writersdigest.com.

The Musician's Guide to Making & Selling Your Own CDs & Cassettes, by Jana Stanfield, Writer's Digest Books, 4700 E. Galbraith Rd., Cincinnati OH 45236. (800)448-0915. Website: www.writersdigest.com.

Musicians' Phone Book, The Los Angeles Music Industry Directory, Get Yourself Some Publishing, 28336 Simsalido Ave., Canyon Country CA 91351. (805)299-2405. E-mail: mpb@earthlink.net. Website: www.musiciansphonebook.com.

Nashville Music Business Directory, by Mark Dreyer, NMBD Publishing, 9 Music Square S., Suite 210, Nashville TN 37203. (615)826-4141. E-mail: nmbd@nashvilleconnection.com. Website: www.nashvilleconnection.com.

Nashville's Unwritten Rules: Inside the Business of the Country Music Machine, by Dan Daley, Overlook Press, One Overlook Dr., Woodstock NY 12498. (845)679-6838. E-mail: overlook@netstep.net.

National Directory of Independent Record Distributors, P.O. Box 452063, Lake Mary FL 32795-2063. (407)834-8555. E-mail: info@songwriterproducts.com. Website: www.song writerproducts.com.

The Official Country Music Directory, ICMA Music Directory, P.O. Box 271238, Nashville TN 37227.

Radio Stations of America: A National Directory, P.O. Box 452063, Lake Mary FL 32795-2063. (407)834-8555. E-mail: info@songwriterproducts.com. Website: www.songwriterpr oducts.com.

The Real Deal—How to Get Signed to a Record Label from A to Z, by Daylle Deanna Schwartz, Billboard Books, 1695 Oak St., Lakewood NJ 08701. (800)344-7119.

Recording Industry Sourcebook, Music Books Plus, P.O. Box 670, 240 Portage Rd., Lewiston NY 14092. (800)265-8481. Website: www.musicbooksplus.com.

Reharmonization Techniques, by Randy Felts, Berklee Press, 1140 Boylston St., Boston MA 02215. (617)747-2146. E-mail: info@berkleepress.com. Website: www.berkleepress.com.

The Songwriters Idea Book, by Sheila Davis, Writer's Digest Books, 4700 E. Galbraith Rd., Cincinnati OH 45236. (800)448-0915. Website: www.writersdigest.com.

Songwriter's Market Guide to Song & Demo Submission Formats, Writer's Digest Books, 4700 E. Galbraith Rd., Cincinnati OH 45236. (800)448-0915. Website: www.writersdigest.com.

Songwriter's Playground—Innovative Exercises in Creative Songwriting, by Barbara L. Jordan, Creative Music Marketing, 1085 Commonwealth Ave., Suite 323, Boston MA 02215. (617)926-8766.

The Songwriter's Workshop: Harmony, by Jimmy Kachulis, Berklee Press, 1140 Boylston St., Boston MA 02215. (617)747-2146. E-mail: info@berkleepress.com. Website: www.ber kleepress.com.

The Songwriter's Workshop: Melody, by Jimmy Kachulis, Berklee Press, 1140 Boylston St., Boston MA 02215. (617)747-2146. E-mail: info@berkleepress.com. Website: www.ber kleepress.com.

Songwriting and the Creative Process, by Steve Gillette, Sing Out! Publications, P.O. Box 5640, Bethlehem PA 18015-0253. (888)SING-OUT. E-mail: singout@libertynet.org. Website: www.singout.org/sopubs.html.

Songwriting: Essential Guide to Lyric Form and Structure, by Pat Pattison, Berklee Press, 1140 Boylston St., Boston MA 02215. (617)747-2146. E-mail: info@berkleepress.com. Website: www.www.berkleepress.com.

Songwriting: Essential Guide to Rhyming, by Pat Pattison, Berklee Press, 1140 Boylston St., Boston MA 02215. (617)747-2146. E-mail: info@berkleepress.com. Website: www.w ww.berkleepress.com.

The Songwriting Sourcebook: How to Turn Chords Into Great Songs, by Rikky Rooksby, Backbeat Books, 600 Harrison St., San Francisco CA 94107. (415)947-6615. E-mail: books @musicplayer.com. Website: www.backbeatbooks.com.

Resources

The Soul of the Writer, by Susan Tucker with Linda Lee Strother, Journey Publishing, P.O. Box 92411, Nashville TN 37209. (615)952-4894. Website: www.journeypublishing.com.

Successful Lyric Writing, by Sheila Davis, Writer's Digest Books, 4700 E. Galbraith Rd., Cincinnati OH 45236. (800)448-0915. Website: www.writersdigest.com.

This Business of Music Marketing and Promotion, by Tad Lathrop and Jim Pettigrew, Jr., Billboard Books, Watson-Guptill Publications, 770 Broadway, New York NY 10003. E-mail: info@watsonguptill.com.

Tim Sweeney's Guide to Releasing Independent Records, by Tim Sweeney, TSA Books, 31805 Highway 79 S., Temecula CA 92592. (909)303-9506. E-mail: info@tsamusic.com. Website: www.tsamusic.com.

Tim Sweeney's Guide to Succeeding at Music Conventions, by Tim Sweeney, TSA Books, 31805 Highway 79 S., Temecula CA 92592. (909)303-9506. Website: www.tsamusic.com.

Texas Music Industry Directory, Texas Music Office, Office of the Governor, P.O. Box 13246, Austin TX 78711. (512)463-6666. E-mail: music@governor.state.tx.us. Website: www.governor.state.tx.us/music.

Tunesmith: Inside the Art of Songwriting, by Jimmy Webb, Hyperion, 77 W. 66th St., 11th Floor, New York NY 10023. (800)759-0190.

Volunteer Lawyers for the Arts Guide to Copyright for Musicians and Composers, One E. 53rd St., 6th Floor, New York NY 10022. (212)319-2787.

Writing Better Lyrics, by Pat Pattison, Writer's Digest Books, 4700 E. Galbraith Rd., Cincinnati OH 45236. (800)448-0915. Website: www.writersdigest.com.

Writing Music for Hit Songs, by Jai Josefs, Schirmer Trade Books, 257 Park Ave. S., New York NY 10010. (212)254-2100.

The Yellow Pages of Rock, The Album Network, 120 N. Victory Blvd., Burbank CA 91502. (800)222-4382. Fax: (818)955-9048. E-mail: ypinfo@yprock.com.

Web Sites of Interest

The Internet provides a wealth of information for songwriters and performers, and the number of sites devoted to music grows each day. Below is a list of some websites that can offer you information, links to other music sites, contact with other songwriters and places to showcase your songs. Since the online world is changing and expanding at such a rapid pace, this is hardly a comprehensive list. But it gives you a place to start on your journey through the Internet to search for opportunities to get your music heard.

About.com Musicians' Exchange: http://musicians.miningco.com
Site featuring headlines and articles of interest to independent musicians, as well as numerous links.

American Music Center: www.amc.net
Classical/jazz archives, includes a list of composer organizations and contacts.

American Society of Composers, Authors and Publishers (ASCAP) www.ascap.com
Database of performed works in ASCAP's repertoire. Also includes songwriter, performer and publisher information, ASCAP membership information and industry news.

Backstage Commerce: www.backstagecommerce.com
Offers secure online ordering support to artist websites for a commission.

The Bandit A&R Newsletter: www.banditnewsletter.com
Offers newsletter to help musicians target demos and press kits to labels, publishers, managers and production companies actively looking for new talent.

Bandname.com: www.bandname.com
Online band name registry and archive, as well as digital storefront services and classifieds.

Bandstand: www.bandstand.com
Music news and links.

Berklee School of Music: www.berkleemusic.com
Offers online instruction, including a certificate program in songwriting.

The Bard's Crier: http://thebards.net/crier/
A free guerilla music marketing e-zine.

Billboard.com: www.billboard.com
Music industry news and searchable online database of music companies by subscription.

The Blues Foundation: www.blues.org
Information on the foundation, its membership and events.

John Braheny Homepage: www.johnbraheny.com
John Braheny is the author of *The Craft and Business of Songwriting*, and his site features articles, interviews, and a blog with commentary on business and creative issues.

Broadcast Music, Inc. (BMI): www.bmi.com
Offers lists of song titles, songwriters and publishers of the BMI repertoire. Also includes BMI membership information, and general information on songwriting and licensing.

The Buzz Factor: www.thebuzzfactor.com
Offers press kit evaluation, press release writing, guerrilla music marketing, tips and weekly newsletter.

CDBABY: www.cdbaby.com
An online CD store dedicated solely to independent music.

CDFreedom: www.cdfreedom.com
Online CD store for independent musicians.

Chorus America: www.chorusamerica.org
The website of Chorus America, a national service organization for professional and volunteer choruses, including job listings and professional development information.

CPCC: www.under.org/cpcc
Website for the Center for the Promotion of Contemporary Composers.

Creative Musicians Coalition (CMC): www.aimcmc.com
Website of the CMC, an international organization dedicated to the advancement of independent musicians, links to artists, and tips and techniques for musicians.

Ensemble 21: www.ensemble21.com/e21.html
Website of the New York contemporary music performance group dedicated to promotion and performance of new orchestral compositions.

Film Music Network: www.filmmusicworld.com or www.filmmusic.net
Offers new about the fim music world, as well as educational and networking opportunities and an e-mail newsletter.

Fourfront Media and Music: www.knab.com
This site by music industry consultant Christopher Knab offers in-depth information on product development, promotion, publicity and performance.

Garageband.com: www.garageband.com
Online music hosting site where bands can post music and profiles, and then be critiqued by online listeners and industry insiders.

Getsigned.com: www.getsigned.com
Interviews with industry executives, how-to business information and more.

Government Liaison Services: www.trademarkinfo.com
An intellectual property research firm. Offers an online trademark search.

Guitar Nine Records: www.guitar9.com
Offers articles by music professionals and insiders.

Harry Fox Agency: www.harryfox.com
Offers a comprehensive FAQ about licensing songs for use in recording, performance and film.

Independent Artists' Services: www.idiom.com/ ~ upend/
Full of information including searchable databases of bands and booking/touring information and other resources.

Independent Distribution Network: www.idnmusic.com/
Website of independent bands distributing their music, with advice on everything from starting a band to finding labels.

Independent Songwriter Web Magazine: www.independentsongwriter.com
Independent music reviews, classifieds, message board and chat sessions.

Indie-Music.com: http://indie-music.com
Full of how-to articles, record label directory, radio links and venue listing.

Internet Underground Music Archive (IUMA): www.iuma.com
Online musicians community and music hosting site.

Jazz Composers Collective: www.jazzcollective.com
Industry information on composers, projects, recordings, concerts and events.

Jazz Corner: www.jazzcorner.com
Website for musicians and organizations featuring links to 70 websites for jazz musicians and organizations and the Speakeasy, an interactive conference area.

Just Plain Folks: www.jpfolks.com
Online songwriting organization featuring messageboards, lyric feedback forums, member profiles, featured members' music, contact listings, chapter homepages, and an Internet radio station. (See the Just Plain Folks listing in the Organizations section).

Kathode Ray Music: www.kathoderaymusic.com
Specializes in marketing and promotion consultation and offers a business forum, e-newsletter and a free classified ads board.

Li'l Hank's Guide for Songwriters in L.A.: www.halsguide.com
Website for songwriters with information on clubs, publishers, books, etc. as well as links to other songwriting sites.

Los Angeles Goes Underground: http://lagu.somaweb.org
Website dedicated to underground rock bands from Los Angeles and Hollywood.

Lyrical Line: www.lyricalline.com
Offers places to market your songs, critique service, industry news and more.

Lyricist.com: www.lyricist.com
Jeff Mallet's songwriter site offering contests, tips and job opportunities in the music industry.

MI2N (THE MUSIC INDUSTRY NEWS NETWORK): www.mi2n.com
Offers news on happenings in the music industry and career postings.

The Muse's Muse: www.musesmuse.com
Classifieds, catalog of lyric samples, songwriting articles, organizations and chat room.

Resources

Music & Audio Connection: www.musicandaudio.com
Guide to Canadian artists, associations and other resources from Norris-Whitney Communications, Inc.

Music Publishers Association: www.mpa.org
Provides a copyright resource center, directory of member publishers and information on the organization.

Music Yellow Pages: www.musicyellowpages.com
Phone book listings of music-related businesses.

Musicians Assistance Site (MAS): www.musicianassist.com
Features site reviews and databases of venues, contacts, promoters, manufacturers and record labels. Also includes an archive of music business articles, columns, and pre-made contracts and agreements.

The Musicians Guide Through the Legal Jungle: www.legaljungleguide.com/resource.htm
Offers articles on copyright law, music publishing and talent agents.

MySpace.com: www.myspace.com
Social networking site featuring music Web pages for musicians and songwriters.

National Association of Composers USA (NACUSA): www.music-usa.org/nacusa
Website of the organization dedicated to promotion and performance of new music by Americans, featuring a young composers' competition, concert schedule, job opportunities and more.

National Music Publishers Association: www.nmpa.org
The organization's online site with information about copyright, legislation and other concerns of the music publishing world.

Online Rock: www.onlinerock.com
Offers e-mail, marketing and free webpage services. Also features articles, chat rooms, links, etc.

Opera America: www.operaamerica.org
Website of Opera America, featuring information on advocacy and awareness programs, publications, conference schedules and more.

Outersound: www.outersound.com
Information on finding a recording studio, educating yourself in the music industry, and a list of music magazines to advertise in or get reviewed by.

PerformerMag: www.performermag.com
Offers articles, music industry news, classifieds, and reviews.

Public Domain Music: www.pdinfo.com
Articles on public domain works and copyright, including public domain song lists, research resources, tips and a FAQ.

PUMP AUDIO: www.pumpaudio.com
License music for film and TV on a non-exclusive basis. (See the Insider Report with singer/songwriter Bibi Farber on page 160.)

Rhythm Net: www.rhythmnet.com
Online CD store for independent musicians.

Resources

SESAC Inc.: www.sesac.com
Includes SESAC performing rights organization information, songwriter profiles, organization news, licensing information and links to other sites.

Song Shark: www.geocities.com/songshark
Website of information on known song sharks.

Songcatalog.com: www.songcatalog.com
Online song catalog database for licensing.

Songlink: www.songlink.com
Offers opportunities to pitch songs to music publishers for specific recording projects, also industry news.

Songscope.com: www.songscope.com
Online song catalog database for pitching and licensing.

Songwriter Products Ideas & Necessities (SPIN): www.songwriterproducts.com
Offer songwriting tips, tools and accessories, including tapes, CDs, duplication products and music business career packages.

Songwriter's Guild of America (SGA): www.songwritersguild.com
Offers industry news, member services information, newsletters, contract reviews and more.

Songwriter's Resource Network: www.songwritersresourcenetwork.com
Online information and services designed especially for songwriters.

The Songwriting Education Resource: www.craftofsongwriting.com
An educational site for Nashville songwriters offering discussion boards, articles and links.

SongU.com: www.songu.com
Offers online songwriting courses, networking opportunities, e-mail newsletter, and opportunities to pitch songs to industry professionals.

Sonic Bids: www.sonicbids.com
Features an online press kit template with photos, bio, music samples, and a date calendar.

StarPolish: www.starpolish.com
Features articles and interviews on the music industry, as well as the Velvet Rope Forum.

TAXI: www.taxi.com
Independent A&R vehicle that shops tapes to A&R professionals.

United States Copyright Office: http://www.copyright.gov
The homepage for the U.S. copyright office, offering information on registering songs.

Yahoo!: www.yahoo.com/Entertainment/Music/
Use this search engine to retrieve over 20,000 music listings.

Resources

Glossary

A cappella. Choral singing without accompaniment.

AAA form. A song form in which every verse has the same melody; often used for songs that tell a story.

AABA, ABAB. A commonly used song pattern consisting of two verses, a bridge and a verse, or a repeated pattern of verse and bridge, where the verses are musically the same.

A&R Director. Record company executive in charge of the Artists and Repertoire Department who is responsible for finding and developing new artists and matching songs with artists.

A/C. Adult contemporary music.

Advance. Money paid to the songwriter or recording artist, which is then recouped before regular royalty payment begins. Sometimes called ''up front'' money, advances are deducted from royalties.

AFIM. Association for Independent Music (formerly NAIRD). Organization for independent record companies, distributors, retailers, manufacturers, etc.

AFM. American Federation of Musicians. A union for musicians and arrangers.

AFTRA. American Federation of Television and Radio Artists. A union for performers.

AIMP. Association of Independent Music Publishers.

Airplay. The radio broadcast of a recording.

AOR. Album-Oriented Rock. A radio format that primarily plays selections from rock albums as opposed to hit singles.

Arrangement. An adaptation of a composition for a recording or performance, with consideration for the melody, harmony, instrumentation, tempo, style, etc.

ASCAP. American Society of Composers, Authors and Publishers. A performing rights society. (See the Organizations section.)

Assignment. Transfer of rights of a song from writer to publisher.

Audio Visual Index (AVI). A database containing title and production information for cue sheets which are available from a performing rights organization. Currently, BMI, ASCAP, SOCAN, PRS, APRA and SACEM contribute their cue sheet listings to the AVI.

Audiovisual. Refers to presentations that use audio backup for visual material.

Background music. Music used that creates mood and supports the spoken dialogue of a radio program or visual action of an audiovisual work. Not feature or theme music.

b&w. Black and white.

Bed. Prerecorded music used as background material in commercials. In rap music, often refers to the sampled and looped drums and music over which the rapper performs.

Black box. Theater without fixed stage or seating arrangements, capable of a variety of formations. Usually a small space, often attached to a major theater complex, used for workshops or experimental works calling for small casts and limited sets.

BMI. Broadcast Music, Inc. A performing rights society. (See the Organizations section.)

Booking agent. Person who schedules performances for entertainers.

Bootlegging. Unauthorized recording and selling of a song.

Business manager. Person who handles the financial aspects of artistic careers.

Buzz. Attention an act generates through the media and word of mouth.

b/w. Backed with. Usually refers to the B-side of a single.

C&W. Country and western.

Catalog. The collected songs of one writer, or all songs handled by one publisher.

CD. Compact Disc (see below).

CD-R. A recordable CD.

CD-ROM. Compact Disc-Read Only Memory. A computer information storage medium capable of holding enormous amounts of data. Information on a CD-ROM cannot be deleted. A computer user must have a CD-ROM drive to access a CD-ROM.

Chamber music. Any music suitable for performance in a small audience area or chamber.

Chamber orchestra. A miniature orchestra usually containing one instrument per part.

Chart. The written arrangement of a song.

Charts. The trade magazines' lists of the best-selling records.

CHR. Comtemporary Hit Radio. Top 40 pop music.

Collaboration. Two or more artists, writers, etc., working together on a single project; for instance, a playwright and a songwriter creating a musical together.

Compact disc. A small disc (about 4.7 inches in diameter) holding digitally encoded music that is read by a laser beam in a CD player.

Composers. The men and women who create musical compositions for motion pictures and other audio visual works, or the creators of classical music composition.

Co-publish. Two or more parties own publishing rights to the same song.

Copyright. The exclusive legal right giving the creator of a work the power to control the publishing, reproduction and selling of the work. Although a song is technically copyrighted at the time it is written, the best legal protection of that copyright comes through registering the copyright with the Library of Congress.

Copyright infringement. Unauthorized use of a copyrighted song or portions thereof.

Cover recording. A new version of a previously recorded song.

Crossover. A song that becomes popular in two or more musical categories (e.g., country and pop).

Cut. Any finished recording; a selection from a LP. Also to record.

DAT. Digital Audio Tape. A professional and consumer audio cassette format for recording and playing back digitally-encoded material. DAT cassettes are approximately one-third smaller than conventional audio cassettes.

DCC. Digital Compact Cassette. A consumer audio cassette format for recording and playing back digitally-encoded tape. DCC tapes are the same size as analog cassettes.

Demo. A recording of a song submitted as a demonstration of a writer's or artist's skills.

Derivative work. A work derived from another work, such as a translation, musical arrangement, sound recording, or motion picture version.

Distributor. Wholesale marketing agent responsible for getting records from manufacturers to retailers.

Donut. A jingle with singing at the beginning and end and instrumental background in the middle. Ad copy is recorded over the middle section.

E-mail. Electronic mail. Computer address where a company or individual can be reached via modem.

Engineer. A specially-trained individual who operates recording studio equipment.

Enhanced CD. General term for an audio CD that also contains multimedia computer information. It is playable in both standard CD players and CD-ROM drives.

EP. Extended play record or cassette containing more selections than a standard single, but fewer than a standard album.

EPK. Electronic press kit. Usually contains photos, sound files, bio information, reviews, tour dates, etc. posted online. Sonicbids.com is a popular EPK hosting Web site.

Final mix. The art of combining all the various sounds that take place during the recording session into a two-track stereo or mono tape. Reflects the total product and all of the energies and talents the artist, producer and engineer have put into the project.

Fly space. The area above a stage from which set pieces are lowered and raised during a performance.

Folio. A softcover collection of printed music prepared for sale.

Following. A fan base committed to going to gigs and buying albums.

Foreign rights societies. Performing rights societies other than domestic which have reciprocal agreements with ASCAP and BMI for the collection of royalties accrued by foreign radio and television airplay and other public performance of the writer members of the above groups.

Harry Fox Agency. Organization that collects mechanical royalties.

Grammy. Music industry awards presented by the National Academy of Recording Arts and Sciences.

Hip-hop. A dance oriented musical style derived from a combination of disco, rap and R&B.

Hit. A song or record that achieves top 40 status.

Hook. A memorable ''catch'' phrase or melody line that is repeated in a song.

House. Dance music created by remixing samples from other songs.

Hypertext. Words or groups of words in an electronic document that are linked to other text, such as a definition or a related document. Hypertext can also be linked to illustrations.

Indie. An independent record label, music publisher or producer.

Infringement. A violation of the exclusive rights granted by the copyright law to a copyright owner.

Internet. A worldwide network of computers that offers access to a wide variety of electronic resources.

ips. Inches per second; a speed designation for tape recording.

IRC. International reply coupon, necessary for the return of materials sent out of the country. Available at most post offices.

Jingle. Usually a short verse set to music designed as a commercial message.

Lead sheet. Written version (melody, chord symbols and lyric) of a song.

Leader. Plastic (non-recordable) tape at the beginning and between songs for ease in selection.

Libretto. The text of an opera or any long choral work. The booklet containing such text.

Listing. Block of information in this book about a specific company.

LP. Designation for long-playing record played at $33\frac{1}{3}$ rpm.

Lyric sheet. A typed or written copy of a song's lyrics.

Market. A potential song or music buyer; also a demographic division of the record-buying public.

Master. Edited and mixed tape used in the production of records; the best or original copy of a recording from which copies are made.

MD. MiniDisc. A 2.5 inch disk for recording and playing back digitally-encoded music.

Mechanical right. The right to profit from the physical reproduction of a song.

Mechanical royalty. Money earned from record, tape and CD sales.

MIDI. Musical instrument digital interface. Universal standard interface that allows musical instruments to communicate with each other and computers.

Mini Disc. (See **MD** above.)

Mix. To blend a multi-track recording into the desired balance of sound, usually to a 2-track stereo master.

Modem. MOdulator/DEModulator. A computer device used to send data from one computer to another via telephone line.

MOR. Middle of the road. Easy-listening popular music.

MP3. File format of a relatively small size that stores audio files on a computer. Music saved in a MP3 format can be played only with a MP3 player (which can be downloaded onto a computer).

Ms. Manuscript.

Multimedia. Computers and software capable of integrating text, sound, photographic-quality images, animation and video.

Music bed. (See **Bed** above.)

Music jobber. A wholesale distributor of printed music.

Music library. A business that purchases canned music, which can then be bought by producers of radio and TV commercials, films, videos and audiovisual productions to use however they wish.

Music publisher. A company that evaluates songs for commercial potential, finds artists to record them, finds other uses (such as TV or film) for the songs, collects income generated by the songs and protects copyrights from infringement.

Music Row. An area of Nashville, TN, encompassing Sixteenth, Seventeeth and Eighteenth avenues where most of the major publishing houses, recording studios, mastering labs, songwriters, singers, promoters, etc. practice their trade.

NARAS. National Academy of Recording Arts and Sciences.

The National Academy of Songwriters (NAS). The largest U.S. songwriters' association. (See the Organizations section.)

Needle-drop. Refers to a type of music library. A needledrop music library is a licensed library that allows producers to borrow music on a rate schedule. The price depends on how the music will be used.

Network. A group of computers electronically linked to share information and resources.

NMPA. National Music Publishers Association.

One-off. A deal between songwriter and publisher which includes only one song or project at a time. No future involvement is implicated. Many times a single song contract accompanies a one-off deal.

One-stop. A wholesale distributor of who sells small quantities of records to "mom and pop" record stores, retailers and jukebox operators.

Operetta. Light, humorous, satiric plot or poem, set to cheerful light music with occasional spoken dialogue.

Overdub. To record an additional part (vocal or instrumental) onto a basic multi-track recording.

Parody. A satirical imitation of a literary or musical work. Permission from the owner of the copyright is generally required before commercial exploitation of a parody.

Payola. Dishonest payment to broadcasters in exchange for airplay.

Performing rights. A specific right granted by U.S. copyright law protecting a composition from being publicly performed without the owner's permission.

Performing rights organization. An organization that collects income from the public performance of songs written by its members and then proportionally distributes this income to the individual copyright holder based on the number of performances of each song.

Resources

Personal manager. A person who represents artists to develop and enhance their careers. Personal managers may negotiate contracts, hire and dismiss other agencies and personnel relating to the artist's career, review material, help with artist promotions and perform many services.

Piracy. The unauthorized reproduction and selling of printed or recorded music.

Pitch. To attempt to solicit interest for a song by audition.

Playlist. List of songs a radio station will play.

Points. A negotiable percentage paid to producers and artists for records sold.

Producer. Person who supervises every aspect of a recording project.

Production company. Company specializing in producing jingle packages for advertising agencies. May also refer to companies specializing in audiovisual programs.

Professional manager. Member of a music publisher's staff who screens submitted material and tries to get the company's catalog of songs recorded.

Proscenium. Permanent architectural arch in a theater that separates the stage from the audience.

Public domain. Any composition with an expired, lapsed or invalid copyright, and therefore belonging to everyone.

Purchase license. Fee paid for music used from a stock music library.

Query. A letter of inquiry to an industry professional soliciting his interest.

R&B. Rhythm and blues.

Rack Jobber. Distributors who lease floor space from department stores and put in racks of albums.

Rate. The percentage of royalty as specified by contract.

Release. Any record issued by a record company.

Residuals. In advertising or television, payments to singers and musicians for use of a performance.

RIAA. Recording Industry Association of America.

Royalty. Percentage of money earned from the sale of records or use of a song.

RPM. Revolutions per minute. Refers to phonograph turntable speed.

SAE. Self-addressed envelope (with no postage attached).

SASE. Self-addressed stamped envelope.

SATB. The abbreviation for parts in choral music, meaning Soprano, Alto, Tenor and Bass.

Score. A complete arrangement of all the notes and parts of a composition (vocal or instrumental) written out on staves. A full score, or orchestral score, depicts every orchestral part on a separate staff and is used by a conductor.

Self-contained. A band or recording act that writes all their own material.

SESAC. A performing rights organization, originally the Society of European Stage Authors and Composers. (See the Organizations section.)

SFX. Sound effects.

Shop. To pitch songs to a number of companies or publishers.

Single. 45 rpm record with only one song per side. A 12″ single refers to a long version of one song on a 12″ disc, usually used for dance music.

Ska. Fast tempo dance music influenced primarily by reggae and punk, usually featuring horns, saxophone and bass.

SOCAN. Society of Composers, Authors and Music Publishers of Canada. A Canadian performing rights organization. (See the Organizations section.)

Solicited. Songs or materials that have been requested.

Song plugger. A songwriter representative whose main responsibility is promoting uncut songs to music publishers, record companies, artists and producers.

Song shark. Person who deals with songwriters deceptively for his own profit.

SoundScan. A company that collates the register tapes of reporting stores to track the actual number of albums sold at the retail level.

Soundtrack. The audio, including music and narration, of a film, videotape or audiovisual program.

Space stage. Open stage that features lighting and, perhaps, projected scenery.

Split publishing. To divide publishing rights between two or more publishers.

Staff songwriter. A songwriter who has an exclusive agreement with a publisher.

Statutory royalty rate. The maximum payment for mechanical rights guaranteed by law that a record company may pay the songwriter and his publisher for each record or tape sold.

Subpublishing. Certain rights granted by a U.S. publisher to a foreign publisher in exchange for promoting the U.S. catalog in his territory.

Synchronization. Technique of timing a musical soundtrack to action on film or video.

Take. Either an attempt to record a vocal or instrument part, or an acceptable recording of a performance.

Tejano. A musical form begun in the late 1970s by regional bands in south Texas, its style reflects a blended Mexican-American culture. Incorporates elements of rock, country, R&B and jazz, and often features accordion and 12-string guitar.

Thrust stage. Stage with audience on three sides and a stagehouse or wall on the fourth side.

Top 40. The first 40 songs on the pop music charts at any given time. Also refers to a style of music which emulates that heard on the current top 40.

Track. Divisions of a recording tape (e.g., 24-track tape) that can be individually recorded in the studio, then mixed into a finished master.

Trades. Publications covering the music industry.

12″ Single. A 12-inch record containing one or more remixes of a song, originally intended for dance club play.

Unsolicited. Songs or materials that were not requested and are not expected.

VHS. $\frac{1}{2}$″ videocassette format.

Vocal score. An arrangement of vocal music detailing all vocal parts, and condensing all accompanying instrumental music into one piano part.

Website. An address on the World Wide Web that can be accessed by computer modem. It may contain text, graphics and sound.

Wing space. The offstage area surrounding the playing stage in a theater, unseen by the audience, where sets and props are hidden, actors wait for cues, and stagehands prepare to chance sets.

World music. A general music category which includes most musical forms originating outside the U.S. and Europe, including reggae and calypso. World music finds its roots primarily in the Caribbean, Latin America, Africa and the south Pacific.

World Wide Web (WWW). An Internet resource that utilizes hypertext to access information. It also supports formatted text, illustrations and sounds, depending on the user's computer capabilities.

Category
Indexes

The Category Indexes are a good place to begin searching for a market. They break down the listings by section (music publishers, record companies, etc.) and by the type of music they are interested in. For example, if you write country songs, and are looking for a publisher to pitch them, go to the Music Publishers heading and then check the companies listed under the Country subheading. The music categories cover a wide range of variations within each genre, so be sure to read each listing thoroughly to make sure your own unique take on that genre is a good match. Some listings do not appear in these indexes because they did not cite a specific preference. Listings that were very specific, or whose music descriptions don't quite fit into these categories also do not appear. (Category listings for **Music Publishers** begin on this page, **Record Companies** on page 366, **Record Producers** on page 371 and **Managers & Booking Agents** begin on page 376.)

MUSIC PUBLISHERS

Adult Contemporary (also easy listening, middle of the road, AAA, ballads, etc.)

Abalorn Music 82

Allegheny Music Works 84

Antelope Publishing Inc. 84

Baitstring Music 85

Bay Ridge Publishing 86

Big Fish Music Publishing Group 87

Bradley Music, Allan 89

Buckeye Music Group 93

Buried Treasure Music 93

California Country Music 94

Come Alive Communications, Inc. 96

Corelli Music Group 96

Duane Music, Inc. 102

Emstone Music Publishing 104

Gary Music, Alan 106

Hammel Associates, Inc., R.L. 107

Happy Melody 107

Hickory Lane Publishing and Recording 107

High-Minded Moma Publishing & Productions 108

His Power Productions and Publishing 108

Hitsburgh Music Co. 108

Inside Records/OK Songs 109

Ivory Pen Entertainment 109

Lilly Music Publishing 113

Lineage Publishing Co. 113

Many Lives Music Publishers 114

MIDI Track Publishing/ALLRS Music Publishing Co. 116

Montina Music 117

New Rap Jam Publishing, A 118

Pegasus Music 119

Prescription Company 121

Rockford Music Co. 123

Rondor Music International/Almo/Irving Music 124

S.M.C.L. Productions, Inc. 125

Segal's Publications 126
Silicon Music Publishing Co. 126
Tourmaline Music, Inc. 130
Walker Publishing Co. L.L.C. 132
Your Best Songs Publishing 134

Alternative (also modern rock, punk, college rock, new wave, hardcore, new music, industrial, ska, indie rock, garage, etc.)

Alias John Henry Tunes 83
Black Market Entertainment Recordings 88
Cornelius Companies, The 97
Intoxygene Sarl 109
Juke Music 111
Lake Transfer Productions & Music 112
Many Lives Music Publishers 114
Montina Music 117
Naked Jain Records 117
Prescription Company 121
Rondor Music International/Almo/ Irving Music 124
Sandalphon Music Publishing 126
Tourmaline Music, Inc. 130
Unknown Source Music 131
Winston & Hoffman House Music Publishers 134
Zomba Music Publishing 135

Blues

Abalorn Music 82
Bay Ridge Publishing 86
Bearsongs 87
Brandon Hills Music, LLC 89
BSW Records 92
Christopher Publishing, Sonny 95
Dave Music, Jof 97
Duane Music, Inc. 102
Earthscream Music Publishing Co. 102
Many Lives Music Publishers 114
Montina Music 117
New Rap Jam Publishing, A 118
Prescription Company 121

Queen Esther Music Publishers 122
Sandalphon Music Publishing 126
Silicon Music Publishing Co. 126
Sizemore Music 127
Sound Cellar Music 128
Tower Music Group 130

Children's

Brandon Hills Music, LLC 89
Many Lives Music Publishers 114
Piano Press 120
Prescription Company 121
Ren Zone Music 123
Rhythms Productions 123
Segal's Publications 126

Classical (also opera, chamber music, serious music, choral, etc.)

Bourne Co. Music Publishers 89
Emandell Tunes 103
Many Lives Music Publishers 114
Silver Blue Music/Oceans Blue Music 127

Country (also western, C&W, bluegrass, cowboy songs, western swing, honky-tonk, etc.)

Abalorn Music 82
Abear Publishing 82
Acuff-Rose Music 82
Alias John Henry Tunes 83
All Rock Music 83
Allegheny Music Works 84
Americatone International 84
Baird Music Group 85
Baitstring Music 85
Bay Ridge Publishing 86
Beaverwood Audio-Video 87
Big Fish Music Publishing Group 87
Bradley Music, Allan 89
Brandon Hills Music, LLC 89
Branson Country Music Publishing 89
BSW Records 92
Buckeye Music Group 93

Buried Treasure Music 93
California Country Music 94
Cherri/Holly Music 94
Christopher Publishing, Sonny 95
Coal Harbor Music 95
Come Alive Communications, Inc. 96
Copperfield Music Group 96
Cornelius Companies, The 97
Curb Music 97
De Miles Music Company, The Edward 97
Delev Music Company 101
Dream Seekers Publishing 101
Duane Music, Inc. 102
Earitating Music Publishing 102
Earthscream Music Publishing Co. 102
Electric Mule Publishing Company 103
Emandell Tunes 103
EMF Productions 103
Emstone Music Publishing 104
Famous Music Publishing Companies 104
Fricon Music Company 105
Furrow Music 106
G Major Music 106
Gary Music, Alan 106
Glad Music Co. 106
Hammel Associates, Inc., R.L. 107
Hickory Lane Publishing and Recording 107
High-Minded Moma Publishing & Productions 108
Hitsburgh Music Co. 108
Inside Records/OK Songs 109
Jerjoy Music 110
JoDa Music 111
JPMC Music Inc. 111
Juke Music 111
Kaysarah Music 112
Lari-Jon Publishing 112
Lilly Music Publishing 113
Lineage Publishing Co. 113
Lita Music 113

M & T Waldoch Publishing, Inc. 114
Many Lives Music Publishers 114
Markea Music/Gina Pie Music/Si Que Music 115
Marvin Publishing, John Weller 115
Maui Arts & Music Association/Survivor Records/Ten of Diamonds Music 115
MCA Music Publishing 116
McClure & Trowbridge Publishing, Ltd. 116
McCoy Music, Jim 116
MIDI Track Publishing/ALLRS Music Publishing Co. 116
Montina Music 117
Moon June Music 117
New Rap Jam Publishing, A 118
Newbraugh Brothers Music 118
Old Slowpoke Music 119
Orchid Publishing 119
Pegasus Music 119
Peters Music, Justin 120
Phoebob Music 120
Platinum Planet Music, Inc. 120
Portage Music 121
Prescription Company 121
Rainbow Music Corp. 122
Red Sundown Music 123
Rhinestone Cowboy Music 123
Rockford Music Co. 123
Rondor Music International/Almo/Irving Music 124
Rustic Records, Inc Publishing 124
Rustron Music Publishers 124
Saddlestone Publishing 125
Salt Works Music 125
Sandalphon Music Publishing 126
SDB Music Group 126
Segal's Publications 126
Silicon Music Publishing Co. 126
Sizemore Music 127
Sony/ATV Music Publishing 128
Sound Cellar Music 128
Starbound Publishing Co. 128
Still Working Music Group 129

T.C. Productions/Etude Publishing
  Co. 129
Thistle Hill 130
Tourmaline Music, Inc. 130
Tower Music Group 130
Transamerika Musikverlag KG 130
Trio Productions 131
Vaam Music Group 132
Vine Creek Music 132
Walker Publishing Co. L.L.C. 132
Walkerbout Music Group 132
Weaver of Words Music 133
Wilcom Publishing 134
Windswept Music 134
Winston & Hoffman House Music
  Publishers 134
Your Best Songs Publishing 134
Zettitalia Music International 134

**Dance (also house, hi-NRG,
disco, club, rave, techno, trip-
hop, trance, etc.)**
Audio Music Publishers 85
Cherri/Holly Music 94
De Miles Music Company, The Ed-
  ward 97
Delev Music Company 101
Duane Music, Inc. 102
Fresh Entertainment 105
Gary Music, Alan 106
Happy Melody 107
Inside Records/OK Songs 109
Lake Transfer Productions & Music
  112
Lilly Music Publishing 113
M & T Waldoch Publishing, Inc. 114
Makers Mark Gold 114
Many Lives Music Publishers 114
Montina Music 117
Platinum Planet Music, Inc. 120
Prescription Company 121
QUARK, Inc. 121
Rockford Music Co. 123
S.M.C.L. Productions, Inc. 125
Still Working Music Group 129
Succes 129

T.C. Productions/Etude Publishing
  Co. 129
Walkerbout Music Group 132
Winston & Hoffman House Music
  Publishers 134

Folk (also acoustic, Celtic, etc.)
Earitating Music Publishing 102
Kaysarah Music 112
Many Lives Music Publishers 114
Markea Music/Gina Pie Music/Si
  Que Music 115
Montina Music 117
Newbraugh Brothers Music 118
Piano Press 120
Prescription Company 121
Rockford Music Co. 123
Rustron Music Publishers 124

**Instrumental (also background
music, musical scores, etc.)**
Alpha Music Inc. 84
Big Fish Music Publishing Group 87
Cherri/Holly Music 94
CTV Music (Great Britain) 97
De Miles Music Company, The Ed-
  ward 97
Happy Melody 107
JPMC Music Inc. 111
Many Lives Music Publishers 114
Rustron Music Publishers 124
Shawnee Press, Inc. 126
Sinus Musik Produktion, Ulli Weigel
  127
Succes 129
Zettitalia Music International 134

**Jazz (also fusion, bebop, swing,
etc.)**
Alexander Sr. Music 82
Antelope Publishing Inc. 84
Barkin' Foe the Master's Bone 85
Bearsongs 87
His Power Productions and Publish-
  ing 108
Ivory Pen Entertainment 109

Ja/Nein Musikverlag GmbH 109
JPMC Music Inc. 111
Many Lives Music Publishers 114
Montina Music 117
Old Slowpoke Music 119
Perla Music 120
Prescription Company 121
Rainbow Music Corp. 122
Rockford Music Co. 123
Winston & Hoffman House Music
    Publishers 134

Latin (also Spanish, salsa, Cuban, conga, Brazilian, cumbja, rancheras, Mexican, merengue, Tejano, Tex Mex, etc.)

Americatone International 84
Cherri/Holly Music 94
Famous Music Publishing Compa-
    nies 104
Inside Records/OK Songs 109
Many Lives Music Publishers 114
McClure & Trowbridge Publishing,
    Ltd. 116
Supreme Enterprises Int'l Corp. 129

Metal (also thrash, grindcore, heavy metal, etc.)

Abalorn Music 82
Bay Ridge Publishing 86
Intoxygene Sarl 109
M & T Waldoch Publishing, Inc. 114
Sound Cellar Music 128
Your Best Songs Publishing 134

New Age (also ambient)

Abalorn Music 82
Bay Ridge Publishing 86
High-Minded Moma Publishing &
    Productions 108
Intoxygene Sarl 109
Many Lives Music Publishers 114
Maui Arts & Music Association/Sur-
    vivor Records/Ten of Diamonds
    Music 115
Rustron Music Publishers 124

Sinus Musik Produktion, Ulli Weigel
    127
Your Best Songs Publishing 134

Novelty (also comedy, humor, etc.)

Allegheny Music Works 84
Big Fish Music Publishing Group 87
Coal Harbor Music 95
Many Lives Music Publishers 114
Peters Music, Justin 120
Piano Press 120

Pop (also top 40, top 100, popular, chart hits, etc.)

Abalorn Music 82
Allegheny Music Works 84
Audio Music Publishers 85
Baitstring Music 85
Barkin' Foe the Master's Bone 85
Bay Ridge Publishing 86
Big Fish Music Publishing Group 87
Bradley Music, Allan 89
Buried Treasure Music 93
California Country Music 94
Cherri/Holly Music 94
Coal Harbor Music 95
Come Alive Communications, Inc.
    96
Copperfield Music Group 96
Cornelius Companies, The 97
De Miles Music Company, The Ed-
    ward 97
Delev Music Company 101
Dream Seekers Publishing 101
Duane Music, Inc. 102
Earthscream Music Publishing Co.
    102
Emandell Tunes 103
EMF Productions 103
Emstone Music Publishing 104
Fresh Entertainment 105
G Major Music 106
Gary Music, Alan 106
Hammel Associates, Inc., R.L. 107
Happy Melody 107

High-Minded Moma Publishing & Productions 108
His Power Productions and Publishing 108
Inside Records/OK Songs 109
Ivory Pen Entertainment 109
Ja/Nein Musikverlag GmbH 109
JoDa Music 111
JPMC Music Inc. 111
Juke Music 111
Lake Transfer Productions & Music 112
Lineage Publishing Co. 113
M & T Waldoch Publishing, Inc. 114
Makers Mark Gold 114
Manuiti L.A. 114
Many Lives Music Publishers 114
Markea Music/Gina Pie Music/Si Que Music 115
Marvin Publishing, John Weller 115
Maui Arts & Music Association/Survivor Records/Ten of Diamonds Music 115
MIDI Track Publishing/ALLRS Music Publishing Co. 116
Montina Music 117
Music Room Publishing Group, The 117
New Rap Jam Publishing, A 118
Orchid Publishing 119
PeerMusic 119
Pegasus Music 119
Peters Music, Justin 120
Prescription Company 121
QUARK, Inc. 121
Rainbow Music Corp. 122
Red Sundown Music 123
Rockford Music Co. 123
Rustron Music Publishers 124
S.M.C.L. Productions, Inc. 125
Saddlestone Publishing 125
Salt Works Music 125
Sandalphon Music Publishing 126
Segal's Publications 126
Silver Blue Music/Oceans Blue Music 127

Sinus Musik Produktion, Ulli Weigel 127
Sizemore Music 127
Sound Cellar Music 128
Still Working Music Group 129
Succes 129
T.C. Productions/Etude Publishing Co. 129
Thistle Hill 130
Tower Music Group 130
Transamerika Musikverlag KG 130
Twin Towers Publishing Co. 131
Vaam Music Group 132
Walker Publishing Co. L.L.C. 132
Walkerbout Music Group 132
Weaver of Words Music 133
Wengert, Berthold (Musikverlag) 133
Wilcom Publishing 134
Winston & Hoffman House Music Publishers 134
Your Best Songs Publishing 134
Zettitalia Music International 134
Zomba Music Publishing 135

R&B (also soul, black, urban, etc.)

Abalorn Music 82
Alexander Sr. Music 82
Allegheny Music Works 84
Americatone International 84
Audio Music Publishers 85
Baitstring Music 85
Barkin' Foe the Master's Bone 85
Bay Ridge Publishing 86
Black Market Entertainment Recordings 88
Bradley Music, Allan 89
Buckeye Music Group 93
California Country Music 94
Dave Music, Jof 97
De Miles Music Company, The Edward 97
Delev Music Company 101
Duane Music, Inc. 102
EMF Productions 103

Emstone Music Publishing 104
Famous Music Publishing Companies 104
Fresh Entertainment 105
Gary Music, Alan 106
Hammel Associates, Inc., R.L. 107
His Power Productions and Publishing 108
Ivory Pen Entertainment 109
Ja/Nein Musikverlag GmbH 109
JPMC Music Inc. 111
Lake Transfer Productions & Music 112
M & T Waldoch Publishing, Inc. 114
Makers Mark Gold 114
Manuiti L.A. 114
Many Lives Music Publishers 114
Markea Music/Gina Pie Music/Si Que Music 115
Marvin Publishing, John Weller 115
MIDI Track Publishing/ALLRS Music Publishing Co. 116
Montina Music 117
Music Room Publishing Group, The 117
New Rap Jam Publishing, A 118
Old Slowpoke Music 119
PeerMusic 119
Platinum Planet Music, Inc. 120
Prescription Company 121
Queen Esther Music Publishers 122
Rainbow Music Corp. 122
Rondor Music International/Almo/ Irving Music 124
Rustron Music Publishers 124
Saddlestone Publishing 125
Segal's Publications 126
Silver Blue Music/Oceans Blue Music 127
Sizemore Music 127
Starbound Publishing Co. 128
Still Working Music Group 129
T.C. Productions/Etude Publishing Co. 129
Tower Music Group 130
Twin Towers Publishing Co. 131

Unknown Source Music 131
Vaam Music Group 132
Wilcom Publishing 134
Winston & Hoffman House Music Publishers 134
Your Best Songs Publishing 134
Zettitalia Music International 134
Zomba Music Publishing 135

Rap (also hip-hop, bass, etc.)

Audio Music Publishers 85
Barkin' Foe the Master's Bone 85
Black Market Entertainment Recordings 88
Fresh Entertainment 105
Ivory Pen Entertainment 109
Lake Transfer Productions & Music 112
Makers Mark Gold 114
Marvin Publishing, John Weller 115
McClure & Trowbridge Publishing, Ltd. 116
New Rap Jam Publishing, A 118
Queen Esther Music Publishers 122
Silver Blue Music/Oceans Blue Music 127
Unknown Source Music 131
Walkerbout Music Group 132
Winston & Hoffman House Music Publishers 134
Zomba Music Publishing 135

Religious (also gospel, sacred, Christian, church, hymns, praise, inspirational, worship, etc.)

Alexander Sr. Music 82
Allegheny Music Works 84
Audio Music Publishers 85
Barkin' Foe the Master's Bone 85
Beaverwood Audio-Video 87
Big Fish Music Publishing Group 87
Bradley Music, Allan 89
Brandon Hills Music, LLC 89
California Country Music 94
Cherri/Holly Music 94

Coal Harbor Music 95

Come Alive Communications, Inc. 96

Copperfield Music Group 96

Corelli Music Group 96

Cornelius Companies, The 97

Dave Music, Jof 97

Delev Music Company 101

Emandell Tunes 103

EMF Productions 103

G Major Music 106

Hammel Associates, Inc., R.L. 107

His Power Productions and Publishing 108

Hitsburgh Music Co. 108

Ivory Pen Entertainment 109

Jaelius Enterprises 110

JoDa Music 111

JPMC Music Inc. 111

Juke Music 111

Lari-Jon Publishing 112

Lita Music 113

Makers Mark Gold 114

McClure & Trowbridge Publishing, Ltd. 116

McCoy Music, Jim 116

MIDI Track Publishing/ALLRS Music Publishing Co. 116

Montina Music 117

New Rap Jam Publishing, A 118

Newbraugh Brothers Music 118

Orchid Publishing 119

Phoebob Music 120

Queen Esther Music Publishers 122

Saddlestone Publishing 125

Salt Works Music 125

Sandalphon Music Publishing 126

Shawnee Press, Inc. 126

SME Publishing Group 128

Starbound Publishing Co. 128

Tourmaline Music, Inc. 130

Tower Music Group 130

Walkerbout Music Group 132

Wells Music, Angela Baker 133

Rock (also rockabilly, AOR, rock 'n' roll, etc.)

Abalorn Music 82

Alias John Henry Tunes 83

All Rock Music 83

Americatone International 84

Baird Music Group 85

Bay Ridge Publishing 86

Black Market Entertainment Recordings 88

BSW Records 92

Buckeye Music Group 93

California Country Music 94

Christopher Publishing, Sonny 95

Coal Harbor Music 95

De Miles Music Company, The Edward 97

Duane Music, Inc. 102

Earitating Music Publishing 102

Earthscream Music Publishing Co. 102

EMF Productions 103

Famous Music Publishing Companies 104

Gary Music, Alan 106

Hammel Associates, Inc., R.L. 107

Hickory Lane Publishing and Recording 107

High-Minded Moma Publishing & Productions 108

Ja/Nein Musikverlag GmbH 109

JoDa Music 111

Juke Music 111

Lari-Jon Publishing 112

Lilly Music Publishing 113

Lita Music 113

M & T Waldoch Publishing, Inc. 114

Many Lives Music Publishers 114

Marvin Publishing, John Weller 115

McClure & Trowbridge Publishing, Ltd. 116

McCoy Music, Jim 116

Montina Music 117

Music Room Publishing Group, The 117

New Rap Jam Publishing, A 118

Newbraugh Brothers Music 118
Old Slowpoke Music 119
PeerMusic 119
Portage Music 121
Prescription Company 121
Red Sundown Music 123
Rockford Music Co. 123
Rondor Music International/Almo/
    Irving Music 124
Saddlestone Publishing 125
Sandalphon Music Publishing 126
Segal's Publications 126
Silicon Music Publishing Co. 126
Sinus Musik Produktion, Ulli Weigel
    127
Sound Cellar Music 128
Still Working Music Group 129
Succes 129
Thistle Hill 130
Tourmaline Music, Inc. 130
Transamerika Musikverlag KG 130
Twin Towers Publishing Co. 131
Walkerbout Music Group 132
Weaver of Words Music 133
Wilcom Publishing 134
Your Best Songs Publishing 134
Zomba Music Publishing 135

World Music (also reggae, ethnic, calypso, international, world beat, etc.)

Abalorn Music 82
Bay Ridge Publishing 86
Inside Records/OK Songs 109
Kaysarah Music 112
Many Lives Music Publishers 114
Peters Music, Justin 120
Supreme Enterprises Int'l Corp. 129
Transamerika Musikverlag KG 130

RECORD COMPANIES
Adult Contemporary (also easy listening, middle of the road, AAA, ballads, etc.)

ABL Records 142
Allegheny Music Works 142
Avitor Music 148
Banana Records 149
Bolivia Records 150
Bouquet Records 151
Capstan Record Production 152
Lucifer Records, Inc. 167
Minotaur Records 171
Missile Records Film & TV, Inc. 171
Monticana Records 173
P. & N. Records 174
Roll On Records® 178
Rustron-Whimsong Music Produc-
    tions 179
Valtec Productions 185
X.R.L. Records/Music 188

Alternative (also modern rock, punk, college rock, new wave, hardcore, new music, industrial, ska, indie rock, garage, etc.)

AMP Records & Music 143
Astralwerks 144
Avitor Music 148
Banana Records 149
Cleopatra Records 154
Crank! A Record Company 156
Deep South Entertainment 157
Elektra Records 158
Generic Records, Inc. 160
Gonzo! Records Inc. 161
Gotham Records 161
Idol Records Publishing 165
Judgment Entertainment Inc. 166
Metal Blade Records 170
Monticana Records 173
Presence Records 175
Radical Records 176
RAVE Records, Inc. 176
Redemption Records 177
Rotten Records 178
Sandalphon Records 180
Small Stone Records 180
Ton Records 183
Transdreamer Records 184
TVT Records 184
28 Records 184

X.R.L. Records/Music 188
Xemu Records 189

Blues
Avitor Music 148
Big Bear Records 149
Blue Wave 150
BSW Records 151
Cellar Records 153
Chiaroscuro Records 154
Front Row Records 160
Goldwax Record Corporation 161
Monticana Records 173
Parliament Records 174
Rustron-Whimsong Music Productions 179
Sandalphon Records 180
Small Stone Records 180
Surface Records 182
Texas Rose Records 183
Ton Records 183
Topcat Records 183
Warehouse Creek Recording Corp. 186
X.R.L. Records/Music 188

Children's
Avitor Music 148
Awal.com 149
Rustron-Whimsong Music Productions 179

Classical (also opera, chamber music, serious music, choral, etc.)
Arkadia Entertainment Corp. 144
Avitor Music 148
Cambria Records & Publishing 151
Compendia Music Group 156
EMF Records & Affiliates 158
Minotaur Records 171
Tangent® Records 182
Videa Artists International Distribution 186

Country (also western, C&W, bluegrass, cowboy songs, western swing, honky-tonk, etc.)
ABL Records 142
Allegheny Music Works 142
Americatone Records International USA 143
Atlan-Dec/Grooveline Records 145
Avitor Music 148
Blue Gem Records 150
Blue Wave 150
Bolivia Records 150
Bouquet Records 151
BSW Records 151
Capstan Record Production 152
Case Entertainment Group/C.E.G. Records, Inc. 153
Cellar Records 153
Cherry Street Records 154
Coal Harbor Music 155
Collector Records 155
Compadre Records 155
Compendia Music Group 156
Deep South Entertainment 157
EMF Records & Affiliates 158
Front Row Records 160
Generic Records, Inc. 160
Goldwax Record Corporation 161
Hacienda Records & Recording Studio 164
Judgment Entertainment Inc. 166
Lari-Jon Records 166
Mighty Records 171
Missile Records Film & TV, Inc. 171
Monticana Records 173
NBT Records 173
Outstanding Records 174
Pop Record Research 175
Roll On Records® 178
Rustic Records 178
Rustron-Whimsong Music Productions 179
Sandalphon Records 180
Solana Records 181
Sony Music Nashville 181

Sugar Hill Records 182
Surface Records 182
Texas Rose Records 183
UAR Records 185
Valtec Productions 185
Winchester Records 187
X.R.L. Records/Music 188

Dance (also house, hi-NRG, disco, club, rave, techno, trip-hop, trance, etc.)
A.A.M.I. Music Group 142
AMP Records & Music 143
Atlan-Dec/Grooveline Records 145
Avitor Music 148
Awal.com 149
Broken Records International 151
CAPP Records 152
Gig Records 160
Gonzo! Records Inc. 161
Hi-Bias Records Inc. 165
Lucifer Records, Inc. 167
Mighty Records 171
Minotaur Records 171
Missile Records Film & TV, Inc. 171
Monticana Records 173
Neurodisc Records, Inc. 173
P. & N. Records 174
Parliament Records 174
Quark Records 176
RAVE Records, Inc. 176
Robbins Entertainment LLC 177
Sahara Records and Filmworks Entertainment 179
World Beatnik Records 188
X.R.L. Records/Music 188

Folk (also acoustic, Celtic, etc.)
Avitor Music 148
Kill Rock Stars 166
Missile Records Film & TV, Inc. 171
Monticana Records 173
NBT Records 173
Rustron-Whimsong Music Productions 179
Waterdog Music 187

Winchester Records 187
Wind-Up Entertainment 187

Instrumental (also background music, musical scores, etc.)
AMP Records & Music 143
Avitor Music 148
Coal Harbor Music 155
Makoche Recording Company 167
Missile Records Film & TV, Inc. 171
Sahara Records and Filmworks Entertainment 179
Tangent® Records 182

Jazz (also fusion, bebop, swing, etc.)
Americatone Records International USA 143
Ariana Records 144
Arkadia Entertainment Corp. 144
Atlan-Dec/Grooveline Records 145
Avita Records 145
Avitor Music 148
Awal.com 149
Big Bear Records 149
Cherry Street Records 154
Chiaroscuro Records 154
CKB Records/Helaphat Entertainment 154
Coal Harbor Music 155
CPA Records 156
Creative Improvised Music Projects (CIMP) Records 157
EMF Records & Affiliates 158
Fresh Entertainment 159
Goldwax Record Corporation 161
Heads Up Int., Ltd. 165
Hi-Bias Records Inc. 165
Mighty Records 171
Missile Records Film & TV, Inc. 171
Monticana Records 173
Outstanding Records 174
Rustron-Whimsong Music Productions 179
Sahara Records and Filmworks Entertainment 179

Salexo Music 180
Tangent® Records 182
Topcat Records 183
TVT Records 184
World Beatnik Records 188

Latin (also Spanish, salsa, Cuban, conga, Brazilian, cumbja, rancheras, Mexican, merengue, Tejano, Tex Mex, etc.)
Americatone Records International USA 143
Avitor Music 148
EMF Records & Affiliates 158
Hacienda Records & Recording Studio 164
Outstanding Records 174

Metal (also thrash, grindcore, heavy metal, etc.)
Avitor Music 148
Cellar Records 153
Cleopatra Records 154
Metal Blade Records 170
Missile Records Film & TV, Inc. 171
Rotten Records 178
28 Records 184
Wind-Up Entertainment 187

New Age (also ambient)
AMP Records & Music 143
Avitor Music 148
CAPP Records 152
EMF Records & Affiliates 158
Missile Records Film & TV, Inc. 171
Neurodisc Records, Inc. 173
Only New Age Music, Inc. 173
Rustron-Whimsong Music Productions 179
Tangent® Records 182

Novelty (also comedy, humor, etc.)
Avitor Music 148
Rustic Records 178

Pop (also top 40, top 100, popular, chart hits, etc.)
A.A.M.I. Music Group 142
ABL Records 142
Allegheny Music Works 142
Arkadia Entertainment Corp. 144
Avitor Music 148
Awal.com 149
Aware Records 149
Banana Records 149
Blue Gem Records 150
Bolivia Records 150
Broken Records International 151
Candyspiteful Productions 152
CAPP Records 152
Capstan Record Production 152
Case Entertainment Group/C.E.G. Records, Inc. 153
Cellar Records 153
Coal Harbor Music 155
CPA Records 156
Crank! A Record Company 156
Deep South Entertainment 157
Dental Records 158
EMF Records & Affiliates 158
Fresh Entertainment 159
Generic Records, Inc. 160
Goldwax Record Corporation 161
Gonzo! Records Inc. 161
Gotham Records 161
Hacienda Records & Recording Studio 164
Heads Up Int., Ltd. 165
Hi-Bias Records Inc. 165
Idol Records Publishing 165
Judgment Entertainment Inc. 166
Lucifer Records, Inc. 167
Mighty Records 171
Minotaur Records 171
Missile Records Film & TV, Inc. 171
Monticana Records 173
Parliament Records 174
Pop Record Research 175
Quark Records 176
Red Admiral Records 177
Redemption Records 177

Robbins Entertainment LLC 177
Roll On Records® 178
Rustron-Whimsong Music Productions 179
Sahara Records and Filmworks Entertainment 179
Sandalphon Records 180
Solana Records 181
Sonic Unyon Records Canada 181
Surface Records 182
Texas Rose Records 183
Valtec Productions 185
Waterdog Music 187
World Beatnik Records 188
X.R.L. Records/Music 188

R&B (also soul, black, urban, etc.)
ABL Records 142
Allegheny Music Works 142
Arkadia Entertainment Corp. 144
Atlan-Dec/Grooveline Records 145
Avitor Music 148
Blue Gem Records 150
Blue Wave 150
Bolivia Records 150
Candyspiteful Productions 152
Cellar Records 153
Cherry Street Records 154
CKB Records/Helaphat Entertainment 154
CPA Records 156
EMF Records & Affiliates 158
Fresh Entertainment 159
Front Row Records 160
Goldwax Record Corporation 161
Groove Makers' Recordings 164
Heads Up Int., Ltd. 165
Hi-Bias Records Inc. 165
Judgment Entertainment Inc. 166
Lucifer Records, Inc. 167
Monticana Records 173
Parliament Records 174
Pop Record Research 175
Red Admiral Records 177
Roll On Records® 178

Rustron-Whimsong Music Productions 179
Sahara Records and Filmworks Entertainment 179
Sound Gems 181
Topcat Records 183
TVT Records 184
Warehouse Creek Recording Corp. 186
X.R.L. Records/Music 188

Rap (also hip-hop, bass, etc.)
A.A.M.I. Music Group 142
Atlan-Dec/Grooveline Records 145
Avitor Music 148
CKB Records/Helaphat Entertainment 154
CPA Records 156
Fresh Entertainment 159
Generic Records, Inc. 160
Gig Records 160
Goldwax Record Corporation 161
Groove Makers' Recordings 164
Judgment Entertainment Inc. 166
Neurodisc Records, Inc. 173
Parliament Records 174
TVT Records 184
World Beatnik Records 188

Religious (also gospel, sacred, Christian, church, hymns, praise, inspirational, worship, etc.)
ABL Records 142
Allegheny Music Works 142
Atlan-Dec/Grooveline Records 145
Avitor Music 148
Bouquet Records 151
Coal Harbor Music 155
Compendia Music Group 156
CPA Records 156
Fresh Entertainment 159
Goldwax Record Corporation 161
Lari-Jon Records 166
Monticana Records 173
NBT Records 173

Parliament Records 174
Roll On Records® 178
Rustic Records 178
Salexo Music 180
Sandalphon Records 180
Texas Rose Records 183
Warehouse Creek Recording Corp.
   186
Winchester Records 187
Word Records & Music 188

Rock (also rockabilly, AOR, rock 'n' roll, etc.)
A.A.M.I. Music Group 142
Ariana Records 144
Arkadia Entertainment Corp. 144
Atlan-Dec/Grooveline Records 145
Avitor Music 148
Aware Records 149
Blue Gem Records 150
Blue Wave 150
Bouquet Records 151
Broken Records International 151
BSW Records 151
Candyspiteful Productions 152
Capstan Record Production 152
Case Entertainment Group/C.E.G.
   Records, Inc. 153
Cellar Records 153
Chattahoochee Records 153
Cherry Street Records 154
Coal Harbor Music 155
Collector Records 155
Compendia Music Group 156
CPA Records 156
Deep South Entertainment 157
EMF Records & Affiliates 158
Fresh Entertainment 159
Front Row Records 160
Generic Records, Inc. 160
Gig Records 160
Goldwax Record Corporation 161
Gotham Records 161
Idol Records Publishing 165
Judgment Entertainment Inc. 166
Kill Rock Stars 166

Lari-Jon Records 166
Lucifer Records, Inc. 167
Megaforce Records 167
Missile Records Film & TV, Inc. 171
Monticana Records 173
NBT Records 173
Outstanding Records 174
P. & N. Records 174
Presence Records 175
Radical Records 176
Roll On Records® 178
Rotten Records 178
Sandalphon Records 180
Small Stone Records 180
Solana Records 181
Sonic Unyon Records Canada 181
Surface Records 182
Tangent® Records 182
Texas Rose Records 183
Ton Records 183
Transdreamer Records 184
28 Records 184
Valtec Productions 185
Waterdog Music 187
Winchester Records 187
Wind-Up Entertainment 187
X.R.L. Records/Music 188

World Music (also reggae, ethnic, calypso, international, world beat, etc.)
Arkadia Entertainment Corp. 144
Avitor Music 148
Awal.com 149
EMF Records & Affiliates 158
Makoche Recording Company 167
Modal Music, Inc.™ 172
Only New Age Music, Inc. 173
Silver Wave Records 180
Tangent® Records 182
World Beatnik Records 188

RECORD PRODUCERS
Adult Contemporary (also easy listening, middle of the road, AAA, ballads, etc.)
''A'' Major Sound Corporation 194
Aberdeen Productions 194

Human Factor 200
Integrated Entertainment 200
Jay Jay Publishing & Record Co. 201
Jump Productions 201
June Productions Ltd. 201
Monticana Productions 205
Mustrock Productionz Worldwide
    205
Philly Breakdown Recording Co. 207
Prescription Co., The 207
Rustron Music Productions 208
Valtec Productions 213

Alternative (also modern rock, punk, college rock, new wave, hardcore, new music, industrial, ska, indie rock, garage, etc.)

''A'' Major Sound Corporation 194
AIF Music Productions 194
Blues Alley Records 196
Coachouse Music 196
DaVinci's Notebook Records 198
Kane Producer/Engineer, Karen 201
L.A. Entertainment, Inc. 202
Lazy Bones Productions/Record-
    ings, Inc. 202
Mac-Attack Productions 203
Marenco, Cookie 203
Mathews, d/b/a Hit or Myth Produc-
    tions Inc., Scott 204
Monticana Productions 205
Stuart Audio Services 211
Tari, Roger Vincent 212
Westwires Recording 213

Blues

AIF Music Productions 194
Big Bear 196
Coachouse Music 196
Coal Harbor Music 197
Hailing Frequency Music Produc-
    tions 199
Kane Producer/Engineer, Karen 201
Linear Cycle Productions 202
Mega Truth Records 205
Monticana Productions 205

Prescription Co., The 207
Reel Adventures 207
Silver Bow Productions 209
Sound Arts Recording Studio 210
Studio Seven 211
TMC Productions 212
Weisman Production Group, The
    213
Willson, Frank 214
WLM Music/Recording 214

Children's

Prescription Co., The 207
Rustron Music Productions 208
Stuart Audio Services 211

Classical (also opera, chamber music, serious music, choral, etc.)

Marenco, Cookie 203
Satkowski Recordings, Steve 209
World Records 214

Country (also western, C&W, bluegrass, cowboy songs, western swing, honky-tonk, etc.)

Aberdeen Productions 194
ACR Productions 194
AIF Music Productions 194
Allyn, Stuart J. 195
Audio 911 195
Baird Enterprises, Ron 195
Cacophony Productions 196
Coachouse Music 196
Coal Harbor Music 197
Craig Productions, Charlie 197
De Miles, Edward 198
Jay Jay Publishing & Record Co. 201
Kane Producer/Engineer, Karen 201
Lari-Jon Productions 202
Linear Cycle Productions 202
Marenco, Cookie 203
Martin, Pete/Vaam Music Produc-
    tions 204
Mega Truth Records 205
Monticana Productions 205

Pierce, Jim 207
Prescription Co., The 207
Reel Adventures 207
RN'D Distribution, LLC. 208
Rustron Music Productions 208
Segal's Productions 209
Silver Bow Productions 209
Sound Arts Recording Studio 210
Sound Works Entertainment Productions Inc. 210
Sphere Group One 210
SRS Productions/Hit Records Network 211
Stuart Audio Services 211
Studio Seven 211
Swift River Productions 211
TMC Productions 212
Trinity Studio, The 213
Valtec Productions 213
Willson, Frank 214
WLM Music/Recording 214

Dance (also house, hi-NRG, disco, club, rave, techno, trip-hop, trance, etc.)

De Miles, Edward 198
Diamond Entertainment, Joel 199
Final Mix Inc. 199
Jump Productions 201
Mac-Attack Productions 203
Makers Mark Music Productions 203
Mega Truth Records 205
Monticana Productions 205
Neu Electro Productions 205
Prescription Co., The 207
Soul Candy Productions 209
Weisman Production Group, The 213
Westwires Recording 213

Folk (also acoustic, Celtic, etc.)

AIF Music Productions 194
Marenco, Cookie 203
Monticana Productions 205
Rustron Music Productions 208

Sound Works Entertainment Productions Inc. 210
Swift River Productions 211
Westwires Recording 213
World Records 214

Instrumental (also background music, musical scores, etc.)

Jump Productions 201
Mega Truth Records 205
Swift River Productions 211

Jazz (also fusion, bebop, swing, etc.)

Allyn, Stuart J. 195
Big Bear 196
Candyspiteful Productions 196
Coal Harbor Music 197
DAP Entertainment 198
DaVinci's Notebook Records 198
De Miles, Edward 198
Heart Consort Music 200
Marenco, Cookie 203
Mega Truth Records 205
Monticana Productions 205
Philly Breakdown Recording Co. 207
Prescription Co., The 207
RN'D Distribution, LLC. 208
Silver Bow Productions 209
Studio Seven 211
Tari, Roger Vincent 212
Willson, Frank 214
World Records 214

Latin (also Spanish, salsa, Cuban, conga, Brazilian, cumbja, rancheras, Mexican, merengue, Tejano, Tex Mex, etc.)

DeLory and Music Makers, Al 199
Satkowski Recordings, Steve 209

Metal (also thrash, grindcore, heavy metal, etc.)

AIF Music Productions 194

New Age (also ambient)

DaVinci's Notebook Records 198
Heart Consort Music 200

Neu Electro Productions 205
Rustron Music Productions 208
Sphere Group One 210

Novelty (also comedy, humor, etc.)
Jay Jay Publishing & Record Co. 201
Linear Cycle Productions 202
Segal's Productions 209
TMC Productions 212

Pop (also top 40, top 100, popular, chart hits, etc.)
''A'' Major Sound Corporation 194
Aberdeen Productions 194
ACR Productions 194
AIF Music Productions 194
Allyn, Stuart J. 195
Audio 911 195
Blues Alley Records 196
Cacophony Productions 196
Candyspiteful Productions 196
Coachouse Music 196
Craig Productions, Charlie 197
DaVinci's Notebook Records 198
De Miles, Edward 198
DeLory and Music Makers, Al 199
Diamond Entertainment, Joel 199
Final Mix Inc. 199
Human Factor 200
Jump Productions 201
June Productions Ltd. 201
Kane Producer/Engineer, Karen 201
Linear Cycle Productions 202
Mac-Attack Productions 203
Marenco, Cookie 203
Martin, Pete/Vaam Music Productions 204
Mathews, d/b/a Hit or Myth Productions Inc., Scott 204
Monticana Productions 205
Mustrock Productionz Worldwide 205
Neu Electro Productions 205
New Experience Records/Faze 4 Records 206

Philly Breakdown Recording Co. 207
Prescription Co., The 207
Reel Adventures 207
Rustron Music Productions 208
Segal's Productions 209
Silver Bow Productions 209
Soul Candy Productions 209
Sound Arts Recording Studio 210
Sound Works Entertainment Productions Inc. 210
Sphere Group One 210
SRS Productions/Hit Records Network 211
Tari, Roger Vincent 212
Valtec Productions 213
Weisman Production Group, The 213
WLM Music/Recording 214

R&B (also soul, black, urban, etc.)
''A'' Major Sound Corporation 194
ACR Productions 194
Allyn, Stuart J. 195
Candyspiteful Productions 196
DAP Entertainment 198
DaVinci's Notebook Records 198
De Miles, Edward 198
Diamond Entertainment, Joel 199
Final Mix Inc. 199
Hailing Frequency Music Productions 199
Kane Producer/Engineer, Karen 201
L.A. Entertainment, Inc. 202
Lazy Bones Productions/Recordings, Inc. 202
Linear Cycle Productions 202
Makers Mark Music Productions 203
Martin, Pete/Vaam Music Productions 204
Monticana Productions 205
Mustrock Productionz Worldwide 205
New Experience Records/Faze 4 Records 206
Philly Breakdown Recording Co. 207

Prescription Co., The 207
Rustron Music Productions 208
Segal's Productions 209
Weisman Production Group, The
    213
Westwires Recording 213

Rap (also hip-hop, bass, etc.)
Final Mix Inc. 199
Human Factor 200
L.A. Entertainment, Inc. 202
Marenco, Cookie 203
Mustrock Productionz Worldwide
    205
Neu Electro Productions 205
New Experience Records/Faze 4 Re-
    cords 206
Philly Breakdown Recording Co. 207
RN'D Distribution, LLC. 208
Soul Candy Productions 209
Weisman Production Group, The
    213

**Religious (also gospel, sacred,
Christian, church, hymns,
praise, inspirational, worship,
etc.)**
"A" Major Sound Corporation 194
ACR Productions 194
Blues Alley Records 196
Coal Harbor Music 197
DAP Entertainment 198
Hailing Frequency Music Produc-
    tions 199
Jay Jay Publishing & Record Co. 201
L.A. Entertainment, Inc. 202
Lari-Jon Productions 202
Linear Cycle Productions 202
Makers Mark Music Productions 203
Monticana Productions 205
New Experience Records/Faze 4 Re-
    cords 206
Philly Breakdown Recording Co. 207
Pierce, Jim 207
Silver Bow Productions 209
Stuart Audio Services 211

Trinity Studio, The 213
Valtec Productions 213
Weisman Production Group, The
    213
WLM Music/Recording 214

**Rock (also rockabilly, AOR, rock
'n' roll, etc.)**
"A" Major Sound Corporation 194
Aberdeen Productions 194
ACR Productions 194
AIF Music Productions 194
Allyn, Stuart J. 195
Audio 911 195
Baird Enterprises, Ron 195
Cacophony Productions 196
Candyspiteful Productions 196
Coachouse Music 196
Collector Records 197
DaVinci's Notebook Records 198
Hailing Frequency Music Produc-
    tions 199
Human Factor 200
Integrated Entertainment 200
June Productions Ltd. 201
Kane Producer/Engineer, Karen 201
Lari-Jon Productions 202
Lazy Bones Productions/Record-
    ings, Inc. 202
Linear Cycle Productions 202
Mathews, d/b/a Hit or Myth Produc-
    tions Inc., Scott 204
Mega Truth Records 205
Monticana Productions 205
Neu Electro Productions 205
New Experience Records/Faze 4 Re-
    cords 206
Prescription Co., The 207
Reel Adventures 207
RN'D Distribution, LLC. 208
Rustron Music Productions 208
Segal's Productions 209
Silver Bow Productions 209
Soul Candy Productions 209
Sound Arts Recording Studio 210

Sound Works Entertainment Productions Inc. 210
Sphere Group One 210
SRS Productions/Hit Records Network 211
Stuart Audio Services 211
Studio Seven 211
Swift River Productions 211
TMC Productions 212
Valtec Productions 213
Westwires Recording 213
Willson, Frank 214
WLM Music/Recording 214

World Music (also reggae, ethnic, calypso, international, world beat, etc.)
Human Factor 200
Kane Producer/Engineer, Karen 201
Reel Adventures 207
Rustron Music Productions 208
Studio Seven 211
Tari, Roger Vincent 212

MANAGERS & BOOKING AGENTS

Adult Contemporary (also easy listening, middle of the road, AAA, ballads, etc.)
All Star Management 219
Brothers Management Associates 223
First Time Management 229
Hale Enterprises 229
International Entertainment Bureau 232
Knight Agency, Bob 233
Kuper Personal Management/Recovery Recordings 234
Levinson Entertainment Ventures International, Inc. 234
Loggins Promotion 235
Management by Jaffe 235
Prestige Management 238
Richards World Management, Inc., Diane 239

Risavy, Inc., A.F. 240
Rustron-Whimsong Music Productions 240
St. John Artists 244
Skorman Productions, Inc., T. 243
Staircase Promotion 244
Tas Music Co./Dave Tasse Entertainment 245
Wagner Agency, William F. 246
Warner Productions, Cheryl K. 246
Winterland Entertainment Management & Publishing 247
World Wide Management 247
Zane Management, Inc. 248
Zirilli Management, D. 248

Alternative (also modern rock, punk, college rock, new wave, hardcore, new music, industrial, ska, indie rock, garage, etc.)
Bread & Butter Productions 223
Cox Promotions & Management, Stephen 226
Cranium Management 226
DAS Communications, Ltd. 226
First Time Management 229
Freestyle Entertainment 229
Hot Steaming Coffee Films 231
Knight Agency, Bob 233
Kuper Personal Management/Recovery Recordings 234
Loggins Promotion 235
Management by Jaffe 235
On the Level Music! 237
Outlaw Entertainment International 238
Prestige Management 238
Prime Time Entertainment 238
Saffyre Management 241
Sandalphon Management 241
Silver Bow Management 242
Smeltzer Productions, Gary 243
Southeastern Attractions 243
Staircase Promotion 244

Blues

Barnard Management Services (BMS) 221
Blowin' Smoke Productions/Records 222
Blue Wave Productions 222
Concerted Efforts, Inc./Foggy Day Music 225
Countrywide Producers 225
Cox Promotions & Management, Stephen 226
First Time Management 229
Kendall West Agency 232
Kickstart Music Ltd. 232
Knight Agency, Bob 233
Media Management 236
Noteworthy Productions 237
On the Level Music! 237
Rustron-Whimsong Music Productions 240
Sandalphon Management 241
Twentieth Century Promotions 245
Universal Music Marketing 246
World Wide Management 247

Children's

First Time Management 229
Levy Management, Rick 234

Classical (also opera, chamber music, serious music, choral, etc.)

Clousher Productions 224
Countrywide Producers 225
Fiedler Management, B.C. 228
First Time Management 229
Wagner Agency, William F. 246

Country (also western, C&W, bluegrass, cowboy songs, western swing, honky-tonk, etc.)

Air Tight Management 219
All Star Management 219
Allen Entertainment Development, Michael 219
American Bands Management 220

Barnard Management Services (BMS) 221
Bouquet-Orchid Enterprises 223
Bread & Butter Productions 223
Circuit Rider Talent & Management Co. 223
Clousher Productions 224
Coal Harbor Music 224
Concept 2000 Inc. 225
Concerted Efforts, Inc./Foggy Day Music 225
Countrywide Producers 225
Cranium Management 226
D&R Entertainment 226
De Miles Company, The Edward 227
Fenchel Entertainment Agency, Fred T. 228
First Time Management 229
Hale Enterprises 229
Harrell & Associates, M. 231
International Entertainment Bureau 232
J & V Management 232
Kendall West Agency 232
Kickstart Music Ltd. 232
Kitchen Sync 233
Knight Agency, Bob 233
Lari-Jon Promotions 234
Levinson Entertainment Ventures International, Inc. 234
Levy Management, Rick 234
Management Plus 235
Midcoast, Inc. 236
Monterey Artists Peninsula Artists/ Paradigm 237
Noteworthy Productions 237
Outlaw Entertainment International 238
Prime Time Entertainment 238
Pro Talent Consultants 238
Risavy, Inc., A.F. 240
Rothschild Productions Inc., Charles R. 240
Rustron-Whimsong Music Productions 240
Sandalphon Management 241

Serge Entertainment Group 242
Silver Bow Management 242
Skorman Productions, Inc., T. 243
Smeltzer Productions, Gary 243
Southeastern Attractions 243
Sphere Group One 243
Staircase Promotion 244
T.L.C. Booking Agency 245
Texas Sounds Entertainment 245
Twentieth Century Promotions 245
Universal Music Marketing 246
Varrasso Management, Richard 246
Wagner Agency, William F. 246
Warner Productions, Cheryl K. 246
Wemus Entertainment 247
Winterland Entertainment Management & Publishing 247
World Wide Management 247

Dance (also western, C&W, bluegrass, cowboy songs, western swing, honky-tonk, etc.)

Bassline Entertainment, Inc. 221
Clousher Productions 224
Countrywide Producers 225
De Miles Company, The Edward 227
First Time Management 229
Freestyle Entertainment 229
Kendall West Agency 232
Kickstart Music Ltd. 232
Martin Productions, Rick 235
Mega Music Productions 236
Outlaw Entertainment International 238
Richards World Management, Inc., Diane 239
Sound Management Direction 243
Southeastern Attractions 243
Tas Music Co./Dave Tasse Entertainment 245
Varrasso Management, Richard 246
Wood Artist Management, Richard 247
Zane Management, Inc. 248

Folk (also acoustic, Celtic, etc.)

Bread & Butter Productions 223
Concerted Efforts, Inc./Foggy Day Music 225
Countrywide Producers 225
Cox Promotions & Management, Stephen 226
EAO Music Corporation of Canada 227
First Time Management 229
Knight Agency, Bob 233
Noteworthy Productions 237
Rothschild Productions Inc., Charles R. 240
Rustron-Whimsong Music Productions 240
World Wide Management 247
Zane Management, Inc. 248

Instrumental (also background music, musical scores, etc.)

Fiedler Management, B.C. 228
First Time Management 229
Raspberry Jam Music 239
Wagner Agency, William F. 246

Jazz (also fusion, bebop, swing, etc.)

Air Tight Management 219
All Star Management 219
Bacchus Group Productions, Ltd. 220
Blue Cat Agency, The 222
Concept 2000 Inc. 225
Countrywide Producers 225
First Time Management 229
Harrell & Associates, M. 231
International Entertainment Bureau 232
Kendall West Agency 232
Klein, Joanne 233
Knight Agency, Bob 233
Loggins Promotion 235
On the Level Music! 237
Prime Time Entertainment 238
Raspberry Jam Music 239

Richards World Management, Inc.,
    Diane 239
Riohcat Music 240
Rothschild Productions Inc., Charles
    R. 240
Stander Entertainment 244
Tas Music Co./Dave Tasse Enter-
    tainment 245
Universal Music Marketing 246
Wagner Agency, William F. 246
World Wide Management 247
Zane Management, Inc. 248

Latin (also Spanish, salsa, Cuban, conga, Brazilian, cumbja, rancheras, Mexican, merengue, Tejano, Tex Mex, etc.)

Apodaca Promotions Inc. 220
Bacchus Group Productions, Ltd.
    220
Bassline Entertainment, Inc. 221
Blue Cat Agency, The 222
First Time Management 229
Hansen Enterprises, Ltd. 230
Management Plus 235
Mega Music Productions 236
Raspberry Jam Music 239
Texas Sounds Entertainment 245

Metal (also thrash, grindcore, heavy metal, etc.)

Artist Representation and Manage-
    ment 220
First Time Management 229
Outlaw Entertainment International
    238
Raspberry Jam Music 239
WorldSound, LLC 248

New Age (also ambient)

Cox Promotions & Management, Ste-
    phen 226
First Time Management 229
Richards World Management, Inc.,
    Diane 239

Rustron-Whimsong Music Produc-
    tions 240
Serge Entertainment Group 242
Sphere Group One 243
World Wide Management 247

Novelty (also comedy, humor, etc.)

Circuit Rider Talent & Management
    Co. 223
First Time Management 229
Hall Entertainment & Events, Bill 230
T.L.C. Booking Agency 245

Pop (also top 40, top 100, popular, chart hits, etc.)

Alert Music, Inc. 219
All Star Management 219
Allen Entertainment Development,
    Michael 219
Artist Representation and Manage-
    ment 220
Atch Records and Productions 220
Bacchus Group Productions, Ltd.
    220
Bassline Entertainment, Inc. 221
Big J Productions 221
Blue Cat Agency, The 222
Bouquet-Orchid Enterprises 223
Brothers Management Associates
    223
Circuit Rider Talent & Management
    Co. 223
Clockwork Entertainment Manage-
    ment Agency 224
Concept 2000 Inc. 225
Countrywide Producers 225
Cranium Management 226
D&R Entertainment 226
DAS Communications, Ltd. 226
DCA Productions 227
De Miles Company, The Edward 227
Evans Productions, Scott 227
Fenchel Entertainment Agency, Fred
    T. 228
Fiedler Management, B.C. 228

First Time Management 229
Freestyle Entertainment 229
Hale Enterprises 229
Hot Steaming Coffee Films 231
Huge Production, Inc., A 231
Kagan International, Sheldon 232
Kickstart Music Ltd. 232
Kitchen Sync 233
Knight Agency, Bob 233
Levy Management, Rick 234
Loggins Promotion 235
Management by Jaffe 235
Martin Productions, Rick 235
Mayo & Company, Phil 236
Media Management 236
Mega Music Productions 236
Midcoast, Inc. 236
Nik Entertainment Co. 237
Outlaw Entertainment International 238
Prestige Management 238
Pro Talent Consultants 238
Raspberry Jam Music 239
Richards World Management, Inc., Diane 239
Risavy, Inc., A.F. 240
Rothschild Productions Inc., Charles R. 240
Saffyre Management 241
Sandalphon Management 241
Serge Entertainment Group 242
Silver Bow Management 242
Skorman Productions, Inc., T. 243
Sphere Group One 243
Staircase Promotion 244
Stander Entertainment 244
Starkravin' Management 245
Tas Music Co./Dave Tasse Entertainment 245
Wagner Agency, William F. 246
Warner Productions, Cheryl K. 246
Winterland Entertainment Management & Publishing 247
Wood Artist Management, Richard 247
World Wide Management 247

WorldSound, LLC 248
Zane Management, Inc. 248

R&B (also soul, black, urban, etc.)

Allen Entertainment Development, Michael 219
Atch Records and Productions 220
Bacchus Group Productions, Ltd. 220
Barnard Management Services (BMS) 221
Bassline Entertainment, Inc. 221
Big J Productions 221
Blowin' Smoke Productions/Records 222
Bouquet-Orchid Enterprises 223
Bread & Butter Productions 223
Brothers Management Associates 223
Circuit Rider Talent & Management Co. 223
Concept 2000 Inc. 225
Countrywide Producers 225
DAS Communications, Ltd. 226
De Miles Company, The Edward 227
Evans Productions, Scott 227
First Time Management 229
Freestyle Entertainment 229
Hardison International Entertainment Corporation 230
Harrell & Associates, M. 231
Kitchen Sync 233
Knight Agency, Bob 233
Levinson Entertainment Ventures International, Inc. 234
Levy Management, Rick 234
Media Management 236
Precision Management 238
Prestige Management 238
Rainbow Talent Agency 239
Raspberry Jam Music 239
Rustron-Whimsong Music Productions 240
Silver Bow Management 242
Smeltzer Productions, Gary 243

Sound Management Direction 243
Sphere Group One 243
Stander Entertainment 244
Starkravin' Management 245
Tas Music Co./Dave Tasse Entertainment 245
Texas Sounds Entertainment 245
Wood Artist Management, Richard 247
World Wide Management 247
Zane Management, Inc. 248

Rap (also hip-hop, bass, etc.)
Atch Records and Productions 220
Bassline Entertainment, Inc. 221
First Time Management 229
Freestyle Entertainment 229
Hardison International Entertainment Corporation 230
Loggins Promotion 235
Precision Management 238
Richards World Management, Inc., Diane 239

Religious (also gospel, sacred, Christian, church, hymns, praise, inspirational, worship, etc.)
All Star Management 219
Allen Entertainment Development, Michael 219
Atch Records and Productions 220
Bouquet-Orchid Enterprises 223
Circuit Rider Talent & Management Co. 223
Coal Harbor Music 224
Concept 2000 Inc. 225
Countrywide Producers 225
D&R Entertainment 226
Exclesisa Booking Agency 228
Fenchel Entertainment Agency, Fred T. 228
First Time Management 229
Harrell & Associates, M. 231
Lari-Jon Promotions 234
Mayo & Company, Phil 236

Precision Management 238
Sandalphon Management 241
Silver Bow Management 242
Staircase Promotion 244
Warner Productions, Cheryl K. 246

Rock (also rockabilly, AOR, rock 'n' roll, etc.)
Air Tight Management 219
Alert Music, Inc. 219
Allen Entertainment Development, Michael 219
American Bands Management 220
Apodaca Promotions Inc. 220
Artist Representation and Management 220
Barnard Management Services (BMS) 221
Barrett Rock 'n' Roll Enterprises, Paul 221
Big J Productions 221
Blowin' Smoke Productions/Records 222
Blue Cat Agency, The 222
Blue Wave Productions 222
Bouquet-Orchid Enterprises 223
Bread & Butter Productions 223
Brothers Management Associates 223
Clockwork Entertainment Management Agency 224
Clousher Productions 224
Concerted Efforts, Inc./Foggy Day Music 225
Countrywide Producers 225
Cox Promotions & Management, Stephen 226
DAS Communications, Ltd. 226
DCA Productions 227
De Miles Company, The Edward 227
EAO Music Corporation of Canada 227
First Time Management 229
Hale Enterprises 229
Hansen Enterprises, Ltd. 230
Harrell & Associates, M. 231

Hot Steaming Coffee Films 231
Huge Production, Inc., A 231
International Entertainment Bureau
  232
Kendall West Agency 232
Kickstart Music Ltd. 232
Kitchen Sync 233
Knight Agency, Bob 233
Lari-Jon Promotions 234
Levinson Entertainment Ventures
  International, Inc. 234
Loggins Promotion 235
Management by Jaffe 235
Martin Productions, Rick 235
Media Management 236
Mega Music Productions 236
Midcoast, Inc. 236
Nik Entertainment Co. 237
On the Level Music! 237
Outlaw Entertainment International
  238
Prestige Management 238
Pro Talent Consultants 238
Rainbow Talent Agency 239
Raspberry Jam Music 239
Risavy, Inc., A.F. 240
Rothschild Productions Inc., Charles
  R. 240
Rustron-Whimsong Music Produc-
  tions 240
Saffyre Management 241
St. John Artists 244
Sandalphon Management 241
Serge Entertainment Group 242
Silver Bow Management 242
Sound Management Direction 243

Southeastern Attractions 243
Sphere Group One 243
Staircase Promotion 244
Starkravin' Management 245
T.L.C. Booking Agency 245
Tas Music Co./Dave Tasse Enter-
  tainment 245
Universal Music Marketing 246
Varrasso Management, Richard 246
Winterland Entertainment Manage-
  ment & Publishing 247
World Wide Management 247
WorldSound, LLC 248
Zane Management, Inc. 248
Zirilli Management, D. 248

World Music (also reggae, ethnic, calypso, international, world beat, etc.)

Apodaca Promotions Inc. 220
Bacchus Group Productions, Ltd.
  220
Clousher Productions 224
Concerted Efforts, Inc./Foggy Day
  Music 225
Cox Promotions & Management, Ste-
  phen 226
EAO Music Corporation of Canada
  227
First Time Management 229
Harrell & Associates, M. 231
Management Plus 235
Noteworthy Productions 237
Prime Time Entertainment 238
Raspberry Jam Music 239
Stander Entertainment 244
WorldSound, LLC 248

Openness to Submissions Index

Use this index to find companies open to your level of experience. It is recommended to use this index in conjunction with the Category Indexes found on page 358. Once you have compiled a list of companies open to your experience and music, read the information in these listings, paying close attention to the **How to Contact** subhead. (Also see A Sample Listing Decoded on page 11.)

☐ OPEN TO BEGINNERS

Music Publishers

Alexander Sr. Music 82
Alias John Henry Tunes 83
All Rock Music 83
Allegheny Music Works 84
Antelope Publishing Inc. 84
Audio Music Publishers 85
Barkin' Foe the Master's Bone 85
Black Market Entertainment Recordings 88
Bradley Music, Allan 89
Brandon Hills Music, LLC 89
Buckeye Music Group 93
Buried Treasure Music 93
California Country Music 94
Corelli Music Group 96
Dream Seekers Publishing 101
Emandell Tunes 103
Fifth Avenue Media, Ltd. 104
Fresh Entertainment 105
Furrow Music 106
Gary Music, Alan 106
Glad Music Co. 106
Hammel Associates, Inc., R.L. 107
His Power Productions and Publishing 108
Hitsburgh Music Co. 108
Ivory Pen Entertainment 109
Ja/Nein Musikverlag GmbH 109
Jerjoy Music 110
JPMC Music Inc. 111
Kaysarah Music 112
LCS Music Group 113
Lilly Music Publishing 113
M & T Waldoch Publishing, Inc. 114
Material Worth Publishing 115
McCoy Music, Jim 116
Moon June Music 117
Peters Music, Justin 120
Prescription Company 121
QUARK, Inc. 121
R.T.L. Music 122
Red Sundown Music 123
Rustic Records, Inc Publishing 124
Rustron Music Publishers 124
Saddlestone Publishing 125
Salt Works Music 125
Sandalphon Music Publishing 126
Silicon Music Publishing Co. 126
Succes 129
Thistle Hill 130
Transition Music Corporation 131
Walkerbout Music Group 132

Wells Music, Angela Baker 133
Wengert, Berthold (Musikverlag) 133

Record Companies
ABL Records 142
Allegheny Music Works 142
Atlan-Dec/Grooveline Records 145
Banana Records 149
Blue Gem Records 150
Blue Wave 150
Chattahoochee Records 153
Collector Records 155
Crank! A Record Company 156
Creative Improvised Music Projects (CIMP) Records 157
Deep South Entertainment 157
Dental Records 158
Fresh Entertainment 159
Front Row Records 160
Generic Records, Inc. 160
Goldwax Record Corporation 161
Gonzo! Records Inc. 161
Gotham Records 161
Hacienda Records & Recording Studio 164
Hi-Bias Records Inc. 165
Megaforce Records 167
Modal Music, Inc.™ 172
NBT Records 173
Only New Age Music, Inc. 173
P. & N. Records 174
Presence Records 175
Radical Records 176
Red Admiral Records 177
Redemption Records 177
Roll On Records® 178
Rotten Records 178
Rustron-Whimsong Music Productions 179
Sandalphon Records 180
Silvertone Records 180
Solana Records 181
Sonic Unyon Records Canada 181
Tangent® Records 182
Ton Records 183

28 Records 184
UAR Records 185
World Beatnik Records 188
X.R.L. Records/Music 188

Record Producers
Aberdeen Productions 194
ACR Productions 194
AIF Music Productions 194
Blues Alley Records 196
Coachouse Music 196
Coal Harbor Music 197
DAP Entertainment 198
Jay Jay Publishing & Record Co. 201
L.A. Entertainment, Inc. 202
Lazy Bones Productions/Recordings, Inc. 202
Linear Cycle Productions 202
Mac-Attack Productions 203
Mathews, d/b/a Hit or Myth Productions Inc., Scott 204
Neu Electro Productions 205
Nightworks Records 206
Philly Breakdown Recording Co. 207
Prescription Co., The 207
Reel Adventures 207
RN'D Distribution, LLC. 208
Rustron Music Productions 208
Satkowski Recordings, Steve 209
Silver Bow Productions 209
Sound Works Entertainment Productions Inc. 210
SRS Productions/Hit Records Network 211
Studio Seven 211
Tari, Roger Vincent 212
TMC Productions 212
Trinity Studio, The 213
Weisman Production Group, The 213

Managers & Booking Agents
American Bands Management 220
Atch Records and Productions 220
Bassline Entertainment, Inc. 221
Blue Wave Productions 222

Bread & Butter Productions 223
Clockwork Entertainment Management Agency 224
Cox Promotions & Management, Stephen 226
D&R Entertainment 226
Evans Productions, Scott 227
Exclesisa Booking Agency 228
Hardison International Entertainment Corporation 230
Hot Steaming Coffee Films 231
Kickstart Music Ltd. 232
Kuper Personal Management/Recovery Recordings 234
Loggins Promotion 235
Martin Productions, Rick 235
Midcoast, Inc. 236
On the Level Music! 237
Outlaw Entertainment International 238
Precision Management 238
Pro Talent Consultants 238
Raspberry Jam Music 239
Rustron-Whimsong Music Productions 240
St. John Artists 244
Sandalphon Management 241
Silver Bow Management 242
Smeltzer Productions, Gary 243
Universal Music Marketing 246
Winterland Entertainment Management & Publishing 247
Wood Artist Management, Richard 247
Zirilli Management, D. 248

◗ PREFERS EXPERIENCED, BUT OPEN TO BEGINNERS

Music Publishers

Abalorn Music 82
Abear Publishing 82
Acuff-Rose Music 82
Alpha Music Inc. 84
Americatone International 84
Baird Music Group 85
Baitstring Music 85
Bay Ridge Publishing 86
Big Fish Music Publishing Group 87
Branson Country Music Publishing 89
BSW Records 92
Cherri/Holly Music 94
Christmas & Holiday Music 94
Christopher Publishing, Sonny 95
Coal Harbor Music 95
Come Alive Communications, Inc. 96
Cornelius Companies, The 97
Curb Music 97
De Miles Music Company, The Edward 97
Earitating Music Publishing 102
Earthscream Music Publishing Co. 102
Electric Mule Publishing Company 103
EMF Productions 103
Emstone Music Publishing 104
First Time Music (Publishing) U.K. 104
Fricon Music Company 105
G Major Music 106
Goodnight Kiss Music 106
Happy Melody 107
High-Minded Moma Publishing & Productions 108
Inside Records/OK Songs 109
Jaelius Enterprises 110
Juke Music 111
Lake Transfer Productions & Music 112
Lari-Jon Publishing 112
Lineage Publishing Co. 113
Lita Music 113
Makers Mark Gold 114
Many Lives Music Publishers 114
Marvin Publishing, John Weller 115
Maui Arts & Music Association/Survivor Records/Ten of Diamonds Music 115
MCA Music Publishing 116
New Rap Jam Publishing, A 118

Newbraugh Brothers Music 118
Orchid Publishing 119
Piano Press 120
Pollybyrd Publications Limited 121
Queen Esther Music Publishers 122
Rockford Music Co. 123
SDB Music Group 126
Shawnee Press, Inc. 126
Sinus Musik Produktion, Ulli Weigel 127
Sizemore Music 127
SME Publishing Group 128
Sound Cellar Music 128
Starbound Publishing Co. 128
Supreme Enterprises Int'l Corp. 129
T.C. Productions/Etude Publishing Co. 129
Tourmaline Music, Inc. 130
Tower Music Group 130
Transamerika Musikverlag KG 130
Twin Towers Publishing Co. 131
Unknown Source Music 131
Vaam Music Group 132
Vine Creek Music 132
Walker Publishing Co. L.L.C. 132
Weaver of Words Music 133
Wilcom Publishing 134
Windswept Music 134
Winston & Hoffman House Music Publishers 134
Your Best Songs Publishing 134
Zettitalia Music International 134
Zomba Music Publishing 135

Record Companies
A.A.M.I. Music Group 142
Americatone Records International USA 143
AMP Records & Music 143
Audio-Visual Media Productions (formerly First Time Records) 145
Avitor Music 148
Awal.com 149
Big Bear Records 149
Bolivia Records 150
Bouquet Records 151

BSW Records 151
Candyspiteful Productions 152
CAPP Records 152
Capstan Record Production 152
Case Entertainment Group/C.E.G. Records, Inc. 153
Cellar Records 153
Cherry Street Records 154
Chiaroscuro Records 154
CKB Records/Helaphat Entertainment 154
Cleopatra Records 154
Coal Harbor Music 155
Compadre Records 155
Compendia Music Group 156
Drumbeat Indian Arts, Inc. 158
EMF Records & Affiliates 158
Fireant 159
Gig Records 160
Idol Records Publishing 165
Judgment Entertainment Inc. 166
Kill Rock Stars 166
Lari-Jon Records 166
Makoche Recording Company 167
Metal Blade Records 170
Mighty Records 171
Missile Records Film & TV, Inc. 171
Neurodisc Records, Inc. 173
Outstanding Records 174
Parliament Records 174
Pop Record Research 175
PPL Entertainment Group 175
Quark Records 176
Rustic Records 178
Salexo Music 180
Silver Wave Records 180
Silvertone Records 180
Small Stone Records 180
Sound Gems 181
Surface Records 182
Texas Rose Records 183
Topcat Records 183
Transdreamer Records 184
TVT Records 184
Valtec Productions 185

Warehouse Creek Recording Corp. 186

Westpark Music—Records, Production & Publishing 187

Winchester Records 187

Xemu Records 189

Record Producers

''A'' Major Sound Corporation 194

Audio 911 195

Baird Enterprises, Ron 195

Big Bear 196

Candyspiteful Productions 196

Collector Records 197

Craig Productions, Charlie 197

DaVinci's Notebook Records 198

DeLory and Music Makers, Al 199

Hailing Frequency Music Productions 199

Heart Consort Music 200

Human Factor 200

Integrated Entertainment 200

June Productions Ltd. 201

Kane Producer/Engineer, Karen 201

Lari-Jon Productions 202

Makers Mark Music Productions 203

Martin, Pete/Vaam Music Productions 204

Mega Truth Records 205

Mustrock Productionz Worldwide 205

New Experience Records/Faze 4 Records 206

Pierce, Jim 207

Sound Arts Recording Studio 210

Sphere Group One 210

Stuart Audio Services 211

Swift River Productions 211

Valtec Productions 213

Westwires Recording 213

Willson, Frank 214

WLM Music/Recording 214

World Records 214

Managers & Booking Agents

Air Tight Management 219

Alert Music, Inc. 219

All Star Management 219

Allen Entertainment Development, Michael 219

Apodaca Promotions Inc. 220

Artist Representation and Management 220

Big J Productions 221

Blank & Blank 222

Blowin' Smoke Productions/Records 222

Bouquet-Orchid Enterprises 223

Brothers Management Associates 223

Circuit Rider Talent & Management Co. 223

Class Act Productions/Management 224

Clousher Productions 224

Coal Harbor Music 224

Concept 2000 Inc. 225

Concerted Efforts, Inc./Foggy Day Music 225

Countrywide Producers 225

Cranium Management 226

DCA Productions 227

EAO Music Corporation of Canada 227

Feldman & Associates, S.L. 228

Fenchel Entertainment Agency, Fred T. 228

Fiedler Management, B.C. 228

First Time Management 229

Freestyle Entertainment 229

Hale Enterprises 229

Hall Entertainment & Events, Bill 230

Hansen Enterprises, Ltd. 230

J & V Management 232

Kagan International, Sheldon 232

Kendall West Agency 232

Kitchen Sync 233

Klein, Joanne 233

Knight Agency, Bob 233

Lari-Jon Promotions 234

Levinson Entertainment Ventures International, Inc. 234

Management Plus 235

Management Trust Ltd., The 235
Mayo & Company, Phil 236
Media Management 236
Mega Music Productions 236
Nik Entertainment Co. 237
Prestige Management 238
Prime Time Entertainment 238
Rainbow Talent Agency 239
Riohcat Music 240
Risavy, Inc., A.F. 240
Rothschild Productions Inc., Charles
    R. 240
Saffyre Management 241
Sa'Mall Management 241
Siddons & Associates 242
Skorman Productions, Inc., T. 243
Sound Management Direction 243
Southeastern Attractions 243
Sphere Group One 243
Staircase Promotion 244
Stander Entertainment 244
Starkravin' Management 245
T.L.C. Booking Agency 245
Tas Music Co./Dave Tasse Enter-
    tainment 245
Texas Sounds Entertainment 245
Twentieth Century Promotions 245
Varrasso Management, Richard 246
Wagner Agency, William F. 246
Warner Productions, Cheryl K. 246
Wemus Entertainment 247
WorldSound, LLC 248
Zane Management, Inc. 248

❤ OPEN TO PREVIOUSLY PUBLISHED/WELL-ESTABLISHED

Music Publishers

Dave Music, Jof 97
Duane Music, Inc. 102
Markea Music/Gina Pie Music/Si
    Que Music 115
Montina Music 117
Pegasus Music 119
Rhythms Productions 123
Segal's Publications 126

Record Companies

American Recordings 143
Ariana Records 144
Arkadia Entertainment Corp. 144
Astralwerks 144
Broken Records International 151
Cambria Records & Publishing 151
CPA Records 156
Heads Up Int., Ltd. 165
Lucifer Records, Inc. 167
Monticana Records 173
Robbins Entertainment LLC 177

Record Producers

Cacophony Productions 196
Final Mix Inc. 199
Monticana Productions 205
Segal's Productions 209

Managers & Booking Agents

Barrett Rock 'n' Roll Enterprises,
    Paul 221
Blue Cat Agency, The 222
DAS Communications, Ltd. 226
De Miles Company, The Edward 227
Levy Management, Rick 234
Management by Jaffe 235
Noteworthy Productions 237
Serge Entertainment Group 242

⊘ DOES NOT ACCEPT UNSOLICITED MATERIAL

Music Publishers

Bourne Co. Music Publishers 89
Bug Music, Inc. 93
Chrysalis Music Group 95
Copperfield Music Group 96
CTV Music (Great Britain) 97
Disney Music Publishing 101
DreamWorks SKG Music Publishing
    102
EMI Christian Music Publishing 103
EMI Music Publishing 103
Famous Music Publishing Compa-
    nies 104

Hickory Lane Publishing and Recording 107
Intoxygene Sarl 109
Jones Music, Quincy 111
Manuiti L.A. 114
Maverick Music 116
MIDI Track Publishing/ALLRS Music Publishing Co. 116
Music Room Publishing Group, The 117
Naked Jain Records 117
Old Slowpoke Music 119
PeerMusic 119
Perla Music 120
Phoebob Music 120
Portage Music 121
Rainbow Music Corp. 122
Ren Zone Music 123
Rhinestone Cowboy Music 123
Rondor Music International/Almo/Irving Music 124
S.M.C.L. Productions, Inc. 125
Silver Blue Music/Oceans Blue Music 127
Sony/ATV Music Publishing 128
Still Working Music Group 129
Trio Productions 131
Universal Music Publishing 131
Warner/Chappell Music, Inc. 133

Record Companies
Angel Records 143
Arista Records 144
Atlantic Records 145
Avita Records 145
Aware Records 149
Capitol Records 152
Columbia Records 155
Cosmotone Records 156
Curb Records 157
DreamWorks Records 158
Elektra Records 158
Epic Records 159
Groove Makers' Recordings 164

Interscope/Geffen/A&M Records 165
Island/Def Jam Music Group 166
J Records 166
Maverick Records 167
MCA Nashville 167
RAVE Records, Inc. 176
Razor & Tie Entertainment 176
RCA Records 176
Reprise Records 177
Sahara Records and Filmworks Entertainment 179
Sony Music 181
Sony Music Nashville 181
Sugar Hill Records 182
Tommy Boy Records 183
Universal Records 185
Verve Music Group, The 185
Videa Artists International Distribution 186
Virgin Records 186
Warner Bros. Records 186
Waterdog Music 187
Wind-Up Entertainment 187
Word Records & Music 188

Record Producers
Allyn, Stuart J. 195
De Miles, Edward 198
Diamond Entertainment, Joel 199
Marenco, Cookie 203
Soul Candy Productions 209

Managers & Booking Agents
Bacchus Group Productions, Ltd. 220
Barnard Management Services (BMS) 221
Harrell & Associates, M. 231
Huge Production, Inc., A 231
International Entertainment Bureau 232
Richards World Management, Inc., Diane 239
Sendyk, Leonard & Co. Inc. 242
World Wide Management 247

Film & TV Index

This index lists companies who place music in motion pictures and TV shows (excluding commercials). To learn more about their film/TV experience, read the information under **Film & TV** in their listings. It is recommended to use this index in conjunction with the Openness to Submissions Index beginning on page 383.

Music Publishers

Alexander Sr. Music 82
Alpha Music Inc. 84
Big Fish Music Publishing Group 87
BSW Records 92
Cherri/Holly Music 94
Christmas & Holiday Music 94
CTV Music (Great Britain) 97
De Miles Music Company, The Edward 97
Famous Music Publishing Companies 104
First Time Music (Publishing) U.K. 104
Fresh Entertainment 105
Goodnight Kiss Music 106
Intoxygene Sarl 109
Jaelius Enterprises 110
Lilly Music Publishing 113
Manuiti L.A. 114
Markea Music/Gina Pie Music/Si Que Music 115
MIDI Track Publishing/ALLRS Music Publishing Co. 116
Naked Jain Records 117
Old Slowpoke Music 119

QUARK, Inc. 121
Rainbow Music Corp. 122
S.M.C.L. Productions, Inc. 125
Saddlestone Publishing 125
Silver Blue Music/Oceans Blue Music 127
Sinus Musik Produktion, Ulli Weigel 127
Still Working Music Group 129
Succes 129
Tower Music Group 130
Transamerika Musikverlag KG 130
Weaver of Words Music 133
Winston & Hoffman House Music Publishers 134
Zettitalia Music International 134

Record Companies

CAPP Records 152
Sahara Records and Filmworks Entertainment 179

Record Producers

De Miles, Edward 198
Human Factor 200
Mustrock Productionz Worldwide 205

Sphere Group One 210

Managers & Booking Agents
Hansen Enterprises, Ltd. 230
Stander Entertainment 244
Wagner Agency, William F. 246

Advertising, Audiovisual & Commercial Music Firms
D.S.M. Producers Inc. 253
Disk Productions 253
Entertainment Productions, Inc. 254
TRF Production Music Libraries 255

Geographic Index

This Geographic Index will help you locate companies by state, as well as those in countries outside of the U.S. It is recommended to use this index in conjunction with the Openness to Submissions Index on page 383. Once you find the names of companies in this index you are interested in, check the listings within each section for addresses, phone numbers, contact names and submission details.

ALABAMA
Music Publishers
Baitstring Music 85
Unknown Source Music 131
Walker Publishing Co. L.L.C. 132

Record Companies
Bolivia Records 150

Managers & Booking Agents
Southeastern Attractions 243

Organizations
Alabama Songwriter's Guild 294

ALASKA
Record Producers
Nightworks Records 206

ARIZONA
Record Companies
Ariana Records 144
Candyspiteful Productions 152
Drumbeat Indian Arts, Inc. 158

Record Producers
Candyspiteful Productions 196

Organizations
Arizona Songwriters Association 298

ARKANSAS
Music Publishers
G Major Music 106

Advertising, Audiovisual & Commercial Music Firms
Cedar Crest Studio 253

Play Producers & Publishers
Arkansas Repertory Theatre 257

CALIFORNIA
Music Publishers
Audio Music Publishers 85
Big Fish Music Publishing Group 87
Bradley Music, Allan 89
Bug Music, Inc. 93
California Country Music 94
CAPP Records 152
Cherri/Holly Music 94
Christmas & Holiday Music 94
Chrysalis Music Group 95
Disney Music Publishing 101
DreamWorks SKG Music Publishing 102
Duane Music, Inc. 102
Emandell Tunes 103
EMI Music Publishing 103

Famous Music Publishing Companies 104
Fricon Music Company 105
Goodnight Kiss Music 106
Jones Music, Quincy 111
Lake Transfer Productions & Music 112
Manuiti L.A. 114
Maverick Music 116
Music Room Publishing Group, The 117
Naked Jain Records 117
PeerMusic 119
Piano Press 120
Pollybyrd Publications Limited 121
Ren Zone Music 123
Rhythms Productions 123
Rondor Music International/Almo/ Irving Music 124
Silver Blue Music/Oceans Blue Music 127
Sony/ATV Music Publishing 128
Supreme Enterprises Int'l Corp. 129
Twin Towers Publishing Co. 131
Vaam Music Group 132
Warner/Chappell Music, Inc. 133
Wilcom Publishing 134
Winston & Hoffman House Music Publishers 134
Zettitalia Music International 134
Zomba Music Publishing 135

Record Companies

ABL Records 142
American Recordings 143
Arista Records 144
Atlantic Records 145
Awal.com 149
Blue Gem Records 150
Cambria Records & Publishing 151
Capitol Records 152
Chattahoochee Records 153
Cleopatra Records 154
Columbia Records 155
Crank! A Record Company 156
Curb Records 157

DreamWorks Records 158
Elektra Records 158
EMF Records & Affiliates 158
Epic Records 159
Gonzo! Records Inc. 161
Gotham Records 161
Interscope/Geffen/A&M Records 165
Island/Def Jam Music Group 166
Maverick Records 167
Metal Blade Records 170
Only New Age Music, Inc. 173
Outstanding Records 174
Parliament Records 174
PPL Entertainment Group 175
RCA Records 176
Redemption Records 177
Reprise Records 177
Roll On Records® 178
Rotten Records 178
Solana Records 181
Ton Records 183
28 Records 184
Universal Records 185
Valtec Productions 185
Verve Music Group, The 185
Virgin Records 186
Warner Bros. Records 186

Record Producers

Cacophony Productions 196
Diamond Entertainment, Joel 199
Final Mix Inc. 199
Hailing Frequency Music Productions 199
L.A. Entertainment, Inc. 202
Linear Cycle Productions 202
Marenco, Cookie 203
Martin, Pete/Vaam Music Productions 204
Mathews, d/b/a Hit or Myth Productions Inc., Scott 204
Mega Truth Records 205
Prescription Co., The 207
SRS Productions/Hit Records Network 211

Valtec Productions 213
Weisman Production Group, The 213

Managers & Booking Agents
Barnard Management Services (BMS) 221
Blowin' Smoke Productions/Records 222
Blue Cat Agency, The 222
Class Act Productions/Management 224
Cox Promotions & Management, Stephen 226
Kitchen Sync 233
Levinson Entertainment Ventures International, Inc. 234
Loggins Promotion 235
Media Management 236
Prestige Management 238
Prime Time Entertainment 238
Pro Talent Consultants 238
Saffyre Management 241
Sa'Mall Management 241
Sendyk, Leonard & Co. Inc. 242
Siddons & Associates 242
Stander Entertainment 244
Starkravin' Management 245
Varrasso Management, Richard 246
Wagner Agency, William F. 246
Zirilli Management, D. 248

Advertising, Audiovisual & Commercial Music Firms
Entertainment Productions, Inc. 254

Play Producers & Publishers
French, Inc., Samuel 262
Los Angeles Designers' Theatre 257
Players Press, Inc. 263
Shakespeare Santa Cruz 259
Ten-Minute Musicals Project, The 259
West End Artists 260

Classical Performing Arts
BRAVO! L.A. 267
Chamber Orchestra of South Bay/ Carson-Dominiquez Hills Symphony 269
Lamarca American Variety Singers 271
Mancini Institute Orchestra, Henry 271
San Francisco Girls Chorus 273

Contests & Awards
Blank Theatre Company Young Playwrights Festival, The 278
L.A. Designers' Theatre Music Awards 283
NACUSA Young Composers' Competition 285
Ten-Minute Musicals Project, The 290
Unisong International Song Contest 291

Organizations
Academy of Country Music 294
American Society of Composers, Authors and Publishers (ASCAP) 295
Broadcast Music, Inc. (BMI) 300
California Lawyers for the Arts 300
CLW Music Award, The 279
Los Angeles Music Network 309
Musicians Contact 310
National Association of Composers/ USA (NACUSA), The 311
San Diego Songwriters Guild 314
San Francisco Folk Music Club 314
SESAC Inc. 315

Workshops & Conferences
ASCAP West Coast/Lester Sill Songwriter's Workshop 323
Film Music Network 305
Hollywood Reporter/Billboard Film & TV Music Conference 325

Songwriters Guild Foundation, The 329

Ten-Minute Musicals Project, The 330

West Coast Songwriters Conference 331

COLORADO
Record Companies
Case Entertainment Group/C.E.G. Records, Inc. 153

Silver Wave Records 180

Play Producers & Publishers
Contemporary Drama Service 261

Pioneer Drama Service 263

Contests & Awards
Delta Omicron International Composition Competition 281

Rocky Mountain Folks Festival Songwriter Showcase 289

Telluride Troubadour Contest 290

CONNECTICUT
Music Publishers
Antelope Publishing Inc. 84

Record Companies
Generic Records, Inc. 160

Pop Record Research 175

Record Producers
Audio 911 195

Managers & Booking Agents
Air Tight Management 219

Martin Productions, Rick 235

Rustron-Whimsong Music Productions 240

Classical Performing Arts
Connecticut Choral Artists/Concora 269

Organizations
Connecticut Songwriters Association 303

Pop Record Research 313

Workshops & Conferences
Independent Music Conference 325

DELAWARE
Advertising, Audiovisual & Commercial Music Firms
Ken-Del Productions Inc. 254

DISTRICT OF COLUMBIA
Record Producers
Human Factor 200

Classical Performing Arts
Master Chorale of Washington 272

Contests & Awards
Fulbright Scholar Program, Council for International Exchange of Scholars 281

Mid-Atlantic Song Contest 284

Monk International Jazz Composers Competition, Thelonious 285

Nestico Award, Sammy/USAF Band Airmen of Note 285

U.S.-Japan Creative Artists Exchange Fellowship Program 291

FLORIDA
Music Publishers
Emstone Music Publishing 104

Rustron Music Publishers 124

Record Companies
CPA Records 156

Neurodisc Records, Inc. 173

Rustron-Whimsong Music Productions 179

Record Producers
Jay Jay Publishing & Record Co. 201

Mac-Attack Productions 203

Rustron Music Productions 208

Satkowski Recordings, Steve 209

Sphere Group One 210

Managers & Booking Agents

Concept 2000 Inc. 225
Evans Productions, Scott 227
Levy Management, Rick 234
Mega Music Productions 236
Rustron-Whimsong Music Productions 240
Skorman Productions, Inc., T. 243
Sound Management Direction 243

Advertising, Audiovisual & Commercial Music Firms

D.S.M. Producers Inc. 253

Play Producers & Publishers

Eldridge Publishing Co., Inc. 262

Classical Performing Arts

Piccolo Opera Company Inc. 272

Contests & Awards

U.S.A. Songwriting Competition 291

Organizations

All Songwriters Network (ASN) 294
Broadcast Music, Inc. (BMI) 300
International Songwriters Guild 307
North Florida Christian Music Writers Association 312

Workshops & Conferences

Winter Music Conference Inc. 331

Retreats & Colonies

Bonk Festival of New Music 324

GEORGIA
Music Publishers

Black Market Entertainment Recordings 88
Fresh Entertainment 105
Orchid Publishing 119

Record Companies

Atlan-Dec/Grooveline Records 145
Bouquet Records 151
Fresh Entertainment 159

Goldwax Record Corporation 161

Managers & Booking Agents

Bouquet-Orchid Enterprises 223
Serge Entertainment Group 242

Advertising, Audiovisual & Commercial Music Firms

Anderson Communications 252

Classical Performing Arts

Atlanta Pops Orchestra 266

Organizations

Broadcast Music, Inc. (BMI) 300

Retreats & Colonies

Hambidge Center, The 333

HAWAII
Music Publishers

Maui Arts & Music Association/Survivor Records/Ten of Diamonds Music 115

Organizations

Hawai'i Songwriters Association 306

Retreats & Colonies

Virginia Center for the Creative Arts 334

ILLINOIS
Music Publishers

De Miles Music Company, The Edward 97
Dream Seekers Publishing 101
Jerjoy Music 110
Kaysarah Music 112
Sound Cellar Music 128

Record Companies

Aware Records 149
Broken Records International 151
Cellar Records 153
Modal Music, Inc.™ 172

Sahara Records and Filmworks Entertainment 179
UAR Records 185
Waterdog Music 187

Record Producers
Coachouse Music 196
De Miles, Edward 198
Neu Electro Productions 205

Managers & Booking Agents
Bacchus Group Productions, Ltd. 220
De Miles Company, The Edward 227
Risavy, Inc., A.F. 240

Advertising, Audiovisual & Commercial Music Firms
Qually & Company Inc. 255

Play Producers & Publishers
Dramatic Publishing Company, The 261

Classical Performing Arts
Wheaton Symphony Orchestra 275

Contests & Awards
Cunningham Commission for Youth Theatre 281
Kinley Memorial Fellowship, Kate Neal 283

Organizations
American Society of Composers, Authors and Publishers (ASCAP) 295
Chicago Dance and Music Alliance 302

INDIANA
Music Publishers
Hammel Associates, Inc., R.L. 107

Managers & Booking Agents
Hale Enterprises 229
Harrell & Associates, M. 231

International Entertainment Bureau 232

Classical Performing Arts
Anderson Symphony Orchestra 266
Carmel Symphony Orchestra 268

Organizations
Just Plain Folks Music Organization 307

IOWA
Music Publishers
JoDa Music 111

Record Producers
Heart Consort Music 200

Managers & Booking Agents
Fenchel Entertainment Agency, Fred T. 228

Play Producers & Publishers
Heuer Publishing Co. 262

Workshops & Conferences
Davidson's Writer's Seminar, Peter 324

KANSAS
Music Publishers
Dave Music, Jof 97

KENTUCKY
Play Producers & Publishers
Aran Press 260

Contests & Awards
Y.E.S. Festival of New Plays 291

LOUISIANA
Music Publishers
EMF Productions 103

Managers & Booking Agents
Big J Productions 221

Advertising, Audiovisual & Commercial Music Firms
Disk Productions 253

Classical Performing Arts
Acadiana Symphony Orchestra 265

Organizations
Louisiana Songwriters Association 309

Workshops & Conferences
Cutting Edge Music Business Conference 324
Shiznit Music Conference, The 328

MAINE
Record Producers
Stuart Audio Services 211

MARYLAND
Music Publishers
Ivory Pen Entertainment 109

Record Companies
Banana Records 149

Managers & Booking Agents
Noteworthy Productions 237

Classical Performing Arts
Susquehanna Symphony Orchestra 274

Organizations
North American Folk Music and Dance Alliance 311

Workshops & Conferences
Baltimore Songwriters Association 299
Folk Alliance Annual Conference 325

MASSACHUSETTS
Music Publishers
Segal's Publications 126

Record Producers
Segal's Productions 209

Managers & Booking Agents
Clockwork Entertainment Management Agency 224
Concerted Efforts, Inc./Foggy Day Music 225
Huge Production, Inc., A 231

Advertising, Audiovisual & Commercial Music Firms
Communications for Learning 253
Lapriore Videography 254

Plays Producers & Publishers
Baker's Plays 260
Freelance Press, The 262

Classical Performing Arts
Boston Philharmonic, The 267

Contests & Awards
ALEA III International Composition Prize 277

Organizations
Boston Songwriters Workshop, The 300

Workshops & Conferences
Music Business Solutions/Career Building Workshops 326
NEMO Music Showcase & Conference 327

MICHIGAN
Record Companies
RAVE Records, Inc. 176
Small Stone Records 180

Record Producers
World Records 214

Managers & Booking Agents
J & V Management 232

Play Producers & Publishers
Thunder Bay Theatre 260

Classical Performing Arts
Adrian Symphony Orchestra 265
Birmingham-Bloomfield Symphony
    Orchestra 267
Cantata Academy 268

Workshops & Conferences
Lamb's Retreat for Songwriters 326

Retreats & Colonies
Isle Royale National Park Artist-in-
    Residence Program 334
Northwood University Alden B. Dow
    Creativity Center 334

MINNESOTA
Music Publishers
Portage Music 121

Managers & Booking Agents
Artist Representation and Manage-
    ment 220

Contests & Awards
Bush Artist Fellows Program 278

Organizations
American Composers Forum 295
Minnesota Association of Songwrit-
    ers 310

MISSISSIPPI
Music Publishers
Abalorn Music 82
Bay Ridge Publishing 86

Record Companies
Avitor Music 148
Missile Records Film & TV, Inc. 171

Rustic Records 178

Managers & Booking Agents
Exclesisa Booking Agency 228

Play Producers & Publishers
Carey College Dinner Theatre, Wil-
    liam 257

MISSOURI
Music Publishers
Lineage Publishing Co. 113

Record Companies
Capstan Record Production 152

Managers & Booking Agents
Staircase Promotion 244

Classical Performing Arts
Heartland Men's Chorus 269

Contests & Awards
Columbia Entertainment Company's
    Jackie White Memorial Children's
    Playwriting Contest 280

MONTANA
Classical Performing Arts
Billings Symphony 267

Organizations
College Music Society, The 303

NEBRASKA
Music Publishers
Lari-Jon Publishing 112

Record Companies
Lari-Jon Records 166

Record Producers
Lari-Jon Productions 202

Managers & Booking Agents
Lari-Jon Promotions 234

Classical Performing Arts
Soli Deo Gloria Cantorum 274

NEVADA
Music Publishers
Americatone International 84
Pollybyrd Publications Limited 121

Record Companies
Americatone Records International
    USA 143

Record Producers
Sound Works Entertainment Produc-
    tions Inc. 210

Managers & Booking Agents
Freestyle Entertainment 229
Hansen Enterprises, Ltd. 230

Organizations
Las Vegas Songwriters Association,
    The 308

NEW HAMPSHIRE
Record Producers
Reel Adventures 207

Retreats & Colonies
MacDowell Colony, The 334

NEW JERSEY
Music Publishers
Gary Music, Alan 106
Perla Music 120
T.C. Productions/Etude Publishing
    Co. 129

Record Companies
Gig Records 160
Lucifer Records, Inc. 167
Presence Records 175

Record Producers
Tari, Roger Vincent 212

Managers & Booking Agents
Brothers Management Associates
    223
Sphere Group One 243

Classical Performing Arts
American Boychoir, The 265
Aureus Quartet 266
Duo Clasico 269

Workshops & Conferences
Appel Farm Arts and Music Festival
    323

NEW YORK
Music Publishers
Alpha Music Inc. 84
BMG Music Publishing 88
BMG Music Publishing 88
Bourne Co. Music Publishers 89
Bug Music, Inc. 93
EMI Music Publishing 103
Famous Music Publishing Compa-
    nies 104
Fifth Avenue Media, Ltd. 104
Material Worth Publishing 115
MIDI Track Publishing/ALLRS Mu-
    sic Publishing Co. 116
Prescription Company 121
QUARK, Inc. 121
Rainbow Music Corp. 122
Rockford Music Co. 123
Sony/ATV Music Publishing 128
Warner/Chappell Music, Inc. 133
Zomba Music Publishing 135

Record Companies
Angel Records 143
Arista Records 144
Arkadia Entertainment Corp. 144
Astralwerks 144
Atlantic Records 145
Blue Wave 150
Chiaroscuro Records 154
Columbia Records 155
Creative Improvised Music Projects
    (CIMP) Records 157
Dental Records 158
Elektra Records 158
Epic Records 159

Interscope/Geffen/A&M Records
  165
Island/Def Jam Music Group 166
J Records 166
Mighty Records 171
Quark Records 176
Radical Records 176
Razor & Tie Entertainment 176
RCA Records 176
Robbins Entertainment LLC 177
Silvertone Records 180
Sony Music 181
Tommy Boy Records 183
Transdreamer Records 184
TVT Records 184
Universal Records 185
Verve Music Group, The 185
Videa Artists International Distribu-
  tion 186
Virgin Records 186
Warner Bros. Records 186
Wind-Up Entertainment 187
Xemu Records 189

Record Producers
AIF Music Productions 194
Allyn, Stuart J. 195
Mustrock Productionz Worldwide
  205
Prescription Co., The 207

Managers & Booking Agents
Bassline Entertainment, Inc. 221
Blue Wave Productions 222
DAS Communications, Ltd. 226
DCA Productions 227
Hot Steaming Coffee Films 231
Klein, Joanne 233
Knight Agency, Bob 233
Management by Jaffe 235
Nik Entertainment Co. 237
On the Level Music! 237
Rainbow Talent Agency 239
Raspberry Jam Music 239
Richards World Management, Inc.,
  Diane 239

Rothschild Productions Inc., Charles
  R. 240
Wood Artist Management, Richard
  247
World Wide Management 247

**Advertising, Audiovisual &
Commercial Music Firms**
Fine Art Productions/Richie Suraci
  Pictures, Multimedia, Interactive
  254
TRF Production Music Libraries 255

Play Producers & Publishers
Directors Company, The 257
French, Inc., Samuel 262
Open Eye Theater, The 258
Primary Stages 258

Classical Performing Arts
Amherst Saxophone Quartet 265
Touring Concert Opera Co. Inc. 274

Contests & Awards
AGO/ECS Publishing Award in Cho-
  ral Composition 277
Artists' Fellowships 277
European International Competition
  for Composers/IBLA Music Foun-
  dation 281
Holtkamp-AGO Award in Organ
  Composition 283
Lennon Songwriting Contest, The
  John 284
Mazumdar New Play Competition,
  Maxim 284
Pulitzer Prize in Music 289
Rodgers Awards, Richard 290
Rome Prize Competition Fellowship
  290
SESAC Inc. 315

Organizations
American Music Center, Inc. 295
American Society of Composers, Authors and Publishers (ASCAP)
  295

Association of Independent Music
    Publishers 299
Black Rock Coalition, The 299
Broadcast Music, Inc. (BMI) 300
Dramatists Guild of America, Inc.,
    The 304
Field, The 304
Meet the Composer 310
National Academy of Popular Music
    (NAPM) 311
Opera America 312
Outmusic 313

Workshops & Conferences
ASCAP Musical Theatre Workshop
    323
BMI-Lehman Engel Musical Theatre
    Workshop 323
CMJ Music Marathon, MusicFest &
    FilmFest 324
Genesius Theatre Group 325
National Academy of Popular Music
    Songwriting Workshop Program
    327
Songwriters Guild Foundation, The
    329

NORTH CAROLINA
Record Companies
Deep South Entertainment 157
Fireant 159
Salexo Music 180
Sugar Hill Records 182

Record Producers
WLM Music/Recording 214

Organizations
Central Carolina Songwriters Associ-
    ation (CCSA) 302

Workshops & Conferences
Swannanoa Gathering—Contempo-
    rary Folk Week, The 330

Retreats & Colonies
Brevard Music Center 333

NORTH DAKOTA
Record Companies
Makoche Recording Company 167

OHIO
Music Publishers
Alexander Sr. Music 82
Barkin' Foe the Master's Bone 85
Buckeye Music Group 93
Marvin Publishing, John Weller 115
New Rap Jam Publishing, A 118
Salt Works Music 125

Record Companies
Heads Up Int., Ltd. 165
Tangent® Records 182

Record Producers
DAP Entertainment 198
New Experience Records/Faze 4 Re-
    cords 206

Managers & Booking Agents
All Star Management 219
Concept 2000 Inc. 225

Classical Performing Arts
Lithopolis Area Fine Arts Associa-
    tion 271

Workshops & Conferences
Undercurrents 331

OKLAHOMA
Music Publishers
Branson Country Music Publishing
    89
Furrow Music 106
Old Slowpoke Music 119
SME Publishing Group 128

Record Companies
Cherry Street Records 154

Record Producers
Studio Seven 211

Managers & Booking Agents
D&R Entertainment 226

Contests & Awards
Billboard Song Contest 278

Organizations
Oklahoma Songwriters & Composers
    Association 312

OREGON
Music Publishers
Earitating Music Publishing 102
High-Minded Moma Publishing &
    Productions 108
Moon June Music 117

Contests & Awards
Great American Song Contest 282
Portland Songwriters Association
    Annual Songwriting Competition
    289

Organizations
Central Oregon Songwriters Associa-
    tion 302
Portland Songwriters Association
    314

PENNSYLVANIA
Music Publishers
Baird Music Group 85
Come Alive Communications, Inc.
    96
Makers Mark Gold 114
Shawnee Press, Inc. 126

Record Companies
Judgment Entertainment Inc. 166
Megaforce Records 167
Sound Gems 181

Record Producers
Baird Enterprises, Ron 195
Integrated Entertainment 200
Makers Mark Music Productions 203
Philly Breakdown Recording Co. 207
Westwires Recording 213

Managers & Booking Agents
Blank & Blank 222
Clousher Productions 224
Countrywide Producers 225
Hall Entertainment & Events, Bill 230
Zane Management, Inc. 248

Advertising, Audiovisual &
Commercial Music Firms
Advertel, Inc. 252

Play Producers & Publishers
Prince Music Theater 259

Classical Performing Arts
Hershey Symphony Orchestra 270
Singing Boys of Pennsylvania 273

Contests & Awards
CRS National Composers Competi-
    tion 280
Gaul Composition Contest, Harvey
    282

Organizations
Pittsburgh Songwriters Association
    313

RHODE ISLAND
Managers & Booking Agents
Twentieth Century Promotions 245

Organizations
Rhode Island Songwriters' Associa-
    tion 314

TENNESSEE
Music Publishers
Abear Publishing 82
Acuff-Rose Music 82

Alias John Henry Tunes 83
Beaverwood Audio-Video 87
Bug Music, Inc. 93
Buried Treasure Music 93
Chrysalis Music Group 95
Coal Harbor Music 95
Copperfield Music Group 96
Cornelius Companies, The 97
Curb Music 97
Electric Mule Publishing Company 103
EMI Christian Music Publishing 103
Famous Music Publishing Companies 104
Hitsburgh Music Co. 108
Juke Music 111
Lita Music 113
Markea Music/Gina Pie Music/Si Que Music 115
MCA Music Publishing 116
NSAI Song Camps 328
Peters Music, Justin 120
Phoebob Music 120
Platinum Planet Music, Inc. 120
Red Sundown Music 123
Rhinestone Cowboy Music 123
Rustic Records, Inc Publishing 124
SDB Music Group 126
Sizemore Music 127
Sony/ATV Music Publishing 128
Still Working Music Group 129
Thistle Hill 130
Tourmaline Music, Inc. 130
Tower Music Group 130
Trio Productions 131
Universal Music Publishing 131
Vine Creek Music 132
Walkerbout Music Group 132
Warner/Chappell Music, Inc. 133
Windswept Music 134

Record Companies
Arista Records 144
Atlantic Records 145
Avita Records 145
Capitol Records 152
Coal Harbor Music 155
Columbia Records 155
Compendia Music Group 156
Curb Records 157
DreamWorks Records 158
Epic Records 159
Island/Def Jam Music Group 166
MCA Nashville 167
RCA Records 176
Sony Music Nashville 181
Warner Bros. Records 186
Word Records & Music 188

Record Producers
Aberdeen Productions 194
Craig Productions, Charlie 197
DeLory and Music Makers, Al 199
Pierce, Jim 207
Swift River Productions 211

Managers & Booking Agents
Allen Entertainment Development, Michael 219
Circuit Rider Talent & Management Co. 223
Hardison International Entertainment Corporation 230
Midcoast, Inc. 236
Monterey Artists Peninsula Artists/ Paradigm 237
Riohcat Music 240
Warner Productions, Cheryl K. 246

Play Producers & Publishers
Playhouse on the Square 258

Contests & Awards
American Songwriter Lyric Contest 277
NSAI/CMT Annual Song Contest 285
Playhouse on the Square New Play Competition 289

Organizations
American Society of Composers, Authors and Publishers (ASCAP) 295

Broadcast Music, Inc. (BMI) 300
Gospel Music Association 305
International Bluegrass Music Association (IBMA) 306
Knoxville Songwriters Association 308
Memphis Songwriters' Association 310
Nashville Songwriters Association International (NSAI) 310
SESAC Inc. 315

Workshops & Conferences
Nashville Music Festival 327
NSAI Songwriters Songposium 328
Songwriters Guild Foundation, The 329

Retreats & Colonies
Tunesmith Summer & Winter Seminars 330

TEXAS
Music Publishers
BSW Records 92
Christopher Publishing, Sonny 95
Earthscream Music Publishing Co. 102
Glad Music Co. 106
His Power Productions and Publishing 108
Jaelius Enterprises 110
LCS Music Group 113
Silicon Music Publishing Co. 126
Starbound Publishing Co. 128

Record Companies
Arista Records 144
BSW Records 151
CKB Records/Helaphat Entertainment 154
Compadre Records 155
Cosmotone Records 156
Front Row Records 160
Groove Makers' Recordings 164
Hacienda Records & Recording Studio 164

Idol Records Publishing 165
Surface Records 182
Texas Rose Records 183
Topcat Records 183
World Beatnik Records 188

Record Producers
ACR Productions 194
RN'D Distribution, LLC. 208
Sound Arts Recording Studio 210
TMC Productions 212
Trinity Studio, The 213
Willson, Frank 214

Managers & Booking Agents
American Bands Management 220
Apodaca Promotions Inc. 220
Atch Records and Productions 220
Bread & Butter Productions 223
Kendall West Agency 232
Kuper Personal Management/Recovery Recordings 234
Management Plus 235
Smeltzer Productions, Gary 243
Texas Sounds Entertainment 245
Universal Music Marketing 246
Wemus Entertainment 247

Classical Performing Arts
Hermann Sons German Band 270

Contests & Awards
Grassy Hill Kerrville New Folk Competition 282

Organizations
Austin Songwriters Group 299
Country Music Association of Texas 303
Dallas Songwriters Association 303
Fort Worth Songwriters Association 305
Houston Fort Bend Songwriters Association 306

Workshops & Conferences
I Write the Songs 325
Kerrville Folk Festival 326

Retreats & Colonies
South by Southwest Music Conference 330

VERMONT
Music Publishers
JPMC Music Inc. 111

Workshops & Conferences
Manchester Music Festival 326

Retreats & Colonies
Dorset Colony House 333

VIRGINIA
Music Publishers
Weaver of Words Music 133

Record Companies
Warehouse Creek Recording Corp. 186

Managers & Booking Agents
Precision Management 238

Contests & Awards
Henrico Theatre Company One-Act Playwriting Competition 283

Organizations
Aaron Enterprises Songwriters Group 294

WASHINGTON
Music Publishers
Corelli Music Group 96
Your Best Songs Publishing 134

Record Companies
Kill Rock Stars 166

Record Producers
Lazy Bones Productions/Recordings, Inc. 202

Managers & Booking Agents
T.L.C. Booking Agency 245
WorldSound, LLC 248

Classical Performing Arts
Orchestra Seattle/Seattle Chamber Singers 272

Organizations
Pacific Northwest Songwriters Association 313

WEST VIRGINIA
Music Publishers
McCoy Music, Jim 116
Newbraugh Brothers Music 118

Record Companies
NBT Records 173
Winchester Records 187

Record Producers
Blues Alley Records 196

WISCONSIN
Music Publishers
M & T Waldoch Publishing, Inc. 114

Managers & Booking Agents
St. John Artists 244
Tas Music Co./Dave Tasse Entertainment 245

AUSTRALIA
Managers & Booking Agents
Cranium Management 226

BELGIUM
Music Publishers
Happy Melody 107
Inside Records/OK Songs 109
Succes 129

Record Producers
Jump Productions 201

CANADA
Music Publishers
Hickory Lane Publishing and Recording 107
Lilly Music Publishing 113
Many Lives Music Publishers 114
Montina Music 117
S.M.C.L. Productions, Inc. 125
Saddlestone Publishing 125

Record Companies
Hi-Bias Records Inc. 165
Monticana Records 173
P. & N. Records 174
Sonic Unyon Records Canada 181

Record Producers
"A" Major Sound Corporation 194
DaVinci's Notebook Records 198
Kane Producer/Engineer, Karen 201
Monticana Productions 205
Silver Bow Productions 209
Soul Candy Productions 209

Managers & Booking Agents
Alert Music, Inc. 219
EAO Music Corporation of Canada 227
Feldman & Associates, S.L. 228
Fiedler Management, B.C. 228
Kagan International, Sheldon 232
Management Trust Ltd., The 235
Outlaw Entertainment International 238
Silver Bow Management 242
Winterland Entertainment Management & Publishing 247

Advertising, Audiovisual & Commercial Music Firms
Moore Compositions, Patrick 255

Classical Performing Arts
Arcady 266
Canadian Opera Company 268
Vancouver Chamber Choir 275

Organizations
Association des Professionel.le.s de la chanson et de la musique 299
Canada Council for the Arts/Conseil des Arts du Canada 301
Canadian Academy of Recording Arts & Sciences (CARAS) 301
Canadian Country Music Association 301
Canadian Musical Reproduction Rights Agency Ltd. 302
Manitoba Audio Recording Industry Association (MARIA) 309
Pacific Music Industry Association 313
SOCAN (Society of Composers, Authors and Music Publishers of Canada) 315

Workshops & Conferences
Canadian Music Week 324
North by Northeast Music Festival and Conference 327
Orford Festival 328

FRANCE
Music Publishers
Intoxygene Sarl 109

GERMANY
Music Publishers
Ja/Nein Musikverlag GmbH 109
Sinus Musik Produktion, Ulli Weigel 127
Transamerika Musikverlag KG 130
Wengert, Berthold (Musikverlag) 133

Record Companies
Westpark Music—Records, Production & Publishing 187

HOLLAND
Music Publishers
All Rock Music 83

Record Companies
Collector Records 155

IRELAND
Retreats & Colonies
Guthrie Centre, The Tyrone 333

JAPAN
Contests & Awards
U.S.-Japan Creative Artists Exchange Fellowship Program 291

THE NETHERLANDS
Record Companies
A.A.M.I. Music Group 142

Record Producers
Collector Records 197

NEW ZEALAND
Music Publishers
Pegasus Music 119

PUERTO RICO
Organizations
American Society of Composers, Authors and Publishers (ASCAP) 295
Broadcast Music, Inc. (BMI) 300

UNITED KINGDOM
Music Publishers
Bearsongs 87
CTV Music (Great Britain) 97
First Time Music (Publishing) U.K. 104
R.T.L. Music 122

Record Companies
AMP Records & Music 143
Audio-Visual Media Productions (formerly First Time Records) 145
Big Bear Records 149
X.R.L. Records/Music 188

Record Producers
Big Bear 196
June Productions Ltd. 201

Managers & Booking Agents
Kickstart Music Ltd. 232

Organizations
American Society of Composers, Authors and Publishers (ASCAP) 295
Broadcast Music, Inc. (BMI) 300
Guild of International Songwriters & Composers, The 306
International Songwriters Association Ltd. 307
SESAC Inc. 315

General Index

Use this index to locate specific markets and resources. Also, we list companies that appeared in the 2005 edition of *Songwriter's Market*, but do not appear this year. Instead of page numbers beside these markets you will find two-letter codes in parentheses that explain why these markets no longer appear. The codes are (**ED**)—Editorial Decision, (**NS**)—Not Accepting Submissions, (**NR**)No (or late) Response to Listing Request, (**OB**)—Out of Business, (**RR**)—Removed by Listing's Request, (**UC**)—Unable to Contact.

A

A.A.M.I. Music Group 142
"A" Major Sound Corporation 194
A&A Mersier Trucking Entertainment (NR)
Aaron Enterprises Songwriters Group 294
Abalorn Music 82
Abear Publishing 82
Aberdeen Productions 194
ABL Records 142
Academy of Country Music 294
Acadiana Symphony Orchestra 265
ACR Productions 194
Acuff-Rose Music 82
Ad Agency, The 252
Adrian Symphony Orchestra 265
Advertel, Inc. 252
AGO/ECS Publishing Award in Choral Composition 277
AIF Music Productions 194
Air Tight Management 219
Alabama Songwriter's Guild 294
ALEA III International Composition Prize 277
Alert Music, Inc. 219
Alexander Sr. Music 82
Alias John Henry Tunes 83
All Rock Music 83

All Songwriters Network (ASN) 294
All Star Management 219
All Star Talent Agency (NR)
Allegheny Music Works 84, 142
Allen Entertainment Development, Michael 219
Alliance Theatre (NR)
Allisongs Inc. (NR)
Allyn, Stuart J. 195
Alpha Music Inc. 84
AMAS Musical Theatre, Inc. (NR)
American Artists Entertainment (NR)
American Bands Management 220
American Boychoir, The 265
American Composers Forum 295
American Music Center, Inc. 295
American Musical Theatre Of San Jose (NR)
American Recordings 143
American Society of Composers, Authors and Publishers (ASCAP) 295
American Songwriter Lyric Contest 277
Americatone International 84
Americatone Records International USA 143
Amherst Saxophone Quartet 265

Amok Artists Agency (OB)
AMP Records & Music 143
Anderson Communications 252
Anderson Symphony Orchestra 266
Angel Records 143
Annual One-Act Playwrighting Contest (NR)
Antelope Publishing Inc. 84
Apodaca Promotions Inc. 220
Appel Farm Arts and Music Festival 323
Aran Press 260
Arcady 266
Arcady Music Festival (NR)
Arden Theatre Company (NR)
Ariana Records 144
Arista Records 144
Arizona Songwriters Association 298
Arkadia Entertainment Corp. 144
Arkansas Repertory Theatre 257
Artist Representation and Management 220
Artists' Fellowships 277
ASCAP Musical Theatre Workshop 323
ASCAP West Coast/Lester Sill Songwriter's Workshop 323
Asolo Theatre Company (NR)
Association des Professionel.le.s de la chanson et de la musique 299
Association of Independent Music Publishers 299
Astralwerks 144
Atch Records and Productions 220
Atlan-Dec/Grooveline Records 145
Atlanta Pops Orchestra 266
Atlanta Young Singers Of Callanwolde, The (NR)
Atlantic Records 145
Audio 911 195
Audio Music Publishers 85
Audio-Visual Media Productions (formerly First Time Records) 145
Aureus Quartet 266
Austin Songwriters Group 299
Avita Records 145
Avitor Music 148
Awal.com 149
Aware Records 149

B

Bacchus Group Productions, Ltd. 220
Backstreet Booking (NR)
Bagatelle Music Publishing Co. (NR)
Bailiwick Repertory (NR)
Baird Enterprises, Ron 195
Baird Music Group 85
Baitstring Music 85
Baker's Plays 260
Baker's Plays High School Playwriting Contest (NR)
Baltimore Songwriters Association 299
Banana Records 149
Barkin' Foe the Master's Bone 85
Barnard Management Services (BMS) 221
Barrett Rock 'n' Roll Enterprises, Paul 221
Barter Theatre (NR)
Bassline Entertainment, Inc. 221
Bay Ridge Publishing 86
Bearsongs 87
Beaverwood Audio-Video 87
Belmont Records (NR)
Big Bear 196
Big Bear Records 149
Big Fish Music Publishing Group 87
Big Heavy World (NR)
Big J Productions 221
Bill Detko Management (NR)
Billboard Song Contest 278
Billings Symphony 267
Birmingham Children's Theatre (NR)
Birmingham-Bloomfield Symphony Orchestra 267
Bixio Music Group & Associates/Idm Music (NR)
Black Market Entertainment Recordings 88
Black Rock Coalition, The 299
Black Stallion Country, Inc. (NR)
Black Stallion Country Publishing (NR)
Blank & Blank 222
Blank Theatre Company Young Playwrights Festival, The 278

Blowin' Smoke Productions/Records 222

Blowing Rock Stage Company, The (NR)

Blue Cat Agency, The 222

Blue Gem Records 150

Blue Wave 150

Blue Wave Productions 222

Blues Alley Records 196

BMG Music Publishing 88

BMI-Lehman Engel Musical Theatre Workshop 323

BMX Entertainment (NR)

Bolivia Records 150

Bonk Festival of New Music 324

Boston Philharmonic, The 267

Boston Songwriters Workshop, The 300

Boulevard Music & Publishing (NR)

Bouquet Records 151

Bouquet-Orchid Enterprises 223

Bourne Co. Music Publishers 89

BRAVO! L.A. 267

Bradley Music, Allan 89

Brandon Hills Music, LLC 89

Branson Country Music Publishing 89

Bread & Butter Productions 223

Brevard Music Center 333

BRg Music Works (NR)

Brian Song Music Corp. (NS)

Bristol Riverside Theatre (NR)

Broadcast Music, Inc. (BMI) 300

Broken Records International 151

Brothers Management Associates 223

BSW Records 92, 151

Buckeye Music Group 93

Bug Music, Inc. 93

Bugle Publishing Group (NR)

Buried Treasure Music 93

Bush Artist Fellows Program 278

Buxton Walker P/L (RR)

Byrdcliffe Arts Colony (NR)

C

Cacophony Productions 196

Calgary Boys Choir (NR)

California Country Music 94

California Lawyers for the Arts 300

Cambria Records & Publishing 151

Canada Council for the Arts/Conseil des Arts du Canada 301

Canadian Academy of Recording Arts & Sciences (CARAS) 301

Canadian Country Music Association 301

Canadian Music Week 324

Canadian Musical Reproduction Rights Agency Ltd. 302

Canadian Opera Company 268

Candyspiteful Productions 152, 196

Cantata Academy 268

Cantrax Recorders 252

Capitol Records 152

CAPP Records 152

Capstan Record Production 152

Carey College Dinner Theatre, William 257

Carmel Symphony Orchestra 268

Carson City Symphony (NR)

Case Entertainment Group/C.E.G. Records, Inc. 153

Cedar Crest Studio 253

Cellar Records 153

Celt Musical Services, Jan (NR)

Center For The Promotion Of Contemporary Composers (NR)

Central Carolina Songwriters Association (CCSA) 302

Central Oregon Songwriters Association 302

Chamber Orchestra of South Bay/Carson-Dominiquez Hills Symphony 269

Charlotte Philharmonic Orchestra (NR)

Chattahoochee Records 153

Chattanooga Girls Choir (NR)

Cherri/Holly Music 94

Cherry Street Records 154

Cheyenne Symphony Orchestra (NR)

Chiaroscuro Records 154

Chicago Dance and Music Alliance 302

Christmas & Holiday Music 94

Christopher Publishing, Sonny 95

Chrysalis Music Group 95

Cinevue/Steve Postal Productions (NR)

Circa '21 Dinner Playhouse (NR)

Circuit Rider Talent & Management Co. 223

CKB Records/Helaphat Entertainment 154

Class Act Productions/Management 224

Clearwind Publishing (NR)

Cleopatra Records 154

Clockwork Entertainment Management Agency 224

Clousher Productions 224

CLW Music Award, The 279

CMJ Music Marathon, MusicFest & FilmFest 324

Coachouse Music 196

Coal Harbor Music 95, 155, 197, 224

Col. Buster Doss Presents (NR)

Cold Creek Records (CCR) (NR)

Collector Records 155, 197

College Music Society, The 303

Colorado Music Association (NR)

Columbia Entertainment Company's Jackie White Memorial Children's Playwriting Contest 280

Columbia Records 155

Come Alive Communications, Inc. 96

Commonwealth Opera Inc. (NR)

Communications for Learning 253

Compadre Records 155

Compendia Music Group 156

Comstock Records Ltd. (RR)

Concept 2000 Inc. 225

Concerted Efforts, Inc./Foggy Day Music 225

Connecticut Choral Artists/Concora 269

Connecticut Songwriters Association 303

Conscience Music (RR)

Contemporary Drama Service 261

Copperfield Music Group 96

Coppin, Johnny/Red Sky Records (NR)

Corelli Music Group 96

Cornelius Companies, The 97

Cosmotone Records 156

Country Legends Association (NR)

Country Music Association of Texas 303

Countrywide Producers 225

Cox Promotions & Management, Stephen 226

CPA Records 156

Craig Productions, Charlie 197

Cranium Management 226

Crank! A Record Company 156

Crawfish Productions (NR)

Creative Improvised Music Projects (CIMP) Records 157

Creative Soul (NR)

Creative Star Management (NR)

Creede Repertory Theatre (NR)

Cringe Music 97

CRS National Composers Competition 280

CTV Music (Great Britain) 97

Cunningham Commission for Youth Theatre 281

Cupit Music Group (NR)

Cupit Productions, Jerry (NR)

Curb Music 97

Curb Records 157

Cutting Edge Music Business Conference 324

D

D.S.M. Producers Inc. 253

DAP Entertainment 198

Dale Productions, Alan (NR)

Dallas Songwriters Association 303

D&R Entertainment 226

DAS Communications, Ltd. 226

Dave Music, Jof 97

Davidson's Writer's Seminar, Peter 324

DaVinci's Notebook Records 198

dbF A Media Company (NR)

DCA Productions 227

De Miles Company, The Edward 227

De Miles, Edward 198

De Miles Music Company, The Edward 97

Deary Me Records (OB)

Deep South Entertainment 157

Delev Music Company 101

Del-Fi Records, Inc. (RP)

DeLory and Music Makers, Al 199
Delta Omicron International Composition Competition 281
Dental Records 158
Desert Chorale (NR)
Diamond Entertainment, Joel 199
Directors Company, The 257
Discmedia (NR)
Discos Fuentes/Miami Records & Edimusica USA (NR)
Disk Productions 253
Disney Music Publishing 101
Divine Industries (NR)
DM Records Group (NR)
Dorset Colony House 333
Dramatic Publishing Company, The 261
Dramatists Guild of America, Inc., The 304
Dream Seekers Publishing 101
DreamWorks Records 158
DreamWorks SKG Music Publishing 102
Drumbeat Indian Arts, Inc. 158
Duane Music, Inc. 102
Duo Clasico 269
Dwell Records (NR)

E
EAO Music Corporation of Canada 227
Earitating Music Publishing 102
Earthscream Music Publishing Co. 102
Egyptianman Productions (NR)
Eldridge Publishing Co., Inc. 262
Electric Mule Publishing Company 103
Elektra Records 158
Ellis International Talent Agency, The (NR)
Emandell Tunes 103
EMF Productions 103
EMF Records & Affiliates 158
EMI Christian Music Publishing 103
EMI Music Publishing 103
Emstone Music Publishing 104
Ensemble Theatre (NR)
Enterprize Records-Tapes (NS)
Entertainment Productions, Inc. 254

Entourage Music Group (NR)
Epic Records 159
Esquire International (NR)
European International Competition for Composers/IBLA Music Foundation 281
European Union Chamber Orchestra (NR)
Evans Productions, Scott 227
Exclesisa Booking Agency 228

F
Famous Music Publishing Companies 104
Feldman & Associates, S.L. 228
Fenchel Entertainment Agency, Fred T. 228
Fiedler Management, B.C. 228
Field, The 304
Fifth Avenue Media, Ltd. 104
Film Music Network 305
Final Mix Inc. 199
Fine Art Productions/Richie Suraci Pictures, Multimedia, Interactive 254
Fireant 159
First Time Management 229
First Time Music (Publishing) U.K. 104
Flying Heart Records (NR)
Folk Alliance Annual Conference 325
Fort Worth Songwriters Association 305
Freelance Press, The 262
Freestyle Entertainment 229
French, Inc., Samuel 262
Fresh Entertainment 105, 159
Fricon Music Company 105
Front Row Records 160
Fulbright Scholar Program, Council for International Exchange of Scholars 281
Furrow Music 106

G
G Major Music 106
Garrett Entertainment, Marty (NR)
Gary Music, Alan 106
Gaslight Theatre, The (NR)

Gaul Composition Contest, Harvey 282

Geer Theatricum Botanicum, The Will (NR)

Generic Records, Inc. 160

Genesius Theatre Group 325

Gig Records 160

Glad Music Co. 106

Godtland Management, Inc., Eric (NR)

Gold & Associates, Inc. (NS)

Goldwax Record Corporation 161

Gonzo! Records Inc. 161

Goodnight Kiss Music 106

Gospel Music Association 305

Gospel/Christian Songwriters Group (NR)

Gotham Records 161

Grassy Hill Kerrville New Folk Competition 282

Great American Song Contest 282

Greater Grand Forks Symphony Orchestra (NR)

Groove Makers' Recordings 164

Gueststar Entertainment Agency (NR)

Gueststar Records, Inc. (NR)

Guild of International Songwriters & Composers, The 306

Gurley & Co. (NS)

Guthrie Centre, The Tyrone 333

H

Hacienda Records & Recording Studio 164

Hailing Frequency Music Productions 199

Hale Enterprises 229

Hall Entertainment & Events, Bill 230

Hambidge Center, The 333

Hammel Associates, Inc., R.L. 107

Hansen Enterprises, Ltd. 230

Happy Melody 107

Hardison International Entertainment Corporation 230

Harrell & Associates, M. 231

Hawai'i Songwriters Association 306

Heads Up Int., Ltd. 165

Heart Consort Music 200

Heart Music, Inc. (NR)

Heartland Men's Chorus 269

Helena Symphony (NR)

Hendersonville Symphony Orchestra (NR)

Henrico Theatre Company One-Act Playwriting Competition 283

Hermann Sons German Band 270

Hershey Symphony Orchestra 270

Heuer Publishing Co. 262

Hi-Bias Records Inc. 165

Hickory Lane Publishing and Recording 107

High-Minded Moma Publishing & Productions 108

His Power Productions and Publishing 108

Hitsburgh Music Co. 108

Hodges Associates, Inc. (NR)

Hollywood Records (NR)

Hollywood Reporter/Billboard Film & TV Music Conference 325

Holtkamp-AGO Award in Organ Composition 283

Home Town Hero's Publishing 109

Horizon Management Inc. (ED)

Horizon Theatre Co. (NR)

Hot Steaming Coffee Films 231

Hottrax Records (NR)

Houston Fort Bend Songwriters Association 306

Hudson Valley Philharmonic (NR)

Huge Production, Inc., A 231

Human Factor 200

I

I Write the Songs 325

Idol Records Publishing 165

Imaginary Records (NR)

Independent Music Conference 325

Indiana Opera Theatre/Macallister Awards For Opera Singers (NR)

Inside Records/OK Songs 109

Integrated Entertainment 200

International Bluegrass Music Association (IBMA) 306

International Entertainment Bureau 232

International Songwriters Association Ltd. 307

International Songwriters Guild 307

Interscope/Geffen/A&M Records 165
Intoxygene Sarl 109
Irish Music Rights Organisation (NR)
Island Culture Music Publishers (NR)
Island/Def Jam Music Group 166
Isle Royale National Park Artist-in-Residence Program 334
Ivory Pen Entertainment 109

J

J & V Management 232
J Records 166
Jae Enterprises, Jana (NR)
Jae Music, Jana (NR)
Jaelius Enterprises 110
James Management, Roger (NR)
Ja/Nein Musikverlag GmbH 109
Janoulis Productions, Alexander/Big Al Jano Productions (NR)
Jay Jay Publishing & Record Co. 201
Jericho Sound Lab (NR)
Jerjoy Music 110
Jerome Composers Commissioning Program (RR)
JoDa Music 111
Jones Music, Quincy 111
JPMC Music Inc. 111
Judgment Entertainment Inc. 166
Juke Music 111
Jump Productions 201
June Productions Ltd. 201
Jupiter Records (NR)
Just Plain Folks Music Organization 307

K

Kagan International, Sheldon 232
Kalani Oceanside Retreat (NR)
K&R's Recording Studios (NR)
Kane Producer/Engineer, Karen 201
Kaupp Records (NR)
Kaupps & Robert Publishing Co. (NR)
Kaysarah Music 112
Kendall West Agency 232
Ken-Del Productions Inc. 254
Kentucky Opera (NR)
Kerrville Folk Festival 326

Kickstart Music Ltd. 232
Kill Rock Stars 166
Kingston Records And Talent (NR)
Kingston Records (NR)
Kinley Memorial Fellowship, Kate Neal 283
Kitchen Sync 233
Klein, Joanne 233
Knight Agency, Bob 233
Knoxville Songwriters Association 308
Kuper Personal Management/Recovery Recordings 234

L

L.A. Designers' Theatre Music Awards 283
L.A. Entertainment, Inc. 202
La Jolla Playhouse (NR)
Lake Transfer Productions & Music 112
Lamarca American Variety Singers 271
Lamb's Retreat for Songwriters 326
Landmark Communications Group (NR)
Lapriore Videography 254
Lari-Jon Productions 202
Lari-Jon Promotions 234
Lari-Jon Publishing 112
Lari-Jon Records 166
Lark Record Productions, Inc. (NR)
Lark Talent & Advertising (NR)
Las Vegas Songwriters Association, The 308
Lawrence, Ltd., Ray (NR)
Lazy Bones Productions/Recordings, Inc. 202
LCS Music Group 113
Lennon Songwriting Contest, The John 284
Levinson Entertainment Ventures International, Inc. 234
Levy Management, Rick 234
Lilly Music Publishing 113
Lima Symphony Orchestra (NR)
Lineage Publishing Co. 113
Linear Cycle Productions 202
Lita Music 113

Lithopolis Area Fine Arts Association 271
Live-Wire Management (NR)
Living Eye Productions Ltd. (NR)
Lock (NR)
Loggins Promotion 235
Los Angeles Designers' Theatre 257
Los Angeles Music Network 309
Louisiana Songwriters Association 309
Lucifer Records, Inc. 167
Luick & Country Music Showcase Intl. Associates, Harold (NR)
Lyric Opera Of Chicago (NR)

M

M & T Waldoch Publishing, Inc. 114
Mac-Attack Productions 203
MacDowell Colony, The 334
Magic Message Music (NR)
Magic Theatre (NR)
Makers Mark Gold 114
Makers Mark Music Productions 203
Makoche Recording Company 167
Malaco Records (NR)
Mallof, Abruzino & Nash Marketing (NR)
Management by Jaffe 235
Management Plus 235
Management Trust Ltd., The 235
Manchester Music Festival 326
Mancini Institute Orchestra, Henry 271
Manhattan Theatre Club (NR)
Manitoba Audio Recording Industry Association (MARIA) 309
Manuiti L.A. 114
Many Lives Music Publishers 114
Marenco, Cookie 203
Markea Music/Gina Pie Music/Si Que Music 115
Martin, Pete/Vaam Music Productions 204
Martin Productions, Rick 235
Marvin Publishing, John Weller 115
Master Chorale of Washington 272
Material Worth Publishing 115
Mathews, d/b/a Hit or Myth Productions Inc., Scott 204

Maui Arts & Music Association/Survivor Records/Ten of Diamonds Music 115
Maverick Music 116
Maverick Records 167
Mayo & Company, Phil 236
Mazumdar New Play Competition, Maxim 284
Mazur Entertainment/Mazur Public Relations (NR)
MCA Nashville 167
MCA Music Publishing 116
McClure & Trowbridge Publishing, Ltd. 116
McCoy Music, Jim 116
McJames Music Inc. (NR)
McKnight Visiting Composer Program (RR)
Media Management 236
Meet the Composer 310
Mega Music Productions 236
Mega Truth Records 205
Megaforce Records 167
Memphis Songwriters' Association 310
Mento Music Group (NR)
Metal Blade Records 170
Metro Talent Group, Inc. (NR)
Mid-Atlantic Song Contest 284
Midcoast, Inc. 236
MIDI Track Publishing/ALLRS Music Publishing Co. 116
Mighty Records 171
Milwaukee Youth Symphony Orchestra (NR)
Minnesota Association of Songwriters 310
Minotaur Records 171
Missile Records Film & TV, Inc. 171
Mixed Blood Theatre Co. (NR)
Modal Music, Inc.™ 172
Monk Family Music Group (NR)
Monk International Jazz Composers Competition, Thelonious 285
Monterey Artists Peninsula Artists/Paradigm 237
Monticana Productions 205
Monticana Records 173
Montina Music 117
Moon June Music 117

Moore Compositions, Patrick 255
Moores Opera Center (NR)
Music Business Solutions/Career
    Building Workshops 326
Music Library: Editors Choice Music
    Library (NR)
Music Marketing & Promotions (NR)
Music Room Publishing Group, The
    117
Musicians Contact 310
Must Have Music (NR)
Mustrock Productionz Worldwide
    205

N

NACUSA Young Composers' Com-
    petition 285
Naked Jain Records 117
Nashville Music Festival 327
Nashville Songwriters Association
    International (NSAI) 310
Nation Records Inc. (NR)
National Academy of Popular Music
    (NAPM) 311
National Academy of Popular Music
    Songwriting Workshop Program
    327
National Association of Composers/
    USA (NACUSA), The 311
National Society Of Men And
    Women Of The Music Business
    (NR)
NBT Records 173
NEMO Music Showcase & Confer-
    ence 327
Nervous Publishing (NR)
Nervous Records (NR)
Nestico Award, Sammy/USAF Band
    Airmen of Note 285
Neu Electro Productions 205
Neurodisc Records, Inc. 173
New Experience Records/Faze 4 Re-
    cords 206
New Harmony Project, The (NR)
New Music West (NR)
New Rap Jam Publishing, A 118
New Repertory Theatre (NR)
New York State Theatre Institute
    (NR)
New York Theatre Workshop (NR)

Newbraugh Brothers Music 118
Newcreature Music (NR)
Nightmare Records (NR)
Nightworks Records 206
Nik Entertainment Co. 237
Norfolk Chamber Music Festival
    (NR)
North American Folk Music and
    Dance Alliance 311
North by Northeast Music Festival
    and Conference 327
North Florida Christian Music Writ-
    ers Association 312
North Shore Music Theatre (NR)
Northwood University Alden B. Dow
    Creativity Center 334
Norton Rubble & Mertz, Inc. Adver-
    tising (NS)
Noteworthy Productions 237
NSAI Song Camps 328
NSAI Songwriters Songposium 328
NSAI/CMT Annual Song Contest 285

O

OCP Publications (NR)
Odyssey Theatre Ensemble (NR)
Oglio Records (NR)
Oklahoma Songwriters & Composers
    Association 312
Old Slowpoke Music 119
Omni Communications (NR)
On the Level Music! 237
Only New Age Music, Inc. 173
Open Eye Theater, The 258
Opera America 312
Opera Memphis (NR)
Orchestra Seattle/Seattle Chamber
    Singers 272
Orchid Publishing 119
Orford Festival 328
Outlaw Entertainment International
    238
Outmusic 313
Outstanding Records 174

P

P. & N. Records 174
Pacific Music Industry Association
    313

Pacific Northwest Songwriters Association 313
Paint Chip Records (NS)
Palmetto Mastersingers (NR)
Panio Brothers Label (NR)
Parker, Patty (RR)
Parliament Records 174
PeerMusic 119
Pegasus Music 119
Perla Music 120
Peters Music, Justin 120
Philly Breakdown Recording Co. 207
Phoebob Music 120
Piano Press 120
Piccolo Opera Company Inc. 272
Pierce, Jim 207
Pioneer Drama Service 263
Pittsburgh Songwriters Association 313
Plateau Music (NR)
Platinum Planet Music, Inc. 120
Playbones Records (NR)
Players Press, Inc. 263
Playhouse on the Square 258
Playhouse on the Square New Play Competition 289
Playwrights' Arena (NR)
Playwrights Horizons (NR)
PMG Records (NR)
Pollybyrd Publications Limited 121
Poole Agency Limited, Gordon (NR)
Pop Record Research 175, 313
Portage Music 121
Portland Songwriters Association 314
Portland Songwriters Association Annual Songwriting Competition 289
PPL Entertainment Group 175
Pravda Records (NR)
Precision Management 238
Prejippie Music Group (NR)
Prescription Co., The 207
Prescription Company 121
Presence Records 175
Prestige Management 238
Primary Stages 258
Prime Time Entertainment 238
Prince Music Theater 259
Princeton Symphony Orchestra (NR)
Prism Saxophone Quartet (NR)
Pro Talent Consultants 238
Pulitzer Prize in Music 289

Q
Qually & Company Inc. 255
QUARK, Inc. 121
Quark Records 176
Queen Esther Music Publishers 122

R
R.J. Music (NR)
R.T.L. Music 122
Radical Records 176
Rainbow Music Corp. 122
Rainbow Talent Agency 239
Rampion Visual Productions (NR)
Raspberry Jam Music 239
RAVE Records, Inc. 176
Razor & Tie Entertainment 176
RBI Entertainment/Bases Loaded Music/Winning Pitch Music (NR)
RCA Records 176
Red Admiral Records 177
Red Sky Records (NR)
Red Sundown Music 123
Redemption Records 177
Reel Adventures 207
Ren Zone Music 123
Repertory Theatre Of St. Louis, The (NR)
Reprise Records 177
RH Power And Associates, Inc. (NR)
Rhinestone Cowboy Music 123
Rhode Island Songwriters' Association 314
Rhythms Productions 123
Richards World Management, Inc., Diane 239
Ridge Music Corp. (NR)
Ridgewood Symphony Orchestra (NR)
Riohcat Music 240
Risavy, Inc., A.F. 240
RN'D Distribution, LLC. 208
Road Records (NR)
Robbins Entertainment LLC 177
Rock Of Ages Productions (NR)
Rockford Music Co. 123

Rocky Mountain Folks Festival Song-writer Showcase 289
Rodeo Video, Inc. (NR)
Rodgers Awards, Richard 290
Roll On Records® 178
Rome Prize Competition Fellowship 290
Rondor Music International/Almo/Irving Music 124
Rothschild Productions Inc., Charles R. 240
Rotten Records 178
Rustic Records 178
Rustic Records, Inc Publishing 124
Rustron Music Productions 208
Rustron Music Publishers 124
Rustron-Whimsong Music Productions 179
Rustron-Whimsong Music Productions 240

S
S.M.C.L. Productions, Inc. 125
Sabteca Music Co. (NR)
Sabteca Record Co. (NR)
Sacramento Master Singers (NR)
Saddlestone Publishing 125
Saffyre Management 241
Safire Records (NR)
Sahara Records and Filmworks Entertainment 179
St. John Artists 244
St. Louis Chamber Chorus (NR)
Salexo Music 180
Salt Works Music 125
Sa'Mall Management 241
San Diego Songwriters Guild 314
San Francisco Folk Music Club 314
San Francisco Girls Chorus 273
Sandalphon Management 241
Sandalphon Music Publishing 126
Sandalphon Records 180
Satellite Music (NR)
Satkowski Recordings, Steve 209
SDB Music Group 126
Segal's Productions 209
Segal's Publications 126
Sendyk, Leonard & Co. Inc. 242
Serge Entertainment Group 242
SESAC Inc. 315

Shakespeare Santa Cruz 259
Shawnee Press, Inc. 126
Shenandoah International Playwrights (NR)
Shiznit Music Conference, The 328
Siddons & Associates 242
Siegel Entertainment Ltd. (NR)
Siegel Music Companies (NR)
Silicon Music Publishing Co. 126
Silver Blue Music/Oceans Blue Music 127
Silver Bow Management 242
Silver Bow Productions 209
Silver Wave Records 180
Silvertone Records 180
Sin Klub Entertainment, Inc. (NR)
Singing Boys of Pennsylvania 273
Sinus Musik Produktion, Ulli Weigel 127
Sitka Center For Art & Ecology (NR)
Sizemore Music 127
Skorman Productions, Inc., T. 243
Small Stone Records 180
SME Publishing Group 128
Smeltzer Productions, Gary 243
Smithsonian Folkways Recordings (NR)
SOCAN (Society of Composers, Authors and Music Publishers of Canada) 315
Society of Composers & Lyricists 315
Society Of Composers, Inc. (NR)
SODRAC Inc. 315
Solana Records 181
Soli Deo Gloria Cantorum 274
Sonar Records & Production (NR)
Songwriters and Poets Critique 316
Songwriters Association of Washington 316
Songwriters Guild Foundation, The 329
Songwriters Guild of America, The 316
Songwriters of Oklahoma 317
Songwriters of Wisconsin International 317
Songwriters Resource Network 317
Sonic Unyon Records Canada 181
Sony Music 181
Sony Music Nashville 181

General Index

General Index

Sony/ATV Music Publishing 128
Soter Associates Inc. (NR)
Soul Candy Productions 209
Sound Arts Recording Studio 210
Sound Cellar Music 128
Sound Gems 181
Sound Management Direction 243
Sound Works Entertainment Productions Inc. 210
South by Southwest Music Conference 330
Southeast Texas Bluegrass Music Association (OB)
Southeastern Attractions 243
Southeastern Composers League (NR)
Southern Songwriters Guild, Inc. (NR)
Southland Records, Inc. (NR)
Southwest Celtic Music Association (NR)
Southwest Virginia Songwriters Association 317
Space Coast Pops, Inc. (NR)
SPARS (Society of Professional Audio Recording Services) (NR)
Sphere Group One 210, 243
SPNM—Promoting New Music 318
SRS Productions/Hit Records Network 211
Stage One (NR)
Stages Repertory Theatre (NR)
Staircase Promotion 244
Standard Music Publishing (NR)
Stander Entertainment 244
Starbound Publishing Co. 128
Starkravin' Management 245
Steinman Management, Obi (NR)
Still Working Music Group 129
Strictly Forbidden Artists (OB)
Stuart Audio Services 211
Stuart Music Co., Jeb (NR)
Studio Seven 211
Succes 129
Sugar Hill Records 182
Supreme Enterprises Int'l Corp. 129
Sureshot Records (NR)
Surface Records 182
Susquehanna Symphony Orchestra 274

Swannanoa Gathering—Contemporary Folk Week, The 330
Swift River Productions 211
Swine Palace Productions (NR)

T
T.C. Productions/Etude Publishing Co. 129
T.L.C. Booking Agency 245
Tada! (NR)
Talbot Music Group (NR)
Tangent® Records 182
Tari, Roger Vincent 212
Tas Music Co./Dave Tasse Entertainment 245
Telluride Troubadour Contest 290
Ten-Minute Musicals Project, The 259, 290, 330
Tennessee Songwriters International, The 318
Texas Accountants & Lawyers for the Arts 318
Texas Music Cafe (NR)
Texas Music Office 319
Texas Rose Records 183
Texas Sounds Entertainment 245
Theatre Three, Inc. (NR)
Theatre West Virginia (NR)
Theatreworks/USA (NR)
Theodore Presser Co. (NR)
Third Wave Productions Limited (NS)
Third Wave Productions Ltd. (NR)
Thistle Hill 130
Thunder Bay Theatre 260
Tiki Enterprises, Inc. (NR)
TMC Productions 212
Tommy Boy Records 183
Ton Records 183
Topcat Records 183
Toronto Mendelssohn Choir (NR)
Toronto Musicians' Association 319
Toucabaca Music (NR)
Touring Concert Opera Co. Inc. 274
Tourmaline Music, Inc. 130
Tower Music Group 130
Trac Record Co. (NR)
Transamerika Musikverlag KG 130
Transdreamer Records 184
Transition Music Corporation 131

TRF Production Music Libraries 255
Triangle Talent, Inc. (NR)
Trinity Studio, The 213
Trio Productions 131
Tulsa Opera Inc. (NR)
Tunesmith Summer & Winter Seminars 330
TVT Records 184
Twentieth Century Promotions 245
28 Records 184
Twin Towers Publishing Co. 131

U

U.S.A. Songwriting Competition 291
U.S.-Japan Creative Artists Exchange Fellowship Program 291
U.S.-Mexico Fund For Culture (NR)
UAR Records 185
Umpire Entertainment Enterprizes (NS)
Undercurrents 331
Unisong International Song Contest 291
Universal Music Marketing 246
Universal Music Publishing 131
Universal Records 185
Unknown Source Music 131
Utopian Empire Creativeworks (NR)

V

Vaam Music Group 132
Valiant Records & Management (NS)
Valtec Productions 185, 213
Van Pol Management, Hans (NR)
Vancouver Chamber Choir 275
Varrasso Management, Richard 246
Verve Music Group, The 185
Victory Music (NR)
Videa Artists International Distribution 186
Video I-D, Inc. (NR)
Vine Creek Music 132
Virgin Records 186
Virginia Center for the Creative Arts 334
Virginia Opera (NR)
Virginia Stage Company (NR)
Vis/Aid Marketing/Associates (NR)
Volunteer Lawyers for the Arts 319

W

Wagner Agency, William F. 246
Walker Publishing Co. L.L.C. 132
Walkerbout Music Group 132
Walnut Street Theatre (NR)
Warehouse Creek Recording Corp. 186
Warner Bros. Records 186
Warner Productions, Cheryl K. 246
Warner/Chappell Music, Inc. 133
Washington Area Music Association 319
Waterdog Music 187
Weaver of Words Music 133
Weisman Production Group, The 213
Wells Music, Angela Baker 133
Wemar Music Corp. (NR)
Wemus Entertainment 247
Wengert, Berthold (Musikverlag) 133
West Coast Ensemble; Musical Stairs (NR)
West Coast Ensemble (NR)
West Coast Songwriters 320
West Coast Songwriters Conference 331
West End Artists 260
Westbeth Theatre Center (NR)
Western Wind Workshop In Ensemble Singing (NR)
Westpark Music—Records, Production & Publishing 187
Westwires Recording 213
Wheaton Symphony Orchestra 275
White Cat Music (RR)
Wilcom Publishing 134
Wilder Artists' Management, Shane (NR)
Wilder Music, Shane (NR)
Williams Management, Yvonne (OB)
Willson, Frank 214
Wilma Theater, The (NR)
Winchester Records 187
Windswept Music 134
Wind-Up Entertainment 187
Wings Theatre Co. (NR)
Winston & Hoffman House Music Publishers 134

Winter Music Conference Inc. 331
Winterland Entertainment Management & Publishing 247
Wisconsin Alliance For Composers (NR)
WLM Music/Recording 214
Women in Music 320
Wood Artist Management, Richard 247
Woolly Mammoth Theatre (NR)
Word Records & Music 188
World Beatnik Records 188
World Records 214
World Wide Management 247
WorldSound, LLC 248

X
X.R.L. Records/Music 188
Xemu Records 189

Y
Y.E.S. Festival of New Plays 291
Young Composers Awards (RR)
Young Country Records/Plain Country Records (NR)
Your Best Songs Publishing 134

Z
Zane Management, Inc. 248
Zettitalia Music International 134
Zirilli Management, D. 248
Zomba Music Publishing 135

Songwriter's Market
Feedback

If you have a suggestion for improving *Songwriter's Market*, or would like to take part in a reader survey we conduct from time to time, please make a photocopy of this form (or cut it out of the book), fill it out, and return it to:

Songwriter's Market Feedback
4700 East Galbraith Road
Cincinnati, OH 45236
Fax: (513) 531-2686

○ **Yes!** I'm willing to fill out a short survey by mail or online to provide feedback on *Songwriter's Market* or other books on songwriting.

○ **Yes!** I have a suggestion to improve *Songwriter's Market* (attach a second sheet if more room is necessary):

_____
_____
_____
_____
_____
_____
_____
_____
_____

Name: _____
Address: _____
City: _____ State: _____ Zip: _____
Phone: _____ Fax: _____
E-mail: _____ Web site: _____

I am a

○ songwriter
○ performing songwriter
○ musician
○ other: _____